An introduction from Steve

In the book's preface, you'll find more detail about the story of *Reflect & Relate*, its overall approach, and all the exciting changes in the fourth edition (see pp. vii–xxi). Here, however, I focus on *teaching*. First, I am going to share some of the ways that I use the text in my classes. Every feature and activity in the book is designed to be adapted in multiple ways—depending on the teaching goals of the instructor, the learning styles and abilities of the students, and the class format. I hope that sharing some of the things that I do in my classes will spark ideas for how you might use the book in your own classroom. Second, an Activity Guide on pages T-17–T-39, revised and expanded for the fourth edition, features a collection of activities and assignments submitted by fellow interpersonal communication instructors from all over the country. I always find it helpful, inspiring, and a bit humbling to see (and borrow!) the amazing innovations that other teachers come up with for how best to engage students. Finally, special instructor annotations in every chapter (the ones in blue) suggest even more ways to incorporate videos, activities, Web sites, group work, assignments, and discussions into your courses. These annotations were created by Dr. Alicia Alexander (Southern Illinois University Edwardsville), and my most heartfelt thanks goes out to her for sharing these ideas with us.

I hope that the *Instructor's Annotated Edition* proves helpful to you and beneficial to your students. I also would love to hear what you are doing in your classes. Your feedback and suggestions inspire me and directly influence *Reflect & Relate*. Please feel free to drop me a line at **smcc911@uab.edu** so we can talk shop about interpersonal communication teaching. I'm on Facebook as well, so you can contact me that way if you prefer!

Warmly,

Steve McCornack

How I use chapter-opening vignettes…

The chapter openers for *Reflect & Relate* respond directly to concerns raised by my students. They tell me they want vignettes that grab their attention and preview each chapter's content. But more than anything else, my students want *real* stories—not hypothetical situations like "Imagine Jane and John are in a relationship." As one former student said, "I don't care if it's history or a movie or a book, I want it to feel real—if it doesn't feel real, how can I trust it?"

For example, Chapter 1, Introducing Interpersonal Communication, begins with the story of how author Melissa Seligman uses various communication media to maintain her marriage and family relationships during her husband's military deployments. After reading a national editorial that Melissa wrote, I knew her story was one that students could relate to—whether they have a family member, friend, or romantic partner in the military, or they're geographically separated from a loved one. I contacted Melissa and invited her to collaborate on a chapter opener, and she generously agreed. The result is a powerful, poignant, and authentic narrative framing the theme of Chapter 1 and the text as a whole: *the communication choices we make determine the personal, interpersonal, and relationship outcomes that follow.*

> The Melissa Seligman story isn't the only chapter-opener collaboration. I also worked with radio personality and producer Vy Higginsen (Chapter 4), Dean of "Santa School" Jennifer Andrews (Chapter 6), and Olympic gold medalist Brenda Villa (Chapter 11) to create stories illustrating the importance of interpersonal communication in shaping and improving relationships.
>
> —SM

In my classes, I use this vignette as the springboard for a one-page critical self-reflection paper. I have students read Melissa's story and focus on the section in which she chooses between lying to her husband about how things are going on the home front or telling him the truth. Then I have them identify an interpersonal incident in their own lives in which they faced a similar choice. These events might include, for example, disclosure of faded romantic feelings, conflict with a family member, or intervention with a friend suffering from substance abuse. I then have them briefly describe the event (one paragraph) and answer four questions: (1) Why did you make the communication choice that you did? (2) How competent was your communication—that is, was the media you chose (e.g., text, e-mail, phone, face-to-face) and the words you used appropriate, effective, and ethical? (3) What outcomes resulted from your communication? (4) What, if anything, could you have thought, said, and done differently to improve your outcome? This assignment sets the tone for the class by compelling students to critically self-reflect, relate course content to real-life challenges, and drill deep into the theme of the book: choices, communication, and outcomes.

The relevance and pedagogical utility of chapter openers is further reinforced through the end-of-chapter *Postscript*. This brings students back to the opening vignette and shows how it links to the main points of the chapter. The *Postscript* then challenges students once more to consider how the chapter connects to them, their lives, and their relationships, helping to reinforce their self-reflection skills.

POSTSCRIPT

We began this chapter with a military wife struggling to juggle the competing demands of raising her children and maintaining her marriage. Melissa Seligman uses multiple media to stay connected with her husband during his combat deployments. At the same time, she has learned that computers, phones, and care packages are merely tools. The most important thing is open, honest, and loving communication.

How do you stay close with loved ones who a[re] distant? What tough communication choices have [you] faced in these relationships?

The story of Melissa Seligman's struggle remi[nds] us of an inescapable truth that forms the foundati[on of] this book. Our close relationships are *the* most important things in our lives, and it's our choices regarding how we communicate that determine whether these relationships survive and thrive, or fade away.

> I like the <u>Postscript</u> at the end of each chapter because it connects to the chapter-opening vignette.
>
> —SM

NEW coverage I'm excited about…

My students—like yours—are a constant source of inspiration and innovation for me. How they approach the course material and relate it to their own lives not only connects them to the class but provides me with insight into what topics they find most relevant—and correspondingly, what issues I should address in my book and classroom.

Using their feedback, comments and suggestions from reviewers, and the conversations I've had with students and teachers alike at conferences and through e-mail and Facebook, I opted to cover a host of new topics in the fourth edition. Most significantly, this fourth edition has a brand-new chapter on culture (Chapter 5) that supplements the *Focus on Culture* boxes throughout the text and coverage of culture in other chapters. While I was working on the fourth edition, my philosophy was "culture—broad *and* deep." In order to accurately reflect the profound impact that culture has on students' lives, I decided to devote this chapter to deeply exploring topics such as individualism and collectivism, uncertainty avoidance, power distance, masculinity and femininity, cultural views of time, co-cultures, prejudice, ethnocentrism, and world-mindedness.

> When deciding what new topics to cover, I thought about the areas my own students express interest in. This influenced the fourth edition's separate chapter on culture and coverage of subjects like online competence and the effect of social media on communication.
>
> —SM

T-4

Second, the new edition spotlights the latest theories and research related to a host of topics important to our students. These include online competence, the impact of mobile devices on intimacy and disclosure, self-concept clarity, empathy mind-sets, anxiety and emotional contagion, overcoming prejudice, improving intercultural competence, the neuroscience of romantic passion, and blended families, to name just a few. The fourth edition also features three new *Self-Quizzes* in the print text and three new *Self-Quizzes* on LaunchPad, which help get students thinking about key concepts in the text. For example, when I teach culture in my classes, I have students take the *Self-Quiz* "Are You World-Minded or Ethnocentric?" to get them thinking about their cultural attitudes. This *Self-Quiz* can also be used as the basis for a written self-reflection assignment or as an in-class discussion activity.

The Self-Quiz feature adapts various diagnostic scales from communication and social psychology so that students can gain insight into themselves and their communication. Some of these quizzes give students an additional avenue for exploring issues of culture, gender, or technology (like the one shown from p. 154).

—SM

T-5

My capstone feature: *Making Relationship Choices*...

Unique to *Reflect & Relate,* the *Making Relationship Choices* feature presents a challenging interpersonal situation and then helps students reason through it by drawing on all the knowledge and skills they've acquired from the text (not just one theory or concept). In the fourth edition, *Making Relationship Choices* has been greatly expanded, including new professionally shot videos and multimedia content on LaunchPad, to make the experience more engaging than ever before.

For an example of how it works, see the *Making Relationship Choices* in Chapter 1 (pp. 30–31). This feature involves Kaitlyn, a friend who posts potentially damaging photos of herself on Facebook, and then lashes out when someone suggests she might want to take the photos down. The situation is designed to test students' competence to the utmost: How do you communicate appropriately, effectively, and ethically toward someone who is behaving badly toward you? Using the new five-part process, students read about the situation, think critically about it, and compose a response to Kaitlyn. Next, students go to

> *Making Relationship Choices* presents students with realistic and complex situations that are similar to those they may face in their everyday lives.
>
> —SM

making relationship choices

Dealing with a Difficult Friend

1 BACKGROUND

Communicating competently is challenging, especially when close relationship partners provoke us. When problematic encounters happen online, it makes dealing with them even more difficult. Read the case study in Part 2; then, drawing on all you know about interpersonal communication thus far, work through the problem-solving model in Part 3.

▶ Visit LaunchPad to check out the other side of the story (Part 4). For the best experience, complete all parts in LaunchPad: **macmillanhighered.com /reflectrelate4e**.

2 CASE STUDY

Kaitlyn, Cort, and you have been best friends for years. The three of you are inseparable, and people joke that you're more like triplets than friends. After high school, you and Cort become college housemates. Kaitlyn can't afford tuition yet, so she stays in your hometown to work and save money. Despite the distance, the three of you stay in daily contact.

Recently, however, things have changed. Kaitlyn has been hanging out with people you consider shady. She's been drinking heavily and boasting about her all-night binges. You try to be supportive, but you're worried.

You awake one Sunday to find that one of Kaitlyn's new friends has tagged her in a series of Facebook photos documenting their latest party adventure. Kaitlyn has added a comment that reads, "A new low is reached—I *LUV* it!!" Surfing through the pictures, you see Kaitlyn drinking until she passes out. Several photos show her friends laughing and posing with her while she's unconscious. In one image, they've drawn a smiley face on her forehead with a Sharpie. Looking at these photos, you're heartsick with humiliation for your friend. Why would Kaitlyn hang with people like that? But you also can't understand why she would comment on these pictures rather than insist on having them deleted. What if her family saw them? or her employers? You e-mail her, telling her she should have the photos deleted, and saying that you're worried about her behavior and her choice of new friends. She doesn't respond.

That night, you're studying with Cort. When Cort steps out to get some food, a message alert sounds on his phone. It's a text from Kaitlyn. You know you shouldn't read it, but your curiosity gets the best of you. It's a rage message, in which Kaitlyn blasts you for prying into her business, for judging her, for thinking you're better than her, and for telling her what to do. It's personal, profane, and *very* insulting.

You feel sick to your stomach. You love Kaitlyn, but you're also furious with her. How could she say such horrible things when all you were trying to do was help? As you sit there stewing, another text to Cort from Kaitlyn comes in. "Where r u? Text me back! I want to talk w/ u about our nosy, o-so-perfect friend!"

T-6

LaunchPad and watch a professionally shot video in which Kaitlyn explains her side of the story. This feature—Part 4, "The Other Side"—is brand new in the fourth edition, and it forces students to consider alternative points of view and to realize that there are two sides to every interpersonal encounter. Finally, in Part 5, students get a chance to reconsider their initial response to Kaitlyn, now that they have heard her side of the story.

As is clear from the first *Making Relationship Choices* onward, these situations don't lend themselves to one easy, obvious, or correct solution. Many of them are no-win situations, in which students must decide among various options to find the optimal outcome. These features make for lively and intense classroom interactions. Students often feel strongly, at first, that their solutions are the best and only options, only to realize otherwise when watching "The Other Side" videos and discussing with other students in class.

Overall, the revised *Making Relationship Choices* is a unique and comprehensive feature that immerses students in interpersonal situations like never before. The feature enhances students' communication competence by getting them to think about interpersonal conflicts in new ways.

> *The unique five-step process in "Your Turn" helps students learn how to reason through problems, not just react.*
> —SM

YOUR TURN

Think about all you've learned thus far about interpersonal communication. Then work through the following five steps. Remember, there are no "right" answers, so think hard about what is the *best* choice! (P.S. Need help? See the *Helpful Concepts* list.)

step 1
Reflect on yourself. What are your thoughts and feelings in this situation? What assumptions are you making about Kaitlyn and her communication? Are your assumptions accurate?

step 2
Reflect on your partner. Put yourself in Kaitlyn's shoes. How is she thinking and feeling? Are her views valid?

step 3
Identify the optimal outcome. Think about your relationship and communication with Kaitlyn and all that has happened. What's the best, most constructive relationship outcome possible? Consider what's best for you and for Kaitlyn.

step 4
Locate the roadblocks. Taking into consideration your own and Kaitlyn's thoughts and feelings and all that has happened in this situation, what obstacles are preventing you from achieving the optimal outcome?

step 5
Chart your course. What can you say to Kaitlyn to overcome the roadblocks you've identified and achieve your optimal outcome?

HELPFUL CONCEPTS
I-Thou and I-It, 13
Relationship information, 13–15
The irreversibility of interpersonal communication, 16
Ethics, 23–24
Improving your online competence, 24–27

> *All-new, professionally shot videos on LaunchPad reveal the other character's side of the story, helping students build empathy.*
> —SM

4 THE OTHER SIDE

Visit LaunchPad to watch a video in which Kaitlyn tells her side of the case study story. As in many real-life situations, this is information to which you did not have access when you were initially crafting your response in Part 3. The video reminds us that even when we do our best to offer competent responses, there is always another side to the story that we need to consider.

My favorite examples…

Throughout the text, examples precede, rather than follow, discussions of almost every major topic. This structure helps students comprehend concepts, understand how they apply to real life, and remember them over time. Perhaps even more important, the variety of example topics makes the book more engaging and fun to read!

In-text examples come from pop culture and current events, my own experiences, history, TV shows, movies, and books. No matter the origin of the examples, students relate to them because of how authentic they are. To illustrate, one of the most dramatic examples in the fourth edition appears in Chapter 12 on friendships (see pp. 372–373). A student of mine, Ashlee (not her real name), volunteered the incident for inclusion in my text (she had originally written about it for a class paper). Ashlee's friendship with Rachel (also a pseudonym) came apart when Ashlee saw a text message she wasn't supposed to—an all-too-common occurrence. In the text message, Rachel mocked Ashlee's intelligence and integrity, and viciously attacked her boyfriend's ethnicity.

With my students, I use the Ashlee example as the basis for a journal exercise: What friendship betrayals have you experienced? How has technology contributed to these betrayals? What were the consequences of these situations? How have these experiences changed your relationships? I like to couple this discussion with the betrayal content that follows on pages 373–374, the friendship rules on pages 369–370, and the *Skills Practice* on page 374. Many students later share with me that the assignment caused them to reassess their own friendships, especially how damaging it can be to talk (or text) about friends behind their backs.

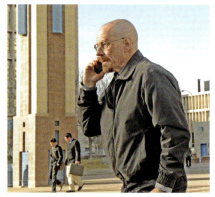

> I frequently use examples from the media and pop culture that resonate with students. These can include anything from the TV show *Breaking Bad* (Chapter 7) to human rights activist Malala Yousafzai (Chapter 5) to *SpongeBob SquarePants* (Chapter 12).
>
> —SM

My take on the LaunchPad video feature . . .

I'm very excited to announce that for the first time, *Reflect & Relate*'s extensive online video collection is fully integrated with LaunchPad, the new course platform: **macmillanhighered.com /reflectrelate4e**. In every chapter, video features— look for this icon ⓞ —prompt students to go to LaunchPad and watch one of the more than 90 clips, including over 20 professionally shot videos new to the fourth edition, that illustrate concepts from the text. These brief clips (most are under a minute long) bring key interpersonal ideas to life, giving students an additional avenue for understanding the course. The accompanying questions challenge students to reflect on what they see and relate the lessons to their own lives. This combination makes each video a self-contained activity that is easy to assign as the basis for journals, reflection papers, or even in-class discussions.

To help you get the most out of these videos, there are activity and assignment suggestions in the *Instructor's Annotated Edition* as well as a dedicated section in the Instructor's Resource Manual (which is also available on LaunchPad). For example, in Chapter 5 on page 144, the video feature for individualism points students to a clip of college seniors discussing their plans after they graduate. When I use this in my class, I start by giving students an assignment to watch the video and answer the reflection questions in a journal. Then I show the video in class and ask the following questions: Do you agree or disagree with the attitudes and views expressed by the students in the video? Do you value your personal goals more highly than the needs of your family and your community? To what extent do you think your answers are affected by your culture? How do you think people in different cultures might answer differently? Not only does this integrate a powerful visual (the video) with active learning (group discussion), but it functions to solidify students' understanding of the comprehensive new content in the chapter on culture (Chapter 5).

This icon indicates which key concepts have online videos. Look for the icon in the Contents and in every chapter. You can also see a complete list on the last page of the book.

—SM

T-9

How I use Self-Reflections...

The *Self-Reflection* marginal feature helps students learn one of the more important skills of the interpersonal communication class: improved self-awareness through thinking critically about their communication and behaviors. These features (keyed to specific lines of text) give students an opportunity to pause in their reading and reflect on how the content relates to their own experiences, thoughts, feelings, and relationships.

For example, I commonly use the *Self-Reflection* questions on page 204 (following an excerpt from Alice Sebold's *The Lovely Bones*)—"Consider a recent instance in which a relationship of yours suddenly changed direction, either for better or for worse. What was said that triggered this turning point? How did the words that were exchanged impact intimacy?"—to get students reflecting on how deeply language is intertwined with our relationship trajectories. Almost every major relational turning point is rooted in words exchanged during an interpersonal encounter. To help students wrap their minds around this, I use an in-class activity in which we list common high-impact "turning points" that are language based, and sort them into two categories—those that increase intimacy ("positive") and those that decrease it ("negative"). Common examples students come up with are marriage proposals, infidelity confessions, pregnancy announcements, and illness disclosures. Often interesting complexities arise. When the disclosure of love comes "too early" in a relationship, is it positive or negative? Is the admission of addiction a negative or a positive? What about when infidelity is disclosed to a partner who was looking for an excuse to end the relationship anyway?

I also use the Self-Reflection features as the basis for journal assignments and reflection papers.

—SM

Ways I assign *Skills Practices*...

In addition to leading students toward becoming more critically self-aware, another goal of the course is for students to improve their interpersonal skills. To help students apply what they are learning in class to their own lives, the *Skills Practice* marginal exercises provide them with simple, straightforward activities to do at home. To better reflect how today's students communicate, at least one *Skills Practice* feature in every chapter helps students with their online communication skills. Sometimes I also use the *Skills Practice* features to start class discussions, debating with students about whether they achieved their desired outcomes or whether alternative behaviors would have been better choices.

Consider the *Skills Practice* on page 90 in Chapter 3 that occurs adjacent to the example from the movie *Mud*, illustrating how students (like the main character in the movie) can reconsider and modify initial negative impressions they have formed. This simple exercise provides students with powerful tools for reshaping and reevaluating their impressions. Learning this skill can also help students overcome their tendency to negatively stereotype others.

I designed the Self-Reflection and the Skills Practice features to help students with two key aspects of the course: self-awareness and improved skills.

—SM

My integrated approach to gender and culture coverage…

My goal in covering gender and culture is to make these vital topics a *focus* of the text and *integral* to it. Student attention is consistently drawn to these essential topics because they appear in every chapter—in the narrative, examples, features, and even the photo program. Additionally, the fourth edition features a brand-new chapter that focuses exclusively on culture. In this way, the text's coverage of culture is both broad *and* deep.

Students often come to class thinking they already know all about the differences between the genders because of information they've learned from depictions in pop culture. *Reflect & Relate* pushes students to think beyond these simple stereotypes by challenging them to consider the complexities of gender socialization and the intriguing similarities and differences that both separate and unite the genders.

In covering culture, I want *all* students to be able to see themselves in this book and view themselves as close to, rather than distant from, culturally diverse others. So *Reflect & Relate* embraces a uniquely broad and inclusive definition of culture, including points of cultural distinction that many texts avoid—for example, age, religion, ability, and socioeconomic class—as well as more traditional touchstones of culture, such as nationality, ethnicity, and sexual orientation. In addition to the integrated coverage throughout the text, the *Focus on Culture* boxes help facilitate in-class discussions, while the new culture chapter (Chapter 5) provides in-depth coverage of key cultural concepts.

Immediately after birth, we begin a lifelong process of gender socialization
Allan Grant/Time & Life Pictures/Getty Images

Some of my favorite sections on gender are the image of gender socialization on page 45, the complex relationship between gender and perception on pages 81–83, and the discussion about gender and "practical" love on page 289.

—SM

T-12

I consider the *perception of ingroup/outgroup differences* in Chapter 3 (pp. 79–81) one of the most important pieces of culture content because it is the cause of most difficult cross-cultural encounters. I have students interview two people from their lives: one whom they consider culturally different from themselves (outgroup) and one whom they consider culturally similar (ingroup). For the ingroup interview, students must unveil significant points of difference in beliefs, attitudes, values, and background. For the outgroup interview, students must discover substantial points of similarity.

Students report this assignment to be a "mind blower" because of three common outcomes: (1) they discover substantial points of difference between themselves and their ingrouper; (2) they discover previously unrecognized points of commonality between themselves and their outgrouper; and (3)—most importantly—they end up realizing that the points of similarity they share with both parties are more substantial than the points of difference. Even for the rare cases in which perceived outgroup differences are reinforced, students typically still walk away with a more refined understanding, tolerance, and acceptance of such differences because the encounter allows them to discover the common *humanity* that we all share.

---

focus on CULTURE

Men Just Don't Listen!

The belief that men are listening-challenged is widespread. Linguist Deborah Tannen (1990a) posits that the perception of male listening incompetence stems from several sources, including men facing away rather than toward people when listening, making dismissive comments in response to disclosures, changing conversational topics too rapidly, and listening silently rather than providing vocal back-channel cues such as "Mm-hmm" and "Yeah." But at a broader level, Tannen believes that male listening is symptomatic of *cultural* differences between the sexes. As she elaborates,

> For women, intimacy is the fabric of relationships, and talk is the thread from which it is woven. Bonds between boys are based less on talking, more on doing things together. Boys' groups are more hierarchical, so boys must struggle to avoid the subordinate position. This may play a role in women's complaints that men don't listen. Some men really don't like to listen, because being the listener makes them feel one-down, like a child listening to adults.

What's the solution? Tannen recommends that men and women view "their differences as cross-cultural rather than right or wrong."

Cognitive scientists and communication scholars offer an alternative view. Analyzing data from dozens of studies, brain researcher Daniel Voyer (2011) found only small differences between the sexes in their listening, so small that they can't be generalized to individual women and men.

Communication researchers Daena Goldsmith and Patricia Fulfs (1999) examined every sex difference suggested by Tannen and found no scientific evidence supporting them. After reviewing existing communication studies, scholar Kathryn Dindia (2006) agreed with Fulfs and Goldsmith, concluding that "the empirical evidence indicates that differences between women and men are minimal by any measure." Dindia noted that "North American girls and boys are raised in the same culture, but that culture teaches them that they are very different. In spite of this, they turn out remarkably similar." Dindia goes on to suggest a different metaphor for thinking about sex differences. When it comes to interpersonal communication and listening, "Men are from North Dakota, women are from South Dakota. Women and men do not come from different planets or different cultures, they come from neighboring states."

discussion questions

- Do men and women grow up in different communication cultures, as Tannen suggests? Or, as Dindia argues, is it the same culture, in which they are repeatedly taught about how different they are?
- In your experience, do men and women listen differently? If so, what differences have you observed? Is one sex inherently better at listening than the other, or is it a matter of individual style rather than a general sex difference?

---

that just because a person is female or male means that she or he will always listen—or expect you to listen—in certain ways. Take your cue from the person you are talking with.

CULTURE AND LISTENING STYLES

Culture powerfully shapes the use and perception of listening styles. What's considered effective listening by one culture is often perceived as ineffective by others, something you should always keep in mind when communicating with people from other cultures. For example, in individualistic cultures such as the

177

I use the Focus on Culture feature by breaking students up into groups and having them read through the feature and answer the discussion questions. (Students are generally more willing to discuss sensitive topics in smaller groups at first.) Then each group presents its answers, creating a broad discussion about the role of culture in communication.

—SM

How I cover online communication…

Communicating online and via technology (whether through social networking sites, texting, or webcam) is a natural part of our—and our students'—everyday lives. Consequently, every chapter in the fourth edition of *Reflect & Relate* includes sections, examples, or features devoted to interpersonal communication and technology.

Expanding on the groundbreaking work of the third edition, I continued to include the latest research on this topic from top scholars in online communication, including Emil Bakke (Gjøvik University College, Norway), Andrew K. Przybylski and Netta Weinstein (University of Essex, UK), and Erin Ruppel (University of Wisconsin, Milwaukee).

Chapter 10 discusses how technology influences romantic attraction, including the challenge of moving from an online relationship to an offline one.

—SM

Perhaps my favorite online example is found in Chapter 2, related to online self-presentation (pp. 51–52). I start by sharing my own experience of selecting a Facebook profile photo. This seemingly small decision nets large consequences, as I discovered when I posted a photo that others found worrisome. I use this example to encourage my students to analyze *their* profile photos. What do they want the images to say about their selves? How have others responded? I have students craft a one-page paper, answering the *Self-Reflection* on page 52 and sharing their experiences from trying the *Skills Practice* on page 54. Students tell me that this assignment helps enhance their understanding of how people commonly distort their online self-presentations.

> This Facebook example helps show students that everyone needs to work to improve their online self-presentation—even me!
>
> —SM

T-15

Plug into our new online course space.

LaunchPad brings together content and tools that help you manage your course materials, classes, and students. You'll love how much easier it is to get the job done.

I'm so excited about LaunchPad; I can't wait to use the video resources and LearningCurve adaptive quizzing!

—SM

Get content

LaunchPad is preloaded with media: the *e-book for Reflect & Relate*; more than 90 videos illustrating interpersonal concepts, including over 20 professionally shot videos that are brand new to the fourth edition; LearningCurve adaptive quizzing; a downloadable Test Bank, Instructor's Resource Manual, and lecture slides; and an easy-to-use interface that allows you to customize your course as you see fit.

Customize

LaunchPad is completely customizable. Add or remove content from our vast library of quizzes, videos (your own or those embedded from sites like YouTube), and e-book pages. Reorder your course by moving chapters around. Choose what to assign to your students, and customize your course table of contents and calendar.

Assign

Easily create assignments around any of the content in LaunchPad, including sections from the e-book, chapter summaries, quizzes, and videos.

Use video

The video resource section makes it easy to upload, embed, comment on video, and create video assignments for the individual student, for groups, and for the whole class—a great way to encourage discussion.

Assess

Get and stay on top of individual and classroom performance with powerful testing, tracking, grading, and organizing tools.

How do you get it?

LaunchPad is available on its own or bundled with the print text for a significant discount. For packaging and pricing information, contact your Bedford rep: **macmillanhighered.com/Catalog/ContactUs**.

Activity Guide

Edited by Alicia Alexander
Southern Illinois University Edwardsville

Preparing a new class or revamping teaching methods can require a lot of creative energy and output. As a jumping-off point, the following pages include activity ideas submitted by interpersonal communication teachers from around the country. These activities are loosely organized around the chapter order of *Reflect & Relate*, Fourth Edition, but many can be used throughout the semester, so be sure to check them all out. For even more ideas, look through the annotations in the margins of the textbook as well as the activities in the online Instructor's Resource Manual available on LaunchPad: **macmillanhighered.com/reflectrelate4e**.

Browsing through the entire guide will reveal a range of creative and fun ideas for activities and assignments. However, if you have less time and want to quickly locate an activity for a specific topic—say, emotions or culture—the chart below lists which activities relate to each chapter in *Reflect & Relate*. (The numbers in the Related Activities column correspond to the numbered activities in the guide.)

A big thank-you to everyone who submitted such amazing activities!

Chapter	Related Activities
First Week of Class	1, 2
1: Introducing Interpersonal Communication	3, 4, 9, 17
2: Considering Self	1, 17
3: Perceiving Others	5, 8, 17
4: Experiencing and Expressing Emotions	4, 6
5: Understanding Culture	2, 7, 15
6: Listening Actively	8, 10
7: Communicating Verbally	4, 8, 9, 17
8: Communicating Nonverbally	2, 4, 8, 10, 17
9: Managing Conflict and Power	4, 12, 13
10: Relationships with Romantic Partners	13, 16
11: Relationships with Family Members	13, 14, 15, 16
12: Relationships with Friends	13, 16
Appendix: Relationships in the Workplace	13

1. Uniquely in Common

Submitted by: Julie Cajigas, The University of Akron

Related Topics: The first week of class or self-disclosure (Ch. 2)

Objective: To break the ice, help students get to know one another, and facilitate self-disclosure in the classroom

Activity: Break the class into small groups of five to seven students. Each group has 20 minutes to create a list of things that *every* member of the group has in common and a list of things that are unique to only *one* person in the group. For example, every member of a group might have ridden a roller coaster, but only one member of the group may have visited Ireland. Each group should select one member to record all the common and unique items.

The goal is to create the most extensive list possible. (You can make it a contest, in which the group with the longest list "wins.") Encourage groups to come up with the most interesting commonalities and unique characteristics. Be sure to tell students to think outside the box to find unique characteristics. You can offer a few personal examples to help them get their brains in gear (e.g., "I played in Scottish fiddle competitions when I was younger" or "I've been stung by a jellyfish").

This activity is great because it gives students an opportunity to practice self-disclosure and is a fun challenge, not only to find things a group has 100 percent in common but also to find things that are unique to only one member. It also helps create a bond among the students early on in the class, which makes discussions throughout the class more fruitful and open.

Materials Needed: Paper and pencils/pens

2. Communication Scavenger Hunt

Submitted by: Alicia Alexander, Southern Illinois University Edwardsville

Related Topics: The first few weeks of class, culture (Ch. 5), and nonverbal communication (Ch. 8)

Objective: To help students orient themselves to the university and to the class. This activity also helps students get to know one another a bit better and can help students find ways to apply specific concepts.

Activity: Place students in groups of four and give them a list of approximately 20 items to locate for a university scavenger hunt. This activity can take an entire class period or could be completed outside of class over an extended period. The task involves having groups of students "compete" to find all the items you have compiled on your scavenger hunt list. You might have students collect such things as an article from a communication journal, a picture of a romantic couple or a small group, and so forth. Or if you want to use this exercise to teach students about nonverbal messages, you could ask students to take photos of various emotional expressions, examples of different workplace/organizational environments, examples of bumper stickers, or pictures of tattoos. I have often asked students to find my office on their scavenger hunt and to put a friendly note on the door to show that they know how to find my office. It is fun to come back to a door full of Post-It notes, and I have found that it encourages students to visit my office in the future. I have also requested that they take pictures of their team during the hunt to build team cohesiveness. These pictures can be part of the scavenger hunt requirements (e.g., take a picture of your team in the library) or a way of documenting their team efforts and enjoyment (e.g., team selfie). For fun, you can offer various awards, such as the team with the most items, the most creative means of finding items, or the best team cohesiveness.

Students enjoy having the opportunity to step outside the classroom to complete the activity. However, you could just as easily create a version of the activity that can be done in the classroom or an online version in which all scavenger hunt items can be discovered on the Internet. For example, they might have to locate an article online about improving workplace friendships, find a blog on balancing work and family life, or find a research article on relationship maintenance in families. The variations and possibilities for this activity are virtually endless. You can truly tailor the hunt to fit just about any of your course goals.

Materials Needed: Each student needs a list of scavenger hunt items to find. It also helps if they have a phone or similar device for taking photos or videos as proof of their finds.

3. Feedback Illustration: A Drawing Activity

Submitted by: Julie Cajigas, The University of Akron

Related Topics: Communication models and feedback (Ch. 1)

Objective: To teach students about feedback and the role it plays in communication. By limiting students' ability to give feedback, they can see how much we depend on feedback to respond to and tailor our own communication.

Activity: Give each student a white sheet of paper and ask them to draw a picture of anything they would like, as complicated or as simple as they want. It can be any size and in the center, top, bottom, or corner of the page. Ask them not to show one another their drawings. Then split students into teams of two and designate each member as A or B. First, Student A will look at his or her own paper and tell Student B how to replicate his or her exact drawing. The goal is to create a drawing as similar as possible to Student A's original without looking at it. Student B will attempt to replicate it on a second sheet of paper. During this first round, Student B MAY NOT give any feedback, visually or verbally, to the student who is giving the instructions. After this step is completed, the two drawings should be pinned or taped up on a wall or board for everyone to see. Next, Student B will look at his or her own drawing and tell Student A how to replicate it exactly. The goal again is to create a drawing as similar as possible to Student B's original. This time, however, Student A is allowed to give the other student feedback during instructions, including asking questions. Tape or pin this round's drawings beneath each team's round-one drawings.

You can debrief the activity with the following discussion questions ask questions for the class: Was it easier to draw with or without the ability to ask questions? Did the accuracy of the drawings improve the second time? Was there any noise (psychological or physical) that impeded the drawing process? What does this tell us about feedback?

Materials Needed: Each student needs two plain sheets of paper and a pencil or pen.

4. Bad Habits We Learn from Facebook

Submitted by: Curt VanGeison, St. Charles Community College

Related Topics: Communication and technology (Chs. 1, 4, 7, 8, 9)

Objective: To get students thinking about the impact of technology on communication and how communicating through social media differs from face-to-face communication.

Activity: Ask students to break into small groups of four or five. Instruct them to brainstorm in their groups a list of 10 bad habits that people learn from Facebook. These habits should highlight some of the ill effects or pitfalls that can occur from Facebook use. Encourage students to consider how these bad habits might influence how others perceive them. You might want to provide a couple of examples to jump-start the process:

Example #1: Too much information (TMI). Many people overshare information about their personal lives on Facebook.

Example #2: Poor time management. It is very easy to lose track of one's time while socializing on Facebook, and hours at a time can be lost without even realizing it.

Allow 10–15 minutes for students to brainstorm. Afterwards, each group should share their lists with the rest of the class. You should anticipate some of the following responses:

- inappropriate friending
- posting of inappropriate photos
- indiscriminate downloading
- poor grammar skills
- not safeguarding personal information
- using Facebook as a channel for terminating relationships

Next, engage the class in a discussion about the bad habits that have been generated by asking some of the following questions:

- Which of these bad habits pertain to you?
- How might these habits influence how other people perceive you? For example, maybe the information you have posted will be looked at by a future employer.
- What is your perception of people who have these habits?
- What can be done to prevent or break these habits?

Materials Needed: Students need paper to write on and a pencil or pen.

Activity Guide   T-21

5. Halo or Horns?

Submitted by: Curt VanGeison, St. Charles Community College

Related Topics: Perception, Gestalts, and halo and horn effects (Ch. 3)

Objective: To teach students about the power of the halo effect and the horn effect, and to illustrate how these effects influence our perception of others.

Activity: Before class, create a slide-show presentation with images of various well-known people (politicians, famous athletes, movie stars, and so on). Some suggested people to use: Betty White, Lindsay Lohan, Stephen Colbert, Hillary Clinton, Michael Vick, Lady Gaga, Ellen DeGeneres, Paris Hilton, Justin Bieber, Taylor Swift, Ray Rice, Madonna, Jimmy Fallon, Oprah Winfrey, Kim Kardashian, Kanye West, and Tiger Woods.

In class, break students up into groups of four or five. Then show them the slides. As you show each image, give students one or two minutes to discuss in their groups whether their Gestalt of the pictured individual is representative of the halo effect or the horn effect. At the end of class, have each group share its responses with the whole class. Are there any figures who are polarizing—that is, some students apply the halo effect while others apply the horn effect? Conversely, are there any figures about whom the whole class is more or less in agreement? Ask students: What do these results tell you about how we perceive other people?

Materials Needed: A slide-show presentation of famous people (or, as an alternative, you could use handouts with photos of various famous people).

6. Mixed-Matched Emotions

Submitted by: Alicia Alexander, Southern Illinois University Edwardsville

Related Topics: Types of emotions, expressing emotions, and emotional intelligence (Ch. 4)

Objective: To help students understand the complexity of emotions. This activity encourages students to decipher the different types of emotions and reflect on the ways in which each is expressed. It also challenges students' emotional intelligence.

Activity: This activity was inspired by the board game Moods, which encourages players to accurately display their moods with a variety of interesting statements. To use in the classroom, students will work in groups to perform a selected statement based on a selected emotion.

Place students in groups of four or five, and give each group an envelope labeled "emotions" and an envelope labeled "statements." Students should also be given a sheet listing all the possible emotions in the envelope to reference during the game. You may want to take some time to define and discuss each emotion on the sheet before beginning the activity.

Tell students to take turns drawing one emotion and one statement from each envelope. Be sure other group members cannot see what was drawn until after the performance. Each student will take a turn performing the statement using the emotion drawn. For example, a student performer may select the statement, "I studied really hard for my exam today," and select the emotion "disappointment." The challenge of this game is that often the emotion drawn can be difficult to enact when it does not typically match the statement given (e.g., "I won the lottery" expressed with a sad emotional tone). Encourage students to use their voice, gestures, and facial expressions to best convey the emotion. Although group members may ask the student to repeat the performance, a statement can only be performed twice.

Group members should try to guess the emotion displayed by the performer based on the provided list of all possible emotions. Students should record their guess before the performer reveals the correct emotion. For fun and competition, students can keep score and give themselves points for each time they correctly identify a performer's emotion. Be sure each group member has a chance to perform at least once, and complete as many rounds as desired.

To debrief the activity as a class, you can discuss the following questions: What cues did you use to determine the emotion portrayed? What made this exercise challenging? Was it easier when the emotion naturally matched the statement, or more difficult? Are some group members harder to interpret? What emotions seemed very similar or very different from one another? Did you notice any blended emotions? What have you learned about your emotional intelligence from this activity?

Materials Needed: Each group will need two envelopes: one with 20 emotions written on separate slips of paper, and one with 15 statements written on separate slips of paper. Each student will also need a list of the Mixed-Matched Emotions Statements (noted below) to record their guesses on. Note: You may want to create your own list of statements or emotions that better suits your institution or students.

Mixed-Matched Emotions Statements

(To be cut into slips and placed in each group's "Statements" envelope)

1. I'm moving next year.
2. X is the best college.
3. I'm studying X major.
4. I love living in/near X city.
5. My cell phone is the best.
6. I eat pizza every day.
7. In my spare time, I like to X.
8. My boyfriend/girlfriend asked me to marry him/her.
9. I'm going out of town next weekend.
10. I have a paper due tomorrow.
11. My boyfriend/girlfriend broke up with me.
12. I have two wonderful roommates.
13. I'm taking two classes this summer.
14. My parents gave me this watch for my birthday.
15. Interpersonal communication is my favorite class.

Mixed-Matched Emotions

(To be cut into slips and placed in each group's "Emotions" envelope)

1. Surprise	8. Relieved	15. Nervous
2. Hope	9. Embarrassed	16. Confused
3. Grateful	10. Disappointed	17. Sad
4. Happy	11. Scared	18. Jealous
5. Love	12. Hate	19. Hurt
6. Excited	13. Worried	20. Guilty
7. Proud	14. Angry	

7. The Whole World as 100 People

Submitted by: Ashley Fitch Blair, Union University

Related Topics: Culture, communication, and perception (Ch. 3)

Objective: This exercise provides a nonthreatening shared experience that exposes perceptions about the world, as well as the accuracy of those perceptions. Students tend to be sharply divided between those who see the world in a very positive light and those who see the world in a decidedly negative light. This contrast can lead to great discussions about the formation and accuracy of our perceptions. Since the exercise also incorporates small-group discussion, it provides a great opportunity to discuss personal credibility and the influence others have on our perceptions.

Activity: In our hyperconnected world, it is sometimes difficult for students to differentiate between their perceptions and reality. The Whole World as 100 People asks the question: If we could shrink the earth's population to a village of precisely 100 people, with all the existing human ratios remaining the same, what would it look like?

Have students fill out The Whole World as 100 People worksheet (p. T-24) on their own. Then break them up into small groups so they have the opportunity to compare answers and make changes if they wish. Finally, bring the class back together to discuss the answers. Use the provided answer key for instructors to guide this discussion.

Materials Needed: The Whole World as 100 People worksheet (p. T-24) for students and the answer key for the instructor

Note: To encourage further discussion either before or after your students have completed the activity, consider showing a video that contemplates existing human ratios in a similar way, like the one found here: www.miniature-earth.com.

Name: _____
Date: _____
Section: _____

The Whole World as 100 People

WORKSHEET FOR STUDENTS

Directions: Make your best educated guess for each column below.

If we could shrink the earth's population to a village of precisely 100 people, with all the existing human ratios remaining the same, it would look like this:

_____ out of 100 would be unable to read

_____ out of 100 would suffer from malnutrition

_____ out of 100 would not have electricity

_____ out of 100 would have a college education

_____ out of 100 would be cell-phone subscribers

_____ out of 100 would live on less than 2 U.S. dollars a day

---

The following groups should each total 100 people:

_____ Asians

_____ Europeans

_____ North, South, & Central Americans

_____ Africans

_____ Female
_____ Male

_____ Urban dwellers
_____ Rural dwellers

_____ Christian
_____ Muslim
_____ Hindu
_____ Buddhist
_____ Other
_____ Atheist/Not identified with any religion

_____ 0–14-year-olds
_____ 15–64-year-olds
_____ 65+ year-olds

"The Whole World as 100 People" worksheet by Ashley Fitch Blair, Union University, as published in *Reflect & Relate,* Fourth Edition, by Steven McCornack

Answer Key for the Instructor

- **18** out of 100 would be unable to read
- **17** out of 100 would suffer from malnutrition
- **24** out of 100 would not have electricity
- **1** out of 100 would have a college education
- **34** out of 100 would be cell-phone subscribers
- **53** out of 100 would live on less than 2 U.S. dollars a day

The following groups should each total 100 people:

- **61** Asians
- **12** Europeans
- **14** North, South, & Central Americans
- **13** Africans

- **50** Female
- **50** Male

- **47** Urban dwellers
- **53** Rural dwellers

- **31** Christian
- **21** Muslim
- **14** Hindu
- **6** Buddhist
- **12** Other
- **16** Atheist/Not identified with any religion

- **20** 0–14-year-olds
- **66** 15–64-year-olds
- **14** 65+ year-olds

8. "Tell Me No Lies!": Deciphering Nonverbal Cues of Deception

Submitted by: Judith Vogel, Des Moines Area Community College

Related Topics: Communicating verbally (Ch. 7), communicating nonverbally (Ch. 8), perceiving others (Ch. 3), and listening (Ch. 6)

Objective: To identify the nonverbal cues typically associated with deceptive communication; to realize that some people are very good liars and that communicators should not rely just on nonverbal cues to determine if others are being truthful; and to use techniques such as perception-checking, asking questions, and evaluating verbal content to help verify truthfulness

Activity: Ask students to get into small groups of three or four. Tell them to share with their group either what they did last weekend or what they plan to do the coming weekend. Students must decide individually whether to tell the truth or to make up a lie (and should keep that decision to themselves). The other students in the group must listen and decide if the stories are the truth or lies. Students may ask questions of each storyteller. When everyone has had an opportunity to share, students announce which group members they think were telling the truth and which ones they think were lying. Then each student reveals if he or she was telling the truth or lying. After the revelations, the whole class can discuss why they felt their classmates were being truthful or not. Several of the typical nonverbal cues associated with lying should be mentioned. The surprise comes when some students are able to effectively lie to their classmates with few or no deceptive cues. That generates another discussion on not relying completely on nonverbal deceptive cues to decide if a person is telling the truth or lying and on identifying other techniques to discern truth tellers from liars.

9. Using Language Effectively

Submitted by: Rick Hogrefe, Crafton Hills College

Related Topics: Verbal communication (Ch. 7) and communication competence (Ch. 1)

Objective: To help students gain an awareness of the power of language by evaluating less interpersonally competent messages and crafting more interpersonally competent statements

Activity: In this activity, students analyze relational communication statements that are filled with examples of "I," "you," and "we" language errors, and other less interpersonally competent language. This is an engaging exercise because the statements are realistic but have upwards of 8 to 10 language errors. Give each student the Using Language Effectively worksheet (p. T-27), and ask them to read through the statements on their own. Then place students in small groups and have each group work on one statement and present their conclusions and revised statements to the class.

Materials Needed: The Using Language Effectively worksheet on page T-27

Name: _____
Date: _____
Section: _____

Using Language Effectively

WORKSHEET FOR STUDENTS

Directions: For each of the following statements, identify the words in the message that make it an example of incompetent communication, and then rewrite the statement to make it a more interpersonally competent message.

1. . . . to a classmate

"I'm kind of angry. That test . . . it was so unfair. The instructor should curve the grades, don't you think? But you always do well."

2. . . . to your roommate

"You are such a pig! This place is a total mess. You never take the trash out, and I always end up doing the dishes."

3. . . . to your younger brother

"I don't mean to be bossy, but you really need to pay closer attention to the road. They will never pass someone who drives like that."

4. . . . to a waitress

"Excuse me. Excuse me, ma'am! I have been waiting here patiently, but you continue to ignore me. I would sort of like some help."

5. . . . to your boss

"It was impossible. I thought your instructions were clear, but once I started the work, it was a total disaster. You should have done it yourself."

6. . . . to your neighbor

"You make me so mad. You never return things that you borrow. You should ask someone else for it. . . . Fine. Yes, I will lend you the drill, but I want it back tomorrow."

7. . . . to your instructor

"I hate to say this, sir. I wanted to finish the assignment, but I had a family situation and they would not let me get my work done. You understand, don't you?"

"Using Language Effectively" worksheet by Rick Hogrefe, Crafton Hills College, as published in *Reflect & Relate*, Fourth Edition, by Steven McCornack

10. Are You Connecting? The Power of Eye Contact

Submitted by: Lisa Miczo, Western Illinois University

Related Topics: Nonverbal communication (Ch. 8) and listening (Ch. 6)

Objective: To encourage students to understand the importance of nonverbal communication, specifically how powerful eye contact is in interactions with others

Activity: Ask students to converse with a partner for three two-minute increments (approximately six minutes total), changing their rate of eye contact at each two-minute mark. During the first two minutes, students will converse normally. This is relatively easy, unless someone suffers from communication anxiety. At the two-minute mark, interrupt briefly and tell them to converse over the next two minutes using uninterrupted direct eye contact. Warn them that this may be difficult, but you'd like them to give it their best effort. Students will squirm, look away, smile or laugh nervously, and so forth. Some may even refuse to follow directions because they are so uncomfortable. What this demonstrates is how aware we are when people ARE or ARE NOT looking at us and what a big difference it makes in how we relate to them and how we perceive they are responding to us. After those two minutes, interrupt them again and tell them to continue to converse normally for another two minutes, but this time with NO eye contact. This is also difficult, with students often "checking" to see if their partner is even looking at them because it feels so awkward. Students will often state that they suddenly found it difficult to actually hear what their partner was saying when they weren't looking at him or her. We don't realize how much information we get from another's facial expression, eye movement, and lip movement, but all these stimuli (and our attendance to them) influence how much we receive in the conversation and conversely, just how much we're missing.

After the conversations, you can guide a class discussion about how this activity influenced students' understanding of communication competence, appropriateness and effectiveness of eye contact, and the ways in which eye contact can confirm or disconfirm relational partners.

11. Artifact Application

Submitted by: Mary Haslerud Opp, University of North Dakota

Related Topics: Can be used throughout the semester

Objective: To help students understand course concepts by tying the material to their daily lives. This can increase interest in course concepts and help facilitate relationships in the classroom.

Activity: For each chapter, ask students to bring in to share with the rest of the class an "artifact." This is anything that relates to the material for the chapter, such as a short clip from a movie or television show, a song, a poem, a cartoon, or a story from their own life. It is usually helpful to remind students that their artifacts need to be acceptable to share in a classroom and follow any applicable institutional guidelines. When you get to the part of the chapter where their "artifact" applies, students should raise their hand and explain the artifact and how it ties in to the chapter. They should be able to show their artifact and explain its relevance in two minutes or less.

Materials Needed: Students' artifacts and any materials needed to display them (e.g., iPad, DVD player, or CD player). While many students will have their own personal electronic devices with which to display artifacts, it may be best to have DVD and CD players available for students who do not.

12. Identifying Approaches to Conflict

Submitted by: Ann Gross, Napa Valley College

Related Topics: Managing conflict, power, and interpersonal competence (Ch. 9)

Objective: To help students realize that most people are uncomfortable with conflict and that people often share approaches to conflict, from avoidance to aggression. This activity allows students to talk about a personal issue in a very open and nonthreatening way.

Activity: Collect several cross-cultural images that express a range of emotions. These could include pictures ranging from lightning storms and shark attacks to Betty Boop, a Buddha face, a group of people white-water rafting, Einstein sticking out his tongue, a boxer with gloves on, Bashful (one of Snow White's Seven Dwarfs), a charging elephant, an ostrich with its head in the sand, and so on. The idea is to provide enough variety so that every student is sure to find at least one image that resonates with his or her own experience. Spread out the images and have students choose one or two that represent their approach to conflict or how they feel/act when they get into conflict situations. Place students in a circle so that everyone can see one another and ask students to share their image and explain why they chose it. After everyone has shared, talk about the range of responses to conflict, from avoidance to humor, attack, and so forth. This leads to a discussion about how uncomfortable most of us are with conflict and why we need to learn more constructive ways to resolve conflicts. You can also ask students to discuss any trends about how people deal with conflict. Students love the exercise, and it allows them to share personal reactions in a clear and manageable way.

Materials Needed: Postcards, magazine photos, or pictures taken from online sources

13. Appropriate Apologies

Submitted by: Joyce Carey, Normandale Community College

Related Topics: Conflict (Ch. 9) and relationship maintenance (Chs. 10–12 and Appendix)

Objective: To help students learn the appropriate steps needed for a good apology

Activity: Ask students to think about a real situation in which they did something that they needed to apologize for. This could be something recent or in the past. Based on that situation, students will create an apology card. They may make their own, find a greeting card program online, or just rewrite a previous card they have received. Students should write out their apology (usually four to five lines) on the inside of the card. Students should use The Apology worksheet (p. T-31) to help them create a competent apology.

It is important to recognize that students have different artistic talents. When conducting this activity, you should inform your students that they will not be judged on their creativity or artistic abilities. Instead, the purpose of making the card is to help students express their ideas and connect with the person they wronged.

Materials Needed: The Apology worksheet on page T-31

Name: _____
Date: _____
Section: _____

The Apology

WORKSHEET FOR STUDENTS

An apology involves accepting responsibility for behavior while asking to be pardoned. Apologies are usually expected in predicaments that harm other people, and failing to apologize when others expect it makes the situation worse. Communicating an effective apology is a great skill for relationships.

Benefits of Apology

For the apology receiver:

- The person harmed can begin to heal emotionally.
- Apology helps the one hurt to move past anger and stop being stuck in the past.
- Apology opens the door to forgiveness by allowing the recipient to feel empathy for the wrongdoer.
- Apology creates the feeling that the wrongdoer is no longer a personal threat.

For the apology giver:

- Apologizing usually causes the giver to feel humiliated and thus acts as a deterrent to repeating the act.
- Remorse and shame can be debilitating for the wrongdoer, so admitting the wrong and taking responsibility for one's actions helps get rid of esteem-robbing guilt.

Assignment

Create a greeting card containing an apology for a real situation—something you did. You may make your own, find a greeting card program online, or just rewrite a previous card you have received.

Write out your apology (usually 4–5 lines) on the inside of the card. Remember these hints when writing your card:

- Make a clear statement of the action you are apologizing for.
- Clearly admit that you were wrong.
- Make a sincere expression of remorse.
- Make sure to offer an appropriate compensation or promise to change.
- Create a greeting card that is neat and creative.

"The Apology" worksheet by Joyce Carey, Normandale Community College, as published in *Reflect & Relate*, Fourth Edition, by Steven McCornack

14. Portrayals of Families in the Media

Submitted by: Alicia Alexander, Southern Illinois University Edwardsville

Related Topics: Relationships with family members, types of families, communication norms, dialectics, and relationship maintenance (Ch. 11)

Objective: To help students learn about the different types of family relationships. This activity also helps students apply various communication concepts to mediated examples of family relationships.

Activity: Give each student one copy of the Portrayals of Families in the Media worksheet on page T-33 and one copy of the Discussion Questions worksheet on page T-34. Have students read over the instructions at the top of the sheet, and ask them to think on their own about each category of family relationship types in the media for about a minute. Then place students in groups of four or five to complete the worksheet. In their groups, students should brainstorm for media portrayals of each of the family relationship types. For example, students might mention Alan as a single father on *Two and a Half Men* or Cam and Mitchell as an example of a gay family on *Modern Family*. In addition to writing the media examples, students should comment on the communication norms in each relationship role. For example, they might mention if the family experiences closeness, conflict, authoritative parenting styles, rigid boundaries, and so forth. Once the group has come up with at least a few examples for each relationship type, they should discuss the four questions on the Discussion Questions worksheet.

Ask each group to pick one example of each relationship type to share with the class. Then have each group choose a representative to share the group's responses to the four discussion questions. You can follow up with a class discussion of the following questions: Do you believe the media accurately portrays family communication today? Why or why not? What relationship type in families would you like to see more of in the media today? You will likely find that students have strong opinions about the media's inaccurate or accurate portrayals of families.

Materials Needed: Each student needs a copy of the Portrayals of Families in the Media worksheet (p. T-33) as well as the Discussion Questions worksheet (p. T-34) and a pen or pencil.

Name: _____
Date: _____
Section: _____

Portrayals of Families in the Media

WORKSHEET FOR STUDENTS

Directions: With your group members, brainstorm media portrayals of each of the following relationship types in families. Try to come up with at least one television or film example for each category. In addition to writing down media examples, you should comment on the communication norms common for each relationship role. Once you have completed your list, work with your group to record your responses on the Discussion Questions worksheet.

Relationship	1970s	1980s	1990s	2000–2010	2010–present
Father					
Mother					
Children					
Single-Parent					
Stepfamilies					
Extended Families					
Family Friends					
Inter ethnic Families					
Gay or Lesbian Families					

Name: _____
Date: _____
Section: _____

Discussion Questions for Portrayals of Families in the Media

WORKSHEET FOR STUDENTS

1. Which family relationship type was the hardest to find in the media? Which was the easiest? Why do you think that was the case?

2. What types of relationship maintenance strategies are used in the examples that you listed?

3. What dialectical tensions did you observe in the examples that you listed?

4. How does the media's portrayal of each relationship type in families differ from the earlier time periods to the later time periods?

15. Family Fun Food Day

Submitted by: Alicia Alexander, Southern Illinois University Edwardsville

Related Topics: Family communication (Ch. 11) and culture and communication (Ch. 5)

Objective: To encourage students to share and learn about family traditions and culture

Activity: Family Fun Food Day is an enjoyable activity to do as a way to celebrate the end of the semester. The event involves having students bring in a food item to share that represents a family ritual or tradition or their cultural heritage.

I give my students the following instructions and an index card: "Please bring a dish to share with the class (approximately 30 people) that represents a food ritual in your family. The dish could be a dessert, a side dish, candy, a drink (nonalcoholic, of course!), or any other food that has special meaning to your family. It can be something that represents your culture, a birthday, Christmas, Hanukkah, Thanksgiving, or any other celebration or ritual that your family recognizes. It can be store bought or handmade, depending on your culinary skills! I've had students make homemade pies from scratch, and I've had students bring store-bought chips and salsa. I even had a student bring McDonald's chicken nuggets to represent his grandma's famous fried chicken. Please bring your food along with a filled-out index card. On the front side of the card, you should provide your name and a short explanation of why this food item is special to your family. On the back side of the card, please write the name of the food, main ingredients, and any possible food allergens (e.g., peanuts). I will bring plates, napkins, and utensils, but please bring a special serving utensil if needed for your dish."

On the day of the event, I usually try to move the desks into a big circle to represent a large family dining table. While eating all of the delicious food, we go around the room, giving each student an opportunity to explain what they brought and the story behind the food. Once everyone has enjoyed the food, I like to ask the following discussion questions to the class or ask them to share their personal answers to the following questions in small groups:

1. Based on the class presentations of the food items, what themes can you identify?
2. How does food serve as a source of meaning-making in families?
3. What patterns of "dinner talk" are there in families (e.g., parents speak only, question and answer, very little conversation, "highs and lows" for the day)?
4. What rules are associated with food in families?
5. What roles are associated with food in families?
6. How does food contribute to the organization of families?
7. What elements of cultural identities are evident in the stories told about food?

8. How does food bond and connect generations?
9. What new discoveries did you make about food, family, and culture during this activity?

Materials Needed: Napkins, plates, silverware, cups, and materials for cleanup. You will also need index cards for the student's story of the food item and recipe or ingredient list.

16. Exploring Relationships

Submitted by: Joyce Carey, Normandale Community College

Related Topics: Relationships such as friendship, family, or romantic (Chs. 10–12)

Objective: To encourage students to explore their relationships and to understand how each relationship has unique differences in communication

Activity: Provide each student with five index cards. Students should write the name of a person with whom they have an important relationship on one side of each card. Tell students that they will share information about the people they list with a small group, as this may affect what names they choose to write down. Students will rank how important these relationships are by putting the card with the name of the person who is LEAST IMPORTANT to them on top. The second least important person should be second from the top, and so on. The bottom card in the pile should be the name of the person that is MOST IMPORTANT to students.

Then divide students into groups of five or six. Each group member will turn over their cards (starting with the top one) and answer the following questions about their relationship with that person:

Card #1 (Top)

- What type of relationship is this? (How many types of relationships can you come up with as a group?)
- Describe your communication with the person listed. What are the key subjects you typically discuss?

Card #2

- If this relationship was a movie, what would it be called? Why?
- What are the positive and negative aspects of this relationship?

Card #3

- How do you feel when you are around this person?
- What does this person confirm about how you feel about yourself?
- On a scale of 1 to 10 (1 = superficial information, 10 = deep disclosure), how much do you disclose to this person?

Card #4

- What needs does this relationship fulfill for you?
- How intimate do you consider this relationship? Why? How is that intimacy expressed?

Card #5 (Bottom)

- How would your life be different if you didn't have this relationship?
- How is your disclosure with this person different from that with the person on Card #1?
- What do you like and dislike about the way you and this person communicate with each other?

Materials Needed: Five index cards per student. (Students could also just tear a piece of paper into five slips.)

17. Analyzing Political Debates

Submitted by: Susan Kilgard, Anne Arundel Community College

Related Topics: Communication competence and communication models (Ch. 1), self-presentation (Ch. 2), perception (Ch. 3), cooperative verbal communication (Ch. 7), and nonverbal communication (Ch. 8)

Objective: Though rehearsed media events like political debates are not typically interactions we would define as "interpersonal communication," they allow students a fascinating opportunity to extend their study of human communication using scholarly perspectives. Since this activity covers a variety of topics, students will understand how interpersonal concepts work together in everyday life and even in a mass communication context.

Activity: This is an extra-credit assignment in my course during presidential election years, but it could also be easily transitioned during any semester into a paper assignment or class discussion by accessing previous political debates online. Students receive the Analyzing Political Debates worksheet (p. T-38) to guide their reports.

Materials Needed: Analyzing Political Debates worksheet on page T-38

Name: _____
Date: _____
Section: _____

Analyzing Political Debates

WORKSHEET FOR STUDENTS

Directions: You must watch an entire presidential or primary debate and then write an analysis paper. (For more information about potential debates, refer to the Commission on Presidential Debates: www.debates.org.) In your paper, you must answer three out of the following five questions:

1. **Mediated vs. face-to-face communication:** A study by communications researchers William Benoit and Glenn Hansen (*Communication Research Reports*, Spring 2004) examined how U.S. voters use different media to learn about candidates, since very few of us actually get a chance to communicate with candidates interpersonally. These scholars studied all the presidential campaigns from 1952 through 2000 and found that for learning about candidates, the

   - use of **newspapers** has **dropped** over time.
   - use of **radio** has **dropped** over time.
   - use of **debates** has **dropped** over time.
   - use of **television** had no clear trend over time.
   - use of **magazines** had no clear trend over time.
   - use of **political discussion with others** has **increased significantly** over time.

   Based on the debate you just watched, why do you think the interpersonally based method of learning about candidates was the only one to become more popular with American voters between 1952 and 2000? Why do you adhere to that opinion? Also, discuss how the newest generation of voters (citizens turning 18 recently or in the near future) might prefer to learn about the candidates, including ways of receiving information that these two researchers did not include in their study. This answer should be approximately one typed page.

   For Questions 2–5: Make each key term **bold** and <u>underlined</u> in your paper. One typed page minimum per item.

2. Use **five** of the following key terms to reflect on any aspect(s) of the debate you just watched:

channel	context	self-monitoring
communication competence	feedback	field of experience
message	noise	

3. Use **five** of the following key terms to reflect on any aspect(s) of the debate you just watched:

face	mask	interpretation
interpersonal impressions	selection	empathy
attributions	organization	

4. Use **five** of the following key terms to reflect on any aspect(s) of the debate you just watched:

cooperative verbal communication	speech acts	communication accommodation theory
denotative language	"I" language	"we" language
connotative language	"you" language	

5. Use **five** of the following key terms to reflect on any aspect(s) of the debate you just watched:

power	kinesics	physical appearance
vocalics	emblems	
proxemics	mixed messages	

"Analyzing Political Debates" worksheet by Susan Kilgard, Anne Arundel Community College, as published in *Reflect & Relate*, Fourth Edition, by Steven McCornack

18. Making Relationship Choices and You

Submitted by: Alicia Alexander, Southern Illinois University Edwardsville

Related Topics: *Making Relationship Choices* feature throughout all chapters; this activity should take place near the end of the semester

Objective: To build empathy in students and encourage them to reflect on what they've learned during the semester

Activity: This activity is for instructors who assign the *Making Relationship Choices* (*MRC*) feature for each chapter throughout the semester. The activity should take place near the end of the course, after students have read and watched all of the *MRCs*. Ask students to choose the one *MRC* feature that they personally relate to the most or that resonates with them the most. Then split students into groups of four or five and have them discuss. Each student should talk about why he or she chose that *MRC* feature, how he or she relates to the situation in the *MRC*, and what real-life experiences he or she has had that are similar.

Materials Needed: No materials are needed in class, but students should come prepared, having watched all the *MRC* videos and completed all the *MRC* activities.

What is your best friend/sister/coworker/dad REALLY thinking?

Making Relationship Choices videos take communication to the next level

The *Making Relationship Choices* feature has been expanded to include new, professionally shot videos of challenging interpersonal situations and self-assessment questions on LaunchPad, making the experience even more engaging. Now you'll be able to:

- **Read** the *Making Relationship Choices* background in the text or e-book.
- **React** to the situation.
- **Watch** a video called "The Other Side," which shows an alternative point of view.
- **Consider** that there are two sides to every encounter.
- **Reevaluate** your initial response through self-assessment questions.
- **Build** a deeper sense of empathy and understanding.

▶ How would you react to your best friend who's been making some questionable choices and posting about it on Facebook?

▶ What's the deal with the guy in your study group who's always late to meetings and doesn't seem to take the group seriously?

◀ Things have been tense between you and your brother since your grandmother died—and now he's not even speaking to you.

◀ Your cousin Britney crashed her car and dropped out of college…. Ugh.

▶ You've never been that close with your dad, but things got worse last weekend.

▶ Your friend Karina is back from the Peace Corps, but she's not the same.

Making Relationship Choices by chapter

Chapter 1: Introducing Interpersonal Communication: Kaitlyn's story
Chapter 2: Considering Self: Jonathan's story
Chapter 3: Perceiving Others: Dylan's story
Chapter 4: Experiencing and Expressing Emotions: Sam's story
Chapter 5: Understanding Culture: Mom's story
Chapter 6: Listening Actively: Ana's story
Chapter 7: Communicating Verbally: Britney's story
Chapter 8: Communicating Nonverbally: Dakota's story
Chapter 9: Managing Conflict and Power: Devdas's story
Chapter 10: Relationships with Romantic Partners: Javi's story
Chapter 11: Relationships with Family Members: Dad's story
Chapter 12: Relationships with Friends: Karina's story

Reflect & Relate

an introduction to interpersonal communication

Reflect & Relate

an introduction to interpersonal communication

FOURTH EDITION

Steven McCornack
The University of Alabama at Birmingham

Instructor's Annotations by Alicia Alexander
Southern Illinois University Edwardsville

Instructor's Annotated Edition

Bedford/St. Martin's
A Macmillan Education Imprint

Boston • New York

For Bedford/St. Martin's

Vice President, Editorial, Macmillan Higher Education Humanities: Edwin Hill
Publisher for Communication: Erika Gutierrez
Development Manager: Susan McLaughlin
Senior Developmental Editor: Lorraina Morrison
Project Editor: Won McIntosh
Production Manager: Joe Ford
Marketing Manager: Kayti Corfield
Editorial Assistant: Will Stonefield
Director of Rights and Permissions: Hilary Newman
Senior Art Director: Anna Palchik
Text Design: Jerilyn Bockorick
Cover Design: John Callahan
Cover Images: © Tetra Images/Getty Images; © Hemera Technologies/Getty Images
Composition: Cenveo Publisher Services
Printing and Binding: RR Donnelley and Sons

Copyright © 2016, 2013, 2010, 2007 by Bedford/St. Martin's

All rights reserved. No part of this book may be reproduced, stored in a retrieval system, or transmitted in any form or by any means, electronic, mechanical, photocopying, recording, or otherwise, except as may be expressly permitted by the applicable copyright statutes or in writing by the Publisher.

Manufactured in the United States of America.

0   9   8   7   6   5
f   e   d   c   b   a

For information, write: Bedford/St. Martin's, 75 Arlington Street, Boston, MA 02116 (617-399-4000)

ISBN 978-1-4576-9718-0 (Student Edition)
ISBN 978-1-319-01967-9 (Loose-leaf Edition)
ISBN 978-1-4576-9719-7 (Instructor's Annotated Edition)

Acknowledgments

Test Your Self-Monitoring, p. 23 Mark Snyder, adapted from "Self-monitoring of expressive behavior," *Journal of Personality and Social Psychology,* 1974, Volume 30, Issue 4 (Oct). Copyright © 1974 by the American Psychological Association. Used by permission of the American Psychological Association.

Credo of the National Communication Association, p. 24 *The Credo of the National Communication Association.* Reprinted with permission of the National Communication Association.

The Big Five Personality Traits (OCEAN), p. 84 O. P. John and Sanjay Srivastava, from *The Big-Five Trait Taxonomy: History, Measurement, and Theoretical Perspectives.* Reprinted by permission of Dr. Oliver P. John.

Making You Noise, p. 339 Francesca Bell, "Making You Noise." First appeared in *Nimrod.* Copyright © Francesca Bell. Used by permission of the author.

Art acknowledgments and copyrights appear on the same page as the art selections they cover. It is a violation of the law to reproduce these selections by any means whatsoever without the written permission of the copyright holder.

At the time of publication, all Internet URLs published in this text were found to accurately link to their intended Web site. If you do find a broken link, please forward the information to will.stonefield@macmillan.com so that it can be corrected for the next printing.

preface

One of the greatest blessings we all experience as teachers of interpersonal communication is the chance to connect with an array of interesting, complicated, and diverse people. Each term, a new window of contact opens. As we peer through it on that first day, we see the faces of those who will comprise our class. They are strangers to us at that moment—an enigmatic group distinguished only by visible differences in skin, hair, and mode of dress. But over the weeks that follow, they become individuated *people*. We learn the names that symbolize their now-familiar faces, as well as their unique cultural identities: the intersection of ethnicity, gender identity, sexual orientation, religion, nationality, age, and economic background that comprises each of them. And because it's an *interpersonal* class, we also learn their *stories*: the tragedies that linger in sadness etched upon their brows; the aspirations that urge them to lean forward in knowledge-anticipation. Then the term ends, the window closes, and the shade is drawn. All that remains are the afterimages imprinted on the retina of our memories: Alex, who came out of the closet—but only to you; Sonia, who struggled to surmount stereotypes of her Pakistani ancestry; Lourdes, who, as the first in her family to attend college, brought to your class all the hopes and dreams of multiple generations.

This seemingly limitless breadth of cultural variation should evoke a sense of unbridgeable distance. But instead, these people whom we come to call *our* students share a common bond that serves to connect them: *they all want to improve their relationships.* They bring to our classes romantic heartbreaks, battles with family members, and betrayals of friends; and they look to us to give them practical, relevant knowledge that will empower them to choose wisely in dealing with these challenges. The skills and knowledge that we provide transform their lives in powerful, constructive ways. The legacy of such impact is found in their e-mails and Facebook messages to us months, and even years, later: "I just wanted you to know that your class changed my life."

It is this combination of cultural diversity, commonality in goals and concerns, and potential for transformative impact that compelled me to write *Reflect & Relate,* Fourth Edition. But to understand the fourth edition, you need to know the backstory of the editions that precede it. When I wrote the first edition of *Reflect & Relate,* I wanted to provide my fellow teachers and their students with a textbook that was welcoming, friendly, personal, trustworthy, and practical— a book that was rock solid in content, represented the finest of new and classic scholarship in our discipline, and provided a clear sense of the field as a domain of scientific endeavor, not just "common sense." I also wanted a book that didn't read like a typical textbook but was so engaging that students might read through entire chapters before they realized they had done so. And, of course, my core mission: a book that didn't just tell students what to do but taught students *how* to systematically reason through interpersonal communication challenges. Students could walk away from reading it knowing how to solve their own problems and flexibly adapt to dynamic changes in contexts and relationships. I also had a very particular view of how I wanted to treat *culture*. Given that cultural variation permeates nearly every aspect of our interpersonal lives, I wanted to have cultural content integrated seamlessly *throughout* the text, rather than sequestered into a single chapter.

As the years have gone by, however, I've come to realize that coverage of culture within the book should reflect our (and our students') *true* experience of culture. Culture isn't just *broadly* disseminated *across* our daily lives; *culture runs deep*. Our cultural backgrounds play a fundamental role in shaping our perceptions, our emotions, our communication, and our relationships. This idea of "culture broad *and* deep" served as the guiding metaphor for my revision: cover cultural applications across all chapters, but also have a chapter devoted to deeply exploring culture. The single biggest change returning users will find in this edition is the inclusion of a new culture chapter, where they'll find classic and new scholarship related to the impact of cultural difference on interpersonal communication and relationships, including coverage of collectivism and individualism, uncertainty avoidance, power distance, masculinity and femininity, prejudice, ethnocentrism, and world-mindedness.

At the same time, the fourth edition also contains a ton of new and recent research representing the very best of interpersonal scholarship, including coverage of online competence, the impact of mobile devices on intimacy and disclosure, self-concept clarity, empathy mind-sets, anxiety and emotional contagion, the neuroscience of romantic passion, and blended families. Scores of new examples—*Girls*, *Breaking Bad*, and *The Babadook*, to name a few—will resonate with students and illustrate key concepts for them. Meanwhile, the new *Instructor's Annotated Edition* offers more instructional support than ever before.

Also new to the fourth edition is the exciting evolution of the flagship feature of the book: *Making Relationship Choices*. Traditionally, this exercise has challenged students with a perplexing case study in which they must reason through to an optimal solution. For this edition of *Reflect & Relate*, we have added a potent and provocative twist: students read the "story" of the situation and generate a communicative solution, but *then* they have the opportunity to go online and see "The Other Side" of the story, as told in a video recording by the other person in the situation. Subsequently, students can revisit their initial thought on a solution to assess whether it's still the most competent way of dealing with the situation. This feature provides an unprecedented opportunity for students to build and refine their perspective-taking and empathy skills.

I'm thrilled about all that *Reflect & Relate*, Fourth Edition has to offer you and your students, and I would love to hear what you think about this new edition. Please feel free to drop me a line at **smcc911@uab.edu** or on Facebook so that we can chat about the book and the course, or just talk shop about teaching interpersonal communication.

What's New in the Fourth Edition?

The Fourth Edition of *Reflect & Relate* is truly modern and digital-forward, covering the most important topics in interpersonal communication and connecting them to digital media.

- **Culture! Expanded coverage of culture in a new chapter, and *Focus on Culture* features throughout all chapters.** Since culture permeates every aspect of interpersonal communication, *Reflect & Relate*, Fourth Edition, devotes a chapter to this vital topic. This chapter explores the definitions of *culture* and *co-cultures*, and also dives into specific topics, such as emotional displays, views of time, overcoming prejudice, communication accommodation, and regional dialects. Culture is also covered in other chapters, both in text sections and in *Focus on Culture* boxes, addressing the importance of students being aware of how culture influences interpersonal communication.

- **New videos for the *Making Relationship Choices* feature now help students see a different point of view.** Unique to *Reflect & Relate*, the *Making Relationship Choices* feature presents a challenging interpersonal situation and then helps students reason through it by drawing on the knowledge and skills they've acquired from the text and the course. In the fourth edition, *Making Relationship Choices* has been expanded to include brand-new, professionally shot videos and multimedia content on LaunchPad to make the experience even more engaging. Each video shows the communication partner's point of view; the confessional-style videos express the thoughts and feelings of your best friend, your sister, your coworker, your dad, and other important people in your life. Raw and emotional, the videos provide a window into what the other person is really thinking, and help students practice perspective-taking and build empathy.

- **Extensive coverage of computer-mediated communication** meets students where they are: online. Our modes of communication are changing. Whether via app, text, tweet, or note, learning appropriate digital communication skills is vital to successful communication. Specific examples dedicated to computer-mediated communication help students refine and improve their pervasive use of communication technologies.

- **Access to LaunchPad, a dynamic and easy-to-use platform.** LaunchPad makes instructors' lives easier by putting everything in one place, combining the full e-book with carefully chosen videos, quizzes, activities, instructor's resources, and LearningCurve adaptive quizzing. LaunchPad allows instructors to create reading, video, or quiz assignments in seconds, as well as VideoTools that enable students to embed their own videos or custom content. Instructors can also keep an eye on their students' progress throughout the semester.

(From top to bottom) Amy Eckert/Getty Images; © Mika/Corbis; China Photos/Getty Images; © David Grossman/The Image Works

ix

Reflect & Relate offers lots of new content in areas that interest students the most

Topics like multitasking online, the impact of mobile devices on intimacy and disclosure, social media, and supportive communication can be found in every chapter. This new content reflects issues of concern for today's students and represents the very best scholarship within the field of interpersonal communication.

- **Current, powerful stories and images hook students' interest.** *Reflect & Relate* is full of new, current, and relatable examples that students will want to read. The text and photo program pulls from pop culture—everything from *Scandal*, *Orange Is the New Black*, and *The Dallas Buyer's Club* to *Game of Thrones*—as well as current events and real stories from the author and his students to provide content that resonates with students and is easy to show and discuss in class.

- **New chapter openers feature a diverse group of contributors who share compelling** stories about the impact of interpersonal communication in everyday life. New openers include an interview with the dean of a "Santa School," Jennifer Andrews, on the important role of listening; and an exploration of the friendships in *SpongeBob SquarePants*. The chapter openers share appealing stories that students can look to, learn from, and use to transform their own lives and relationships.

Flagship Features

Reflect & Relate Offers an Accessible, Innovative Look at the Discipline

- ***Reflect & Relate* presents a fresh perspective on interpersonal communication.** Discussions of classic and cutting-edge scholarship from interpersonal communication, psychology, sociology, philosophy, and linguistics are woven together. Unlike other texts, *Reflect & Relate* continues to focus on how these concepts are linked to interpersonal communication and how communication skills can be improved.

- ***Reflect & Relate* balances current topics with classic coverage.** The text integrates coverage of social media, workplace bullying, multitasking online, and other novel topics with familiar topics like self-awareness, conflict approaches, and nonverbal communication codes.

- **Integrated discussions on culture and gender appear in every chapter.** *Reflect & Relate* treats individual and cultural influences as integral parts of the story by discussing the myths and realities of how race, gender, ethnicity, sexual orientation, religion, and age shape communication. In the fourth edition, new examples and updated coverage include the differences between high- and low-context cultures, and how gender equality and inequality around the world influence power.

- *Reflect & Relate* **offers clear explanations, engaging examples, and an attractive art program.** The text is truly a page-turner, engaging students' interest with compelling writing. Nearly every major concept is illustrated with examples drawn from pop culture, history, current events, and everyday life—examples that reflect the diversity of students themselves in terms of age, gender, lifestyle, occupation, and culture. Meanwhile, the appealing and pedagogically sound art program works with the examples to grab students' attention and focus them on the subject at hand.

Reflect & Relate Helps Students Look More Deeply at Themselves—and Develop Skills for a Lifetime

- *Self-Reflection* **questions foster critical self-awareness.** Self-awareness is essential for competent communication, and carefully placed *Self-Reflection* questions show students how to examine their own experiences and communication in light of theory and research. As a result, students gain a better understanding of concepts—such as emotional intelligence, stereotyping, and relationship ethics—and of themselves. They also learn the habit of ongoing critical self-reflection, which can lead to better communication outcomes.

- *Skills Practice* **exercises strengthen students' abilities.** Every chapter includes three *Skills Practice* exercises—one devoted to online communication—that give step-by-step instruction on practical skills, such as appropriately self-disclosing and interpreting nonverbal codes. *Skills Practice* activities are specifically designed to make it easy for students to implement them in their everyday lives.

- *Focus on Culture* **boxes and** *Self-Quiz* **exercises help students gain knowledge about their own communication.** *Focus on Culture* boxes challenge students to think about how the influence of their own culture shapes their communication. Rooted in research, *Self-Quiz* exercises help students analyze their strengths and weaknesses so that they can focus on how to improve their communication.

Reflect & Relate Helps Students Improve Their Relationships

- **Romantic, family, friend, and workplace relationships are explored.** Tailoring communication strategies to specific relationships is both essential and challenging, so *Reflect & Relate* devotes three full chapters and an appendix to these key communication contexts, giving students in-depth knowledge along with practical strategies for using communication to improve their relationships. Special emphasis is given to relationship maintenance—a key relational concern many students bring to the classroom.

- **Unique** *Making Relationship Choices* **case studies take application to a new level.** These activities challenge students to draw on their knowledge when facing difficult relationship issues and to create their own solutions.

(From top to bottom) SHONDALAND/ABC STUDIOS/THE KOBAL COLLECTION; Jessica Miglio/© Netflix/Everett Collection; Anne Marie Fox/© Focus Features/Everett Collection; Helen Sloan/© HBO/Courtesy: Everett Collection

xi

Instead of just asking students "What would you do?" or offering them solutions, *Making Relationship Choices* teaches students how to systematically reason through problems in order to generate their own constructive solutions. Students walk step-by-step through realistic scenarios—critically self-reflecting, considering others' perspectives, determining best outcomes, and identifying potential roadblocks—to make informed communication decisions. They then have the opportunity to experience "The Other Side" of the story by going online to hear and see a first-person account of the situation by watching a video. Becoming aware of both sides of the story allows students to reevaluate their initial reaction and response.

A Multifaceted Digital Experience Brings It All Together

LaunchPad helps students learn, study, and apply communication concepts.

Digital resources for *Reflect & Relate* are available in LaunchPad, a dynamic new platform that combines a collection of relevant video clips, self-assessments, e-book content, and LearningCurve adaptive quizzing in a simple design. LaunchPad can be packaged at a significant discount with *Reflect & Relate*, or it can be purchased separately.

- **NEW *Making Relationship Choices* videos** help students see "The Other Side" of the scenario, helping them develop empathy.

- **LearningCurve provides adaptive quizzing and a personalized learning program.** In every chapter, call-outs prompt students to tackle the game-like LearningCurve quizzes to test their knowledge and reinforce learning of the material. Based on research as to how students learn, LearningCurve motivates students to engage with course materials, while the reporting tools let you see what content students have mastered, allowing you to adapt your teaching plan to their needs.

- **LaunchPad videos help students see concepts in action and encourage self-reflection.** The LaunchPad video feature connects theories in the text with online video illustrations that help students understand interpersonal communication. Videos, including new clips on Culture and Mediated Communication, help students *see* theory in action, while accompanying reflection questions help them *apply* it to their own experiences. More than 70 video activities are easily assignable and make useful journal prompts or discussion starters. An interactive feature, each video activity includes two reflection questions that encourage students to consider how the concepts may impact their own relationships and lives. For ideas on how to integrate video into your course, see the *Instructor's Annotated Edition* and the Instructor's Resource Manual. To access the videos, and for a complete list of available clips, see page 458 or visit **macmillanhighered.com/reflectrelate4e**.

- **VideoTools makes it easy to create assignments and evaluate videos.** The functionality of VideoTools enables instructors to create video assignments. Instructors and students can add video, use time-based comments to discuss video, and assess video using rubrics.

Digital and Print Formats

Whether it's print, digital, or a value option, choose the best format for you. For more information on these resources, please visit the online catalog at **macmillanhighered.com/reflectrelate4e/catalog**.

LaunchPad for *Reflect & Relate* is a new platform that dramatically enhances teaching and learning. LaunchPad combines the full e-book, videos, quizzes and self-assessments, instructor's resources, and LearningCurve adaptive quizzing. To get access to all multimedia resources, package LaunchPad at a significant discount with a print book or order LaunchPad on its own.

***Reflect & Relate* is available as a print text.** To get the most out of the book, package LaunchPad at a significant discount with the text.

The Loose-leaf Edition of *Reflect & Relate* features the same print text in a convenient, budget-priced format, designed to fit into any three-ring binder. The loose-leaf version can be packaged at a significant discount with LaunchPad.

***Reflect & Relate* e-book option.** The e-book *for Reflect & Relate* includes the same content as the print book and allows students to add their own notes and highlight important information. Instructors can customize the e-book by adding their own content and deleting or rearranging the chapters.

Resources for Students and Instructors

For more information on these resources or to learn about package options, please visit the online catalog at **macmillanhighered.com/reflectrelate4e/catalog**.

Resources for Students

The Essential Guide to Intercultural Communication, by Jennifer Willis-Rivera (University of Wisconsin, River Falls). This brief and useful guide offers an overview of key communication areas—including perception, verbal and nonverbal communication, interpersonal relationships, and organizations—from a uniquely intercultural perspective.

***The Essential Guide to Group Communication*, Second Edition**, by Dan O'Hair (University of Kentucky) and Mary Wiemann (Santa Barbara City College). This concise and incisive text explains the role of group communication within organizations and other settings, and contains useful guidelines for acting as an effective leader, avoiding groupthink, and achieving optimal results.

The Essential Guide to Rhetoric, by William M. Keith (University of Wisconsin, Milwaukee) and Christian O. Lundberg (University of North Carolina, Chapel Hill). Written by two leaders in the communication field, this concise guide combines concrete, relevant examples with jargon-free language to provide an accessible and balanced overview of key historical and contemporary rhetorical theories.

Media Career Guide: Preparing for Jobs in the 21st Century, **Tenth Edition**, by Sherri Hope Culver (Temple University). Practical, student friendly, and revised to include the most recent statistics on the job market, this guide includes a comprehensive directory of media jobs, practical tips, and career guidance for students considering a major in the media industry.

Resources for Instructors

For more information or to order or download the instructor's resources, please visit the online catalog. The Instructor's Resource Manual, Test Bank, and lecture slides are also available on LaunchPad: **macmillanhighered.com/reflectrelate4e**.

Instructor's Annotated Edition for Reflect & Relate, **Fourth Edition,** edited by Alicia Alexander (Southern Illinois University Edwardsville). A valuable resource for instructors with any level of experience, the comprehensive *Instructor's Annotated Edition* provides more than 120 suggestions for activities and assignments, recommendations for videos and Web sites that illustrate course concepts, and tips for starting in-class discussions. In addition, a special introduction from author Steven McCornack at the front of the *Instructor's Annotated Edition* provides insight into how the book works, while the Activity Guide—a collection of classroom activities submitted by interpersonal communication instructors around the country—is sure to spark ideas for innovative activities in your classroom.

Online Instructor's Resource Manual for Reflect & Relate, **Fourth Edition,** by Curt VanGeison (St. Charles Community College), Joseph Ortiz (Scottsdale Community College), and Marion Boyer (Kalamazoo Valley Community College, Emeritus). The comprehensive Instructor's Resource Manual is available on LaunchPad and from the Instructor Resources tab at **macmillanhighered.com/reflectrelate/catalog**. It includes teaching notes on managing an interpersonal communication course, organization, and assessment; sample syllabi; advice on addressing ESL and intercultural issues; and tips for using the pedagogical features of *Reflect & Relate*. In addition, a teaching guide provides suggestions for implementing the book's thorough coverage of cultural issues. Every chapter also includes lecture outlines and class discussion starters, class and group exercises, assignment suggestions, video and music recommendations, and Web site links.

Computerized Test Bank for Reflect & Relate, **Fourth Edition,** by Charles J. Korn (Northern Virginia Community College). Available on LaunchPad and from the Instructor Resources tab at **macmillanhighered.com/reflectrelate/catalog**, the

Test Bank is one of the largest for the introductory interpersonal communication course, with more than 100 multiple-choice, true/false, short-answer, and essay questions for every chapter. This easy-to-use Test Bank also identifies the level of difficulty for each question, includes the number of the page on which the answer is found, and connects every question to a learning objective.

Teaching Interpersonal Communication, **Second Edition,** by Elizabeth J. Natalle (University of North Carolina–Greensboro) and Alicia Alexander (Southern Illinois University Edwardsville). Written by award-winning instructors, this essential resource provides all the tools instructors need to develop, teach, and manage a successful interpersonal communication course. New and seasoned instructors alike will benefit from the practical advice, scholarly insight, suggestions for integrating research and practice into the classroom—as well as the new chapter dedicated to teaching online.

Coordinating the Communication Course: A Guidebook, **by Deanna Fassett and John Warren.** This guidebook offers the most practical advice on every topic central to the coordinator/director role. Starting with setting a strong foundation, this professional resource continues on with thoughtful guidance, tips, and best practices on such crucial topics as creating community across multiple sections, orchestrating meaningful assessment, and hiring and training instructors. Model course materials, recommended readings, and insights from successful coordinators make this resource a must-have for anyone directing a course in communication.

Lecture slides for *Reflect & Relate* provide support for important concepts addressed in each chapter, including graphics of key figures and questions for class discussion. The slides are available for download on LaunchPad and from the Instructor Resources tab at **macmillanhighered.com/reflectrelate/catalog**.

Acknowledgments

I would like to thank everyone at Bedford/St. Martin's who was involved in this project and whose support made it possible, especially Macmillan Higher Education Vice President of Editorial Edwin Hill, Publisher Erika Gutierrez, Development Manager Susan McLaughlin, and Managing Editor Elise Kaiser. A very special shout-out goes to Senior Editor Lorraina Morrison and Freelance Editor Karen Schultz Moore for all their unflagging optimism, brilliant insights, and perseverance. I could not have done it without you two! Thanks to the editorial team who worked with me throughout the process: Senior Media Editor Tom Kane, Editor Alexis Smith, Associate Editor Catherine Burgess, and Editorial Assistant Will Stonefield. The book also would not have come together without the efforts of Project Editor Won McIntosh, who oversaw the book's tight schedule; the watchful eyes of Production Manager Joe Ford; and stunning photo research by Susan McDermott Barlow. The enthusiasm and support from the marketing team is particularly appreciated: Director of Marketing Sandy Lindelof, Marketing Manager Thomas Digiano, Marketing Assistant Alex Kaufman, and the entire sales force of Bedford/St. Martin's. Thanks to the video production team: Director Kaliya Warren, Director of Photography Shadi Best, and all of the talented actors!

On a more personal level, I want to thank all those who assisted me with the book during its development, and all those who collaborated with me in contributing their extraordinary stories to the text: Melissa Seligman, Vy Higginsen, Jennifer Andrews, Brenda Villa, Eric Staib, Leigh-Anne Goins, Vivian Derr, and Silvia Amaro. I would like to thank my undergraduate and graduate mentors, Malcolm Parks and Barbara O'Keefe, for instilling within me a fierce love of our discipline and a deep respect for the sacred endeavor that is undergraduate teaching. Thanks to my parents, Connie and Bruce McCornack, for raising me to value reading, books, and the unparalleled power of engaging human narrative—both spoken and written. Thanks to my boys—Kyle, Colin, and Conor—who have blessed and enriched my life more than words on a page could ever express. And most of all, I want to thank my unfailing source for relevant and interesting examples, Kelly Morrison. Your exceptional skill in the classroom, and the broad and deep generosity that marks your interactions with others in the world at large, are a constant source of inspiration for me as a teacher, spouse, parent, and human being.

Throughout the development of this textbook, hundreds of interpersonal communication instructors voiced their opinion through surveys, focus groups, and reviews of the manuscript, and I thank them all.

For the fourth edition: Christine Armstrong, *Northampton County Area Community College, Monroe Campus*; Courtney Atkins, *Union County College*; Diane Badzinski, *Colorado Christian University*; Patrick Barton, *Lone Star College*; Cassandra Carlson, *University of Wisconsin, Madison*; Allison Edgley, *Union County College*; Zach Frohlich, *Tarrant County College, Northwest Campus*; David Fusani, *Erie Community College*; Valerie Manno Giroux, *University of Miami*; Annette Hamel, *Western Michigan University*; Cherlyn Kipple, *Union County College*; Melanie Lea, *Bossier Parish Community College*; Susan McDaniel, *Loyola Marymount University*; Neil Moura, *MiraCosta College*; Ruth Spillberg, *Curry College*; Lindsay Timmerman, *University of Wisconsin, Madison*; Curt VanGeison, *St. Charles Community College*.

For the third edition: Ashley Fitch Blair, *Union University*; Angela Blais, *University of Minnesota, Duluth*; Deborah Brunson, *University of North Carolina, Wilmington*; Cassandra Carlson, *University of Wisconsin, Madison*; Kristin Carlson, *University of Minnesota, Duluth*; Janet Colvin, *Utah Valley University*; Andrew Cuneo, *University of Wisconsin, Milwaukee*; Melissa Curtin, *University of California, Santa Barbara*; Paige Davis, *Cy-Fair College*; Sherry Dewald, *Red Rocks Community College*; Marcia D. Dixson, *Indiana University–Purdue*

University, Fort Wayne; Jean Farrell, *University of Maryland*; David Gaer, *Laramie County Community College*; Jodi Gaete, *Suffolk County Community College*; Carla Gesell-Streeter, *Cincinnati State Technical and Community College*; Valerie Manno Giroux, *University of Miami;* Neva Gronert, *Arapahoe Community College*; Katherine Gronewold, *North Dakota State University;* Virginia Hamilton, *University of California, Davis*; Kristin Haun, *University of Tennessee, Knoxville*; Doug Hurst, *St. Louis Community College, Meramec*; Nicole Juranek, *Iowa Western Community College*; Janice Krieger, *Ohio State University*; Gary Kuhn, *Chemekata Community College*; Melanie Lea-Birck, *Bossier Parish Community College*; Myra Luna Lucero, *University of New Mexico*; Sorin Nastasia, *Southern Illinois University Edwardsville*; David Naze, *Prairie State College*; Gretchen Norling, *University of West Florida*; Laura Oliver, *University of Texas, San Antonio*; Lance Rintamaki, *University at Buffalo*; Jeanette Ruiz, *University of California, Davis*; Rebecca Sailor, *Aims Community College*; Alan H. Shiller, *Southern Illinois University Edwardsville*; Mara Singer, *Red Rocks Community College*; Jamie Stech, *Iowa Western Community College*; Deborah Stieneker, *Arapahoe Community College*; Kevin Stoller, *Indiana University–Purdue University, Fort Wayne*; Renee Strom, *St. Cloud State University*; Deatra Sullivan-Morgan, *Elmhurst College*; Marcilene Thompson-Hayes, *Arkansas State University*; Lindsay Timmerman, *University of Wisconsin, Milwaukee*; Curt VanGeison, *St. Charles Community College*; Charles Veenstra, *Dordt College*; Jamie Vega, *Full Sail University*; Judith Vogel, *Des Moines Area Community College*; Thomas Wagner, *Xavier University*.

For the second edition: Michael Laurie Bishow, *San Francisco State University*; Angela Blais, *University of Minnesota, Duluth*; Judy DeBoer, *Inver Hills Community College*; Greg Gardner, *Rollins College*; Jill Gibson, *Amarillo College*; Betsy Gordon, *McKendree University*; Robert Harrison, *Gallaudet University*; Brian Heisterkamp, *California State University, San Bernardino*; Eileen Hemenway, *North Carolina State University*; Yanan Ju, *Connecticut State University*; Beverly Kelly, *California Lutheran University;* Howard Kerner, *Polk Community College*; Karen Krumrey-Fulks, *Lane Community College*; Karen Krupar, *Metro State College of Denver*; Gary Kuhn, *Chemeketa Community College*; Victoria Leonard, *College of the Canyons*; Annie McKinlay, *North Idaho College*; Michaela Meyer, *Christopher Newport University*; Maureen Olguin, *Eastern New Mexico University, Roswell*; James Patterson, *Miami University*; Evelyn Plummer, *Seton Hall University*; Laurie Pratt, *Chaffey College*; Narissra M. Punyanunt-Carter, *Texas Tech University*; Thomas Sabetta, *Jefferson Community College*; Bridget Sampson, *California State University, Northridge*; Cami Sanderson, *Ferris State University*; Rhonda Sprague, *University of Wisconsin, Stevens Point*; Robert Steinmiller, *Henderson State University*; Deborah Stieneker, *Arapahoe Community College*; Anita J. Turpin, *Roanoke College*; Inci Ozum Ucok, *Hofstra University*; Paula Usrey, *Umpqua Community College*; Charles Veenstra, *Dordt College*; Sylvia Walters, *Davidson Community College*; Michael Xenos, *University of Wisconsin, Madison*; Phyllis Zrzavy, *Franklin Pierce University*.

For the first edition: A special thank-you goes to the dedicated members of the editorial board, whose commitment to the project was surpassed only by their help in shaping the book: Kathy Adams, *California State University, Fresno*; Stuart Bonnington, *Austin Peay State University*; Marion Boyer, *Kalamazoo Valley Community College*; Tamala Bulger, *University of North Carolina*; Stephanie Coopman, *San Jose State University*; Susan Drucker, *Hofstra University*; Greg Gardner, *Rollins College*; Kathleen Henning, *Gateway Technical College*; Sarah Kays, *DeVry Institute*; Charles J. Korn, *Northern Virginia Community College*; Karen Krumrey-Fulks, *Lane Community College*; Gary Kuhn, *Chemeketa Community College*; Anna Martinez, *Reedley College*; Elizabeth J. Natalle, *University of North Carolina, Greensboro*; Randall Pugh, *Montana State University*; Marta Walz, *Elgin Community College*; and Cherie White, *Muskingum Area Technical College*.

I would also like to thank everyone else who participated in this process: **Alabama:** Robert Agne, *Auburn University*; Jonathan Amsbary, *University of Alabama*; Angela Gibson Wible, *Shelton State Community College*; Bill Huddleston, *University of North Alabama*; James Vickrey, *Troy State University*. **Arizona:** Anneliese Harper, *Scottsdale Community College*; Douglas Kelley, *Arizona State University, West*; Fred Kester, *Yavapai College, Prescott*; Mark Lewis, *Phoenix College*; Joseph Ortiz, *Scottsdale Community College*. **Arkansas:** Patricia Amason, *University of Arkansas*; Jason Hough, *John Brown University*; Robert Steinmiller, *Henderson State University*. **California:** Katherine Adams, *California State University, Fresno*; Susan Childress, *Santa Rosa Junior College*; Stephanie J. Coopman, *San Jose State University*; Kristin Gatto Correia, *San Francisco State University*; Eve-Anne Doohan, *University of San Francisco*; Jeannette Duarte, *Rio Hondo College*; Anne Duran, *California State University, Bakersfield*; William Eadie, *San Diego State University*; Allison Evans, *California State University, Bakersfield*; G. L. Forward, *Point Loma Nazarene University*; Kimberly Hubbert, *Cerritos College*; Annika Hylmö, *Loyola Marymount University*; Cynthia Johnson, *College of the Sequoias*; Beverly Kelley, *California Lutheran University*; William Kelly, *University of California, Los Angeles*; Randall Koper, *University of the Pacific*; Victoria Leonard, *College of the Canyons*; Ben Martin, *Santa Monica College*; Anna Martinez, *Reedley College*; Lawrence Jerome McGill, *Pasadena City College*; William F. Owen, *California State University, Sacramento*; Laurie Pratt, *Fullerton College*; Catherine Puckering, *University of California, Davis*; Jose Rodriguez, *California State University, Long Beach*; Teresa Turner, *Shasta College*; Jennifer Valencia, *San Diego Miramar College*; Richard Wiseman, *California State University, Fullerton*. **Colorado:** Eric Aoki, *Colorado State University*; Diane Blomberg, *Metropolitan State College of Denver*; Cheryl McFarren, *Arapahoe Community College*; Susan Pendell, *Colorado State University*; Dwight Podgurski, *Colorado Christian University*. **Connecticut:** Yanan Ju, *Central Connecticut State University*; Hugh McCarney, *Western Connecticut State University*; William Petkanas, *Western Connecticut State University*; Terri Toles-Patkin, *Eastern Connecticut State University*; C. Arthur VanLear, *University of Connecticut*; Kathryn Wiss, *Western Connecticut State University*. **Florida:** Kenneth Cissna, *University of South Florida*; Ed Coursey,

Palm Beach Community College; Susan S. Easton, *Rollins College*; Greg Gardner, *Rollins College*; Katherine Nelson, *Barry University*; Maria Roca, *Florida Gulf Coast University*; Ann Scroggie, *Santa Fe Community College*. **Georgia:** Allison Ainsworth, *Gainesville College*; Marybeth Callison, *University of Georgia*; Michael H. Eaves, *Valdosta State University*; Pamela Hayward, *Augusta State University*; Gail Reid, *University of West Georgia*; Jennifer Samp, *University of Georgia*. **Hawaii:** Chiung Chen, *Brigham Young University, Hawaii*; Cailin Kulp O'Riordan, *University of Hawaii, Manoa*; Alan Ragains, *Windward Community College*. **Idaho:** Robyn Bergstrom, *Brigham Young University, Idaho*; Marcy Horne, *Lewis-Clark State College*; Annie McKinlay, *North Idaho College*. **Illinois:** Leah Bryant, *De Paul University*; Tim Cole, *De Paul University*; James Dittus, *Elgin Community College*; Katy Fonner, *Northwestern University*; Daena Goldsmith, *University of Illinois, Urbana-Champaign*; Sarah Strom Kays, *DeVry Institute*; Betty Jane Lawrence, *Bradley University*; Jody Littleton, *Parkland College*; Jay Martinson, *Nazarene University*; Lisa Miczo, *Western Illinois University*; Willona Olison, *Northwestern University*; Michael Purdy, *Governors State University*; Lesa Stern, *Southern Illinois University Edwardsville*; Marta Walz, *Elgin Community College*. **Indiana:** Austin Babrow, *Purdue University*; Rebecca Bailey, *Valparaiso University*; Alexandra Corning, *University of Notre Dame*; John Greene, *Purdue University*; Krista Hoffmann-Longtin, *Indiana University–Purdue University, Indianapolis*; Irwin Mallin, *Indiana University–Purdue University, Fort Wayne*; Janet Morrison, *Ivy Tech State College*; James H. Tolhuizen, *Indiana University Northwest*; Ralph Webb, *Purdue University*. **Iowa:** Julie Simanski, *Des Moines Area Community College*; Erik Stroner, *Iowa Central Community College*; Charles Veenstra, *Dordt College*. **Kansas:** David Sherlock, *Independence Community College*; Richard Stine, *Johnson County Community College*. **Kentucky:** Chuck Bryant, *University of Kentucky*; Joy Hart, *University of Louisville*; Mona Leonard, *Jefferson Community College*; Tracy Letcher, *University of Kentucky*; Gregory Rickert, *Bluegrass Community and Technical College*; Kandi L. Walker, *University of Louisville*. **Louisiana:** Terry M. Cunconan, *Louisiana Tech University*; Karen Fontenot, *Southeastern Louisiana University*; Loretta L. Pecchioni, *Louisiana State University*. **Maine:** Julie Zink, *University of Southern Maine*. **Maryland:** Laura Drake, *University of Maryland*; Linda Heil, *Harford Community College*; Audra McMullen, *Towson University*; Susan Ondercin, *Carroll Community College*. **Massachusetts:** Linda Albright, *Westfield State College*; Clea Andreadis, *Middlesex Community College*; Jonathan Bowman, *Boston College*; Elise Dallimore, *Northeastern University*; Joe Klimavich, *Worcester State College*; Michael Milburn, *University of Massachusetts, Boston*; Derrick TePaske, *Framingham State College*; Nancy Willets, *Cape Cod Community College*. **Michigan:** Patricia Amason, *Ferris State University*; Isolde Anderson, *Hope College*; Julie Apker, *Western Michigan University*; Steve Bennett, *Washtenaw Community College*; Marion Boyer, *Kalamazoo Valley Community College*; James Cantrill, *Northern Michigan University*; Robert Loesch, *Ferris State University*; Jennifer Hubbell Ott, *Kalamazoo Valley Community College*; Dennis Patrick, *Eastern Michigan University*; Cami Sanderson-Harris, *Ferris State University*; Sandi Smith, *Michigan State*

University; Patricia Sotirin, *Michigan Technical University*. **Minnesota:** Angela Lynn Blais, *University of Minnesota, Duluth*; Christa Brown, *Minnesota State University, Mankato*; Kari Frisch, *Central Lakes College*; Lori Halverson-Wente, *Rochester Community and Technical College*; Ascan Koerner, *University of Minnesota, Twin Cities*; Mariangela Maguire, *Gustavus Adolphus College*; Minda Orina, *University of Minnesota, Twin Cities*; Patricia Palmerton, *Hamline University*; Daniel Paulnock, *Saint Paul College*; Karri Pearson, *Normandale Community College*; R. Jeffrey Ringer, *St. Cloud State University*; Dan West, *Rochester Community and Technical College*. **Missouri:** Leigh Heisel, *University of Missouri, St. Louis*; Lynette Jachowicz, *Maple Woods Community College*; Virgil Norris, *Park University*; Jennifer Summary, *Southeast Missouri State University*. **Montana:** Randall Pugh, *Montana State University, Billings*; Julie Robinson, *Montana State University, Billings*. **Nebraska:** Karla Jensen, *Nebraska Wesleyan University*; Chad M. McBride, *Creighton University*; Lisa Schreiber, *Dana College*. **New Hampshire:** Phyllis Zrzavy, *Franklin Pierce College*. **New Jersey:** Keith Forrest, *Atlantic Cape Community College*; Rebecca Sanford, *Monmouth University*; Madeline Santoro, *Union County College*. **New Mexico:** Candace Maher, *University of New Mexico*; Virginia McDermott, *University of New Mexico*; Kevin Mitchell, *Eastern New Mexico University*; Pamela Stovall, *University of New Mexico, Gallup*. **New York:** Priya Banerjee, *State University of New York, Brockport*; Rex Butt, *Bronx Community College*; Joseph S. Coppolino, *Nassau Community College*; Susan Drucker, *Hofstra University*; Diane Ferrero-Paluzzi, *Iona College*; Douglas Gaerte, *Houghton College*; Andrew Herman, *State University of New York, Geneseo*; Patricia Iacobazzo, *John Jay College*; Anastacia Kurylo, *Manhattan Marymount College*; Michael Lecesse, *State University of New York, New Paltz*; Linda Reese, *College of Staten Island*; Gordon Young, *Kingsborough Community College*. **North Carolina:** Melissa Atkinson, *Surry Community College*; Alessandra Beasley, *Wake Forest University*; Tamala Bulger, *University of North Carolina, Wilmington*; Allison Carr, *Davidson County Community College*; James Manning, *Western Carolina State University*; Nina-Jo Moore, *Appalachian State University*; Elizabeth J. Natalle, *University of North Carolina, Greensboro*; Chris Poulos, *University of North Carolina, Greensboro*; Melinda Sopher, *North Carolina State University*. **Ohio:** Yemi Akande, *John Carroll University*; Carolyn Anderson, *University of Akron*; Christina S. Beck, *Ohio University*; Kathleen Clark, *University of Akron*; Rozell Duncan, *Kent State University*; David Foster, *University of Findlay*; Stephen Haas, *University of Cincinnati*; William Harpine, *University of Akron*; Kathryn C. Maguire, *Cleveland State University*; Lisa Murray-Johnson, *Ohio State University*; Artemio Ramirez, *Ohio State University*; Deleasa Randall-Griffiths, *Ashland University*; Teresa Sabourin, *University of Cincinnati*; Teresa Thompson, *University of Dayton*; John Warren, *Bowling Green State University*; Cherie White, *Muskingum Area Technical College (now Zane State College)*. **Oklahoma:** Penny Eubank, *Oklahoma Christian University*; Billy Wolfe Jr., *University of Oklahoma*. **Oregon:** Nick Backus, *Western Oregon University*; Cynthia Golledge, *Portland Community College, Sylvania*; Karen Krumrey-Fulks, *Lane Community College*; Gary Kuhn, *Chemeketa Community College*; Paula Usrey, *Umpqua Community College*. **Pennsylvania:** Mary Badami, *Bloomsburg University of Pennsylvania*;

Janet Bodenman, *Bloomsburg University of Pennsylvania*; Denise Danford, *Delaware County Community College*; Joseph Donato, *Harrisburg Area Community College, Lebanon*; Karen Lada, *Delaware County Community College*; David Paterno, *Delaware County Community College*; Elaine Zelley, *La Salle University*. **South Carolina:** Merissa Ferrara, *College of Charleston*; Charmaine Wilson, *University of South Carolina, Aiken*. **Tennessee:** Stuart Bonnington, *Austin Peay State University*; Katherine Hendrix, *University of Memphis*. **Texas:** Shae Adkins, *North Harris College*; Richard Bello, *Sam Houston State University*; Ceilidh Charleson-Jennings, *Collin County Community College*; Karen Daas, *St. Mary's University*; Jill Gibson, *Amarillo College*; Marian Houser, *Texas State University, San Marcos*; Shelly D. Lane, *Collin County Community College*; Laurie Metcalf, *Texas A&M University*; Mark Morman, *Baylor University*; John Nicholson, *Angelo State University*; James Pauff, *Tarleton State University*; Frank G. Pérez, *University of Texas, El Paso*; Lori Peterson, *St. Edward's University*; Narissra Punyanunt-Carter, *Texas Tech University*; Juliann Scholl, *Texas Tech University*; Susan Selk, *El Paso Community College*; Barbara Yancy-Tooks, *El Paso Community College*. **Utah:** Matthew Barton, *Southern Utah University*; Brian Heuett, *Southern Utah University*. **Vermont:** Genevieve Jacobs, *Champlain College*. **Virginia:** Melissa Aleman, *James Madison University*; Jill Jurgens, *Old Dominion University*; Charles J. Korn, *Northern Virginia Community College, Manassas*; Melanie Laliker, *Bridgewater College*; Michaela Meyer, *Christopher Newport University*; Thomas Morra, *Northern Virginia Community College, Annandale*; Nan Peck, *Northern Virginia Community College, Annandale*; Jeffrey Pierson, *Bridgewater College*; James Roux, *Lynchburg College*. **Washington:** Mara Adelman, *Seattle University*; Margaret Kreiner, *Spokane Community College*; Mark Murphy, *Everett Community College*; Roxane Sutherland, *Clark College*. **Washington, D.C.:** Robert Harrison, *Gallaudet University*; Clay Warren, *George Washington University*. **West Virginia:** Robert Bookwalter, *Marshall University*; Matthew Martin, *West Virginia University*. **Wisconsin:** Cheri Campbell, *University of Wisconsin, Waukesha*; Valerie Hennen, *Gateway Technical College*; Craig Hullett, *University of Wisconsin, Madison*; Rebecca Imes, *Carroll College*; Carol Knudson, *Gateway Technical College*; Lindsay Timmerman, *University of Wisconsin, Milwaukee*.

Finally, no textbook is created by one person. Thank you to the interpersonal communication discipline and its students.

brief contents

1 Introducing Interpersonal Communication 2

part one / Interpersonal Essentials

2 Considering Self 34
3 Perceiving Others 68
4 Experiencing and Expressing Emotions 100

part two / Interpersonal Skills

5 Understanding Culture 132
6 Listening Actively 160
7 Communicating Verbally 188
8 Communicating Nonverbally 220
9 Managing Conflict and Power 250

part three / Interpersonal Relationships

10 Relationships with Romantic Partners 284
11 Relationships with Family Members 324
12 Relationships with Friends 354
Appendix Relationships in the Workplace 384

Preface vii

1
Introducing Interpersonal Communication 2

What Is Communication? 6
   Defining Communication 6
   Understanding Communication Models 8

What Is Interpersonal Communication? 10
   Defining Interpersonal Communication 11
   Principles of Interpersonal Communication 13
   Motives for Interpersonal Communication 16
   Research in Interpersonal Communication 19

What Is Interpersonal Communication Competence? 20
   Understanding Competence 21
   Self-Quiz: Test Your Self-Monitoring 23
   Improving Your Competence Online 24

Issues in Interpersonal Communication 27
   Culture 27
   Gender and Sexual Orientation 27
   Focus on Culture: Intercultural Competence 29
   Online Communication 29
   The Dark Side of Interpersonal Relationships 29
   Making Relationship Choices: Dealing with a Difficult Friend 30

The Journey Ahead 32

Chapter Review 33

LaunchPad For LearningCurve adaptive quizzing and over 100 videos to help you understand key concepts, go to LaunchPad:
macmillanhighered.com/reflectrelate4e

(Image at top) Photo by Virginia Hagin

XXV

part one / Interpersonal Essentials

2
Considering Self 34

The Components of Self 37
   Self-Awareness 37
   Self-Concept 39
   Self-Quiz: Test Your Self-Concept Clarity 40
   Self-Esteem 40
   Focus on Culture: How Does the Media Shape Your Self-Esteem? 43

The Sources of Self 43
   Gender and Self 44
   Family and Self 44
   Culture and Self 46

Presenting Your Self 48
   Maintaining Your Public Self 50
   The Importance of Online Self-Presentation 51
   Improving Your Online Self-Presentation 54

The Relational Self 55
   Opening Your Self to Others 55
   Your Hidden and Revealed Self 58
   Disclosing Your Self to Others 59

Improving Your Self 63
   Making Relationship Choices: Workplace Self-Disclosure 64

Chapter Review 67

LaunchPad For LearningCurve adaptive quizzing and over 100 videos to help you understand key concepts, go to LaunchPad: macmillanhighered.com/reflectrelate4e

3
Perceiving Others 68

Perception as a Process 71
   Selecting Information 72
   Organizing the Information You've Selected 72
   Interpreting the Information 73
   Reducing Uncertainty 77

Influences on Perception 79
   Perception and Culture 79
   Perception and Gender 81
   Focus on Culture: Perceiving Race 83
   Perception and Personality 83

(Top to bottom) Photo by Scott Rosenfeld; AP Photo/Wide World

Contents   xxvii

Forming Impressions of Others 86
  Constructing Gestalts 87
  Calculating Algebraic Impressions 89
  Using Stereotypes 90

Improving Your Perception of Others 92
  Offering Empathy 92
  Self-Quiz: Test Your Empathy 93
  Checking Your Perception 94

Practicing Responsible Perception 95
  ▶ **Making Relationship Choices:** Balancing Impressions and Empathy 96

Chapter Review 99

🅛 LaunchPad   For LearningCurve adaptive quizzing and over 100 videos to help you understand key concepts, go to LaunchPad: macmillanhighered.com/reflectrelate4e

4
Experiencing and Expressing Emotions 100

The Nature of Emotion 103
  Defining Emotion 103
  Feelings and Moods 105
  Types of Emotions 107
  Focus on Culture: Happiness across Cultures 108

Forces Shaping Emotion 109
  Personality 110
  Gender 112

Managing Your Emotional Experience and Expression 112
  Emotional Intelligence 113
  Managing Your Emotions After They Occur 114
  Preventing Emotions 115
  Reappraising Your Emotions 116

Emotional Challenges 117
  Anger 117
  Self-Quiz: Test Your Chronic Hostility 118
  Online Communication and Empathy Deficits 119
  Passion 121
  Grief 122

Living a Happy Emotional Life 126
  ▶ **Making Relationship Choices:** Managing Anger and Providing Support 128

Chapter Review 131

Photo by G.N. Miller/MaMa Foundation
Gospel for Teens

🅛 LaunchPad   For LearningCurve adaptive quizzing and over 100 videos to help you understand key concepts, go to LaunchPad: macmillanhighered.com/reflectrelate4e

xxviii   Contents

part two / Interpersonal Skills

5
Understanding Culture 132

What Is Culture? 135
   Culture Defined 136
   Co-Cultures 137
   Focus on Culture: Millennials and Technology 139
   Prejudice 141

Cultural Influences on Communication 143
   Individualism versus Collectivism 143
   Uncertainty Avoidance 144
   Power Distance 145
   High and Low Context 147
   Emotion Displays 148
   Masculinity versus Femininity 149
   Views of Time 151

Creating Intercultural Competence 152
   World-Mindedness 152
   Attributional Complexity 153
   Communication Accommodation 153
   Self-Quiz: Are You World-Minded or Ethnocentric? 154

Embracing Difference 155
   ▶ **Making Relationship Choices:** Parent-Child Culture Clash 156

Chapter Review 159

LaunchPad   For LearningCurve adaptive quizzing and over 100 videos to help you understand key concepts, go to LaunchPad: macmillanhighered.com/reflectrelate4e

6
Listening Actively 160

Listening: A Five-Step Process 163
   Receiving 164
   Attending 165
   Self-Quiz: Multitasking and Attention 166
   Understanding 167
   Responding 168
   Recalling 170

The Five Functions of Listening 171
   Listening to Comprehend 171

(Top to bottom) John Tlumacki/The Boston Globe via Getty Images; © Mary Evans Picture Library/The Image Works

Listening to Discern   172
Listening to Analyze   172
Listening to Appreciate   172
Listening to Support   173
Adapting Your Listening Purpose   173

Understanding Listening Styles   173

Four Listening Styles   174
Gender Differences in Listening Styles   176
Culture and Listening Styles   177
Focus on Culture: Men Just Don't Listen!   177

Preventing Incompetent Listening   178

Selective Listening   178
Eavesdropping   180
Pseudo-Listening   181
Aggressive Listening   181
Narcissistic Listening   182

The Gift of Active Listening   183

▶ **Making Relationship Choices:** Listening When You Don't Want To   184

Chapter Review   187

LaunchPad   For LearningCurve adaptive quizzing and over 100 videos to help you understand key concepts, go to LaunchPad: macmillanhighered.com/reflectrelate4e

7
Communicating Verbally   188

Characteristics of Verbal Communication   191

Language Is Symbolic   191
Language Is Governed by Rules   193
Language Is Flexible   193
Language Is Cultural   194
Language Evolves   195

Functions of Verbal Communication   196

Sharing Meaning   197
Shaping Thought   197
Naming   199
Focus on Culture: Challenging Traditional Gender Labels   200
Performing Actions   201
Crafting Conversations   201
Managing Relationships   203

Cooperative Verbal Communication   204

Understandable Messages   205

Washington Crossing the Delaware River, 25th December 1776, 1851 (oil on canvas) (copy of an original painted in 1848), Leutze, Emanuel Gottlieb (1816–68)/Metropolitan Museum of Art, New York, USA/The Bridgeman Art Library

xxx   Contents

    Using "I" Language   207
    Using "We" Language   208
    Gender and Cooperative Verbal Communication   208

Barriers to Cooperative Verbal Communication   209
    Verbal Aggression   210
    Deception   211
    Self-Quiz: Test Your Deception Acceptance   212
    Defensive Communication   213
    Communication Apprehension   214

The Power of Verbal Communication   215
    Making Relationship Choices: Dealing with Difficult Truths   216

Chapter Review   219

LaunchPad For LearningCurve adaptive quizzing and over 100 videos to help you understand key concepts, go to LaunchPad: macmillanhighered.com/reflectrelate4e

8
Communicating Nonverbally   220

Principles of Nonverbal Communication   223
    Nonverbal Communication Uses Multiple Channels   224
    Nonverbal Communication Is More Ambiguous   224
    Nonverbal Communication Has Fewer Rules   224
    Nonverbal Communication Has More Meaning   225
    Nonverbal Communication Is Influenced by Culture   225
    Nonverbal Communication Is Influenced by Gender   226
    Nonverbal Communication Is Liberated Through Technology   228
    Nonverbal and Verbal Combine to Create Communication   229

Nonverbal Communication Codes   229
    Communicating Through Body Movements   230
    Communicating Through Voice   232
    Communicating Through Touch   234
    Focus on Culture: Touch and Distance   235
    Communicating Through Personal Space   236
    Communicating Through Physical Appearance   237
    Communicating Through Objects   238
    Communicating Through the Environment   239

Functions of Nonverbal Communication   239
    Expressing Emotion   240
    Conveying Meanings   241
    Presenting Self   241
    Managing Interactions   242
    Defining Relationships   243

The Beaver Family, 1907. Whyte Museum of the Canadian Rockies, #V527, by Mary Schaffer, Photographer

Contents   xxxi

    Self-Quiz: Test Your Nonverbal Dominance Knowledge   245

Competently Managing Your Nonverbal Communication   245
    ▶ **Making Relationship Choices:** Dealing with Mixed Messages   246

Chapter Review   249

🚀 **LaunchPad**   For LearningCurve adaptive quizzing and over 100 videos to help you understand key concepts, go to LaunchPad: macmillanhighered.com/reflectrelate4e

9
Managing Conflict and Power   250

Conflict and Interpersonal Communication   253
    What Is Conflict?   253
    Conflict in Relationships   255

Power and Conflict   256
    Power's Defining Characteristics   257
    Power Currencies   259
    Power and Gender   260
    Power and Culture   260

Handling Conflict   261
    Approaches to Handling Conflict   262
    Gender and Handling Conflict   266
    Culture and Handling Conflict   267
    Focus on Culture: Accommodation and Radical Pacifism   267
    Technology and Handling Conflict   268

Conflict Endings   270
    Short-Term Conflict Resolutions   271
    Long-Term Conflict Outcomes   273

Challenges to Handling Conflict   274
    Self-Enhancing Thoughts   274
    Destructive Messages   275
    Self-Quiz: Test Your Understanding of Destructive Thoughts   275
    Serial Arguments   276
    Physical Violence   277
    Unsolvable Disputes   278

Managing Conflict and Power   279
    ▶ **Making Relationship Choices:** Dealing with Family Conflict   280

Chapter Review   283

🚀 **LaunchPad**   For LearningCurve adaptive quizzing and over 100 videos to help you understand key concepts, go to LaunchPad: macmillanhighered.com/reflectrelate4e

Photo by Erin Patrice O'Brien

part three / Interpersonal Relationships

10
Relationships with Romantic Partners 284

Defining Romantic Relationships 287
  Liking and Loving 287
  Different Types of Romantic Love 288
  Key Elements of Romantic Relationships 290

Romantic Attraction 293
  Proximity 293
  Physical Attractiveness 294
  Similarity 295
  Reciprocal Liking 296
  Resources 296
  Technology and Romantic Attraction 297

Relationship Development and Deterioration 298
  Coming Together 298
  Coming Apart 301

Maintaining Romantic Relationships 303
  Maintenance Strategies 304
  Maintaining Romance across Distance 308
  Deciding Whether to Maintain 309

The Dark Side of Romantic Relationships 311
  Betrayal 312
  Self-Quiz: How Often Do You Betray Romantic Partners? 312
  Jealousy 315
  Focus on Culture: Infidelity Internationally 316
  Relational Intrusion 316
  Dating Violence 318

The Hard Work of Successful Love 319
  Making Relationship Choices: Managing Jealousy about a Partner's Ex 320

Chapter Review 323

LaunchPad For LearningCurve adaptive quizzing and over 100 videos to help you understand key concepts, go to LaunchPad: macmillanhighered.com/reflectrelate4e

© TopFoto/The Image Works

Contents   xxxiii

11
Relationships with Family Members   324

Defining Family   327
   Defining Characteristics of Family   328
   Types of Families   329
   Family Stories   331

Communicating in Families   334
   Communication Dimensions   335
   Family Communication Patterns   335

Maintaining Family Relationships   337
   Maintenance Strategies for Families   338
   Technology and Family Maintenance   339
   Dealing with Family Dialectics   340
   Focus on Culture: Autonomy and Class: Helicopter Parents   342

Family Relationship Challenges   344
   Stepfamily Transition   344
   Parental Favoritism   346
   Self-Quiz: How Much Family Favoritism Exists?   347
   Interparental Conflict   348

The Primacy of Family   349
   ▶ **Making Relationship Choices:** Struggling with Family Transitions   350

Chapter Review   353

🎯 **LaunchPad**   For LearningCurve adaptive quizzing and over 100 videos to help you understand key concepts, go to LaunchPad: macmillanhighered.com/reflectrelate4e

12
Relationships with Friends   354

The Nature of Friendship   357
   Friendship Defined   357
   Friendship Functions   359
   Friendship across the Life Span   360
   Friendship, Culture, and Gender   361
   Friendship and Technology   361

xxxiv   Contents

Types of Friendships   363
Best Friends   363
Cross-Category Friendships   364
Focus on Culture: Cross-Orientation Male Friendships   367

Maintaining Friendships   368
Following Friendship Rules   369
Maintenance Strategies for Friends   370

Friendship Challenges   372
Betrayal   373
Geographic Separation   374
Self-Quiz: Friendship Distance-Durability   376
Attraction: Romance and FWB Relationships   376

The Importance of Friends   379
▶ **Making Relationship Choices:** Choosing between Friends   380

Chapter Review   383

LaunchPad   For LearningCurve adaptive quizzing and over 100 videos to help you understand key concepts, go to LaunchPad: macmillanhighered.com/reflectrelate4e

Appendix
Relationships in the Workplace   384

The Nature of Workplace Relationships   A-1
The Culture of the Workplace   A-1
Networks in the Workplace   A-2
Organizational Climates   A-4
Technology in the Workplace   A-6

Peer Relationships   A-7
Types of Peer Relationships   A-7
Maintaining Peer Relationships   A-9

Mixed-Status Relationships   A-10
Managing Up   A-11
Communicating with Subordinates   A-12
Focus on Culture: The Model Minority Myth   A-13
Maintaining Mixed-Status Relationships   A-15

Challenges to Workplace Relationships   A-16
Workplace Bullying   A-17
Workplace Romances   A-19
Sexual Harassment   A-20

Workplace Relationships and Human Happiness A-22

Review A-24

LaunchPad For LearningCurve adaptive quizzing and over 100 videos to help you understand key concepts, go to LaunchPad: macmillanhighered.com/reflectrelate4e

Glossary G-1
References R-1
Name Index I-1
Subject Index I-9

from the reviewers

"Students say *Reflect & Relate* is their favorite textbook. They love the popular culture examples (books, movies, TV shows)."

Valerie Manno Giroux
University of Miami

"I found myself spending hours reading and thinking about the material, especially the opening vignettes and the *Making Relationship Choices* features—two strengths of the text."

Diane Bazinski
Colorado Christian University

"*Reflect & Relate* is an ideal textbook for an introductory course in interpersonal communication. The author has compiled a thoughtful presentation of the importance of interpersonal communication in our daily lives."

Curt VanGeison
St. Charles Community College

"*Reflect & Relate* is up-to-date and current, showing great images from past and present, which bring both historical culture and popular culture to life."

Allison Edgley
Union County College

about the author

"I believe that the most important thing a textbook can teach students is how to make better communication decisions so that they can build happier and healthier interpersonal relationships."

Steven McCornack grew up in Seattle, Washington, in the years before Microsoft and Amazon. For as long as he can remember, he has been fascinated with how people create, maintain, and disband close relationships, especially the challenges confronting romantic couples. As an undergraduate at the University of Washington, he pursued this passion by studying with Malcolm "Mac" Parks, who inspired Steve to devote his life to interpersonal communication, teaching, and research.

Steve moved to the Midwest in 1984, pursuing his graduate studies under the tutelage of Barbara O'Keefe at the University of Illinois, where he received his master's degree and his PhD. After twenty-seven years at Michigan State University, Steve moved to the South, where he is now a Full Professor at the University of Alabama Birmingham. Steve has published more than 30 articles in leading communication journals and has received several prestigious awards and fellowships related to undergraduate teaching, including the Lilly Endowment Teaching Fellowship, the Amoco Foundation Excellence-in-Teaching Award, the MSU All-University Teacher/Scholar Award, and the MSU Alumni Association Undergraduate Teaching Award. Steve was the 2013 recipient of the National Communication Association's Donald H. Ecroyd Award for Outstanding Teaching in Higher Education.

To Steve, authoring *Reflect & Relate* represents the culmination of 30 years of devout interest in how best to share knowledge of interpersonal communication theory and research with undergraduate students. His courses are some of the most popular on campus. Other than his love of teaching, Steve's principal passions are his family (wife Kelly and three redheaded sons, Kyle, Colin, and Conor), playing and listening to music, yoga, Kona coffee, his Subaru WRX, and meditation.

For Kelly, Kyle, Colin, and Conor:

"You know how everyone's always saying, 'seize the moment'? I don't know, I'm kinda thinkin' it's the other way around—you know, like, the moment seizes us."

"Yeah, yeah, I know. It's constant—the moments. It's just, it's like, it's always 'right now,' you know?"

—*Boyhood* (2014)

Reflect & Relate

an introduction to interpersonal communication

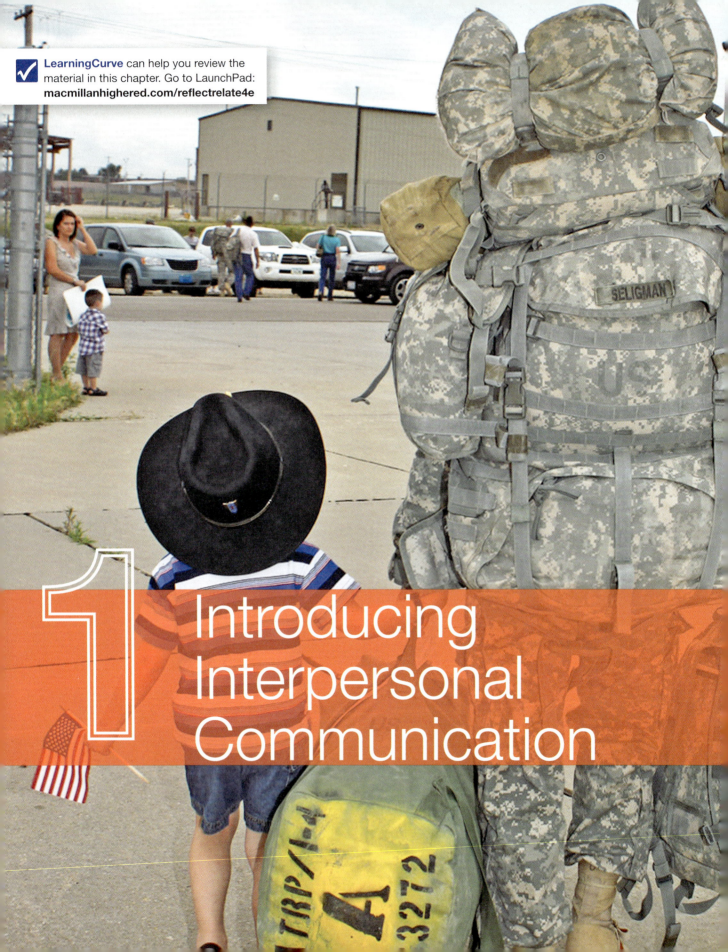

She is home with the kids, who are alternating between angry and clingy.[1] She's trying to cook dinner, but the smoke detector keeps blaring, causing the dog to bark. Sure enough, it's at this moment that the phone rings. Glancing at the caller ID, she sees it is the caller she'd hoped for. She answers, because despite the chaos around her, this could be their last conversation. He says, "I've been waiting in line for two hours to talk, and I only have ten minutes. I've had a really bad day and miss you all." What should she say? Choice #1: *Lie*. Tell him everything's fine, and mask her frustration with coolness. But he'll sense her aloofness and leave the conversation worrying about why she is distracted. Is she angry with him? Having an affair? Choice #2: *Be honest*. Tell him that things are chaotic, and ask whether he can talk to the kids for a minute while she clears her head.

Military wife, author, and *New York Times* columnist Melissa Seligman has lived this scene many times during her husband's combat deployments. She has learned to choose the second path because of the inescapable connection between communication choices and relationship outcomes. As she describes, "When a family member is gone for *a year* at a time, how can you sustain closeness? How do you maintain a three-dimensional marriage in a two-dimensional state? The only way is through open, honest, and loving communication."

---

[1] All information that follows is adapted from a personal interview with the author, July 2011. Published with permission from Melissa Seligman.

Virginia Hagin

1 / Introducing Interpersonal Communication

The Seligmans use multiple media to maintain intimacy, including webcams and exchanging videos, e-mails, phone calls, and letters. Melissa notes, "This way, we have a rounded communication relationship. We even send care packages of leaves, sand, pine needles, or pieces of fabric with cologne or perfume, to awaken the senses and cement the memories we have of each other." They also journal, then read each other's writings when they are reunited. The journals "have the dates, circumstances, and what went unsaid in the day-to-day minutiae of our lives. They are our way of staying connected when ripped apart."

Melissa Seligman uses similarly diverse communication in her professional work with military support groups. "In my working life, I am on Facebook, Skype, and Web conference calls all the time. Texting. Instant-messaging. All of these are essential." But she also is mindful of the limits of technology, recognizing the importance of tailoring the medium to the task. "Technology cannot sustain a relationship, and relying on it to do so will create chaos. Rather, choosing the technology that best suits an individual's relationship is the key."

Through years of experience, Melissa Seligman and her family have learned to cope with intense versions of the challenges we *all* face in our relationships. How can I better manage my anger and frustration? What can I do to maintain closeness with those I love? How can I communicate in a way that's both honest *and* kind? In 2010, she and coauthor Christina Piper released a children's book, *A Heart Apart*, which helps young children cope with the absence of military parents. When she is asked to reflect on the importance of communication, Melissa thinks of the next generation: "Children need to know and understand that anger and sadness go along with missing someone. They must be taught the importance of communication, and how to communicate well. This sets them up for success when their emotions begin to flow. Feelings are not right or wrong—it's what you choose to do with them that counts. Teaching our children to communicate well is the best gift we can give them."

My wife and I are out to dinner with our three grown sons—Kyle, Colin, and Conor—and our best friends, Tim and Hee Sun, whom we haven't seen since they moved to Korea. The conversation between us flows freely as we drift through discussions of personal events, past stories, politics, world affairs, and even online gaming—a passion Tim shares with my boys. The intimacy of the interaction is enhanced by us going "unplugged"; we've all placed our phones off the table. Nevertheless, the boys succumb to technological temptation when their entrées arrive, snapping photos of their food, which they post to Twitter, Instagram, and Facebook so that their friends and girlfriends can share in the festivities. As the evening ends, phones are retrieved from handbags and pockets, selfies are taken to lock down the memory, and texts are sent to absent family and friends to spread our happiness outward. All in all, it's one of those life events during which you count the minutes as precious yet bittersweet because they pass too quickly.

As I'm driving home, it flashes into my mind that regardless of the particulars, the peak moments of relationship joy that punctuate our lives are created through interpersonal communication. It's not the dinners, the fireworks, the sunsets, or the concerts that connect us to others. Those things are just, well, *things*. Instead, it's our communication. We use interpersonal communication to build, maintain, and even end relationships with romantic partners, family members, friends, coworkers, and acquaintances. We do this through tweeting, texting, instant-messaging, social networking site posts and chats, e-mail, face-to-face interactions, and phone calls. And we switch back and forth between these various forms fluidly, effortlessly.

But regardless of how we're communicating, where, or with whom, one fact inescapably binds us: *the communication choices we make determine the personal, interpersonal, and relationship outcomes that follow*. When we communicate well, we create desirable outcomes, such as positive emotions, satisfying relationships, and encounters that linger as happy memories. When we communicate poorly, we generate negative outcomes, such as interpersonal conflict, dissatisfaction with a relationship, and bitter lament over things that shouldn't have been said. By studying interpersonal communication, you can acquire knowledge and skills to boost your interpersonal competence. This will help you build and maintain satisfying relationships and, ultimately, improve your quality of life.

In this chapter, we begin our study of interpersonal communication. You'll learn:

- What communication is and the different models for communication
- The nature of interpersonal communication, the role it plays in relationships, and the needs and goals it helps us fulfill
- How to improve your interpersonal communication competence, both online and off
- Major issues related to the study of interpersonal communication

---

chapter outline

6
What Is Communication?

10
What Is Interpersonal Communication?

20
What Is Interpersonal Communication Competence?

27
Issues in Interpersonal Communication

32
The Journey Ahead

Chapter Theme

The story of this chapter is the story of the text: our communication choices determine our relationship outcomes. We can't control how others behave toward us, but we can improve our *own* decision making and the communication that flows from these decisions. When we choose to communicate appropriately, effectively, and ethically with others, our relationships benefit. Learning the knowledge and skills necessary for competent interpersonal communication is essential for ensuring our happiness and that of others.

Assignment: Competence on the Job

To show students how communication skills apply to the workplace, bring several job descriptions to class that include "strong communication skills" as a major requirement. Ask students, "What are communication skills?" and generate a large list of their responses. Discuss how these skills are needed for various careers. Then ask students to write an essay introducing themselves and explaining how their communication skills will apply to their career aspirations.

self-reflection

Is good communication just common sense? Does experience communicating *always* result in better communication? When you think about all the communication and relational challenges you face in your daily life, what do you think would help you improve your communication skills?

▶ Whether we are watching a movie, going to school, visiting with friends, or starting a new romance, communication plays a significant role in our everyday experiences. JoJo Whilden/©Weinstein Company/Courtesy Everett Collection

What Is Communication?

How we create and exchange messages with others

It was the first minute of the first day of the very first communication class I ever taught. I had just finished defining *communication*, when a student raised her hand with a puzzled look on her face. "I understand your definition," she said, "but isn't this all just common sense?" Her question has stuck with me all these years because it highlights an important starting point for learning about communication. We all come to communication classes with a lifetime of hands-on experience communicating. This leads some to think that they have little new to learn. But personal experience isn't the same as systematic training. When you're formally educated about communication, you gain knowledge that goes far beyond your intuition, allowing you to broaden and deepen your skills as a communicator. It's like any form of expertise. You know how to kick a ball, and you've likely done so hundreds, maybe thousands, of times since you were little. But does that mean you have the knowledge and skills to play in the World Cup? Of course not.

My goal for this text is to provide you with the knowledge and skills to make you a World Cup interpersonal communicator. This process begins by answering a basic question: what *is* communication?

DEFINING COMMUNICATION

The National Communication Association (n.d.), a professional organization representing communication teachers and scholars in the United States, defines **communication** as the process through which "people use messages to generate meanings within and across contexts, cultures, channels, and media." This definition highlights the five features that characterize communication.

First, communication is a *process* that unfolds over time through a series of interconnected actions carried out by the participants. For example, your friend tweets that she is going out to a movie, you text her back to see if she wants you to join her, and so forth. Because communication is a process, everything you say and do affects what is said and done in the present and in the future.

Second, those engaged in communication (*communicators*) use *messages* to convey meaning. A **message** is the "package" of information that is transported during communication. When people exchange a series of messages, the result is called an **interaction** (Watzlawick, Beavin, & Jackson, 1967).

Third, communication occurs in a seemingly endless variety of **contexts,** or situations. We communicate with others at sporting events, while at work, and in our homes. In each context, a host of factors influences how we communicate, such as how much time we have, how many people are in the vicinity, and whether the setting is personal or professional. Think about it: you probably communicate with your romantic partner differently when you're in class than when you're watching a movie at home and snuggling on the couch.

Fourth, people communicate through various *channels*. A **channel** is the sensory dimension along which communicators transmit information. Channels can be auditory (sound), visual (sight), tactile (touch), olfactory (scent), or oral (taste). For example, your manager at work smiles while complimenting your job performance (visual and auditory channels). A visually impaired friend reads a message you left her, touching the Braille letters with her fingertips (tactile). Your romantic partner shows up at your house exuding an alluring scent and carrying delicious takeout, which you then share together (olfactory and oral).

Fifth, to transmit information, communicators use a broad range of **media**—tools for exchanging messages. Consider the various media used by Melissa Seligman and her husband, described in our chapter opener. Webcams, cell phones, texting, e-mail, letters, face-to-face interaction—all of these media and more can be used to communicate. And we often use multiple media channels simultaneously—for example, texting while checking our Facebook page. (See Figure 1.1 for common media forms.)

🔸 Today we have access to more types of media than ever before. Technologies like tablets and smartphones offer new ways for us to communicate, but they also pose new communication challenges. pixdeluxe/Getty Images

Media Note: Inappropriate Media Channels

In season 6, episode 6, of *Sex and the City*, Carrie's boyfriend breaks up with her by leaving a Post-it on her laptop that reads, "I'm sorry. I can't. Don't hate me." Discuss how this scene illustrates appropriate or inappropriate use of media channels for various types of messages. Have students debate similar situations. For example, is it appropriate to fire someone over the phone? Is it acceptable to break up in a text?

Text-messaging (SMS)

Face-to-face interaction

Social networking sites

E-mail

Talking on the phone

figure 1.1 **Five Most Common Forms of Communication Media Used by College Students**

Sources: Dean (2011) and Lenhart, Purcell, Smith, & Zickuhr (2010).

8   chapter 1 / Introducing Interpersonal Communication

UNDERSTANDING COMMUNICATION MODELS

▶ **Teaching Tip: The Video Feature**
The Video feature prompts students to view brief and fun online videos that illustrate book concepts. Each video is paired with reflection questions to encourage critical thinking. These video activities are easy to assign as journal entries or homework, to use in class discussions, or even to use as the basis for student response videos. For more on how to use the Video feature and for a complete list of videos, please see page 496 or visit LaunchPad: macmillanhighered.com/reflectrelate4e.

Think about all the different ways you communicate each day. You text your sister to check in. You give a speech in your communication class to an engaged audience. You exchange a knowing glance with your best friend at the arrival of someone you mutually dislike. Now reflect on how these forms of communication differ from one another. Sometimes (like when texting) you create messages and send them to receivers, the messages flowing in a single direction, from origin to destination. In other instances (like when speaking in front of your class) you present messages to recipients, and the recipients signal to you that they've received and understood them. Still other times (like when you and your best friend exchange a glance) you mutually construct meanings with others, with no one serving as "sender" or "receiver." These different ways of experiencing communication are reflected in three models that have evolved to describe the communication process: the linear model, the interactive model, and the transactional model. As you will see, each of these models has both strengths and weaknesses. Yet each also captures something unique and useful about the ways you communicate in your daily life.

macmillanhighered.com/reflectrelate4e

Noise
Watch this clip online to answer the questions below.

What examples of noise can you identify in this video? What sensory channels did they occur on? What type(s) of sensory channel(s) distract you the most? Why?

Want to see more? Check out LaunchPad for clips on **channel** and the **linear communication model**.

Linear Communication Model   According to the **linear communication model,** communication is an activity in which information flows in one direction, from a starting point to an end point (see Figure 1.2). The linear model contains several components (Lasswell, 1948; Shannon & Weaver, 1949). In addition to a *message* and a *channel*, there must be a **sender** (or senders) of the message—the individual(s) who generates the information to be communicated, packages it into a message, and chooses the channel(s) for sending it. There also is **noise**—factors in the environment that impede messages from reaching their destination. Noise includes anything that causes our attention to drift from messages—such as poor reception during a cell-phone call or the smell of fresh coffee nearby. Last, there must be a **receiver**—the person for whom a message is intended and to whom the message is delivered.

Interactive Communication Model   The **interactive communication model** also views communication as a process involving senders and receivers (see

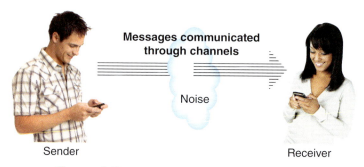

figure 1.2 **Linear Model of Communication**

chapter 1 / Introducing Interpersonal Communication   9

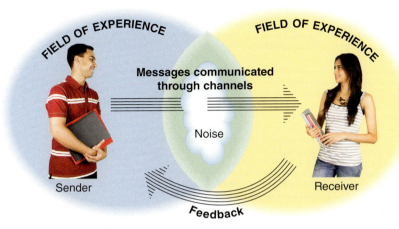

figure 1.3 **Interactive Model of Communication**

Figure 1.3). However, according to this model, transmission is influenced by two additional factors: feedback and fields of experience (Schramm, 1954). **Feedback** is composed of the verbal and nonverbal messages (such as eye contact, utterances such as "Uh-huh," and nodding) that recipients convey to indicate their reaction to communication. **Fields of experience** consist of the beliefs, attitudes, values, and experiences that each participant brings to a communication event. People with similar fields of experience are more likely to understand each other while communicating than are individuals with dissimilar fields of experience.

Transactional Communication Model The **transactional communication model** (see Figure 1.4) suggests that communication is fundamentally multidirectional. That is, each participant equally influences the communication behavior of the other participants (Miller & Steinberg, 1975). From the transactional perspective, there are no "senders" or "receivers." Instead, all the parties constantly exchange verbal and nonverbal messages and feedback, *collaboratively* creating

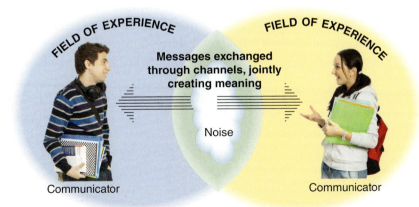

figure 1.4 **Transactional Model of Communication**

▶ **Assignment: Communication Models and Misunderstandings**
Have students watch the LaunchPad video clips on the **linear communication model**, **noise**, and the **transactional communication model**. Ask students to write a short paper describing a misunderstanding or difficult conversation that they had in a close relationship. Have them analyze the conversation using each specific component of one of the models. Did the misunderstanding occur because you came from different fields of experience? Did one of you use an inappropriate channel? What noise made the conversation more challenging? Did you use appropriate feedback?

▶ **Video**
macmillanhighered.com /reflectrelate4e

Transactional Communication Model
Watch this clip online to answer the questions below.

Can you think of situations in which you jointly created meaning with another person? How did this happen? In what ways are these situations different from ones that follow the interactive communication model?

table 1.1 Communication Models

Model	Examples	Strength	Weakness
Linear	Twitter, text and instant-messaging, e-mail, wall posts, scripted public speeches	Simple and straightforward	Doesn't adequately describe most face-to-face or phone conversations
Interactive	Classroom instruction, group presentations, team/coworker meetings	Captures a broad variety of communication forms	Neglects the active role that receivers often play in constructing meaning
Transactional	Any encounter (most commonly face-to-face) in which you and others jointly create communication meaning	Intuitively captures what most people think of as interpersonal communication	Doesn't apply to many forms of online communication, such as Twitter, e-mail, Facebook posts, and text-messaging

meanings (Streek, 1980). This may be something as simple as a shared look between friends, or it may be an animated conversation among close family members in which the people involved seem to know what the others are going to say before it's said.

These three models represent an evolution of thought regarding the nature of communication, from a relatively simplistic depiction of communication as a linear process to one that views communication as a complicated process that is mutually crafted. However, these models don't necessarily represent "good" or "bad" ways of thinking about communication. Instead, each of them is useful for thinking about different forms of communication. See Table 1.1 for more on each model.

What Is Interpersonal Communication?

Interpersonal communication impacts our relationships

My students frequently comment that they can't believe how relevant interpersonal communication scholarship is to their everyday lives. After all, we cover (and this book will discuss) self-esteem, jealousy, anger, conflict, betrayal, love, friendship, and healthy close relationships, to name just a few topics. Students often find themselves using this material to analyze everyone they know—driving roommates, lovers, family, and friends crazy in the process!

Of course, interest in interpersonal communication has existed since the dawn of recorded history. In fact, one of the earliest texts ever written—the maxims of the Egyptian sage Ptah Hotep (2200 B.C.E.)—was essentially a guidebook for enhancing interpersonal skills (Horne, 1917). Ptah Hotep encouraged people to be truthful, kind, and tolerant in their communication. He urged active listening, especially for situations in which people lack experience, because "to not do so is to embrace ignorance." He also emphasized mindfulness in word choice, noting that "good words are more difficult to find than emeralds."

DEFINING INTERPERSONAL COMMUNICATION

Why has learning about interpersonal communication always been considered so valuable? Because knowledge of interpersonal skills is essential for maintaining healthy interpersonal *relationships*. For most people, having happy relationships with romantic partners, friends, family members, and coworkers is of the utmost importance (Myers, 2002).

The link that exists between relationships and interpersonal communication is clearly illustrated by our definition: **interpersonal communication** is a dynamic form of communication between two (or more) people in which the messages exchanged significantly influence their thoughts, emotions, behaviors, and relationships. This definition has four important implications. First, interpersonal communication differs from some other forms of communication—such as office memos, e-mail spam, and formal lectures or speeches—because it's *dynamic*. That is, communication is constantly in motion and changing over time, unlike the carefully planned messages that dominate advertisements, professional journalism, and formal public speeches. For example, consider a Skype interaction you have with a sibling who lives overseas. The first few moments may be awkward or tense as you strive to reconnect with each other. This tension is reflected in long pauses between short sentences. Then one of you cracks a joke, and the whole exchange suddenly feels warmer. Just a few minutes later, as you realize you have to end the encounter, the conversation slows, and the mood shifts yet again to sadness and regret, as each of you tries to delay the inevitable disconnection.

Second, most interpersonal communication is *transactional*; both parties contribute to the meaning. For example, you and a romantic partner share an intimate dinner, jointly reminiscing about past times together and exchanging expressions of affection fluidly back and forth. But some interpersonal communication isn't transactional. You know that your sister is feeling depressed over a breakup, so you send her a consoling text message in the middle of her workday. You don't expect her to respond, and she doesn't because she's busy. There's no feedback and no interplay between you and your sister. Instead, there is a sender (you), a message (your expression of support), and a receiver (your sister), making it a linear encounter, albeit an interpersonal one.

Third, interpersonal communication is primarily **dyadic**—it involves pairs of people, or *dyads*. You chat with your daughter while driving her to school, or you exchange a series of Facebook messages with a long-distance friend. Of course, some interpersonal communication may involve more than just two people. For instance, several family members converse at once while sitting around the dinner table, or a group of friends talk while enjoying an evening out. The dyadic nature of interpersonal communication allows us to distinguish it from **intrapersonal communication**—communication involving only one person, in the form of talking out loud to oneself or having a mental "conversation" inside one's head.

Finally, and perhaps most importantly, interpersonal communication creates *impact*: it changes participants' thoughts, emotions, behaviors, and relationships. The impact on relationships is one of the most profound and unique effects created through interpersonal communication. When we interpersonally communicate, we

---

self-reflection

How do *you* define *interpersonal communication*? Can interpersonal communication happen between more than two people? Can it happen through tweets, texts, or e-mails? Or is it the content of what is discussed that makes communication interpersonal? What types of communication are *not* interpersonal?

forge meaningful bonds with others, easing the distance that naturally arises from differences between people. We don't have to agree with everything another person says and does, but to communicate competently with others, we need to approach them with an open mind and a welcoming heart, affording them the same attention and respect we expect for ourselves. According to philosopher Martin Buber (1965), we then perceive our relationship with that person as **I-Thou.**

In contrast, when we focus on our differences, refuse to accept or even acknowledge rival viewpoints as legitimate, and communicate in ways that emphasize our own supposed superiority over others, the distance between us and others increases to the point where it becomes impenetrable. As a consequence, we increasingly perceive our relationships as **I-It:** we regard other people as "objects which we observe, that are there for our use and exploitation" (Buber, 1965, p. 24). The more we view others as objects, the greater is the likelihood that we'll communicate with them in disrespectful, manipulative, or exploitative ways. When we treat others this way, our relationships deteriorate.

Interpersonal communication contrasts sharply with **impersonal communication**—exchanges that have a negligible perceived impact on our thoughts, emotions, behaviors, and relationships. For example, you're watching TV with your lover, and one of you casually comments on an advertisement that is annoying. Within most close relationships, at least some communication has this impersonal quality. But we can shift to interpersonal at a moment's notice. A while after the ad commentary, you snuggle up to your partner and murmur, "I love you." You're rewarded by warm eye contact, a tender smile, and a gentle hug—all signs that your message has had a significant impact on your partner.

Highlighting the mental, emotional, behavioral, and relational impact of interpersonal communication reinforces the central theme of this text: *the communication choices we make determine the personal, interpersonal, and relationship outcomes that follow.* Through communicating interpersonally with others, you can change your own feelings and thoughts about both yourself and others; alter others' opinions of you; cause heartbreak or happiness; incite hugs or hostility; and create, maintain, or dissolve relationships. This power makes your interpersonal communication choices critically important.

PRINCIPLES OF INTERPERSONAL COMMUNICATION

Now that you know the definition of interpersonal communication, we can expand our understanding of how it functions in our daily lives by looking at several principles suggested by scholars, based on decades of research and theory development. These principles are affirmed repeatedly throughout our text, and each one suggests practical insights into how you can improve your interpersonal communication choices, skills, and relationships.

Interpersonal Communication Conveys Both Content and Relationship Information During every interpersonal encounter, people simultaneously exchange two types of information (Watzlawick et al., 1967). *Content information*

---

skills practice

I-Thou Communication
Shifting your communication from I-It to I-Thou

❶ Think of someone you have to interact with regularly but with whom you have an I-It relationship.

❷ Identify the qualities that cause you to see this person as different from or inferior to you.

❸ Analyze these differences. Are they really a cause for concern?

❹ Identify similarities you have with this person.

❺ Develop a plan for communicating with this person in ways that accept and respect differences while appreciating and emphasizing similarities.

Media Note: Buber and The Big Bang Theory
To illustrate Buber's concept of I-It, play a clip from season 3, episode 3, of the TV show *The Big Bang Theory* that features the characters Sheldon and Penny. Sheldon uses classical conditioning to train Penny to behave in certain ways. Unbeknownst to Penny, Sheldon tosses a chocolate to her every time she behaves appropriately in his eyes. Ask students: In what ways is Sheldon exploiting Penny? How is he disrespecting or manipulating her?

◉ Whether an encounter is interpersonal depends on those people participating in it. Some only consider an encounter interpersonal if they gain new knowledge, make different decisions, or forge an I-Thou connection. Others consider an encounter interpersonal if information is conveyed. When do you think an encounter is interpersonal? AP Photo/Mark Lennihan

is the actual meaning of the words you utter. *Relationship information* consists of signals indicating how each of you views your relationship. These signals may indicate whether you consider yourself superior, equal, or inferior to the other person and whether you see the relationship as intimate, acquainted, or estranged.

You convey content information directly through spoken or written words, but you communicate relationship information primarily through nonverbal cues. These cues can include vocal tone, pitch, and volume; facial expression and eye contact; hand gestures; position in relation to the listener; and posture. For instance, imagine that you're FaceTiming with your mom about whether or not you're coming home for Thanksgiving. She wants you to visit, but you'd rather stay at school and work the weekend to earn money. She says, "Everyone else in the family is coming, and so we hope you can make it, too," with a friendly tone and welcoming smile. Now imagine the exact same situation—except this time she is frowning, using a loud and demanding voice, and pointing her finger at you. In both scenarios, the content information is identical—she uses exactly the same words—but very different relationship information is conveyed. In the first scenario, your mom indicates both equality and affection, suggesting a hopeful invitation. In the second, she communicates superiority and anger, implying criticism of your priorities and demanding your attendance.

Relationship information strongly influences how people interpret content information (Watzlawick et al., 1967). In the preceding example, you will likely look much more to your mom's actions than her words in deciding how she feels about you and the relationship. During most interpersonal encounters, however, people aren't consciously aware of the relationship information being delivered. You don't usually sit there thinking, "Gee, what's this person trying to convey to me about how she sees our relationship?" Relationship information becomes most obvious when it's unexpected or when it suggests that the sender's view of the relationship is different from the receiver's. For example, a new acquaintance says something overly intimate to you, or a roommate starts ordering you around as if he's your boss. When such events occur, we often experience annoyance or anxiety ("Who does he think he is?!"). That's why it's important to communicate relationship information in ways that are sensitive to and respectful of others' impressions of the relationship while staying true to your own relationship feelings.

Because relationship information influences how people interpret content information, it can be considered a specific form of **meta-communication**—communication about communication (Watzlawick et al., 1967). Meta-communication includes any message, verbal or nonverbal, that has as its central focus the meaning of communication—everything from discussion of previous comments ("I actually was joking when I sent you that text message") to exchanged glances between friends questioning how a message should be interpreted ("What did he mean when he said that?"). During interpersonal encounters, meta-communication helps us understand each other's communication, giving us additional guidance regarding how messages should be perceived.

Interpersonal Communication Can Be Intentional or Unintentional   During interpersonal encounters, people attach meaning to nearly everything you say and do—whether you intend to send a message or not. Scholars express this as the axiom, "One cannot not communicate" (Watzlawick et al., 1967, p. 51). In most situations, you intend certain meanings, and people understand you. Sometimes, however, people read meanings into behaviors that you didn't intend as communicative. In such instances, interpersonal communication *has* occurred, even though it was unintentional. For example, imagine that you greet a friend of yours, "Hey,

self-reflection

Consider an instance in which you didn't intend to communicate a message but someone saw your behavior as communication. How did this person misinterpret your behavior? What were the consequences? What did you say and do to correct the individual's misperception?

◁ In the movie *Crazy, Stupid, Love*, a conversation between estranged couple Cal and Emily Weaver changes from distant to intimate to hostile. What experience have you had in handling changing relationship information within a single encounter? How has it influenced your communication choices?
Ben Glass/© Warner Bros. Pictures/Courtesy Everett Collection

how's it going?" She greets you back, "Hi, good to see you!" So far so good—both messages were intentional, and both were interpreted correctly. But then, as your friend tells you about her new boyfriend, your contact lens gets displaced. It's the third time it's happened that day, so you sigh loudly in frustration and move your eyes to try to get it back into position. Your friend, seeing this, thinks you're sighing and rolling your eyes *as a message* about her boyfriend, and gets angry, "Oh, so you disapprove of him? Why!?" Whether you like it or not, interpersonal communication *has* occurred, even though it was unintentional. To avoid such misunderstandings, keep this simple rule in mind: when you're interacting with others, most of what you say and do will be perceived as communication.

Interpersonal Communication Is Irreversible   Every time you communicate interpersonally, you and the other person affect your future communication and the quality of your relationship. Take the way you answer your cell phone when your brother calls. The ringtone prompts you to look at the incoming number. Your warm and enthusiastic "Hi!" or terse "Yeah?" depends on how you feel about him. Your answer, in turn, influences how the caller responds. And his response further affects your next comment.

This interconnectedness of action makes all interpersonal communication irreversible. By tweeting, posting a message on someone's Facebook timeline, sending a text, leaving a voice-mail message, or expressing a thought out loud during a face-to-face encounter, you set in motion the series of outcomes that follow. Simply put, once you've said something, you can't take it back. This is why it's important to think carefully before you communicate. Ask yourself, Is what I'm about to say going to lead to outcomes I want? If the answer is no, revise your message accordingly.

Interpersonal Communication Is Dynamic   When you interact with others, your communication and all that influences it—perceptions, thoughts, feelings, and emotions—are constantly in flux. This has several practical implications. First, no two interactions with the same person will ever be identical. People with whom we once interacted effortlessly and joyfully can seem difficult to talk with during our next encounter. Those we once felt awkward around may become our closest confidants.

Second, no two moments within the *same* interaction will ever be identical. The complex combination of perceptions, thoughts, moods, and emotions that fuels our interpersonal communication choices is constantly changing. For instance, you meet your long-distance romantic partner at the airport, and for the first few minutes after reuniting you both feel joyous. But half an hour later, while driving home, you suddenly find yourselves at a loss for things to talk about. As the minutes pass, the tension increases as you both silently ponder, "What happened?"

MOTIVES FOR INTERPERSONAL COMMUNICATION

In the movie *Cast Away* (2000), Tom Hanks plays FedEx executive Chuck Noland, who survives a plane crash at sea, only to find himself alone on an uncharted island. Noland must improvise his survival, learning how to obtain food and fresh

---

self-reflection

Think of an encounter in which you said something and then immediately regretted it. What effect did your error have on you? on the other person or people involved? on your relationship? How could you have expressed the same information differently to avoid negative outcomes?

self-reflection

Recall an interaction that took a sudden turn for the worse. How did each person's communication contribute to the change in the interaction's quality? What did you say or do to deal with the problem?

chapter 1 / Introducing Interpersonal Communication

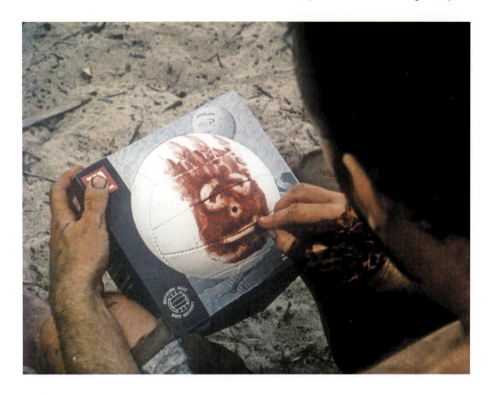

◐ Human beings are fundamentally social creatures, with a powerful need to have interpersonal contact with others. Chuck Noland, stranded alone on an island, carries out one-sided "conversations" with Wilson the volleyball to fulfill his social needs. Dreamworks/Photofest

water, build a shelter, and create fire. But by far his biggest challenge is dealing with his isolation from others. Realizing that he will be presumed dead by all who knew him and likely live out the rest of his days alone on the island, Noland sinks into despair. To emotionally save himself, he creates a friend with whom he can interact: a volleyball named Wilson. Wilson becomes his constant companion, to whom he talks incessantly.

Since *Cast Away*'s release more than a decade ago, "Wilson the volleyball" has become iconic. Numerous YouTube videos spoof Noland's conversations with Wilson; you can buy Wilson T-shirts, tote bags, and coffee mugs; and in 2014 the Myrtle Beach Pelicans—a minor league branch team of the Texas Rangers—tried to lure pro football star Russell Wilson to its baseball roster by creating a *Cast Away*-style video with "Wilson" as a football. But beneath the satire and silliness lies a deeper truth about our basic nature. We may be able to *physically* survive without interpersonal communication with others, but we can't *mentally* and *emotionally* endure such isolation. Interpersonal communication isn't trivial or incidental; it fulfills a profound human need for connection that we all possess. Of course, it helps us achieve more mundane practical goals as well.

Interpersonal Communication and Human Needs   Psychologist Abraham Maslow (1970) suggested that we seek to fulfill a hierarchy of needs in our daily lives. When the most basic needs (at the bottom of the hierarchy) are fulfilled, we turn our attention to pursuing higher-level ones. Interpersonal communication allows us to develop and foster the interactions and relationships that help us fulfill all of these needs. At the foundational level are *physical needs*, such as air, food, water, sleep, and shelter. If we can't satisfy these needs, we prioritize them

Discussion Prompt: Communication Is Irreversible

Ask students to think about what life would be like if we all had a DVR for our daily lives. What if they could hit Pause when needed? What would they record if they couldn't be present? Would they like to hit Fast Forward or Rewind? Have them consider times when they have thought, "I wish I could take that back" after communicating something they regretted. Then, in pairs or as a class, have them discuss the power of irreversibility.

⚪ Each interpersonal interaction we have shapes our future communication. Before expressing a potentially hurtful thought, consider what outcomes you're setting in motion. BananaStock/Getty Images

over all others. Once physical needs are met, we concern ourselves with *safety needs*—such as job stability and protection from violence. Then we seek to address *social needs*: forming satisfying and healthy emotional bonds with others.

Next are *self-esteem* needs, the desire to have others' respect and admiration. We fulfill these needs by contributing something of value to the world. Finally, we strive to satisfy *self-actualization needs* by articulating our unique abilities and giving our best in our work, family, and personal life.

Interpersonal Communication and Specific Goals In addition to enabling us to meet fundamental needs, interpersonal communication helps us meet three types of goals (Clark & Delia, 1979). During interpersonal interactions, you may pursue one or a combination of these goals. The first—**self-presentation goals**—are desires you have to present yourself in certain ways, so that others perceive you as being a particular type of person. For example, you're conversing with a roommate who's just been fired. You want him to know that you're a supportive friend, so you ask what happened, commiserate, and offer to help him find a new job.

You also have **instrumental goals**—practical aims you want to achieve or tasks you want to accomplish through a particular interpersonal encounter. If you want to borrow your best friend's prized Porsche for the weekend, you might remind her of your solid driving record and your sense of responsibility to persuade her to lend you the car.

Finally, you use interpersonal communication to achieve **relationship goals**—building, maintaining, or terminating bonds with others. For example, if you succeed in borrowing your friend's car for the weekend and accidentally drive it into a nearby lake, you will likely apologize profusely and offer to pay for repairs to save your friendship.

Discussion Prompt: Specific Goals of Students

Ask students to consider how they use interpersonal communication to achieve self-presentation, instrumental, and relationship goals. For example, have them reflect on a first date: Did you try to present yourself to your date's friends or parents in a certain way (presentation)? Did you try to persuade your roommate to borrow his or her car for the date (instrumental)? Did you offer to pay for dinner or the movie or use other romantic gestures to intensify the bond (relationship)?

RESEARCH IN INTERPERSONAL COMMUNICATION

The goal of this textbook is to provide you with knowledge regarding interpersonal communication that will help you improve your communication choices, skills, and relationships. But to be useful, knowledge has to be trustworthy. That means it must be based on solid research and theory. How does this come about?

When you conduct *research*, you formulate a question, then try to answer it through careful observation or the creation of a controlled "test" or experiment. When you develop *theory*, you formulate propositions (statements) about your interests, then identify factors relevant to them and how those factors interrelate (Chaffee & Berger, 1987).

To illustrate how research and theory give rise to interpersonal communication knowledge, let's walk through an example. Imagine that you post a message in one of your favorite online discussion groups. Within hours, you find a couple of *flames*—inappropriately aggressive online messages that most people wouldn't communicate face-to-face. You're shocked and confused, but you want to know why this happened. So you decide to do some research and develop a theory.

Communication scholars typically take one of two approaches when conducting research and developing theory. Through *qualitative approaches*, they make careful observations, identify patterns in what they're seeing, and try to determine the principles behind their observations (Znaniecki, 1934). If you opted to study flaming qualitatively, you would follow several steps (Katz, 1983). First, you would carefully define what you meant by *flaming* based on observation of various flame messages. You would consider questions such as: What characteristics of an online message make it a "flame"? How is flaming

"Aren't you supposed to be doing research on why employees goof off?"

Frank Cothern/The New Yorker Collection/The Cartoon Bank

different from other negative messages? Once you had a clear definition of flaming, you would formulate tentative *hypotheses*—predictions that describe the relationship between your phenomenon of interest and other related factors. For example, you might hypothesize that flaming is more likely to occur in certain discussion forums than in others or that certain types of messages are especially likely to trigger flames. Then you would test your hypotheses by observing multiple instances of flaming in online discussion groups. If your observations consistently confirmed your hypotheses, you would conclude that your hypotheses were likely correct. If your observations disconfirmed your hypotheses, you would revise your hypotheses until they matched your observations. Then you would create a set of propositions describing the nature of flaming and the factors that influence it. These propositions would constitute your flame theory.

Whereas qualitative approaches begin with observation and description and then move to development of theory, *quantitative approaches* follow the opposite order. Researchers first propose a theory, then formulate hypotheses based on that theory, and finally test those hypotheses by conducting an experiment. For example, to study flaming from a quantitative perspective, you might first read previous research on flaming. You would then select an existing theory or create your own. From this theory, you would choose specific hypotheses and design and conduct a controlled test of them. For example, you might hypothesize that anonymity boosts flaming frequency and conduct a study in which people are provided with either anonymous or identifiable accounts. If the results from the controlled test support your hypothesis, you would consider your theory plausible. If the results do not match the hypothesis, you would reject the hypothesis and view your theory as suspect.

Many people view qualitative and quantitative approaches as opposites or even rivals, but both are equally valid for the study of interpersonal communication. Qualitative approaches are especially well suited for learning the details, nuances, and richness of real-life communication patterns. Quantitative approaches are excellent for determining the frequency of various communication behaviors, as well as systematically testing the influence of various factors on such behaviors (Pomerantz, 1990).

skills practice

Using Research Methods Online
How to analyze online communication challenges with research

❶ Think of a problem you commonly face when communicating with others online—such as encountering someone whose messages are consistently rude or vague.

❷ Identify the factors that seem to cause the problem, and formulate a hypothesis.

❸ Carefully observe encounters in which the problem arises, testing if the factors in your hypothesis are really the causes.

❹ Identify ways you can change, control, or improve the factors that cause the problem.

❺ Implement these changes; then see if the problem is resolved. If not, repeat the process until a solution is found.

Discussion Prompt: Competent Communicators

The text discusses Chef from *South Park* as an example of someone who strives to be a competent communicator. Ask students to think of someone they consider to be a competent communicator. What skills does that person use to communicate effectively? How is his or her communication effective, appropriate, and ethical?

What Is Interpersonal Communication Competence?

Competence matters the most during difficult situations

For nine seasons of *South Park*, Jerome "Chef" McElroy (voiced by the late, great R&B singer Isaac Hayes) was the only adult trusted and respected by the show's central characters: Kyle, Stan, Kenny, and Cartman. In a routine interaction, the boys—while waiting on the school lunch line—would share their concerns and seek Chef's counsel. He would do his best to provide appropriate, effective, and ethical advice, often bursting into song. Of course, given his reputation as a ladies' man, the boys frequently asked him for advice regarding relationships and sex. Chef would answer in vague and allusive ways, trying to remain child appropriate but ending up completely unintelligible. In other instances he'd get carried away, singing about his sexual exploits before remembering his audience. But despite occasional lapses in effectiveness and appropriateness, Chef consistently was the most ethical, kind, and compassionate adult in a show populated by insecure, self-absorbed, and outright offensive characters.

Many of us can think of a Chef character in our own lives—someone who, even if he or she occasionally errs, always *strives* to communicate competently. Often, this person's efforts pay off; competent communicators report more relational satisfaction (including happier marriages), better psychological and physical health, and higher levels of educational and professional achievement than others (Spitzberg & Cupach, 2002).

Although people who communicate competently report positive outcomes, they don't all communicate in the same way. No one recipe for competence exists. Communicating competently will help you achieve more of your interpersonal goals, but it doesn't guarantee that all of your relationship problems will be solved.

Throughout this text, you will learn the knowledge and skills necessary for strengthening your interpersonal competence. In this chapter, we explore what competence means and how to improve your competence online. Throughout later chapters, we examine how you can communicate more competently across various situations, and within romantic, family, friendship, and workplace relationships.

Jerome "Chef" McElroy's style may have been unconventional, but he strived for competence in his communication with the boys of *South Park*. © Comedy Central/Courtesy Everett Collection

UNDERSTANDING COMPETENCE

Interpersonal communication competence means consistently communicating in ways that are *appropriate* (your communication follows accepted norms), *effective* (your communication enables you to achieve your goals), and *ethical* (your communication treats people fairly) (Spitzberg & Cupach, 1984; Wiemann, 1977). Acquiring knowledge of what it means to communicate competently is the first step in developing interpersonal communication competence (Spitzberg, 1997).

The second step is learning how to translate this knowledge into **communication skills**—repeatable goal-directed behaviors and behavioral patterns that you routinely practice in your interpersonal encounters and relationships (Spitzberg & Cupach, 2002). Both steps require *motivation* to improve your communication. If you are strongly motivated to do so, you can master the knowledge and skills necessary to develop competence.

Appropriateness The first characteristic of competent interpersonal communication is **appropriateness**—the degree to which your communication matches situational, relational, and cultural expectations regarding how people should communicate. In any interpersonal encounter, norms exist regarding what people should and shouldn't say, and how they should and shouldn't act. For example, in

self-reflection

Think of an interpersonal encounter in which different people expected very different things from you in your communication. How did you choose which expectations to honor? What were the consequences of your decision? How could you have communicated in a way perceived as appropriate by everyone in the encounter?

🔸 Labor leader César Chávez spent most of his life speaking out for America's poorest farm laborers. Whether speaking with union volunteers or powerful politicians, Chávez's interpersonal communication competence allowed him to translate his personal intentions into actions that changed the world. Arthur Schatz/Time Life Pictures/Getty Images

South Park, Chef commonly struggled when the boys asked him to talk about topics that aren't considered appropriate for children. Part of developing your communication competence is refining your sensitivity to norms and adapting your communication accordingly. People who fail to do so are perceived by others as incompetent communicators.

We judge how appropriate our communication is through **self-monitoring:** the process of observing our own communication and the norms of the situation in order to make appropriate communication choices. Some individuals closely monitor their own communication to ensure they're acting in accordance with situational expectations (Giles & Street, 1994). Known as *high self-monitors*, they prefer situations in which clear expectations exist regarding how they're supposed to communicate, and they possess both the ability and the desire to alter their behaviors to fit any type of social situation (Oyamot, Fuglestad, & Snyder, 2010). In contrast, *low self-monitors* don't assess their own communication or the situation (Snyder, 1974). They prefer encounters in which they can "act like themselves" by expressing their values

▶ Video

macmillanhighered.com
/reflectrelate4e

Self-Monitoring
Watch this clip online to answer the questions below.

Does this video show a low self-monitor or a high self-monitor? Please explain your reasoning. Have you ever changed your behavior after self-monitoring? If so, under what circumstances?

and beliefs, rather than abiding by norms (Oyamot et al., 2010). As a consequence, high self-monitors are often judged as more adaptive and skilled communicators than low self-monitors (Gangestad & Snyder, 2000).

One of the most important choices you make related to appropriateness is when to use mobile devices and when to put them away. Certainly, cell phones and tablets allow us to quickly and efficiently connect with others. However, when you're interacting with people face-to-face, the priority should be your conversation with them; if you prioritize your device over the person in front of you, you run the risk of being perceived as inappropriate. This is not a casual choice: research documents that simply having cell phones out on a table—but not using them—during face-to-face conversations significantly reduces perceptions of relationship quality, trust, and empathy compared to having conversations with no phones present (Przybylski & Weinstein, 2012). To avoid this, put your mobile devices away at the beginning of any interaction.

While communicating appropriately is a key part of competence, *overemphasizing* appropriateness can backfire. If you focus exclusively on appropriateness and always adapt your communication to what others want, you may end up forfeiting your freedom of communicative choice to peer pressure or fears of being perceived negatively (Burgoon, 1995).

Effectiveness The second characteristic of competent interpersonal communication is **effectiveness:** the ability to use communication to accomplish the three types of interpersonal goals discussed earlier (self-presentation, instrumental, and relationship). There's rarely a single communicative path for achieving all

Test Your Self-Monitoring

Place a check mark next to the statements you agree with. Then count the total number of statements you checked to see if you're a high or low self-monitor.

To take this quiz online, visit LaunchPad: **macmillanhighered.com/reflectrelate4e**.

_____ I find it easy to imitate others' behavior.

_____ When I'm uncertain how to act during an interpersonal encounter, I look to others' behaviors for cues.

_____ I would probably make a good actor.

_____ In different situations and with different people, I often act like a very different person.

_____ Even if I'm not enjoying myself, I often behave as if I'm having a good time.

_____ I find it easy to change my behavior to suit different people and situations.

_____ I sometimes appear to others to be experiencing deeper emotions than I really am.

_____ I'm pretty good at making other people like me.

_____ I'm not always the person I appear to be.

Note: This *Self-Quiz* is adapted from the self-monitoring scale provided by Snyder (1974).

Scoring: 0–4 indicates you're probably a low self-monitor; 5–9 suggests you're a high self-monitor.

---

of these goals, and sometimes you must make trade-offs. For example, a critical part of maintaining satisfying close relationships is the willingness to occasionally sacrifice instrumental goals to achieve important relationalship goals. Suppose you badly want to see a movie tonight, but your romantic partner needs your emotional support to handle a serious family problem. Would you say, "I'm sorry you're feeling bad—I'll call you after I get home from the movie" (emphasizing your instrumental goals)? Or would you say, "I can see the movie some other time—tonight I'll hang out with you" (emphasizing your relationship goals)? The latter approach, which facilitates relationship health and happiness, is obviously more competent.

Ethics The final defining characteristic of competent interpersonal communication is **ethics**—the set of moral principles that guide our behavior toward others (Spitzberg & Cupach, 2002). At a minimum, we are ethically obligated to avoid intentionally hurting others through our communication. By this standard, communication that's intended to erode a person's self-esteem, that expresses intolerance or hatred, that intimidates or threatens others' physical well-being, or that expresses violence is unethical and therefore incompetent (Parks, 1994).

To truly be an ethical communicator, however, we must go beyond simply not doing harm. During every interpersonal encounter, we need to strive to treat others with respect, and communicate with them honestly, kindly, and positively (Englehardt, 2001). For additional guidelines on ethical communication, review the "Credo for Ethical Communication" on page 24.

We are all capable of competence in contexts that demand little of us—situations in which it's easy to behave appropriately, effectively, and ethically. True competence is developed when we consistently communicate competently

self-reflection

Is the obligation to communicate ethically absolute or situation-dependent? That is, are there circumstances in which it's ethical to communicate in a way that hurts someone else's feelings? Can one be disrespectful or dishonest and still be ethical? If so, in what kinds of situations?

Media Note: Self-Monitoring in *Mean Girls*
In the film *Mean Girls*, the main character, Cady Heron, uses high self-monitoring to fit in with the popular girls, known as the Plastics. To see an example, have students watch the scene in which the Plastics are complaining about their physical imperfections and Cady feels compelled to join in on the self-deprecation when she says, "I have really bad breath in the morning." Ask students if they have been in a situation like this before. Do they see themselves as high or low self-monitors? If students are familiar with the film, you can also discuss how self-monitoring eventually causes problems for Cady.

across *all* situations that we face—contexts that are uncertain, complex, and unpleasant, as well as those that are simple, comfortable, and pleasant. One of the goals of this book is to arm you with the knowledge and skills you need to meet challenges to your competence with confidence.

IMPROVING YOUR COMPETENCE ONLINE

Much of our interpersonal interaction is **online communication:** connecting with others by means of new media, including social networking sites, e-mail, text- or instant-messaging, Snapchat, Skype, chatrooms, and even massively multiplayer video games like *World of Warcraft* (Walther & Parks, 2002). Online communication enables us to meet and form friendships and romances with people we wouldn't encounter otherwise, and it helps us maintain established relationships (Howard, Rainie, & Jones, 2001). This is especially important for people who are geographically separated. For example, friends who are thousands of miles apart can routinely text each other and maintain a sense that they are actually proximic (Baym et al., 2012). In fact, we can predict quality and strength of interpersonal relationships by the frequency of technology use: relational partners who talk for longer periods of time on their cell phones and text each other more often typically have stronger, closer relationships (Licoppe, 2003).

Given how often we use technology to interpersonally communicate, building *online competence* becomes extremely important. A host of factors—including

Credo of the National Communication Association

The National Communication Association (NCA) is the largest professional organization representing communication instructors, researchers, practitioners, and students in the United States. In 1999, the NCA Legislative Council adopted this "Credo for Ethical Communication" (National Communication Association, 1999).

- We advocate truthfulness, accuracy, honesty, and reason as essential to the integrity of communication.

- We endorse freedom of expression, diversity of perspective, and tolerance of dissent to achieve informed and responsible decision making.

- We strive to understand and respect other communicators before evaluating and responding to their messages.

- We promote communication climates of caring and mutual understanding that respect the unique needs and characteristics of individual communicators.

- We condemn communication that degrades people through distortion, intimidation, coercion, and violence, or expression of intolerance and hatred.

- We are committed to the courageous expression of personal convictions in pursuit of fairness and justice.

- We advocate sharing information, opinions, and feelings when facing significant choices while also respecting privacy and confidentiality.

- We accept responsibility for the short- and long-term consequences for our own communication and expect the same of others.

chapter 1 / Introducing Interpersonal Communication

Signs of the social networking times. joyoftech.com by Nitrozac & Snaggy © 2007 Geek Culture

comfort with mobile devices and beliefs about their usefulness for achieving goals—impact whether or not someone will be a competent online communicator (Bakke, 2010). People who are confident learning new apps tend to be better online communicators because they use new media frequently and have fun doing it (Bakke, 2010). But beyond these factors, what can you do to improve your online competence? Based on years of research, scholar Malcolm Parks offers five suggestions (see Table 1.2 on p. 26).[2]

1. *Choose your medium wisely.* An essential part of online competence is knowing when to communicate online versus offline. For many interpersonal goals, online communication is more effective. Text-messaging a friend to remind her of a coffee date makes more sense than dropping by her workplace, and it's probably quicker and less disruptive than calling her. E-mail may be best when dealing with problematic people or certain types of conflicts. That's because you can take time to think and carefully draft and revise responses before sending them—something that isn't possible during face-to-face interactions.

   But online communication is not the best medium for giving in-depth, lengthy, and detailed explanations of professional or personal dilemmas, or for conveying weighty relationship decisions. Despite the ubiquity of online communication, many people still expect important news to be shared in person. Most of us would be surprised if a spouse revealed a long-awaited pregnancy through e-mail, or if a friend disclosed a cancer relapse through a text message.

Media Note: Understanding Competence
Show students the first few minutes of the popular *MADtv* skit "Can I Have Your Number?" (available online). Before playing the clip, advise students to analyze the character Darrell's appropriateness, effectiveness, and ethics. After viewing the clip, have students discuss how the three components of competence were violated.

---

[2] Personal communication with author, May 13, 2008. This material was developed specifically for this text and published with permission of Dr. Malcolm Parks; it may not be reproduced without the written consent of Dr. Parks and the author.

2. *Don't assume that online communication is always more efficient.* Matters of relational significance or issues that evoke strong emotional overtones are more effectively and ethically handled in person or over the phone. But so, too, are many simple things—like deciding when to meet and where to go to lunch. Many times, a one-minute phone call or a quick, face-to-face exchange can save several minutes of texting.

3. *Presume that your posts are public.* You may be thinking of the laugh you'll get from friends when you post the funny picture of you drunkenly hugging the houseplant on Instagram or Facebook. But what about family members, future in-laws, or potential employers who see the picture? That clever joke you made about friend A in an e-mail to friend B—what if B forwards it to C who then forwards it to A? Even if you have privacy settings on your personal page, what's to stop authorized-access friends from downloading your photos and posts and distributing them to others? Keep this rule in mind: anything you've sent or posted online can potentially be seen by anyone.

4. *Remember that your posts are permanent.* The things you say online are like old TV shows: they hang around as reruns forever. Old texts, tweets, e-mails, photographs, videos, and blogs—all of these may still be accessible years later. As just one example, everything you have ever posted on Facebook is stored on its server, whether you delete it from your profile or not. And Facebook legally reserves the right to sell your content, as long

> **Media Note: Incompetent Online Communication**
>
> Lamebook.com compiles real, incompetent comments, statuses, and pictures that people have posted on Facebook. Before showing students, view the site and choose some specific examples to share with your class (note: because these are authentic, some are not suitable for in-class viewing). Have students consider the following questions: Do you see yourself as effective, appropriate, and ethical in your own online communication? What lessons about your own online communication can you learn from Lamebook?

table 1.2 Online Communication Competence

Online Competence Suggestion	Best Practices Suggestion
1. Choose your medium wisely.	*Online* is best for quick reminders, linear messages, or messages that require time and thought to craft. *Offline* is best for important information: engagements, health issues, etc.
2. Don't assume that online communication is always more efficient.	If your message needs a quick decision or answer, a phone call or face-to-face conversation may be best. Use online communication if you want the person to have time to respond.
3. Presume that your posts are public.	If you wouldn't want a message published for public consumption, don't post/send it online.
4. Remember that your posts are permanent.	Even after you delete something, it still exists on servers and may be accessible.
5. Practice the art of creating drafts.	Don't succumb to the pressure to respond to e-mails immediately. Taking your time will result in a more competent message.

as it deletes personally identifying information (such as your name) from it. One of my students learned this the hard way when he saw a personal family photo he had uploaded to Facebook packaged as the sample photo in a gift frame at a local store. Think before you post.

5. *Practice the art of creating drafts.* Get into the habit of saving text and e-mail messages as "drafts," then revisiting them later and editing them as needed for appropriateness, effectiveness, and ethics. Because online communication makes it easy to flame, many of us impetuously fire off messages that we later regret. Sometimes the most competent online communication is none at all—the result of a process in which you compose a text, save it as a draft, but delete it after reviewing it and realizing that it's incompetent.

Issues in Interpersonal Communication

Adapting to influences on interpersonal communication

As we move through the twenty-first century, scholars and students alike increasingly appreciate how important interpersonal communication is in our daily lives and relationships. Moreover, they're recognizing the impact of societal changes, such as diversity and technological innovation. To ensure that the field stays current with social trends, communication scholars have begun exploring the issues of culture, gender and sexual orientation, online communication, and the dark side of interpersonal relationships.

skills practice

Online Competence
Become a more competent online communicator.

❶ Before communicating online, ask yourself if the information is important or complicated, or if it requires a negotiated decision. If so, call or communicate face-to-face instead.

❷ Don't share content you consider private. Anything you tweet, text, e-mail, or post can be exported elsewhere by anyone who has access to it.

❸ Save messages as drafts, then revisit them later, checking appropriateness, effectiveness, and ethics.

❹ When in doubt, delete— don't send!

CULTURE

In this text, we define *culture* broadly and inclusively as an established, coherent set of beliefs, attitudes, values, and practices shared by a large group of people (Keesing, 1974). Culture includes many different types of large-group influences, such as nationality, ethnicity, religion, gender, sexual orientation, physical and mental abilities, and even age. We learn our cultural beliefs, attitudes, and values from parents, teachers, religious leaders, peers, and the mass media (Gudykunst & Kim, 2003). As our world gets more diverse, scholars and students must consider cultural differences when discussing interpersonal communication theory and research, and how communication skills can be improved.

Throughout this book, and particularly in Chapter 5, we examine differences and similarities across cultures and consider their implications for interpersonal communication. As we cover this material, critically examine the role that culture plays in your own interpersonal communication and relationships.

GENDER AND SEXUAL ORIENTATION

Gender consists of social, psychological, and cultural traits generally associated with one sex or the other (Canary, Emmers-Sommer, & Faulkner, 1997). Unlike biological sex, which we're born with, gender is largely learned. Gender influences how people communicate interpersonally, but scholars disagree about how. For example, you may have read in popular magazines or heard on TV that

28   chapter 1 / Introducing Interpersonal Communication

▲ Understanding how culture, gender, and sexual orientation can influence interpersonal communication will help you communicate more effectively. (Clockwise from top left) Danny Lehman/Corbis; Heiko Meyer/laif/Redux Pictures; Kelvin Murray/Getty Images; Carl De Keyzer/Magnum Photos

women are more "open" communicators than men, and that men "have difficulty communicating their feelings." But when these beliefs are compared with research and theory on gender and interpersonal communication, it turns out that differences (and similarities) between men and women are more complicated than the popular stereotypes suggest. Throughout this book, we discuss such stereotypes and look at scholarly research on the impact of gender on interpersonal communication.

Each of us also possesses a **sexual orientation:** an enduring emotional, romantic, sexual, or affectionate attraction to others that exists along a continuum ranging from exclusive homosexuality to exclusive heterosexuality and that includes various forms of bisexuality (APA Online, n.d.). You may have heard that gays and lesbians communicate in ways different from "straights" or that each group builds, maintains, and ends relationships in distinct ways. But as with common beliefs about gender, research shows that same-gender and opposite-gender relationships are formed, maintained, and dissolved in similar ways. We also discuss these assumptions about sexual orientation throughout this text.

Intercultural Competence

When GM first began marketing the Chevy Nova in South America, it sold few cars. Why? Because *no va* means "it won't go" in Spanish. When Coke first began selling in China, its attempt to render *Coca-Cola* in Mandarin (*Ke-kou-ke-la*) translated as "bite the wax tadpole!"

Intercultural communication challenges aren't limited to language. The "hook 'em horns" gesture (index and pinky finger raised) used by Texas football fans means "your wife is cheating on you" in Italy. And simply pointing at someone with your index finger is considered rude in China, Japan, Indonesia, and Latin America.

Throughout this text, we discuss cultural differences in communication and how you can best adapt to them. Such skills are essential, given that hundreds of thousands of college students choose to pursue their studies overseas, international travel is increasingly common, and technology continues to connect people worldwide. As a starting point for building your intercultural competence, consider these suggestions:

1. Think globally. If the world's population was reduced in scale to 1,000 people, only 56 would be from Canada, Mexico, and the United States.

2. Learn appropriateness. Take the time to learn the practices of other cultures before interacting with their people.

3. Be respectfully inquisitive. When you're unsure about how to communicate, politely ask. People will view you as competent—even if you make mistakes—when you sincerely try to learn and abide by their cultural expectations.

4. Use simple language. Avoid slang and jargon. A phrase like "Let's cut to the chase" may make sense if you're originally from Canada or the United States, but it won't necessarily be understood elsewhere.

5. Be patient with yourself and others. Becoming interculturally competent is a lifelong journey, not a short-term achievement.

discussion questions

- How has *your* cultural background shaped how you communicate with people from other cultures?
- What's the biggest barrier that keeps people of different cultures from communicating competently with each other?

ONLINE COMMUNICATION

Radical changes in communication technology have had a profound effect on our ability to interpersonally communicate. Mobile devices keep us in almost constant contact with friends, family members, colleagues, and romantic partners. Our ability to communicate easily and frequently, even when separated by geographic distance, is further enhanced through *online communication*. In this book, we treat such technologies as tools for connecting people interpersonally—tools that are now thoroughly integrated into our lives. In each chapter, you'll find frequent mention of these technologies as they relate to the chapter's specific topics.

THE DARK SIDE OF INTERPERSONAL RELATIONSHIPS

Interpersonal communication strongly influences the quality of our interpersonal relationships, and the quality of those relationships in turn affects how we feel about our lives. When our involvements with lovers, family, friends, and coworkers are satisfying and healthy, we feel happier in general (Myers, 2002). But the fact that relationships can bring us joy obscures the fact that relationships, and the interpersonal communication that occurs within them, can often be destructive.

making relationship choices

Dealing with a Difficult Friend

BACKGROUND

Communicating competently is challenging, especially when close relationship partners provoke us. When problematic encounters happen online, it makes dealing with them even more difficult. Read the case study in Part 2; then, drawing on all you know about interpersonal communication thus far, work through the problem-solving model in Part 3.

 Visit LaunchPad to check out the other side of the story (Part 4). For the best experience, complete all parts in LaunchPad: **macmillanhighered.com /reflectrelate4e**.

2 CASE STUDY

Kaitlyn, Cort, and you have been best friends for years. The three of you are inseparable, and people joke that you're more like triplets than friends. After high school, you and Cort become college housemates. Kaitlyn can't afford tuition yet, so she stays in your hometown to work and save money. Despite the distance, the three of you stay in daily contact.

Recently, however, things have changed. Kaitlyn has been hanging out with people you consider shady. She's been drinking heavily and boasting about her all-night binges. You try to be supportive, but you're worried.

You awake one Sunday to find that one of Kaitlyn's new friends has tagged her in a series of Facebook photos documenting their latest party adventure. Kaitlyn has added a comment that reads, "A new low is reached—I *LUV* it!!" Surfing through the pictures, you see Kaitlyn drinking until she passes out. Several photos show her friends laughing and posing with her while she's unconscious. In one image, they've drawn a smiley face on her forehead with a Sharpie. Looking at these photos, you're heartsick with humiliation for your friend. Why would Kaitlyn hang with people like that? But you also can't understand why she would comment on these pictures rather than insist on having them deleted. What if her family saw them? or her employers? You e-mail her, telling her she should have the photos deleted, and saying that you're worried about her behavior and her choice of new friends. She doesn't respond.

That night, you're studying with Cort. When Cort steps out to get some food, a message alert sounds on his phone. It's a text from Kaitlyn. You know you shouldn't read it, but your curiosity gets the best of you. It's a rage message, in which Kaitlyn blasts you for prying into her business, for judging her, for thinking you're better than her, and for telling her what to do. It's personal, profane, and *very* insulting.

You feel sick to your stomach. You love Kaitlyn, but you're also furious with her. How could she say such horrible things when all you were trying to do was help? As you sit there stewing, another text to Cort from Kaitlyn comes in. "Where r u? Text me back! I want to talk w/ u about our nosy, o-so-perfect friend!"

3 YOUR TURN

Think about all you've learned thus far about interpersonal communication. Then work through the following five steps. Remember, there are no "right" answers, so think hard about what is the *best* choice! (P.S. Need help? See the *Helpful Concepts* list.)

step 1
Reflect on yourself. What are your thoughts and feelings in this situation? What assumptions are you making about Kaitlyn and her communication? Are your assumptions accurate?

step 2
Reflect on your partner. Put yourself in Kaitlyn's shoes. How is she thinking and feeling? Are her views valid?

step 3
Identify the optimal outcome. Think about your relationship and communication with Kaitlyn and all that has happened. What's the best, most constructive relationship outcome possible? Consider what's best for you and for Kaitlyn.

step 4
Locate the roadblocks. Taking into consideration your own and Kaitlyn's thoughts and feelings and all that has happened in this situation, what obstacles are preventing you from achieving the optimal outcome?

step 5
Chart your course. What can you say to Kaitlyn to overcome the roadblocks you've identified and achieve your optimal outcome?

HELPFUL CONCEPTS
I-Thou and I-It, 13
Relationship information, 13–15
The irreversibility of interpersonal communication, 16
Ethics, 23–24
Improving your online competence, 24–27

4 THE OTHER SIDE

Visit LaunchPad to watch a video in which Kaitlyn tells her side of the case study story. As in many real-life situations, this is information to which you did not have access when you were initially crafting your response in Part 3. The video reminds us that even when we do our best to offer competent responses, there is always another side to the story that we need to consider.

Online Self-Quiz: The Dark Side of Interpersonal Relationships. To take this self-quiz, visit LaunchPad: macmillanhighered.com /reflectrelate4e

Teaching Tip: National Communication Association
Encourage your students to visit the National Communication Association's Web site at natcom.org to find a wealth of information on the field of communication. Students can find brief articles about cutting-edge communication research and information on careers in communication.

In studying interpersonal communication, you can learn much by looking beyond constructive encounters to the types of damaging exchanges that occur all too frequently in life. *The greatest challenges to your interpersonal communication skills lie not in communicating competently when it is easy to do so but in practicing competent interpersonal communication when doing so is difficult.* Throughout the text, we will discuss many of the negative situations that you may experience, as well as recommendations for how to deal with them.

The Journey Ahead

Studying communication is the first step toward improving it

Interpersonal communication is our primary vehicle for exchanging meaning, connecting emotionally, and building relationships with others. This makes it essential that we base our interpersonal decisions on the best knowledge to which we have access. No one would consider making choices about collegiate majors, future careers, or monetary interests without first gathering the most trustworthy information available. Interpersonal communication should be no different.

This chapter—which introduces key definitions and important principles—will start you on your journey into the study of interpersonal communication. As we travel together through interpersonal essentials, skills, and relationships, the transformative potential of your interpersonal communication will become apparent.

POSTSCRIPT

We began this chapter with a military wife struggling to juggle the competing demands of raising her children and maintaining her marriage. Melissa Seligman uses multiple media to stay connected with her husband during his combat deployments. At the same time, she has learned that computers, phones, and care packages are merely tools. The most important thing is open, honest, and loving communication.

How do you stay close with loved ones who are distant? What tough communication choices have you faced in these relationships?

The story of Melissa Seligman's struggle reminds us of an inescapable truth that forms the foundation for this book. Our close relationships are *the* most important things in our lives, and it's our choices regarding how we communicate that determine whether these relationships survive and thrive, or fade away.

chapter review

LaunchPad for *Reflect & Relate* offers videos and encourages self-assessment through adaptive quizzing. Go to **macmillanhighered.com/reflectrelate4e** to get access to:

- LearningCurve Adaptive Quizzes
- Video clips that help you understand interpersonal communication

key terms

- communication, 6
- message, 7
- interaction, 7
- contexts, 7
- channel, 7
- media, 7
- linear communication model, 8
- sender, 8
- noise, 8
- receiver, 8
- interactive communication model, 8
- feedback, 9
- fields of experience, 9
- transactional communication model, 9
- interpersonal communication, 11
- dyadic, 11
- intrapersonal communication, 11
- I-Thou, 13
- I-It, 13
- impersonal communication, 13
- meta-communication, 15
- self-presentation goals, 18
- instrumental goals, 18
- relationship goals, 18
- interpersonal communication competence, 21
- communication skills, 21
- appropriateness, 21
- self-monitoring, 22
- effectiveness, 22
- ethics, 23
- online communication, 24
- gender, 27
- sexual orientation, 28

You can watch brief, illustrative videos of these terms and test your understanding of the concepts in LaunchPad.

key concepts

What Is Communication?

- The **message** is the basic unit of **communication.** We exchange messages during **interactions** with others, **contexts** shape how we create and interpret messages, and messages are conveyed through a variety of **channels** and **media.**
- The **linear communication model** describes the components necessary for communication to occur. The **interactive communication model** adds **feedback** and **fields of experience.** The **transactional communication model** presents the notion that communication participants collaboratively create meaning.

What Is Interpersonal Communication?

- **Dyadic** communication allows us to distinguish interpersonal communication from **intrapersonal communication.**
- Interpersonal communication changes, and is changed by, participants' emotions, thoughts, behavior, and relationships.
- Interpersonal communication is characterized by four principles: it has content and relationship information, it can be intentional or unintentional, it's irreversible, and it's dynamic. It can be used for fulfilling a hierarchy of needs and pursuing **self-presentation, instrumental,** and **relationship goals.**

What Is Interpersonal Communication Competence?

- **Interpersonal communication competence** means communicating with others in ways that are appropriate, effective, and ethical.
- People use **self-monitoring** to observe and judge the appropriateness of their communication as it relates to norms.
- People who demonstrate **effectiveness** in achieving their interpersonal goals are interpersonally competent.
- For competent **online communication,** choose your medium wisely, don't assume online communication is always more efficient, presume your posts are public, remember that your posts are permanent, and practice the art of creating drafts.

Issues in Interpersonal Communication

- Relevant topics include culture, **gender** and **sexual orientation,** online communication, and the dark side of interpersonal relationships.

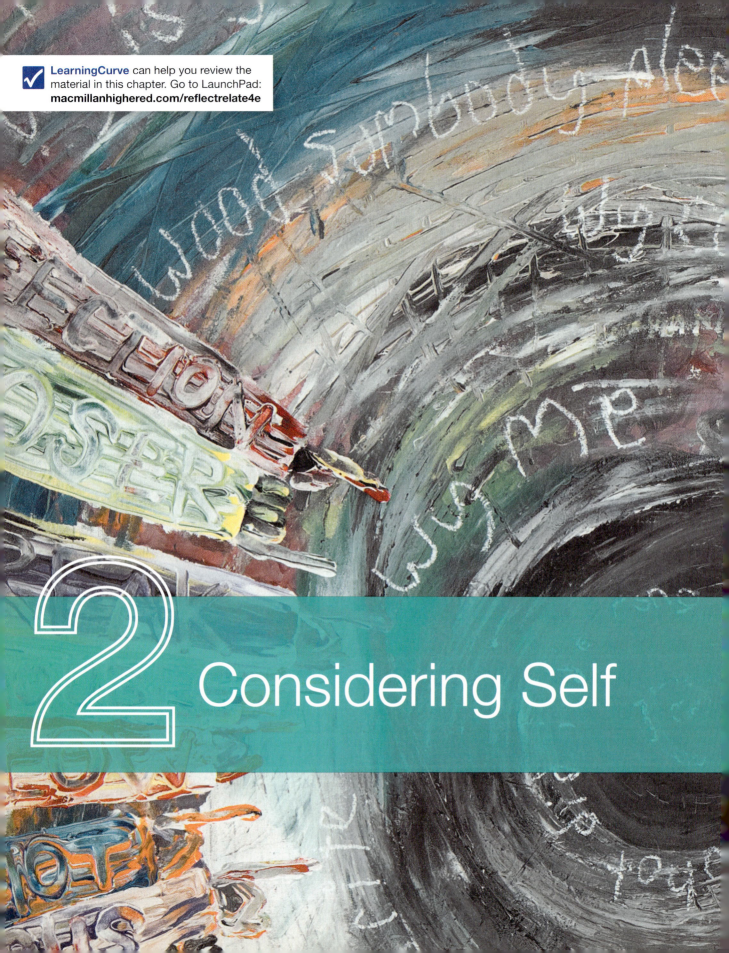

> By deepening your self-understanding, you can begin to clarify your thoughts and feelings about your self.

Artist Eric Staib describes his 2002 painting *labeled* as a self-portrait. "It depicts my feelings about how my peers saw me when I was growing up. The hands pointing, words said under people's breath. You can tell what they're thinking: you're an idiot, you're stupid, you're a joke."[1]

By the time Eric was in third grade, he knew he was different. Whereas his classmates progressed rapidly in reading and writing, Eric couldn't make sense of words on the written page. But it wasn't until fifth grade that Eric was finally given a label for his difference: learning disabled, or LD. The LD label stained Eric's sense of self, making him feel ashamed. His low self-esteem spread outward, constraining his communication and relationships. "My whole approach was *Don't get noticed!* I'd slouch down in class, hide in my seat. And I would never open up to people. I let nobody in."

Frustrated with the seemingly insurmountable challenges of reading and writing, Eric channeled intense energy into art. By eleventh grade, Eric had the reading and writing abilities of a fifth grader but managed to pass his classes through hard work and artistic ability. He graduated from high school with a D average.

---

[1] All information presented regarding artist Eric Staib was provided with his permission, from an interview conducted by the author in February 2005.

35

2 / Considering Self

Photo by Scott Rosenfeld

Many of Eric's peers with learning disabilities had turned to substance abuse and dropped out of school, but Eric pursued his education further, taking classes at a local community college. There, something happened that transformed his view of his self, his self-esteem, and the entire course of his life. While taking his first written exam of the semester, Eric knew the answers, but he couldn't write them down. No matter how hard he focused, he couldn't convert the knowledge in his head into written words. Rather than complete the exam, he wrote the story of his disability on the answer sheet, including his struggles with reading and writing and the pain associated with being labeled LD. He turned in his exam and left. Eric's professor took his exam to the college dean, and the two of them called Eric to the dean's office. They told him, "You need help, and we're going to help you." Their compassion changed Eric's life. Eric's professor arranged for Eric to meet with a learning specialist, who immediately diagnosed him as dyslexic. As Eric explains, "For the first time in my life, I had a label for myself other than 'learning disabled.' To me, the LD label meant I couldn't learn. But dyslexia was different. It could be overcome. The specialist taught me strategies for working with my dyslexia, and gave me my most important tool—my Franklin Spellchecker—to check spellings. But most importantly, I was taught that it was OK to be dyslexic."

Armed with an improving sense of self, Eric went from hiding to asserting himself, "from low self-esteem to being comfortable voicing my opinion, from fear to confidence." That confidence led him to transfer to a Big Ten university, where he graduated with a degree in studio arts, percussion, and horticulture. He subsequently earned a postgraduate degree in K–12 art education, graduating with a straight-A average.

Eric Staib is now an art instructor in the Midwest and was a 2006 recipient of the Robert Rauschenberg Foundation Power of Art Award, given to the top arts educators in the country each year. He also teaches instructors how to use art to engage students with learning disabilities. What means the most to him is the opportunity to pass down the legacy of his personal transformation. "When I think about my dyslexia, it's really incredible. What was my greatest personal punishment is now the most profound gift I have to offer to others."

Every word you've ever spoken during an encounter, every act of kindness or cruelty you've committed, has the same root source—your self. When you look inward, you are peering into the wellspring from which all your interpersonal actions flow. But even as your self influences your interpersonal communication, it is shaped by your communication as well. Through communicating with others, we learn who we are, what we're worth, and how we should act. This means that the starting point for improving your communication is to understand your self. In this way, you can begin to clarify your thoughts and feelings about your self; comprehend how these are linked to your interpersonal communication; and develop strategies for enhancing your sense of self, your communication skills, and your interpersonal relationships.

In this chapter, we explore the source of all interpersonal communication: the self. You'll learn:

- The components of self, as well as how critical self-reflection can be used to improve your communication skills and your self-esteem
- The ways in which gender, family, and culture shape your sense of self
- How to present and maintain a positive self when interacting with others
- The importance of online self-presentation
- The challenges of managing the self in relationships, including suggestions for successful self-disclosure

chapter outline

37
The Components of Self

43
The Sources of Self

48
Presenting Your Self

55
The Relational Self

63
Improving Your Self

Chapter Theme

This chapter is the first of three that examine the foundational factors influencing our communication decision making: self, perception, and emotion. We will discus how the labels placed on us by ourselves and others shape our sense of self. The labels we embrace impact not just our private selves—self-concept, self-esteem, and capacity for critical self-reflection—but our public selves as well, in what we disclose to others and how we form relationships.

The Components of Self

Your self is the driving force of your communication

At Delphi in ancient Greece, the temple of the sun-god Apollo was adorned with the inscription *Gnothi se auton*—"Know thyself." According to legend, when one of the seven sages of Greece, Chilon of Sparta, asked Apollo, "What is best for people?" the deity responded with that simple admonition. More than 2,500 years later, these words still ring true, especially in the realm of interpersonal communication and relationships. To understand our interactions with others and the bonds we forge, we must first comprehend ourselves. But what exactly is "thyself" that we need to know?

The **self** is an evolving composite of self-awareness, self-concept, and self-esteem. Although each of us experiences the self as singular ("*This* is who I am"), it is actually made up of three distinct yet integrated components that evolve continually over time, based on your life experiences.

SELF-AWARENESS

Self-awareness is the ability to view yourself as a unique person distinct from your surrounding environment and to reflect on your thoughts, feelings, and behaviors. According to sociologist George Herbert Mead (1934), self-awareness helps you have a strong sense of your self because during interpersonal encounters, you monitor your own behaviors and form impressions of who you are from

37

▶ Our self-concept is influenced by our beliefs about how others view us.
Paul Bradbury/Getty Images

Assignment: Social Comparison
Have students brainstorm a list of socioeconomic expectations they have for people in specific age groups (career, marital status, income, living arrangement, for 18- to 25-year-olds or 40- to 50-year-olds). Then discuss the following questions: How are these expectations generated? What role do the media play in shaping these expectations? How do these expectations shape self-esteem?

▶ **Video**

macmillanhighered.com
/reflectrelate4e

Social Comparison
Watch this clip online to answer the questions below.

What aspects of your self are you more likely to compare with others? How does this impact your self-awareness?

Want to see more? Check out LaunchPad for a clip on **self-fulfilling prophecies.**

such observations. For example, your best friend texts you that she has failed an important exam. You feel bad for her, so you text her a comforting response. Your self-awareness of your compassion and your observation of your kindhearted message lead you to think, "I'm a caring and supportive friend."

As we're watching and evaluating our own actions, we also engage in **social comparison:** observing and assigning meaning to others' behavior and then comparing it with ours. Social comparison has a particularly potent effect on self when we compare ourselves to people we wish to emulate. When we compare favorably when measured against respected others, we think well of ourselves; when we don't compare favorably, we think less of ourselves.

You can greatly enhance your interpersonal communication by practicing a targeted kind of self-awareness known as *critical self-reflection*. To engage in critical self-reflection, ask yourself the following questions:

- What am I thinking and feeling?
- Why am I thinking and feeling this way?
- How am I communicating?
- How are my thoughts and feelings influencing my communication?
- How can I improve my thoughts, feelings, and communication?

The ultimate goal of critical self-reflection is embodied in the last question: How can I *improve*? Improving your interpersonal communication is possible only when you accurately understand how your self drives your communication behavior. In the remainder of this chapter, and in the marginal *Self-Reflection* exercises you'll find throughout this book, we help you make links between your self and your communication.

SELF-CONCEPT

Self-concept is your overall perception of who you are. Your self-concept is based on the beliefs, attitudes, and values you have about yourself. *Beliefs* are convictions that certain things are true—for example, "I'm an excellent student." *Attitudes* are evaluative appraisals, such as "I'm happy with my appearance." *Values* represent enduring principles that guide your interpersonal actions—for example, "I think it's wrong to . . ."

Your self-concept is shaped by a host of factors, including your gender, family, friends, and culture (Vallacher, Nowak, Froehlich, & Rockloff, 2002). As we saw in the opening story about Eric Staib, one of the biggest influences on your self-concept is the labels others put on you. How do others' impressions of you shape your self-concept? Sociologist Charles Horton Cooley (1902) argued that it's like looking at yourself in the "looking glass" (mirror). When you stand in front of it, you consider your physical appearance through the eyes of others. Do they see you as attractive? overweight? too tall or too short? Seeing yourself in this fashion—and thinking about how others must see you—has a powerful effect on how you think about your physical self. Cooley noted that the same process shapes our broader self-concept: it is based in part on your beliefs about how others see you, including their perceptions and evaluations of you ("People think I'm talented, and they like me") and your emotional response to those beliefs ("I feel good/bad about how others see me"). Cooley referred to the idea of defining our self-concepts through thinking about how others see us as the **looking-glass self**.

Some people have clear and stable self-concepts; that is, they know exactly who they are, and their sense of self endures across time, situations, and relationships. Others struggle with their identity, remaining uncertain about who they really are, what they believe, and how they feel about themselves. The degree to which you have a clearly defined, consistent, and enduring sense of self is known as **self-concept clarity** (Campbell et al., 1996), and it has a powerful effect on your outlook, health, and happiness. Research suggests that people who have a stronger, clearer, sense of self (i.e., higher self-concept clarity) have higher self-esteem, are less likely to experience negative emotions (both in response to stressful situations and in general), and are less likely to experience chronic depression (Lee-Flynn, Pomaki, DeLongis, Biesanz, & Puterman, 2011). In simple terms, high self-concept clarity helps you weather the unpredictability and instability of the world around you. To test *your* self-concept clarity, take the *Self-Quiz* on page 40.

In considering your self-concept and its impact on your interpersonal communication, keep two implications in mind. First, because your self-concept consists of deeply held beliefs, attitudes, and values, changing it is difficult. Once you've decided you're a compassionate person, for example, you'll likely perceive yourself that way for a long time (Fiske & Taylor, 1991).

Second, our self-concepts often lead us to make **self-fulfilling prophecies**—predictions about future interactions that lead us to behave in ways that ensure the interaction unfolds as we predicted. Some self-fulfilling prophecies set positive events in motion. For instance, you may see yourself as professionally capable and highly skilled at communicating, which leads you to predict job interview success. During an interview, your prophecy of success leads you to communicate in a calm

self-reflection

Consider your looking-glass self. What kinds of labels do your friends use to describe you? your family? How do you feel about others' impressions of you? In what ways do these feelings shape your interpersonal communication and relationships?

Assignment: The Looking-Glass Self

While discussing the looking-glass self, ask students to engage in Think-Ink-Pair-Share on the following statement: "I'm not who I think I am. I'm not who you think I am. I am who I think you think I am." Thus, students should think about the statement on their own, write down their ideas, discuss them with a partner, and then share their ideas with the class.

self-QUIZ

Test Your Self-Concept Clarity

High self-concept clarity means that your sense of self is clear and enduring. Low self-concept clarity means that you struggle with your identity and who you really are. To test your self-concept clarity, simply check the items with which you agree; then tally the total number of items you checked and use the key at the bottom.

To take this quiz online, visit LaunchPad: macmillanhighered.com/reflectrelate4e.

_____ My beliefs about myself rarely conflict with one another.

_____ I don't spend a lot of time wondering about what kind of person I really am.

_____ I seldom experience conflict between the different aspects of my personality.

_____ My beliefs about myself hardly ever change.

_____ If I were asked to describe my personality, my description would be the same from one day to the next.

_____ In general, I have a clear sense of who I am and what I am.

_____ It is easy for me to make up my mind about things because I know what I want.

Note: This *Self-Quiz* is adapted from Campbell et al. (1996, p. 151).

Scoring: 0–3 indicates low self-concept clarity (you remain uncertain about who you really are, what you believe, and how you feel about yourself). 4–7 indicates high self-concept clarity (you have a clear sense of self that endures across time, situations, and relationships).

skills practice

Self-Fulfilling Prophecies
Overcoming negative self-fulfilling prophecies

❶ Identify a communication problem you experience often (e.g., social anxiety).

❷ Describe situations in which it occurs, including what you think, say, and do.

❸ Use critical self-reflection to identify how your thoughts and feelings shape your communication.

❹ List things you could say and do that would generate positive results.

❺ In similar situations, block negative thoughts and feelings that arise, and focus your attention on practicing the positive behaviors you listed.

and confident fashion, which impresses the interviewers. In turn, their reaction confirms your prophecy. Other self-fulfilling prophecies set negative events in motion. I once had a friend who believed he was unattractive and undesirable. Whenever we went out to parties, his self-concept would lead him to predict interpersonal failure. He would then spend the entire time in a corner staring morosely into his drink. Needless to say, no one tried to talk to him. At the end of the evening, he'd say, "See, I told you no one would want to talk to me!"

SELF-ESTEEM

Self-esteem is the overall value, positive or negative, that we assign to ourselves. Whereas self-awareness prompts us to ask, "Who am I?" and self-concept is the answer to that question, self-esteem is the answer to the follow-up question, "Given who I am, what's my evaluation of my self?" When your overall estimation of self is negative, you'll have a meager sense of self-worth and suffer from low self-esteem. When your evaluation of self is positive, you'll enjoy high self-esteem.

Your self-esteem strongly shapes your interpersonal communication, relationships, and physical and mental health (Pyszczynski, Greenberg, Solomon, Arndt, & Schimel, 2004). People with high self-esteem report greater life satisfaction; communicate more positively with others; experience more happiness in their relationships; and exhibit greater leadership ability, athleticism, and academic performance than do people with low self-esteem (Fox, 1997, 1992). High self-esteem also helps insulate people from stress and anxiety (Lee-Flynn et al., 2011).

chapter 2 / Considering Self   41

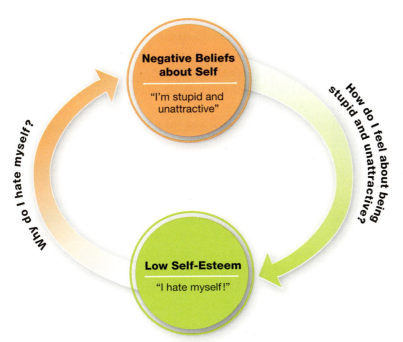

figure 2.1 **Low Self-Esteem: A Vicious Cycle**

By contrast, people with low self-esteem are more likely to believe that friends and romantic partners think negatively of them (Gaucher et al., 2012) and, as a consequence, are less likely to share their thoughts and feelings with others. This lack of expressivity ultimately undermines their close relationships (Gaucher et al., 2012). In addition, low self-esteem individuals experience negative emotions and depression more frequently (Orth, Robius, Trzesniewski, Maes, & Schmitt, 2009), resulting in destructive feedback loops like the one depicted in Figure 2.1.

Measuring Up to Your Own Standards The key to bolstering your self-esteem is understanding its roots. **Self-discrepancy theory** suggests that your self-esteem is determined by how you compare to two mental standards (Higgins, 1987). The first is your *ideal self*, the characteristics (mental, physical, emotional, material, and spiritual) that you want to possess—the "perfect you." The second is your *ought self*, the person others wish and expect you to be. This standard stems from expectations of your family, friends, colleagues, and romantic partners as well as cultural norms. According to self-discrepancy theory, you feel happy and content when your perception of your self matches both your ideal and your ought selves (Katz & Farrow, 2000). However, when you perceive your self to be inferior to both your ideal and your ought selves, you experience a discrepancy and are likely to suffer low self-esteem (Veale, Kinderman, Riley, & Lambrou, 2003).

Research looking at self-discrepancy theory suggests three things to consider (Halliwell & Dittmar, 2006; Phillips & Silvia, 2005). First, women report larger ideal self-discrepancies than do men. This isn't surprising, given the degree to which women are deluged with advertising and other media emphasizing unattainable standards for female beauty (see *Focus on Culture* on p. 43). Second, for both men and women, self-discrepancies impact a host of specific emotions and

Assignment: Self-Fulfilling Prophecies
Have students watch the LaunchPad video clip on self-fulfilling prophecies, then write a short journal entry comparing the outcomes of a positive and a negative self-fulfilling prophecy they have experienced. Have them consider the common steps of a self-fulfilling prophecy. Then have them answer the following: What impact do your self-fulfilling prophecies have on your interactions? How have they affected your relationships? What have you done (or can you do) to reduce the impact of your negative self-fulfilling prophecies?

Discussion Prompt: Body Image and the Media
Ask students if they believe exposure to the media influences the way they feel about themselves. Do the media have an impact on their self-esteem (e.g., ads or TV shows with beautiful characters and impressive lifestyles)? Then cite Pavica Sheldon's (2010) survey of 224 college students, which revealed that while perfectionism and media use were not related to students' body image, higher family and peer pressure and a higher score on perfectionism influenced women to compare themselves to the models in fashion magazines and on television. Thus, family and peer messages have a strong influence on our body image.

Blogger and magazine editor Tavi Gevinson is a role model for many teen girls in the United States. Her online magazine, *Rookie*, hosts articles about fashion and feminism to help her readers understand issues of women's representation in the media.
Glynis Selina Arban/Contour by Getty Images

feelings linked to self-esteem. For instance, people who have substantial ideal and ought self-discrepancies are more likely to report feeling dejected, disappointed, hopeless, and upset about themselves. Finally, self-discrepancies are most apparent and impactful to us in situations in which we become consciously self-aware: looking in a mirror, watching ourselves on video, or getting direct feedback from others. After watching an unflattering video clip of yourself posted online or getting an unsatisfactory employee evaluation, you may suddenly feel that you're "not the kind of person you should be"—resulting in negative emotions and plummeting self-esteem.

This latter finding suggests an important relationship implication. If you live your life surrounded by people who constantly criticize you, belittle you, or call attention to your flaws, you are more likely to have wider self-discrepancies and lower self-esteem. Alternatively, if your social network supports you and praises you for your unique abilities, your self-discrepancies will diminish and your self-esteem will rise. Thus, *a critical part of maintaining your life happiness and self-esteem is avoiding or limiting contact with people who routinely tear you down and surrounding yourself with people who build you up.*

What's more, it doesn't matter whether you *think* you're immune to others' opinions. Research looking at people who said that they couldn't "care less" about what other people think of them found that their self-esteem was just as strongly impacted by approval and criticism as people who reported valuing others' opinions (Leary et al., 2003). In short, receiving others' approval or criticism will boost or undermine your self-esteem whether you think it will or not.

Improving Your Self-Esteem Your self-esteem can start to improve only when you reduce discrepancies between your self and your ideal and ought selves. How can you do this? Begin by assessing your self-concept. Make a list of the beliefs, attitudes, and values that make up your self-concept. Be sure to include both positive and negative attributes. Then think about your self-esteem. In reviewing the list you've made, do you see yourself positively or negatively?

Next, analyze your ideal self. Who do you wish you were? Is this ideal attainable, or is it unrealistic? If it is attainable, what would you have to change to become this person? If you made these changes, would you be satisfied with yourself, or would your expectations for yourself simply escalate further?

Third, analyze your ought self. Who do others want you to be? Can you ever become the person others expect? What would you have to do to become this person? If you did all of these things, would others be satisfied with you, or would their expectations escalate?

Fourth, revisit and redefine your standards. This step requires intense, concentrated effort over a long period of time. If you find that your ideal and ought selves are realistic and attainable, move to the final step. If you decide that your

focus on CULTURE

How Does the Media Shape Your Self-Esteem?

Korean American comedian Margaret Cho describes herself as a "trash-talkin' girl comic." In this excerpt from her one-woman show *The Notorious C.H.O.*, she offers her thoughts on self-esteem:

> You know when you look in the mirror and think, "Oh, I'm so fat, I'm so old, I'm so ugly"? That is not your authentic self speaking. That is billions upon billions of dollars of advertising—magazines, movies, billboards—all geared to make you feel bad about yourself so that you'll take your hard-earned money and spend it at the mall. When you don't have self-esteem, you will hesitate before you do anything. You will hesitate to go for the job you really want. You will hesitate to ask for a raise. You will hesitate to defend yourself when you're discriminated against. You will hesitate to vote. You will hesitate to dream. For those of us plagued with low self-esteem, improving [it] is truly an act of revolution! (Custudio, 2002)

Cho is right. We live in an "appearance culture," a society that values and reinforces extreme, unrealistic ideals of beauty and body shape (Thompson, Heinberg, Altabe, & Tantleff-Dunn, 1999). In an appearance culture, standards for appearance are defined through digitally enhanced images of bodily perfection produced by the mass media (Field et al., 1999). When we internalize media standards of the perfect body and perfect beauty, we end up despising our own bodies and craving unattainable perfection (Jones, Vigfusdottir, & Lee, 2004). This results in low self-esteem, depression, and, in some cases, self-destructive behaviors such as eating disorders (Harrison, 2001).

discussion questions

- Consider your own body. How have images of ideal beauty in magazines and on TV influenced your ideas about what constitutes an attractive body?
- How do your feelings about your body affect your self-esteem? How do they affect your interpersonal communication and relationships?

---

ideal and ought selves are unrealistic and unattainable, redefine these standards so that each can be attainable through sustained work. If you find yourself unable to abandon unrealistic and unattainable standards, don't be afraid to consult with a professional therapist or another trusted resource for assistance.

Finally, create an action plan for resolving any self-discrepancies. Map out the specific actions necessary to eventually attain your ideal and ought selves. Frame your new standards as a list of goals, and post them in your planner, cell phone, personal Web page, bedroom, or kitchen to remind yourself of these goals. Since self-esteem can't be changed in a day, a week, or even a month, establish a realistic time line. Then implement this action plan in your daily life, checking your progress as you go.

The Sources of Self

Outside forces influence your view of self

For most of us, critical self-reflection isn't a new activity. After all, we spend much of our daily lives looking inward, so we feel that we know our selves. But this doesn't mean that our sense of self is entirely self-determined. Instead, our selves are shaped by at least three powerful outside forces: gender, family, and culture.

Assignment: Positive Self-Esteem

Give students a handout with a T-shirt shape on it. Ask them to take it home and create a design emphasizing positive self-esteem. Students can be creative with colors, words, and art. Encourage them to come up with their own sayings or include existing quotations that promote positive self-esteem. For example, Eleanor Roosevelt said, "No one can make you feel inferior without your consent." T-shirt designs could be used for group discussion or for short introductory presentations by each student.

The sources of self include your gender, your family, and your culture.
(Left to right) Ronnie Kaufman/Larry Hirshowitz/Getty Images; Caroline Penn/Panos Pictures; commerceandculturestock/Getty Images

Media Note: Gender Role Socialization and Children

Ask students to watch the "Interviews with Kids on Gender Roles" (found on YouTube) that shows an experiment in which young children are asked to identify a variety of gender role expectations by pointing to the girl or boy doll (e.g., "Who takes care of the babies?"). Then ask students to report on their reactions to the video. Were they surprised by the findings? What impact does gender role socialization have on children today?

self-reflection

What lessons about gender did you learn from your family when you were growing up? from your friends? Based on these lessons, what aspects of your self did you bolster—or bury—given what others deemed appropriate for your gender? How did these lessons affect how you interpersonally communicate?

GENDER AND SELF

Arguably the most profound outside force shaping our sense of self is our *gender*—the composite of social, psychological, and cultural attributes that characterize us as male or female (Canary, Emmers-Sommer, & Faulkner, 1997). It may strike you as strange to see gender described as an "outside force." Gender is innate, something you're born with, right? Actually, scholars distinguish gender, which is largely learned, from *biological sex*, which we're born with. Each of us is born with biological sex organs that distinguish us anatomically as male or female. However, our gender is shaped over time through our interactions with others.

Immediately after birth, we begin a lifelong process of gender socialization, learning from others what it means personally, interpersonally, and culturally to be "male" or "female." Girls are typically taught feminine behaviors, such as sensitivity to one's own and others' emotions, nurturance, and compassion (Lippa, 2002). Boys are usually taught masculine behaviors, learning about assertiveness, competitiveness, and independence. As a result of gender socialization, men and women often end up forming comparatively different self-concepts (Cross & Madson, 1997). For example, women are more likely than men to perceive themselves as connected to others and to assess themselves based on the quality of these interpersonal connections. Men are more likely than women to think of themselves as a composite of their individual achievements, abilities, and beliefs—viewing themselves as separate from other people. However, this doesn't mean that all men and all women think of themselves in identical ways. Many men and women appreciate and embrace both feminine and masculine characteristics in their self-concepts.

FAMILY AND SELF

When we're born, we have no self-awareness, self-concept, or self-esteem. As we mature, we become aware of ourselves as unique and separate from our environments and begin developing self-concepts. Our caregivers play a crucial role in

chapter 2 / Considering Self 45

◔ Immediately after birth, we begin a lifelong process of gender socialization.
Allan Grant/Time & Life Pictures/Getty Images

this process, providing us with ready-made sets of beliefs, attitudes, and values from which we construct our fledgling selves. We also forge emotional bonds with our caregivers, and our communication and interactions with them powerfully shape our beliefs regarding the functions, rewards, and dependability of interpersonal relationships (Bowlby, 1969; Domingue & Mollen, 2009).

These beliefs, in turn, help shape two dimensions of our thoughts, feelings, and behavior: attachment anxiety and attachment avoidance (Collins & Feeney, 2004). *Attachment anxiety* is the degree to which a person fears rejection by relationship partners. If you experience high attachment anxiety, you perceive yourself as unlovable and unworthy—thoughts that may result from being ignored or even abused during childhood. Consequently, you experience chronic fear of abandonment in your close relationships. If you have low attachment anxiety, you feel lovable and worthy of attention—reflections of a supportive and affectionate upbringing. As a result, you feel comfortable and confident in your intimate involvements.

Attachment avoidance is the degree to which someone desires close interpersonal ties. If you have high attachment avoidance, you'll likely experience little interest in intimacy, preferring solitude instead. Such feelings may stem from childhood neglect or an upbringing that encouraged autonomy. If you experience low attachment avoidance, you seek intimacy and interdependence with others, having learned in childhood that such connections are essential for happiness and well-being.

Four attachment styles derive from these two dimensions (Collins & Feeney, 2004; Domingue & Mollen, 2009). **Secure attachment** individuals are low on both anxiety and avoidance: they're comfortable with intimacy and seek close ties with others. Secure individuals report warm and supportive relationships, high self-esteem, and confidence in their ability to communicate. When relationship problems arise, they move to resolve them and are willing to solicit support from others. In addition, they are comfortable with sexual intimacy and are unlikely to engage in risky sexual behavior.

Preoccupied attachment adults are high in anxiety and low in avoidance: they desire closeness but are plagued with fear of rejection. They may use sexual contact to satisfy their compulsive need to feel loved. When faced with relationship challenges, preoccupied individuals react with extreme negative emotion and a lack of trust ("I know you don't love me!"). These individuals often have difficulty maintaining long-term involvements.

People with low anxiety but high avoidance have a **dismissive attachment** style. They view close relationships as comparatively unimportant, instead prizing and prioritizing self-reliance. Relationship crises evoke hasty exits ("I don't need this kind of hassle!"), and they are more likely than other attachment styles to engage in casual sexual relationships and to endorse the view that sex without love is positive.

Finally, **fearful attachment** adults are high in both attachment anxiety *and* avoidance. They fear rejection and tend to shun relationships. Fearful individuals can develop close ties if the relationship seems to guarantee a lack of rejection, such as when a partner is disabled or otherwise dependent on them. But even then, they suffer from a chronic lack of faith in themselves, their partners, and the relationship's viability.

CULTURE AND SELF

At the 1968 Summer Olympics, U.S. sprinter Tommie Smith won the men's 200-meter gold medal, and teammate John Carlos won the bronze. During the medal ceremony, as the American flag was raised and "The Star-Spangled Banner" played, both runners closed their eyes, lowered their heads, and raised black-gloved fists. Smith's right fist represented black power, and Carlos's left fist represented black unity (Gettings, 2005). The two fists, raised next to each other, created an arch of black unity and power. Smith wore a black scarf around his neck for black pride, and both men wore black socks with no shoes, representing African American poverty. These symbols and gestures, taken together, clearly spoke of the runners' allegiance to black culture and their protest of the poor treatment of African Americans in the United States (see the photo on p. 47).

Assignment: Self and Social Expectations
Place students in groups and have them generate a list of social expectations suggested by television programs. Each group should focus on a different demographic, such as age, gender, sexual orientation, race, or political affiliation. After sharing their lists with the class, students should individually complete a one-minute reaction paper to the discussion or, for homework, write a short paper about how they can personally relate to the expectations discussed in class.

Tommie Smith and John Carlos's protest at the 1968 Summer Olympics showed how they identified with the African American culture of the time. Allan Grant/Time & Life Pictures/Getty Images

Many Euro-Americans viewed Smith and Carlos's behavior at the ceremony as a betrayal of "American" culture. Both men were suspended from the U.S. team and even received death threats. Over time, however, people of all American ethnicities began to sympathize with their protest. Thirty years later, in 1998, Smith and Carlos were commemorated in an anniversary celebration of their protest.

In addition to gender and family, our culture is a powerful source of self. *Culture* is an established, coherent set of beliefs, attitudes, values, and practices shared by a large group of people (Keesing, 1974). If this strikes you as similar to our definition of *self-concept*, you're right; culture is like a collective sense of self shared by a large group of people.

Thinking of culture in this way has three important implications. First, culture includes many types of large-group influences, including your nationality as well as your ethnicity, religion, gender, sexual orientation, physical ability, and even age. We learn our cultural beliefs, attitudes, and values from parents, teachers, religious leaders, peers, and the mass media (Gudykunst & Kim, 2003). Second, most of us belong to more than one culture simultaneously—possessing the beliefs, attitudes, and values of each. Third, the various cultures to which we belong sometimes clash. When they do, we often have to choose the culture to which we pledge our primary allegiance.

We'll be discussing culture in greater depth in Chapter 5, where we'll consider some of the unique variables of culture that help to define us and communicate our selves to others.

self-reflection

When you consider your own cultural background, to which culture do you "pledge allegiance"? How do you communicate this allegiance to others? Have you ever suffered consequences for openly communicating your allegiance to your culture? If so, how?

Presenting Your Self

Managing your self both online and off

Rick Welts is one of the most influential people in professional basketball.[2] He created the NBA All-Star Weekend and is cofounder of the women's professional league, the WNBA. For years he served as the NBA's executive vice president and chief marketing officer, and he is now president of the Golden State Warriors. But throughout his entire sports career—40 years of ascension from ball boy to executive—he lived a self-described "shadow life," publicly playing the role of a

---

[2]All of the information that follows regarding Welts is adapted from Barry (2011).

◐ Cultural identity is part of a sophisticated definition of self, as Professor Alfred Guillaume Jr. passionately describes: "I am a 50-year-old American. I am black, Roman Catholic, and Creole. . . . The segregated South wanted me to believe that I was inferior. The Catholic Church taught me that all of God's people were equal. My French Creole heritage gave me a special bond to Native Americans, to Europeans, and to Africans. This is the composite portrait of who I am. I like who I am and can imagine being no other." (Left to right) West Rock/Getty Images; © Image Source/Alamy; © John Elk III/Alamy; Exotica.im 15/Alamy; © Paul A. Souders/Corbis; © David R. Frazier Photolibrary, Inc./Alamy

straight male while privately being gay. The lowest point came when his long-time partner died and Welts couldn't publicly acknowledge his loss. Instead, he took only two days off from work—telling colleagues that a friend had died—and for months compartmentalized his grief. In early 2011, following his mother's death, he came out publicly. As Welts described, "I want to pierce the silence that envelops the subject of being gay in men's team sports. I want to mentor gays who harbor doubts about a sports career, whether on the court or in the front office. But most of all, I want to feel whole, authentic."

In addition to our private selves, the composite of our self-awareness, self-concept, and self-esteem, each of us also has a public self—the self we present to others (Fenigstein, Scheier, & Buss, 1975). We actively create our public selves through our interpersonal communication and behavior.

In many encounters, our private and public selves mirror each other. At other times, they seem disconnected. In extreme instances, like that of Rick Welts, we may intentionally craft an inauthentic public self to hide something about our private self we don't want others to know. But regardless of your private self, it is your public self that your friends, family members, and

◐ Rick Welts was ultimately able to reconcile his private self with his public self. What parts of your private self do you keep hidden from public view? Photo AP/The Arizona Republic, Michael Chow

Video
macmillanhighered.com
/reflectrelate4e

Mask
Watch this clip online to answer the questions below.

When, if ever, have you chosen to use a mask to veil your private self or emotions? What motivates you to use a mask? Do you think others use masks for similar reasons?

Want to see more? Check out LaunchPad for a clip on **face.**

Assignment: Mask
Ask students to watch the LaunchPad video clip on **mask,** and then place them in small groups for a point-of-view analysis. Encourage students to analyze the video by looking at the interaction from each person's perspective and address the following: What type(s) of masks would you present if you were the loser in this situation? the winner? When have you displayed such a mask? Why? Groups can share their findings with the class.

romantic partners hold dear. Most (if not all) of others' impressions of you are based on their appraisals of your public self. People know and judge the "you" who communicates with them, not the "you" you keep inside. Thus, managing your public self is a crucial part of competent interpersonal communication.

MAINTAINING YOUR PUBLIC SELF

Renowned sociologist Erving Goffman (1955) noted that whenever you communicate with others, you present a public self—your **face**—that you want others to see and know. You actively create and present your face through your communication. Your face can be anything you want it to be—"perky and upbeat," "cool and level-headed," or "tough as nails." We create different faces for different moments and relationships in our lives, such as our face as a parent, college student, coworker, or homeless-shelter volunteer.

Sometimes your face is a **mask,** a public self designed to strategically veil your private self (Goffman, 1959). Masks can be dramatic, such as when Rick Welts hid his grief over the loss of his longtime partner. Or masks can be subtle—the parent who acts calm in front of an injured child so the youngster doesn't become frightened. Some masks are designed to inflate one's estimation in the eyes of others. One study found that 90 percent of college students surveyed admitted telling at least one lie to impress a person they were romantically interested in (Rowatt, Cunningham, & Druen, 1998). Other masks are crafted so that people underestimate us and our abilities (Gibson & Sachau, 2000), like acting disorganized or unprepared before a debate in the hope that your opponent will let her guard down.

Regardless of the form our face takes—a genuine representation of our private self, or a mask designed to hide this self from others—Goffman argued that we often form a strong emotional attachment to our face because it represents the person we most want others to see when they communicate with and relate to us.

Sometimes after we've created a certain face, information is revealed that contradicts it, causing us to lose face (Goffman, 1955). Losing face provokes feelings of shame, humiliation, and sadness—in a word, **embarrassment.** For example, singer Katy Perry stakes her career on appearing glamorous, fashionable, and sexy. In December 2010, however, her then husband—comedian Russell Brand—tweeted a photo of her that contradicted her carefully crafted image: Perry just waking up, without makeup. The singer was understandably upset and embarrassed.

While losing face can cause intense embarrassment, this is not the only cost. When others see us lose face, they may begin to question whether the public self with which they're familiar is a genuine reflection of our private self. For example, suppose your workplace face is "dedicated, hardworking employee." You ask your boss if there's extra work to be done, help fellow coworkers, show up early, stay late, and so forth. But if you tell your manager that you need your afternoon schedule cleared to work on an urgent report and then she sees you playing *World of Warcraft* on your computer, she'll undoubtedly view your actions as inconsistent with your communication. Your face as the "hardworking employee" will be called into question, as will your credibility.

Because losing face can damage others' impressions of you, maintaining face during interpersonal interactions is extremely important. How can you effectively maintain face?[3] Use words and actions consistent with the face you're trying to craft. From one moment to the next and from one behavior to the next, your interpersonal communication and behaviors must complement your face. Make sure your communication and behaviors mesh with the knowledge that others already have about you. If you say or do things that contradict what others know is true about you, they'll see your face as false. For example, if your neighbor knows you don't like him because a friend of yours told him so, he's likely to be skeptical the next time you adopt the face of "friendly, caring neighbor" by warmly greeting him.

Finally, for your face to be maintained, your communication and behavior must be reinforced by objects and events in the surrounding environment—things over which you have only limited control. For example, imagine that your romantic partner is overseas for the summer, and you agree to video chat regularly. Your first scheduled chat is Friday at 5 p.m. But when you're driving home Friday afternoon, your car breaks down. Making things worse, your phone goes dead because you forgot to charge it, so there is no way to contact your partner. By the time you get home and online, your partner has already signed off, leaving a perplexed message regarding your "neglect." To restore face, you'll need to explain what happened.

Of course, all of us fall from grace on occasion. What can you do to regain face following an embarrassing incident? Promptly acknowledge that the event happened, admit responsibility for any of your actions that contributed to the event, apologize for your actions and for disappointing others, and move to maintain your face again. Apologies are fairly successful at reducing people's negative impressions and the anger that may have been triggered, especially when such apologies avoid excuses that contradict what people know really happened (Ohbuchi & Sato, 1994). People who deny their inconsistencies or who blame others for their lapses are judged much more harshly.

THE IMPORTANCE OF ONLINE SELF-PRESENTATION

One of the most powerful vehicles for presenting your self online is your profile photo. Whether it's on Facebook, Twitter, LinkedIn, Google, Tumblr, Flickr, Foursquare, or any other site, this image, more than any other, represents who you are to others. When I first built my Facebook profile, the photo I chose was one taken at a club, right before my band went onstage. For me, it depicted the "melancholy artist" that I consider part of my self-concept. But presenting my self online in this fashion was a disaster. Within hours of posting it, I was flooded with messages from students, colleagues, and even long-lost friends:

---

[3] All of the information that follows regarding how to successfully maintain face is adapted from Goffman (1955).

self-reflection

Recall an embarrassing interpersonal encounter. How did you try to restore your lost face? Were you successful? If you could relive the encounter, what would you say and do differently?

Assignment: Face Conflicts

Ask students to generate a list of the faces they present—that is, how they want others to see and know them (e.g., "I want to be considered generous and loving"). Then have them create another list of the faces someone close to them maintains (e.g., a best friend who sees herself as a "peacekeeper"). Ask students to think about a time when they had a conflict with that person because of a face issue. What makes face conflicts difficult to resolve? Why is face so important in close relationships?

skills practice

Apologizing
Creating a skillful apology

❶ Watch for instances in which you offend or disappoint someone.

❷ Acknowledge the incident and admit your responsibility, face-to-face (if possible) or by phone.

❸ Apologize for any harm you have caused.

❹ Avoid pseudo-apologies that minimize the event or shift accountability, like "I'm sorry you overreacted" or "I'm sorry you think I'm to blame."

❺ Express gratitude for the person's understanding if he or she accepts your apology.

🔸 The freedom to create an online identity can cause discord if people think it doesn't match your offline persona. In the top inset is the photo I first posted to Facebook. In the bottom inset is the "happier" one that I replaced the first one with.

"Are you OK?" "Did someone die?" I quickly pulled the photo and replaced it with a more positive one—a sunny image of me and my boys taken atop a mountain near Sun Valley. Now I use the melancholy photo only rarely, as accompaniment to a sad or an angry status update.

Presenting the Self Online Online communication provides us with unique benefits and challenges for self-presentation. When you talk with others face-to-face, people judge your public self on your words as well as what you look like—your age, gender, clothing, facial expressions, and so forth. Similarly, during a phone call, vocal cues such as tone, pitch, and volume help you and your conversation partner draw conclusions about each other. But during online interactions, the amount of information communicated—visual, verbal, and nonverbal—is radically restricted and more easily controlled. We carefully choose our photos and edit our tweets, text messages, e-mail, instant messages, and profile descriptions. We selectively self-present in ways that make us look good, without having to worry about verbal slipups, uncontrollable nervous habits, or physical disabilities that might make people judge us (Parks, 2007).

People routinely present themselves online (through photos and written descriptions) in ways that amplify positive personality characteristics such as warmth, friendliness, and extraversion (Vazire & Gosling, 2004). For instance, photos posted on social networking sites typically show groups of friends, fostering

self-reflection

Have you ever distorted your self-presentation online to make yourself appear more attractive and appealing? If so, was this ethical? What were the consequences—for yourself and others—of creating this online mask?

the impression that the person in the profile is likable, fun, and popular (Ellison, Steinfield, & Lampe, 2007). These positive and highly selective depictions of self generally work as intended. Viewers of online profiles tend to form impressions of a profile's subject that match the subject's intended self-presentation (Gosling, Gaddis, & Vazire, 2007). So, for example, if you post profile photos and descriptions in an attempt to portray your self as "wild" and "hard partying," this is the self that others will likely perceive.

The freedom that online communication allows us in flexibly crafting our selves comes with an associated cost: unless you have met someone in person, you will have difficulty determining whether their online self is authentic or a mask. Through misleading profile descriptions, fake photos, and phony screen names, people communicating online can assume identities that would be impossible for them to maintain in offline encounters (Rintel & Pittam, 1997). On online dating sites, for example, people routinely distort their self-presentations in ways designed to make them more attractive (Ellison, Heino, & Gibbs, 2006). Some people may also "gender swap" online, portraying themselves as female when they're male, or vice versa—often by posting fake photos (Turkle, 1995). For this reason, scholars suggest that you should never presume the gender of someone you interact with online if you haven't met the person face-to-face, even if he or she has provided photos (Savicki, Kelley, & Oesterreich, 1999).

Celebrities are notorious for making poor online communication choices for which they must later apologize. In 2014, actor Jason Biggs created a firestorm of controversy after he posted a joking tweet following the crash of a Malaysian airliner and the deaths of all 295 people aboard, "Anyone wanna buy my Malaysian Airlines frequent flier miles?" How would your online profile and posts be judged if reported in the mainstream media? Ben Pruchnie/GC Images/Getty Images

Evaluating the Self Online Because of the pervasiveness of online masks, people often question the truthfulness of online self-presentations, especially overly positive or flattering ones. *Warranting theory* (Walther & Parks, 2002) suggests that when assessing someone's online self-descriptions, we consider the **warranting value** of the information presented—that is, the degree to which the information is supported by other people and outside evidence (Walther, Van Der Heide, Hamel, & Schulman, 2008). Information that was obviously crafted by the person, that isn't supported by others, and that can't be verified offline has *low warranting value*, and most people wouldn't trust it. Information that's created or supported by others and that can be readily verified through alternative sources on- and offline has *high warranting value* and is consequently perceived as valid. So, for example, news about a professional accomplishment that you tweet or post on Facebook will have low warranting value. But if the same information is also featured on your employer's Web site, its warranting value will increase (Walther et al., 2008). Similarly, photos you take and post of yourself will have less warranting value than similar photos of you taken and posted by others, especially if the photos are perceived as having been taken without your knowledge, such as candid shots (Walther et al., 2008).

Not surprisingly, the warranting value of online self-descriptions plummets when they are directly contradicted by others. Imagine that Jane, a student in your communication class, friends you on Facebook. Though you don't know her especially well, you accept and, later, check out her page. In the content that Jane has provided, she presents herself as quiet, thoughtful, and reserved. But messages from her friends on her Facebook timeline contradict this, saying things like, "You were a MANIAC last night!" and "u r a wild child!" Based on this information, you'll likely disregard Jane's online self-presentation and judge her instead as sociable and outgoing, perhaps even "crazy" and "wild."

Research shows that when friends, family members, coworkers, or romantic partners post information on your page, their messages shape others' perceptions of you more powerfully than your own postings do, especially when their postings contradict your self-description (Walther et al., 2008). This holds true not just for personality characteristics such as extraversion (how outgoing you are) but also for physical attractiveness. One study of Facebook profiles found that when friends posted things like, "If only I was as hot as you" or (alternatively) "Don't pay any attention to those jerks at the bar last night; beauty is on the inside," such comments influenced others' perceptions of the person's attractiveness more than the person's own description of his or her physical appeal (Walther et al., 2008).

IMPROVING YOUR ONLINE SELF-PRESENTATION

Taken as a whole, the research and theory about online self-presentation suggests three practices for improving your online self-presentation. First, keep in mind that online communication is dominated by visual information, such as text, photos, and videos. Make wise choices in the words and images you select to present yourself to others. For example, many women managers know they're more likely than their male peers to be judged solely on appearance, so they post photos of themselves that convey professionalism (Miller & Arnold, 2001).

Second, always remember the important role that warranting value plays in shaping others' impressions of you. The simple rule is that *what others say about you online is more important than what you say about your self*. Consequently, be wary of allowing messages and timeline postings on your personal Web pages that contradict the self you want to present, or that cast you in a negative light—even if you think such messages and postings are cute, funny, or provocative. If you want to track what others are posting about you away from your personal pages, set up a Google Alert or regularly search for your name and other identifying keywords. This will allow you to see what information, including photos, others are posting about you online. When friends, family members, coworkers,

---

Assignment: Analyzing Warranting Value

Ask students to view their own and others' Facebook profiles or blogs and examine the ways in which self is presented online. Have students answer the following questions in a journal or essay about warranting value: What posts could have low warranting value, and why? What posts have high warranting value, and why? Do they feel that the posts are an accurate representation of themselves or the other person?

skills practice

Your Online Self
Maintaining your desired online face

❶ Describe your desired online face (e.g., "I want to be seen as popular, adventurous, and attractive").

❷ Critically compare this description with your profiles, photos, and posts. Do they match?

❸ Revise or delete content that doesn't match your desired face.

❹ Repeat this process for friends' postings on your personal pages.

❺ In your future online communication—tweeting, texting, e-mailing, and posting—present yourself only in ways that mesh with your desired face.

or romantic partners post information about you that disagrees with how you wish to be seen, you can (politely) ask them to delete it.

Finally, subject your online self-presentation to what I call *the interview test*: ask yourself, Would I feel comfortable sharing all elements of this presentation—photos, personal profiles, videos, blogs—in a job interview? If your answer is no, modify your current online self-presentation immediately. In a survey of 1,200 human resources professionals and recruiters, 78 percent reported using search engines to screen candidates, while 63 percent reported perusing social networking sites (Balderrama, 2010).

The Relational Self

Sharing your self can foster intimacy

One of the reasons we carefully craft the presentation of our self is to create interpersonal relationships. We present our self to acquaintances, coworkers, friends, family members, and romantic partners, and through our interpersonal communication, relationships are fostered, maintained, and sometimes ended. Within each of these relationships, how close we feel to one another is defined largely by how much of our self we reveal to others, and vice versa.

Managing the self in interpersonal relationships isn't easy. Exposing our self to others can make us feel vulnerable, provoking tension between how much to reveal versus how much to veil. Even in the closest of relationships, certain aspects of the self remain hidden—from our partners as well as ourselves.

OPENING YOUR SELF TO OTHERS

In the movie *Shrek*, the ogre Shrek forges a friendship with a likable but occasionally irksome donkey (Adamson & Jenson, 2001). As their acquaintanceship deepens to friendship, Shrek tries to explain the nature of his inner self to his companion:

> **SHREK:** For your information, there's a lot more to ogres than people think!
> **DONKEY:** Example . . . ?
> **SHREK:** Example . . . OK . . . Um . . . Ogres . . . are like onions.
> **DONKEY:** They stink?
> **SHREK:** Yes . . . NO!
> **DONKEY:** Or they make you cry?
> **SHREK:** No!
> **DONKEY:** Oh . . . You leave 'em out in the sun and they get all brown and start sprouting little white hairs!
> **SHREK:** No! Layers! Onions have layers—OGRES have layers! Onions have layers! You get it!? We both have layers!
> **DONKEY:** Ooohhhh . . . you both have layers . . . oh. You know, not everybody likes onions . . . CAKE! Everybody loves cakes! Cakes have layers!

Dreamworks LLC/The Kobal Collection

Discussion Prompt: Social Penetration Theory
Ask your students to consider interactions in which another's self-disclosures did not fit the predictable patterns of social penetration theory. For example, you meet someone on an airplane and within an hour you seem to have quickly passed the first two layers and begin discussing the core characteristics. Why do we sometimes bypass the typical patterns of disclosure? What role does the norm of reciprocity play in these interactions? How do you feel in these interactions?

Shrek was not the first to use the onion as a metaphor for self. In fact, the idea that revealing the self to others involves peeling back or penetrating layers was first suggested by psychologists Irwin Altman and Dalmas Taylor (1973) in their **social penetration theory.** Like Shrek, Altman and Taylor envisioned the self as an "onion-skin structure," consisting of sets of layers.[4]

At the *outermost, peripheral layers* of your self are demographic characteristics such as birthplace, age, gender, and ethnicity (see Figure 2.2). Discussion of these characteristics dominates first conversations with new acquaintances: What's your name? What's your major? Where are you from? In the *intermediate layers* reside your attitudes and opinions about music, politics, food, entertainment, and other such matters. Deep within the "onion" are the *central layers* of your self—core characteristics such as self-awareness, self-concept, self-esteem, personal values, fears, and distinctive personality traits. We'll discuss these in more detail in Chapter 3.

The notion of layers of self helps explain the development of interpersonal relationships, as well as how we distinguish between casual and close involvements. As relationships progress, partners communicate increasingly personal information to each other. This allows them to mutually penetrate each other's peripheral, then intermediate, and finally central selves. Relationship development is like slowly pushing a pin into an onion: it proceeds layer by layer, without skipping layers.

The revealing of selves that occurs during relationship development involves both breadth and depth. *Breadth* is the number of different aspects of self each

---

[4]Although Altman and Taylor use *personality* to describe the self, they define it in terms of self-concept and self-esteem, and use the terms *personality* and *self* interchangeably throughout their text (1973, pp. 17–19).

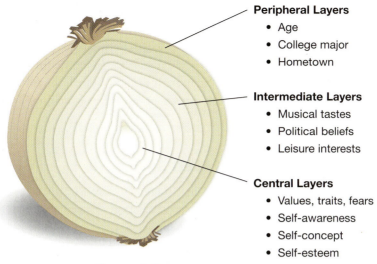

figure 2.2 **The Layers of Self**

partner reveals at each layer—the insertion of more and more pins into the onion, so to speak. *Depth* involves how deeply into each other's self the partners have penetrated: have you revealed only your peripheral self, or have you given the other person access into your intermediate or central selves as well?

Although social penetration occurs in all relationships, the rate at which it occurs isn't consistent. For example, some people let others in quickly, while others never grant access to certain elements of their selves no matter how long they know a person. The speed with which people grant each other access to the broader and deeper aspects of their selves depends on a variety of factors,

○ The ability to share our selves with someone else feels like a rare experience, but when the opportunity arises, information flows more freely, and greater relational intimacy develops.
Cathy Yeulet/123RF.com

Online Self-Quiz: Discover Your Attachment Style. To take this self-quiz, visit LaunchPad: macmillanhighered.com/reflectrelate4e

including the attachment styles discussed earlier in the chapter. But in all relationships, depth and breadth of social penetration is intertwined with **intimacy:** the feeling of closeness and "union" that exists between us and our partners (Mashek & Aron, 2004). The deeper and broader we penetrate into each other's selves, the more intimacy we feel; the more intimacy we feel, the more we allow each other access to broad and deep aspects of our selves (Shelton, Trail, West, & Bergsieker, 2010).

YOUR HIDDEN AND REVEALED SELF

The image of self and relationship development offered by social penetration theory suggests a relatively straightforward evolution of intimacy, with partners gradually penetrating broadly and deeply into each other's selves over time. But in thinking about our selves and our relationships with others, two important questions arise: First, are we really aware of all aspects of our selves? Second, are we willing to grant others access to all aspects of our selves?

We can explore possible answers to these questions by looking at the model of the relational self called the Johari Window (see Figure 2.3), which suggests that some "quadrants" of our selves are open to self-reflection and

Quadrant I	Quadrant II
Public Area Aspects of your self that you and others are aware of. Includes everything you openly disclose—from music and food preferences to religious beliefs and moral values.	**Blind Area** Facets of your self that are readily apparent to others through your interpersonal communication but that you're not aware of. Includes strengths that you may not see in yourself or character flaws that don't mesh with your self-concept.
Quadrant III	Quadrant IV
Hidden Area Parts of your self that you're aware of but that you hide from most others. These include destructive thoughts, impulses, fantasies, and disturbing life experiences that don't fit comfortably with your public self or your own self-concept.	**Unknown Area** Aspects of your self that you and others aren't aware of, such as unconscious motives and impulses that strongly influence your interpersonal communication and relationships. While you can't gain access to your unknown area through critical self-reflection, you can indirectly infer aspects of your unknown area by observing consistent patterns in your own behavior.

figure 2.3 **The Johari Window**

sharing with other people, while others remain hidden—to both ourselves and others.

During the early stages of an interpersonal relationship and especially during first encounters, our *public area* of self is much smaller than our *hidden area*. As relationships progress, partners gain access to broader and deeper information about their selves; consequently, the public area expands, and the hidden area diminishes. The Johari Window provides us with a useful alternative metaphor to social penetration. As relationships develop, we don't just let people "penetrate inward" to our central selves; we let them "peer into" more parts of our selves by revealing information that we previously hid from them.

As our interpersonal relationships develop and we increasingly share previously hidden information with our partners, our *unknown* and *blind* quadrants remain fairly stable. By their very nature, our unknown areas remain unknown throughout much of our lives. And for most of us, the blind area remains imperceptible. That's because our blind areas are defined by our deepest-rooted beliefs about ourselves—those beliefs that make up our self-concepts. Consequently, when others challenge us to open our eyes to our blind areas, we resist.

To improve our interpersonal communication, we must be able to see into our blind areas and then change the aspects within them that lead to incompetent communication and relationship challenges. But this isn't easy. After all, how can you correct misperceptions about yourself that you don't even know exist or flaws that you consider your greatest strengths? Delving into your blind area means challenging fundamental beliefs about yourself—subjecting your self-concept to hard scrutiny. The goal of this is to overturn your most treasured personal misconceptions. Most people accomplish this only over a long period of time and with the assistance of trustworthy and willing relationship partners.

DISCLOSING YOUR SELF TO OTHERS

In Eowyn Ivey's novel, *The Snow Child* (2012), Mabel and Jack are a couple mired in grief following the death of their only child. Early in the story, Mabel's depression leads her to attempt suicide by walking across a newly frozen river, presuming she'll break through the ice and drown. Instead, the ice holds, and she survives. Later, over dinner, she struggles to share her experience—and her despair—with Jack.

> "I went to the river today," she said. She waited for him to ask why she would do such a thing. Maybe then she could tell him. He gave no indication he had heard her. "It's frozen all the way across to the cliffs," she said in a near whisper. Her eyes down, her breath shallow, she waited, but there was only Jack's chewing. Mabel looked up and saw his windburned hands and the crow's feet that spread at the corners of his downturned eyes. She

self-reflection

Consider your "blind area" of self. What strengths might you possess that you don't recognize? What character flaws might exist that don't mesh with your self-concept? How can you capitalize on these strengths and mend your flaws so that your interpersonal communication and relationships improve?

Assignment: PostSecret and Disclosure

PostSecret is an ongoing art project that asks people to mail in their secrets anonymously on homemade postcards (postsecret.com). While your class is discussing self-disclosure, give students notecards and envelopes and have them create their own "post secrets" and turn them in to you anonymously in the sealed envelope. Tell students to be as creative as they like. Display the secrets on a board and discuss how some individuals disclose more intimate information, while others' secrets seem less risky. Discuss the potential personal, professional, and relational risks of revealing secrets.

couldn't remember the last time she had touched that skin, and the thought ached like loneliness in her chest. Then she spotted a few strands of silver in his reddish-brown beard. When had they appeared? So he, too, was graying. Each of them fading away without the other's notice. "That ice isn't solid yet," Jack said from across the table. "Best to stay off it." Mabel swallowed, cleared her throat. "Yes. Of course."[5]

We all can think of situations in which we've struggled with whether to share deeply personal thoughts, feelings, or experiences with others. Revealing private information about ourselves is known as **self-disclosure** (Wheeless, 1978), and it plays a critical role in interpersonal communication and relationship development. According to the **interpersonal process model of intimacy,** the closeness we feel toward others in our relationships is created through two things: self-disclosure and responsiveness of listeners to disclosure (Reis & Patrick, 1996). Relationships are intimate when *both* partners share private information with each other *and* each partner responds to the other's disclosures with understanding, caring, and support (Reis & Shaver, 1988).

Four practical implications flow from this model. First, like Mabel and Jack in *The Snow Child*, you can't have intimacy in a relationship without disclosure and supportiveness. If you, like Mabel, view a friend, family member, or lover as being nonsupportive, you likely won't disclose private thoughts and feelings to that person, and your relationship will be less intimate as a result. Second, if listeners are nonsupportive *after* a disclosure, the impact on intimacy can be devastating. Think about an instance in which you shared something personal with a friend, but he or she responded by ridiculing or judging you. How did this reaction make you feel? Chances are, it substantially widened the emotional distance between the two of you. Third, just because you share your thoughts and feelings with someone doesn't mean that you have an intimate relationship. For example, if you regularly chat with a classmate and tell her all of your secrets, but she never does the same in return, your relationship isn't intimate, it's one sided. In a similar fashion, tweeting or posting personal thoughts and feelings and having people read them doesn't create intimate relationships. Intimacy only exists when both people are sharing with and supporting each other.

And finally, not all disclosures boost intimacy. Research suggests that one of the most damaging events that can happen in interpersonal relationships is a partner's sharing information that the other person finds inappropriate and perplexing (Planalp & Honeycutt, 1985). This is especially true in relationships in which the partners are already struggling with a challenging problem or experiencing a painful transition. For example, during divorce proceedings, parents commonly disclose negative and demeaning

▶ **Video**

macmillanhighered.com/reflectrelate4e

Self-Disclosure
Watch this clip online to answer the questions below.

Do you ever find it easier to self-disclose to a stranger? Why or why not? How much self-disclosure do you expect from a close friend, and when, if ever, is it too much?

---

[5]Adapted from Ivey (2012, p. 10).

information about each other to their children. The parents may see this sharing as stress-relieving or "cathartic" (Afifi, McManus, Hutchinson, & Baker, 2007). But these disclosures only intensify the children's mental and physical distress and make them feel caught between the two parents (Koerner, Wallace, Lehman, & Raymond, 2002).

Differences in Disclosure Researchers have conducted thousands of self-disclosure studies over the past 40 years (Tardy & Dindia, 1997). These studies suggest five important facts regarding how people self-disclose.

First, in any culture, people vary widely in the degree to which they self-disclose. Some people are naturally transparent whereas others are more opaque (Jourard, 1964). Trying to force someone who has a different idea of self-disclosure than yours to open up or be more discreet not only is presumptuous but can damage the relationship (Luft, 1970).

○ Contrary to stereotypes, men are fully capable of self-disclosure and forming close emotional bonds with other men. Amy Eckert/Getty Images

Second, people across cultures differ in their self-disclosure. For instance, people of Asian descent tend to disclose less than people of European ancestry. Japanese disclose substantially less than Americans in both friendships and romantic relationships, and they view self-disclosure as a less important aspect of intimacy development than do Americans (Barnlund, 1975). In general, Euro-Americans tend to disclose more frequently than just about any other cultural group, including Asians, Hispanics, and African Americans (Klopf, 2001).

Third, people disclose differently online than they do face-to-face, and such differences depend on the intimacy of the relationship. When people are first getting to know each other, they typically disclose more quickly, broadly, and deeply when interacting online than face-to-face. One reason for this is that online encounters lack nonverbal cues (tone of voice, facial expressions), so the consequences of such disclosure seem less noticeable, and words take on more importance and intensity than those exchanged during face-to-face interactions (Joinson, 2001). The consequence is that we often overestimate the intimacy of online interactions and relationships with acquaintances or strangers. However, as relationships mature and intimacy increases, the relationship between communication medium and disclosure reverses. Individuals in close relationships typically use online communication for more trivial exchanges (such as coordinating schedules, updating each other on mundane daily events, and so forth), and reserve their deeper, more meaningful discussions for when they are face-to-face (Ruppel, 2014).

⬆ A key aspect to understanding your self is to practice critical self-reflection by analyzing what you are thinking and feeling, why, and how this is influencing your communication. This can help you improve your communication and your relationships. Even John F. Kennedy took time for reflection in the Oval Office during his presidency. Time & Life Pictures/Getty Images

To help ensure competent online disclosure, scholar Malcolm Parks offers the following advice: *Be wary of the emotionally seductive qualities of online interaction.*[6] Disclose information slowly and with caution. Remember that online communication is both public and permanent; hence, *secrets that you tweet, post, text, or e-mail are no longer secrets*. Few experiences in the interpersonal realm are more uncomfortable than "post-cyber-disclosure panic"—that awful moment when you wonder who else might be reading the innermost thoughts you just revealed in an e-mail or a text message to a friend (Barnes, 2001).

Fourth, self-disclosure appears to promote mental health and relieve stress (Tardy, 2000). When the information is troubling, keeping it inside can escalate your stress levels substantially, resulting in problematic mental and physical symptoms and ailments (Pennebaker, 1997; Kelly & McKillop, 1996). Of course, the flip side of disclosing troubling secrets to others is that people might react negatively and you might be more vulnerable.

Finally, and importantly, little evidence exists that supports the stereotype that men can't disclose their feelings in relationships. In close same-sex friendships, for example, both men and women disclose deeply and broadly (Shelton et al., 2010). And in cross-sex romantic involvements, men often disclose at levels equal to or greater than their female partners (Canary et al., 1997). At the same time, however, both men and women feel more comfortable disclosing to female than to male recipients (Dindia & Allen, 1992). Teenagers are more likely to disclose to mothers and best female friends than to fathers and best male friends—suggesting that adolescents may perceive females as more empathic and understanding than males (Garcia & Geisler, 1988).

Competently Disclosing Your Self Based on all we know about self-disclosure, how can you improve your disclosure skills? Consider these recommendations for competent self-disclosure:

- **Follow the advice of Apollo: know your self.** Before disclosing, make sure that the aspects of your self you reveal to others are aspects that you want to reveal and that you feel certain about. This is especially important when disclosing intimate feelings, such as romantic interest. When you disclose feelings about others directly to them, you affect their lives and relationship

---

[6]Personal communication with author, May 13, 2008. This material was developed specifically for this text and published with permission of Dr. Malcolm Parks; it may not be reproduced without the written consent of Dr. Parks and the author.

decisions. Consequently, you're ethically obligated to be certain about the truth of your own feelings before sharing them with others.

- **Know your audience.** Whether it's a Facebook timeline post or an intimate conversation with a friend, think carefully about how others will perceive your disclosure and how it will impact their thoughts and feelings about you. If you're unsure of the appropriateness of a disclosure, don't disclose. Instead of disclosing, talk more generally about the issue or topic first, gauging the person's level of comfort with the conversation before revealing deeper information.

- **Don't force others to self-disclose.** We often presume it's good for people to open up and share their secrets, particularly those that are troubling them. Although it's perfectly appropriate to let someone know you're available to listen, it's unethical and destructive to force or cajole others into sharing information against their will. People have reasons for not wanting to tell you things—just as you have reasons for protecting your own privacy.

- **Don't presume gender preferences.** Don't fall into the trap of thinking that because someone is a woman she will disclose freely, or that because he's a man he's incapable of discussing his feelings. Men and women are more similar than different when it comes to disclosure. At the same time, be mindful of the tendency to feel more comfortable disclosing to women. Don't presume that because you're talking with a woman it's appropriate for you to freely disclose.

- **Be sensitive to cultural differences.** When interacting with people from different backgrounds, disclose gradually. As with gender, don't presume disclosure patterns based on ethnicity. Just because someone is Asian doesn't mean he or she will be more reluctant to disclose than someone of European descent.

- **Go slowly.** Share intermediate and central aspects of your self gradually and only after thorough discussion of peripheral information. Moving too quickly to discussion of your deepest fears, self-esteem concerns, and personal values not only increases your sense of vulnerability but may make others uncomfortable enough to avoid you.

Improving Your Self

[The self constantly evolves]

One of the greatest gifts we possess is our capacity for self-awareness. Through self-awareness, we can ponder the kind of person we are, what we're worth, where we come from, and how we can improve. We can craft face and strive to maintain it. We can openly disclose some aspects of our selves and protect other aspects. And all the while, we can stand apart from our selves, critically reflecting on our interpersonal communication and relationship decisions: was I right or was I wrong?

---

self-reflection

During your childhood, to which family member did you feel most comfortable disclosing? Why? Of your friends and family right now, do you disclose more to women or men, or is there no difference? What does this tell you about how gender has guided your disclosure decisions?

Media Note: Disclosing Self in Forming Relationships

In season 5, episode 9, of the TV show *King of Queens*, titled "Connect Four," the main characters Doug and Carrie go on a double date to a basketball game with a friend and his new girlfriend. The conversation between the new girlfriend and Carrie illustrates how inappropriate self-disclosure can have a harmful effect on interpersonal relationships. Have students discuss how they felt when others disclosed inappropriate information to them.

Discussion Prompt: Improving Self

Have students think about times they have engaged in self-sabotage or crippling self-talk—for example, "I must be perfect" or "I must please everyone." Talk about the implications of these statements on their self-concepts and interpersonal relationships. Encourage students to replace each of these statements with more realistic and positive statements to improve self-esteem.

making relationship choices

Workplace Self-Disclosure

1 BACKGROUND

Workplace connections are essential to happiness and success on the job. But they can also be tricky, especially when it comes to disclosing personal information. To understand how you might competently manage such a relationship challenge, read the case study in Part 2; then, drawing on all you know about interpersonal communication, work through the problem-solving model in Part 3.

 Visit LaunchPad to check out the other side of the story (Part 4). For the best experience, complete all parts in LaunchPad: **macmillanhighered.com/reflectrelate4e**.

2 CASE STUDY

You and Jonathan are friendly work rivals. Jonathan is very competitive and always tries to outperform you. At the same time, he has been a reliable workplace friend who goes out of his way to assist you. For instance, several times when you got behind on projects, he stepped in to help you out so that you could make your deadlines. You appreciate Jonathan as a colleague but also as a friend whose company you've come to enjoy.

Your rivalry with Jonathan heated up last year, when you were both up for the same promotion. Jonathan really wanted it; you ended up getting it. In the aftermath, he congratulated you but was visibly upset for several weeks, and your interactions with him during that period were pretty strained.

One of your new job responsibilities is mentoring new hires, and you are assigned to mentor Lennon. Within a few days, it becomes clear that you and Lennon are romantically attracted to each other. This is a problem because your workplace has strict rules about employee romances, particularly across status lines. At the same time, you're not *technically* Lennon's supervisor, and Lennon will be assigned to a different unit when your mentorship ends.

The two of you start secretly dating. You're nervous because your supervisor, Sharon, is a stickler about company policies. You two are careful to mask your feelings while you're at work, but it's difficult. You're pretty sure that a few of your colleagues are whispering behind your back. On the other hand, the "forbidden" nature of your affair adds to the passion!

A few days later, you join Jonathan for lunch. He smiles and asks, "So, how long have you been dating Lennon?" When you dodge the question, he says, "Don't worry, I won't say a word!" You decide to disclose the truth because you've been dying to tell someone and you know you can trust him.

The following Monday, Sharon demands to see you in her office. She tells you that she has determined you have violated company policy regarding romantic relationships, and as a result, she is letting you go. Returning to your office in shock, you cross paths with Jonathan, who takes one look at your face and asks what happened. When you tell him, he gives you a hug and says, "This is terrible! How could this have happened?!"

3 YOUR TURN

Think about all you've learned thus far about interpersonal communication. Then work through the following five steps. Remember, there are no "right" answers, so think hard about what is the *best* choice! (P.S. Need help? See the *Helpful Concepts* list.)

step 1
Reflect on yourself. What are your thoughts and feelings in this situation? What assumptions are you making about Jonathan and his behavior? about your other colleagues? Are your assumptions accurate?

step 2
Reflect on your partner. Put yourself in Jonathan's shoes. What is he thinking and feeling in this situation? What about your other colleagues?

step 3
Identify the optimal outcome. Think about your communication and relationship with Jonathan and all that has happened. What's the best, most constructive outcome possible? Consider what's best for you and for Jonathan.

step 4
Locate the roadblocks. Taking into consideration your own and Jonathan's thoughts and feelings and all that has happened in this situation, what obstacles are preventing you from achieving the optimal outcome?

step 5
Chart your course. What can you say to Jonathan to overcome the roadblocks you've identified and achieve your optimal outcome?

HELPFUL CONCEPTS
Face and masks, **49–50**

Maintaining face, **51**

Recommendations for competent self-disclosure, **62–63**

4 THE OTHER SIDE

Visit LaunchPad to watch a video in which Jonathan tells his side of the case study story. As in many real-life situations, this is information to which you did not have access when you were initially crafting your response in Part 3. The video reminds us that even when we do our best to offer competent responses, there is always another side to the story that we need to consider.

At the same time, we're often hampered by the beliefs, attitudes, and values we hold about our selves. Our self-concepts can trap us in destructive self-fulfilling prophecies. Whether imposed by gender, culture, or family, the standards we embrace suggesting who we should be are often unattainable. When we inevitably fall short of these standards, we condemn our selves, destroying our own self-esteem.

But our selves are not static. We constantly evolve, so we always have the opportunity to improve our selves and enhance our interpersonal communication and relationships. Through dedicated and focused effort, we can learn to avoid destructive self-fulfilling prophecies and resolve discrepancies between our self-concepts and standards that damage our self-esteem. We can also maintain face and disclose our selves competently to others. The starting point for improving our selves is the same as it ever was, summed up in the advice mythically offered to Chilon by Apollo: know thyself.

POSTSCRIPT

Look again at the painting *labeled*. Note that this work of art isn't simply a portrait of the pain and isolation felt by one artist suffering from dyslexia. It embraces all of us. We've all had fingers pointed and names hurled at us.

What metaphorical fingers point at you? Are some of those fingers your own? What names go with them? How do these shape the ways in which you communicate with others and make choices in your relationships?

This chapter began with a self-portrait of suffering—an artist stigmatized in youth by labels. But we can all draw inspiration from Eric Staib's story. Each of us possesses the uniquely human capacity to turn our personal punishments into profound gifts, just as Eric did.

LaunchPad for *Reflect & Relate* offers videos and encourages self-assessment through adaptive quizzing. Go to **macmillanhighered.com/reflectrelate4e** to get access to:

 LearningCurve Adaptive Quizzes

 Video clips that help you understand interpersonal communication

key terms

- self, 37
- self-awareness, 37
- ▶ social comparison, 38
- self-concept, 39
- looking-glass self, 39
- self-concept clarity, 39
- ▶ self-fulfilling prophecies, 39
- self-esteem, 40
- self-discrepancy theory, 41
- secure attachment, 46
- preoccupied attachment, 46
- dismissive attachment, 46
- fearful attachment, 46
- ▶ face, 50
- ▶ mask, 50
- embarrassment, 50
- warranting value, 53
- social penetration theory, 56
- intimacy, 58
- ▶ self-disclosure, 60
- interpersonal process model of intimacy, 60

▶ You can watch brief, illustrative videos of these terms and test your understanding of the concepts in LaunchPad.

key concepts

The Components of Self

- The root source of all interpersonal communication is the **self,** an evolving composite of **self-awareness, self-concept,** and **self-esteem.**
- We make sense of ourselves and our communication by comparing our behaviors with those of others. **Social comparison** has a pronounced impact on our sense of self when the people to whom we're comparing ourselves are those we admire.
- Our **self-concept** is defined in part through our **looking-glass self.** When we have a clearly defined, consistent, and enduring sense of self, we possess **self-concept clarity.**
- It is challenging to have positive self-esteem while living in a culture dominated by images of perfection. **Self-discrepancy theory** explains the link between these standards and our feelings about our selves, and ways we can overcome low self-esteem.

The Sources of Self

- When our families teach us gender lessons, they also create emotional bonds with us that form the foundation for various attachment styles, including **secure, preoccupied, dismissive,** and **fearful attachment.**
- Many of us identify with more than one culture and can be thrust into situations in which we must choose a primary cultural allegiance.

Presenting Your Self

- The **face** we present to others is the self that others perceive and evaluate. Sometimes our face reflects our inner selves, and sometimes we adopt **masks.**
- Information posted about you online has higher **warranting value** than what you post directly.

The Relational Self

- According to **social penetration theory,** we develop relationships by delving deeper and more broadly into different layers of self. The more we reveal, the more **intimacy** we feel with others.
- Revealing private information about ourselves to others is **self-disclosure,** which, along with the responsiveness of listeners to such disclosure, makes up the **interpersonal process model of intimacy.**

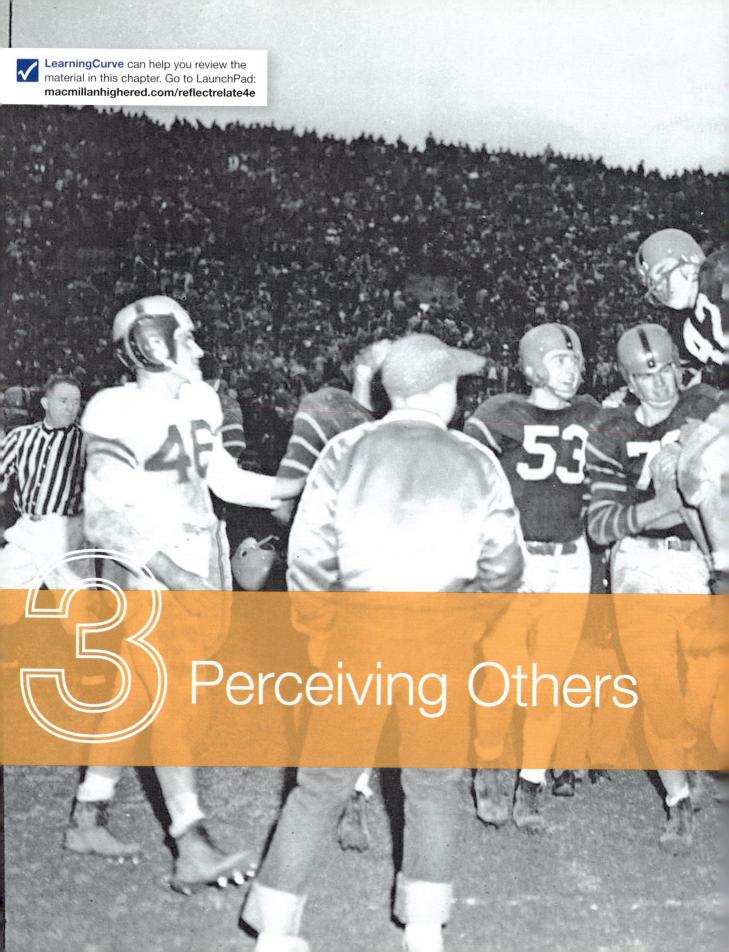

3 Perceiving Others

LearningCurve can help you review the material in this chapter. Go to LaunchPad: macmillanhighered.com/reflectrelate4e

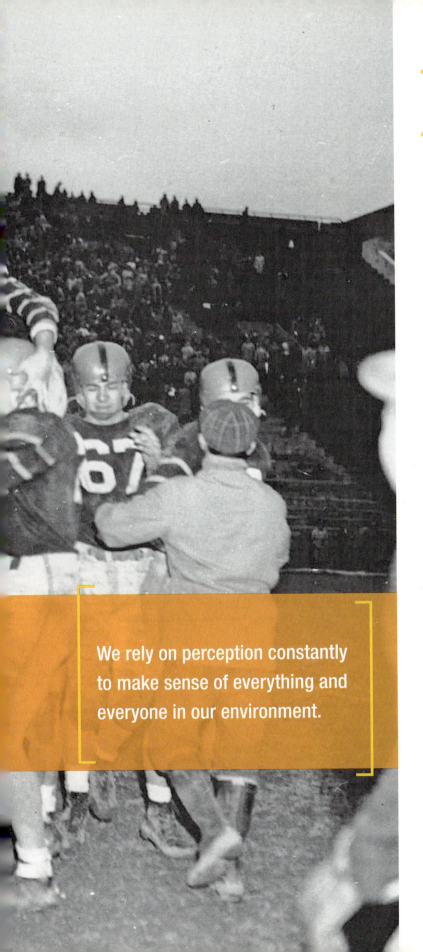

> We rely on perception constantly to make sense of everything and everyone in our environment.

In November 1951, the Dartmouth College football team traveled to Princeton University to play the final game of the season.[1] For Princeton, the contest had special significance: it was the farewell performance of its All-American quarterback, Heisman Trophy winner Dick Kazmaier. Princeton had an 18–1 record at home during Kazmaier's tenure, and they walked onto their turf that day undefeated for the season.

From the opening kickoff, it was a brutal affair. Kazmaier suffered a hit late in the second quarter that broke his nose, caused a concussion, and forced him from the field. In retaliation, Princeton defenders knocked two consecutive Dartmouth quarterbacks out of the game, one of them with a broken leg. Several fights erupted, and referees' flags filled the afternoon air, most of them signaling "roughing." Although Princeton prevailed, both sides left the stadium bitter about the on-field violence.

In the days that followed, perceptions of the game diverged wildly, depending on scholastic allegiance. Princeton supporters denounced Dartmouth's "dirty play," and the *Daily Princetonian* decried Dartmouth for "deliberately attempting to cripple Kazmaier." The Dartmouth student paper countered, accusing Princeton's coach of urging his players to "get" the Dartmouth quarterbacks.

Perceptual differences weren't limited to players and attendees. A Dartmouth alumnus in

---
[1] The information that follows is adapted from Hastorf & Cantril (1954) and Palmer Stadium (2008).

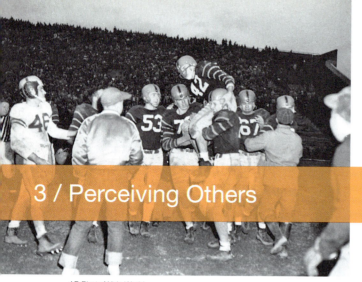

AP Photo/Wide World

3 / Perceiving Others

the Midwest heard reports of his team's "disgusting" play and requested a copy of the game film. After viewing it, he sent a telegram to the university: "Viewing of the film indicates considerable cutting of important parts. Please airmail the missing excerpts." Why did he believe that the film had been edited? Because when he watched it, he didn't perceive *any* cheap shots by his team.

Intrigued by the perceptual gulf between Princeton and Dartmouth devotees, two psychologists—Albert Hastorf from Dartmouth and Hadley Cantril from Princeton—teamed up to study reactions to the game. What they found was striking. After viewing the game film, students from both schools were asked, "Who instigated the rough play?" Princeton students overwhelmingly blamed Dartmouth, while Dartmouth students attributed the violence to both sides. When questioned about whether Dartmouth had intentionally injured Kazmaier, Princeton students said yes; Dartmouth students said no. And when asked about penalties, Dartmouth students perceived both teams as committing the same number. Princeton students said Dartmouth committed twice as many as Princeton. Though the two groups saw the same film, they perceived two very different games.

Although Hastorf and Cantril examined rival perceptions of a historic college football game, their results tell us much about the challenges we face in responsibly perceiving other people. Each of us perceives the "games," "cheap shots," and "fights" that fill our lives in ways skewed to match our own beliefs and desires. All too often we fail to consider that others feel just as strongly about the "truth" of their viewpoints as we do about ours. Every time we perceive our own behavior as beyond reproach and others' as deficient, see others as exclusively to blame for conflicts, or neglect to consider alternative perspectives and feelings, we are exactly like the Dartmouth and Princeton fans who could perceive only the transgressions of the *other* team.

But competent interpersonal communication and healthy relationships are not built on belief in perceptual infallibility. Instead, they are founded on recognition of our perceptual limitations, constant striving to correct perceptual errors, and sincere effort invested in considering others' viewpoints.

Perception is our window to the world. Everything we experience while interacting with others is filtered through our perception. While information seems to enter our conscious minds without bias, our perception is not an objective lens. Instead, it's a product of our own mental creation. When we perceive, we actively create the meanings we assign to people, their communication, and our relationships, and we look to our perception—not reality itself—to guide our interpersonal communication and relationship decisions. This is why it's essential to understand how perception works. By honing our awareness of the perception process, we can improve our interpersonal communication and forge better relationships.

In this chapter, we explore how you can improve your perception to become a better interpersonal communicator. You'll learn:

- How the perception process unfolds, and which perceptual errors you need to watch for
- The influence that gender and personality have in shaping your perception of others and your interpersonal communication
- How you form impressions of others, and the benefits and limitations of the methods you use
- Strategies for improving your perceptual accuracy

chapter outline

71 Perception as a Process

79 Influences on Perception

86 Forming Impressions of Others

92 Improving Your Perception of Others

95 Practicing Responsible Perception

Chapter Theme
The focus of this chapter is that we see what we already believe. Although our perception seems unfiltered and objective, it is neither. Instead, we perceive people in ways that skew to squarely fit our extant beliefs. We also fall prey to errors in attributions and impressions that lead us to communicate poorly. To become more competent interpersonal communicators, we must understand how perception works and learn to routinely offer empathy and check our perception.

Perception as a Process

[Perception helps us understand our world]

In the movie *Inception*, Dom Cobb—played by Leonardo DiCaprio—enters others' unconscious minds while they're asleep and steals their thoughts. Since living inside others' dreams can lead one to confuse dream states with reality, Cobb has a totem that he keeps with him always—a toy top that allows him to tell quickly whether he's dreaming or awake. When he is within a dream state, the top spins endlessly, whereas when he is awake, it spins for a few moments, then wobbles and falls.

Like Dom Cobb, each of us has a totem we trust to tell us what's real and what isn't: *our perception*. **Perception** is the process of selecting, organizing, and interpreting information from our senses. We rely on perception constantly to make sense of everything and everyone in our environment. Perception begins when we select information on which to focus our attention. We then organize the information into an understandable pattern inside our minds and interpret its meaning. Each activity influences the other: our mental organization of information shapes how we interpret it, and our interpretation of information influences how we

▶ In the movie *Inception*, Dom Cobb's totem helps him distinguish what is real and what is not. Stephen Vaughan/© Warner Bros./Everett Collection

figure 3.1 **The Process of Perception**

mentally organize it. (See Figure 3.1) Let's take a closer look at the perception process.

SELECTING INFORMATION

It's finals week, and you're in your room studying for a difficult exam. Exhausted, you decide to take a break and listen to some music. You don your headphones, press play, and close your eyes. Suddenly you hear a noise. Startled, you open your eyes and remove your headphones to find that your housemate has just yanked open your bedroom door. "I've been yelling at you to pick up your phone for the last five minutes," she snaps. "What's going on?!"

The first step of perception, **selection,** involves focusing attention on certain sights, sounds, tastes, touches, or smells in our environment. Consider the housemate example. Once you hear her enter, you would likely select her communication as the focus of your attention. The degree to which particular people or aspects of their communication attract our attention is known as **salience** (Fiske & Taylor, 1991). When something is salient, it seems especially noticeable and significant. We view aspects of interpersonal communication as salient under three conditions (Fiske & Taylor, 1991). First, communication is salient if the communicator behaves in a visually and audibly stimulating fashion. A housemate yelling and energetically gesturing is more salient than a quiet, motionless housemate. Second, communication becomes salient if our goals or expectations lead us to view it as significant. Even a housemate's softly spoken phone announcement will command our attention if we are anticipating an important call. Last, communication that deviates from our expectations is salient. An unexpected verbal attack will always be more salient than an expected one.

ORGANIZING THE INFORMATION YOU'VE SELECTED

Once you've selected something as the focus of your attention, you take that information and structure it into a coherent pattern in your mind, a phase of the perception process known as **organization** (Fiske & Taylor, 1991). For example, imagine that a cousin is telling you about a recent visit to your hometown. As she

Discussion Prompt: The Process of Perception

To demonstrate how we select and interpret information, bring photographs of people in formal and casual clothes to class and ask students to imagine that they are candidates for a specific job. (You can choose the job or allow students to do so.) Ask students to answer a series of questions about the people in each photo based on their observations: What is the person's education level, potential for success, likability, intelligence, and so on? Discuss how students made these judgments based on a simple photo.

shares her story with you, you select certain bits of her narrative on which to focus your attention based on salience, such as a mutual friend she saw during her visit or a favorite old hangout she went to. You then organize your own representation of her story inside your head.

During organization, you engage in **punctuation,** structuring the information you've selected into a chronological sequence that matches how you experienced the order of events (Watzlawick, Beavin, & Jackson, 1967). To illustrate punctuation, think about how you might punctuate the sequence of events in our housemate example. You hear a noise, open your eyes, see your housemate in your room, and then hear her yelling at you. But two people involved in the same interpersonal encounter may punctuate it in very different ways. Your housemate might punctuate the same incident by noting that your ringing cell phone in the common area was disrupting her studying, and despite her efforts to get your attention, you never responded.

If you and another person organize and punctuate information from an encounter differently, the two of you may well feel frustrated with each other. Disagreements about punctuation, and especially disputes about who started unpleasant encounters, are a common source of interpersonal conflict (Watzlawick et al., 1967). For example, your housemate may contend that "you started it" because she told you to get your phone but you ignored her. You may believe that "she started it" because she barged into your room without knocking.

We can avoid perceptual misunderstandings that lead to conflict by understanding how our organization and punctuation of information differ from those of other people. One helpful way to forestall such conflicts is to practice asking others to share their views of encounters. You might say, "Here's what I saw, but that's just my perspective. What do *you* think happened?"

INTERPRETING THE INFORMATION

As we organize information we have selected into a coherent mental model, we also engage in **interpretation,** assigning meaning to that information. We call to mind familiar information that's relevant to the current encounter, and we use that information to make sense of what we're hearing and seeing. We also create explanations for why things are happening as they are.

Using Familiar Information   We make sense of others' communication in part by comparing what we currently perceive with knowledge that we already possess. For example, I proposed to my wife by surprising her after class. I had decorated her apartment with several dozen roses and carnations, was dressed in my best (and only!) suit, and was spinning "our song" on her turntable—the Spinners' "Could It Be I'm Falling in Love." When she opened the door and I asked her to marry me, she immediately interpreted my communication correctly. But how, given that she had never been proposed to before? Because she knew from friends, family members, movies, and television shows what a marriage proposal looks and sounds like. Drawing on this familiar information, she correctly figured out what I was up to and (thank goodness!) accepted my proposal.

macmillanhighered.com
/reflectrelate4e

Punctuation
Watch this clip online to answer the questions below.

How does punctuation influence each person's perception and communication in the video? How might the previous communication between two people influence how each would punctuate a situation between a parent and a child or between romantic partners?

Assignment: Punctuation

Play the LaunchPad video clip on **punctuation** for the class and ask them to get into small groups for a role play. Groups should create their own scenarios in which punctuation was perceived differently among the people involved, leading to problematic interactions. After the groups' performances, discuss how each situation could have been improved.

self-reflection

Recall a conflict in which you and a friend disagreed about "who started it." How did you punctuate the encounter? How did your friend punctuate it? If each of you punctuated differently, how did those differences contribute to the conflict? If you could revisit the situation, what might you say or do differently to resolve the dispute?

○ People familiar with marriage traditions have many marriage-related schemata in their minds, including a schema for "proposal" consisting of roses, nice attire, a diamond ring, and a partner on bended knee. Such schemata help us make sense of events when we experience them. (Left to right) © Royalty-Free/Corbis; Steve Cukrov/Shutterstock; Royalty-Free/Corbis; Hero Images/Corbis

Discussion Prompt: Schemata
A fun way to illustrate schemata is to read aloud a list of words for students to memorize, organized around a "movie" schema, *without* actually giving them the word *movie*. Instead, give them a list of 10 words—*popcorn, soda,* and *comedy* and so on—and see how many repeat back the word *movie* without actually having heard it. Students are often surprised to find their thoughts focused on a word that was not explicitly mentioned.

Assignment: Attribution Theories
Ask students to write a brief synopsis of a recent time someone snapped at them or was rude in a computer-mediated interaction. Students should identify the possible internal and external attributions that could be made for their own and the other person's behavior. Students should also name potential attribution errors that may have contributed to this situation (the fundamental attribution error, self-serving bias, etc.). How could the situation have been improved?

The knowledge we draw on when interpreting interpersonal communication resides in **schemata,** mental structures that contain information defining the characteristics of various concepts, as well as how those characteristics are related to each other (Macrae & Bodenhausen, 2001). Each of us develops schemata for individual people, groups of people, places, events, objects, and relationships. In the previous example, my wife had a schema (the singular form of *schemata*) for "marriage proposal," and that enabled her to correctly interpret my actions.

Because we use familiar information to make sense of current interactions, our interpretations reflect what we presume to be true. For example, suppose you're interviewing for a job with a manager who has been at the company for 18 years. You'll likely interpret everything she says in light of your knowledge about "long-term employees." This knowledge includes your assumption that "company veterans generally know insider information." So, when your interviewer talks in glowing terms about the company's future, you'll probably interpret her comments as credible. Now imagine that you receive the same information from someone who has been with the company only a few weeks. Based on your perception of him as "new employee" and on the information you have in your "new employee" schema, you may interpret his message as naïve speculation rather than expert commentary, even if his statements are accurate.

Creating Explanations In addition to drawing on our schemata to interpret information from interpersonal encounters, we create explanations for others' comments or behaviors, known as **attributions.** Attributions are our answers to the *why* questions we ask every day. "Why didn't my partner return my text message?" "Why did my best friend share that horrible, embarrassing photo of me on Instagram?"

Consider an example shared with me by a friend, Sarah. She had finished teaching for the semester and was out of town and off line for a week. When she returned home and logged on to her e-mail, she found a week-old note from Janet, a student who had failed her course, asking Sarah if there was anything she could do to improve her grade. She also found a second e-mail from Janet, dated a few days later, accusing Sarah of ignoring her:

From: Janet [mailto:janet@school.edu]
Sent: Friday, May 15, 2015 10:46 AM
To: Professor Sarah
Subject: FW: Grade

Maybe my situation isn't a priority to you, and that's fine, but a response e-mail would've been appreciated! Even if all you had to say was "there's nothing I can do." I came to you seeking help, not a hand-out!—Janet.[2]

Put yourself in Janet's shoes for a moment. What attributions did Janet make about Sarah's failure to respond? How did these attributions shape Janet's communication in her second e-mail? Now consider this situation from Sarah's perspective. If you were in her shoes, what attributions would you make about Janet, and how would they shape how you interpreted her e-mail?

Attributions take two forms, internal and external (see Table 3.1). *Internal attributions* presume that a person's communication or behavior stems from internal causes, such as character or personality. For example, "My professor didn't respond to my e-mail because she doesn't care about students" or "Janet sent this message because she's rude." *External attributions* hold that a person's communication is caused by factors unrelated to personal qualities: "My professor didn't respond to my e-mail because she hasn't checked her messages yet" or "Janet sent this message because I didn't respond to her first message."

People are especially susceptible to the fundamental attribution error when communicating electronically, as when texting.
© David Grossman/The Image Works

table 3.1 Internal versus External Attributions

Communication Event	Internal Attribution	External Attribution
Your romantic partner doesn't reply after you send a flirtatious text message.	"My partner doesn't care about me."	"My partner is probably too busy to respond."
Your unfriendly coworker greets you warmly.	"My coworker is friendlier than I thought."	"Something unusual must have happened to make my coworker act so friendly."
Your friend ridicules your taste in music.	"My friend has an unpredictable mean streak."	"My friend must be having a really bad day."

---

[2]This is an example e-mail contributed to the author by a professional colleague, with all identifying information removed to protect the identity of the student in question.

self-reflection

Recall a fight you've had with parents or other family members. Why did they behave as they did? What presumptions did they make about you and your behavior? When you assess both your and their attributions, are they internal or external? What does this tell you about the power and prevalence of the fundamental attribution error?

skills practice

Improving Online Attributions

Improving your attributions while communicating online

1. Identify a negative tweet, text, e-mail, or Web posting you've received.

2. Consider why the person sent the message.

3. Write a response based on this attribution, and save it as a draft.

4. Think of and list other possible, external causes for the person's message.

5. Keeping these alternative attributions in mind, revisit and reevaluate your response draft, editing it as necessary to ensure competence before you send or post it.

Like schemata, the attributions we make influence powerfully how we interpret and respond to others' communication. For example, if you think Janet's e-mail was caused by her having a terrible day, you'll likely interpret her message as an understandable venting of frustration. If you think her message was caused by her personal rudeness, you'll probably interpret the e-mail as inappropriate and offensive.

Given the dozens of people with whom we communicate each day, it's not surprising that we often form invalid attributions. One common mistake is the **fundamental attribution error,** the tendency to attribute others' behaviors solely to internal causes (the kind of person they are) rather than to the social or environmental forces affecting them (Heider, 1958). For example, communication scholar Alan Sillars and his colleagues found that during conflicts between parents and teens, both parties fall prey to the fundamental attribution error (Sillars, Smith, & Koerner, 2010). Parents commonly attribute teens' communication to "lack of responsibility" and "desire to avoid the issue," whereas teens attribute parents' communication to "desire to control my life." All these assumptions are internal causes. These errors make it harder for teens and parents to constructively resolve their conflicts, something we discuss more in Chapter 9.

The fundamental attribution error is so named because it is the most prevalent of all perceptual biases, and each of us falls prey to it (Langdridge & Butt, 2004). Why does this error occur? Because when we communicate with others, they dominate our perception. They—not the surrounding factors that may be causing their behavior—are most salient for us. Consequently, when we make judgments about why someone is acting in a certain way, we overestimate the influence of the person and underestimate the significance of his or her immediate environment (Heider, 1958; Langdridge & Butt, 2004).

The fundamental attribution error is especially common during online interactions (Shedletsky & Aitken, 2004). Because we aren't privy to the rich array of environmental factors that may be shaping our communication partners' messages—all we perceive is words on a screen—we're more likely to interpret others' communication as stemming solely from internal causes (Wallace, 1999). As a consequence, when a tweet, text message, Facebook post, e-mail, or chat message is even slightly negative in tone, we're very likely to blame that negativity on bad character or personality flaws. Such was the case when Sarah presumed that Janet was a rude person based on her e-mail.

A related error is the **actor-observer effect,** the tendency of people to make external attributions regarding their own behaviors (Fiske & Taylor, 1991). Because our mental focus during interpersonal encounters is on factors external to us—especially the person with whom we're interacting—we tend to credit these factors as causing our own communication. This is particularly prevalent during unpleasant interactions. Our own impolite remarks during family conflicts, for example, are viewed as "reactions to their hurtful communication" rather than "messages caused by our own insensitivity."

However, we don't always make external attributions regarding our own behaviors. In cases in which our actions result in noteworthy success, either personal or professional, we typically take credit for the success by making an internal attribution, a tendency known as the **self-serving bias** (Fiske & Taylor, 1991). Suppose you've successfully persuaded a friend to lend you her car for the weekend. In this case, you will probably attribute this success to your charm and persuasive skill rather than to luck or your friend's generosity. The self-serving bias is driven by *ego protection*: by crediting ourselves for our life successes, we can feel happier about who we are.

Clearly, attributions play a powerful role in how we interpret communication. For this reason, it's important to consider the attributions you make while you're interacting with others. Check your attributions frequently, watching for the fundamental attribution error, the actor-observer effect, and the self-serving bias. If you think someone has spoken to you in an offensive way, ask yourself if it's possible that outside forces—including *your own behavior*—could have caused the problem. Also keep in mind that communication (like other forms of human behavior) rarely stems from *only* external *or* internal causes. It's caused by a combination of both (Langdridge & Butt, 2004).

Finally, when you can, check the accuracy of your attributions by asking people for the reasons behind their behavior. When you've made attribution errors that lead you to criticize or lose your patience with someone else, apologize and explain your mistake to the person. After Janet learned that Sarah hadn't responded because she had been out of town and offline, Janet apologized. She also explained why her message was so terse: she thought Sarah was intentionally ignoring her. Upon receiving Janet's apology, Sarah apologized also. She realized that she, too, had succumbed to the fundamental attribution error by wrongly presuming that Janet was a rude person.

REDUCING UNCERTAINTY

When intercultural communication scholar Patricia Covarrubias (2000) was a young girl, she and her family immigrated to the United States from Mexico. On her first day of school in her adoptive country, Patricia's third-grade teacher, Mrs. Williams, led her to the front of the classroom to introduce her to her

Teaching Tip
Students can watch videos and answer questions about **self-serving bias** and **Uncertainty Reduction Theory** in LaunchPad.

▶ When we are uncertain about other people's behavior, we can learn more about them by observing them, by asking their friends about them, or by interacting with them directly. This helps us make decisions about our future communication with them. (Top to bottom) Cultura/Luc Beziat/Getty Images; Jonas Ingerstedt/Getty Images; David R. Frazier/The Image Works

new classmates. Growing up in Mexico, her friends and family called her *la chiquita* (the little one) or *mi Rosita de Jerico* (my rose of Jericho), but in the more formal setting of the classroom, Patricia expected her teacher to introduce her as Patricia Covarrubias, or perhaps Patricia. Instead, Mrs. Williams, her hand gently resting on Patricia's shoulder, turned to the class and said, "Class, this is *Pat*."

Patricia was dumbfounded. In her entire life, she had never been Pat, nor could she understand why someone would call her Pat. As she explains, "In one unexpected moment, all that I was and had been was abridged into three-letter, bottom-line efficiency" (Covarrubias, 2000, pp. 10–11). And although Mrs. Williams was simply trying to be friendly—using an abbreviation most Euro-Americans would consider informal—Patricia was mortified. The encounter bolstered her feeling that she was an outsider in an uncertain environment.

In most interpersonal interactions, the perception process unfolds in a rapid, straightforward manner. But sometimes we find ourselves in situations in which people communicate in perplexing ways. In such contexts, we experience *uncertainty*, the anxious feeling that comes when we can't predict or explain someone else's communication.

Uncertainty is common during first encounters with new acquaintances, when we don't know much about the people with whom we're communicating. According to **Uncertainty Reduction Theory,** our primary compulsion during initial interactions is to reduce uncertainty about our communication partners by gathering enough information about them that their communication becomes predictable and explainable (Berger & Calabrese, 1975). When we reduce uncertainty, we're inclined to perceive people as attractive and likable, talk further, and consider forming relationships with them (Burgoon & Hoobler, 2002).

Uncertainty can be reduced in several ways, each of which has advantages and disadvantages (Berger & Bradac, 1982). First, you can observe how someone interacts with others. Known as *passive strategies*, these approaches can help you predict how he or she may behave when interacting with you, reducing your uncertainty. Examples include observing someone hanging out with friends at a party or checking out someone's Facebook profile. Second, you can try *active strategies* by asking other people questions about someone you're interested in. You might find someone who knows the person you're assessing and then get him or her to disclose as much information as possible about that individual. Be aware, though, that this poses risks: the target person may find out that you've been asking questions. That could embarrass you and upset the target. In addition, third-party information may not be accurate. Third, and perhaps most effective, are *interactive strategies*: starting a direct interaction with the person you're interested in. Inquire where the person is from, what he or she does for a living, and what interests he or she has. You should also disclose personal information about yourself. This enables you to test the other person's reactions to you. Is the person intrigued or bored? That information can help you reduce your uncertainty about how to communicate further.

Assignment: Uncertain Interactions

Ask students to write a short paper or journal entry describing someone in their network whom they perceive as unpredictable in their interactions. How has this person's behavior increased their uncertainty? How has this unpredictability affected their communication and relationship? What strategies could be used to reduce their uncertainty?

self-reflection

When do you use passive strategies to reduce your uncertainty? active strategies? interactive strategies? Which do you prefer, and why? What ethical concerns influence your own use of passive and active strategies?

Influences on Perception

Culture, gender, and personality affect perception

A sense of directness dominates the perceptual process. Someone says something to us, and with lightning speed we focus our attention, organize information, and interpret its meaning. Although this process seems unmediated, powerful forces outside our conscious awareness shape our perception during every encounter, whether we're communicating with colleagues, friends, family members, or lovers. Three of the most powerful influences on perception are culture, gender, and personality.

PERCEPTION AND CULTURE

Your cultural background influences your perception in at least two ways. Recall from Chapter 1 that *culture* is an established, coherent set of beliefs, attitudes, values, and practices shared by a large group of people. Whenever you interact with others, you interpret their communication in part by drawing on information from your schemata. But your schemata are filled with the beliefs, attitudes, and values you learned in your own culture (Gudykunst & Kim, 2003). Consequently, people raised in different cultures have different knowledge in their schemata, so they interpret one another's communication in very different ways. Competent interpersonal communicators recognize this fact. When necessary and appropriate, they check the accuracy of their interpretation by asking questions such as, "I'm sorry, could you clarify what you just said?"

Second, culture affects whether you perceive others as similar to or different from yourself. When you grow up valuing certain cultural beliefs, attitudes, and values as your own, you naturally perceive those who share these with you as fundamentally similar to yourself—people you consider **ingroupers** (Allport, 1954). You may consider individuals from many different groups as your ingroupers as long as they share substantial points of cultural commonality with you, such as nationality, religious beliefs, ethnicity, socioeconomic class, or political views (Turner, Hogg, Oakes, Reicher, & Wetherell, 1987). In contrast, you may perceive people who aren't similar to yourself as **outgroupers.**

Perceiving others as ingroupers or outgroupers is one of the most important perceptual distinctions we make. We often feel passionately connected to our ingroups, especially when they are tied to central aspects of our self-concepts, such as sexual orientation, religious beliefs, or ethnic heritage. Consequently, we are more likely to give valued resources, such as money, time, and effort, to those who are perceived as ingroupers versus those who are outgroupers (Castelli, Tomelleri, & Zogmaister, 2008). Basically, we like, and want to support, people who are "like" us.

We also are more likely to form positive interpersonal impressions of people we perceive as ingroupers (Giannakakis & Fritsche, 2011). One study of 30 ethnic groups in East Africa found that members of each group perceived ingroupers'

Media Note: Ingroupers and Outgroupers
The award-winning movie *The Help* (2011) provides a fictional depiction of the interracial challenges faced in Mississippi in the 1960s during the early stages of the civil rights movement. The film chronicles the plight of black women working as maids for white women in Jackson. Have students discuss the ways the characters fall into both ingrouper and outgrouper status and how that influences their communication.

self-reflection

Consider people in your life whom you view as outgroupers. What points of difference lead you to see them that way? How does their outgrouper status shape your communication toward them? Is there anything you could learn about them that would lead you to judge them as ingroupers?

⬥ Ingroupers or outgroupers? It depends on your point of view. As psychologist Marilynn Brewer (1999) describes, "The very factors that make ingroup attachment and allegiance important to individuals also provide a fertile ground for antagonism and distrust of those outside the ingroup boundaries" (p. 442). Fancy Collection/SuperStock

communication as substantially more trustworthy, friendly, and honest than outgroupers' communication (Brewer & Campbell, 1976). Similarly, when we learn that ingroupers possess negative traits, such as stubbornness or narrow-mindedness, we're likely to dismiss the significance of this revelation, instead ascribing these traits to human nature (Koval, Laham, Haslam, Bastian, & Whelan, 2012). Discovering the same characteristics in outgroupers is likely to trigger a strong negative impression. And in cases in which people communicate in rude or inappropriate ways, you're substantially more inclined to form negative, internal attributions if you perceive them as outgroupers (Brewer, 1999). So, for example, if a cashier chides you for attempting to break a large bill but he's wearing a T-shirt emblazoned with a message advocating your beliefs and values, you're likely to make an external attribution: "He's just having a bad day." The same communication coming from someone who is proudly displaying chestwide messages attacking your beliefs will likely provoke a negative, internal attribution: "What a jerk! He's just like all those other people who believe that stuff!"

While categorizing people as ingroupers or outgroupers, it's easy to make mistakes. For example, even if people dress differently than you do, they may hold beliefs, attitudes, and values similar to your own. If you assume they're outgroupers based on surface-level differences, you may communicate with them in ways that prevent you from getting to know them better.

PERCEPTION AND GENDER

Get your family or friends talking about gender differences, and chances are you'll hear most of them claim that men and women perceive interpersonal communication differently. They may insist that "men are cool and logical," while "women see everything emotionally." But the relationship between gender and perception is much more complex. For example, through magnetic resonance imaging (MRI) and positron emission tomography (PET), we have learned that the structure of the brain's cerebral cortex differs in men and women (Frederikse, Lu, Aylward, Barta, & Pearlson, 1999). Researchers maintain that this difference enables men to perceive time and speed more accurately than women do and to mentally rotate three-dimensional figures more easily. The difference in cerebral cortex structure allows women to understand and manipulate spatial relationships between objects more skillfully than men do and to more accurately identify others' emotions. Women also have a greater ability to process information related to language simultaneously in both of the brain's frontal lobes, resulting in higher scores on tests of language comprehension and vocabulary (Schlaepfer et al., 1995).

But whether variation in brain structure actually translates into differences in interpersonal communication is hotly debated among scholars. Linguist Deborah Tannen (1990) argues that men and women perceive and produce communication in vastly different ways. For example, Tannen suggests that when problems arise, men focus on solutions, and women offer emotional support. Consequently, women perceive men's solutions as unsympathetic, and men perceive women's needs for emotional support as unreasonable. In contrast, researchers from communication and psychology argue that men and women are actually more similar than different in how they interpersonally communicate (Hall, Carter, & Horgan, 2000). Researchers Dan Canary, Tara Emmers-Sommer, and Sandra Faulkner (1997) reviewed data from over 1,000 gender studies and found that if you consider all the factors that influence our communication and compare their impact, only about 1 percent of people's communication behavior is caused by gender. They concluded that when it comes to interpersonal communication, "men and women respond in a similar manner 99% of the time" (p. 9).

Despite the debate over differences, we know one thing about gender and perception for certain: people are socialized to *believe* that men and women communicate differently. Within Western culture, people believe that women talk

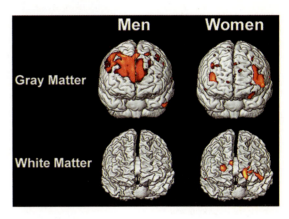

● Professor Richard Haier of the University of California, Irvine, led a study that showed that men use the gray matter part of the brain more, while women use more white matter. However, the study points out that there is no difference in intellectual performance between men and women. They just think differently.
www.livescience.com

**Media Note:
Perception and Gender**
Have students watch the trailer for *How to Lose a Guy in 10 Days* and discuss how the movie portrays perceptions about women and men communicating differently in relationships. Are these perceptions correct? What makes us form these perceptions?

more about their feelings than men do, talk about "less important" issues than men do (women "gossip," whereas men "discuss"), and generally talk more than men do (Spender, 1984). But in one of the best-known studies of this phenomenon, researchers found that this was more a matter of perception than real difference (Mulac, Incontro, & James, 1985). Two groups of participants were given the same speech. One group was told that a man had authored and presented the speech, while the other was told that a woman had written and given it. Participants who thought the speech was a woman's perceived it as having more "artistic quality." Those who believed it was a man's saw the speech as having more "dynamism." Participants also described the "man's" language as strong, active, and aggressive, and the "woman's" language as pleasing, sweet, and beautiful, despite the fact that the speeches were identical.

🟠 Despite popular beliefs, most researchers from communication and psychology argue that men and women are more similar than different in how they interpersonally communicate. As researchers Dindia & Allen (1992) put it, "It's time to stop perpetuating the myth that there are large sex differences in men's and women's self-disclosure."
Fox Photos/Getty Images

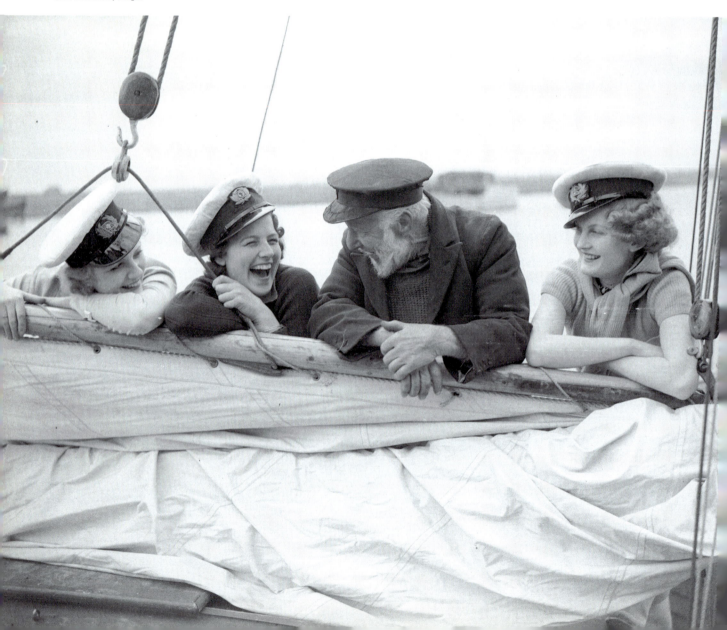

focus on CULTURE

Perceiving Race

Race is a way we classify people based on common ancestry or descent and is almost entirely judged by physical features (Lustig & Koester, 2006). Once we perceive race, other perceptual judgments follow, most notably the assignment of people to ingrouper versus outgrouper status (Brewer, 1999). People we perceive as being the "same race" we see as being ingroupers. Their communication is perceived more positively than the communication of people of "other races," and we're more likely to make positive attributions about their behavior.

Not surprisingly, the perception of racial categories is more salient for people who suffer racial discrimination than for those who don't. Consider the experience of Canadian professor Tara Goldstein (2001). She asked students in her teacher education class to sort themselves into "same race" groups for a discussion exercise. Four black women immediately grouped together; several East Asian students did the same. But the white students were perplexed. One shouted, "All Italians—over here!" while another inquired, "Any other students of Celtic ancestry?" One white female approached Dr. Goldstein and said, "I'm not white; I'm Jewish." Following the exercise, the white students commented that they had never been sorted by their whiteness and didn't perceive themselves or one another as white.

The concept of whiteness has been investigated only recently. Whiteness can often seem "natural" or "normal" to individuals who are white, but for scholars interested in whiteness and for people of color, it means privilege. In her book *White Privilege*, Peggy McIntosh (1999) lists 26 privileges that she largely takes for granted and that result from her skin color. For example, as a white person, McIntosh is able to swear, dress in secondhand clothes, or not answer e-mail without having members of her race or other races attribute these behaviors to bad morals, poverty, or computer illiteracy. This perception of verbal and nonverbal communication may seem mundane, but as McIntosh says, it is part of white privilege, "an invisible package of unearned assets which I can count on cashing in each day, but about which I was meant to remain oblivious" (p. 79).

discussion questions

- What race do you identify with? How does your race affect your perception of ingrouper versus outgrouper communication? How does your race affect other people's perception of your communication?
- Is race an ethical way to perceive how others communicate? Do you think some races have more or less privilege in their interpersonal communication? If so, why?

Given our tendency to presume broad gender differences in communication, can we improve the accuracy of our perception? Yes, if we challenge the assumptions we make about gender and if we remind ourselves that both genders' approaches to communication are more similar than different. The next time you find yourself thinking, "Oh, she said that because she's a woman" or "He sees things that way because he is a man," question your perception. Are these people really communicating differently because of their gender, or are you simply perceiving them as different based on *your* beliefs about their gender?

PERCEPTION AND PERSONALITY

When you think about the star of a hit television show, a cartoon aardvark isn't usually the first thing to come to mind. But as any one of the 10 million weekly viewers of PBS's *Arthur* will tell you, the appeal of the show is more than just the title character. It is the breadth of personalities displayed across the entire cast,

Characters from the television show *Arthur* exhibit a range of personality traits that influence how they perceive the world around them as well as how we perceive them.
© 2000 Marc Brown Studios

allowing us to link each of them to people in our own lives. Sue Ellen loves art, music, and world culture, while the Brain is studious, meticulous, and responsible. Francine loves interacting with people, especially while playing sports, and Buster is laid-back, warm, and friendly to just about everyone. D.W. drives Arthur crazy with her moods, obsessions, and tantrums, while Arthur—at the center of it all—combines all of these traits into one appealing, complicated package.

table 3.2 The Big Five Personality Traits (OCEAN)

Personality Trait	Description
Openness	The degree to which a person is willing to consider new ideas and take an interest in culture. People high in openness are more imaginative, creative, and interested in seeking out new experiences than those low in openness.
Conscientiousness	The degree to which a person is organized and persistent in pursuing goals. People high in conscientiousness are methodical, well organized, and dutiful; those low in conscientiousness are less careful, less focused, and more easily distracted. Also known as *dependability*.
Extraversion	The degree to which a person is interested in interacting regularly with others and actively seeks out interpersonal encounters. People high in extraversion are outgoing and sociable; those low in extraversion are quiet and reserved.
Agreeableness	The degree to which a person is trusting, friendly, and cooperative. People low in agreeableness are aggressive, suspicious, and uncooperative. Also known as *friendliness*.
Neuroticism	The degree to which a person experiences negative thoughts about oneself. People high in neuroticism are prone to insecurity and emotional distress; people low in neuroticism are relaxed, less emotional, and less prone to distress. Also known as *emotional stability*.

In the show *Arthur*, we see embodied in animated form the various dispositions that populate our real-world interpersonal lives. And when we think of these people and their personalities, visceral reactions are commonly evoked. We like, loathe, or even love people based on our perception of their personalities and how their personalities mesh with our own.

Clearly, personality shapes how we perceive others, but what exactly is it? **Personality** is an individual's characteristic way of thinking, feeling, and acting, based on the traits—enduring motives and impulses—that he or she possesses (McCrae & Costa, 2001). Contemporary psychologists argue that although thousands of personalities exist, each is composed of only five primary traits, referred to as the "Big Five" (John, 1990). These are openness, conscientiousness, extraversion, agreeableness, and neuroticism (see Table 3.2 on p. 84). A simple way to remember them is the acronym *OCEAN*. The degree to which a person possesses each of the Big Five traits determines his or her personality (McCrae, 2001).

Prioritizing Our Own Traits When Perceiving Others Our perception of others is strongly guided by the personality traits we see in ourselves and how we evaluate these traits. If you're an extravert, for example, another person's extraversion becomes salient to you when you're communicating with him or her. Likewise, if you pride yourself on being friendly, other people's friendliness becomes your perceptual focus.

But it's not just a matter of focusing on certain traits to the exclusion of others. We evaluate people positively or negatively in accordance with how we feel about our own traits. We typically like in others the same traits we like in ourselves, and we dislike in others the traits that we dislike in ourselves.

To avoid this preoccupation with your own traits, carefully observe how you focus on other people's traits and how your evaluation of these traits reflects your own feelings about yourself. Strive to perceive people broadly, taking into consideration all of their traits and not just the positive or negative ones that you share. Then evaluate them and communicate with them independently of your own positive and negative self-evaluations.

Generalizing from the Traits We Know Another effect that personality has on perception is the presumption that because a person is high or low in a certain trait, he or she must be high or low in other traits. For example, say that I introduce you to a friend of mine, Shoshanna. Within the first minute of interaction, you perceive her as highly friendly. Based on your perception of her high friendliness, you'll likely also presume that she is highly extraverted, simply because high friendliness and high extraversion intuitively seem to go together. If people you've known in the past who were highly friendly and extraverted also were highly open, you may go further, perceiving Shoshanna as highly open as well.

Your perception of Shoshanna was created using **implicit personality theories,** personal beliefs about different types of personalities and the ways in which traits cluster together (Bruner & Taguiri, 1954). When we meet people for the first time, we use implicit personality theories to perceive just a little

Online Self-Quiz: What Kind of Personality Do You Have? To take this self-quiz, visit LaunchPad: macmillanhighered.com /reflectrelate4e

self-reflection

What personality traits do you like in yourself? When you see these traits in others, how does that impact your communication toward them? How do you perceive people who possess traits you don't like in yourself? How do these perceptions affect your relationships with them?

Discussion Prompt: Generalizing Traits

To demonstrate implicit personality theories, ask students to fill in the blanks: "Craig is smart, funny, and ____." Lisa is opinionated, argumentative, and ____." Then have students create their own phrase for "a significant other" and challenge the class (or a small group) to fill in the blank. Discuss how presuming specific personality traits can lead to communicating in inappropriate and ineffective ways.

about an individual's personality and then presume a great deal more, making us feel that we know the person and helping to reduce uncertainty. At the same time, making presumptions about people's personalities is risky. Presuming that someone is high or low in one trait because he or she is high or low in others can lead you to communicate incompetently. For example, if you presume that Shoshanna is high in openness, you might mistakenly presume she has certain political or cultural beliefs, leading you to say things to her that cut directly against her actual values, such as, "Don't you just hate when people mix religion and politics?" However, Shoshanna might respond with, "No, actually I think that government should be based on scriptural principles."

Forming Impressions of Others

Perception creates impressions that may evolve over time

When we use perception to size up other people, we form **interpersonal impressions**—mental pictures of who people are and how we feel about them. All aspects of the perception process shape our interpersonal impressions: the information we select as the focus of our attention, the way we organize this information, the interpretations we make based on knowledge in our schemata and our attributions, and even our uncertainty.

Given the complexity of the perception process, it's not surprising that impressions vary widely. Some impressions come quickly into focus. We meet a person and immediately like or dislike him or her. Other impressions form slowly, over a series of encounters. Some impressions are intensely positive, others neutral, and still others negative. But regardless of their form, interpersonal impressions exert a profound impact on our communication and relationship choices. To illustrate this impact, imagine yourself in the following situation.

It's summer, and you're at a lake, hanging out with friends. As you lie on the beach, the man pictured in the photo at left approaches you. He introduces himself as "Ted" and tells you that he's waiting for some friends who were supposed to help him load his sailboat onto his car. He is easy to talk to, is friendly, and has a nice smile. His left arm is in a sling, and he casually mentions that he injured it playing racquetball. Because his arm is hurting and his friends are missing, he asks if you would help him with his boat. You say, "Sure." You walk with him to the parking lot, but when you get to Ted's car, you don't see a boat. When you ask him where his boat is, he says, "Oh! It's at my folks' house, just up the hill. Do you mind going with me? It'll just take a couple of minutes." You tell him you can't go with him because your friends will wonder where you are. "That's OK," Ted says cheerily, "I should have told you it wasn't in the parking lot. Thanks for bothering anyways." As the two of you walk back to the beach, Ted repeats his apology and expresses gratitude for your willingness to help him. He's polite and strikes you as sincere.

© Bettmann/Corbis

Discussion Prompt: Misperceptions

Ask students to think about the wrong impressions that people may have, or have had, of them. Then have them share these misperceptions with a partner and discuss the ways they affect interpersonal interactions. Students should share their "true self" with their partner. Additionally, you could ask students to present their partner to the class as a means of introduction and to dispel any misperceptions students may have of each other.

Think about your encounter with Ted, and all that you've perceived. What's your impression of him? What traits besides the ones you've observed would you expect him to have? What do you predict would have happened if you had gone with him to his folks' house to help load the boat? Would you want to play racquetball with him? Would he make a good friend? Does he interest you as a possible romantic partner?

The scenario you've read actually happened. The description is drawn from the police testimony of Janice Graham, who was approached by Ted at Lake Sammamish State Park, near Seattle, Washington, in 1974 (Michaud & Aynesworth, 1989). Graham's decision not to accompany Ted saved her life. Two other women—Janice Ott and Denise Naslund—were not so fortunate. Each of them went with Ted, who raped and murdered them. Friendly, handsome, and polite, Ted was none other than Ted Bundy, one of the most notorious serial killers in U.S. history.

Thankfully, most of the interpersonal impressions we form don't have life-or-death consequences. But all impressions do exert a powerful impact on how we communicate with others and whether we pursue relationships with them. For this reason, it's important to understand how we can flexibly adapt our impressions to create more accurate and reliable conceptions of others.

CONSTRUCTING GESTALTS

One way we form impressions of others is to construct a **Gestalt,** a general sense of a person that's either positive or negative. We discern a few traits and, drawing on information in our schemata, arrive at a judgment based on these traits. The result is an impression of the person as a whole rather than as the sum of individual parts (Asch, 1946). For example, suppose you strike up a conversation with the person sitting next to you at lunch. The person is funny, friendly, and attractive—characteristics associated with positive information in your schemata. You immediately construct an overall positive impression ("I like this person!") rather than spending additional time weighing the significance of his or her separate traits.

Gestalts form rapidly. This is one reason why people consider first impressions so consequential. Gestalts require relatively little mental or communicative effort. Thus, they're useful for encounters in which we must render quick judgments about others with only limited information—a brief interview at a job fair, for instance. Gestalts are also useful for interactions involving casual relationships (contacts with acquaintances or service providers) and contexts in which we are meeting and talking with a large number of people in a small amount of time (business conferences or parties). During such exchanges, it isn't possible to carefully scrutinize every piece of information we perceive about others. Instead, we quickly form broad impressions and then mentally walk away from them. But this also means that Gestalts have significant shortcomings.

The Positivity Bias
In 1913, author E. H. Porter published a novel titled *Pollyanna*, about a young child who was happy nearly all of the time. Even when

Discussion Prompt: Positivity and Negativity Bias

Ask your students which popular media figures they perceive to be subject to the positivity and negativity bias. Students will likely produce many examples of celebrities who "can do no wrong" or who "will never get things right," such as *Golden Girls* actress Betty White or singer Miley Cyrus. Have students consider how they formed such impressions and how perceptions are formed differently. How does culture, gender, or personality affect perception?

self-reflection

Think of someone for whom you have a negative Gestalt. How did the negativity effect shape your impression? Now call to mind personal flaws or embarrassing events from your past. If someone learned of this information and formed a negative Gestalt of you, would his or her impression be accurate? fair?

Assignment: Halo and Horn Effects

Ask students to watch the LaunchPad video clips on **halo effect** and **horn effect** and then find another example of either from a media source. Students should analyze their example based on these questions: What effects (positive or negative) do the halo effect or horn effect have on the relationships in the example? How could the communication and relationships be improved?

---

faced with horrible tragedies, Pollyanna saw the positive side of things. Research on human perception suggests that some Pollyanna exists inside each of us (Matlin & Stang, 1978). Examples of *Pollyanna effects* include people believing pleasant events are more likely to happen than unpleasant ones, most people deeming their lives "happy" and describing themselves as "optimists," and most people viewing themselves as "better than average" in terms of physical attractiveness and intellect (Matlin & Stang, 1978; Silvera, Krull, & Sassler, 2002).

Pollyanna effects come into play when we form Gestalts. When Gestalts are formed, they are more likely to be positive than negative, an effect known as the **positivity bias.** Let's say you're at a party for the company where you just started working. During the party, you meet six coworkers for the first time and talk with each of them for a few minutes. You form a Gestalt for each. Owing to the positivity bias, most or all of your Gestalts are likely to be positive. Although the positivity bias is helpful in initiating relationships, it can also lead us to make bad interpersonal decisions, such as when we pursue relationships with people who turn out to be unethical or even abusive.

The Negativity Effect When we create Gestalts, we don't treat all information that we learn about people as equally important. Instead, we place emphasis on the negative information we learn about others, a pattern known as the **negativity effect.** Across cultures, people perceive negative information as more informative about someone's "true" character than positive information (Kellermann, 1989). Though you may be wondering whether the negativity effect contradicts Pollyanna effects, it actually derives from them. People tend to believe that positive events, information, and personal characteristics are more commonplace than negative events, information, and characteristics. So when we learn something negative about another person, we see it as unusual. Consequently, that information becomes more salient, and we judge it as more truly representative of a person's character than positive information (Kellermann, 1989).

Needless to say, the negativity effect leads us away from accurate perception. Accurate perception is rooted in carefully and critically assessing everything we learn about people, then flexibly adapting our impressions to match these data. When we weight negative information more heavily than positive, we perceive only a small part of people, aspects that may or may not represent who they are and how they normally communicate.

Halos and Horns Once we form a Gestalt about a person, it influences how we interpret that person's subsequent communication and the attributions we make regarding that individual. For example, think about someone for whom you've formed a strongly positive Gestalt. Now imagine that this person discloses a dark secret: he or she lied to a lover, cheated on exams, or stole from the office. Because of your positive Gestalt, you may dismiss the significance of this behavior, telling yourself instead that the person "had no choice" or "wasn't acting normally." This tendency to positively interpret what someone says or does because we have a positive Gestalt of them is known as the **halo effect** (see Table 3.3 on p. 89).

table 3.3 The Halo and Horn Effects

The Halo Effect

Impression	Behavior	Attribution
Person we like :)	Positive behavior	Internal
Person we like :)	Negative behavior	External

The Horn Effect

Person we dislike :(	Positive behavior	External
Person we dislike :(	Negative behavior	Internal

Note: Information in this table is adapted from Guerin (1999).

The counterpart of the halo effect is the **horn effect,** the tendency to negatively interpret the communication and behavior of people for whom we have negative Gestalts (see Table 3.3). Call to mind someone you can't stand. Imagine that this person discloses the same secret as the individual previously described. Although the information in both cases is the same, you would likely chalk up this individual's unethical behavior to bad character or lack of values.

CALCULATING ALGEBRAIC IMPRESSIONS

A second way we form interpersonal impressions is to develop **algebraic impressions** by carefully evaluating each new thing we learn about a person (Anderson, 1981). Algebraic impressions involve comparing and assessing the positive and negative things we learn about a person in order to calculate an overall impression, then modifying this impression as we learn new information. It's similar to solving an algebraic equation, in which we add and subtract different values from each side to compute a final result.

Consider how you might form an algebraic impression of Ted Bundy from our earlier example. At the outset, his warmth, humor, and ability to chat easily with you strike you as "friendly" and "extraverted." These traits, when added together, lead you to calculate a positive impression: friendly + extraverted = positive impression. But when you accompany Bundy to the parking lot and realize his boat isn't there, you perceive this information as deceptive. This new information—Ted is a liar—immediately causes you to revise your computation: friendly + extraverted + potential liar = negative impression.

When we form algebraic impressions, we don't place an equal value on every piece of information in the equation. Instead, we weight some pieces of information more heavily than others, depending on the information's *importance* and its *positivity* or *negativity*. For example, your perception of potential romantic partners' physical attractiveness, intelligence, and personal values will likely carry more weight when calculating your impression than their favorite color or breakfast cereal.

▶ **Video**

macmillanhighered.com
/reflectrelate4e

Halo Effect
Watch this clip online to answer the questions below.

When have you made a perceptual error based on the halo effect? How would you suggest reducing the halo effect in hiring practices?

Want to see more? Check out LaunchPad for clips on **horn effect** and **algebraic impressions.**

Teaching Tip
Students can watch a video and answer questions about **algebraic impressions** in LaunchPad.

skills practice

Algebraic Impressions
Strengthen your ability to use algebraic impressions.

❶ When you next meet a new acquaintance, resist forming a general positive or negative Gestalt.

❷ Instead, observe and learn everything you can about the person.

❸ Then make a list of his or her positive and negative traits, and weigh each trait's importance.

❹ Form an algebraic impression based on your assessment, keeping in mind that this impression may change over time.

❺ Across future interactions, flexibly adapt your impression as you learn new information.

As this discussion illustrates, algebraic impressions are more flexible and accurate than Gestalts. For encounters in which we have the time and energy to ponder someone's traits and how they add up, algebraic impressions offer us the opportunity to form refined impressions of people. We can also flexibly change them every time we receive new information about people. But since algebraic impressions require a fair amount of mental effort, they aren't as efficient as Gestalts. In unexpected encounters or casual conversations, such mental calculations are unnecessary and may even work to our disadvantage, especially if we need to render rapid judgments and act on them.

USING STEREOTYPES

A final way we form impressions is to categorize people into social groups and then evaluate them based on information we have in our schemata related to these groups (Bodenhausen, Macrae, & Sherman, 1999). This is known as **stereotyping,** a term first coined by journalist Walter Lippmann (1922) to describe overly simplistic interpersonal impressions. When we stereotype others, we replace the subtle complexities that make people unique with blanket assumptions about their character and worth based solely on their social group affiliation.

We stereotype because doing so streamlines the perception process. Once we've categorized a person as a member of a particular group, we can apply all of the information we have about that group to form a quick impression (Bodenhausen et al., 1999). For example, suppose a friend introduces you to Conor, an Irish transfer student. Once you perceive Conor as "Irish," beliefs that you might hold about Irish people could come to mind: they love to tell exaggerated stories (the blarney), have bad tempers, like to drink, and are passionate about soccer. Mind you, none of these assumptions may be accurate about Irish people or relevant to Conor. But if this is what you *believe* about the Irish, you'll keep it in mind during your conversation with Conor and look for ways to confirm your beliefs.

As this example suggests, stereotyping frequently leads us to form flawed impressions of others. One study of workplace perception found that male supervisors who stereotyped women as "the weaker sex" perceived female employees' work performance as deficient and gave women low job evaluations, regardless of the women's actual job performance (Cleveland, Stockdale, & Murphy, 2000). A separate study examining college students' perceptions of professors found a similar biasing effect for ethnic stereotypes. Euro-American students who stereotyped Hispanics as "laid-back" and "relaxed" perceived Hispanic professors who set high expectations for classroom performance as "colder" and "more unprofessional" than Euro-American professors who set identical standards (Smith & Anderson, 2005).

△ In the movie *Mud* (2012), Ellis at first believes that Mud is a dangerous and untrustworthy fugitive. However, as Ellis learns more about Mud's past, his perceptions of him evolve from distrust to a close friendship. How have you used algebraic impressions to get closer to or distance yourself from a friend?
Everest Entertainment/The Kobal Collection

chapter 3 / Perceiving Others 91

▶ Whom do you see in this photograph of Tupac Shakur—a famous African American male? a rapper who was popular in the 1990s? a gangster who died in a hail of gunfire? or perhaps a man who was named after an Inca chief, who studied ballet and acting, and whose mother required him as a young boy to read the *New York Times*? The LIFE Picture Collection/Getty Images

Stereotyping is almost impossible to avoid. Researchers have documented that categorizing people in terms of their social group affiliation is the most common way we form impressions, more common than either Gestalts or algebraic impressions (Bodenhausen et al., 1999). Why? Social group categories such as race and gender are among the first things we notice about others upon meeting them. As a consequence, we often perceive people in terms of their social group membership before any other impression is even possible (Devine, 1989). The Internet provides no escape from this tendency. Without many of the nonverbal cues and additional information that can distinguish a person as a unique individual, people communicating online are even more likely than those communicating face-to-face to form stereotypical impressions when meeting others for the first time (Spears, Postmes, Lea, & Watt, 2001).

Most of us presume that our beliefs about groups are valid. As a consequence, we have a high degree of confidence in the legitimacy of our stereotypical impressions, despite the fact that such impressions are frequently flawed (Brewer, 1993). We also continue to believe in stereotypes even when members of a stereotyped group repeatedly behave in ways that contradict the stereotype. In fact, contradictory behavior may actually *strengthen* stereotypes. For example, if you think of Buddhists as quiet and contemplative and meet a talkative and funny Buddhist, you may dismiss his or her behavior as atypical and not worthy of your attention (Seta & Seta, 1993). You'll then actively seek examples of behavior that confirm the stereotype to compensate for the uncertainty that the unexpected behavior aroused (Seta & Seta, 1993). As a result, the stereotype is reinforced.

You can overcome stereotypes by critically assessing your beliefs about various groups, especially those you dislike. Then educate yourself about these groups. Pick several groups you feel positively or negatively about. Read a variety of materials about these groups' histories, beliefs, attitudes, values, and behaviors. Look for similarities and differences between people affiliated with these groups and yourself. Finally, when interacting with members of these groups, keep in mind that just because someone belongs to a certain group, it doesn't necessarily mean that all of the defining characteristics of that group apply to that person. Since each of us simultaneously belongs to multiple social groups, don't form a narrow and biased impression of someone by slotting him or her into just one group.

self-reflection

Think of an instance in which you perceived someone stereotypically based on the information the person posted online (photos, profile information, tweets). How did the information affect your overall impression of him or her? your communication with the person? What stereotypes might others form of you, based on *your* online postings?

Improving Your Perception of Others

Explore empathy, world-mindedness, and perception-checking

Discussion Prompt: Empathy vs. Sympathy
Explain that empathy focuses on perspective-taking and empathic concern, while sympathy is an expression of support. Ask students to share a time when they had difficulty expressing empathy to someone. What strategies did they use to convey social support? What made the interaction difficult? How would they improve their approach in future interactions?

Teaching Tip
Students can watch a video and answer questions about **empathy** in LaunchPad.

Malcolm X is most remembered for his fiery rhetoric denouncing white racism and his rejection of nonviolent protest as a means for dealing with oppression. Less well known is the marked change in his perception and communication that occurred following his visit to Saudi Arabia. He traveled to Mecca for a traditional Muslim hajj, or pilgrimage. During his visit, he worshipped, ate, socialized, and slept in the same room with white Muslims. In doing so, he was shocked to discover that despite their differences in skin color, they all shared similar degrees of religious devotion. The experience was a revelation and led him to reassess his long-standing belief in an unbridgeable racial divide between whites and blacks. As he explained in a letter home: "on this pilgrimage, what I have seen and experienced has forced me to rearrange my thought-patterns and toss aside some of my previous conclusions" (Malcolm X, 1964).

Malcolm's transformation suggests important lessons for everyone interested in improving perception and communication. He came to appreciate others' perspectives and feel a strong emotional kinship with those he previously disparaged based on skin color. He also freely called into question his own perceptual accuracy by critically assessing his prior judgments and correcting those found to deviate from "the reality of life." These changes reveal two ways we can improve our perception and interpersonal communication: offering empathy, and checking our perception.

OFFERING EMPATHY

Empathy is one of our most valuable tools for communicating competently with others (Campbell & Babrow, 2004). The word *empathy* comes from the Greek word *empatheia*, meaning "feeling into." When we experience **empathy,** we "feel into" others' thoughts and emotions, making an attempt to both understand their perspectives and be aware of their feelings in order to identify with them (Kuhn, 2001).

Empathy consists of two components. The first is *perspective-taking*—the ability to see things from someone else's vantage point without necessarily

🔸 Malcolm X's perception changed after 1964, as shown in this quote: "I believe in recognizing every human being as a human being, neither white, black, brown, nor red—when you are dealing with humanity as one family, it's just one human being marrying another human being, or one human being living around or with another human being." (Left) AP/Wide World Photos; (right) Bettmann/Corbis

Test Your Empathy

self-QUIZ

Read these statements, marking the ones with which you agree. Total up your check marks, and interpret your score below.

To take this quiz online, visit LaunchPad: macmillanhighered.com/reflectrelate4e.

Perspective-Taking

_____ Before I criticize a person, I try to imagine how I would view the situation in his or her place.

_____ I believe there are two sides to every question, and I try to look at both sides.

_____ I find it easy to see things from another person's point of view.

_____ I try to look at everybody's side of a disagreement before I make a decision.

_____ When I am upset with someone, I usually try to put myself in his or her shoes for a while.

Empathic Concern

_____ When I see a person being taken advantage of, I feel protective toward him or her.

_____ I often have tender, concerned feelings for people who seem less fortunate than I.

_____ I would describe myself as a pretty softhearted person.

_____ Other people's misfortunes disturb me a great deal.

_____ I am often touched by the things that I see happen to people around me.

Note: This *Self-Quiz* is adapted from Stiff et al. (1988).

Scoring: For each section, a score of 0–1 indicates that you have low empathy, 2–3 indicates moderate empathy, and 4–5 indicates high empathy.

experiencing that person's emotions (Duan & Hill, 1996). The second is *empathic concern*—becoming aware of how the other person is feeling, experiencing a sense of compassion regarding the other person's emotional state, and perhaps even experiencing some of his or her emotions yourself (Stiff, Dillard, Somera, Kim, & Sleight, 1988).

We often think of empathy as an automatic process beyond our control, something we either feel or don't feel (Schumann, Zaki, and Dweck, 2014). Consequently, we excuse ourselves from being empathic toward outgroupers or people we dislike. But recent research suggests that whether we feel empathy toward others depends largely on our **empathy mind-set**—our beliefs about whether empathy is something that can be developed and controlled (Schumann et al., 2014). People who view empathy as developable and controllable are capable of feeling empathy for a broad range of others—even within interpersonally challenging contexts, such as during conflicts, when arguing about political beliefs, or when asked to listen to a grief story told by an outgroup member (Schumann et al., 2014). Those who believe empathy is an uncontrollable, natural response have difficulty experiencing empathy within such challenging encounters.

But experiencing empathy isn't sufficient in itself to improve your interpersonal communication and relationships. You also must convey your empathy to

skills practice

Enhancing Empathy

Improving your ability to experience and express empathy

❶ Identify a challenging interpersonal encounter.

❷ As the encounter unfolds, consider how the other person is viewing you and the interaction.

❸ Think about the emotions he or she is feeling.

❹ Communicate perspective-taking, avoiding "I know" messages.

❺ Express empathic concern, letting the person know you value his or her feelings.

❻ Disclose your own feelings.

△ Empathy is one of the most powerful tools for strengthening interpersonal relationships. Can you think of a time when you used empathy effectively to comfort a friend or family member? © Mika/Corbis

others. To competently communicate the perspective-taking part of empathy, let others know that you're genuinely interested in hearing their viewpoints ("I'd love to get your impression"), and tell them that you think their views are important and understandable ("Seeing it from your side makes a lot of sense"). To communicate empathic concern, disclose to others that you care about them and their feelings ("I hope you're doing OK"). Share with them your own emotions regarding their situation ("I feel terrible that you're going through this"). Competently conveying empathy isn't just something to be strived for as a matter of principle; it's a recommendation packed with practical benefits. Recent research on perceived perspective-taking, for example, suggests that when others believe that you are taking their perspective, they are more likely to perceive you as relatable, to like you, and to help you when you are in need (Goldstein, Vezich, & Shapiro, 2014).

Importantly, avoid using "I know" messages (as in "I know just how you feel"). Even if you make such comments with kind intentions, others will likely view you as presumptuous and perhaps even patronizing, especially if they suspect that you don't or can't feel as they do. For example, when people suffer a great loss—such as the death of a loved one—many don't believe that anyone else could feel the depth of anguish they're experiencing. Saying "I know how you feel" isn't helpful under these conditions.

CHECKING YOUR PERCEPTION

The second way to improve your perception is through **perception-checking,** a five-step process in which you apply all that you've learned in this chapter to your perception of others.

1. *Check your punctuation.* People punctuate encounters in different ways, often disagreeing on "who/what started it" or "who/what ended it." When you experience a conflict, be aware of your own punctuation and keep in mind that other people may see things differently. Remember to ask others to share their punctuation with you.

2. *Check your knowledge.* Your perception of others is only as accurate as the information you have in your schemata. Never presume that you know the "truth" about what others "really" mean or what they're "really" like. When in doubt, ask others to explain their meaning to you.

3. *Check your attributions.* Avoid the common temptation to attribute others' communication and behavior exclusively to internal causes, such as character or personality. Remember that all behavior—including interpersonal communication—stems from a complex combination of internal and external forces.

4. *Check perceptual influences.* Reflect on how culture, gender, and personality shape your perception of others. Are you perceiving others as ingroupers or outgroupers? If so, on what basis? How is this perception affecting your communication? your relationships?

5. *Check your impressions.* Reflect on your impressions as you're forming them. If you find yourself making Gestalts, realize that your Gestalts may bias your perception of subsequent information you learn about a person. Resist stereotyping, but also realize that it's difficult to avoid, given the natural human tendency to categorize people into groups upon first meeting. Strive to create flexible impressions, thoughtfully weighing new information you learn about a person and reshaping your overall impression based on new data.

Perception-checking is an intense mental exercise. Mastering it takes time and effort, but the ability to critically check your own perception goes, as Malcolm X wrote, "hand in hand with every form of intelligent search for truth," whether the truth is personal, interpersonal, or universal. When you routinely perception-check, errors are corrected and perception becomes more accurate, balanced, and objective. As a result, you will make fewer communication blunders, and you will be able to tailor your communication to people as they really are, making your messages more sensitive and effective. The ultimate result will also be perceptual: *others* seeing *you* as a competent communicator.

Practicing Responsible Perception

Perception affects every interpersonal encounter

We experience our interpersonal reality—the people around us, our communication with them, and the relationships that result—through the lens of perception. But perception is a product of our own creation, metaphorical clay we can shape in whatever ways we want. At each stage of the perception process, we make choices that empower us to mold our perception in constructive or destructive ways. What do I select as the focus of my attention? What attributions do I make? Do I form initial impressions and cling to them in the face of contradictory evidence? Or do I strive to adapt my impressions of others as I learn new information about them? The choices we make at each of these decision points feed directly into how we communicate with and relate to others. When we negatively stereotype people, for example, or refuse to empathize with someone because he or she is an outgrouper, we immediately destine ourselves to incompetent communication.

To improve our interpersonal communication and relationship decisions, we must practice responsible perception. This means routinely perception-checking and correcting errors. It means striving to adjust our impressions of people as we get to know them better. It means seizing control of our empathy, seeing those who populate our interpersonal world through eyes of empathy, emotionally reaching out to them, and communicating this perspective-taking

making relationship choices

Balancing Impressions and Empathy

BACKGROUND

Forging constructive, collaborative work relationships with people whom we judge to be outgroupers is a challenge, particularly when we've formed negative impressions of them and they behave in questionable ways. To understand how you might competently manage such a relationship challenge, read the case study in Part 2; then, drawing on all you know about interpersonal communication, work through the problem-solving model in Part 3.

 Visit LaunchPad to check out the other side of the story (Part 4). For the best experience, complete all parts in LaunchPad: **macmillanhighered.com/reflectrelate4e**.

2 CASE STUDY

Your professor assigns a group project that will count for a significant portion of your final course grade.[1] Each group member gets two grades for the project: one for the group presentation and one for individual contribution. The professor selects you as a group leader. Your responsibilities include making sure that each group member gets his or her work done and telling the professor what grade you think each person deserves. The professor will evaluate you in part based on your skill as group leader.

At your first group meeting, everyone is on time except Dylan. He apologizes and says that "something came up." As everyone introduces themselves, it becomes clear that Dylan's tardiness isn't his only difference from you and the others. He's wearing a shirt emblazoned with extreme political slogans, viewpoints opposed to yours. It quickly becomes clear that his religious beliefs are dissimilar as well. The more you talk with him, the more you dislike him.

Despite your distaste for Dylan, the meeting goes well. The project you all decide on is interesting and provocative. A ton of research needs to be done, but split several ways you *might* get it done—if everyone does his or her fair share. If even one person fails to follow through, however, it will be a disaster. You exit the meeting excited but anxious.

As the project progresses, Dylan seldom makes it to meetings on time and skips one meeting entirely. At that meeting, two members petition you to remove him from the group, but others argue for keeping him. You decide to give Dylan another chance. A few hours later, Dylan e-mails you an apology, saying he's been "dealing with family problems." He offers to do extra research to make amends, and you gladly accept his offer, as you're stressed about getting the project done.

It's Thursday afternoon. The group's in-class presentation is next Tuesday. The plan is to rehearse tomorrow afternoon, then use the weekend to do any final tweaking that needs to be done. Your phone rings, and it's Dylan. He says, "I am so sorry; my family situation has been holding me back. Can I have more time to finish my research?"

[1] Situation adapted from the "Ron" situation developed by O'Keefe (1988).

3 YOUR TURN

Think about all you've learned thus far about interpersonal communication. Then work through the following five steps. Remember, there are no "right" answers, so think hard about what is the *best* choice! (P.S. Need help? See the *Helpful Concepts* list.)

step 1
Reflect on yourself. What are your thoughts and feelings in this situation? What attributions are you making about Dylan and his behavior? Are your attributions accurate, or are they shaded by your impressions of him?

step 2
Reflect on your partner. Using perspective-taking and empathic concern, put yourself in Dylan's shoes. What is he thinking and feeling in this situation?

step 3
Identify the optimal outcome. Think about your communication and relationship with Dylan as well as the situation surrounding the group project (including your leadership responsibilities). What's the best, most constructive relationship outcome possible? Consider what's best for you and for Dylan.

step 4
Locate the roadblocks. Taking into consideration your own and Dylan's thoughts and feelings and all that has happened in this situation, what obstacles are keeping you from achieving the optimal outcome?

step 5
Chart your course. What can you say to Dylan to overcome the roadblocks you've identified and achieve your optimal outcome?

HELPFUL CONCEPTS
Attribution errors, **76–77**
Uncertainty-reducing strategies, **78**
Ingroupers and outgroupers, **79–81**
Negativity effect, **88**
Algebraic impressions, **89–90**
Empathy, **92–94**
Perception-checking, **94–95**

4 THE OTHER SIDE

▶ Visit LaunchPad to watch a video in which Dylan tells his side of the case study story. As in many real-life situations, this is information to which you did not have access when you were initially crafting your response in Part 3. The video reminds us that even when we do our best to offer competent responses, there is always another side to the story that we need to consider.

and empathic concern in open, appropriate ways. Practicing responsible perception means not just mastering the knowledge of perception presented in these pages but also translating this intellectual mastery into active practice during every interpersonal encounter. We all use perception as the basis for our communication and relationship decisions. But when we practice *responsible* perception, the natural result is more competent communication and wiser relationship choices.

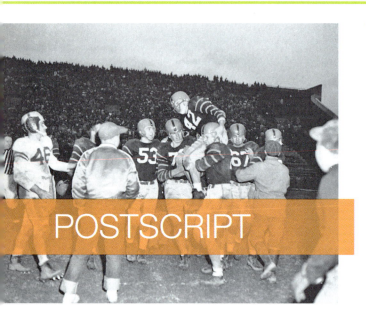

POSTSCRIPT

We began this chapter with an account of a football game marked by brutality and accusations of unfair play and an examination of its perceptual aftermath. Following the Dartmouth-Princeton game, fans from both sides felt the opposition had played dirty and that their own team had behaved honorably. Although there was only one game, fans perceived two radically different contests.

When you observe the "game film" of your own life, how often do you perceive others as instigating all of the rough play and penalties you've suffered while seeing yourself as blameless? Do you widen the perceptual gulf between yourself and those who see things differently? Or do you seek to bridge that divide by practicing and communicating empathy?

More than 60 years ago, two teams met on a field of play. Decades later, that game—and people's reactions to it—remind us of our own perceptual limitations and the importance of overcoming them. Although we'll never agree with everyone about everything that goes on around us, we can strive to understand one another's viewpoints much of the time. In doing so, we build lives that connect us to others rather than divide us from them.

LaunchPad for *Reflect & Relate* offers videos and encourages self-assessment through adaptive quizzing. Go to **macmillanhighered.com /reflectrelate4e** to get access to:

 LearningCurve
Adaptive Quizzes

 Video clips that help you understand interpersonal communication

key terms

- perception, 71
- selection, 72
- salience, 72
- organization, 72
- ▶ punctuation, 73
- interpretation, 73
- schemata, 74
- attributions, 74
- fundamental attribution error, 76
- actor-observer effect, 76
- ▶ self-serving bias, 77
- ▶ Uncertainty Reduction Theory, 78
- ingroupers, 79
- outgroupers, 79
- personality, 85
- implicit personality theories, 85
- interpersonal impressions, 86
- Gestalt, 87
- positivity bias, 88
- negativity effect, 88
- ▶ halo effect, 88
- ▶ horn effect, 89
- ▶ algebraic impressions, 89
- stereotyping, 90
- ▶ empathy, 92
- empathy mind-set, 93
- perception-checking, 94

▶ You can watch brief, illustrative videos of these terms and test your understanding of the concepts in LaunchPad.

key concepts

Perception as a Process

- We make sense of our interpersonal world through **perception,** and engage in **selection, organization,** and **interpretation** of information received from our senses.
- We interpret the meaning of communication by drawing on known information stored in our mental **schemata.** We make **attributions** regarding why people said and did certain things but sometimes fall prey to the **fundamental attribution error,** the **actor-observer effect,** or the **self-serving bias.**
- According to **Uncertainty Reduction Theory,** we commonly experience uncertainty during first encounters with new acquaintances.

Influences on Perception

- Culture and gender play major roles in shaping our perception of communication.
- **Personality** influences our perception of the traits we possess and how we perceive the traits of others. **Implicit personality theories** guide our perceptions of others' personalities.

Forming Impressions of Others

- When we perceive others, we form **interpersonal impressions.** Sometimes we create general **Gestalts,** which are quite often positive, thanks to the **positivity bias.**
- The **negativity effect** plays a role in shaping how we perceive information we learn about others.
- Forming strong positive or negative Gestalts sometimes leads to a **halo effect** or a **horn effect,** causing us to perceive subsequent information we learn about people in distorted ways.
- The most accurate and refined impressions of others are **algebraic impressions.** When we calculate our impressions based on individual traits, we're more likely to see people as they really are and adapt our communication accordingly.
- The most common form of interpersonal impression is **stereotyping.**

Improving Your Perception of Others

- When you can take the perspective of others and experience empathic concern toward them, your communication becomes more sensitive and adaptive.
- Responsible perception is rooted in **perception-checking,** routinely questioning your perceptions and correcting errors that may lead to ineffective communication.

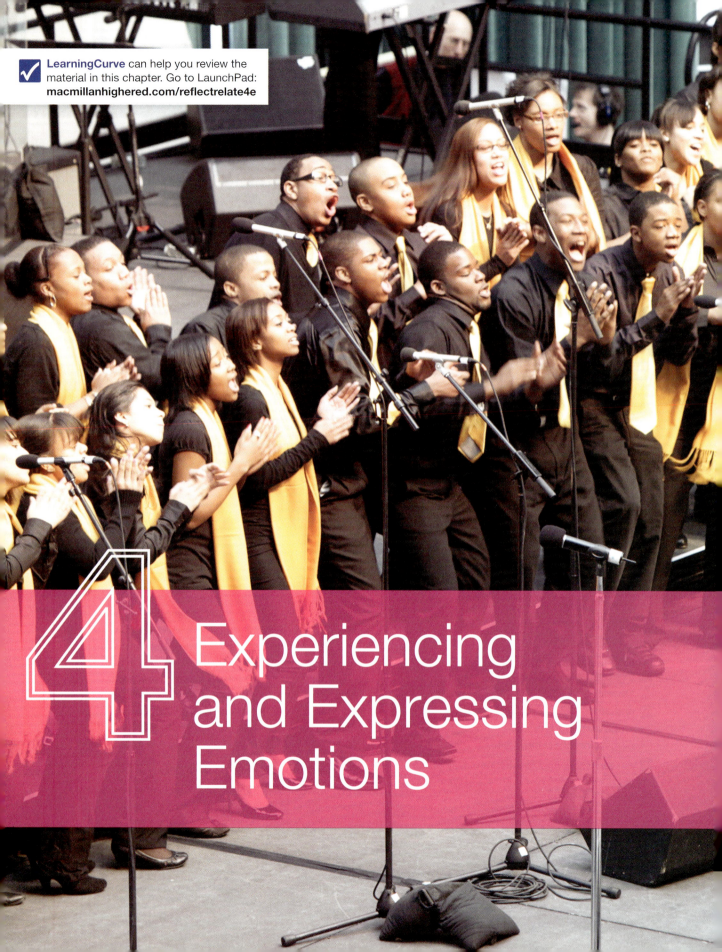

> Emotion fills our lives with meaning.

When radio personality and producer Vy Higginsen created the nonprofit Gospel for Teens program, her mission was to teach teens gospel music.[1] Higginsen and a group of volunteer instructors met weekly with kids ages 13 to 19, honing their vocal skills and sharing with them the history of gospel. As Higginsen notes, "The lyrics of gospel songs provide courage, inner strength, and hope for a better life in the future." But she quickly found that her program wouldn't only be about introducing gospel to a generation more versed in rap and hip-hop. Instead, Gospel for Teens would become a powerful vehicle for helping teens manage intense and challenging emotions.

Higginsen originally instituted a simple rule governing emotions and program participation: *leave the baggage at the door*. As she describes, "The teen years are a vulnerable time in kids' lives, and they are dealing with shyness, anxiety, trauma, and family dysfunction. Many students are uncomfortable about their physical appearance and self-esteem based on the peers around them. Some are overcome with anxiety from their home life, school, and thoughts of their futures." To keep difficult emotions from hindering performances, Higginsen began each singing session by having participants stand up and shake their hands, arms, legs, and feet, physically purging themselves of emotional constraints. As she

---

[1]The information that follows is adapted from a personal interview with the author, October 2011, and www.mamafoundation.org, retrieved October 12, 2011. Interview content published with permission of Vy Higginsen.

4 / Experiencing and Expressing Emotions

G.N. Miller/MaMa Foundation, Gospel for Teens

instructed, "Any worry, any pain, any problem with your mother, your father, your sister, your brother, the boyfriend, the girlfriend, I want that out now of your consciousness. That's your baggage; leave the bags outside because *this* time is for you!"

But Higginsen's "no baggage" policy was abandoned when the cousin of one of her most talented students was shot and killed. Higginsen realized that many program participants had suffered similar tragedies, and that her class could provide a forum within which students could safely share their stories, their pain, and their grief with one another—working together to begin healing. As she describes, "Our teens are living a very adult life—their friends and family are getting murdered, dying from diseases and drugs—and it's leaving emotional scars on them.

They need something uplifting in their lives. So I decided to allow the students to bring their baggage in. I invited the students to share what was happening in their worlds. I wasn't trying to fix their situations, because I couldn't, but their being heard was a profound step in their being healed. It made our choir realize we are not alone in our experience. We made a connection—emotionally, personally, and interpersonally."

Whereas Higginsen once encouraged students to leave their emotions at the door, she now realizes that the experience of singing and sharing the experience of singing with others provides students with a powerful vehicle for managing negative emotions in positive ways. "I would like the teens to take away the idea that we have emotions yet we are not our emotions. We can recover and thrive by changing our mind and rechanneling our energy through music, art, service, acceptance, meditation, and practice. In simple terms, we can rechannel the negative to the positive and use this as an opportunity for excellence. Gospel music has the power to empower and transform. More than anything, I want my students to know that joy, hope, faith, and goodness are possible."

Emotion fills our lives with meaning (Berscheid & Peplau, 2002). To experience emotion is to feel alive, and to lack emotion is to view life itself as colorless and meaningless (Frijda, 2005). Because emotion is so important, we feel compelled to express our emotional experiences to others through communication. And when we share our emotions with others, they transition from private and personal to profoundly interpersonal. It's at this point that choice becomes relevant. We may not be able to select our emotions before they arise, but we can choose how to handle and convey them after they occur. When we intelligently manage and competently communicate emotional experiences, our relationship satisfaction and overall life happiness increase. When we don't, our relationships suffer, and these lapses are reflected in relationships and lives torn by anger and sadness.

In this chapter, we examine the most personal and interpersonal of human experiences—emotion. You'll learn:

- The important differences between emotions, feelings, and moods, as well as the best approaches to managing negative moods
- Ways in which gender and personality influence emotion
- Why improving your emotional intelligence can help you more competently manage your experience and expression of emotion
- How to deal with emotional challenges, such as managing anger, communicating empathy online, handling fading romantic passion, and suffering grief.

chapter outline

103 The Nature of Emotion

109 Forces Shaping Emotion

112 Managing Your Emotional Experience and Expression

117 Emotional Challenges

126 Living a Happy Emotional Life

The Nature of Emotion

Distinguishing between emotions, feelings, and moods

Take a moment and recall the most recent emotion you felt. What comes to mind? For most people, it's a hot emotion—that is, a physically and mentally intense experience, like joy, anger, or grief, during which your palms sweated, your mouth felt dry, and your heart pounded (Berscheid & Regan, 2005). When we are asked to translate these emotions into words, we use vivid physical metaphors. Joy makes "our hearts leap," while anger makes "our blood boil." Grief is "a living hell" (Frijda, 2005). Understanding what emotions are and how they differ from feelings and moods are the first steps in better managing our emotions.

DEFINING EMOTION

Scholarly definitions of emotion mirror our everyday experiences. **Emotion** is an intense reaction to an event that involves interpreting event meaning, becoming physiologically aroused, labeling the experience as emotional, managing reactions, and communicating through emotional displays and disclosures (Gross, Richards, & John, 2006). This definition highlights the five key features of

Chapter Theme: Understanding and Intelligently Managing Emotions

Emotions profoundly shape our thoughts and perceptions. Yet we often underestimate the impact that they have on our communication. What's more, when we experience unpleasant emotions—such as anger or grief—we typically manage them by suppression or venting. Neither of these responses yields constructive outcomes. Understanding how emotions impact our interpersonal decision making, and learning how to intelligently manage them, are essential interpersonal competencies.

▶ Emotions are not just internally felt but also expressed through body language, gestures, facial expressions, and other physical behaviors. Raul Arboleda/AFP/Getty Images

emotion. First, emotion is reactive, triggered by our perception of outside events (Cacioppo, Klein, Berntson, & Hatfield, 1993). A friend telling you that her cancer is in remission leads you to experience joy. Receiving a scolding text message from a parent triggers both your surprise and your anger. When an emotion-inducing event occurs, we engage in the same perceptual process as we do with other types of interpersonal events—selecting, organizing, and interpreting information related to that event. As we interpret the event's meaning, we decide whether the incident is positive, neutral, negative, or somewhere in between, triggering corresponding emotions (Smith & Kirby, 2004).

A second feature of emotion is that it involves physiological arousal in the form of increased heart rate, blood pressure, and adrenaline release. Many researchers consider arousal *the* defining feature of emotion, a belief mirrored in most people's descriptions of emotion as "intense" and "hot" (Berscheid, 2002).

Third, to experience emotion, you must become aware of your interpretation and arousal as "an emotion"—that is, you must consciously label them as such (Berscheid, 2002). For example, imagine that a friend posts an embarrassing photo of you on Instagram. Upon discovering it, your face grows hot, your breathing quickens, and you become consciously aware of these physical sensations. This awareness, combined with your assessment of the situation, causes you to label your experience as the emotion "anger."

Fourth, how we each experience and express our emotions is constrained by historical, cultural, relational, and situational norms governing what is and isn't appropriate (Metts & Planalp, 2002). As a consequence, once we become aware that we're experiencing an emotion, we try to manage that experience and express that emotion in ways we consider acceptable. We may allow our emotion to dominate our thoughts and communication, try to channel it in constructive ways, or suppress our emotion completely. Emotion management results from

self-reflection

Recall an emotional event in a close relationship. What specific action triggered your emotion? How did you interpret the triggering event? What physical sensations resulted? What does this tell you about the link between events, mind, and body that is the basis of emotional experience?

the recognition that the totally unrestrained experience and expression of emotion will lead to negative consequences.

Finally, when emotion occurs, the choices you make regarding emotion management are reflected outward in your verbal and nonverbal displays in the form of word choices, exclamations or expletives, facial expressions, body posture, and gestures (Mauss, Levenson, McCarter, Wilhelm, & Gross, 2005). The communicative nature of emotion is so fundamental that people developed emoticons to represent emotional expressions in mediated communication, such as text messages and e-mail.

Another way in which emotion is communicative is by talking about our emotional experiences with others, a form of communication known as **emotion-sharing.** Much of interpersonal communication consists of disclosing emotions, talking about them, and pondering them. Studies on emotion-sharing suggest that people share between 75 and 95 percent of their emotional experiences with at least one other person, usually a spouse, parent, or friend (Frijda, 2005). The people with whom we share our emotions generally enjoy being confided in. Often, they share the incident with others, weaving a socially intimate network of emotion-sharing. The teens in the Gospel for Teens program (described in our chapter opener) use emotion-sharing to connect with one another and collaboratively work together to heal their individual experiences of grief and anger.

Sometimes emotion-sharing leads to **emotional contagion**—when the experience of the same emotion rapidly spreads from one person to others. Emotional contagion can be positive, such as when the joy you experience over an unexpected job promotion spreads to your family members as you tell them about it. At other times, emotional contagion can be negative. For instance, interacting with people who are anxious can cause an increase in your own anxiety level—even in cases in which you don't share their worries or feel personally concerned about their well-being (Parkinson & Simons, 2012). In extreme instances, emotional contagion can be disastrous. Such was the case in the 1903 stampede in Chicago's Iroquois Theater. A small fire broke out, and although it was quickly extinguished, people's fear of the fire swept rapidly from person to person throughout the crowd, causing a panicked stampede that killed more than 500 people (Brown, 1965).

FEELINGS AND MOODS

We often talk about emotions, feelings, and moods as if they are the same thing. But they're not. **Feelings** are short-term emotional reactions to events that generate only limited arousal; they do not typically trigger attempts to manage their experience or expression (Berscheid, 2002). We experience dozens, if not hundreds, of feelings daily—most of them lasting only a few seconds or minutes. An attractive stranger casts you an approving smile, causing you to feel momentarily flattered. A friend texts you unexpectedly when you're trying to study, making you feel briefly annoyed. Feelings are like small emotions. Common feelings include gratitude, concern, pleasure, relief, and resentment.

Whereas emotions occur occasionally in response to substantial events, and feelings arise frequently in response to everyday incidents, **moods** are low-intensity states—such as boredom, contentment, grouchiness, or serenity—that are not

---

self-reflection

With whom do you share your emotional experiences? Does such sharing always have a positive impact on your relationships, or does it cause problems at times? What ethical boundaries govern emotion-sharing?

Assignment: Emotion-Sharing

Ask students to create a list of significant others—parents, siblings, boyfriend/girlfriend, spouse, roommate, and so forth. Then have them indicate on a scale of 1 = "least likely" to 5 = "most likely" their likelihood of sharing their emotional experiences with each person on their list. How does the relationship type affect their likelihood of sharing? Does relational history have an impact? What other factors influence emotion-sharing?

Assignment: Emotional Contagion

Have students watch the LaunchPad video clip on **emotional contagion,** then place them in groups to generate a list of examples of positive emotional contagion (joy, excitement) and negative emotional contagion (disappointment, anger) in different relationship types (workplace, friendship, family, etc.). Follow up with a discussion on the potential relational outcomes for different types of emotional contagion.

○ Some strategies for improving moods work better than others. What strategies have you used to successfully pull yourself out of a bad mood? (Left) Blasius Erlinger/Getty Images; (right) AP Photo/Pat Sullivan

caused by particular events and typically last longer than feelings or emotions (Parkinson, Totterdell, Briner, & Reynolds, 1996). Positive or negative, moods are the slow-flowing emotional currents in our everyday lives. We can think of our frequent, fleeting feelings and occasional intense emotions as riding on top of these currents, as displayed in Figure 4.1.

Moods powerfully influence our perception. People who describe their moods as "good" are more likely than those in bad moods to form positive impressions of others (Forgas & Bower, 1987); are more likely than those in bad moods to perceive new acquaintances as "sociable," "honest," "giving," and "creative" (Fiedler, Pampe, & Scherf, 1986); and are more likely to fall prey to the fundamental attribution error (Forgas, 1998)—attributing others' behaviors to internal rather than external causes (see Chapter 3). Taken together, these findings suggest that people in positive moods aren't especially good perceivers. Why? Because they tend to selectively focus only on things that seem positive and rewarding (Tamir & Robinson, 2007), and they don't process information thoughtfully. In simple terms, when you're happy, you tend to skim along the perceptual surface and not deeply ponder things (Hunsinger, Isbell, & Clore, 2012).

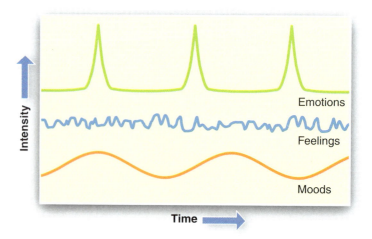

figure 4.1 **The Flow of Emotions, Feelings, and Moods**

Our moods also influence our communication, including how we talk with partners in close relationships (Cunningham, 1988). People in good moods are significantly more likely to disclose relationship thoughts and concerns to close friends, family members, and romantic partners. In contrast, people in bad moods typically prefer to *not* communicate, instead preferring to sit and think, be left alone, and avoid social and leisure activities (Cunningham, 1988).

Despite the perceptual shortcomings associated with positive mood states, most people prefer positive moods because negative moods are so unpleasant (Thayer, Newman, & McClain, 1994). Unfortunately, some of the most commonly practiced strategies for improving bad moods—drinking alcohol or caffeinated beverages, taking recreational drugs, and eating—are also the least effective and may actually worsen your bad mood (Thayer et al., 1994). More effective strategies for improving bad moods are ones that involve active expenditures of energy, especially strategies that combine relaxation, stress management, mental focus and energy, and exercise. The most effective strategy of all appears to be rigorous physical exercise (Thayer et al., 1994). Sexual activity does not seem to consistently elevate mood.

self-reflection

How do you behave toward others when you're in a bad mood? What strategies do you use to better your mood? Are these practices effective in elevating your mood and improving your communication in the long run, or do they merely provide a temporary escape or distraction?

TYPES OF EMOTIONS

Take a moment and look at the emotions communicated by the people in the photos on pages 108–109. How can you discern the emotion expressed in each picture? One way to distinguish between different types of emotions is to examine consistent patterns of facial expressions, hand gestures, and body postures that characterize specific emotions. By considering these patterns, scholars have identified six **primary emotions** that involve unique and consistent behavioral displays across cultures (Ekman, 1972). The six primary emotions are surprise, joy, disgust, anger, fear, and sadness.

Some situations provoke especially intense primary emotions. In such cases, we often use different words to describe the emotion, even though what we're experiencing is simply a more intense version of the same primary emotion (Plutchik, 1980). For instance, receiving a gift from a romantic partner may cause intense joy that we think of as "ecstasy," just as the passing of a close relative will likely trigger intense sadness that we label as "grief" (see Table 4.1).

Discussion Prompt: Brainstorming for Emotions

Ask students to brainstorm an exhaustive list of emotions; be sure to share their ideas on the board or screen so that the entire class can keep track as the discussion progresses. When they run out of ideas, analyze the list with the following questions: Which are primary emotions, and which are their high-intensity counterparts? How are they expressed differently? Which of these emotions are blended?

table 4.1 Intense Primary Emotions

Primary Emotion	High-Intensity Counterpart
Surprise	Amazement
Joy	Ecstasy
Disgust	Loathing
Anger	Rage
Fear	Terror
Sadness	Grief

In other situations, an event may trigger two or more primary emotions simultaneously, resulting in an experience known as **blended emotions** (Plutchik, 1993). For example, imagine that you borrow your romantic partner's phone and accidentally access a series of flirtatious texts between your partner and someone else. You'll likely experience jealousy, a blended emotion because it

focus on CULTURE

Happiness across Cultures

A Chinese proverb warns, "We are never happy for a thousand days, a flower never blooms for a hundred" (Myers, 2002, p. 47). Although most of us understand that our positive emotions may be more passing than permanent, we tend to presume that greater joy lies on the other side of various cultural fences. If only we made more money, lived in a better place, or even were a different age or gender, *then* we would truly be happy. But the science of human happiness has torn down these fences, suggesting instead that happiness is interpersonally based.

Consider class, the most common cultural fence believed to divide the happy from the unhappy. Studies suggest that wealth actually has little effect on happiness. Across countries and cultures, happiness is unaffected by the gain of additional money once people have basic human rights, safe and secure shelter, sufficient food and water, meaningful activity with which to occupy their time, and worthwhile relationships.

What about age? The largest cross-cultural study of happiness and age ever conducted, which examined 170,000 people in 16 countries, found no difference in reported happiness and life satisfaction based on age (Myers, 2002). And gender? Differences in gender account for less than 1 percent in reported life happiness (Michalos, 1991; Wood, Rhodes, & Whelan, 1989). Men and women around the globe all report roughly similar levels of happiness. Even population density drops as a predictor of joy: people in rural areas, towns, suburbs, and big cities report similar levels of happiness (Crider, Willits, & Kanagy, 1991).

When asked, "What is necessary for your happiness?" people overwhelmingly cite satisfying close relationships with family, friends, and romantic partners at the top of their lists (Berscheid & Peplau, 2002). Faith also matters. Studies over the past 20 years in both Europe and the United States have repeatedly documented that people who are religious are more likely to report being happy and satisfied with life than those who are nonreligious (Myers, 2002). Finally, living a healthy life breeds joy. The positive effect of exercise on mood extends to broader life satisfaction: people who routinely exercise report substantially higher levels of happiness and well-being than those who don't (Myers, 2002).

discussion questions

- What are your own sources of happiness and life satisfaction?
- Do you agree that interpersonal relationships, spiritual beliefs, and healthy living are the most essential ingredients for happiness?

◐ According to studies performed by psychologist Paul Ekman (1972), people around the world associate the same facial expressions with particular feelings. Part of improving your interpersonal communication is to recognize others' emotions. Can you identify the ones displayed in each of these photographs? (From left to right, the emotions shown are joy, surprise, anger, disgust, fear, and sadness.) (Left to right) Kiratsinh Jadeja/Getty Images; George Marks/Stringer/Getty Images; Digital Vision/Getty Images; Howard Kingsnorth/Getty Images; Richard Kalvar/Magnum Photos; Lauren Rosenbaum/Getty Images

combines the primary emotions anger, fear, and sadness (Guerrero & Andersen, 1998): in this case, *anger* at your partner, *fear* that your relationship may be threatened, and *sadness* at the thought of potentially losing your partner to a rival. Other examples of blended emotions include contempt (anger and disgust), remorse (disgust and sadness), and awe (surprise and fear) (Plutchik, 1993).

While North Americans often identify six primary emotions—surprise, joy, love, anger, fear, and sadness (Shaver, Wu, & Schwartz, 1992)—some cultural variation exists. For example, in traditional Chinese culture, shame and sad love (an emotion concerning attachment to former lovers) are primary emotions. Traditional Hindu philosophy suggests nine primary emotions: sexual passion, amusement, sorrow, anger, fear, perseverance, disgust, wonder, and serenity (Shweder, 1993).

Forces Shaping Emotion

[Personality and gender affect emotion]

In the movie *Bridesmaids* (2011), Annie is a woman struggling to overcome the failure of her beloved small business, Cake Baby, as well as her breakup with her boyfriend, Ted, who continues to lead her on. Annie's sadness and sense of hopelessness lead her to seek comfort from her best friend, Lillian, whose own life is on the upswing because of her recent engagement. Lillian asks Annie to be her maid of honor, but the situation quickly devolves as Annie's anxieties and neuroses cause a series of emotional displays, culminating in her ruining a "girls weekend together" and causing a jealous scene at Lillian's bridal shower.

Surrounding Annie throughout the story are several other vivid characters. Becca is perpetually upbeat and perky; Helen—Annie's primary rival for Lillian's affections—is fanatically conscientious; Rita, Lillian's cousin, is always sarcastic and negative. Adding to the dispositional mix is Nathan, a warm and friendly state trooper who exempts Annie from a traffic ticket and subsequently tries to romance her. But dominating the group is Megan, who is outgoing to the point of aggressiveness. When Annie succumbs to her sadness, it is Megan who lifts her up:[2]

Annie: I can't get off the couch, I got fired from my job, I got kicked out of my apartment, I can't pay any of my bills, I don't have any friends. . . .

---

[2]Adapted from Mumulo & Wiig (2011).

 Video
macmillanhighered.com/reflectrelate4e

Blended Emotions
Watch this clip online to answer the questions below.

What blended emotions is the woman in the video experiencing? What type of situation could cause this? What types of communication situations make you experience blended emotions? Why?

Want to see more? Check out LaunchPad for a clip on **emotional contagion.**

Discussion Prompt: Hurt as an Emotional Blend

Vangelisti, Maguire, Alexander, & Clark (2007) suggest that hurt is a blended emotion of sadness, anger, and fear of being vulnerable to harm. Hurt happens when someone says or does something that causes emotional pain. Ask students to write a short journal entry recalling an incident in which someone hurt them and explaining why it hurt. Did it hurt more when it was intentional or unintentional? How did they effectively deal with the hurt?

109

▲ The characters in *Bridesmaids* display many intense emotions, leading to frequent and sometimes explosive conflicts between them. Suzanne Hanover/© Universal Pictures/Courtesy Everett Collection

Megan: You know what I find interesting, Annie? That you have no friends. You know why that's interesting? Here's a friend standing directly in front of you trying to talk to you, and you choose to talk about the fact that you don't have any friends. No, I don't think you want any help; you just want to have a little pity party. I think Annie wants a little pity party. I'm life, is life bothering you Annie? . . . Fight back for your life!

As with the characters in *Bridesmaids*, our emotions and their expression just seem to happen: an incident occurs, an emotion arises, and we communicate accordingly. But although emotions seem unfiltered and immediate, powerful forces shape how we experience and express them. Two of the most influential of these forces are personality and gender.

PERSONALITY

Personality exerts a pronounced impact on our emotions. Recall the Big Five personality traits described in Chapter 3—openness, conscientiousness, extraversion, agreeableness, and neuroticism (or OCEAN). Of these five, three strongly influence our experience and communication of emotion (Pervin, 1993). The first is *extraversion*, the degree to which one is outgoing and sociable versus quiet and reserved. High-extraversion people experience positive emotions more frequently than do low-extraversion people, which appears to be due to enhanced sensitivity to positive events. Put simply, high-extraversion people look for happiness in their everyday lives, focusing their attention more on positive events than on negative (Larsen & Ketelaar, 1991). They also rate themselves as better able to cope with stress and more skilled at managing their emotional communication than are low-extraversion people (Lopes, Salovey, Cote, & Beers, 2005). In *Bridesmaids*, we see this trait in Megan when she discusses her success in overcoming a challenging high school experience by working hard and believing in herself, leading her to land a high-ranking government job (with the "highest possible security clearance").

Another personality trait that influences emotion is *agreeableness*. Like Nathan in *Bridesmaids*, people high in agreeableness (who are trusting, friendly, and cooperative) report being happier in general, better able to manage stress, and more skilled at managing their emotional communication than are low-agreeable people. High-agreeable people also score substantially higher on measures of emotion management and are rated by their peers as having superior emotion management skills (Lopes et al., 2005).

The tendency to think negative thoughts about oneself, known as *neuroticism*, also affects emotional experience and expression. High-neurotic people, like Annie in *Bridesmaids*, focus their attention primarily on negative events (Larsen & Ketelaar, 1991). Consequently, they report more frequent negative emotions than do low-neurotic people and rate themselves as less happy overall. They also describe themselves as less skilled at emotional communication, and they test lower on scientific measures of emotion management than do low-neurotic people (Lopes et al., 2005).

Although these findings seem to suggest that highly neurotic people are doomed to lives of negative emotion, this isn't necessarily the case. Psychologist Albert Ellis (1913–2007) dedicated much of his professional life to helping neurotics change their self-defeating beliefs. Ellis believed that much of neurosis and its accompanying emotional states—sadness, anger, and anxiety—is tied to three extreme, irrational beliefs: "I must be outstandingly competent or I am worthless," "Others must treat me considerately or they are absolutely rotten," and "The world should always give me happiness or I will die" (Ellis & Dryden, 1997). Ellis developed **Rational Emotive Behavior Therapy (REBT)** as a way for therapists to help neurotic patients systematically purge themselves of such beliefs.

If you find yourself habitually plagued by negative thoughts similar to those mentioned above, you can use Ellis's five steps on your own to change your thoughts and the negative emotions that flow from them. First, call to mind common situations that cause you to be upset. Second, identify irrational beliefs about your self and others that are tied to these situations. Third, consider the emotional, behavioral, and relational consequences that you suffer as a result of these beliefs—negative outcomes that you would like to change. Fourth, critically challenge these beliefs, disputing their validity. Is there really any support for these beliefs? What evidence contradicts them? What is the worst thing that can happen if you abandon these beliefs? The best thing that can happen? Finally, identify more accurate and realistic beliefs about yourself, others, and the world

self-reflection

To what degree are you extraverted, agreeable, and neurotic? How have these traits affected your emotions? your relationships? Are these traits, and their impact, enduring and permanent, or can they be changed in ways that will improve your interpersonal communication?

at large that lead to more positive emotional, behavioral, and relational outcomes, and embrace these beliefs fully.

Clearly, your degree of extraversion, agreeableness, and especially neuroticism influences how often you experience positive and negative emotions and how effectively you manage and communicate these emotions. At the same time, keep in mind that personality is merely one of many pieces that make up the complex puzzle that is emotion. Part of becoming a competent emotional communicator is learning how your personality traits shape your emotional experience and expression, and treating personality-based emotion differences in others with sensitivity and understanding.

GENDER

Like personality, gender also impacts our experience of emotions. Across cultures, women report experiencing more sadness, fear, shame, and guilt than men, while men report feeling more anger and other hostile emotions (Fischer, Rodriguez Mosquera, van Vianen, & Manstead, 2004). In Western cultures, gender differences in emotion derive in part from differences in how men and women orient to interpersonal relationships (Brody & Hall, 2000). Women are more likely than men to express emotions that support relationships and suppress emotions that assert their own interests over another's (Zahn-Waxler, 2001). As a consequence, women may feel sadness more often than men because sadness, unlike anger, isn't directed outward at another person; thus, it doesn't threaten relationships. Sadness communicates personal vulnerability and signals the need for comforting from others, much the way Annie seeks comfort from Lillian in *Bridesmaids* by leaving her lengthy voice-mail messages about the assorted messes in her life. By contrast, anger conveys a motivation to achieve one's own goals or to take satisfaction in one's success over another's (Chaplin, Cole, & Zahn-Waxler, 2005).

Though men and women may experience emotions with different frequency and express them differently, when they experience the same emotions, there is no difference in the intensity of the emotion experienced (Fischer et al., 2004). Whether it's anger, sadness, joy, or disgust, men *and* women experience these emotions with equal intensity.

Managing Your Emotional Experience and Expression

Dealing with emotions before, while, and after they occur

It's arguably the most well-known psychology experiment.[3] Over a six-year period, Stanford psychologist Walter Mischel brought 653 young children from the university's Bing Nursery School into a room and offered them a tasty

---

[3]The information that follows is adapted from Goleman (2007b); Lehrer (2009); and Shoda, Mischel, & Peake (1990).

treat of their choice: marshmallow, Oreo cookie, or pretzel stick. But he also presented them with a dilemma. If they could resist eating the treat while he stepped out for several minutes, they would get a second treat as a reward. The children were then left alone. The experiment was a simple test of impulse control: the ability to manage one's emotional arousal, excitement, and desire. Most of the kids gave in and ate the treat, usually in less than three minutes. But about 30 percent held out. Years later, Mischel gathered more data from the same children, who were then in high school. He was stunned to learn that their choices in the experiment predicted a broad range of outcomes. Children who had waited were more socially skilled, were better able to cope with stress, were less likely to have emotional outbursts when frustrated, were better able to deal with temptations, and had closer, more stable friendships than those who hadn't waited. They also had substantially higher SAT scores. Why was "the marshmallow test" such a powerful predictor of long-term personal and interpersonal outcomes? Because it taps a critical skill: the ability to constructively manage emotions. As Mischel notes, "If you can deal with hot emotions in the face of temptation, then you can study for the SAT instead of watching television. It's not just about marshmallows."

Can you recall a time when you had to resist an emotional impulse or desire, like in the marshmallow study? What was the outcome of this event? © Quinn Kirk/Terry Wild Stock

EMOTIONAL INTELLIGENCE

Managing your emotions is part of **emotional intelligence:** the ability to interpret emotions accurately and to use this information to manage emotions, communicate them competently, and solve relationship problems (Gross & John, 2002). People with high degrees of emotional intelligence typically possess four skills:

1. Acute understanding of their own emotions
2. Ability to see things from others' perspectives and have a sense of compassion regarding others' emotional states (*empathy*)
3. Aptitude for constructively managing their own emotions
4. Capacity for harnessing their emotional states in ways that create competent decision making, communication, and relationship problem solving (Kotzé & Venter, 2011)

Given that emotional intelligence (EI) involves understanding emotions coupled with the ability to manage them in ways that optimize interpersonal competence, it's not surprising that people with high EI experience a broad range of positive outcomes. For example, within leadership positions, people with high EI are more likely than low EI people to garner trust, inspire followers, and be perceived as having integrity (Kotzé & Venter, 2011). High EI individuals are less likely than low EI people to bully people or use violence to get what they want

**Media Note:
Emotional Intelligence**
Comedies often portray characters that have an inability to interpret their emotions or manage them competently. Examples include the movies *Anchorman* and *Bruce Almighty* and the hit TV shows *Family Guy* and *The Big Bang Theory*, in which the main characters, Peter Griffin and Sheldon Cooper, often lack emotional intelligence. Share clips with students and have them discuss which of the four skills of emotional intelligence the characters lack.

Online Self-Quiz: Assessing Your Emotional Intelligence. To take this self-quiz, visit LaunchPad: macmillanhighered.com/reflectrelate4e

Assignment: Managing Emotions

Ask students to write a short paper articulating the ways in which they will manage their emotions in their current or future careers. Does their desired or chosen occupation require more suppression than others? What challenges can arise when suppressing emotions at work?

self-reflection

Consider your own use of suppression and venting. What leads you to choose one or the other strategy? Are there limits to how often you vent or how long you suppress? What ethical considerations arise related to each strategy?

(Mayer, Salovey, & Caruso, 2004). High EI people even find it easier to forgive relational partners who have wronged them because of their strong empathy and skill at emotion management (Hodgson & Wertheim, 2007).

Of the skills that constitute emotional intelligence, emotion management is arguably the most important one to improve because—as demonstrated by Mischel's research—it directly influences your communication choices and the outcomes that result (Lopes, Salovey, Cote, & Beers, 2005). How? Put bluntly, *if you can't manage your emotions, you can't communicate competently.* **Emotion management** involves attempts to influence which emotions you have, when you have them, and how you experience and express them (Gross, Richards, & John, 2006). Emotions naturally trigger attempts to manage them. Consequently, the practical issue is not whether you will manage your emotions but how you can do so in ways that improve your interpersonal communication and relationships.

MANAGING YOUR EMOTIONS AFTER THEY OCCUR

One strategy for managing emotions is to try to modify or control them after we become aware of them (Gross et al., 2006). An event triggers arousal, interpretation, and awareness of an emotion. We then consciously try to modify our internal experience and outward communication of that emotion.

The two most common ways people manage emotions after they have been triggered are suppression and venting. **Suppression** involves inhibiting thoughts, arousal, and outward behavioral displays of emotion (Richards, Butler, & Gross, 2003). For example, one participant in an emotion management study describes suppressing his communication of happiness and surprise after scoring well on a college paper in which he had invested little effort (Gross et al., 2006):

> I didn't work very hard on this paper so I was surprised. My roommate actually did some work and didn't get a good grade, so he was very down about it. I was very happy inside, but at the same time, I didn't want to show up my roommate because he's my friend. Instead of acting happy and surprised, I kind of put on my academic sad face and said, "Oh, I didn't do well either." (p. 11)

The desire to suppress stems from the recognition that feeling, thinking, and openly communicating certain emotions would be relationally, socially, or culturally inappropriate. Although people sometimes suppress positive emotions, suppression occurs most commonly with negative emotions, especially anger and sadness (Gross et al., 2006). This is because displays of pleasant emotions elicit favorable responses from others, whereas the expression of negative emotions often drives other people away (Argyle & Lu, 1990; Furr & Funder, 1998).

Suppression is the most widely practiced strategy for managing unavoidable and unwanted emotions. But its effectiveness is marginal because you are trying to modify the intense arousal you are already experiencing, the thoughts you are already thinking, and the body's natural inclination to display this arousal and these thoughts in the form of expressions (Lopes et al., 2005).

The inverse of suppression is **venting:** allowing emotions to dominate our thoughts and explosively expressing them (Fuendeling, 1998; Kostiuk & Fouts,

In *Game of Thrones*, Tyrion Lannister is unjustly accused of a crime he didn't commit. He finds it difficult to manage his emotions and, during his trial, vents his rage at his father and the onlookers who ridicule him. Helen Sloan/© HBO/Courtesy: Everett Collection

2002). Venting may be positive, such as when we jump up and shout for joy after learning we got the job we wanted. At other times, we vent negative emotions, such as when we blow up at a spouse or other family member who has been pestering us repeatedly.

PREVENTING EMOTIONS

An alternative to managing emotions after they occur is to prevent unwanted emotions from happening in the first place. Four strategies are commonly used for preventing emotions, the first of which is **encounter avoidance**: staying away from people, places, or activities that you know will provoke emotions you don't want to experience (Gross et al., 2006). For example, you might purposely avoid a particular class that your ex signed up for because seeing him or her always provokes intense and unpleasant emotions within you.

A second preventive strategy is **encounter structuring**: intentionally avoiding specific topics that you know will provoke unwanted emotion during encounters with others. For example, I love my in-laws (honestly!), but my political attitudes are very different from theirs. Early in our acquaintanceship, my father-in-law and I would both get angry whenever we discussed politics. After a few such battles, we agreed to avoid this topic and now structure our encounters so that politics isn't discussed.

A third preventive strategy is **attention focus**: intentionally devoting your attention only to aspects of an event or encounter that you know will not provoke an undesired emotion. Imagine that you're sitting in class, listening to a lecture, but the person sitting behind you keeps getting and sending text messages. To use attention focus, you would actively watch and listen to the professor, letting the sound of the phone text alerts drop beneath conscious awareness so that it doesn't set you off.

▶ Video
macmillanhighered.com/reflectrelate4e

Encounter Structuring
Watch this clip online to answer the questions below.

What kinds of topics are so difficult for you that you avoid them in discussion? When two people in any relationship consistently avoid difficult topics because they are emotionally charged, how might that affect their bond?

Want to see more? Check out LaunchPad for clips on **encounter avoidance** and **reappraisal**.

A fourth way people preventively manage emotion is through **deactivation:** systematically desensitizing yourself to emotional experience (Fuendeling, 1998). Some people, especially after experiencing a traumatic emotional event, decide that they no longer want to feel anything. The result is an overall deadening of emotion. Though the desire to use this strategy is understandable, deactivation can trigger deep depression.

REAPPRAISING YOUR EMOTIONS

Imagine that you (like me) occasionally receive friendly Facebook messages from former romantic partners. You feel ethically obligated to share these messages with your current partner, but you also know that when you do, he or she will respond with nasty remarks about your ex that anger you. How can you best manage the emotions that will arise?

The most fruitful strategy for engaging difficult and unavoidable emotions is **reappraisal:** actively changing how you think about the meaning of emotion-eliciting situations so that their emotional impact is changed (Jackson, Malmstadt, Larson, & Davidson, 2000). To use reappraisal in the previous example, you might think vividly about your partner's positive aspects, your mutual love for each other, and your future together (Richards et al., 2003). As a result, you'll be more likely to communicate positively, with empathy—"I know you don't like my ex, and I can totally understand why; I would feel the same if I were in your shoes."

Reappraisal is effective because you employ it *before* a full-blown emotional reaction commences. This strategy requires little effort compared to trying to suppress or control your emotions after they've occurred. In addition, reappraisal produces interpersonal communication that is partner-focused and perceived as engaged and emotionally responsive (Gross et al., 2006). Across studies, people who are most effective at managing their emotional communication report reappraisal as their primary strategy (John & Gross, 2004).

Reappraisal is accomplished in two steps. First, before or during an encounter that you suspect will trigger an undesired emotion in yourself, *call to mind the positive aspects of the encounter*. If you truly can't think of anything positive about the other person, your relationship, or the situation, focus on seeing yourself as the kind of person who can constructively communicate even during unpleasant encounters with people you ardently dislike. Second, *consider the short- and long-term consequences of your actions*. Think about how communicating positively in the here and now will shape future outcomes in constructive ways.

You can use reappraisal to effectively manage problematic positive emotions as well. Imagine again that you've received a job offer from the company you have long desired to work for. Your roommate, however, hasn't gotten a single interview. Jumping for joy will not help maintain your relationship with him or her. In this case, reappraisal allows you to focus on your roommate's feelings and perspective; you might respond with "I did receive an exciting offer, but I also know that you're going to land somewhere great. It's a tough market right now, but you have so many desirable skills and qualities; any employer would be lucky to have you."

---

skills practice

Using Reappraisal
Managing difficult emotions through reappraisal

① Identify a recurring behavior or event that triggers emotions you'd like to manage more effectively.

② When the behavior or event happens, focus your thoughts on positive aspects of yourself, the other person, your relationship, and the situation.

③ Consider ways to communicate that will foster positive outcomes.

④ Communicate in those ways.

⑤ Observe how your positive thoughts and constructive communication affect the relationship.

Teaching Tip: Reappraisal

Have students watch the LaunchPad video clip on **reappraisal** to better understand this important term and to see how it can be a useful tool for managing emotions. This video clip can also be assigned to individual students or groups for them to write about or discuss how they might use reappraisal in a situation that is currently angering them.

Emotional Challenges

[Intense emotions are the most difficult to handle]

Each day we face personal trials that trigger difficult-to-manage emotions affecting our communication, our relationships, and the quality of our lives. For example, romantic jealousy—which we discuss in Chapter 10—is toxic to interpersonal communication and must be managed effectively for relationships to survive (Guerrero & Andersen, 1998). Likewise, fear—of emotional investment, vulnerability, or long-term commitment—can prevent us from forming intimate connections with others (Mickelson, Kessler, & Shaver, 1997). In the remainder of this chapter, we focus on four such challenges that occur all too frequently in our daily lives: anger, lack of empathy online, passion, and grief.

ANGER

Anger is a negative primary emotion that occurs when you are blocked or interrupted from attaining an important goal by what you see as the improper action of an external agent (Berkowitz & Harmon-Jones, 2004). As this definition suggests, anger is almost always triggered by someone or something external to us and is driven by our perception that the interruption is unfair (Scherer, 2001). So, for example, when your sister refuses to give you a much-needed loan, you're more likely to feel angry if you think she can afford to give you the loan but is simply choosing not to. By contrast, if you think your sister is willing but unable to help you, you'll be less likely to feel anger toward her.

Each of us experiences anger frequently; the average person is mildly to moderately angry anywhere from several times a day to several times a week (Berkowitz & Harmon-Jones, 2004). Perhaps because of its familiarity, we commonly underestimate anger's destructive potential. Anger causes perceptual errors that enhance the likelihood we will respond in a verbally and physically violent fashion toward others (Lemerise & Dodge, 1993). For instance, both men *and* women report the desire to punch, smash, kick, bite, or do similar actions that will hurt others when they are angry (Carlson & Hatfield, 1992). The impact of anger on

Assignment:
Music and Emotions
Music often focuses on specific emotions, especially passion, anger, or grief over a breakup. Ask students to bring the lyrics of one of their favorite songs that relate to passion, anger, or grief (contemporary or classic). Students should write a short paper identifying the emotion the song is about, how that emotion is expressed, and their own emotional reactions to the song.

▼ Anger is our most intense and potentially destructive emotion. Both men and women report the desire to react to anger in similar ways: through verbal outbursts or physical violence.
(Left to right) Richard Schulman/Corbis; Nicholas Asfouri/AFP/Getty Images; Phil Schermeister/Getty Images

self-QUIZ

Test Your Chronic Hostility

Place a check mark next to the statements with which you agree. Count up all your check marks, and then use the scoring key below to interpret your score.

To take this quiz online, visit LaunchPad: **macmillanhighered.com/reflectrelate4e**.

_____ People are always trying to use me for their own selfish purposes.

_____ It's human nature to be immoral and exploitative.

_____ I can't help but feel angry when I consider the rudeness of others.

_____ People seem to enjoy behaving in ways that annoy and provoke me.

_____ It's hard to not blow up at people, given how they're always screwing up.

_____ I get furious just thinking about how inconsiderate most people are.

_____ Most people are manipulative, and they truly sicken me.

Scoring: A score of 0–2 means low hostility. If you've scored in this range, you likely experience anger on an occasional basis, triggered in the normal way by events that you perceive negatively. A score of 3–4 means moderate hostility. If you fall into this range, anger may be an issue of concern in your interpersonal relationships. A score of 5–7 means high hostility. You likely experience anger frequently, and your interpersonal relationships are probably strongly and detrimentally affected by your anger.

---

interpersonal communication is also devastating. Angry people are more likely to argue, make accusations, yell, swear, and make hurtful and abusive remarks (Knobloch, 2005). Additionally, passive-aggressive communication such as ignoring others, pulling away, giving people dirty looks, and using the "silent treatment" are all more likely to happen when you're angry (Knobloch, 2005).

The most frequently used strategy for managing anger is suppression. You bottle it up inside rather than let it out. Occasional suppression can be constructive, such as when open communication of anger would be unprofessional, or when anger has been triggered by mistaken perceptions or attributions. But *always* suppressing anger can cause physical and mental problems: you put yourself in a near-constant state of arousal and negative thinking known as **chronic hostility.** People suffering from chronic hostility spend most of their waking hours simmering in a thinly veiled state of suppressed rage. Their thoughts and perceptions are dominated by the negative. They are more likely than others to believe that human nature is innately evil and that most people are immoral, selfish, exploitative, and manipulative. Ironically, because chronically hostile people believe the worst about others, they tend to be difficult, self-involved, demanding, and ungenerous (Tavris, 1989).

A second common anger management strategy is *venting*, which many people view as helpful and healthy; it "gets the anger out." The assumption that venting will rid you of anger is rooted in the concept of **catharsis,** which holds that openly expressing your emotions enables you to purge them. But in contrast to popular beliefs about the benefits of venting, research suggests that while venting may provide a temporary sense of pleasure, it actually *boosts* anger. One field study of engineers and technicians who were fired from their jobs found that the more individuals vented their anger about the company, the angrier they became (Ebbeson, Duncan, & Konecni, 1975).

To manage your anger, it's better to use strategies such as encounter avoidance, encounter structuring, and reappraisal. In cases in which something or someone has already triggered anger within you, consider using the **Jefferson strategy,** named after the third president of the United States. When a person says or does something that makes you angry, count slowly to 10 before you speak or act (Tavris, 1989). If you are very angry, count slowly to 100; then speak or act. Thomas Jefferson adopted this simple strategy for reducing his own anger during interpersonal encounters.

Although the Jefferson strategy may seem silly, it's effective because it creates a delay between the event that triggered your anger, the accompanying arousal and awareness, and your communication response. The delay between your internal physical and mental reactions and your outward communication allows your arousal to diminish somewhat, including lowering your adrenaline, blood pressure, and heart rate. Therefore, you communicate in a less extreme (and possibly less inappropriate) way than if you had not "counted to 10." A delay also gives you time for critical self-reflection, perception-checking, and empathy. These three skills can help you identify errors in your assessment of the event or person and plan a competent response. The Jefferson strategy is especially easy to use when you're communicating by e-mail or text message, two media that naturally allow for a delay between receiving a message and responding.

ONLINE COMMUNICATION AND EMPATHY DEFICITS

After giving a lecture about stereotypes, I received an e-mail from a student: "Stereotypes are DEMEANING!! People should DENOUNCE them, not TEACH them!!! WHY LECTURE ABOUT STEREOTYPES???" Noting the lack of greeting, capped letters, and excessive punctuation, I interpreted the message as angry. Irritated, I popped back a flippant response, "Uhhhh . . .

Assignment: Jefferson Strategy
Ask students to try the Jefferson strategy the next time they become angry, and have them write a brief paper about the experience. Students should describe the scenario and any outcomes: Did the Jefferson strategy work? Did it defuse their arousal? Did it allow them time for self-reflection, perception-checking, and empathy? How did it help them identify errors in their assessment of their partner or the situation?

⊘ When we communicate face-to-face, we have the advantage of communicating in real time and having feedback from the person with whom we are interacting. Online communication can cause empathy deficits that we may need to compensate for. (Left) © Steve Hix/Somos Images/Corbis; (right) © Michael Doolittle/Alamy

because people often wrongly believe that stereotypes are true?" Hours later, I received a caustic reply: "I think it's really disrespectful of you to treat my question so rudely!! I'M PAYING YOU TO TEACH, NOT MOCK!!!"

You have probably had similar experiences—online encounters in which anger or other emotions were expressed inappropriately, triggering a destructive exchange. In most of these interactions, the messages traded back and forth would never have been expressed face-to-face.

Why are we more likely to inappropriately express our emotions online? Two features of online interaction—asynchronicity and invisibility—help explain this phenomenon (Suler, 2004). Much of our online communication is *asynchronous*. That is, we don't interact with others in real time but instead exchange messages (such as tweets, texts, e-mails, or Facebook postings) that are read and responded to at later points. When communicating asynchronously, it's almost as if time is magically suspended (Suler, 2004). We know that there *will* likely be responses to our messages, but we choose when (and if) we view those responses. This predisposes us to openly express emotions that we might otherwise conceal if we knew the response would be immediate.

Online communication also provides us with a sense of *invisibility*. Without sharing a physical context with the people with whom we're communicating, we feel as if we're not really there—that people can't really see or hear us. Consequently, we feel distant from the consequences of our messages.

Recent brain research suggests that our sense of invisibility when communicating online may have a neurological basis. Recall from Chapter 1 that *feedback* consists of the verbal and nonverbal messages recipients convey to indicate their reaction to communication. Now remember our definition of *empathy* from Chapter 3: the ability to experience others' thoughts and emotions. Research documents that the same part of the brain that controls empathy—the orbitofrontal cortex—also monitors feedback (Goleman, 2006). This means that our ability to experience empathy is neurologically tied to our ability to perceive feedback (Beer, John, Scabini, & Knight, 2006). During face-to-face and phone encounters, we constantly track the feedback of others, watching their facial expressions, eye contact, and gestures, and listening to their tone of voice. This enables us to feel empathy for them, to consider what they're thinking and feeling about our communication. When we see or hear people react negatively to something we're saying, we can instantly modify our messages in ways that avoid negative consequences.

Now consider what happens when we lack feedback—such as when we're communicating online. Without the ability to perceive others' immediate responses to our communication, it's difficult for us to experience empathy and to adjust our communication in ways that maintain appropriateness (Goleman, 2007a). We're less able to *perspective-take* (see the situation and our communication from our partner's point of view) and to feel *empathic concern* (experience his or her emotions and feelings). Consequently, we're more likely to express negative emotions—especially anger—in blunt, tactless, and inappropriate ways. We may shout at others by using capped letters and exclamation points, or we may say things we'd never say over the phone or face-to-face. Complicating matters further, people on the receiving end of our communication have the same deficit. Their online messages are less sensitive, less tactful, and maybe even more

self-reflection

Recall an online encounter in which you inappropriately expressed emotion. How did lack of empathy shape your behavior? Would you have communicated the same way face-to-face? What does this tell you about the relationship between feedback, empathy, and emotional expression?

offensive than their offline messages. *Without feedback, we have difficulty experiencing empathy and gauging the appropriateness of our emotional expression.*

What can you do to experience and express emotions more competently online? First, compensate for the online empathy deficit by investing intense effort into perspective-taking and empathic concern.

Second, communicate these aspects of empathy directly to your online partners, following suggestions from Chapter 3. Integrate into your online messages questions that seek the other person's perspectives, such as "What's your view on this situation?" Validate their views when they provide them: "You make a lot of sense." Communicate empathic concern by saying things like "I hope you're doing OK." If you receive what looks like an angry message, convey that you recognize the other person is angry and that you feel bad about it: "I feel really terrible that you're so upset."

Third, expect and be tolerant of any aggressive messages you receive, accepting that such behavior is a natural outcome of the online environment rather than evidence that other people are mean or rude. Finally, avoid crafting and sending angry online messages in the heat of the moment. You might craft a response, wait 24 hours to cool off, revisit it, assess it in terms of empathy, and then modify or even delete it if it's inappropriate.

PASSION

Few emotions fascinate us more than romantic passion. Thousands of Web sites, infomercials, books, and magazine articles focus on how to create, maintain, or recapture passion. Feeling passion toward romantic partners seems almost obligatory in Western culture, and we often decide to discard relationships when passion fades (Berscheid & Regan, 2005). At the same time, most of us recognize that passion is fleeting and distressingly fragile (Berscheid, 2002).

Passion is a blended emotion, a combination of surprise and joy coupled with a number of positive feelings, such as excitement, amazement, and sexual attraction. People who elicit passion in us are those who communicate in ways

skills practice

Managing Anger Online
Responding competently during an online encounter in which you're angry

❶ Identify a message or post that triggers anger.

❷ Before responding, manage your anger.

❸ Practice perspective-taking and empathic concern toward the message source.

❹ Craft a response that expresses empathy, and save it as a draft.

❺ Later, review your message, revise it as necessary, and then send it.

◁ In *Scandal*, the professional relationship between Olivia Pope and President Grant develops into a passionate love affair. However, their romance leads to serious relational problems when the president's wife learns about his infidelity.
Shondaland/ABC Studios/The Kobal Collection

Media Note:
Frozen **and True Love**

In the film *Frozen*, Princess Anna is forbidden by her sister, Elsa, to marry Prince Hans because she has only known him for one day. Elsa's desire is to protect Anna because she assumes that true love develops over time rather than at first sight. Ask your students to discuss the connections between passion and long-lasting love. Have they ever fallen in love "at first sight," or do they know anyone who has? Can true love really happen at first sight?

self-reflection

How has passion changed over time in your romantic relationships? What have you and your partners done to deal with these changes? Is passion a necessary component of romance, or is it possible to be in love without passion?

that deviate from what we expect (triggering surprise and amazement), whom we interpret positively (generating joy and excitement), and whom we perceive as physically pleasing (leading to sexual attraction).

If passion necessarily involves joy, excitement, and sexual attraction, why would we consider passion a *challenging* emotion? Because passion stems in large part from surprise. Consequently, the longer and better you know someone, the less passion you will experience toward that person on a daily basis (Berscheid, 2002). In the early stages of romantic involvements, our partners communicate in ways that are novel and positive. The first time our lovers invite us on a date, kiss us, or disclose their love, all are surprising events and intensely passionate. But as partners become increasingly familiar with each other, their communication and behavior do, too. Things that were once perceived as unique become predictable. Partners who have known each other intimately for years may be familiar with almost all the communication behaviors in each other's repertoires (Berscheid, 2002). Consequently, the capacity to surprise partners in dramatic, positive, and unanticipated ways is diminished (Hatfield, Traupmann, & Sprecher, 1984).

Because passion derives from what we perceive as surprising, you can't engineer a passionate evening by carefully negotiating a dinner or romantic rendezvous. You or your partner might experience passion if an event is truly unexpected, but jointly planning and then acting out a romantic candlelight dinner together or spending a weekend in seclusion cannot recapture passion for both you and your partner. When it comes to passion, the best you can hope for in long-term romantic relationships is a warm afterglow (Berscheid, 2002). However, this is not to say that you can't maintain a happy *and* long-term romance; maintaining this kind of relationship requires strategies that we discuss in Chapter 10.

GRIEF

Carlos Arredondo and Lu Jun first met on a 2013 cruise honoring those impacted by the Boston Marathon bombings—including heroes, survivors, and their families. Jun lost his daughter, Lingzi, on that fateful April day; Arredondo is a civilian hero of the bombings who knows about loss from the deaths of his two sons—one from combat in Iraq and the other from suicide. Although they have little else in common, they share the bond of grief. As Arredondo noted: "Sometimes I don't need to say anything to him. . . . I give him a hug, or touch his shoulders, or shake hands. We sit on the bus together. Hopefully that makes him feel comfort" (Wedge & Sherman, 2014). Arredondo and Jun were not the only ones who found comfort on the cruise. Other passengers had the opportunity to talk with one another about the Boston tragedy, the nightmares that still haunt them, and the ways in which their lives have been irreparably altered by loss—whether it be of loved ones, mobility, the ability to hear, or a general sense of safety and well-being. Arredondo explained: "There's been a few moments where I shared my experience with some of them, and they help me out, to get it off my chest. And I've been listening to a few stories myself. I hope I help out as well. Like family. Like an old friend. It's amazing how this works" (Wedge & Sherman, 2014).

◉ This photograph taken by Arko Datta shows a woman mourning a relative who was killed in the 2004 tsunami in South Asia. It won the World Press Photo Foundation Spot News award in 2005.
© Arko Datta/Reuters/Corbis

The intense sadness that follows a substantial loss, known as **grief,** is something each of us will experience. We cannot maintain long-term, intimate involvements with other mortal beings without at some point losing loved ones to death. But grief isn't only about mortality. You're likely to experience grief in response to *any* type of major loss. This may include parental (or personal) divorce, physical disability due to injury (as was the case for many of the Boston Marathon victims), romantic relationship breakup, loss of a much-loved job, or even the destruction or misplacing of a valued object, such as an engagement ring or a treasured family heirloom.

Managing grief is enormously and uniquely taxing. Unlike other negative emotions such as anger, which is typically triggered by a onetime, short-lived event, grief stays with us for a long time—triggered repeatedly by experiences linked with the loss.

Managing Your Grief

No magic pill can erase the suffering associated with a grievous loss. It seems ludicrous to think of applying strategies such as reappraisal, encounter structuring, or the Jefferson strategy to such pain. Grief is a unique emotional experience, and none of the emotion management strategies discussed in this chapter so far can help you.

Instead, you must use *emotion-sharing*: talking about your grief with others who are experiencing or have experienced similar pain, or people who are skilled at providing you with much-needed emotional support and comfort. Participating in a support group for people who have suffered similar losses can encourage you to share your emotions. When you share your grief, you feel powerfully connected with others, and this sense of connection can be a source of comfort, as it was for Arredondo, Jun, and the other cruise passengers whose lives were

Assignment: Ineffective Supportive Communication

Ask students to Think-Ink-Pair-Share on some sort of grief they have experienced in their lifetime, and discuss these questions: What are some examples of incompetent support communication people provided during their grief? Did they include such sayings as "I know just how you feel" or "It could be worse"? How did this communication make them feel? What would have been more effective?

 Video

macmillanhighered.com/reflectrelate4e

Supportive Communication
Watch this clip online to answer the questions below.

What supportive messages are given in this video? How successful are they? If you had to comfort someone grieving, how would you convey supportive communication?

forever changed by tragedy and loss. You also gain affirmation that the grief process you're experiencing is normal. For example, a fellow support-group participant who also lost his mother to cancer might tell you that he, too, finds Mother's Day a particularly painful time. Finally, other participants in a support group can help you remember that grief does get gradually more bearable over time.

For those of us without ready access to face-to-face support groups, online support offers a viable alternative. Besides not requiring transportation and allowing access to written records of any missed meetings, online support groups also provide a certain degree of anonymity for people who feel shy or uncomfortable within traditional group settings (Weinberg, Schmale, Uken, & Wessel, 1995). You can interact in a way that preserves some degree of privacy. This is an important advantage, as many people find it easier to discuss sensitive topics online than face-to-face, where they run the risk of embarrassment (Furger, 1996).

Comforting Others The challenges you face in helping others manage their grief are compounded by the popular tendency to use suppression for managing sadness. The decision to use suppression derives from the widespread belief that it's important to maintain a stoic bearing, a "stiff upper lip," during personal tragedies (Beach, 2002). However, a person who uses suppression to manage grief can end up experiencing stress-related disorders, such as chronic anxiety or depression. Also, the decision to suppress can lead even normally open and communicative people to stop talking about their feelings. This places you in the awkward position of trying to help others manage emotions that they themselves are unwilling to admit they are experiencing.

The best way you can help others manage their grief is to engage in **supportive communication**—sharing messages that express emotional support and that offer personal assistance (Burleson & MacGeorge, 2002). Competent support messages convey sincere expressions of sympathy and condolence, concern for the other person, and encouragement to express emotions. Incompetent support messages tell a person how he or she *should* feel or indicate that the individual is somehow inadequate or blameworthy. Communication scholar and social support expert Amanda Holmstrom offers seven suggestions for improving your supportive communication.[4]

1. *Make sure the person is ready to talk.* You may have amazing support skills, but if the person is too upset to talk, don't push it. Instead, make it clear that you care and want to help, and that you'll be there to listen when he or she needs you.

2. *Find the right place and time.* Once a person *is* ready, find a place and a time conducive to quiet conversation. Avoid distracting settings such as parties, where you won't be able to focus, and find a time of the day where neither of you has other pressing obligations.

3. *Ask good questions.* Start with open-ended queries such as "How are you feeling?" or "What's on your mind?" Then follow up with more targeted

---

[4]The content that follows was provided to the author by Dr. Amanda Holmstrom and published with permission. The author thanks Dr. Holmstrom for her contribution.

◬ A candlelight vigil can be a powerful source of comfort and connection for those grieving similar losses. AP Photo/Jessica Hill

questions based on the response, such as "Are you eating and sleeping OK?" (if not, a potential indicator of depression) or "Have you connected with a support group?" (essential to emotion-sharing). Don't assume that because you've been in a similar situation, you know what someone is going through. Refrain from saying "I know just how you feel."

Importantly, *if you suspect a person is contemplating suicide, ask him or her directly about it*. Say, "Have you been thinking about killing yourself?" or "Has suicide crossed your mind?" People often mistakenly think that direct questions such as these will push someone over the edge, but in fact it's the opposite. Research suggests that someone considering suicide *wants* to talk about it but believes that no one cares. If you ask direct questions, a suicidal person typically *won't* be offended or lie but instead will open up to you. Then you can encourage the person to seek counseling. Someone *not* considering suicide will express surprise at the question, often laughing it off with a "What? No way!"

4. *Legitimize, don't minimize.* Don't dismiss the problem or the significance of the person's feelings by saying things such as "It could have been worse," "Why are you so upset?!" or "You can always find another lover!" Research shows that these comments are unhelpful. Instead, let the person know that it's normal and OK to feel as he or she does.

5. *Listen actively.* Show the person that you are interested in what is being said. Engage in good eye contact, lean toward him or her, and say "Uh-huh" and "Yeah" when appropriate.

6. *Offer advice cautiously.* We want to help someone who is suffering, so we often jump right in and offer advice. But many times that's not helpful or

skills practice

Supportive Communication
Skillfully providing emotional support

❶ Let the person know you're available to talk, but don't force an encounter.

❷ Find a quiet, private space.

❸ Start with general questions, and work toward more specific questions. If you think he or she might be suicidal, ask directly.

❹ Assure the person that his or her feelings are normal.

❺ Show that you're attending closely to what is being said.

❻ Ask before offering advice.

❼ Let the person know you care!

even wanted. Advice is best when it's asked for, when the advice giver has relevant expertise or experience (e.g., a relationship counselor), or when it advocates actions the person can actually do. Advice is hurtful when it implies that the person is to blame or can't solve his or her own problems. When in doubt, ask if advice would be appreciated—or just hold back.

7. *Show concern and give praise.* Let the person know you genuinely care and are concerned about his or her well-being ("I am *so* sorry for your loss; you're really important to me"). Build the person up by praising his or her strength in handling this challenge. Showing care and concern helps connect you to someone, while praise will help a person feel better.

> **Media Note:**
> *This Emotional Life*
> Show a clip from PBS's *This Emotional Life* TV series, in which Elizabeth Gilbert, the author of *Eat, Pray, Love,* discusses "porcupine love" as a way of understanding relationships and happiness. Then have your students do a one-minute freewrite detailing their reactions to the clip. (All "The Meaning of Happiness" clips can be found here: pbs.org/thisemotionallife/perspective/meaning-happiness)

Living a Happy Emotional Life

[Interpersonal connections determine our joy]

We all live lives rich in relationships and punctuated with emotion. Lovers arrive, bringing gifts of passion and tenderness, and then exit, marking their passage with anger and sadness. Children flash into being, evoking previously unimaginable exhilaration and exhaustion. Friends and family members tread parallel paths, sharing our emotions, and then pass on, leaving grief and memories in their wake.

Across all our relationship experiences, what balances out our anger and grief is our joy. All human beings share the capacity to relish intense joy and the desire to maintain such happiness in an impermanent and ever-changing world. Also universal is the fact that our personal joy is determined by the quality of our interpersonal connections. When our relationships with family, friends, coworkers, and romantic partners are happy, we are happy, and when they're not, we're not.

Yet joy doesn't drop magically from the sky into our hearts and minds and stay there. *We* create joy—through every decision we make and every thought, word, and deed. When we manage our emotional experiences and communication poorly, the interpersonal sorrows we wreak on others reflect back on us in the form of personal unhappiness. When we steadfastly and skillfully manage our emotions, the positive relationship outcomes we create multiply and, with them, our happiness and the joy of those who surround us.

Damon Winter/The New York Times/Redux Pictures

[*We* create joy—through every decision we make and every thought, word, and deed.]

making relationship choices

Managing Anger and Providing Support

1 BACKGROUND

Managing your anger and providing supportive communication are two skills that can clash when you're trying to support someone who is making you angry. To understand how you might competently manage such a relationship challenge, read the case study in Part 2; then, drawing on all you know about interpersonal communication, work through the problem-solving model in Part 3.

 Visit LaunchPad to check out the other side of the story (Part 4). For the best experience, complete all parts in LaunchPad: **macmillanhighered.com /reflectrelate4e**.

2 CASE STUDY

You're the oldest sibling in a close family in which everyone freely expresses their emotions. Of all your siblings, you share an especially close bond with Sam, the youngest. When Sam accepts a scholarship out of state, you're sad to see him go, but you're excited for his future and take comfort in the daily texts you exchange.

Shortly after Sam moves away, your grandmother (Nana) has a heart attack. Doctors initially think she will make a full recovery, so you text Sam and tell him not to worry. However, her condition suddenly worsens, and she passes away. Everyone is grief-stricken, but Sam is devastated. He is the only one in your immediate family who didn't see her before she died.

When Sam arrives for the funeral, he seems sullen and bitter. But so much is going on that you don't get a chance to talk with him at length. Before you know it, he has left. Following the funeral, Sam rebuffs your attempts to communicate with him. He doesn't return your texts, and after several messages he finally e-mails you, "leave me alone!" You become increasingly worried about how he is dealing with his grief. You leave Sam a voice mail telling him that you're coming to visit. Despite receiving no response, you go anyway.

Arriving after several hours of grueling travel, you are shocked to find Sam unwelcoming. Scowling, he says, "What are you *doing* here? I thought I told you to leave me alone." You start getting angry. After all, you spent a good portion of your savings to get there, and you made the trip out of love and concern. As you try to manage your anger by using the Jefferson strategy, Sam attacks: "Oh, I get it. This is the big 'ease your conscience' trip. You figure that if you comfort me, I'll feel better about you lying to me about Nana's condition. Well, it's not going to work. I didn't get to see her before she died, and it's your fault, so why don't you take your self-serving concern and go home!" He slams the door in your face.

You're left standing on the porch, furious. Do you make the several-hour trip home, heeding Sam's request even though you know he said it out of anger? Or do you pursue your original plan of trying to help Sam deal with his grief?

3 YOUR TURN

Think about all you've learned thus far about interpersonal communication. Then work through the following five steps. Remember, there are no "right" answers, so think hard about what is the *best* choice! (P.S. Need help? See the *Helpful Concepts* list.)

step 1
Reflect on yourself. What are your thoughts and feelings in this situation? Are your impressions and attributions accurate?

step 2
Reflect on your partner. Using perspective-taking and empathic concern, put yourself in Sam's shoes. What is he thinking and feeling in this situation?

step 3
Identify the optimal outcome. Think about your communication and relationship with Sam as well as the situation surrounding Nana's death. What's the best, most constructive relationship outcome possible? Consider what's best for you and for Sam.

step 4
Locate the roadblocks. Taking into consideration your own and Sam's thoughts and feelings and all that has happened in this situation, what obstacles are keeping you from achieving the optimal outcome?

step 5
Chart your course. What can you say to Sam to overcome the roadblocks you've identified and achieve your optimal outcome?

HELPFUL CONCEPTS
Gender and emotion, **112**

Emotion management strategies, **114–116**

Anger, **117–119**

Grief, **122–126**

Supportive communication, **124–126**

4 THE OTHER SIDE

▶ Visit LaunchPad to watch a video in which Sam tells his side of the case study story. As in many real-life situations, this is information to which you did not have access when you were initially crafting your response in Part 3. The video reminds us that even when we do our best to offer competent responses, there is always another side to the story that we need to consider.

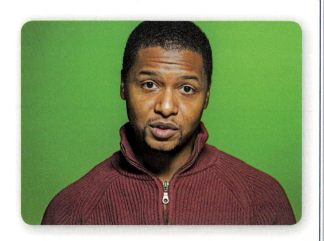

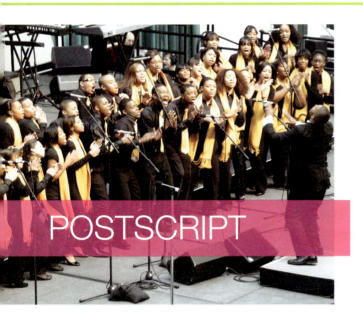

POSTSCRIPT

We began this chapter with the story of a woman committed to transforming the lives of teenagers. Vy Higginsen founded Gospel for Teens in part to create a musical refuge for young people to escape their emotional turmoil. But she quickly learned that her students' emotions couldn't be suppressed, and that through sharing their emotions with one another they could more quickly heal their wounds of anger and grief.

How do you manage the emotional challenges of your life? Do you leave your baggage at the door, burying your emotions? Or do you let your baggage in, sharing your emotions with others?

The story of Vy Higginsen and her students reminds us that although we have emotions, we are not our emotions. It's our capacity to constructively manage the emotions we experience, and communicate them in positive ways, that makes hope and goodness in our lives possible.

LaunchPad for *Reflect & Relate* offers videos and encourages self-assessment through adaptive quizzing. Go to **macmillanhighered.com/reflectrelate4e** to get access to:

 LearningCurve Adaptive Quizzes

 Video clips that help you understand interpersonal communication

key terms

- emotion, 103
- emotion-sharing, 105
- ▶ emotional contagion, 105
- feelings, 105
- moods, 105
- primary emotions, 107
- ▶ blended emotions, 108
- Rational Emotive Behavior Therapy (REBT), 111
- emotional intelligence, 113
- emotion management, 114
- suppression, 114
- venting, 114
- ▶ encounter avoidance, 115
- ▶ encounter structuring, 115
- attention focus, 115
- deactivation, 116
- ▶ reappraisal, 116
- anger, 117
- chronic hostility, 118
- catharsis, 118
- Jefferson strategy, 119
- passion, 121
- grief, 123
- ▶ supportive communication, 124

▶ You can watch brief, illustrative videos of these terms and test your understanding of the concepts in LaunchPad.

key concepts

The Nature of Emotion

- **Emotion** is the most powerful of human experiences and involves thoughts, physiological arousal, and communication. Emotions are so significant that we feel compelled to engage in **emotion-sharing** with our relationship partners.
- Emotions are rare compared to **feelings,** which occur often and typically arise and decay with little conscious awareness. **Moods** endure longer than feelings or emotions and affect our perception and communication.
- Six **primary emotions** exist based on patterns of nonverbal behavior: surprise, joy, disgust, anger, fear, and sadness. Sometimes we experience more than one primary emotion simultaneously; the result is **blended emotions.**

Forces Shaping Emotion

- Personality plays a powerful role in shaping our experience and expression of emotion.
- Gender contributes to our experience and expression of emotion, often due to the different ways men and women typically orient themselves in interpersonal relationships.

Managing Your Emotional Experience and Expression

- Effective **emotion management** is a critical part of **emotional intelligence.** Emotions are usually managed after they have occurred with **suppression** and **venting.** Strategies used for preventing emotions before they occur include **encounter avoidance, encounter structuring, attention focus,** and **deactivation.**
- Of all the strategies available to people for managing emotions, the most effective is **reappraisal.**

Emotional Challenges

- **Anger** is difficult to manage, given its intensity. People who manage anger through suppression can develop **chronic hostility.** Providing a time delay between the onset of anger and your communicative response, known as the **Jefferson strategy,** can be especially effective during online communication.
- Most people experience intense **passion** in the early stages of their involvements, and then a steady decline the longer the relationship endures.
- Managing your own **grief** is best accomplished through emotion-sharing, whereas providing **supportive communication** is the best approach for aiding others in overcoming their grief.

chapter review

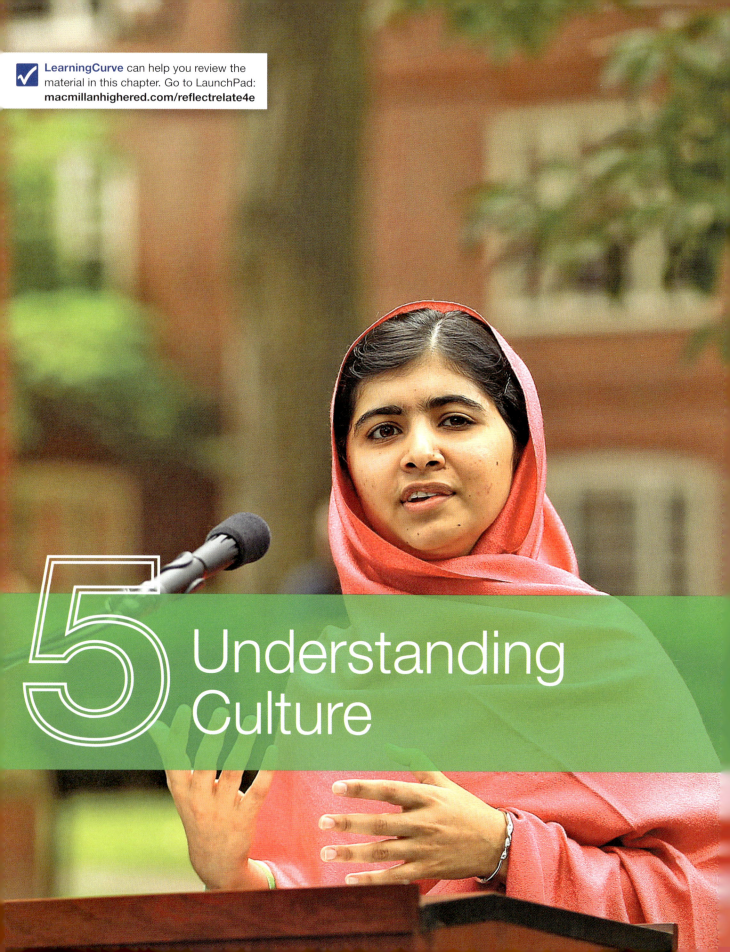

5 Understanding Culture

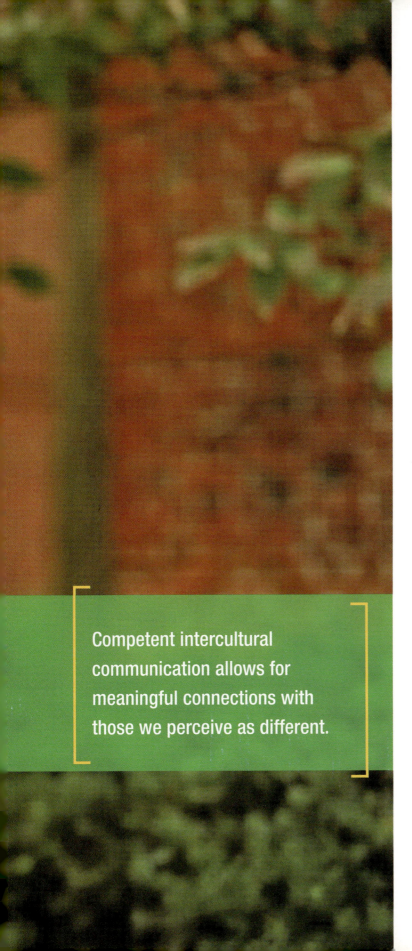

Malala Yousafzai grew up in the Swat Valley of Pakistan. Her father, Ziauddin, was a poet and the owner of a chain of local schools. He also was an outspoken activist on behalf of women's rights and the importance of education for girls. From the time Malala was very young, her father treated her as someone special, encouraging her to stay up late to discuss politics with him, long after her two brothers and mother had gone to bed.

Malala's life changed dramatically when the Taliban seized control of the Swat Valley. They began systematically attacking and destroying girls' schools, and women in the community were banned from going to the local market or even leaving their houses. Malala found such imprisonment intolerable, and—with her father's support—she began blogging under an assumed name about her experiences, even though she was only 11 years old. However, when her true identity was publicly revealed, she didn't retreat into hiding. Instead, she became an activist. As she describes,

> Why should I wait for someone else to help us? Why don't I raise my voice; why don't we speak up for our rights? The girls of Swat, they spoke up for their rights. I started writing [a] diary; I spoke on every media channel I could and I raised my voice on every platform and I said, "I need to tell the world what is happening."[1]

[**Competent intercultural communication allows for meaningful connections with those we perceive as different.**]

---

[1] All quotes adapted from interview by Jon Stewart, October 10, 2013, www.youtube.com/watch?v=gjGL6YY6oMs

John Tlumacki/The Boston Globe via Getty Images

5 / Understanding Culture

Early in 2012, a friend came to Malala and said that when she had Googled Malala's name, a death threat from the Taliban popped up as a search result. Malala didn't initially believe it, but when she saw it for herself, her first concern was for her *father*, not herself. She figured that he would be a more likely target, given that she was only a child. But the more she thought about a possible attack on her, the more she became convinced that, when facing her killer, she would talk with him rather than fight him.

> I started thinking that if a Talib comes to kill me, what would you do? Then I would reply to myself, Malala, just take a shoe and hit him! But then I said, if you hit a Talib, then there would be no difference between you and the Talib. You must not treat others with cruelty, but through peace and through dialogue. Then I said, I would tell him how important education is and that I want education for [his] children as well, and I would tell him, "That's what I want to tell you, now do what you want."

On October 9, 2012, on her way home from school, a man boarded the bus Malala was riding in and opened fire on her and her friends. Although she almost died from her wounds, her commitment to dialogue between peoples separated by difference remains unfazed. Since the attack and her lengthy, difficult recovery, Malala has traveled the world as a global ambassador, advocating on behalf of women, education, equality, and cultural tolerance. As she details,

> Going to school is not only learning about different subjects; it teaches you communication, it teaches you how to live a life. You learn about equality because students are provided the same benches; they sit equally. It teaches students how to live with others together, how to accept each other's language, how to accept each other's traditions and each other's religion. It teaches us justice, respect, and how to live together.

Let's face it: not all of us are as stunningly heroic as Malala Yousafzai. I'm most certainly not! Nor will many of us achieve the accolades she has. Malala gave a speech at the United Nations on her 16th birthday, July 12, 2013; has a best-selling autobiography, *I Am Malala* (2013); was awarded the European Sakharov Prize for Freedom of Thought in 2013; and is the youngest recipient ever of the Nobel Peace Prize (2014). At the same time, each of us has within us the capacity for acts of interpersonal heroism that mirror Malala's anticipated approach for dealing with her assassin: "You must not treat others with cruelty, but through peace and through dialogue." When facing those who seem separated from us by cultural distance—who we don't understand, who make us uncomfortable, or whom we may even feel threatened by—*the* most important thing we can do is not lash out at them with a metaphorical "shoe" but, instead, engage them in dialogue marked by compassion, tolerance, and respect. When we do so, we embrace intercultural communication competence, creating the possibility for connections with, rather than separation from, culturally diverse others.

In this chapter, you'll learn:

- The defining characteristics of culture
- What co-cultures are and their role in communication
- The impact of prejudice on communication
- The ways cultural differences influence how people communicate
- How to improve your intercultural communication competence

> **Chapter outline**
>
> **135**
> What Is Culture?
>
> **143**
> Cultural Influences on Communication
>
> **152**
> Creating Intercultural Competence
>
> **155**
> Embracing Difference

What Is Culture?

Culture affects communication constantly

As our world gets more diverse, understanding culture and cultural differences in interpersonal communication becomes increasingly important. Consider, for example, cultural diversity in the United States. In 2012, for example, the Census Bureau reported that for the first time in history, more than 50 percent of all U.S. births were nonwhite—including Latino, Asian, African American, and mixed-raced children. This means that nonwhite minorities, as a group, are now the *majority*. International student enrollments in the United States are also on the rise (Institute of International Education, 2011); consequently, your college classmates are just as likely to be from Singapore as from Seattle. Plus, with all the digital devices available, we have easy access to people around the world. This enables us to conduct business and personal relationships on a global level in a way never possible before. As just one example, I routinely Skype with faculty friends in Korea, the Netherlands, France, and Brazil, although keeping track of the time differences is a challenge! As our daily encounters increasingly cross cultural lines, making us more aware of diversity, the question arises: what exactly *is* culture? Understanding the nature of culture, how it's different from co-cultures, and how prejudice can impact our interpersonal communication is the starting point for building intercultural communication competence.

Chapter Theme
The focus of this chapter is to understand the connections between communication and culture. Students will come to understand that culture is learned, lived, and communicated. Further, students will learn the many different definitions and layers of culture. To become more competent interpersonal communicators, we must understand how culture influences communication, recognize and overcome prejudices, embrace world-mindedness, practice attributional complexity, and accommodate our communication appropriately.

○ Culture is so integrated into your everyday life, it is easy to overlook how it can inform everything you see, hear, or believe. How do the activities and images shown relate to your culture or not? What other aspects of your culture make you *you*?
(Clockwise from top left) CamBuff/Getty Images; Chris McGrath/Getty Images; © Justin Lane/EPA/Corbis; © Alex Neely/Demotix/Corbis

CULTURE DEFINED

As defined in Chapter 1, **culture** is an established, coherent set of beliefs, attitudes, values, and practices shared by a large group of people (Keesing, 1974). Culture includes many types of influences, such as your nationality, ethnicity, religion, gender, sexual orientation, physical abilities, and even age. But what really makes a culture a "culture" is that it's widely shared. This happens because cultures are learned, communicated, layered, and lived.

self-reflection

Recall a childhood memory of learning about your culture. What tradition or belief did you learn about? Who taught you this lesson? What impact did this have on your understanding of your culture?

Culture Is Learned   You learn your cultural beliefs, attitudes, and values from many sources, including your parents, teachers, religious leaders, peers, and the mass media (Gudykunst & Kim, 2003). This process begins at birth, through customs such as choosing a newborn's name, taking part in religious ceremonies, and selecting godparents or other special guardians. As you mature, you learn deeper aspects of your culture, including the history behind certain traditions: why unleavened bread is eaten during Jewish Passover, for instance, or why certain days are more auspicious than others. When I was young, Halloween was all about trick-or-treating and competing with my brother to see who could get the most candy. But as I aged, my parents shared with me the rich history behind such practices, and how they date back to ancient Celtic celebrations of the new year. You also learn how to participate in rituals—everything from blowing out the candles on a birthday cake to lighting Advent candles. In most societies, teaching children to understand, respect, and practice their culture is considered an essential part of child rearing. When I raised my three boys, I shared with them the history of Halloween just as my parents had done with me.

Culture Is Communicated Each culture has its own practices regarding how to communicate, and these can widely differ from one another (Whorf, 1952). To illustrate, when I was an undergraduate, I became good friends with Amid, who was originally from Iran. Despite our friendship, our interpersonal communication behaviors would often clash because of cultural differences. For example, in his culture, he was taught, when talking with friends, "stand close enough to smell their breath." I, on the other hand, grew up in the United States, where expectations on personal distance are to stay at least an arm's length away, even with friends. (We'll discuss nonverbal communication, including personal space, in more detail in Chapter 8.) So, whenever Amid and I would talk, he would sidle closer, coming to within a few inches of my face. I would then step back, at which point he would step closer, and I would step back—resulting in a little "dance of distance"! At this point, we'd usually notice what we were doing and laugh about it.

Culture Is Layered Many of us belong to more than one culture. This means we experience multiple layers of culture simultaneously, as various traditions, heritages, and practices are recognized and held as important. My family heritage, for example, is Scottish, Irish, and Swiss German. But each of us prioritizes the different layers of our ancestry differently. My brother takes our Scottish ancestry *very* seriously, attending the Scottish Highland Games in Washington State (where he lives) every year. My mom, on the other hand, thinks of herself as primarily Swiss German, and even made a pilgrimage to our hereditary hometown of Breitenbach, in Switzerland. In contrast, I think of myself as Irish (largely because I love Irish music!), and I celebrate various Irish holidays. My dad keeps us all grounded by reminding us that we're really all "mutts," and that *all* of these facets of our cultural heritage are important.

Culture Is Lived Culture affects everything about how you live your life. It influences the neighborhoods you live in; the means of transportation you use; the way you think, dress, talk, and even eat. Its impact runs so deep that it is often taken for granted. At the same time, culture is often a great source of personal pride. Many people consciously live in ways that celebrate their cultural heritage through such behaviors as wearing a Muslim hijab, placing a Mexican flag decal on their car, or greeting others with the Thai gesture of the Wai (hands joined in prayer, heads bowed).

CO-CULTURES

As societies become more culturally diverse, awareness of how various cultures, and groups of people within them, interact increases. In any society, there's

---

Discussion Prompt: Communicating Culture

One might say that "all communication is enculturated, and all culture is communicated." Encourage a class discussion on this phrase. Ask students what the phrase means to them, in their own words. How does their understanding of this phrase differ from that of other students in the class?

self-reflection

Have you ever encountered a situation in which your communication behaviors and those of someone from a different culture clashed? How did you respond? What cultural factors played a role? Were you able to overcome the difficulty?

Assignment: Introducing Culture

Ask students to bring a cultural artifact that represents a layer of their culture to share with the class or in small groups. For example, a student might want to share a piece of jewelry that shows her Irish ancestry or to display something from a co-culture to which he belongs (e.g., his church, a Greek organization, the LGBT community). Students can briefly explain the item and articulate how this layer of their culture influences their communication.

Discussion Prompt: Co-cultures

Ask students to brainstorm all of the co-cultures to which they belong. Then, as a class, generate a large list on the board or screen to demonstrate and discuss all of the different co-cultural influences that affect communication in just one class of students.

△ Co-cultures come in many different forms. Do you identify with any of the co-cultures shown in the images above? What specific aspects make the pictured people seem similar or dissimilar to you? How does this classification influence your communication? *(Left to right) MyLoupe/UIG via Getty Images; Robert Nicholas/Getty Images; Kuzma/Shutterstock; © Tom Miner/The Image Works*

self-reflection

Which of your co-cultures is most important in shaping your sense of self? Which ones are less important? (For example, you may identify strongly as a Latina but not identify as strongly as a Catholic.) Why? Are there ever situations in which your different co-cultural identities clash with one another?

▶ **Teaching Tip: Assimilation**

The concept of **assimilation** can be challenging for students, especially those who feel pressure from loved ones to "choose" between cultures. The LaunchPad video clip on assimilation presents a comfortable and low-pressure scenario in which one woman learns how to assimilate into one aspect of the culture in which she is currently teaching. Showing this clip in class can lead to a deeper discussion of the topic for the entire class or small groups.

usually a group of people who have more *power* than others—that is, the ability to influence or control people and events. (We'll discuss power in more detail in Chapter 9.) Having more power in a society comes from controlling major societal institutions, such as banks, businesses, the government, and legal and educational systems. According to **Co-cultural Communication Theory,** the people who have more power within a society determine the *dominant culture,* because they get to decide the prevailing views, values, and traditions of the society (Orbe, 1998). Consider the United States. Throughout its history, wealthy Euro-American men have been in power. When the United States was first founded, the only people allowed to vote were landowning males of European ancestry. Now, more than 200 years later, Euro-American men still make up the vast majority of U.S. Congress and Fortune 500 CEOs. As a consequence, what is thought of as "American culture" is tilted toward the interests, activities, and accomplishments of these men.

Members of a society who don't conform to the dominant culture—by way of language, values, lifestyle, or even physical appearance—often form what are called **co-cultures**: that is, they have their own cultures that *co-exist* within a dominant cultural sphere (Orbe, 1998). Co-cultures may be based on age, gender, social class, ethnicity, religion, mental and physical ability, sexual orientation, and other unifying elements, depending on the society (Orbe, 1998). U.S. residents who are not members of the dominant culture—people of color, women, members of the LGBTQ community, and so forth—exist as distinct co-cultures, with their own political lobbying groups, Web sites, magazines, and television networks (such as Lifetime, BET, Telemundo, and Here TV).

Because members of co-cultures are (by definition) different from the dominant culture, they develop and use numerous communication practices that help them interact with people in the culturally dominant group (Ramirez-Sanchez, 2008). These differ from one another, depending on whether the co-cultural members engage in **assimilation** or are attempting to be accepted into the dominant culture. Alternatively, they might get the dominant culture to *accommodate* their co-cultural identity or *separate* themselves from the dominant culture altogether. For example, they might use overly polite language with individuals from the dominant culture, and suppress reactions when such people make offensive

focus on CULTURE

Millennials and Technology

Older adults like to say that "Millennials"—people born between the years 1980 and 2000—are completely different from previous generations in their beliefs, attitudes, values, and communication practices. As *New York Times* columnist Sheila Marikar (2013) jests, "You know them when you see them. They are tapping on their smartphones, strolling into work late and amassing Instagram followers faster than a twerking cat." But are Millennials so different from others as to constitute a distinct *culture*? The largest-scale study of Millennials ever conducted suggests that the answer may be yes (Pew Research Center, 2010).

For one thing, the majority of Millennials (61 percent) believe that they *are* a distinct and unique group. The data support this self-perception along many indicators: Millennials are more likely than members of previous generations to report close relationships with their parents; less likely to get married in their 20s; and more likely to have body piercings in places other than earlobes. But the primary point of generational difference is technology. On virtually every measure of Internet and cell-phone use—including texting, tweeting, posting videos and photos, e-mail, and wireless use—Millennials score substantially higher than older adults. For example, 75 percent of Millennials have personal profiles on social networking sites, compared to only one-third of older adults. And the younger the Millennial, the higher the use, especially with regard to texting.

But it's not just their *use* of technology that sets Millennials culturally apart; it's their *view* of it. Millennials are more likely than other generations to say that technology connects family and friends, rather than creates isolation and distance. And Millennials are much more likely than other generations to be tethered to their cell phones. A whopping 83 percent of Millennials place their cell phones on, or right next to, their beds while sleeping, a number far higher than that of older adults. As the Pew Research Center report (2010) concludes, Millennials "are history's first 'always connected' generation. Steeped in digital technology and social media, they treat their multi-tasking hand-held gadgets almost like a body part" (p. 8).

discussion questions

- Given that culture is "an established, coherent set of beliefs, attitudes, values, and practices shared by a large group of people," are Millennials a distinct culture? If so, what are their principal points of cultural uniqueness? If they are not a distinct culture, why not?
- Does technological literacy, and attitudes toward technology, create a cultural divide between people?

---

comments. They might try to excel in all aspects of their professional and personal lives to counteract negative stereotypes about their co-culture. They might attempt to act, look, and talk like members of the dominant culture, or even openly disparage their own co-culture. Alternatively, members of a co-culture might quietly but clearly express their co-cultural identity through appearance, actions, and words; they might even conform to negative stereotypes in an exaggerated way to shock and scare members from the dominant culture.

How might these communication practices work in real life? Imagine that an African American couple moves to a largely Euro-American suburb. They socialize primarily with their white neighbors, never displaying any indication of their African American heritage other than their skin color. Meanwhile, their son dresses in sagging pants, wears a do-rag, and blasts gangsta rap through Beats headphones. Through these behaviors, he actively strives to conform to

Immigrants often form new co-cultures in their country of immigration, which can lead to conflict between their communities and the dominant culture.

In April 2013, the students of Wilcox County High School in Georgia took matters into their own hands and organized the school's first integrated prom, overcoming the prejudice that had previously resulted in years of racially segregated celebrations. © Maria Izaurralde/Zuma Press

stereotypes about young black males. Despite their differences, all these behaviors have the same goal: managing the tension between African American co-culture and the dominant Euro-American culture.

As discussed in Chapter 3, our perceptions of shared attitudes, beliefs, and values based on cultural and co-cultural affiliations can lead us to classify those who are similar to us as *ingroupers* and those who are different as *outgroupers*. This, however, can be a dangerous trap. Just because someone shares a particular co-culture with you (say, your race or sexual orientation), it doesn't mean that you are truly the same. For example, you and a classmate might both be "white" (the same race), but you may be Irish Catholic and she may be Russian Jewish, with a host of different ethnic and religious factors that affect your interpersonal communication. In fact, you may be more similar to an Asian American classmate who shares your religious dedication and your socioeconomic background.

PREJUDICE

Because people tend to shy away from interacting with outgroupers, they may rely on stereotypes to form judgments about them. As you learned in Chapter 3 (pp. 68–99), *stereotypes* are a way to categorize people into a social group and then evaluate them based on information you have related to this group. Stereotypes play a big part in how you form impressions about others during the perception process. This is especially true for racial and gender characteristics, since they are among the things you notice first when encountering others. But when stereotypes reflect rigid attitudes toward groups and their members, they become **prejudice** (Ramasubramanian, 2010).

Because prejudice is rooted in stereotypes, it can vary depending on whether those stereotypes are positive or negative. According to the **Stereotype Content Model** (Fiske, Cuddy, Glick, & Xu, 2002), prejudice centers on two judgments

Assignment: Dealing with Prejudices

Assign students to write a journal entry or short paper about a time they had to deal with any type of prejudice (ageism, sexism, racism, ableism, etc.). Place students in small groups to discuss their experiences. They may find themselves surprised that each person has faced some type of prejudice in his or her life, helping to build empathy and understanding.

chapter 5 / Understanding Culture 141

Granger, NYC — All rights reserved

skills practice

Addressing Prejudice
Become a less prejudiced communicator.

❶ Recognize that we all have prejudices, even if they seem harmless (as in "Men who watch football are lazy").

❷ Commit to having an open mind about individuals belonging to groups about which you hold prejudiced beliefs.

❸ Seek interpersonal communication encounters with members of these groups. Get to know individuals, and don't be afraid to ask questions.

❹ Evaluate your own communication. Do you communicate with group members in ways that set them up to confirm your prejudiced beliefs?

made about others: how warm and friendly they are and how competent they are. These judgments create two possible kinds of prejudice: *benevolent* and *hostile*.

Benevolent prejudice occurs when people think of a particular group as inferior but also friendly and competent. For instance, someone judges a group as "primitive," "helpless," and "ignorant" but attributes their "inferiority" to forces beyond their control, such as lack of education, technology, or wealth (Ramasubramanian, 2010). Thus, although the group is thought of negatively, it also triggers feelings of sympathy (Fiske et al., 2002). If you ever find yourself thinking about a group of people who you consider "inferior" but who you also think could improve themselves "if only they knew better," you're engaging in benevolent prejudice.

Hostile prejudice happens when people have negative attitudes toward a group of individuals whom they see as unfriendly and incompetent (Fiske et al., 2002). Someone demonstrating hostile prejudice might see the group's supposed incompetence as intrinsic to the people: "They're naturally lazy," "They're all crazy zealots," or "They're mean and violent." People exhibiting hostile prejudice often believe that the group has received many opportunities to improve ("They've been given so much") but that their innate limitations hold them back ("They've done nothing but waste every break that's been given to them"). Someone who sees a group in these terms can communicate with contempt.

Prejudice, no matter what form, is destructive and unethical. Benevolent prejudice leads you to communicate with others in condescending and disrespectful ways. Hostile prejudice is the root of every exclusionary "ism": racism, sexism, ageism, classism, ableism, and so on.

Becoming a competent interpersonal communicator requires that you work to overcome prejudices that might influence your communication. However, even if you don't treat people in a prejudiced way, that doesn't necessarily mean you're not prejudiced. Prejudice is rooted in deeply held negative *beliefs* about particular groups (Ramasubramanian, 2010). If you think you have prejudiced beliefs, use the empathy and perception-checking guidelines discussed in Chapter 3 (pp. 93–95) to help you evaluate and change these views. Learn about the cultures and groups you have prejudiced beliefs about. During interactions, ask members of these groups questions about themselves and listen actively to the answers. This will ease the uncertainty and anxiety you may feel around others who are culturally different from you (Berger & Calabrese, 1975). Finally, be open to new people and experiences; this can result in quality relationships that break down prejudicial barriers.

If you've been on the receiving end of prejudice, try not to generalize your experience with that one person (or persons) to all members of the same group. Just because someone of a certain age, gender, ethnicity, or other cultural group behaves badly doesn't mean that all members of that group do. One of the bitter ironies of prejudice is that it often triggers prejudice as a reaction in the people who have been unfairly treated. This is not to excuse the prejudice or poor communication of others but to help you avoid adding to the vicious cycle of prejudicial communication.

Cultural Influences on Communication

Recognizing important cultural factors in communication

The hit TV show *Modern Family* focuses on a California clan whose members have different cultural backgrounds. Euro-American patriarch Jay is married to the (much younger) Gloria, who is originally from Colombia. In addition to their child together, Jay serves as stepfather to Gloria's son Manny. Jay's children from a previous marriage also have families of their own. His son Mitchell and his partner, Cam, have an adopted daughter from Vietnam, while Jay's daughter, Claire, and her goofy husband, Phil, have three biological children. Given this diversity, interpersonal exchanges between the characters routinely cross lines of age, gender, ethnicity, and sexual orientation—sometimes at the same time! Not surprisingly, a lot of miscommunication stemming from these differences occurs. For example, Gloria speaks with a Colombian accent and often tangles up her English words. On Halloween, she tells Jay he's "going to be a gargle." Manny chimes in to clarify, "She means, 'gargoyle.'" Later, when a box of Jesus figurines is mysteriously delivered to their house, Jay realizes the error: he had told Gloria to call his secretary and order a box of baby *cheeses*.

⬤ Gloria Delgado-Pritchett, played by Sofia Vergara, is a Colombian woman whose cultural norms often conflict with those of her American-born family members. How do you navigate situations in which culture blurs the line of understanding between yourself and others? © ABC/Photofest

Shows like *Modern Family* poke lighthearted fun at cultural differences in interpersonal communication. However, the real-world distinctions between cultures can be profound. Scholars suggest that seven cultural characteristics shape our interpersonal communication: individualism versus collectivism, uncertainty avoidance, power distance, high and low context, emotion displays, masculinity versus femininity, and views of time. To build intercultural communication competence, you need to understand these differences. At the same time, keep in mind that while each of these distinctions is presented as polar opposites (high versus low; this versus that), most cultures—and people within them—fall somewhere in between the extremes.

INDIVIDUALISM VERSUS COLLECTIVISM

In **individualistic cultures,** people tend to value independence and personal achievement. Members of these cultures are encouraged to focus on themselves and their immediate family (Hofstede, 2001), and individual achievement is praised as the highest good (Waterman, 1984). Examples of individualistic countries include the United States, Canada, New Zealand, and Sweden (Hofstede, 2001).

Discussion Prompt: Individualism and Collectivism in Daily Interactions
To help students understand the impact of these cultural characteristics on interactions and relationships, ask them to meet in small groups to define individualism and collectivism in their own words. Then have them discuss the many ways in which these characteristics influence various aspects of their daily lives, such as their view on responsibility, their perspective on success, their beliefs about leadership, their attitude about family, and their communication style in different settings.

⚠ In what ways does the popular trend of posting selfies exemplify the individualistic culture of the United States? How does this differ from the more group-oriented activities seen in a collectivistic culture? (Left) © Jo Kirchherr/Westend61/Corbis; (right) China Photos/Getty Images

▶ Video

macmillanhighered.com /reflectrelate4e

Individualism
Watch this clip online to answer the questions below.

Do you have higher regard for your personal goals and dreams than you do for the needs and desires of your family and community? How might your answer be affected by the culture in which you were raised?

Want to see more? Check out LaunchPad for a clip on **collectivism.**

By contrast, in **collectivistic cultures,** people emphasize group identity ("we" rather than "me"), interpersonal harmony, and the well-being of in-groups (Park & Guan, 2006). If you were raised in a collectivistic culture, you were probably taught that it's important to belong to groups or "collectives" that look after you in exchange for your loyalty. In collectivistic cultures, people emphasize the goals, needs, and views of groups over those of individuals, and define the highest good as cooperation with others rather than individual achievement. Collectivistic countries include Guatemala, Pakistan, Korea, and Japan (Hofstede, 2001).

Differences between individualistic and collectivistic cultures can powerfully influence people's behaviors, including which social networking sites they use and how they use them. For instance, people in collectivistic cultures tend to use sites that emphasize group connectedness, whereas those in individualistic cultures tend to use sites that focus on self-expression (Barker & Ota, 2011). American Facebook users devote most of their time on the site describing their own actions and viewpoints as well as personally important events. They also post controversial status updates and express their personal opinions, even if these trigger debate. Japanese users of mixi, meanwhile, carefully edit their profiles so they won't offend anyone (Barker & Ota, 2011). While American Facebook users often post photos of themselves alone doing various activities, mixi users tend to write in diaries that are shared with their closest friends, boosting ingroup solidarity (Barker & Ota, 2011).

UNCERTAINTY AVOIDANCE

Cultures vary in how much they tolerate and accept unpredictability, known as **uncertainty avoidance.** As scholar Geert Hofstede explains, "The fundamental issue here is how a society deals with the fact that the future can never be known: should we try to control the future or just let it happen?"[1] In *high-uncertainty-avoidance cultures* (such as Mexico, South Korea, Japan, and Greece), people place

---

[1] The Hofstede Centre, National Culture, Uncertainty Avoidance Index (UAI), Retrieved July 10, 2013, from http://geert-hofstede.com/national-culture.html

▲ In high-uncertainty-avoidance cultures, social roles and job assignments tend to be very clearly defined. By contrast, people in low-uncertainty-avoidance cultures learn from a young age to embrace innovation and more fluid social roles.
(Left) Sozaijiten/Datacraft/Getty Images; (right) Christopher Futcher/Getty Images

a lot of value on control. They define rigid rules and conventions to guide all beliefs and behaviors, and they feel uncomfortable with unusual or innovative ideas. People from such cultures want structure in their organizations, institutions, relationships, and everyday lives (Hofstede, 2001). For example, a coworker raised in a high-uncertainty-avoidance culture would expect everyone assigned to a project to have clear roles and responsibilities, including a designated leader. In his research on organizations, Hofstede found that in high-uncertainty-avoidance cultures, people commit to organizations for long periods of time, expect their job responsibilities to be clearly defined, and strongly believe that organizational rules should not be broken (2001, p. 149). Children raised in such cultures are taught to believe in cultural traditions and practices without ever questioning them.

In *low-uncertainty-avoidance cultures* (such as Jamaica, Denmark, Sweden, and Ireland), people put more emphasis on letting the future happen without trying to control it (Hofstede, 2001). They care less about rules, they tolerate diverse viewpoints and beliefs, and they welcome innovation and change. They also feel free to question and challenge authority. In addition, they teach their children to think critically about the beliefs and traditions they're exposed to, rather than automatically following them. Examples of low-uncertainty avoidance cultures include Singapore, Jamaica, and Denmark.

As with each of these cultural distinctions, most countries and people within them fall somewhere between high and low. For instance, both the United States and Canada are moderately uncertainty-avoidant. How does this translate into cultural values? Within both countries, people generally value innovation and new ideas (especially with regard to technology) while emphasizing the importance of laws, rules, and clear guidelines governing behavior, particularly within the workplace.

POWER DISTANCE

The degree to which people in a particular culture view the unequal distribution of power as acceptable is known as **power distance** (Hofstede, 1991, 2001). In

self-reflection

Consider your own presence on social media (e.g., Facebook, Twitter, Instagram). Does how you portray yourself through social media suggest collectivism or individualism? Does your online portrayal match or clash with how you think of yourself offline?

Assignment: Uncertainty Avoidance in Student Groups

Ask your students to Think-Ink-Pair-Share about ways in which they would overcome the challenges of working on a group project with a student from a culture with a different orientation toward uncertainty avoidance. What strategies could they use to ensure that the group works in a way that is comfortable for all members while achieving the group's goals?

self-reflection

What's your own view of power distance? Are you comfortable communicating with individuals who are better educated or more established than you are? For example, can you chat openly with a professor you admire? How does your cultural or co-cultural identity mesh with your personal feelings about power distance?

high-power-distance cultures, it's considered normal and even desirable for people of different social and professional status to have different levels of power (Ting-Toomey, 2005). In such cultures, people give privileged treatment and extreme respect to those in high-status positions (Ting-Toomey, 1999). They also expect individuals of lesser status to behave humbly, especially around people of higher status, who are expected to act superior.

In *low-power-distance cultures*, people in high-status positions try to minimize the differences between themselves and lower-status persons by interacting with them in informal ways and treating them as equals (Oetzel et al., 2001). For instance, a high-level marketing executive might chat with the cleaning service workers in her office and invite them to join her for a coffee break. See Figure 5.1 for examples of high- and low-power-distance cultures.

Power distance affects how people deal with interpersonal conflict. In low-power-distance cultures, people with little power may still choose to engage in conflict with high-power people. What's more, they may do so *competitively*, confronting high-power people and demanding that their goals be met. For

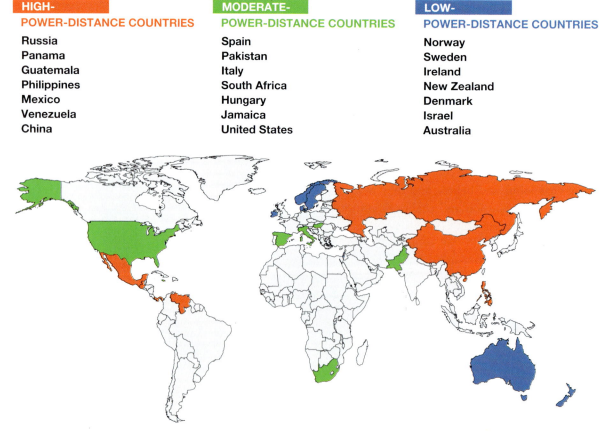

figure 5.1 Power Distance across Countries
Source: Hofstede (2009). Retrieved May 16, 2011, from www.geert-hofstede.com/index.shtml

instance, employees may question management decisions and suggest that alternatives be considered, or townspeople may attend a meeting and demand that the mayor address their concerns. These behaviors are much less common in high-power-distance cultures (Bochner & Hesketh, 1994), where low-power people are more likely to either *avoid* conflict with high-power people or *accommodate* them when conflict arises. (For more insight on how people approach conflict, see Chapter 9, pp. 262–266.)

Power distance also influences how people communicate in close relationships, especially families. In traditional Mexican culture, for instance, the value of *respeto* (respect) emphasizes power distance between younger people and their elders (Delgado-Gaitan, 1993). As part of *respeto*, children are expected to defer to elders' authority and to avoid openly disagreeing with them. In contrast, many Euro-Americans believe that once children reach adulthood, power in family relationships should be balanced, with children and their elders treating one another as equals (Kagawa & McCornack, 2004).

HIGH AND LOW CONTEXT

Cultures can also be described as *high* or *low context*. In **high-context cultures,** such as China, Korea, and Japan, people presume that others within the culture will share their viewpoints and thus perceive situations (contexts) in very much the same way. (High-context cultures are often collectivistic as well.) Consequently, people in such cultures often talk indirectly, using hints or suggestions to convey meanings—the presumption being that because individuals share the same contextual view, they automatically know what another person is trying to say. Relatively vague, ambiguous language—and even silence—is frequently used, and there's no need to provide a lot of explicit information within messages.

In **low-context cultures,** people tend *not* to presume that others share their beliefs, attitudes, and values. So they strive to be informative, clear, and direct in their communication (Hall & Hall, 1987). Many low-context cultures are also individualistic; as a result, people openly express their views and try to persuade others to accept them (Hall, 1976, 1997a). Within such cultures, which include Germany, Scandinavia, Canada, and the United States, people work to make important information obvious, rather than hinting or implying.

How does the difference between high-context and low-context cultures play out in real-world encounters? Consider the experiences of my friend and former graduate student Naomi Kagawa, who is now a Japanese communication professor. Growing up in Japan, a high-context culture, Naomi learned to reject requests by using words equivalent to *OK* or *sure* in order to maintain the harmony of the encounter. These words, however, are accompanied by subtle vocal tones that *imply* no. Because all members of the culture understand this practice, they recognize that such seeming assents are actually rejections. In contrast, in the United States—a low-context culture—people don't share similar knowledge and beliefs, so they spell things out much more explicitly. People

macmillanhighered.com/reflectrelate4e

Low Power Distance
Watch this clip online to answer the questions below.

How comfortable would you be offering a manager or professor feedback—particularly negative or constructive feedback? How might your culture affect your response?

Want to see more? Check out LaunchPad for a clip on **high power distance.**

Discussion Prompt: High-Context and Low-Context Cultures
Ask students to envision a business deal between a corporation from a high-context culture and one from a low-context culture. What differences are they likely to face in their communication style as they negotiate terms? What challenges would they expect to encounter? How might they overcome these challenges?

Online Self-Quiz: Collectivism, Uncertainty Avoidance, and Power Distance: Where Do You Stand? To take this self-quiz, visit LaunchPad: macmillanhighered.com/reflectrelate4e

often come right out and say no, then apologize and explain why they can't grant the request. When Naomi first visited the United States, this difference caused misunderstandings in her interpersonal interactions. She rejected unwanted requests by saying "OK," only to find that people presumed she was consenting rather than refusing. And she was surprised, even shocked, when people rejected her requests by explicitly saying no.

EMOTION DISPLAYS

In all cultures, norms exist regarding how people should and shouldn't express emotion. These norms are called **display rules:** guidelines for when, where, and how to manage emotion displays appropriately (Ekman & Friesen, 1975). Display rules govern very specific aspects of your nonverbal communication, such as how broadly you should smile, whether or not you should scowl when angry, and the appropriateness of shouting out loud in public when you're excited. (For more discussion of this, see Chapter 8 on nonverbal communication.) Children learn such display rules and, over time, internalize them to the point where following these rules seems normal. This is why you likely think of the way you express emotion as natural, rather than as something that has been socialized into you through your culture (Hayes & Metts, 2008).

Because of differences in socialization and traditions, display rules vary across cultures (Soto, Levenson, & Ebling, 2005). Take the two fastest-growing ethnic groups in the United States—Mexican Americans and Chinese Americans (Buriel & De Ment, 1997). In traditional Chinese culture, people prioritize emotional control and moderation; intense emotions are considered dangerous and are even thought to cause illness (Wu & Tseng, 1985). This belief shapes communication in close relationships. Chinese American couples don't openly express positive emotions toward each other as often as Euro-American couples do (Tsai & Levenson, 1997). Meanwhile, in traditional Mexican culture, people openly express emotion, even more so than people in Euro-American cultures (Soto et al., 2005). For people of Mexican descent, the experience, expression, and deep discussion of emotions provide some of life's greatest rewards and satisfactions.

When families immigrate to a new society, the move often provokes tension over which display rules to follow. People more closely oriented to their cultures of origin continue to communicate their emotions in traditional ways. Others—usually the first generation of children born in the new society—may move away from traditional forms of emotional expression (Soto et al., 2005). For example, Chinese Americans who adhere strongly to traditional Chinese culture openly display fewer negative emotions than do those who are Americanized (Soto et al., 2005). Similarly, Mexican Americans with strong ties to traditional Mexican culture express intense negative emotion more openly than do Americanized Mexican Americans.

Keep such differences in mind when interpersonally communicating with others. An emotional expression—such as a loud shout of intense joy—might

---

skills practice

Negotiating Display Rules
Learn how to competently manage emotions in various situations and encounters.

❶ Consider context. Keep in mind that specific contexts also have display rules. For example, some workplaces may demand strict emotional control.

❷ Observe others. Consider how your communication partners regulate emotion, being careful not to judge them as "cold" or "overly emotional."

❸ Adapt accordingly. Ensure that your communication mirrors what is appropriate for the context and your communication partners.

❹ Evaluate your behavior. Consider how your displays of emotion may have helped or hindered achievement of your desired outcomes.

Discussion Prompt: Display Rules
Play the LaunchPad video clip on **display rules** to begin a conversation about the appropriateness of displays of emotion. In the broader American culture, in what contexts are public displays of affection appropriate? Inappropriate? How do co-cultures differ in their display rules regarding public affection? What other emotional displays are considered taboo in various contexts?

chapter 5 / Understanding Culture   149

◯ Extreme circumstances can cause people to ignore the usual display rules of their culture. In the United States, men are generally socialized not to express vulnerable emotions in public, but this father had a powerful grief response when he saw his son's name at the North Pool of the 9/11 Memorial in New York City.
Justin Lane/AFP/Getty Images

be considered shocking and inappropriate in some cultures but perfectly normal and natural in others. Similarly, openly crying or wailing loudly with grief at a funeral service might be expected within some cultures and prohibited in others. At the same time, don't presume that all people from the same culture necessarily share the same expectations. As much as possible, adjust your expression of emotion to match the style of the individuals with whom you're interacting.

MASCULINITY VERSUS FEMININITY

Another dimension along which cultures differ that impacts interpersonal communication is the degree to which masculine, versus feminine, values are emphasized. **Masculine cultural values** include the accumulation of material wealth as an indicator of success, assertiveness, and personal achievement. Within highly masculine cultures, people are taught that competition is the highest good; people who "win" or who are "the best in their field" are looked up to as heroes. "Beating out the competition" and "having a competitive edge" are emphasized throughout schooling, in politics, and within professional life. So, for example, if you and a coworker who is a single mother both apply for the same promotion—one that will result in a substantial raise—but you decide to

Media Note: Emotion Displays

Have your students watch clips from the movie *My Big Fat Greek Wedding*, which depicts the romantic relationship between a Greek woman, Toula, and a non-Greek man, Ian. Ask your students to discuss the ways in which Toula's Greek family displays their emotions differently from Ian's more stoic, upper-class American family.

Media Note: Views of Time

Have your students watch the TED talk by Guillaume Gevrey titled "What Time Is it?" in the Connecting Cultures series (available on YouTube). In his presentation, he discusses the story of how he lost his job due to different perceptions of time and time management. Ask your students to discuss their own experiences in which they faced conflict over different time orientations.

withdraw your application because you think she needs the money more than you do, members of a masculine culture would be highly perplexed by your choice.

In contrast, **feminine cultural values** emphasize compassion and cooperation. Within feminine cultures, emphasis is placed on caring for the weak and underprivileged and boosting the quality of life for all people. To borrow from the previous example, members of a feminine culture would greatly respect and admire the decision to bow out of a competition for a promotion to help a coworker whom you judge as having greater need than you.

Examples of masculine cultures include Japan, Hungary, Venezuela, and Italy; feminine cultures include Sweden, Norway, the Netherlands, and Denmark. The United States rates as a substantially masculine country (62 out of 100 on the masculinity index), whereas Canada is moderately masculine (around 10 points below the United States). See Figure 5.2 for a comparison of the cultural values in the United States and Sweden.

Importantly, whether a culture is masculine, feminine, or somewhere in between impacts both men and women in very real ways. For example, feminine cultures typically offer lengthy paid or partially paid leaves from work following the birth or adoption of a child—in some cases, for more than a *year*. Within masculine cultures, such extended leaves would be unimaginable. The masculinity or femininity of a culture also shapes very specific aspects of communication. For example, managers in masculine cultures are expected to be decisive and authoritarian; managers in feminine cultures are expected to focus more on the process of decision making and the achievement of consensus between involved parties.

figure 5.2 Comparing Masculine and Feminine Cultural Values in the United States and Sweden

The bar graph represents the scores for the United States and Sweden, based on Geert Hofstede's Cultural Survey. According to the Hofstede Centre's Web site, "The fundamental issue here is what motivates people, wanting to be the best (masculine) or liking what you do (feminine)." As you can see from the graph, the United States has a much higher score on masculinity than Sweden. See the chart for more explanation.

Source: http://geert-hofstede.com/index.php

VIEWS OF TIME

Cultures also vary in terms of how people view time. Scholar Edward Hall distinguished between two time orientations: monochronic (*M-time*) and polychronic (*P-time*) (1997b). People who have a **monochronic time orientation** view time as a precious resource. It can be saved, spent, wasted, lost, or made up, and it can even run out. If you're an M-time person, "spending time" with someone or "making time" in your schedule to share activities with him or her sends the message that you consider that person—and your relationship—important (Hall, 1983). You may view time as a gift you give others to show your affection, or as a tool for punishing someone ("I no longer have time for you").

People who have a **polychronic time orientation** don't view time as a resource to be spent, saved, or guarded. They don't consider time of day (what time it is) as especially important or relevant to daily activities. Instead, they're flexible when it comes to time, and they believe that harmonious interaction with others is more important than "being on time" or sticking to a schedule.

Differences in time orientation can create problems when people from different cultures make appointments with each other (Hall, 1983). For example, those with an M-time orientation, such as many Americans, Canadians, Swiss, and Germans, often find it frustrating if P-time people show up for a meeting after the scheduled start time. In P-time cultures, such as those in Arabian, African, Caribbean, and Latin American countries, people think that arriving 30 minutes or more after a meeting's scheduled start is perfectly acceptable and that it's OK to change important plans at the last minute.

You can boost your intercultural competence by understanding other people's views of time. Learn about the time orientation of a destination or country before you travel there. For example, before my family and I traveled to St. Martin in the French West Indies, we learned that it was a P-time culture. So, at the end of our trip, I planned accordingly. When we needed a cab to pick us up at the hotel at 10:30 in the morning, I told the cabdriver to be there by 9:45. Sure enough, at around 10:25 he rolled up—almost exactly the amount of lateness that I had anticipated!

Also, respect others' time orientations. If you're an M-time person interacting with a P-time individual, don't suddenly dash off to your next appointment because you feel you have to stick to your schedule. Your communication partner will likely think you're rude. If you're a P-time person interacting with an M-time partner, realize that he or she may get impatient with a long, leisurely conversation or see a late arrival to a meeting as inconsiderate. In addition, avoid criticizing or complaining about behaviors that stem from other people's time

◐ In M-time societies like the United States, being "on time" is highly valued. A businessperson who is late to an important meeting may face serious consequences, such as losing face with his or her peers or even getting fired. FPG/Archive Photos/Getty Images

skills practice

Understanding Time Orientation

Become more mindful of the way you and your communication partners communicate with time.

❶ Learn about different time orientations. Perhaps your roommate isn't just a stickler about her bedtime; she may simply be on M-time!

❷ Accommodate others. Don't rush your P-time grandmother off the phone when she's telling you about her week. Call her when your schedule allows for a leisurely conversation.

❸ Avoid criticizing. Time is just one dimension of intercultural communication. Your high- or low-context or individualistic or collectivistic communication style can confuse someone, as much as you can be frustrated by another's time orientation.

In the film *Gran Torino*, Walt realizes that his previous beliefs were racist only when he allows himself to experience his neighbors' culture. How has learning about someone's culture changed or enhanced your impressions for the better?
© Warner Brothers/Everett Collection

orientations. Instead, accept the fact that people view time differently, and be willing to adapt your own expectations and behaviors accordingly.

Creating Intercultural Competence

Being mindful of and adapting to cultural difference

In the award-winning movie *Gran Torino*, Clint Eastwood plays Walt, a bitter, racist widower who lives alone in Michigan, estranged from his sons. Despite his bigoted attitudes, Walt strikes up a friendship with two Hmong teens who live next door, Sue and Thao, after he saves Thao from a gang beating. To help Walt communicate more competently with the Hmong, Sue teaches him some simple cultural rules: Never touch a Hmong on the head because they believe that the soul resides there. Don't look a Hmong straight in the eye; they consider it rude. Don't be surprised if a Hmong smiles when he or she is embarrassed; that's how they handle that emotion. In return, Walt teaches Thao how to interpersonally interact during a job interview with an American construction foreman: "Look him straight in the eye, and give a firm handshake!" He even instructs Thao on the art of trading teasing insults with American male friends. As these unlikely friendships deepen, Walt (to his astonishment) realizes he has more in common with his neighbors than with his own family.

Like Walt, Thao, and Sue, you will likely form lasting bonds with people who come from cultures vastly different from your own. The gateway to such connections is **intercultural competence,** the ability to communicate appropriately, effectively, and ethically with people from diverse backgrounds. You can strengthen your intercultural competence by applying the following practices: world-mindedness, attributional complexity, and communication accommodation.

WORLD-MINDEDNESS

When you possess **world-mindedness,** you demonstrate acceptance and respect toward other cultures' beliefs, values, and customs (Hammer, Bennett, & Wiseman, 2003). You can practice world-mindedness in three ways. First, accept others' expression of their culture or co-culture as a natural element in their interpersonal communication, just as your communication reflects your cultural background (Chen & Starosta, 2005). Second, avoid any temptation to judge others' cultural beliefs, attitudes, and values as "better" or "worse" than your own. Third, treat people from all cultures with respect.

This can be especially challenging when differences seem impossible to bridge or when the other person's beliefs, attitudes, and values conflict with your

---

Assignment: World-Mindedness

Have students research and write a paper about a remarkable person who has demonstrated world-mindedness through specific efforts to improve intercultural relations. This can be someone from the present or the past. (You might want to generate a list to inspire students by offering the names of individuals you admire or by visiting the list of "Remarkable People" offered at worldminded.com). What can we learn from the efforts of this individual?

own. But practicing world-mindedness means more than just tolerating cultural differences you find perplexing or problematic. Instead, treat all people with respect by being kind and courteous in your communication. You can also preserve others' personal dignity by actively listening to and asking questions about viewpoints that may differ from yours.

World-mindedness is the opposite of **ethnocentrism,** the belief that one's own cultural beliefs, attitudes, values, and practices are superior to others'. Ethnocentrism is not the same thing as pride in your cultural heritage, or patriotism. You can be culturally proud, or patriotic, and not be ethnocentric. Instead, ethnocentrism is a *comparative evaluation*: ethnocentric people view their own culture or co-culture as the standard against which all other cultures should be judged, and they often have contempt for other cultures (Neulip & McCroskey, 1997; Sumner, 1906). Consequently, such people tend to see their own communication as competent and that of people from other cultures as incompetent.

ATTRIBUTIONAL COMPLEXITY

When you practice **attributional complexity,** you acknowledge that other people's behaviors have complex causes. To develop this ability, observe others' behavior and analyze the various forces influencing it. For example, rather than deciding that a classmate's reserved demeanor or limited eye contact means she's unfriendly, consider the possibility that these behaviors might reflect cultural differences.

Also, learn as much as you can about different cultures and co-cultures, so you can better understand people's interpersonal communication styles and preferences. Experiencing other cultures through observation, travel, or interaction is a great way to sharpen your intercultural communication competence (Arasaratnam, 2006).

In addition, routinely use *perception-checking* to avoid attributional errors, and regularly demonstrate *empathy* to identify with others. In situations where the cultural gaps between you and others seem impossibly wide, try to see things from their perspective. Consider the motivations behind their communication. Examine how people from diverse backgrounds make decisions, and compare their approaches to yours. Finally, ask others to explain the reasons for their behavior, and then accept and validate their explanations ("That makes sense to me") rather than challenge them ("You've got to be kidding!"). Avoid making statements like "I know that people like you act this way because you think that . . . ," because you'll only come across as presumptuous.

COMMUNICATION ACCOMMODATION

A final way to enhance your intercultural competence is to adjust your interpersonal communication to mesh with the behaviors of people from other cultures. According to **communication accommodation theory,** people are especially motivated to adapt their communication when they seek social approval, when they wish to establish relationships with others, and when they view others' language use as appropriate (Giles, Coupland, & Coupland, 1991). In contrast, people tend to accentuate differences between their communication and others' when they wish to convey emotional distance and disassociate themselves from others. Research

Teaching Tip: Attributional Complexity
You can show or assign the video clip on **attributional complexity** to help students better understand this term and how the practice of it can improve their intercultural and interpersonal communication competence.

self-reflection

Think of an encounter in which you failed to engage in perception-checking while interacting with someone from a different culture. What happened as a result? What might you have done differently to improve the situation and outcomes?

self-QUIZ

Are You World-Minded or Ethnocentric?

World-mindedness and ethnocentrism are opposing viewpoints. To see which orientation best fits your own view of culture and the world, simply put a check next to each statement with which you agree. Then total up the number of check marks for each category to see which viewpoint most aligns with your own. For the best results, be as honest as possible in representing your own attitudes.

To take this quiz online, visit LaunchPad: **macmillanhighered.com/reflectrelate4e**.

World-Minded

_____ Lifestyles in other cultures are just as valid as those in my culture.

_____ People in my culture could learn a lot from people in other cultures.

_____ I respect the values and customs of other cultures.

_____ I have many friends from different cultures.

_____ I am very interested in the values and customs of other cultures.

Ethnocentric

_____ Most other cultures are backward compared to my culture.

_____ My culture should be the role model for other cultures.

_____ I am not interested in the values and customs of other cultures.

_____ I dislike interacting with people from different cultures.

_____ I have little respect for the values and customs of other cultures.

Note: This *Self-Quiz* is adapted from the work of Neuliep (2002).

Scoring: 0–1 low, 2–3 moderate, 4–5 high. If you score the same for both categories (world-minded and ethnocentric), it simply means that you believe certain elements of both viewpoints.

suggests that people who use communication accommodation are perceived as being more competent (Coupland, Giles, & Wiemann, 1991; Giles et al., 1991).

How does this work in practice? Try adapting to other people's communication preferences (Bianconi, 2002). During interpersonal interactions, notice how long a turn people take when speaking, how quickly they speak, how direct they

▶ One way to enhance world-mindedness, practice attributional complexity, and try communication accommodation is to travel and experience other cultures firsthand. What experiences do you have with traveling in other cultures, and what did you learn from your interactions with the people? Bill Bachmann/Photoshot/Newscom

table 5.1 Creating Intercultural Communication Competence

- Understand the many factors that create people's cultural and co-cultural identities.
- Be aware of the different cultural influences on interpersonal communication: individualism versus collectivism, uncertainty avoidance, power distance, high and low context, emotional displays, masculinity versus femininity, and views of time.
- Embrace world-mindedness to genuinely accept and respect others' cultures.
- Practice attributional complexity to consider the possible cultural influences on your and others' interpersonal communication.
- Use communication accommodation when building and maintaining relationships with people from different cultural backgrounds.

are, and how much they appear to want to talk compared to you. You may also need to learn and practice cultural norms for nonverbal behaviors, including eye contact, head touching, and handshaking, such as those Sue taught Walt in *Gran Torino*. At the same time, avoid imitating other people's dialects, accents, or word choices. Most people consider such imitation inappropriate and insulting.

For an overview of ways to create intercultural communication competence, see Table 5.1, which pulls together everything you've learned in this chapter.

Embracing Difference

[Intercultural communication is a gift]

People are almost unimaginably diverse in their cultural beliefs, values, and practices. And as the interpersonal world becomes increasingly connected through technology, rarely does a day go by when we don't engage people who are culturally different from us. It might be as simple as passing someone on the street who is dressed in religious garb, indicating that their religious beliefs are different from yours. It might be getting takeout from an ethnic restaurant, only to find that you're the sole person of your ethnicity there. It might even be a more culturally immersive experience, such as taking part in a study abroad or serving in the military overseas.

Across all of these points of intercultural contact, our natural inclination is to perceive *distance*. When we see or speak with someone who is culturally different, we often immediately think, "He is nothing like me!" or "She and I could never share anything in common!" This perception of distance between ourselves and diverse others feeds a host of associated interpersonal judgments and behaviors, including the use of stereotypes, awkward or incompetent communication, and, more negatively, prejudice.

It takes a radical shift in perspective to not flinch and pull away when faced with difference but to embrace it. Yes, it's true that people are different in their cultural beliefs, traditions, values, and communication; and such differences are deep, not superficial. But *difference doesn't mean distance*. It just means . . . difference! People who are culturally different from us may share profound

self-reflection

Think of an encounter in which you tried to communicate with someone from a different culture using communication accommodation, but you did so inappropriately. How were you judged as a result? What might you have done differently to improve the encounter?

making relationship choices

Parent-Child Culture Clash

1 BACKGROUND

Communicating across cultural boundaries can be challenging, especially when those boundaries involve differences between children and their elders within the same family. To understand how you might competently manage such a relationship challenge, read the case study in Part 2; then, drawing on all you know about interpersonal communication, work through the problem-solving model in Part 3.

 Visit LaunchPad to check out the other side of the story (Part 4). For the best experience, complete all parts in LaunchPad: **macmillanhighered.com/reflectrelate4e**.

2 CASE STUDY

You're a first-generation American, the only child of parents who have deep ties to their home culture. Your mother was never openly affectionate, but when you were growing up, she let you know in many indirect ways that she loved you. But after your father died, that changed. She became coldly authoritarian, and throughout your teen years she bossed you around mercilessly.

Your mother's cultural beliefs about parental power have become triggers for resentment since you left for college. She chose your major, based on "your obligation to support her in the future," and even scheduled all your classes your freshman year. You went along with her wishes to preserve harmony, but you resent the fact that you are living the life she wants rather than your own. You've come to believe that she has no regard for, or interest in, *your* dreams and desires.

This past year, three things have happened that may divide you two further. First, you started going to a campus church with some of your American friends, rather than continuing your culture's religious practices. Although you initially did this as a secret protest against your mother, you've enjoyed the experience.

Second, you met Devin. Devin is Euro-American, and he impresses you by being outgoing, warm, and funny. You two start dating, but—like the church thing—you don't tell your mom, because she would *never* approve. Third, through hanging out with Devin and your other American friends, you begin to question your cultural practices regarding parental power. This comes to a head when, with Devin's encouragement, you enroll in a couple of interesting electives. These classes make you realize you want to change majors and pursue a very different career path.

Visiting home one weekend, your mother abruptly broaches the topic of your future: "You seem to be drifting from our traditions recently, and this must stop. You're almost done with school, and you're no longer a child. The time has come for you to do what is expected of you. I have talked with your uncle about hiring you when you graduate, and he has agreed. And your grandparents back home have made arrangements with another family, our long-time friends, for you to marry one of their children. So, your future is set, and you *will* bring great honor to this family!"

3 YOUR TURN

Think about all you've learned thus far about interpersonal communication. Then work through the following five steps. Remember, there are no "right" answers, so think hard about what is the *best* choice! (P.S. Need help? See the *Helpful Concepts* list.)

step 1
Reflect on yourself. What are your thoughts and feelings in this situation? Are your impressions and attributions accurate?

step 2
Reflect on your partner. Using perspective-taking and empathic concern, put yourself in your mother's shoes. What is she thinking and feeling in this situation?

step 3
Identify the optimal outcome. Think about your communication and relationship with your mother, as well as the situation surrounding your college experience and future. What's the best, most constructive relationship outcome possible? Consider what's best for you and for your mother.

step 4
Locate the roadblocks. Taking into consideration your own and your mother's thoughts and feelings and all that has happened in this situation and in your home life, what obstacles are keeping you from achieving the optimal outcome?

step 5
Chart your course. What can you say to your mother to overcome the roadblocks you've identified and achieve your optimal outcome?

> **HELPFUL CONCEPTS**
>
> Individualistic and collectivistic cultures, **143**
> Uncertainty avoidance, **144**
> Power distance, **145**
> Display rules, **148**
> World-mindedness, **152**
> Attributional complexity, **153**
> Communication accommodation theory, **153**

4 THE OTHER SIDE

Visit LaunchPad to watch a video in which your mother tells her side of the case study story. As in many real-life situations, this is information to which you did not have access when you were initially crafting your response in Part 3. The video reminds us that even when we do our best to offer competent responses, there is always another side to the story that we need to consider.

points of commonality, upon which valuable and impactful encounters and relationships can be built. When we embrace the cultural differences of others, metaphorically pulling diverse others closer rather than pushing them away, a host of personal and interpersonal benefits immediately open up before us. These include the possibility of new friendships, romances, and professional alliances; an enriched understanding of other cultures and co-cultures; and, ultimately, a more refined view of ourselves and how we fit into the rich tapestry of life that constitutes the human interpersonal world.

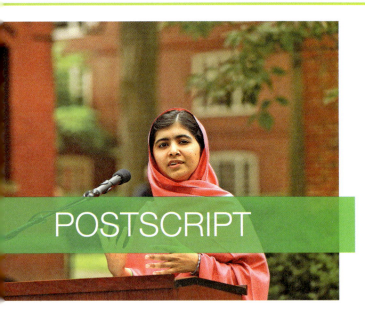

POSTSCRIPT

We began this chapter with a teen blogger who became the youngest person in history to win a Nobel Prize. When the Taliban took over the valley in which she lived, Malala Yousafzai refused to be cowed by their threats, even though it meant the possibility of her own death. And when she spoke out publicly on behalf of women and girls, she took a stand for people everywhere who are oppressed by cultural intolerance.

What struggles have you faced related to your cultural identity? Have you ever experienced threats because of who you are and the culture you're from? Did you lift your voice in challenge, or silently acquiesce?

Malala's courage in the face of extreme adversity reminds us of the triumphant power of tolerance. When we treat those who are culturally different from us with kindness, fairness, and respect, we bridge those aspects that would divide us, and honor the humanity that unites us.

LaunchPad for *Reflect & Relate* offers videos and encourages self-assessment through adaptive quizzing. Go to **macmillanhighered.com/reflectrelate4e** to get access to:

 LearningCurve
Adaptive Quizzes

 Video clips that help you understand interpersonal communication

key terms

culture, 136
Co-cultural Communication Theory, 138
co-cultures, 138
▶ assimilation, 138
prejudice, 141
Stereotype Content Model, 141
▶ individualistic cultures, 143
▶ collectivistic cultures, 144
uncertainty avoidance, 144
▶ power distance, 145
▶ high-context cultures, 147
▶ low-context cultures, 147
▶ display rules, 148
masculine cultural values, 149
feminine cultural values, 150
monochronic time orientation, 151
polychronic time orientation, 151
intercultural competence, 152
world-mindedness, 152
ethnocentrism, 152
▶ attributional complexity, 153
communication accommodation theory, 153

▶ You can watch brief, illustrative videos of these terms and test your understanding of the concepts in LaunchPad.

key concepts

What Is Culture?

- Our sense of **culture** is deeply influenced by our nationality, ethnicity, religion, gender, and many other factors. According to **Co-cultural Communication Theory**, members of assorted **co-cultures** may get the dominant culture to accommodate their co-cultural identity, **assimilate** into the dominant culture, or separate themselves entirely from it.

- The **Stereotype Content Model** contends that our prejudiced views, rooted in stereotypes, cause us to see other groups benevolently or with hostility.

Cultural Influences on Communication

- Whether we grow up within **individualistic cultures** or **collectivistic cultures** strongly influences the extent to which we value personal achievements and independence over group identity. Similarly, the directness or indirectness of our communication is impacted by our experience with **high-** and **low-context cultures.**

- Our level of **uncertainty avoidance** determines our acceptance of life's unpredictability. The **display rules** we learn growing up help us decide when, where, and how to appropriately communicate our emotions.

- Whether and how we will confront people of different social status is affected by the **power distance** of our culture, just as our culture's **masculine cultural values** and **feminine cultural values** impact the importance we place on personal achievement, assertiveness, compassion, and cooperation.

Creating Intercultural Competence

- We demonstrate **world-mindedness** by accepting others' expressions of their culture as part of their interpersonal communication, avoiding the temptation to judge others, and treating others with respect. This is the opposite of **ethnocentrism,** a significant barrier to intercultural competence.

- We develop **attributional complexity** by observing others' behavior and analyzing the various forces influencing it.

- **Communication accommodation theory** encourages us to adapt our communication to gain approval and establish relationships, as long as we avoid imitating others' accents or dialects.

chapter review

✓ **LearningCurve** can help you review the material in this chapter. Go to LaunchPad: macmillanhighered.com/reflectrelate4e

6 Listening Actively

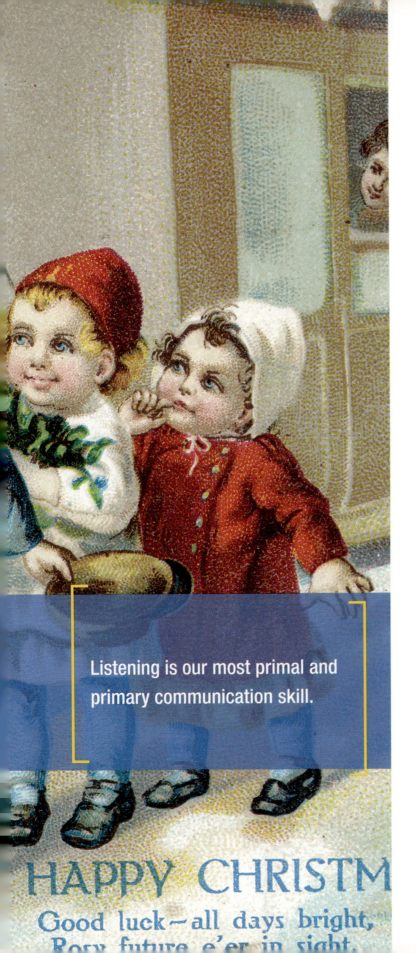

He is arguably the best-known listener in the world. If you see a jolly older man with a long white beard, all dressed in red, his name immediately leaps to mind. Each holiday season, millions of children around the world line up and wait for the opportunity to share their thoughts, feelings, and material desires with him. And they all count on Santa to do one thing at that special moment: *listen*.

Santa Claus is actually a synthesis of several historical figures. His name derives from the Dutch pronunciation ("Sinterklass") of Saint Nicholas, a fourth-century Christian bishop with a reputation for generous gift-giving. His "flying through the sky" comes from the Norse god Odin, who rode storms astride his eight-legged horse—the precursor to Santa's eight reindeer. His look stems largely from Father Christmas, who has welcomed in the British holiday season with festivities for hundreds of years. But how did Santa come to be such a good *listener*?

The practice of Santa listening to children can be credited in part to James Edgar, a Scottish immigrant who owned a dry goods store in the late 1800s. As Edgar himself noted, "I have never been able to understand why the great gentleman lives so far away . . . only able to see the children one day a year. He should live closer to them." To resolve this, Edgar, in 1890, donned a custom-made red suit and began interacting with children in his store each winter.

> Listening is our most primal and primary communication skill.

© Mary Evans Picture Library/The Image Works

6 / Listening Actively

Soon the practice spread nationwide, and with it, the need for formally training such Santas. The central communication facet of this training is *active listening*. As Jennifer Andrews, who currently serves as Santa's Lead Elf and Dean of Victor Nevada's Santa School in Alberta, Canada, describes, "I always teach the Santae (plural of Santa) to recognize their vital role as a listener. Santa is an icon, and one of his main roles is to listen to kids; big and little alike. Santa's ability to listen gives children a safe outlet to confide in, make requests of, and tell him things that frighten them."

Of course, Santa doesn't just sit passively; he actively provides feedback as well. As Andrews details, "Parents put a lot of stock in Santa and how he will weigh in on their children's behavior. Santa is known for asking the children if they have been naughty or nice and then listens for their answers. Regardless of the answer, he will often give a brief counsel; encouraging them to always try harder and then waits and again listens, this time for their wishes."

At the same time, Santa can't grant every wish that is heard. Andrews notes, "Santa is a safe zone for kids, and while children do make material requests of Santa, they also make more heart-wrenching requests as well: to have a mom or dad come home or find employment; or have a loved one find good health again. I train the Santae to be active listeners, but never to make promises. One of Santa's best responses is to say, 'Santa will do his best' or, for the more difficult situations, 'Santa can do many things but not all things; some things are out of Santa's reach, too.' That being said, Santa's job is to truly, actively, and empathically listen; and a visit with him—when you think of it—it is very much akin to a child coming home."

We've all had that experience, whether it was with a parent, a pastor, a priest, a rabbi, or a close friend—that moment when another human being listened to us so attentively and compassionately that we felt liberated to bare our souls. *Active listening* does indeed create a safe zone within which we can share our innermost thoughts and feelings with others, an experience akin to coming home. And when we embrace the potential power of active listening for ourselves—taking the time to truly listen to other people—we transcend our own thoughts, ideas, and beliefs, and begin to directly experience their words and worlds (McNaughton, Hamlin, McCarthy, Head-Reeves, & Schreiner, 2007). By focusing our attention, tailoring our listening to the situation, and letting others know we understand them, we move beyond the personal and create the *interpersonal*. The result is improved relationships (Bunkers, 2010).

In this chapter, we discuss how to build your active listening skills. You'll learn:

- The five stages of the listening process and strategies for improving your listening skills
- The many functions of listening
- The advantages and disadvantages of different listening styles
- Ways to avoid common forms of incompetent listening

chapter outline

163 Listening: A Five-Step Process

171 The Five Functions of Listening

173 Understanding Listening Styles

178 Preventing Incompetent Listening

183 The Gift of Active Listening

Listening: A Five-Step Process

Listening draws on auditory and visual cues

The scares in horror movies almost always begin with sounds. In my favorite scary film of all, *The Babadook* (2014), the stage is set for future fright when a mother and son read a children's story about a monster who announces his arrival with three loud knocks—Dook! Dook! Dook!—only to hear those knocks for real on their own front door. Similar sonic scenes haunt such films as *The Conjuring* (2013), *Paranormal Activity* (2007), and *The Exorcist* (1973). As we sit in the comfort of movie theaters or living rooms, feeling our blood pressure rising, we listen intently to these sounds, trying to understand them and imagining how we would respond if we were in similar situations.

Horror screenwriters use sounds to trigger fear because they know the powerful role that listening plays in our lives. Listening is our most primal and primary communication skill: as children, we develop the ability to listen long before we learn how to speak, read, or write. And as adults, we spend more time listening than we do in any other type of communication activity (Wolvin & Coakley, 1996). But what is often overlooked is that listening is a complex process. **Listening** involves receiving, attending to, understanding, responding to, and recalling sounds and visual images (Wolvin & Coakley, 1996). When you're listening to someone, you draw on both auditory and visual cues. In addition to spoken messages, behaviors such as head nodding, smiling, gestures, and eye contact affect how you listen to others and interpret their communication. The

Chapter Theme

We often think of listening as a passive activity, something that just happens. But listening is arguably our most powerful communicative skill in terms of how much we gain from it and depend on it. Listening actively requires us to focus attention, train memory, adapt listening styles, and avoid incompetent listening. When we do so, we move beyond subjectivity to forge interpersonal connections with others.

In *The Babadook*, Amelia and her son, Samuel, read about the monster's signature three knocks, which triggers a powerful fear response when they hear the real knocks on their door later. Whenever we hear a sound, we go through a process to help us figure out what we heard and how to respond. © IFC Midnight/Everett Collection

self-reflection

Think of the most recent instance in which you were truly frightened. What triggered your fear? Was it a noise you heard, something someone told you, or something you saw? What does this tell you about the primacy of listening in shaping intense emotions?

process of listening also unfolds over time, rather than instantaneously, through the five steps discussed here.

RECEIVING

You're Skyping with your brother, who is in the military, stationed overseas. As he talks, you listen to his words and observe his behavior. How does this process happen? As you observe him, light reflects off his skin, clothes, and hair and travels through the lens of your eye to your retina, which sends the images through the optic nerve to your brain, which translates the information into visual images, such as your brother smiling or shaking his head, an effect called *seeing*. At the same time, sound waves generated by his voice enter your inner ear, causing your eardrum to vibrate. These vibrations travel along acoustic nerves to your brain, which interprets them as your brother's words and voice tone, an effect known as **hearing**.

Together, seeing and hearing constitute **receiving**, the first step in the listening process. Receiving is critical to listening—you can't listen if you don't "see" or hear the other person. Unfortunately, our ability to receive is often hampered by *noise pollution*, sound in the surrounding environment that obscures or distracts our attention from auditory input. Sources of noise pollution include crowds, road and air traffic, construction equipment, and music.

Although noise pollution is inescapable, especially in large cities, some people intentionally expose themselves to intense levels of noise pollution. This can result in *hearing impairment*, the restricted ability to receive sound input across the humanly audible frequency range. For example, research suggests that more than 40 percent of college students have measurable hearing impairment due to loud music in bars, home stereos, headphones, and concerts, but only 8 percent believe that it is a "big problem" compared with other health issues (Chung, Des Roches, Meunier, & Eavey, 2005). One study of rock and jazz musicians found that 75 percent suffered substantial hearing loss from exposure to chronic noise pollution (Kaharit, Zachau, Eklof, Sandsjo, & Moller, 2003).

You can enhance your ability to receive—and improve your listening as a result—by becoming aware of noise pollution and adjusting your interactions accordingly. Practice monitoring the noise level in your environment during your interpersonal encounters, and notice how it impedes your listening. When possible, avoid interactions in loud and noisy environments, or move to quieter locations when you wish to exchange important information with others. If you enjoy loud music or live concerts, always use ear protection to ensure your auditory safety. As a lifelong musician, I myself never practice, play a gig, or attend a concert without earplugs.

ATTENDING

Attending, the second step in the listening process, involves devoting attention to the information you've received. If you don't attend to information, you can't go on to interpret and understand it, or respond to it (Kahneman, 1973). The extent to which you attend to received information is determined largely by its *salience*—the degree to which it seems especially noticeable and significant. As discussed in Chapter 3, we view information as salient when it's *visually or audibly stimulating*, *unexpected*, or *personally important* (Fiske & Taylor, 1991). We have only limited control over salience; whether people communicate in stimulating, unexpected, or important ways is largely determined by them, not us. However, we do control our attention level. To improve your attention, consider trying two things: limiting your multitasking and elevating your attention.

Limiting Multitasking Online One way to improve attention is to limit the amount of time you spend each day *multitasking online*—using multiple forms of technology at once, each of which feeds you an unrelated stream of information (Ophir, Nass, & Wagner, 2012). An example of such multitasking is writing a class paper on your computer while also tweeting on your phone, Facebook chatting with several friends, watching TV, playing an online computer game, and texting family members. Stanford psychologist Clifford Nass has found that habitual multitaskers are extremely confident in their ability to perform at peak levels on the tasks they simultaneously juggle (Glenn, 2010). However, their confidence is misplaced. Multitaskers perform substantially worse on tasks compared with individuals who focus their attention on only one task at a time (Ophir et al., 2012). As a specific example, college students who routinely surf social networking sites and text while they are doing their homework suffer substantially lower overall GPAs than do students who limit their multitasking while studying (Juncoa & Cotton, 2012).

Why is limiting multitasking online important for improving attention? Because multitasking erodes your capacity for sustaining focused attention (Jackson, 2008). Cognitive scientists have discovered that our brains adapt to the tasks we regularly perform during our waking hours, an effect known as *brain plasticity* (Carr, 2010). In simple terms, we "train our brains" to be able to do certain things through how we live our daily lives. People who spend much of their time, day after day, shifting attention rapidly between multiple forms of technology train their brains to focus attention only in brief bursts. The consequence is that they lose the ability to focus attention for long periods of time on just one task (Jackson, 2008). For example, one study of high school and college students found that habitual multitaskers couldn't focus their attention on a single task for more

▶ Repeated exposure to intense levels of noise pollution can result in hearing impairment. Guitarist Pete Townshend of the Who, after years of exposure to his own noise pollution, can no longer hear spoken words during normal conversations. © Neal Preston/Corbis

---

Discussion Prompt: The Difference between Hearing and Listening
People often say "I heard you," yet they are not actually listening. To get students thinking about listening actively, ask them to discuss the differences between listening and hearing. Reinforce the idea that hearing is a passive activity, while listening is a purposeful active behavior.

Discussion Prompt: Attending and Instructions
Give students step-by-step instructions for a task without allowing them to write anything down (drawing something specific, simple origami). After determining how well students accomplished the task, explain the importance of attending when given instructions. Discuss the negative perceptions we have of people who can't follow instructions.

self-QUIZ: Multitasking and Attention

This quiz gauges how multitasking between various forms of technology can divide your attention and how your ability to focus may suffer as a result. Read each statement below and mark the ones with which you agree. Use your score to assess the degree to which your attention is divided.

To take this quiz online, visit LaunchPad: **macmillanhighered.com/reflectrelate4e**.

_____ At any one time, I typically have multiple forms of technology turned on, including my phone and computer.

_____ If I focus my attention on just one task, I find that my mind quickly starts drifting to other stuff, such as who is messaging me, or what is happening online.

_____ Even during class or while I'm at work, I stay connected to and communicate with others through text, e-mail, cell phone, or the Internet.

_____ When I spend too much time doing any one thing, I get bored.

_____ Text messages, cell-phone calls, e-mail, and online posts frequently interrupt activities I am trying to focus on and perform.

_____ I spend much of my day switching rapidly between multiple activities and apps, including Facebook, text, e-mail, games, schoolwork, and Web surfing.

_____ I feel that I am more easily distracted now than I was just a few years ago.

Note: This *Self-Quiz* is adapted from Bane (2010).

Scoring: If you agree with 0–2 of these, your attention is not divided by multitasking, and you likely find it easy to concentrate on one thing for extended periods of time. If you agree with 3–4 of these, you have moderately divided attention and may be experiencing challenges with focusing attention. If you agree with 5–7 of these, you spend much of your time multitasking and likely find it challenging to focus your attention on just one thing.

Assignment: Assessing Your Attention

Have students write a self-assessment paper that analyzes their ability to elevate attention in one of their close relationships. Students should reflect on influences on their attention (hunger, stress) and specific settings that are more difficult for listening to their partner (restaurants, while watching TV). Finally, they should suggest how they will overcome the "attention gap" when listening to this individual.

than five minutes at a time without checking social networking sites or phone messages (Rosen, Carrier, & Cheever, 2013). What's more, habitual multitaskers set themselves up for distraction: they routinely have multiple apps running, which enhances the likelihood of distraction (Rosen et al., 2013).

Not surprisingly, habitual multitaskers have great difficulty listening, as listening requires extended attention (Carr, 2010). Limiting your multitasking and spending at least some time each day focused on just one task (such as reading, listening to music, or engaging in prayer or meditation), without technological distractions, help train your brain to be able to sustain attention. In addition, when you're in a high-stakes setting, one in which important information is being shared, it's essential that you limit access to and use of multiple apps, to avoid the attention impairment that comes with simply having such distractions present (Rosen et al., 2013). To gauge the degree to which multitasking has impacted your attention, take the *Self-Quiz* "Multitasking and Attention."

Elevating Attention The second thing you can try to improve your attention is to elevate it, by following these steps (Marzano & Arredondo, 1996). First, develop awareness of your attention level. During interpersonal interactions, monitor how your attention naturally waxes and wanes. Notice how various factors, such as fatigue, stress, or hunger, influence your attention. Second, take note of encounters in which you *should* listen carefully but that seem to trigger low levels of attention. These might include interactions with parents, teachers, or work managers, or situations such as family get-togethers, classroom lectures, or work meetings. Third, consider the optimal level of attention required for adequate listening during these encounters. Fourth, compare the level of attention you observed in yourself versus the level of attention that is required, identifying the attention gap that needs to be bridged for you to improve your attention.

Finally, and most important, elevate your level of attention to the point necessary to take in the auditory and visual information you're receiving. You can do this in several ways. Before and during an encounter, boost the salience of the exchange by reminding yourself of how it will impact your life and relationships. Take active control of the factors that may diminish your attention. When possible, avoid important encounters when you are overly stressed, hungry, ill, fatigued, or under the influence of alcohol; such factors substantially impair attention. If you have higher energy levels in the morning or early in the week, try to schedule attention-demanding activities and encounters during those times. If you find your attention wandering, practice **mental bracketing**—systematically putting aside thoughts that aren't relevant to the interaction at hand. When irrelevant thoughts arise, let them pass through your conscious awareness and drift away, without allowing them to occupy your attention fully.

UNDERSTANDING

While serving with her National Guard unit in Iraq, Army Specialist Claudia Carreon suffered a traumatic brain injury (TBI).[1] The injury wiped her memory clean. She could no longer remember major events or people from her past, including her husband and her 2-year-old daughter. However, because she seemed physically normal, her TBI went unnoticed and she returned to duty. A few weeks later, Carreon received an order from a commanding officer, but she couldn't understand it and shortly afterward forgot it. She was subsequently demoted for "failure to follow an order." When Army doctors realized that she wasn't being willfully disobedient but instead simply couldn't understand or remember orders, her rank was restored, and Carreon was rushed to the Army's Polytrauma Center in Palo Alto, California. Now Carreon, like many other veterans who have suffered TBIs, carries with her captioned

---

[1]The information that follows is adapted from www.braininjurymn.org/library/archive/NewWarsHallmarkInjury.pdf, retrieved October 12, 2011.

▶ Some people who have long-term memory impairment use captioned photos to supplement their memory. Without this help, they would not be able to compare new information with previous knowledge, prohibiting them from fully understanding the messages they receive. Jose Luis Pelaez Inc/Getty Images

skills practice

Elevating Attention
Focusing your attention during interpersonal encounters

❶ Identify an important person whom you find it difficult to listen to.

❷ List factors—fatigue, time pressure—that impede your attention when you're interacting with this person.

❸ Before your next encounter with the individual, address factors you can control.

❹ During the encounter, increase the person's salience by reminding yourself of his or her importance to you.

❺ As the encounter unfolds, practice mental bracketing to stay focused on your partner's communication.

photos of loved ones and a special handheld personal computer to help her remember people and make sense of everyday conversations.

The challenges faced by Claudia Carreon illustrate the essential role that memory plays in shaping the third stage of listening. **Understanding** involves interpreting the meaning of another person's communication by comparing newly received information against our past knowledge (Macrae & Bodenhausen, 2001). Whenever you receive and attend to new information, you place it in your **short-term memory**—the part of your mind that temporarily houses the information while you seek to understand its meaning. While the new information sits in your short-term memory, you call up relevant knowledge from your **long-term memory**—the part of your mind devoted to permanent information storage. You then compare relevant prior knowledge from your long-term memory with the new information in your short-term memory to create understanding. In Claudia Carreon's case, her long-term memory was largely erased by her injury. Consequently, whenever she hears new information, she has no foundation from which to make sense of it.

RESPONDING

You're spending the afternoon at your apartment discussing your plans for a cross-country road trip with your friends, John and Sarah. You want them to help you with logistical details as well as ideas for interesting places to visit. As you talk, John looks directly at you, smiles, nods his head, and leans forward. He also asks questions and offers up some kitschy Americana attractions. Sarah, in contrast, seems completely uninterested. She alternates between looking at the people strolling by your living-room window and texting on her phone. She also sits with her body half-turned away from you and leans back in her chair. You become frustrated because it's obvious that John is listening closely and Sarah isn't listening at all.

What leads you to conclude that John is listening and Sarah isn't? It's the way your friends are **responding**—communicating their attention and understanding to you. Responding is the fourth stage of the listening process. When you actively listen, you do more than simply attend and understand. You also convey your attention and understanding to others by clearly and constructively responding through positive feedback, paraphrasing, and clarifying (McNaughton et al., 2007).

Feedback Critical to active listening is using verbal and nonverbal behaviors known as **feedback** to communicate attention and understanding *while* others are talking. Scholars distinguish between two kinds of feedback: positive and negative (Wolvin & Coakley, 1996). When you use positive feedback, like John in our earlier example, you look directly at the person speaking, smile, position your body so that you're facing him or her, avoid using electronic devices, and lean forward. You may also offer **back-channel cues,** verbal and nonverbal behaviors such as nodding and making comments—like "Uh-huh," "Yes," and "That makes sense"—that signal you've paid attention to and understood specific comments (Duncan & Fiske, 1977). All of these behaviors combine to show speakers that you're actively listening. In contrast, people who use negative feedback, like Sarah in our example, send a very different message to speakers: "I'm not interested in

self-reflection

Is the provision of positive feedback limited to face-to-face or phone conversations? How does communicating through mobile devices constrain your ability to provide positive feedback? For example, if a friend shares bad news with you via text message, what can you do to show him or her that you're actively listening?

▲ In many Protestant churches, it is perfectly acceptable for audience members to express their feedback loudly during the minister's sermon by shouting "Amen!" or "Hallelujah!" The same type of positive feedback would be radically inappropriate in a traditional Catholic church. (Left) © Philip Gould/Corbis; (right) © Jason Lee/Reuters/Corbis

paying attention to you or understanding what you're saying." Behaviors that convey negative feedback include avoiding eye contact, turning your body away, looking bored or distracted, using electronic devices, and not using back-channel cues.

The type of feedback we provide while we're listening has a dramatic effect on speakers (Wolvin & Coakley, 1996). Receiving positive feedback from listeners can enhance a speaker's confidence and generate positive emotions. Negative feedback can cause speakers to hesitate, make speech errors, or stop altogether to see what's wrong and why we're not listening.

To effectively display positive feedback during interpersonal encounters, try four simple suggestions (Barker, 1971; Daly, 1975). First, make your feedback obvious. No matter how actively you listen, unless others perceive your feedback, they won't view you as actively listening. Second, make your feedback appropriate. Different situations, speakers, and messages require more or less intensity of positive feedback. Third, make your feedback clear by avoiding behaviors that might be mistaken as negative feedback. For example, something as simple as innocently stealing a glance at your phone to see what time it is might unintentionally suggest that you're bored or wish the person would stop speaking. Finally, always provide feedback quickly in response to what the speaker has just said.

Paraphrasing and Clarifying Active listeners also communicate attention and understanding through saying things *after* their conversational partners have finished their turns—things that make it clear they were listening. One way to do this is by **paraphrasing**, summarizing others' comments after they have finished speaking ("My read on your message is that . . ." or "You seem to be saying that . . ."). This practice can help you check the accuracy of your understanding during both

**Media Note:
Active Listening on *The Office***

In season 9, episode 7, of the TV show *The Office*, Dwight's coworkers try to teach him tips for more effective active listening. The coworkers offer humorous, yet helpful, suggestions on feedback and back-channeling cues to improve Dwight's workplace relationships and sales performance. Discuss the importance of feedback in the listening process.

Teaching Tip: Note Taking and Paraphrasing

Students often struggle with listening carefully and taking accurate class notes while paraphrasing the key ideas. Ask for volunteers to share their notes from a class. Review the notes and encourage the best note takers to share their strategies for success. Students will be surprised by how differently each person takes notes and by how much they can learn from classmates.

skills practice

Responding Online
Responding effectively during online encounters

❶ Identify an online interaction that's important.

❷ During the exchange, provide your conversational partner with immediate, positive feedback to his or her messages, sending short responses like "I agree!" and attaching positive emoticons.

❸ Check your understanding by paraphrasing your partner's longer messages ("My read on your last message is . . .").

❹ Seek clarification regarding messages you don't understand ("I'm having trouble understanding. Would you mind explaining that a bit more?").

---

face-to-face and online encounters. Paraphrasing should be used judiciously, however. Some conversational partners may find paraphrasing annoying if you use it a lot or they view it as contrived. Paraphrasing can also lead to conversational lapses—silences of three seconds or longer that participants perceive as awkward (McLaughlin & Cody, 1982).

Paraphrasing can cause lapses because when you paraphrase, you do nothing to usefully advance the conversational topic forward in new and interesting ways (Heritage & Watson, 1979). Instead, you simply rehash what has already been said. Consequently, the only relevant response your conversational partner can provide is a simple acknowledgment, such as "Yeah" or "Uh-huh." In such cases, a lapse is likely to ensue immediately after, unless one of you has a new topic ready to introduce to advance the conversation. This is an important practical concern for anyone interested in being perceived as interpersonally competent, because the more lapses that occur, the more likely your conversational partner is to perceive you as incompetent (McLaughlin & Cody, 1982). To avoid this perception, always couple your paraphrasing with additional comments or questions that usefully build on the previous topic or take the conversation in new directions.

Of course, on some occasions, we simply don't understand what others have said. In such instances, it's perfectly appropriate to respond by seeking clarification rather than paraphrasing, saying, "I'm sorry, but could you explain that again? I want to make sure I understood you correctly." This technique not only helps you clarify the meaning of what you're hearing but also enables you to communicate your desire to understand the other person.

RECALLING

The fifth stage of listening is **recalling,** remembering information after you've received, attended to, understood, and responded to it. Recalling is a crucial part of the listening process because we judge the effectiveness of listening based on our ability to accurately recall information after we've listened to it (Thomas & Levine, 1994). Think about it: when a romantic partner asks, "Were you listening to me?" how do you demonstrate that you really were actively listening? By recalling everything that was said and reciting it back to your partner. Indeed, practically every scientific measure of listening uses recall accuracy as evidence of listening effectiveness (Janusik, 2007).

Your recall accuracy varies, depending on the situation. When people have no task other than simple memorization, recall accuracy is high. But when people are engaged in activities more complicated than straight memorization, recall accuracy plummets. That's because in such cases, we're receiving a lot of information, which increases the likelihood of perceptual and recall errors. Research on the recall accuracy of criminal eyewitnesses, for instance, has found that people frequently err in their recall of crimes, something most jurors and even the eyewitnesses themselves don't realize (Wells, Lindsay, & Tousignant, 1980). Our recall of interpersonal and relational encounters is not exempt from error. For negative and unpleasant interactions, such as conflicts, we tend to recall our own behavior as positive and constructive and the behavior of others as comparatively negative, regardless of what actually happened (Sillars, Smith, & Koerner, 2010).

How can you enhance your recall ability? One way is to use **mnemonics**, devices that aid memory. For example, when I first starting teaching yoga (more than a decade ago), I would often arrive at the studio only to find that I had forgotten something (my mat, my music, my water, my choreography journal, and so forth). So I created a simple mnemonic: "music-water-keys-mat-book." Now, each and every time before I leave for class, I always say out loud this quick checklist mnemonic, and it ensures that I arrive at my classes ready to teach!

Because listening is rooted in both visual and auditory information, and memory is enhanced by using all five senses, you can bolster your memory of an interpersonal communication encounter by linking information you've listened to with pleasant or even silly visuals, scents, or sounds. To create visual images of an interpersonal encounter, you could write detailed notes or draw diagrams documenting the contents of a conversation. You could also link a new acquaintance's name with a unique physical feature characterizing him or her. Finally, when you develop mnemonics or notes, review them repeatedly, including reciting them out loud, because repetition helps aid memory.

> **self-reflection**
>
> What's an example of a mnemonic you've created? How did you go about constructing it? Has it helped you more effectively recall important information? If not, what could be done to improve its usefulness?

The Five Functions of Listening

Adapting our listening purposes

On the hit NBC show *The Voice*, the judges (including Shakira, Usher, Pharrell Williams, and Gwen Stefani) spend much of each season listening. But they do so in different ways, depending on situational needs. When new contestants audition at the start of the season, the judges listen with their chairs turned away from the singers so that they can carefully scrutinize the quality of the contestants' voices (without being distracted by appearance) in order to determine whom to retain for the competition. Once contestants have been selected, the judges become coaches, and the demands on their listening broaden. They must carefully listen to comprehend what contestants tell them about themselves and their life stories to determine the best way to motivate improvement. When contestants argue against their advice, the judges must listen analytically, looking for ways to attack their reasoning and move them in different directions. When contestants give stunning performances, the judges can listen appreciatively, basking in the vocal talent displayed in that moment. And when contestants break down emotionally, the judges must shift gears yet again, listening supportively and offering encouragement.

The different reasons for listening displayed by the judges on *The Voice* mirror the five common **listening functions**, or purposes for listening, we experience daily: to comprehend, to discern, to analyze, to appreciate, and to support.

> **Discussion Prompt: Recall and the Game of Telephone**
>
> Create a short story that you can use to play the game of telephone. Stories with two or three characters and a list of items work well (e.g., gifts purchased and their prices). Ask four students to go out into the hall while you tell the story to the first student. The first student invites one of the volunteers in from the hall and tells the story to him or her. This continues until the last student in the hall returns and tells the story to the class. After enjoying the garbled message, discuss strategies for improving recall.

LISTENING TO COMPREHEND

Think for a minute about your interpersonal communication class—the course for which this text was assigned. When you're attending class, *why* do you listen to your professor? The answer is so obvious it's silly: you listen so that you can comprehend the information he or she is presenting to you. When you listen for this purpose, you work to accurately interpret and store the information you

◯ Each season on *The Voice*, the judges hold "blind auditions," in which they turn their chairs away from the stage and judge contestants based solely on sound. By relying exclusively on listening, they more accurately form impressions of the singers' voices.
NBC/Photofest

receive, so you can correctly recall it later. Additional examples of this type of listening include listening to a coworker explain how to use a software application at work and listening to a prospective landlord explain your contractual obligations if you sign a lease on an apartment.

LISTENING TO DISCERN

When you listen to discern, you focus on distinguishing one sound from another. The most common form is to listen carefully to someone's vocal tone to assess mood and stress level. For example, if you're concerned that your romantic partner is angry with you, you might listen carefully to the sound of his or her voice, rather than the actual words, to gauge how upset he or she is.

LISTENING TO ANALYZE

When you listen to analyze, you carefully evaluate the message you're receiving, and you judge it. For instance, you might analyze your father's neutral comments about his recent medical checkup, listening for signs of worry so you can determine whether he's hiding serious health problems.

LISTENING TO APPRECIATE

When you listen to appreciate, your goal is simply to enjoy the sounds and sights you're experiencing and then to respond by expressing your appreciation.

Common examples include listening to your child excitedly share her story of the soccer goal she scored or listening while a close friend tells a funny story.

LISTENING TO SUPPORT

You're making lunch in your apartment one afternoon when your best friend calls you. You answer only to hear him sobbing uncontrollably. He tells you that he and his girlfriend just broke up because she cheated on him. He says he needs someone to talk to.

Providing comfort to a conversational partner is another common purpose for listening. To provide support through listening, you must suspend judgment—taking in what someone else says without evaluating it, and openly expressing empathy. Examples include comforting a relative after the death of a spouse or responding with a kind e-mail to a coworker who sends you a message complaining that her boss just criticized her at a team meeting.

ADAPTING YOUR LISTENING PURPOSE

The five functions that listening commonly serves are not mutually exclusive. We change between them frequently and fluidly. You might change your purpose for listening even within the same encounter. For example, you're listening with appreciation at a concert when suddenly you realize one of the musicians is out of tune. You might shift to discerning listening (trying to isolate that particular instrument from the others) and ultimately to listening to analyze (trying to assess whether you are in fact correct about its being out of tune). If the musician happens to be a friend of yours, you might even switch to supportive listening following the event, as she openly laments her disastrous performance!

An essential part of active listening is skillfully and flexibly adapting your listening purposes to the changing demands of interpersonal encounters (Bunkers, 2010). To strengthen your ability to adapt your listening purpose, heighten your awareness of the various possible listening functions during your interpersonal encounters. Routinely ask yourself, "What is my primary purpose for listening at this moment, in this situation? Do I want to comprehend, discern, analyze, appreciate, or support?" Then adjust your listening accordingly. As you do this, keep in mind that for some situations, certain approaches to listening may be unethical or simply inappropriate, like listening to analyze when a relational partner is seeking emotional support.

self-reflection

Recall a situation in which you listened the wrong way. For instance, a friend needed you to listen supportively, but you listened to analyze. What led you to make this error? What consequences ensued from your mistake? What can you do in the future to avoid such listening mishaps?

Understanding Listening Styles

Culture and gender affect listening styles

"If the person you are talking to doesn't appear to be listening, be patient. It may simply be that he has a small piece of fluff in his ear." —A. A. Milne

In the original Winnie-the-Pooh books, the character of Christopher Robin is a consistently empathic listener to whom all the other characters turn for

Though they are only characters from a children's book, Pooh and his friends illustrate the different styles of listening. Do you know people in your life who characterize the listening styles in similar ways? Which style best represents you?
Advertising Archive/Everett Collection

Assignment: Analyzing Your Listening Abilities
Ask students to take the *Self-Quiz* "Discover Your Listening Styles" and write an essay analyzing their results. Which of the listening styles do they use the most often? When do they use different styles? Which style would they like to improve on? Encourage students to conclude the essay with goals and strategies for improving their listening skills.

comfort. Whenever Pooh worries about his own ineptitude ("I am a bear of no brain at all"), Christopher Robin listens and then offers support: "You're the best bear in all the world." In contrast, Owl is Mr. Analytical. He prides himself on being wise and encourages others to bring detailed information and dilemmas to him, even if he often doesn't know the answers. Meanwhile, Rabbit just wants people to get to the point, so he can act on it. He interrupts them if they stray from the purpose of the conversation, pointedly asking, "Does it matter?" Tigger, though good natured, never seems to have the *time* to listen. When the group goes adventuring, Tigger urges the others to "Come on!" and then leaves without waiting to hear their responses.

Winnie-the-Pooh is a billion-dollar-a-year industry, and one of the few fictional characters to have a star on the Hollywood walk of fame.[2] Books about him have been translated into 34 languages. But at the heart of A. A. Milne's stories about Edward Bear (Pooh's real name) is a cast of characters who each have very different listening styles.

FOUR LISTENING STYLES

Like the characters in Milne's beloved tales, we all tend to experience habitual patterns of listening behaviors, known as **listening styles** (Barker & Watson, 2000), which reflect our attitudes, beliefs, and predispositions about listening. In general, four different listening styles exist (Bodie & Worthington, 2010). **Action-oriented listeners** want brief, to-the-point, and accurate messages from others—information they can then use to make decisions or initiate courses of action. Action-oriented listeners can grow impatient when communicating with people they perceive as disorganized, long-winded, or imprecise. For example, when faced with an upset spouse, an action-oriented listener would want information about what caused the problem, so that a solution could be generated. He or she would be less interested in hearing elaborate details of the spouse's feelings.

Time-oriented listeners prefer brief and concise encounters. They tend to let others know in advance exactly how much time they have available for each conversation. Time-oriented listeners want to stick to their allotted schedules and often look at clocks, watches, or phones to ensure this is the case (Bodie & Worthington, 2010).

In contrast, **people-oriented listeners** view listening as an opportunity to establish commonalities between themselves and others. When asked to identify the most important part of effective listening, people-oriented listeners cite

---

[2] The information that follows is adapted from Milne (1926, 1928) and The Page at Pooh Corner, www.pooh-corner.org/index.shtml

concern for other people's emotions. They strive to demonstrate empathy when listening by using positive feedback and offering supportive responses. People-oriented listeners tend to score high on measures of extraversion and overall communication competence (Villaume & Bodie, 2007).

Content-oriented listeners prefer to be intellectually challenged by the messages they receive during interpersonal encounters and enjoy receiving complex and provocative information. Content-oriented listeners often take time to carefully evaluate facts and details before forming an opinion about information they've heard. Of the four listening styles, content-oriented listeners are the most likely to ask speakers clarifying or challenging questions (Bodie & Worthington, 2010).

Our listening styles are learned early in life by observation and interaction with parents and caregivers, gender socialization (learning about how men and women are "supposed" to listen), and cultural values regarding what counts as effective listening (Barker & Watson, 2000). Through constant practice, our listening styles become deeply entrenched as part of our communication routines. As a consequence, most of us use only one or two listening styles in all of our interpersonal interactions (Chesebro, 1999). One study found that 36.1 percent of people reported exclusively using a single listening style across all their interpersonal encounters; an additional 24.8 percent reported that they never use more than two listening styles (Watson, Barber, & Weaver, 1995). We also resist attempts to switch from our dominant styles, even when those styles are ill-suited to the situation at hand. This can cause others to perceive us as insensitive, inflexible, and even incompetent communicators.

To be an active listener, you have to use all four styles, so you can strategically deploy each of them as needed. For example, in situations in which your

macmillanhighered.com/reflectrelate4e

Action-Oriented Listeners
Watch this clip online to answer the questions below.

How does the boss in this video signal his listening style? Be specific. When have you been an action-oriented listener? Why did you choose that approach?

Want to see more? Check out LaunchPad for clips on **time-oriented listeners** and **content-oriented listeners.**

◉ In this photo from the filming of the movie *Selma* (2014), actor David Oyelowo listens to director Ava DuVernay as she explains the type of performance that she wants in a scene. Using a content-oriented listening style can be very effective in work situations in which your primary goal is to comprehend. Atsushi Nishijima/© Paramount Pictures/Everett Collection

Assignment: Listening Styles

Ask students to watch the three LaunchPad clips on **action-oriented listeners, time-oriented listeners,** and **content-oriented listeners** after reading about listening styles on pages 173–176. Students should then write a one-page paper on the listening style that best fits their behavior, answering the following: What style do you use the most? Please provide specific examples to illustrate your understanding of the style. How could you improve your listening skills?

Online Self-Quiz: Discover Your Listening Styles. To take this self-quiz, visit LaunchPad: macmillanhighered.com /reflectrelate4e

self-reflection

Do your preferred listening styles match research on male–female differences? How have your listening styles affected your communication with people of the same gender? the opposite gender?

table 6.1 Active Listening

To be a more active listener, try these strategies:
1. Concentrate on important aspects of encounters and control factors that impede your attention.
2. Communicate your understanding to others in competent and timely ways by providing polite, obvious, appropriate, clear, and quick feedback.
3. Improve your recall abilities by using mnemonics or linking new information to other senses, visuals, or features.
4. Develop an awareness of your primary listening functions in various situations.
5. Practice shifting your listening style quickly, depending on the demands of the encounter.

primary listening function is to provide emotional support—when loved ones want to discuss feelings or turn to you for comfort—you should quickly adopt a people-oriented listening style (Barker & Watson, 2000). Studies document that use of a people-oriented listening style substantially boosts others' perceptions of your interpersonal sensitivity (Chesebro, 1999). In such encounters, use of a content-, time-, or action-oriented style would likely be perceived as incompetent.

By contrast, if your dominant listening function is to comprehend—for instance, during a training session at work—you'll need to use a content-oriented listening style. Similarly, if you're talking with someone who is running late for an appointment or who has to make a decision quickly, you should use a more time- or action-oriented style. For additional tips on how to improve your active listening, see Table 6.1.

GENDER DIFFERENCES IN LISTENING STYLES

Studies have found that women and men differ in their listening-style preferences and practices (Watson et al., 1995). Women are more likely than men to use people-oriented and content-oriented listening styles, and men are more likely to use time-oriented and action-oriented styles. These findings have led researchers to conclude that men (in general) tend to have a task-oriented and hurried approach to listening, whereas women perceive listening as an intellectual, an emotional, and, ultimately, a relational activity.

Keeping these differences in mind during interpersonal encounters is an important part of active listening. When interacting with men, observe the listening styles they display, and adapt your style to match theirs. Don't be surprised if time- or action-oriented styles emerge the most. When conversing with women, follow the same pattern, carefully watching their listening styles and adjusting your style accordingly. Be prepared to quickly shift to more people- or content-oriented styles if needed. But don't automatically assume

focus on CULTURE

Men Just Don't Listen!

The belief that men are listening-challenged is widespread. Linguist Deborah Tannen (1990a) posits that the perception of male listening incompetence stems from several sources, including men facing away rather than toward people when listening, making dismissive comments in response to disclosures, changing conversational topics too rapidly, and listening silently rather than providing vocal back-channel cues such as "Mm-hmm" and "Yeah." But at a broader level, Tannen believes that male listening is symptomatic of *cultural* differences between the sexes. As she elaborates,

> For women, intimacy is the fabric of relationships, and talk is the thread from which it is woven. Bonds between boys are based less on talking, more on doing things together. Boys' groups are more hierarchical, so boys must struggle to avoid the subordinate position. This may play a role in women's complaints that men don't listen. Some men really don't like to listen, because being the listener makes them feel one-down, like a child listening to adults.

What's the solution? Tannen recommends that men and women view "their differences as cross-cultural rather than right or wrong."

Cognitive scientists and communication scholars offer an alternative view. Analyzing data from dozens of studies, brain researcher Daniel Voyer (2011) found only small differences between the sexes in their listening, so small that they can't be generalized to individual women and men. Communication researchers Daena Goldsmith and Patricia Fulfs (1999) examined every sex difference suggested by Tannen and found no scientific evidence supporting them. After reviewing existing communication studies, scholar Kathryn Dindia (2006) agreed with Fulfs and Goldsmith, concluding that "the empirical evidence indicates that differences between women and men are minimal by any measure." Dindia noted that "North American girls and boys are raised in the same culture, but that culture teaches them that they are very different. In spite of this, they turn out remarkably similar." Dindia goes on to suggest a different metaphor for thinking about sex differences. When it comes to interpersonal communication and listening, "Men are from North Dakota, women are from South Dakota. Women and men do not come from different planets or different cultures, they come from neighboring states."

discussion questions

- Do men and women grow up in different communication cultures, as Tannen suggests? Or, as Dindia argues, is it the same culture, in which they are repeatedly taught about how different they are?
- In your experience, do men and women listen differently? If so, what differences have you observed? Is one sex inherently better at listening than the other, or is it a matter of individual style rather than a general sex difference?

---

that just because a person is female or male means that she or he will always listen—or expect you to listen—in certain ways. Take your cue from the person you are talking with.

CULTURE AND LISTENING STYLES

Culture powerfully shapes the use and perception of listening styles. What's considered effective listening by one culture is often perceived as ineffective by others, something you should always keep in mind when communicating with people from other cultures. For example, in individualistic cultures such as the

United States and Canada (and particularly in the American workplace), time-oriented and action-oriented listening styles dominate. People often approach conversations with an emphasis on time limits ("I have only 10 minutes to talk"). Many people also feel and express frustration if others don't communicate their ideas efficiently ("Just say it!").

The value that people from individualistic cultures put on time and efficiency—something we discuss in Chapter 5—frequently places them at odds with people from other cultures. In collectivistic cultures, people- and content-oriented listening is emphasized. In many East Asian countries, for example, Confucian teachings admonish followers to pay close attention when listening, display sensitivity to others' feelings, and be prepared to assimilate complex information—hallmarks of people- and content-oriented listening styles (Chen & Chung, 1997). Studies have found that students from outside the United States view Americans as less willing and patient listeners than individuals who come from Africa, Asia, South America, and southern Europe—regions that emphasize people-oriented listening (Wolvin, 1987).

Preventing Incompetent Listening

Avoiding the most common listening pitfalls

No one is a perfect active listener all the time. At one time or another we all make errors during the listening process, fail to identify the right purpose for listening during an interpersonal encounter, or neglect to use the appropriate listening style. In previous sections of this chapter, we discussed ways to avoid such errors. But being an active listener also means systematically avoiding five notoriously incompetent types of listening.

SELECTIVE LISTENING

A colleague stops by your office to chat and shares exciting news: a coworker to whom you're romantically attracted is similarly interested in you. As your thoughts become riveted on this revelation, the remainder of what he says fades from your awareness, including important information he shares with you about an upcoming project deadline.

Perhaps the greatest challenge to active listening is overcoming **selective listening,** taking in only those bits and pieces of information that are immediately salient during an interpersonal encounter and dismissing the rest. When we selectively listen, we rob ourselves of the opportunity to learn information from others that may affect important personal or professional outcomes, such as a missed project deadline.

Selective listening is difficult to avoid because it is the natural result of fluctuating attention and salience. To overcome selective listening, you shouldn't

---

Media Note:
Selective Listening

During the 2007 Miss Teen USA pageant, Miss Teen South Carolina became a victim of her own selective listening. As she became anxious during her interview, she inappropriately selected information from her stockpile of knowledge and rehearsed answers. Ask students to share their experiences with selective listening. How has this caused them to communicate inappropriately or to make incorrect decisions?

---

self-reflection

What personal and professional consequences have you suffered because of your selective listening? What factors led you to selectively listen in those situations? How could you have overcome those factors to listen more actively?

▶ In the TV show *Girls*, Hannah, Shoshanna, and Jessa suffer frequent conflicts because they fail to actively listen to each other. Josiah Kamau/BuzzFoto/FilmMagic/Getty Images

strive to learn how to listen to everything all at once. Instead, seek to slowly and steadily broaden the range of information you can actively attend to during your encounters with others. The best way to do this is by improving your overall level of attention through practicing the techniques for enhancing attention discussed earlier in this chapter. Through these means, you boost your chances of noticing information that has important short- and long-term consequences for your personal and professional relationships.

EAVESDROPPING

In *Wuthering Heights*, Emily Brontë's classic tale of romance and vengeance, a major turning point occurs when Heathcliff eavesdrops on a conversation between his lover, Catherine, and Nelly, the story's narrator. Heathcliff's interpretation of Catherine's comments cause him to abandon her, setting in motion a tragic series of events that lead to Catherine's death:

> "It would degrade me to marry Heathcliff, now; so he shall never know how I love him; and that, not because he's handsome, Nelly, but because he's more myself than I am. Whatever our souls are made of, his and mine are the same." Ere this speech ended I became sensible of Heathcliff's presence. Having noticed a slight movement, I turned my head, and saw him rise from the bench, and steal out, noiselessly. He had listened till he heard Catherine say it would degrade her to marry him, and then he staid to hear no farther. (Brontë, 1995, p. 80)

We often assume that our conversations occur in isolation and that the people standing, sitting, or walking around the participants can't hear the exchange. But they can. As sociologist Erving Goffman (1979) noted, the presence of other individuals within the auditory and visual range of a conversation should be considered the rule and not the exception. This is the case even with phone conversations, tweeting, e-mail, and texting. Most cell-phone conversations occur with others in the immediate proximity, and tweets, e-mail, and texting are no more secure than old-fashioned postcards.

When people intentionally and systematically set up situations so that they can listen to private conversations, they are **eavesdropping** (Goffman, 1979). People eavesdrop for a host of reasons: desire to find out if someone is sharing personally, professionally, or legally incriminating information; suspicion that others are talking behind their backs; or even simple curiosity. Eavesdropping is both inappropriate and unethical (hence, incompetent) because it robs others of their right to privacy and disrespects their decision to not share certain information with you. Perhaps not surprisingly, the social norms governing this behavior are powerful. If people believe that you eavesdropped on a conversation, they will typically be upset and angry, and they may threaten reprisals.

Eavesdropping can be personally damaging as well. People occasionally say spiteful or hurtful things that they don't really mean simply to impress others, fit in, or draw attention to themselves. As the *Wuthering Heights* example illustrates, if you happen to eavesdrop on such conversations, the result can be personally

---

Media Note: Eavesdropping

Have students view and discuss the popular blog overheardinnewyork.com, created to document parts of conversations that are overheard by passersby in New York City. Discuss whether or not hearing another's conversation unintentionally constitutes eavesdropping. How can eavesdropping lead to misunderstanding and misperceptions?

and relationally devastating—especially if you take pieces of what you've heard out of context. The lesson is clear: don't eavesdrop, no matter how tempting it might be.

PSEUDO-LISTENING

You stayed up late the night before to finish a course paper, and when you finally got to bed, your apartment roommates were being so loud they kept you up most of the rest of the night. Now it's the afternoon and you're sitting in a warm and cozy coffeehouse, listening to your friend tell you a story she's shared with you several times previously. Try as you might, you find yourself fading. But you don't want to embarrass yourself or your friend, so you do your best to play the part of an active listener—maintaining good eye contact, nodding your head, and contributing appropriate responses when needed.

You're engaging in **pseudo-listening,** behaving as if you're paying attention though you're really not. Pseudo-listening is obviously an ineffective way to listen because it prevents you from attending to or understanding information coming from the other person, so you can't recall the encounter later. Pseudo-listening is also somewhat unethical because it's deceptive. To be sure, occasional instances of pseudo-listening to veil fatigue or protect a friend's feelings (such as in our example) are understandable. But if you continually engage in pseudo-listening during your encounters with others, eventually they will realize what's going on and conclude that you're dishonest or disrespectful. Consequently, pseudo-listening should be avoided.

AGGRESSIVE LISTENING

People who engage in **aggressive listening** (also called *ambushing*) attend to what others say solely to find an opportunity to attack their conversational partners. For example, your friend may routinely ask for your opinions regarding fashion and music, but then disparages your tastes when you share them with her. Or your romantic partner may encourage you to share your feelings, but then mocks your feelings when you do share them.

The personal, interpersonal, and relational costs of aggressive listening are substantial. People who consistently use listening to ambush others typically think less favorably about themselves (Infante & Wigley, 1986), experience lower marital satisfaction (Payne & Sabourin, 1990), and may experience more physical violence in their relationships (Infante, Chandler, & Rudd, 1989).

Some people engage in aggressive listening online. Known as **provocateurs,** they post messages designed solely to annoy others. They wait for people to post responses, and then they attack the responses. If the attacks of a provocateur are sophisticated enough, naïve group members may side with him or her against participants who seek to oust the instigator from the group. The result can be a flame war that prompts the site manager to shut down the discussion group—the ultimate victory for a provocateur.

Discussion Prompt: Incompetent Listening
Play the three LaunchPad clips on incompetent listening: **selective listening, aggressive listening,** and **narcissistic listening.** Then place students in groups to create role plays (or their own videos) of eavesdropping and pseudo-listening. Discuss strategies for dealing with all five incompetent listening styles and ways for developing improved active listening skills.

macmillanhighered.com /reflectrelate4e

Aggressive Listening
Watch this clip online to answer the questions below.

How does aggressive listening affect the communication in this scene? Is there a person in your life who regularly uses an aggressive listening style? How do you handle interactions with this person?

Want to see more? Check out LaunchPad for clips on **selective listening** and **narcissistic listening.**

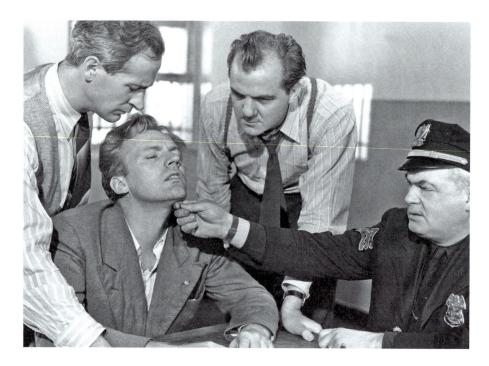

▶ The good cop/bad cop scenario is something we have all seen on television and in movies. The "bad cop" succeeds only if the "good cop" listens well enough to draw information out of the intimidated person both are interrogating. The bad cop's aggressive listening style is unlikely to work on its own. 20th Century Fox/The Kobal Collection/Art Resource

skills practice

Managing Aggressive Listening
Dealing skillfully with an aggressive listener

❶ When someone is using aggressive listening with you, stay calm.

❷ Allow the person to talk, without interruption or challenge.

❸ Express empathy, saying, "I'm sorry you feel that way."

❹ Avoid retaliating with negative comments, as they will only escalate the aggression.

❺ If the person continues to set you up for verbal attacks, end the encounter, saying, "I'm sorry, but I don't feel comfortable continuing this conversation."

If you find yourself habitually listening in an aggressive fashion, combat this type of incompetent listening by discovering and dealing with the root causes of your aggression. Oftentimes, external pressures, such as job stress, relationship challenges, or family problems, can play a role, so be careful to consider all possible causes and solutions for your behavior. Don't hesitate to seek professional assistance if you think it would be helpful. If you're in a personal or professional relationship with someone who uses aggressive listening with you, deal with that person by following the recommendations for addressing verbal aggression outlined in Chapter 7. Limit your interactions when possible, be polite and respectful, and use a people-oriented listening style. Avoid retaliating by using aggressive listening yourself because it will only escalate the aggression.

NARCISSISTIC LISTENING

In Greek mythology, the beautiful nymph Echo falls in love with Narcissus immediately upon seeing him (Bulfinch, 1985). But when she approaches and moves to throw her arms around him, he recoils, telling her that he would rather die than be with her. Heartbroken, Echo flees to the mountains and plots her revenge. She casts a spell on Narcissus, making him fall in love with his own reflected image in a pool. Upon seeing the enchanted image, Narcissus can't tear himself away. He abandons all thought of food and rest, and gazes at himself, entranced, until he finally dies of starvation.

Like its namesake in Greek mythology, **narcissistic listening** is self-absorbed listening: the perpetrator ignores what others have to say and redirects the conversation to him- or herself and his or her own interests. People who engage in narcissistic listening provide positive feedback as long as they are the center of conversational attention, but the moment the topic switches to something other than them, they give negative feedback. In some cases, the negative feedback may be extreme—narcissistic listeners may pout, whine, or even throw tantrums when the conversation switches away from them and onto the other person (Bushman & Baumeister, 1998). To avoid narcissistic listening, allow the conversation to focus on topics other than you and your own interests and offer positive feedback when such topics are discussed.

The Gift of Active Listening

[Active listening creates interpersonal opportunities]

When we are newborns struggling to make sense of a world filled with mysterious noises, we quickly learn to listen. Long before we recognize written words as having meaning, and long before we can produce our own words, we come to understand the words of others. Our lives as interpersonal communicators begin at that point.

It is ironic, then, that this first communicative gift shared by human beings—the gift of listening—poses so many challenges for us when we reach adulthood. We struggle with listening in part because it is exceptionally demanding. Active listening requires dedication to mastering knowledge, hard work in practicing skills, and the motivation to continually improve.

Yet when we surmount the challenges of active listening by focusing our attention, training our memories, adapting our listening styles, and avoiding incompetent listening, an amazing thing happens. The activity that we originally mistook as passive begins to crackle with the energy of opportunity. For when we actively listen, the words and worlds of others wash over us, providing us with rich and unanticipated opportunities to move beyond the constraints of our own thoughts and beliefs and to forge interpersonal connections with others.

self-reflection

How do you feel when people use narcissistic listening with you? Have you ever listened in a narcissistic way? If so, why? Is narcissistic listening always incompetent, or is it acceptable in certain circumstances?

Media Note: Narcissistic Listening

View the clip from *That '70s Show* (season 1, episode 2, "Eric's Birthday") in which Kelso, a narcissistic listener, ignores what his friends are saying and redirects the conversation to himself and his interests. Encourage students to share other examples of narcissistic listeners and reflect on their *own* potential tendencies to engage in narcissistic listening.

○ The ability to listen begins to develop well before we are born and serves us throughout our lives. (Left to right) Bernd Opitz/Getty Images; © Lucidio Studio Inc./Corbis; Somos/Punchstock/Getty Images; Photodisc/Alamy

making relationship choices

Listening When You Don't Want To

1 BACKGROUND

One of the most difficult listening situations you will face is when you feel obligated to listen to information that makes you uncomfortable. To understand how you might competently manage such a relationship challenge, read the case study in Part 2; then, drawing on all you know about interpersonal communication, work through the problem-solving model in Part 3.

 Visit LaunchPad to check out the other side of the story (Part 4). For the best experience, complete all parts in LaunchPad: **macmillanhighered.com /reflectrelate4e**.

2 CASE STUDY

Growing up, you and your twin sister, Ana, were extremely close. As you've gotten older, however, the differences between you two have widened. Ana is a free spirit and never sticks with anything—be it a college major or a romantic interest—for very long. You are much more concerned with conventional notions of success. You plan to finish your degree in four years, have a steady paycheck and a mortgage, and get married before you turn 30.

Lately, you and Ana have been arguing about Ana's friendship with Seneca. You find Seneca to be organized and ambitious, qualities that you hope rub off on Ana. But you still find yourself uncomfortable and awkward around Seneca. Ana says that it's because Seneca is a lesbian and that you have "old-fashioned" values. You get mad at Ana for saying this, but truth be told, you're not entirely sure she's wrong.

Over the past few months, you've started to wonder if Ana might have a romantic interest in Seneca. On several occasions, it seemed as if she wanted to start a conversation with you about this, but in each case, you've dodged the topic or come up with a reason not to listen.

You and Ana are both home on break. One night, Seneca calls the home phone because Ana's cell-phone battery is dead. You yell upstairs to Ana to pick up the cordless phone in her bedroom, but instead of hanging up the other line, you listen in. You know you shouldn't, but your curiosity gets the best of you. After a few minutes, it becomes clear that Ana and Seneca are lovers. What's more, their conversation centers around their decision to move in together after break.

Coming downstairs after the call, Ana finds you in shock. She says, "You should know that I'm moving into Seneca's apartment next semester. She needs a roommate, and I was looking for a place to live anyway."

A million things race through your mind, including your sister's secrecy in not telling you the truth about her relationship with Seneca. Do you tell her you know the truth, even though it will reveal your eavesdropping, and attack her decision? offer support, and tell her that you're finally ready to listen to her? refuse to listen altogether, and change the topic? Seeing your face, Ana scowls and angrily snaps, "Did you hear me? What's your problem!?"

3 YOUR TURN

Think about all you've learned thus far about interpersonal communication. Then work through the following five steps. Remember, there are no "right" answers, so think hard about what is the *best* choice! (P.S. Need help? See the *Helpful Concepts* list.)

step 1
Reflect on yourself. What are your thoughts and feelings in this situation? Are your impressions and attributions accurate?

step 2
Reflect on your partner. Using perspective-taking and empathic concern, put yourself in Ana's shoes. What is she thinking and feeling in this situation?

step 3
Identify the optimal outcome. Think about your communication and relationship with Ana and all that has happened in this situation (including your decision to eavesdrop). What's the best, most constructive relationship outcome possible? Consider what's best for you and for Ana.

step 4
Locate the roadblocks. Taking into consideration your own and Ana's thoughts and feelings and all that has happened in this situation, what obstacles are keeping you from achieving the optimal outcome?

step 5
Chart your course. What can you say to Ana to overcome the roadblocks you've identified and achieve your optimal outcome?

HELPFUL CONCEPTS

Positive and negative feedback, **168–169**

Listening to analyze, **172**

People-oriented listening, **174–175**

Eavesdropping, **180–181**

Psuedo-listening, **181**

4 THE OTHER SIDE

▶ Visit LaunchPad to watch a video in which Ana tells her side of the case study story. As in many real-life situations, this is information to which you did not have access when you were initially crafting your response in Part 3. The video reminds us that even when we do our best to offer competent responses, there is always another side to the story that we need to consider.

POSTSCRIPT

We began this chapter with an iconic gentleman dressed in a red suit. Millions of children around the world line up each year to talk with Santa, and within each of those precious encounters, Santa not only listens but *shows* that he is listening.

Who in your life lines up to wait for a chance to talk with you? When others come to you in anticipation, hoping to be heard, do you offer a metaphorical (or literal) knee to sit on? Do you encourage them, "Tell me . . . ," and then patiently and attentively listen as they share their thoughts, feelings, and desires?

We often count on others to listen to us, forgetting that active listening works both ways. But when we embrace active listening as something that we ourselves do—not just something we count on others to do—we create a safe space within which people will share themselves with us and, through that point of connection, create trust and kinship.

LaunchPad for *Reflect & Relate* offers videos and encourages self-assessment through adaptive quizzing. Go to **macmillanhighered .com/reflectrelate4e** to get access to:

 LearningCurve Adaptive Quizzes

 Video clips that help you understand interpersonal communication

key terms

listening, 163
hearing, 164
receiving, 164
attending, 165
mental bracketing, 167
understanding, 168
short-term memory, 168
long-term memory, 168
responding, 168
feedback, 168
back-channel cues, 168
paraphrasing, 169
recalling, 170
mnemonics, 171
listening functions, 171
listening styles, 174
▶ action-oriented listeners, 174
▶ time-oriented listeners, 174
people-oriented listeners, 174
▶ content-oriented listeners, 175
▶ selective listening, 178
eavesdropping, 180
pseudo-listening, 181
▶ aggressive listening, 181
provocateurs, 181
▶ narcissistic listening, 183

▶ You can watch brief, illustrative videos of these terms and test your understanding of the concepts in LaunchPad.

key concepts

Listening: A Five-Step Process

- **Listening** is an active and complex process. The first step of listening is **receiving,** which involves "seeing" or **hearing** the communication of others.
- A critical part of active listening is **attending** to information by being alert to it. To improve your attention skills, you should limit multitasking, control factors that impede attention, and practice **mental bracketing.**
- **Understanding** the meaning of others' communication requires us to compare information in our **short-term memory** and **long-term memory,** using prior knowledge to evaluate the meaning of new information.
- Active listening requires **responding** to the communication of others in clear and constructive ways. Indications of effective responding include positive **feedback** and the use of **back-channel cues. Paraphrasing** can also help you convey understanding, but if you use it extensively during face-to-face encounters, your partners may find it annoying.
- Listening effectiveness is often measured in terms of our **recalling** ability.

The Five Functions of Listening

- Even during a single interpersonal encounter, you will likely have multiple purposes for listening, known as **listening functions.**
- The five functions are *listening to comprehend*, *listening to discern*, *listening to analyze*, *listening to appreciate*, and *listening to support*.

Understanding Listening Styles

- Most people have one or two dominant **listening styles.** The four most common styles are **people-, action-, content-,** and **time-oriented** listening. Both gender and culture impact listening styles.

Preventing Incompetent Listening

- **Selective listening** is a natural result of fluctuating attention.
- **Eavesdropping** is an especially destructive form of listening and can have serious consequences.
- If you use **pseudo-listening** deliberately to deceive others, you're behaving unethically.
- Some people use **aggressive listening** to attack others.
- People who engage in **narcissistic listening** seek to turn the focus of the conversation back to themselves.

chapter review

7 Communicating Verbally

LearningCurve can help you review the material in this chapter. Go to LaunchPad: macmillanhighered.com/reflectrelate4e

Verbal communication opens doorways to shared understanding, intimacy, and enduring relationships.

"**The game** is pretty near up," George Washington wrote his cousin in 1776.[1] His army had suffered several devastating defeats, and the British had taken New York City. With only 3,000 of his original 20,000 troops remaining, Washington retreated to the Delaware River. There, his troops hunkered down in the snow, sick and fatigued. Ten miles upstream, on the opposing shore, lay the city of Trenton—and a British garrison filled with Hessians (German mercenaries).

The morning of Christmas Eve, Congressman Benjamin Rush paid Washington a visit, hoping to lift his spirits. During their conversation, Washington furiously scribbled on scraps of paper. Seeing one fall to the floor—and thinking perhaps they were notes to loved ones—Rush picked it up. He was surprised to see only three words: "Victory or Death." It was Washington's password to his officers for an assault on Trenton.

Washington's plan was audacious and unprecedented: he would launch a surprise attack on Christmas Day. The risks were enormous. With so few men left, if the ploy failed, the war would be lost, and with it, the dream of a free and independent "United States." The odds of success were minimal. Washington's troops would have to navigate the turbulent, ice-packed river with horses, equipment, and weapons, at night, then hike 10 miles through the snow to attack a heavily fortified encampment filled with highly trained troops.

---

[1] All information in this section is adapted from Randall (1998) and Rothbard (1999).

Washington Crossing the Delaware River, 25th December 1776, 1851 (oil on canvas) (copy of an original painted in 1848), Leutze, Emanuel Gottlieb (1816–68)/ Metropolitan Museum of Art, New York, USA/The Bridgeman Art Library

7 / Communicating Verbally

But Washington had a secret motivational weapon. Five days earlier, intellectual and revolutionary Thomas Paine had penned "The American Crisis," an essay that opened with the following words:

> These are the times that try men's souls. The summer soldier and the sunshine patriot will, in this crisis, shrink from the service of their country; but he that stands it now, deserves the love and thanks of man and woman. Tyranny, like hell, is not easily conquered; yet we have this consolation with us: the harder the conflict, the more glorious the triumph!

Sensing his soldiers' low morale and realizing the power of the spoken word to inspire, Washington ordered officers along the riverbank to read Paine's passage out loud to their troops before they embarked. It worked. Uplifted by the impassioned words, the troops braved the crossing without incurring any losses, despite the giant chunks of ice that surged down the river and rammed their boats.

By 4 a.m. the crossing was complete, and the troops began their cold, treacherous journey to Trenton. It took four hours to march the 10 miles. But when they arrived, they immediately attacked—and caught the sleeping Hessians and their British officers unawares. As they stormed the town, Washington's sleet- and mud-covered troops shouted, "These are the times that try men's souls!"

The battle ended quickly. The Americans suffered only four casualties, whereas 100 Hessians were killed or wounded, over 900 were taken prisoner, and the garrison and all of its weapons and supplies were confiscated. More importantly, a stunning psychological blow had been landed against the British: the "upstart colonists" could fight—and win—after all. In the months that followed, Washington prevailed in a series of similar clashes, ultimately winning the war itself and ensuring the survival of the fledgling nation.

On Christmas Day 1776, a beleaguered general put his faith in the power of verbal communication to motivate forlorn troops to cross an impassable river and attack an impregnable fortress. Centuries later, millions of people live, learn, and love in a country that exists because of those words.

In a life filled with firsts—first kiss, first job, first car—it's a first we don't even remember. But it's celebrated by the people around us, who recognize in that fleeting moment the dawning of a life filled with language. Our first word drops from our mouths as the simplest of monosyllables: "cup," "dog," "ball." But once the sound has left our lips, the path has been irrevocably forged. By age 6, we learn more than 15 new words a day, and our vocabularies have grown to anywhere between 8,000 and 14,000 words (Cole & Cole, 1989). As we master our native tongues, we discover the power of verbal communication. By exchanging words with others through social media, via text message, over the phone, and face-to-face, we share ideas, influence others, and make relationship choices. We also learn that language can serve both constructive and destructive ends. Used constructively, verbal communication opens doorways to shared understanding, intimacy, and enduring relationships. Used destructively, verbal communication can mislead and injure others and damage our relationships.

In this chapter, we examine the nature and role of verbal communication in our lives. You'll learn:

- The defining characteristics of language
- The important functions that verbal communication serves in our interpersonal encounters and relationships
- Principles you can apply to use verbal communication more cooperatively
- The behaviors and actions that undermine cooperative verbal communication—and what can be done about them

chapter outline

191 Characteristics of Verbal Communication

196 Functions of Verbal Communication

204 Cooperative Verbal Communication

209 Barriers to Cooperative Verbal Communication

215 The Power of Verbal Communication

Characteristics of Verbal Communication

Understanding how language works

When we think of what it means to communicate, what often leaps to mind is the exchange of spoken or written language with others during interactions, known as **verbal communication**. Across any given day, we use words to communicate with others in our lives in various face-to-face or mediated contexts. During each of these encounters, we tailor our language in creative ways, depending on whom we're speaking with. We shift grammar, word choices, and sometimes even the entire language itself—for example, firing off a Spanish text message to one friend and an English text to another.

Because verbal communication is defined by our use of language, the first step toward improving our verbal communication is to deepen our understanding of language.

LANGUAGE IS SYMBOLIC

Take a quick look around you. You'll likely see a wealth of images: this book, the surface on which it (or your device) rests, and perhaps your roommate or romantic partner. You might experience thoughts and emotions related to what you're seeing—memories of your roommate asking to borrow your car or feelings of love

self-reflection

How is the language that you use different when talking with professors versus talking to your best friend or romantic partner? Which type of language makes you feel more comfortable or close to the other person? What does this tell you about the relationship between language and intimacy?

part 2 / Interpersonal Skills

▶ Whether face-to-face or online, we exchange verbal communication daily in our interactions with others.
Bloomberg via Getty Images

Chapter Theme
This chapter is about the power of verbal communication to change our lives, our relationships, and the world around us. Our most poignant and painful interpersonal experiences revolve around words shared between us and others. When we use language cooperatively, we lay the foundation on which relationships can be built and sustained. When we fall prey to language pitfalls—such as apprehension, defensive communication, aggression, and deception—we sow the verbal seeds of our own relational destruction.

toward your partner. Now imagine communicating all of this to others. To do so, you need words to represent these things: "roommate," "lover," "borrow," "car," "love," and so forth. Whenever we use items to represent other things, they are considered **symbols.** In verbal communication, words are the primary symbols that we use to represent people, objects, events, and ideas (Foss, Foss, & Trapp, 1991).

All languages are basically giant collections of symbols in the form of words that allow us to communicate with one another. When we agree with others on the meanings of words, we communicate easily. Your friend probably knows exactly what you mean by the word *roommate*, so when you use it, misunderstanding is unlikely. But some words have several possible meanings, making confusion possible. For instance, in English, the word *table* might mean a piece of furniture, an element in a textbook, or a verb referring to the need to end talk ("Let's table this discussion until our next meeting"). For words that have multiple meanings, we rely on the surrounding context to help clarify meaning. If you're in a classroom and the professor says, "Turn to Table 3 on page 47," you aren't likely to search the room for furniture.

LANGUAGE IS GOVERNED BY RULES

When we use language, we follow rules. Rules govern the meaning of words, the way we arrange words into phrases and sentences, and the order in which we exchange words with others during conversations. **Constitutive rules** define word meaning: they tell us which words represent which objects (Searle, 1965). For example, a constitutive rule in the English language is "The word *dog* refers to a domestic canine." Whenever you learn the vocabulary of a language—words and their corresponding meanings—you're learning the constitutive rules for that language.

Regulative rules govern how we use language when we verbally communicate. They're the traffic laws controlling language use—the dos and don'ts. Regulative rules guide everything from spelling ("*i* before *e* except after *c*") to sentence structure ("The article *the* or *a* must come before the noun *dog*") to conversation ("If someone asks you a question, you should answer").

To communicate competently, you must understand and follow the constitutive and regulative rules governing the language you're using. If you don't know which words represent which meanings (constitutive rules), you can't send clear messages to others or understand messages delivered by others. Likewise, without knowing how to form a grammatically correct sentence and when to say particular things (regulative rules), you can't communicate clearly with others or accurately interpret their messages to you.

LANGUAGE IS FLEXIBLE

Although all languages have constitutive and regulative rules, people often bend those rules. Partners in close relationships, for example, often create **personal idioms**—words and phrases that have unique meanings to them (Bell, Buerkel-Rothfuss, & Gore, 1987). One study found that the average romantic couple creates more than a half dozen idioms, the most common being nicknames such as Honeybear or Pookie. Such shared linguistic creativity is both reflective and reinforcing of intimacy and relationship satisfaction. For example, happily married couples report using more idioms than unhappily married couples, and partners in the early stages of marriage (i.e., the honeymoon phase) use the most idioms of all (Bruess & Pearson, 1993).

◐ L. L. Zamenhof invented Esperanto, a constructed language, in the late 19th century. It was intended to be a universal language, one that would permit easy intercultural and international communication. Although Esperanto did not originate with a nationality and remains unaligned with a place or society, it was created in a cultural context that values the goal of universal communication. © Mary Evans Picture Library/The Image Works

◐ We use words as symbols to represent objects, actions, people, places, and ideas. (Left to right) Melinda Fawver/Shutterstock; White Packert/Getty Images; Photodisc/Getty Images; © Joson/zefa/Corbis; Photodisc/Getty Images

Teaching Tip: Personal Idioms and Satisfaction

Dunleavy and Booth-Butterfield (2009) found that couples were more satisfied when partners used personal idioms, and that the use of idioms decreased when a relationship was de-escalating. Further, confrontation, nickname, and teasing-insult idioms had more negative effects on de-escalating couples than on escalating couples. Have students consider their use of personal idioms in any type of past or present close relationship. Do these findings hold true in their relationships? Why does using personal idioms increase relational satisfaction? How were idioms and intimacy linked in their relationships?

LANGUAGE IS CULTURAL

Members of a culture use language to communicate their thoughts, beliefs, attitudes, and values with one another, and thereby reinforce their collective sense of cultural identity (Whorf, 1952). Consequently, the language you speak (English, Spanish, Mandarin, Urdu), the words you choose (proper, slang, profane), and the grammar you use (formal, informal) all announce to others: "This is who I am! This is my cultural heritage!"

Each language reflects distinct sets of cultural beliefs and values. However, a large group of people within a particular culture who speak the same language may, over time, develop their own variations on that language, known as **dialects** (Gleason, 1989). Dialects may include unique phrases, words, and pronunciations (such as accents). Dialects can be shared by people living in a certain region (midwestern, southern, or northeastern United States), people with a common socioeconomic status (upper-middle-class suburban, working-class urban), or people of similar ethnic or religious ancestry (Yiddish English, Irish English, Amish English) (Chen & Starosta, 2005). Within the United States, for example, six regional dialects exist (see Figure 7.1), but the two most easily recognizable are New England and the South (Clopper, Conrey, & Pisoni, 2005). These

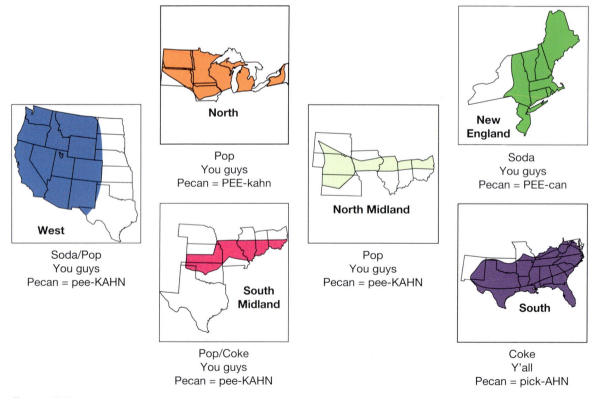

figure 7.1 Regional Dialects in the U.S. These maps show six regions of the United States that have distinct dialects. Three terms are listed beneath each region: First, the regional name for carbonated soft drinks; second, how people in the region refer to "you all" (the second-person plural); and finally, how people in each region pronounce the word "pecan."

Figures adapted from Clopper, C. G., Conrey, B., & Pisoni, D. B. (2005). Text adapted from dialect maps by Joshua Katz, http://spark.rstudio.com/jkatz/SurveyMaps/

two dialects are so distinct that most people can accurately identify them after hearing just one spoken sentence, regardless of whether the speaker is male or female (Clopper et al., 2005).

We often judge others who use dialects similar to our own as *ingroupers*, and we're inclined to make positive judgments about them as a result (Delia, 1972; Lev-Ari & Keysar, 2010). In a parallel fashion, we tend to judge those with dissimilar dialects as *outgroupers*, and make negative judgments about them. Keep this tendency in mind when you're speaking with people who don't share your dialect, and resist the temptation to make negative judgments about them. For additional ideas on dealing with ingroup or outgroup perceptions, see Chapter 3.

Media Note:
Dialectics and Soda Stats
Show your students the map of the United States at http://popvssoda.com/countystats/total-county.html, which demonstrates the various names for soft drinks based on region. Take a poll of your class to find out what word they use (*soda, Coke, pop*). What other words are regional for your students? Discuss the uniqueness of dialects and the perceptions people sometimes have of dialects.

LANGUAGE EVOLVES

Each year, the American Dialect Society selects a Word of the Year. Recent winners include *tweet*, a "short, timely message sent via the Twitter.com service," and *app*, "an abbreviated form of application, a software program for a computer or phone operating system." Even the *Oxford English Dictionary*—the resource that defines the English language—annually announces what new terms have officially been added to the English vocabulary. In 2013, this included the word *selfie* ("a photograph that one has taken of oneself, typically one taken with a smartphone or webcam and uploaded to a social media website").

◬ As technology changes, we add new words to our vocabulary, such as *iPad* and *app*. Meanwhile, other words may become associated with new meanings, such as *tablet* and *tweet*.
Richard B. Levine/Newscom

Many people view language as fixed. But in fact, language constantly changes. A particular language's constitutive rules—which define the meanings of words—may shift. As time passes and technology changes, people add new words to their language (*tweet, app, cyberbullying, sexting, selfie*) and discard old ones. Sometimes people create new phrases, such as *helicopter parent*, that eventually see wide use. Other times, speakers of a language borrow words and phrases from other languages and incorporate them into their own.

Consider how English-speakers have borrowed from other languages: If you tell friends that you want to *take* a *whirl* around the United States, you're using Norse (Viking) words; and if your trip takes you to *Wisconsin, Oregon*, and *Wyoming*, you're visiting places with Native American names.[2] If you stop at a café and request a cup of *tea* along the way, you're speaking Amoy (eastern China), but if you ask the waiter to spike your coffee with *alcohol*, you're using Arabic. If, at the end of the trip, you express an eagerness to return to your *job*,

self-reflection

Which dialect best describes your own speech? Have you ever experienced judgment from others because of the way you speak? How did you respond? If you're being honest, are there dialects that cause you to judge outgroupers negatively? How might you overcome this?

---
[2]The information regarding the origins of these words was obtained from www.krysstal.com/borrow.html (n.d.).

Media Note: Slang Words

In addition to adding new words to its dictionary each year, Merriam-Webster hosts an "open dictionary," where anyone can submit a new word: http://nws.merriam-webster.com/opendictionary/newword_display_recent.php. Share some recent submissions with students, and encourage them to share their own. Have students heard of these new words? Do all students understand and agree on the meaning for each? How do these new words come about, and what role does social media play in spreading them?

you're employing Breton (western France), but if you call in sick and tell your *manager* that you have *influenza*, you're speaking Italian.

A language's regulative rules also change. When you learned to speak and write English, for example, you were probably taught that *they* is inappropriate as a singular pronoun. But before the 1850s, people commonly used *they* as the singular pronoun for individuals whose gender was unknown—for example, "the owner went out to the stables, where they fed the horses" (Spender, 1990). In 1850, male grammarians petitioned the British Parliament to pass a law declaring that all gender-indeterminate references be labeled *he* instead of *they* (Spender, 1990). Since that time, teachers of English worldwide have taught their students that *they* used as a singular pronoun is "not proper."

Functions of Verbal Communication

Language guides our interactions

He was crowned Sportsman of the Century by *Sports Illustrated*, and Sports Personality of the Century by the BBC.[3] He is considered by many to be the greatest boxer of all time, a fact reflected in his nickname, the Greatest. He certainly was the most verbal. Muhammad Ali made a name for himself early in his career by poetically boasting about his abilities ("Your hands can't hit what your eyes can't see!") and trash-talking his opponents. "I'm going to float like a butterfly and sting like a bee," he told then champion Sonny Liston, whom Ali dubbed "the big ugly bear" before defeating him to claim the World Heavyweight title. Ali was just as verbal outside the boxing ring. Early in his professional career, he embraced Islam and subsequently abandoned his birth name of Cassius Clay

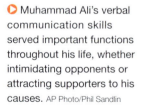

Muhammad Ali's verbal communication skills served important functions throughout his life, whether intimidating opponents or attracting supporters to his causes. AP Photo/Phil Sandlin

---

[3]The information that follows is adapted from Hauser (2006).

because the surname came from his ancestors' slave owners. Years before public sentiment joined him, Ali spoke out repeatedly against the Vietnam War. His refusal to participate in the military draft cost him both his world title and his boxing license (both of which were eventually reinstated). Years later, he continues to be outspoken on behalf of humanitarian causes. His work with UN hunger relief organizations has helped feed tens of millions of people ("Service to others is the rent you pay for your room here on earth"), and he was a United Nations Messenger of Peace and a recipient of the Presidential Medal of Freedom. Whether in the boxing ring or on a charity mission, he has used his prowess with verbal communication to achieve his goals and dreams.

We all use verbal communication to serve many different functions in our daily lives. Let's examine six of the most important of these, all of which strongly influence our interpersonal communication and relationships.

SHARING MEANING

The most obvious function verbal communication serves is enabling us to share meanings with others during interpersonal encounters. When you use language to verbally communicate, you share two kinds of meanings. The first is the literal meaning of your words, as agreed on by members of your culture, known as **denotative meaning.** Denotative meaning is what you find in dictionaries—for example, the word *bear* means "any of a family (Ursidae of the order Carnivora) of large heavy mammals of America and Eurasia that have long shaggy hair" (*Merriam-Webster Dictionary*, 2011). When Ali called Sonny Liston "the big ugly bear," he knew Liston would understand the denotative meanings of his words and interpret them as an insult.

But when we verbally communicate, we also exchange **connotative meaning:** additional understandings of a word's meaning based on the situation and the knowledge we and our communication partners share. Connotative meaning is implied, suggested, or hinted at by the words you choose while communicating with others. Say, for example, that your romantic partner has a large stuffed teddy bear that, despite its weathered and worn appearance, is your partner's most prized childhood possession. To convey your love and adoration for your partner, you might say, "You're *my* big ugly bear." In doing so, you certainly don't mean that your lover is big, ugly, or bearlike in appearance! Instead, you rely on your partner understanding your implied link to his or her treasured object (the connotative meaning). Relationship intimacy plays a major role in shaping how we use and interpret connotative meanings while communicating with others (Hall, 1997a): people who know each other extremely well can convey connotative meanings accurately to one another.

SHAPING THOUGHT

In addition to enabling us to share meaning during interpersonal encounters, verbal communication also shapes our thoughts and perceptions of reality. Feminist scholar Dale Spender (1990) describes the relationship between words and our inner world in this way:

Assignment: Denotative and Connotative Meaning
Have students pair up and brainstorm words that have both denotative and connotative meanings. Give them a list of words (*yacht, sailboat,* etc.) or a phrase (*We bought a boat!*) to get them started. Other words, such as *home,* have a very different emotional meaning based on your frame of reference. Have students share the words and their meanings with the class, and then ask the class to consider some problems that may arise in interpersonal communication due to differences in word meanings.

▶ Video

macmillanhighered.com
/reflectrelate4e

Connotative Meaning
Watch this clip online to answer the questions below.

In this video, which of the terms suggested is the most persuasive to you? the least? What connotative meanings do you have for each? How do you use connotative meanings to display intimacy or affection with a family member or a friend?

Want to see more? Check out LaunchPad for a clip on **denotative meaning.**

We see the world through the lens of our language.

ARS/USDA

Discussion Prompt: Language and Thought

Place students in groups and ask them to take a stance on the following question: Does language *shape* our reality, or does language *reflect* our reality? Have students provide examples to support their positions. Students should also discuss how this question relates to the concepts of linguistic determinism and linguistic relativity.

To speak metaphorically, the brain is blind and deaf; it has no direct contact with light or sound. The brain has to interpret: it only deals in symbols and never knows the real thing. And the program for encoding and decoding is set up by the language which we possess. What we *see* in the world around us depends in large part on our language. (pp. 139–140)

Consider an encounter I had at a family gathering. My 6-year-old niece told me that a female neighbor of hers had helped several children escape a house fire. When I commended the neighbor's heroism, my niece corrected me. "Girls can't be *heroes*," she scolded. "Only boys can be *heroes*!" In talking with her further, I discovered she knew of no word representing "brave woman." Her only exposure to *heroine* was through her mother's romantic novels. Not knowing a word for "female bravery," she considered the concept unfathomable: "The neighbor lady wasn't a hero; she just saved the kids."

The idea that language shapes how we think about things was first suggested by researcher Edward Sapir, who conducted an intensive study of Native American languages in the early 1900s. Sapir argued that because language is our primary means of sharing meaning with others, it powerfully affects how we perceive others and our relationships with them (Gumperz & Levinson, 1996). Almost 50 years later, Benjamin Lee Whorf expanded on Sapir's ideas in what has become known as the Sapir-Whorf Hypothesis. Whorf argued that we cannot conceive of that for which we lack a vocabulary—that language quite literally defines the boundaries of our thinking. This view is known as **linguistic determinism.**

chapter 7 / Communicating Verbally 199

Yet different people from different cultures use different languages.

© Joshua Dalsimer/Corbis

As contemporary scholars note, linguistic determinism suggests that our ability to think is "at the mercy" of language (Gumperz & Levinson, 1996). We are mentally constrained by language to think only certain thoughts, and we cannot interpret the world in neutral ways because we always see the world through the lens of our languages.

Both Sapir and Whorf also recognized the dramatic impact that culture has on language. Because language determines our thoughts, and different people from different cultures use different languages, Sapir and Whorf agreed that people from different cultures would perceive and think about the world in very different ways, an effect known as **linguistic relativity.**

NAMING

A third important function of verbal communication is **naming,** creating linguistic symbols for objects. The process of naming is one of humankind's most profound and unique abilities (Spender, 1984). When we name people, places, objects, and ideas, we create symbols that represent them. We then use these symbols during our interactions with others to communicate meaning about these things. Because of the powerful impact language exerts on our thoughts, the decisions we make about what to name things ultimately determine not just the meanings we exchange but also our perceptions of the people, places, and objects we communicate about. This was why Muhammad Ali decided to abandon his birth name of Cassius Clay. He recognized that our names are *the* most

self-reflection

Think about the vocabulary you inherited from your culture for thinking and talking about relationships. What terms exist for describing serious romantic involvements, casual relationships that are sexual, and relationships that are purely platonic? How do these various terms shape your thinking about these relationships?

Discussion Prompt: Naming in Athletic Teams

Pair students up and ask them to discuss their feelings on the current controversy over team names in athletics. Have them brainstorm for controversial names among high school mascots (e.g., the Midgets) and NFL teams (e.g., the Redskins). Do these names serve as appropriate symbols to represent such groups? Should these names be changed? Why or why not? Discuss the power of language and naming to shape our perceptions.

powerful symbols that define who we are throughout our lives, and he wanted a name that represented his Islamic faith while also renouncing the surname of someone who had, years earlier, enslaved his forebears.

As the Ali example suggests, the issue of naming is especially potent for people who face historical and cultural prejudice, given that others outside the group often label them with derogatory names. Consider the case of gays and lesbians. For many years, gays and lesbians were referred to as "homosexual." But as scholar Julia Wood (1998) notes, many people shortened *homosexual* to *homo* and used the new term as an insult. In response, lesbian and gay activists in the 1960s renamed themselves "gay." This move also triggered disputes, however. Antigay activists protested the use of a term that traditionally meant "joyous and lively." Some lesbian activists argued that *gay* meant only men and was therefore exclusionary to women. Many straight people began using "gay" as an insult in the same manner as earlier epithets. In the 2000s, the inclusive label of "LGBTQ" (lesbian, gay, bisexual, transgendered, queer) was created to embrace the entire community. But this name still doesn't adequately represent many people's self-impressions. One study identified over a dozen different names that individuals chose for their sexual orientation and gender identity,

focus on CULTURE

Challenging Traditional Gender Labels

In September 2011, Australia changed its passport policy to allow three gender options on travel documents instead of two: male, female, and indeterminate.[4] The goal was to remove discrimination against transgendered persons. As Australian Senator Louise Pratt described, "It's an important recognition of people's human rights." The same month, Pomona College in California revised its student constitution to remove gendered pronouns. "A lot of students do not identify as 'male' or 'female' and aren't using the pronouns 'he' or 'she,' so we are trying to better represent the student body," said Student Commissioner Sarah Applebaum. "Ideally, this will help promote a more supportive campus for gender-nonconforming, queer, and transgender students."

These changes are part of a larger cultural trend toward challenging traditional language labels for gender and replacing them with "preferred gender pronouns," or PGPs—gender names of a person's own choosing. As Eliza Byard, executive director of the Gay, Lesbian, and Straight Education Network, describes, "More students today than ever are thinking about what gender means and are using language to get away from masculine and feminine gender assumptions." Some of the more creative PGPs currently in use include "ze," "hir," and "hirs."

Although the use of PGPs is global, the motivation for embracing them is deeply personal. PGPs are a way of using language to authentically capture one's true gender identity. "This has nothing to do with your sexuality and everything to do with who you feel like inside," notes Ann Arbor teen Katy Butler. "My PGPs are 'she,' 'her' and 'hers' and sometimes 'they,' 'them' and 'theirs.'"

discussion questions

- What language label do you most commonly use in reference to your gender? Why do you use this label?
- Does this label authentically and comprehensively capture how you think of yourself in terms of gender?

---

[4]The information that follows is adapted from Conlin (2011), McGuirk (2011), and Wu (2011).

including "pansexual," "omnisexual," and "same-gender loving/SGL" (Morrison & McCornack, 2011). Given the way positive names have been turned to negative in the past, some people reject names for nonstraight sexual orientations altogether. As one study respondent put it, "I don't use labels—I'm not a can of soup!" (Morrison & McCornack, 2011).

PERFORMING ACTIONS

A fourth function of verbal communication is that it enables us to take action. We make requests, issue invitations, deliver commands, or even taunt—as Ali did to his competitors. We also try to influence others' behaviors. We want our listeners to grant our requests, accept our invitations, obey our commands, or suffer from our curses. The actions that we perform with language are called **speech acts** (Searle, 1969). (See Table 7.1 for types of speech acts.)

During interpersonal encounters, the structure of our back-and-forth exchange is based on the speech acts we perform (Jacobs, 1994; Levinson, 1985). When your professor asks you a question, how do you know what to do next? You recognize that the words she has spoken constitute a "question," and you realize that an "answer" is expected as the relevant response. Similarly, when your best friend texts you and inquires, "Can I borrow your car tonight?" you immediately recognize his message as a "request." You also understand that two speech acts are possible as relevant responses: "granting" his request ("no problem") or "rejecting" it ("I don't think so").

CRAFTING CONVERSATIONS

A fifth function served by language is that it allows us to craft conversations. Language meanings, thoughts, names, and acts don't happen in the abstract; they occur within conversations. Although each of us intuitively knows what a

Media Note:
The Big Bang Theory
Have students watch the clip from *The Big Bang Theory* in which Sheldon plots out the components of a conversation in his "friendship algorithm" in order to help him develop a friendship with a coworker (season 2, episode 13). Ask students to apply the four characteristics fundamental to conversations to Sheldon's algorithm. Does his algorithm help or hurt his ability to successfully craft conversations?

table 7.1 Types of Speech Acts

Act	Function	Forms	Example
Representative	Commits the speaker to the truth of what has been said	Assertions, Conclusions	"It sure is a beautiful day."
Directive	Attempts to get listeners to do things	Questions, Requests, Commands	"Can you loan me five dollars?"
Commissive	Commits speakers to future action	Promises, Threats	"I will always love you, no matter what happens."
Expressive	Conveys a psychological or emotional state that the speaker is experiencing	Thanks, Apologies, Congratulations	"Thank you so much for the wonderful gift!"
Declarative	Produces dramatic, observable effects	Marriage Pronouncements, Firing Declarations	"From this point onward, you are no longer an employee of this organization."

Note: The information in this table is adapted from Searle (1976).

conversation is, scholars suggest four characteristics fundamental to conversation (Nofsinger, 1999). First, conversations are *interactive*. At least two people must participate in the exchange for it to count as a conversation, and participants must take turns exchanging messages.

Second, conversations are locally managed. *Local management* means that we make decisions regarding who gets to speak when, and for how long, each time we exchange turns. This makes conversation different from other verbal exchanges, such as debate, in which the order and length of turns are decided before the event begins, and drama, in which people speak words that have been written down in advance.

Third, conversation is *universal*. Conversation forms the foundation for most forms of interpersonal communication and for social organization

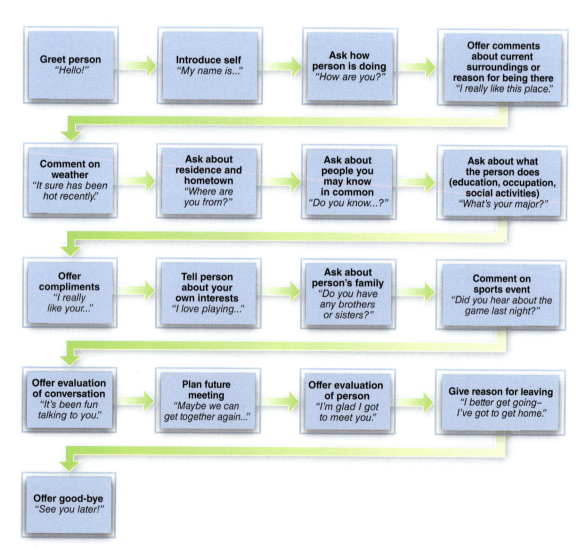

figure 7.2 **Conversational Pattern**

generally. Our relationships and our places in society are created and maintained through conversations.

Fourth, conversations often adhere to *scripts*—rigidly structured patterns of talk. This is especially true in first encounters, when you are trying to reduce uncertainty. For example, the topics that college students discuss when they first meet often follow a set script. Communication researcher Kathy Kellermann (1991) conducted several studies looking at the first conversations of college students and found that 95 percent of the topic changes followed the same pattern regardless of gender, age, race, or geographic region (see Figure 7.2.). This suggests that a critical aspect of appropriately constructing conversations is grasping and following relevant conversational scripts.

Does the fact that we frequently use scripts to guide our conversations mean this type of communication is inauthentic? If you expect more from an exchange than a prepackaged response, scripted communication may strike you as such. However, communication scripts allow us to relevantly *and* efficiently exchange greetings, respond to simple questions and answers, trade pleasantries, and get to know people in a preliminary fashion without putting much active thought into our communication. This saves us from mental exertion and allows us to focus our energy on more involved or important interpersonal encounters.

MANAGING RELATIONSHIPS

In Alice Sebold's (2002) award-winning novel *The Lovely Bones*, Indian high school student Ray Singh is desperately in love with the central character, Susie Salmon. Seeing her sneaking into school late one morning (while he himself is cutting class and hiding out in the school theater), he decides to declare his feelings.

> "You are beautiful, Susie Salmon!" I heard the voice but could not place it immediately. I looked around me. "Here," the voice said. I looked up and saw the head and torso of Ray Singh leaning out over the top of the scaffold above me. "Hello," he said. I knew Ray had a crush on me. He had moved from England the year before, but was born in India. That someone could have the face of one country and the voice of another and then move to a third was too incredible for me to fathom. It made him immediately cool. Plus, he seemed eight hundred times smarter than the rest of us, and he had a crush on me. That morning, when he spoke to me from above, my heart plunged to the floor. (p. 82)

Verbal communication's final, and arguably most profound, function in our lives is to help us manage our relationships. We use language to create relationships by declaring powerful, intimate feelings to others, such as "You are beautiful!" Verbal communication is the principal means through which we maintain our ongoing relationships with lovers, family members, friends, and coworkers (Stafford, 2010). For example, romantic partners who verbally communicate frequently with each other, and with their partners' friends and families, experience less uncertainty in their relationships and are not as likely to break up as those who verbally communicate less often (Parks, 2007). Finally, most of the heartbreaks we'll experience in our lives are preceded by verbal messages that state, in one

---

skills practice

Ensuring Competent First Encounters
Putting Kathy Kellermann's Research on Conversation Scripts into Action

❶ Identify a new acquaintance with whom you would like to interact.

❷ Greet the person, introduce yourself, and ask how he or she is doing.

❸ Discuss current surroundings, the weather, and hometowns.

❹ Ask about interests, school, sports, and social activities, all the while looking for points of commonality and ways to compliment the person.

❺ Raise the possibility of future interaction, express gratitude for the current conversation, and exit with a friendly "Good-bye."

Assignment: Abandoning Scripts
Ask students to identify specific scripts they frequently use with acquaintances, friends, family members, and so on. Then, for an out-of-class experiment, have students deviate from their usual scripts and report back to the class on others' reactions to their behavior. For example, students could hang up at the end of a phone conversation without saying, "Bye, I love you," or launch into a detailed story when a classmate passes in the hall and says, "Hi. How are you?"

▶ Ray creates a deeper, more intimate relationship with Susie when he communicates his love for her in *The Lovely Bones*. Barry Wetcher/© Paramount Pictures/Everett Collection

self-reflection

Consider a recent instance in which a relationship of yours suddenly changed direction, either for better or for worse. What was said that triggered this turning point? How did the words that were exchanged impact intimacy? What does this tell you about the role that language plays in managing relationships?

form or another, "It's over." We'll discuss more about how we forge, maintain, and end our relationships in Chapters 10 through 12, and the Relationships in the Workplace appendix.

Cooperative Verbal Communication

[Creating understandable messages]

Eager to connect with your teenage son, you ask him how his day was when he arrives home from school. But you get only a grunted "Fine" in return, as he quickly disappears into his room to play video games. You invite your romantic partner over for dinner, excited to demonstrate a new recipe. But when you query your partner's opinion of the dish, the response is, "It's interesting." You text your best friend, asking for her feedback on an in-class presentation you gave earlier that day. She responds, "You talked way too fast!"

Although these examples seem widely disparate, they share an underlying commonality: people failing to verbally communicate in a fully cooperative fashion. To understand how these messages are uncooperative, consider their cooperative counterparts. Your son tells you, "It was all right—I didn't do as well on my chem test as I wanted, but I got an A on my history report." Your partner says, "It's good, but I think it'd be even better with a little more salt." Your friend's text message reads, "It went well, but I thought it could have been presented a little slower."

When you use **cooperative verbal communication**, you produce messages that have three characteristics. First, you speak in ways that others can easily understand, using language that is informative, honest, relevant, and clear. Second, you take active ownership for what you're saying by using "I" language. Third, you make others feel included rather than excluded—for example, through the use of "we."

◐ Oral storytelling is an ancient art, one that creates and passes histories and mythologies down from generation to generation. Through blogs and podcasts, this tradition continues to take on new forms.
© George Rodger/Magnum Photos

UNDERSTANDABLE MESSAGES

In his exploration of language and meaning, philosopher Paul Grice noted that cooperative interactions rest on our ability to tailor our verbal communication so that others can understand us. To produce understandable messages, we have to abide by the **Cooperative Principle:** making our conversational contributions as *informative*, *honest*, *relevant*, and *clear* as is required, given the purposes of the encounters in which we're involved (Grice, 1989).

Being aware of situational characteristics is critical to applying the Cooperative Principle. For example, while we're ethically bound to share important information with others, this doesn't mean we *always* should. Suppose a friend discloses a confidential secret to you and your sibling later asks you to reveal it. In this case, it would be unethical to share this information without your friend's permission.

Being Informative

According to Grice (1989), being informative during interpersonal encounters means two things. First, you should present all of the information that is relevant and appropriate to share, given the situation. When a coworker passes you in the hallway and greets you with a quick "How's it going?" the situation requires that you provide little information in return—"Great! How are you?" The same question asked by a concerned friend during a personal crisis creates very different demands; your friend likely wants a detailed account of your thoughts and feelings.

Second, you want to avoid being *too* informative—that is, disclosing information that isn't appropriate or important in a particular situation. A detailed description of your personal woes ("I haven't been sleeping well lately, and my cat is sick . . .") in response to your colleague's quick "How's it going?" query would likely be perceived as inappropriate and even strange.

self-reflection

Recall a situation in which you possessed important information but knew that disclosing it would be personally or relationally problematic. What did you do? How did your decision impact your relationship? Was your choice ethical? Based on your experience, is it always cooperative to disclose important information?

In the BBC series *Sherlock*, Sherlock Holmes is often brutally honest to the point of rudeness when he interacts with his colleague John Watson. Have you ever been too honest or informative in your communication with others? BBC/Photofest

**Assignment:
The Cooperative Principle**
Assign students a short paper reflecting on their own personal use of the Cooperative Principle: Which of these four characteristics do you feel is most important, and why? Describe a time when someone was lacking one of these characteristics in his or her communication. How did you feel when you communicated with this person? Which characteristic do you believe you can improve on in your own communication?

Online Self-Quiz: Test Your Knowledge of Conversational Patterns. To take this self-quiz, visit LaunchPad: macmillanhighered.com /reflectrelate4e

The responsibility to be informative overlaps with the responsibility to be ethical. To be a cooperative verbal communicator, you must share information with others that has important personal and relational implications for them. To illustrate, if you discover that your friend's spouse is having an affair, you're ethically obligated to disclose this information if your friend asks you about it.

Being Honest Honesty is the single most important characteristic of cooperative verbal communication because other people count on the fact that the information you share with them is truthful (Grice, 1989). Honesty means not sharing information that you're uncertain about and not disclosing information that you know is false. When you are dishonest in your verbal communication, you violate standards for ethical behavior, and you lead others to believe false things (Jacobs, Dawson, & Brashers, 1996). For example, if you assure your romantic partner that your feelings haven't changed when in fact they have, you give your partner false hope about your future together. You also lay the groundwork for your partner to make continued investments in a relationship that you already know is doomed.

Being Relevant Relevance means making your conversational contributions responsive to what others have said. When people ask you questions, you provide answers. When they make requests, you grant or reject their requests. When certain topics arise in the conversation, you tie your contributions to that topic. During conversations, you stick with relevant topics and avoid those that aren't. Dodging questions or abruptly changing topics is uncooperative, and in some instances, others may see it as an attempt at deception, especially if you change topics to avoid discussing something you want to keep hidden (McCornack, 2008).

Being Clear Using clear language means presenting information in a straightforward fashion rather than framing it in obscure or ambiguous terms. For example, telling a partner that you like a recipe but that it needs more salt is easier to understand than veiling your meaning by vaguely saying, "It's interesting." But note that using clear language doesn't mean being brutally frank or dumping offensive and hurtful information on others. Competent interpersonal communicators always consider others' feelings when designing their messages. When information is important and relevant to disclose, choose your words carefully to be both respectful *and* clear, so that others won't misconstrue your intended meaning.

Dealing with Misunderstanding Of course, just because you use informative, honest, relevant, and clear language doesn't guarantee that you will be understood by others. When one person misperceives another's verbally expressed thoughts, feelings, or beliefs, **misunderstanding** occurs. Misunderstanding most commonly results from a failure to actively listen. Recall, for example, our discussion of action-oriented listeners in Chapter 6. Action-oriented listeners often become impatient with others while listening and frequently jump ahead to finish other people's (presumed) points (Watson, Barker, & Weaver, 1995). This listening style can lead them to misunderstand others' messages. To overcome this source of misunderstanding, practice the active listening skills described in Chapter 6.

Misunderstanding occurs frequently online, owing to the lack of nonverbal cues to help clarify one another's meaning. One study found that 27.2 percent of respondents agreed that e-mail is likely to result in miscommunication of intent, and 53.6 percent agreed that it is relatively easy to misinterpret an e-mail message (Rainey, 2000). The tendency to misunderstand communication online is so prevalent that scholars suggest the following practices: *If a particular message absolutely must be error-free or if its content is controversial, don't use e-mail or text messaging to communicate it.* Whenever possible, conduct high-stakes encounters, such as important attempts at persuasion, face-to-face. Finally, never use e-mails, posts, or text messages for sensitive actions, such as professional reprimands or dismissals, or relationship breakups (Rainey, 2000).

USING "I" LANGUAGE

It's the biggest intramural basketball game of the year, and your team is down by a point, with five seconds left, when your teammate is fouled. Stepping to the line for two free throws and a chance to win the game, she misses both, and your team loses. As you leave the court, you angrily snap at her, "You really let us down!"

The second key to cooperative verbal communication is taking ownership of the things you say to others, especially in situations in which you're expressing negative feelings or criticism. You can do this by avoiding **"you" language,** phrases that place the focus of attention and blame on other people, such as "*You* let us down." Instead, rearrange your statements so that you use **"I" language,** phrases that emphasize ownership of your feelings, opinions, and beliefs (see Table 7.2). The difference between "I" and "you" may strike you as minor, but it actually has powerful effects: "I" language is less likely than "you" language to trigger defensiveness on the part of your listeners (Kubany, Richard, Bauer, & Muraoka, 1992). "I" language creates a clearer impression on listeners that you're responsible for what you're saying and that you're expressing your own perceptions rather than stating unquestionable truths.

self-reflection

Recall an online encounter in which you thought you understood someone's e-mail, text message, or post, then later found out you were wrong. How did you discover that your impression was mistaken? What could you have done differently to avoid the misunderstanding?

🔻 One downside of our frequent online communication is that it is easy to misunderstand others' messages and to take them as ruder or less clear than intended. If you need a message to be error-free, consider delivering it in person. Jetta Productions/Getty Images

table 7.2 "You" Language versus "I" Language

"You" Language	"I" Language
You make me so angry!	I'm feeling so angry!
You totally messed things up.	I feel like things are totally messed up.
You need to do a better job.	I think this job needs to be done better.
You really hurt my feelings.	I'm feeling really hurt.
You never pay any attention to me.	I feel like I never get any attention.

Video

macmillanhighered.com/reflectrelate4e

"I" Language
Watch this clip online to answer the questions below.

In this video, how do the partners' use of "I" language affect their interaction? Explain your answer. How might the interaction have been different had they used "you" language? Would it have been a more or less productive discussion?

Want to see more? Check out LaunchPad for clips on **"you" language** and **"we" language.**

USING "WE" LANGUAGE

It's Thursday night, and you're standing in line waiting to get into a club. In front of you are two couples, and you can't help but overhear their conversations. As you listen, you notice an interesting difference in their verbal communication. One couple expresses everything in terms of "I" and "you": "What do you want to do later tonight?" "I don't know, but I'm hungry, so I'll probably get something to eat. Do you want to come?" The other couple consistently uses "we": "What should we do later?" "Why don't we get something to eat?"

What effect does this simple difference in pronoun usage—"we" rather than "I" or "you"—have on your impressions of the two couples? If you perceive the couple using "we" as being closer than the couple using "I" and "you," you would be right. "We" is a common way people signal their closeness (Dreyer, Dreyer, & Davis, 1987). Couples who use **"we" language**—wordings that emphasize inclusion—tend to be more satisfied with their relationships than those who routinely rely on "I" and "you" messages (Honeycutt, 1999).

An important part of cooperative verbal communication is using "we" language to express your connection to others. In a sense, "we" language is the inverse of "I" language. We use "I" language when we want to show others that our feelings, thoughts, and opinions are separate from theirs and that we take sole responsibility for our feelings, thoughts, and opinions. But "we" language helps us bolster feelings of connection and similarity, not only with romantic partners but also with anyone to whom we want to signal a collaborative relationship. When I went through my training to become a certified yoga instructor, part of the instruction was to replace the use of "you" with "we" and "let's" during in-class verbal cueing of moves. Rather than saying, "You should lunge forward with your left leg" or "I want you to step forward left," we were taught to say, "*Let's* step forward with *our* left legs." After I implemented "we" language in my yoga classes, my students repeatedly commented on how they liked the "more personal" and "inclusive" nature of my verbal cueing.

GENDER AND COOPERATIVE VERBAL COMMUNICATION

Powerful stereotypes exist regarding what men and women value in verbal communication. These stereotypes suggest that men appreciate informative, honest,

On the television show *Bones*, Dr. Temperance Brennan (Emily Deschanel) is so direct and concise, she often accidentally offends those around her. Dr. Lance Sweets (John Francis Daley), in contrast, uses more indirect language and questions so that people must infer his actual meaning. How do these differences compare to common stereotypes about the ways in which men and women communicate? Richard Foreman/© FOX/EC

relevant, and clear language more than women do. In Western cultures, many people believe that men communicate in a clear and straightforward fashion and that women are more indirect and wordy (Tannen, 1990b). These stereotypes are reinforced powerfully through television, in programs in which female characters often use more polite language than men ("I'm *sorry* to bother you but ..."), more uncertain phrases ("I *suppose* ..."), and more flowery adjectives ("that's *silly*," "oh, how *beautiful*"), and male characters fill their language with action verbs ("let's *get a move on*!") (Mulac, Bradac, & Mann, 1985).

But research suggests that when it comes to language, men and women are more similar than different. For example, data from 165 studies involving nearly a million and a half subjects found that women do not use more vague and wordy verbal communication than men do (Canary & Hause, 1993). The primary determinant of whether people's language is clear and concise or vague and wordy is not gender but whether the encounter is competitive or collaborative (Fisher, 1983). Both women and men use clear and concise language in competitive interpersonal encounters, such as when arguing with a family member or debating a project proposal in a work meeting. Additionally, they use comparatively vaguer and wordier language during collaborative encounters, such as when eating lunch with a friend or relaxing in the evening with a spouse.

Barriers to Cooperative Verbal Communication

[Destructive language can damage relationships]

Walter White is one of the most complicated, manipulative, brilliant, and disturbing characters to ever grace the TV screen. In the critically acclaimed (and ridiculously good!) show *Breaking Bad*, Walter is a high school chemistry teacher who—after being diagnosed with terminal cancer—begins producing

skills practice

Cooperative Language Online
Using cooperative language during an important online interaction

❶ Identify an important online encounter.

❷ Create a rough draft of the message you wish to send.

❸ Check that the language you've used is fully informative, honest, relevant, and clear.

❹ Use "I" language for all comments that are negative or critical.

❺ Use "we" language throughout the message, where appropriate.

❻ Send the message.

▲ In *Breaking Bad*, Walter White's poor verbal communication choices, combined with his prideful and egotistical personality, cause him to transform from high school chemistry teacher to drug kingpin. © AMC/Everett Collection

methamphetamine to raise money to cover his treatment costs and support his family following his anticipated death. As his involvement with the meth industry increases, his moral and ethical corruption deepens, leading him to lie, steal, aggress, and even murder. In season 4, Walt's marriage to Skyler is instantly devastated by one simple disclosure: Walt has been deceiving Skyler about the degree of his criminality. When she expresses fear for his safety, he makes clear that he is not an innocent "high school teacher trying to help his family" but, instead, the perpetrator of evil:

> Who are you talking to right now? Who is it you think you see? Do you know how much I make a year? Even if I told you, you wouldn't believe it. Do you know what would happen if I suddenly decided to stop going into work? A business big enough to be listed on the Nasdaq goes belly up. Disappears. It ceases to exist without me. No, you *clearly* don't know who you're talking to, so let me clue you in. I am not "in danger," Skyler. I *am* the danger! A guy opens his door and gets shot, and you think that of *me*? No! *I am the one who knocks!*

When used cooperatively, language can clarify understandings, build relationships, and bring us closer to others. But language also has the capacity to create divisions between people, and damage or even destroy relationships. Some people, like Walter White in *Breaking Bad*, use verbal communication to aggress on others, deceive them, or defensively lash out. Others are filled with fear and anxiety about interacting and therefore do not speak at all. In this section, we explore the darker side of verbal communication by looking at four common barriers to cooperative verbal communication: verbal aggression, deception, defensive communication, and communication apprehension.

VERBAL AGGRESSION

The most notable aspect of Walter White's infamous "I am the one who knocks!" speech is its ferocity. In fact, he is so scary that his wife, Skyler, shuns him in the aftermath, out of fear for her life. **Verbal aggression** is the tendency to attack others' self-concepts rather than their positions on topics of conversation (Infante & Wigley, 1986). Verbally aggressive people denigrate others' character, abilities, or physical appearance rather than constructively discussing different points of view—for example, Walt condescendingly snarling at Skyler, "You *clearly* don't know who you're talking to, so let me clue you in." Verbal aggression can be expressed not only through speech but also through behaviors, such as physically mocking another's appearance, displaying rude gestures, or assaulting others (Sabourin, Infante, & Rudd, 1993). When such aggression occurs over an extended period of time and is directed toward a particular target, it can evolve into *bullying*.

Why are some people verbally aggressive? At times, such aggression stems from a temporary mental state. Most of us have found ourselves in situations at one time or another in which various factors—stress, exhaustion, frustration or anger, relationship difficulties—converge. As a result, we lose our heads and spontaneously go off on another person. Some people who are verbally aggressive suffer from chronic hostility (see Chapter 4). Others are frequently aggressive because it helps them achieve short-term interpersonal goals (Infante & Wigley, 1986). For example, people who want to cut in front of you in line, win an argument, or steal your parking spot may believe that they stand a better chance of achieving these objectives if they use insults, profanity, and threats. Unfortunately, their past experiences may bolster this belief because many people give in to verbal aggression, which encourages the aggressor to use the technique again.

If you find yourself consistently communicating in a verbally aggressive fashion, identify and address the root causes behind your aggression. Has external stress (job pressure, a troubled relationship, a family conflict) triggered your aggression? Do you suffer from chronic hostility? If you find that anger management strategies don't help you reduce your aggression, seek professional assistance.

Communicating with others who are verbally aggressive is also a daunting challenge. Dominic Infante (1995), a leading aggression researcher, offers three tips. First, avoid communication behaviors that may trigger verbal aggression in others, such as teasing, baiting, or insulting. Second, if you know someone who is chronically verbally aggressive, avoid or minimize contact with that person. For better or worse, the most practical solution for dealing with such individuals is to not interact with them at all. Third, if you can't avoid interacting with a verbally aggressive person, remain polite and respectful during your encounters with him or her. Allow the individual to speak without interruption. Stay calm, and express empathy (when possible). Avoid retaliating with personal attacks of your own; they will only further escalate the aggression. Finally, end interactions when someone becomes aggressive, explaining gently but firmly, "I'm sorry, but I don't feel comfortable continuing this conversation."

DECEPTION

Arguably the most prominent feature of Walter White's communication in *Breaking Bad* is his chronic duplicity. For instance, in season 2, Walt is kidnapped by rival drug lord Tuco and consequently goes missing for several days. In the aftermath, he makes up a story about being in a "fugue state" so that his family doesn't suspect the true reason for his absence.

When most of us think of deception, we think of messages like Walt's to his family, in which one person communicates false information to another ("I was in a fugue state!"). But people deceive in any number of ways, only some of which

Discussion: Types of Lies
Place students in groups and have them discuss the definitions of and differences between half-truths, lies of omission (concealment), and white lies. Do they view all of these concepts as deception? When are these acceptable or unacceptable in relationships? Have the groups provide examples and a rationale for each.

involve saying untruthful things. **Deception** occurs when people deliberately use uninformative, untruthful, irrelevant, or vague language for the purpose of misleading others. The most common form of deception doesn't involve saying anything false at all: studies document that *concealment*—leaving important and relevant information out of messages—is practiced more frequently than all other forms of deception combined (McCornack, 2008).

As noted in previous chapters, deception is commonplace during online encounters. People communicating on online dating sites, posting on social networking sites, and sending messages via e-mail and text message distort and hide whatever information they want, providing little opportunity for the recipients of their messages to check accuracy. Some people provide false information about their backgrounds, professions, appearances, and gender online to amuse themselves, to form alternative relationships unavailable to them offline, or to take advantage of others through online scams (Rainey, 2000).

Deception is uncooperative, unethical, impractical, and destructive. It exploits the belief on the part of listeners that speakers are communicating cooperatively—tricking them into thinking that the messages received are informative, honest, relevant, and clear when they're *not* (McCornack, 2008). Deception is unethical, because when you deceive others, you deny them information

Test Your Deception Acceptance

People vary widely in the degree to which they think deception is an acceptable and appropriate form of verbal communication. To test your deception acceptance, check each statement that you agree with. Then total your checks and compare the result to the scoring key.

To take this quiz online, visit LaunchPad: **macmillanhighered.com/reflectrelate4e**.

_____ You should never tell anyone the real reason you did something unless it is useful to do so.

_____ It is OK to lie to achieve your goals.

_____ What people don't know can't hurt them.

_____ The best way to handle people is to tell them what they want to hear.

_____ It is often better to lie than to hurt someone's feelings.

_____ There is nothing wrong with lying as long as you don't get caught.

_____ In some situations, lying can be the most ethical thing to do.

_____ Honesty isn't always the best policy.

_____ There are many instances in which lying is justified.

_____ Lying can sometimes solve problems more effectively than telling the truth.

Note: This *Self-Quiz* is adapted from the lie acceptability scale developed by Levine, McCornack, and Baldwin Avery (1992).

Scoring: 0–3: Low deception acceptance. You believe that deception is unacceptable no matter the circumstance, and you likely react extremely negatively when you find out people have lied to you. 4–6: Moderate deception acceptance. You believe that deception is acceptable under certain circumstances, and you are probably more accepting when others lie to you. 7–10: High deception acceptance. You believe that deception is an acceptable form of behavior, and you regularly use it to deal with difficult communication and relationship situations.

that may be relevant to their continued participation in a relationship, and in so doing, you fail to treat them with respect (LaFollette & Graham, 1986). Deception is also impractical. Although at times it may seem easier to deceive than to tell the truth (McCornack, 2008), deception typically calls for additional deception. Finally, deception is destructive: it creates intensely unpleasant personal, interpersonal, and relational consequences. The discovery of deception typically causes intense disappointment, anger, and other negative emotions, and frequently leads to relationship breakups (McCornack & Levine, 1990).

At the same time, keep in mind that people who mislead you may not be doing so out of malicious intent. As noted earlier, many cultures view ambiguous and indirect language as hallmarks of cooperative verbal communication. In addition, sometimes people intentionally veil information out of kindness and desire to maintain the relationship, such as when you tell a close friend that her awful new hairstyle looks great because you know she'd be agonizingly self-conscious if she knew how bad it really looked (McCornack, 1997; Metts & Chronis, 1986).

DEFENSIVE COMMUNICATION

A third barrier to cooperative verbal communication is **defensive communication** (or *defensiveness*), impolite messages delivered in response to suggestions, criticism, or perceived slights. For example, at work you suggest an alternative approach to a coworker, but she snaps, "We've *always* done it this way." You broach the topic of relationship concerns with your romantic partner, but he or she shuts you down, telling you to "Just drop it!" People who communicate defensively dismiss the validity of what another person has said. They also refuse to make internal attributions about their own behavior, especially when they are at fault. Instead, they focus their responses away from themselves and on the other person.

Four types of defensive communication are common (Waldron, Turner, Alexander, & Barton, 1993). Through *dogmatic messages*, a person dismisses suggestions for improvement or constructive criticism, refuses to consider other views, and continues to believe that his or her behaviors are acceptable. With *superiority messages*, the speaker suggests that he or she possesses special knowledge, ability, or status far beyond that of the other individual. In using *indifference messages*, a person implies that the suggestion or criticism being offered is irrelevant, uninteresting, or unimportant. Through *control messages*, a person seeks to squelch criticism by controlling the other individual or the encounter (see Table 7.3).

> **Assignment: Defensive Communication**
> Ask students to watch the VideoCentral clip on **defensive communication** and write a short point-of-view analysis. Students should consider the teacher's and the parent's perspectives on the interaction. What does each person hear in the video? How does each person perceive the interaction? What could each person do to improve the interaction? Ask students to discuss times when they have been in similar situations.

table 7.3 Examples of Defensive Communication

Message Type	Example
Dogmatic message	"Why would I change? I've always done it like this!"
Superiority message	"I have more experience and have been doing this longer than you."
Indifference message	"*This* is supposed to interest me?"
Control message	"There's no point to further discussion; I consider this matter closed."

self-reflection

Recall a situation in which you were offered a suggestion, advice, or criticism, and you reacted defensively. What caused your reaction? What were the outcomes of your defensive communication? How could you have prevented a defensive response?

Defensive communication is *interpersonally incompetent* because it violates norms for appropriate behavior, rarely succeeds in effectively achieving interpersonal goals, and treats others with disrespect (Waldron et al., 1993). People who communicate in a chronically defensive fashion suffer a host of negative consequences, including high rates of conflict and lower satisfaction in their personal and professional relationships (Infante, Myers, & Burkel, 1994). Yet even highly competent communicators behave defensively on occasion. Defensiveness is an almost instinctive reaction to behavior that makes us angry—communication we perceive as inappropriate, unfair, or unduly harsh. Consequently, the key to overcoming it is to control its triggering factors. For example, if a certain person or situation invariably provokes defensiveness in you, practice preventive anger management strategies such as encounter avoidance or encounter structuring (see Chapter 4). If you can't avoid the person or situation, use techniques such as reappraisal and the Jefferson strategy (also in Chapter 4). Given that defensiveness frequently stems from attributional errors—thinking the other person is "absolutely wrong" and you're "absolutely right"—perception-checking (Chapter 3) can also help you reduce your defensiveness.

To prevent others from communicating defensively with you, use "I" and "we" language appropriately, and offer empathy and support when communicating suggestions, advice, or criticism. At the same time, realize that using cooperative language is not a panacea for curing chronic defensiveness in another person. Some people are so deeply entrenched in their defensiveness that any language you use, no matter how cooperative, will still trigger a defensive response. In such situations, the best you can do is strive to maintain ethical communication by treating the person with respect. You might also consider removing yourself from the encounter before it can escalate into intense conflict.

COMMUNICATION APPREHENSION

Class Note: Communication Apprehension

Place students in small groups and assign them a common situation that often creates anxiety (e.g., being interviewed for a job, asking someone for a date, or requesting a raise). Ask them to create a role play depicting how they could successfully handle the situation. Then discuss strategies for such occasions: How do you try to conquer that anxiety or fear? What plan actions and plan contingencies should you include? How should you prepare or practice for the occasion to build confidence?

A final barrier to cooperative verbal communication is **communication apprehension**—fear or anxiety associated with interaction, which keeps someone from being able to communicate cooperatively (Daly, McCroskey, Ayres, Hopf, & Ayres, 2004). People with high levels of communication apprehension experience intense discomfort while talking with others and therefore have difficulty forging productive relationships. Such individuals also commonly experience physical symptoms, such as nervous stomach, dry mouth, sweating, increased blood pressure and heart rate, mental disorganization, and shakiness (McCroskey & Richmond, 1987).

Most of us experience communication apprehension at some point in our lives. The key to overcoming it is to develop **communication plans**—mental maps that describe exactly how communication encounters will unfold—*prior* to interacting in the situations or with the people or types of people that cause your apprehension. Communication plans have two elements. The first is *plan actions*, the "moves" you think you'll perform in an encounter that causes you anxiety. Here, you map out in advance the topics you will talk about, the messages you will say in relation to these topics, and the physical behaviors you'll demonstrate.

chapter 7 / Communicating Verbally   215

King George VI of England, played by Colin Firth in *The King's Speech*, overcame his communication apprehension by working with a speech therapist. Have you ever felt anxious when communicating? What strategies did you use to deal with your anxiety? © The Weinstein Company/Everett Collection

The second part of a communication plan is *plan contingencies*, the messages you think your communication partner or partners will present during the encounter and how you will respond. To develop plan contingencies, think about the topics your partner will likely talk about, the messages he or she will likely present, his or her reaction to your communication, and your response to your partner's messages and behaviors.

When you implement your communication plan during an encounter that causes you apprehension, the experience is akin to playing chess. While you're communicating, envision your next two, three, or four possible moves—your plan actions. Try to anticipate how the other person will respond to those moves and how you will respond in turn. The goal of this process is to interact with enough confidence and certainty to reduce the anxiety and fear you normally feel during such encounters.

The Power of Verbal Communication

Language creates our most important moments

We can't help but marvel at the power of verbal communication. Words are our symbolic vehicle for creating and exchanging meanings, performing actions, and forging relationships. We use language to name all that surrounds us, and in turn, the names we have created shape how we think and feel about these things.

But for most of us, the power of language is intensely personal. Call to mind the most important relationship events in your life. When you do, you'll likely find they were not merely accompanied by verbal communication but were defined and created through it. Perhaps it was the first time you said "I love you" to

skills practice

Overcoming Apprehension

Creating communication plans to overcome communication apprehension

❶ Think of a situation or person that triggers communication apprehension.

❷ Envision yourself interacting in this situation or with this person.

❸ List plan actions: topics you will discuss and messages you will present.

❹ List plan contingencies: events that might happen during the encounter, things the other person will likely say and do, and your responses.

❺ Implement your plan the next time you communicate in that situation or with that person.

making relationship choices

Dealing with Difficult Truths

BACKGROUND

Cooperative verbal communicators strive to use appropriate, informative, honest, relevant, and clear language. But in many difficult and complicated relationship situations, deception becomes a tempting alternative. To understand how you might competently manage such a relationship challenge, read the case study in Part 2; then, drawing on all you know about interpersonal communication, work through the problem-solving model in Part 3.

 Visit LaunchPad to check out the other side of the story (Part 4). For the best experience, complete all parts in LaunchPad: macmillanhighered.com/reflectrelate4e.

2 CASE STUDY

Since her early youth, your cousin Britney has always gotten her way. Whenever she wanted something, she would throw a tantrum, and your aunt and uncle would give in. Now she's an adult version of the same child: spoiled and manipulative. Thankfully, you see Britney only during the holidays, and she usually ignores you.

Recently, Britney has had troubles. She dropped out of college and lost her license after totaling the new car her parents bought her. Her drug abuse worsened to the point where her folks forced her into rehab. Despite your dislike of her, you felt sorry for her because you've struggled with your own substance abuse challenges. Now she has apparently recovered and reenrolled in school.

At Thanksgiving, Britney greets you with a big hug and a smile. "How's my favorite cousin?" she gushes. As she talks, your surprise turns to suspicion. She's acting *too* friendly, and you think she may be high. Sure enough, when the two of you are alone, she pulls out a bag of Vicodin tablets. "Do you want some?" she offers, and, when you refuse, says, "Oh, that's right—you're *in recovery*," in a mocking tone. When you ask about rehab, she laughs, "It may have been right for you, but I did it just to shut my parents up." Afterward, you corner your folks and disclose what happened. They counsel silence. If you tell Britney's parents, Britney will lie; everyone in the family will have to take sides, and it will ruin the holiday.

Over dinner, your aunt and uncle praise Britney's recovery. Your aunt then announces that she is rewarding Britney by buying her another car. Your blood boils. Although your aunt and uncle are well intentioned, Britney is deceiving and exploiting them! Noticing your sullen expression, your uncle says, "I'm not sure what's bothering you, but I think it might be envy. Not everyone has Britney's strength of character in dealing with adversity. You could learn a lot from her, don't you think?" Seething in anger, you say nothing, and the conversation moves on. Later, Britney corners you and says, "Thanks for covering for me earlier. But my parents noticed that you were acting weird, and they think something is up. I think they might try to ask you about it. If they do, you won't rat me out, will you?"

YOUR TURN

Think about all you've learned thus far about interpersonal communication. Then work through the following five steps. Remember, there are no "right" answers, so think hard about what is the *best* choice! (P.S. Need help? See the *Helpful Concepts* list.)

step 1
Reflect on yourself. What are your thoughts and feelings in this situation? Are your impressions and attributions accurate?

step 2
Reflect on your partner. Using perspective-taking and empathic concern, put yourself in Britney's shoes. What is she thinking and feeling in this situation?

step 3
Identify the optimal outcome. Think about all the information you have about your communication and relationship with Britney, your relationship with your other family members, and the situation. What's the best, most constructive relationship outcome possible? Consider what's best for you, Britney, and the family.

step 4
Locate the roadblocks. Taking into consideration your own and Britney's thoughts and feelings and all that has happened in this situation, what obstacles are keeping you from achieving the optimal outcome?

step 5
Chart your course. What can you say to Britney to overcome the roadblocks you've identified and achieve your optimal outcome?

HELPFUL CONCEPTS

Being informative, **205–206**

Being honest, **206**

Using "I" and "we" language, **207–208**

Deception, **211–213**

Defensive communication, **213–214**

THE OTHER SIDE

▶ Visit LaunchPad to watch a video in which Britney tells her side of the case study story. As in many real-life situations, this is information to which you did not have access when you were initially crafting your response in Part 3. The video reminds us that even when we do our best to offer competent responses, there is always another side to the story that we need to consider.

a partner or posed the heart-stopping query "Will you marry me?" Maybe it was a doctor declaring "It's a boy!" "It's a girl!" "It's twins!" Or perhaps the relational events that float upward into memory are sadder in nature, the words bitter remnants you wish you could forget: "I don't love you anymore;" "I never want to see you again;" "I'm sorry, but the prognosis is grim."

"With great power comes great responsibility," as the saying goes, and our power to shape and use verbal communication is no different. The words we exchange profoundly affect not only our interpersonal communication and relationships but also those of others. The responsibility we bear because of this power is to communicate cooperatively.

POSTSCRIPT

At the time that General George Washington ordered his officers to read aloud the words of Thomas Paine to their troops, the war to create the United States appeared lost. Washington, along with his officers and soldiers, seemed doomed to certain death. But as they stood on the icy shore of the Delaware River, this simple act of verbal communication—"These are the times that try men's souls . . ."—transformed the mood of the moment. Fatigued men's spirits were uplifted, and the soldiers set out across a seemingly impassable river to triumph in a mission that just a few hours earlier had seemed hopeless.

What words have helped you ford the raging rivers of your life? How have you used verbal communication to inspire others to face their own daunting personal and interpersonal challenges?

More than 200 years ago, a disheartened general borrowed the words of a patriot to raise his soldiers' spirits. In so doing, he created the first link in a chain of events that led to the creation of a country. Now, centuries later, the power of verbal communication to inspire, uplift, embolden, and create is still available to each of us.

LaunchPad for *Reflect & Relate* offers videos and encourages self-assessment through adaptive quizzing. Go to **macmillanhighered.com /reflectrelate4e** to get access to:

 LearningCurve Adaptive Quizzes

 Video clips that help you understand interpersonal communication

key terms

- verbal communication, 191
- symbols, 192
- constitutive rules, 193
- regulative rules, 193
- personal idioms, 193
- dialects, 194
- ▶ denotative meaning, 197
- ▶ connotative meaning, 197
- linguistic determinism, 198
- linguistic relativity, 199
- naming, 199
- speech acts, 201
- cooperative verbal communication, 204
- Cooperative Principle, 205
- honesty, 206
- misunderstanding, 207
- ▶ "you" language, 207
- ▶ "I" language, 207
- ▶ "we" language, 208
- verbal aggression, 210
- deception, 211
- ▶ defensive communication, 213
- communication apprehension, 214
- communication plans, 214

▶ You can watch brief, illustrative videos of these terms and test your understanding of the concepts in LaunchPad.

key concepts

Characteristics of Verbal Communication

- We use **verbal communication** when interacting with others. We employ words as **symbols** to represent people, objects, and ideas.
- Verbal communication is governed by both **constitutive rules** and **regulative rules** that define meanings and clarify conversational structure.
- Partners in close relationships often develop **personal idioms** for each other that convey intimacy. Large groups develop **dialects** that include distinct pronunciations.
- Language constantly changes and evolves.

Functions of Verbal Communication

- When we speak, we convey both **denotative meaning** and **connotative meaning.**
- **Linguistic determinism** suggests that our capacity for thought is defined by our language. People from different cultures experience different realities due to **linguistic relativity.**
- We control language through the power of **naming.**
- Whenever we interact with others, we use language to perform **speech acts.**

Cooperative Verbal Communication

- **Honesty** is the most important characteristic of **cooperative verbal communication.** It requires that you abide by the **Cooperative Principle.** Language should be informative, relevant, and clear to help avoid **misunderstandings.**
- You also should avoid expressing negative evaluations and opinions through **"you" language;** instead, replace it with **"I" language. "We" language** is a good means of fostering a sense of inclusiveness.

Barriers to Cooperative Verbal Communication

- When others display **verbal aggression,** it's best to remain polite or to remove yourself from the encounter.
- The most common form of **deception** is concealment.
- People who use **defensive communication** dismiss the validity of what another person says.
- Some people experience **communication apprehension,** which inhibits them from communicating competently. **Communication plans** can help with overcoming apprehension.

chapter review

8 Communicating Nonverbally

LearningCurve can help you review the material in this chapter. Go to LaunchPad: **macmillanhighered.com/reflectrelate4e**

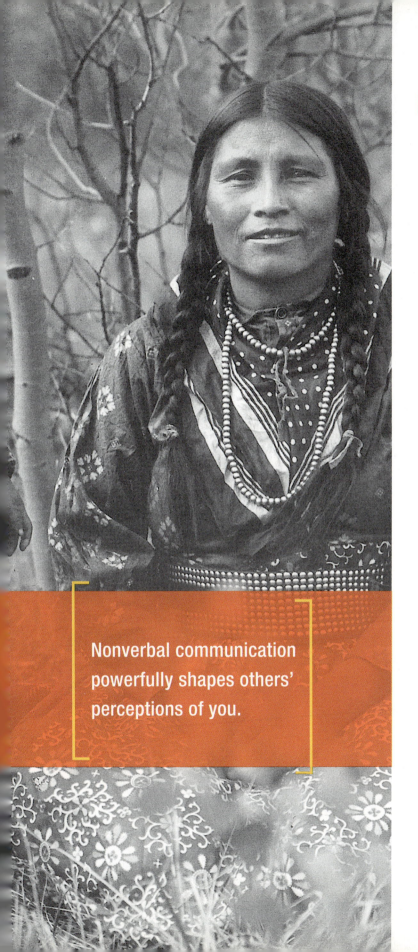

Closely examine this photograph. As you do, try to recall other images of Native Americans from the late 1800s or early 1900s that you've seen. What is different, unique, or interesting about this photo? How does the picture make you feel? What's your impression of the people in it?

I first came upon this image in poster form in my son's preschool classroom, and I was stunned. Intuitively, I found the picture perplexing and provocative, but I couldn't put my finger on precisely why. Seeing me staring at it, the teacher approached me. "Pretty neat, isn't it?" she said. "Yes," I said, "but something about it strikes me as unusual. Do you know what it is?" "Of course," she replied. "They're *smiling*."

By the late 1800s, stereotypical images of Native Americans were being sold as tourist postcards and magazine illustrations (Silversides, 1994). These images depicted Native peoples in full ceremonial dress, astride their horses or posed in front of teepees, scowling fearsomely.

As Cambridge University professor Maria Tippett (1994) notes, "The image one gets throughout this seventy year period is of a blank-faced, stiff, and unengaged people" (p. 2). When I surveyed more than 5,000 photos from this era, I found not a single image portraying Native Americans with smiles—except for this family photo.[1]

> Nonverbal communication powerfully shapes others' perceptions of you.

---

[1] Author review of 5,000 photos in the Curtis Archives, http://curtis.library.northwestern.edu/curtis/toc.cgi

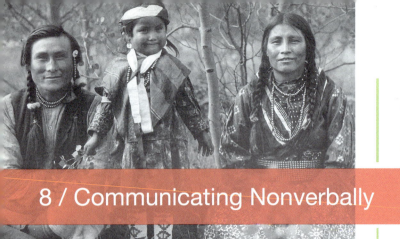

8 / Communicating Nonverbally

The Beaver Family, 1907. Whyte Museum of the Canadian Rockies, #V527, by Mary Schaffer, Photographer.

In contrast, this rare portrait, taken by amateur photographer Mary Schaffer (1861–1939), shows people who, rather than staring blankly into the camera, "communicate with the eyes behind it" (Tippett, 1994). The image has an intriguing history. Schaffer, with her friend Mollie Adams and two guides, were exploring the headwaters of the Saskatchewan and Athabasca Rivers in Canada in late 1907, where they met a band of Stoney Indians who befriended them. Among them were Samson Beaver; his wife, Leah; and their young daughter, Frances, who invited Mary to dinner. After the meal, Mary asked them if she could take their picture, and they agreed.

The Beaver family photo provides a literal and metaphorical snapshot of an interpersonal encounter: the postures, faces, dress, and use of space during a family meeting with a new friend late one sunny afternoon. You can almost feel the fellowship that must have infused the conversation, communicated through Samson's smile, his forward lean, and his direct gaze, all cues conveying intimacy and closeness. If you feel an immediate connection and empathy with Samson, you're not alone. This is a typical human reaction to the sight of a smiling person. A scowling face has quite the opposite effect.

The Beaver family photo reminds us of the universal and transcendent nature of human nonverbal expression and of its powerful role in shaping our impressions of others. A hundred years ago, a family joined new friends to share a meal and something of themselves with one another. Although they're all long since dead, the image of their encounter serves as an enduring reminder of the power of human nonverbal expression to shape our interpersonal communication and relationships.

Learning to manage your nonverbal communication is both important and challenging. It's important because most of the meaning we exchange during interpersonal encounters comes from our nonverbal expressions (Burgoon & Hoobler, 2002). What's more, nonverbal skill is associated with a host of positive outcomes, including high self-esteem, perceptions of attractiveness and popularity by others, and relationship satisfaction (Hodgins & Belch, 2000). It's challenging because nonverbal communication involves many different aspects of behavior, all of which must be considered and controlled simultaneously. When you communicate nonverbally, you manipulate your bodily movements, your voice, and the way you touch others. You also decide how to occupy space and craft your appearance. To do so competently requires knowledge of the various means of nonverbal communication, the ability to shape and adapt nonverbal expression, and the motivation to do so.

In this chapter, we discuss nonverbal communication and offer guidelines for strengthening your skills. You'll learn:

- How nonverbal communication differs from verbal communication
- How culture and gender affect our nonverbal communication
- What the eight codes of nonverbal communication are, and how you can more skillfully use them when interacting with others
- What purposes nonverbal communication serves in our everyday lives
- How to competently manage your nonverbal communication

> **chapter outline**
>
> **223**
> Principles of Nonverbal Communication
>
> **229**
> Nonverbal Communication Codes
>
> **239**
> Functions of Nonverbal Communication
>
> **245**
> Competently Managing Your Nonverbal Communication

Principles of Nonverbal Communication

How nonverbal expression differs from verbal communication

In this book, I define **nonverbal communication** as the intentional or unintentional transmission of meaning through an individual's nonspoken physical and behavioral cues (Patterson, 1995). This definition embraces both intentional and unintentional nonverbal behaviors as communication. Sometimes we do things like yawn, sigh, or grimace and mean nothing by them. But others may interpret these behaviors as acts of communication, and this perception may lead them to respond in ways that affect us, our interpersonal communication, and our relationships. A boss who catches you yawning may express concern that you're "not paying attention," even though you're closely attending to your work. At other times, we intentionally craft nonverbal behaviors to communicate information to others. We add frowning emoticons ☹ to texts, Facebook messages, and e-mails to show family members we're sad, or we look at coworkers to signal we're ready for meetings. We touch other people to signal sympathy or affection, and move closer or farther away from them to indicate intimacy or emotional distance. We arrange and light our offices and homes to convey power or peacefulness, dress and groom ourselves to communicate casualness or formality, and don artifacts such as jewelry and watches to display status and wealth.

Assignment: Unintentional Nonverbal Behaviors
Ask students to journal about a time when unintentional nonverbal communication, such as a sigh, yawn, or slouched posture, has led to miscommunication on the job, with a friend, in a class, or with a loved one. How did they discover that the unintentional behavior was a problem? What did they do to repair the situation?

○ **What comes to mind when you think about nonverbal communication? Is it as subtle as the look in your partner's eyes when you've said something funny? Is it as dramatic as an image from a movie that sticks in your memory?** (Left to right) JoJo Whilden/©Paramount Pictures/Everett Collection; Paramount Pictures/Photofest; Screen Gems/Photofest; Claudette Barius/©Warner Bros/Everett Collection

As you might have gathered, nonverbal communication differs greatly from verbal communication. Let's take a closer look at the key distinctions between nonverbal and verbal forms of expression.

NONVERBAL COMMUNICATION USES MULTIPLE CHANNELS

In contrast with verbal communication, which we transmit through a single channel at a time (the human voice when speaking; written text when online), our nonverbal messages are expressed through multiple channels simultaneously—such as auditory, visual, and tactile. When you talk with a good friend, for example, you simultaneously listen to your friend's tone of voice (auditory); watch your friend's facial expressions, use of eye contact, and hand gestures (visual); and perhaps even touch and receive touch from your friend (tactile). What's more, you do this while also listening to and making sense of your friend's verbal communication.

NONVERBAL COMMUNICATION IS MORE AMBIGUOUS

Nonverbal meanings are more flexible and ambiguous than verbal meanings. A smile can express comfort or contempt, just as a shared glance can convey intimacy or warning—depending on the situation. The ambiguity of nonverbal messages can pose difficulties for interpersonal communication and relationships. For instance, suppose a friend you suspect of harboring romantic feelings for you gives you an extra-long hug. Is he or she just being friendly or signaling romantic interest?

NONVERBAL COMMUNICATION HAS FEWER RULES

Nonverbal communication is more ambiguous than verbal communication because it is governed by fewer rules. As you saw in Chapter 7, you learn literally thousands of constitutive and regulative rules regarding grammar, spelling, pronunciation, and meaning as you master your first and any

Media Note:
Multiple Channels
The video of the behind-the-scenes voice recording of *Frozen* illustrates how vocalics, gestures, and facial expressions work together to create meaning (www.youtube.com/watch?v=SET0DeKtHkc). Point out how the two lead actors use a lot of gestures and facial expressions while recording their voices, even though these nonverbal elements will not be seen in the film. Discuss how other nonverbal elements, such as gestures and facial expressions, can impact vocalics.

additional languages. But consider how rarely you've been instructed in the use of nonverbal communication. To be sure, nonverbal rules do exist, such as "Raise your hand if you want to be called on." However, most of these rules are informal norms—for instance, "It's not polite to stare at people."

NONVERBAL COMMUNICATION HAS MORE MEANING

When we interact with others, we often deduce more meaning from people's nonverbal communication than from their verbal, and we convey more meaning to them through our nonverbal than through our verbal. Suppose you meet someone new at a party and find yourself intrigued. To assess the person's attractiveness, you probably gather a lot more information from his or her facial expressions, eye contact, posture, gestures, vocal tone, clothing, and other nonverbal signals than you do from the person's words. This is particularly true during first encounters because nonverbal communication has a greater impact on our overall impressions of attractiveness than does verbal communication (Zuckerman, Miyake, & Hodgins, 1991).

Whether you intend it or not, your nonverbal communication will transmit meaning to others. © Barbara Peacock/Corbis

Our reliance on nonverbal communication escalates even higher when people display **mixed messages,** verbal and nonverbal behaviors that convey contradictory meanings (Burgoon & Hoobler, 2002). A friend says she "isn't sad," but her slumped shoulders and downturned mouth suggest otherwise. In such cases, we almost always trust the nonverbal messages over the verbal ones. In contrast, when verbal and nonverbal messages align ("Yes, I'm sad" coupled with slumped shoulders and frown), the amount of attention we pay to verbal communication rises (Burgoon & Hoobler, 2002).

NONVERBAL COMMUNICATION IS INFLUENCED BY CULTURE

Nonverbal communication and culture are inextricably linked, in ways we will discuss throughout this chapter. You can wrinkle your brow, use a hand gesture, or speak loudly to make a point, but if people in the culture surrounding you don't understand your behavior, you haven't communicated your message. Consider cultural differences in the meaning of eye contact, for example (Chen & Starosta, 2005). In the United States and Canada, it's considered impolite or even offensive for men to gaze openly at women, but in Italy, people view it as perfectly appropriate. Middle Easterners view gazing as a sign of respect during conversation, but Cambodians see direct eye contact as insulting and an invasion of privacy. Euro-Americans use more eye contact when they're listening than when they're talking, but for African Americans, the opposite often is true.

The tight link between culture and nonverbal communication makes cross-cultural communication difficult to master. Sure, the nonverbal symbols used in

self-reflection

Call to mind an encounter you've experienced in which cultural differences in nonverbal communication proved challenging. In what ways did your cultural practices contribute to the problem? How was the situation resolved? What could you do differently in the future to avoid such dilemmas?

different cultures are easy enough to learn. But familiarity with the full tapestry of cues—perception of touch, appropriateness of gaze, facial expressions—takes much longer. Most people need many years of immersion in a culture before they fully understand the meanings of that culture's nonverbal communication (Chen & Starosta, 2005).

NONVERBAL COMMUNICATION IS INFLUENCED BY GENDER

Try Googling "men and women's body language," and see what pops up. You'll receive *millions* of results. Most are self-help or advice sites that focus on how to tell whether men and women are romantically attracted to you. If you skim through these, you'll see a theme about gender repeatedly expressed: women are better at nonverbal communication than men are. For example, AskMen.com declares, "Women are MUCH better at reading body language than men!" Learnbodylanguage.org claims that women "send five times more body language messages than men," and that their superior nonverbal skills are "engrained in women's DNA from millions of female ancestors dealing with men."

Although online content regarding interpersonal communication and relationships is often inaccurate and stereotypical (like the preceding examples), in the case of gender and nonverbal communication, some posts on popular Web sites are derived from research. Psychologist Judith Hall has examined data from hundreds of gender studies (Hall, Carter, & Horgan, 2000). Her findings suggest four consistent patterns, the first of which matches common wisdom: women *are* better than men at both sending and receiving nonverbal messages (although there's no evidence to suggest that they send "five times more" messages!). Women surpass men at nonverbally communicating in ways receivers can correctly interpret, and women are more accurate than men in their interpretations of others' nonverbal expressions.

Second, women show greater facial expressiveness than men, and they smile more. The difference in smiling stems in part from cultural expectations that women should exhibit only positive and pleasant nonverbal expressions (Spender, 1990). Third, women gaze more at others during interpersonal interactions. This is especially apparent within same-gender conversations, in which mutual gaze occurs much more often between females than between males.

Finally, men are more territorial than women. Men maintain more physical space between themselves and others during encounters. Women tolerate more intrusion into their personal space, give way to others more frequently if space is scarce, and try to take up less space than do men. Women also adopt closer conversational distances during same-gender encounters than do men, prefer side-by-side seating more than men, and perceive crowded situations more favorably.

You can use your knowledge of these differences to improve your nonverbal skills. When interacting with men, be aware that they may prefer greater

self-reflection

Consider content you've read online regarding gender differences in nonverbal communication. Is this information based on reliable research or stereotypes? Does it match or deviate from your own experiences communicating with men and women? What does this tell you about the trustworthiness of this information?

Discussion Prompt: Nonverbal Signals of Attraction

For a fun conversation on the different ways in which nonverbal communication is influenced by gender, take a look online at different tips on recognizing signs of attraction from men and women. Have your students discuss the following: How do men signal that they are interested in you nonverbally? What are women's nonverbal cues of attraction? Which group is better at sending or receiving messages of attraction? Are there differences in the ways those in heterosexual and homosexual relationships communicate attraction?

Ian Berry/Magnum Photos

conversational distance and a less direct gaze than women, and take pains to convey nonverbal messages as clearly as possible. During encounters with women, don't be surprised if they adopt a closer conversational distance, and be sensitive to their likely preference for a more direct gaze and more frequent eye contact. Failing to recognize these differences may result in frustration or misunderstandings.

NONVERBAL COMMUNICATION IS LIBERATED THROUGH TECHNOLOGY

When I walked into the kitchen and found my two youngest sons giggling, I knew they'd been up to something. "What were you doing?" I asked. "Come see!" they gleefully invited. Walking over, I found them watching themselves on YouTube. They had posted a music video of their own creation. The clip was almost entirely nonverbal: it showed them dancing wildly, waving their hands in the air, making funny faces, and pretending (badly) to sing. When I asked them why they had created the video, they said, "Because we want our friends who are gone for the summer to be able to see us!" Sure enough, the rest of the evening was spent checking the number of "views" they had received, and texting their vacationing friends regarding the video.

As recently as 20 years ago, our ability to communicate nonverbally was radically restricted by technology. Phone calls limited us to vocal cues, and communicating on the computer meant seeing words on a screen—nothing else. Only one option existed for experiencing the full tapestry of nonverbal communication: face-to-face interaction. But now, nonverbal communication has been liberated through technology. We can upload and download photos and video clips on our devices. We can interact "face-to-face" through Skype or other webcam programs with loved ones who are separated from us by distance. We can podcast, stream videos, or post photos of ourselves on Instagram, Imgur, or Flickr—then alert all our friends via e-mail, Twitter, texts, and Facebook that our content is available for viewing. As of 2015, over 6 billion hours of video are viewed each month on YouTube ("YouTube Statistics," n.d.).

This shift from technological restriction to liberation has created two notable outcomes. First, whereas we used to have just two communication modes—face-to-face interaction or methods with limited nonverbal content (such as phone calls or text-only online messages)—now we can choose various media that let us hear *and* see others when interacting. Second, we can use these media to better maintain intimate, long-distance relationships. A generation ago, soldiers stationed overseas waited a week (or more) to receive written letters from loved ones back home. Now they can exchange messages rich with verbal and nonverbal expressions in real time via the Web. Like my sons and their YouTube video, friends separated by distance—through summer vacations or unanticipated relocations—can also maintain intimate connections through frequent sharing of video clips and photos.

---

skills practice

Maintaining Online Friendship

Using nonverbal communication online to maintain a friendship

❶ Identify a long-distance friend with whom you haven't communicated recently.

❷ Think of a story or an update that you want to share with that friend.

❸ Compose a message explaining your story that uses nonverbal cues, such as photos or a video of yourself.

❹ Before sending, review your facial expressions, eye contact, body movement, voice, and appearance; make sure they communicate positively what you want to express.

❺ E-mail or post the footage, and see how your friend responds.

NONVERBAL AND VERBAL COMBINE TO CREATE COMMUNICATION

Despite the differences between verbal and nonverbal forms of expression, and the weight we give nonverbal communication when sending and receiving information, both forms are essential. When we interact with others, our verbal and nonverbal behaviors combine to create meaning (Jones & LeBaron, 2002). In everyday encounters, verbal and nonverbal communication are not experienced or expressed separately but are used jointly to create interpersonal communication (Birdwhistell, 1970). Keep this in mind: your skill as a nonverbal communicator goes hand in hand with your skill as a verbal communicator, so you need *both* to communicate competently.

The Internet has expanded the ways in which we can communicate nonverbally. Web sites like BuzzFeed host articles full of eye-catching images and videos, with small amounts of text. *Kay Nietfield/DPA/Newscom*

Nonverbal Communication Codes

[Explore the variety of nonverbal channels]

One reason nonverbal communication contains such rich information is that during interpersonal encounters, we use many different aspects of our behavior, appearance, and surrounding environment simultaneously to communicate meaning. You can greatly strengthen your nonverbal communication skills by understanding **nonverbal communication codes,** the different means used for transmitting information nonverbally (Burgoon & Hoobler, 2002). Scholars distinguish seven nonverbal communication codes, summarized in Table 8.1.

table 8.1 The Seven Codes of Nonverbal Communication

Code	Description
Kinesics	Visible body movements, including facial expressions, eye contact, gestures, and body postures
Vocalics	Vocal characteristics, such as loudness, pitch, speech rate, and tone
Haptics	Duration, placement, and strength of touch
Proxemics	Use of physical distance
Physical appearance	Appearance of hair, clothing, body type, and other physical features
Artifacts	Personal possessions displayed to others
Environment	Structure of physical surroundings

COMMUNICATING THROUGH BODY MOVEMENTS

At age 16, Tyra Banks began doing fashion shows in Europe for designers such as Chanel and Fendi. She subsequently appeared in *Elle* and *Vogue* and was the first African American woman to grace the cover of *GQ*. But what catapulted her to the top of the global modeling industry was not just her beauty; it was her unique self-awareness of, and control over, her body movements. For example, Tyra distinguishes 275 different smiles she uses when modeling, and she teaches her protégés to practice seven basic smiles on her show, *America's Next Top Model*. One of these smiles doesn't involve the mouth at all, just the eyes, which Tyra calls a *smize*. Another smile uses body posture and movement—shifting her shoulder position sideways and downward, and turning her head toward the listener. These different smiles all reflect specific emotions or situations, from anger to surprise.

Tyra Banks's superlative use of nonverbal skill in her modeling exemplifies the power of **kinesics** (from the Greek *kinesis*, meaning "movement")—visible body movements. Kinesics is the richest nonverbal code in terms of its power to communicate meaning, and it includes most of the behaviors we associate with nonverbal communication: facial expressions, eye contact, gestures, and body postures.

◐ Tyra Banks's control over her posture and facial expressions helped her rise to fame. What experiences have you had with people who use facial expressions and body movements to communicate traits such as power, strength, or kindness? Robin Marchant/WireImage/Getty Images

Facial Expression "A person's character is clearly written on the face." As this traditional Chinese saying suggests, the face plays a pivotal role in shaping our perception of others. In fact, some scholars argue that facial cues rank first among all forms of communication in their influence on our interpersonal impressions (Knapp & Hall, 2002). We use facial expressions to communicate an endless stream of emotions, and we make judgments about what others are feeling by assessing their facial expressions. Our use of emoticons (such as ☹ and ☺) to communicate attitudes and emotions online testifies to our reliance on this type of kinesics. The primacy of the face even influences our labeling of interpersonal encounters ("face-to-face") and Web sites devoted to social networking ("Facebook").

Online Self-Quiz: Reading Facial Expressions. To take this self-quiz, visit LaunchPad: macmillanhighered.com /reflectrelate4e

Eye Contact Eye contact serves many purposes during interpersonal communication. We use our eyes to express emotions, signal when it's someone else's turn to talk, and show others that we're listening to them. We also demonstrate our interest in a conversation by increasing our eye contact, or signal relationship intimacy by locking eyes with a close friend or romantic partner.

Eye contact can convey hostility as well. One of the most aggressive forms of nonverbal expression is *prolonged staring*—fixed and unwavering eye contact of several seconds' duration (typically accompanied by a hostile facial expression). Although women seldom stare, men use this behavior to threaten others, invite

chapter 8 / Communicating Nonverbally   231

◐ Within a few days of birth, infants can communicate with caregivers through eye contact.
AP Photo/Ted S. Warren

Discussion Prompt: Eye Contact
Pair students up and instruct them to have a conversation on any topic for about two minutes. Then, stop the conversation and instruct students to continue their conversation with *no* eye contact for two more minutes. Finally, complete one more round, with students maintaining *constant* eye contact. Ask: How did each round make you feel? Which was the most uncomfortable? Did you feel more uncomfortable with partners if they were the same sex or the opposite sex?

aggression (staring someone down to provoke a fight), and assert their status (Burgoon, Buller, & Woodall, 1996).

Gestures Imagine that you're driving to an appointment and someone is riding right on your bumper. Scowling at the offender in your rearview mirror, you're tempted to raise your middle finger and show it to the other driver, but you restrain yourself. The raised finger is an example of a *gesture*, a hand motion used to communicate messages (Streek, 1993). Flipping someone the bird falls into a category of gestures known as **emblems,** which represent specific verbal meanings (Ekman, 1976). With emblems, the gesture and its verbal meaning are interchangeable. You can say the words or use the gesture, and you'll send the same message.

Unlike emblems, **illustrators** accent or illustrate verbal messages. You tell your spouse about a rough road you recently biked, and as you describe the bumpy road you bounce your hand up and down to illustrate the ride.

Regulators control the exchange of conversational turns during interpersonal encounters (Rosenfeld, 1987). Listeners use regulators to tell speakers to keep talking, repeat something, hurry up, or let another person talk (Ekman & Friesen, 1969). Speakers use them to tell listeners to pay attention or to wait longer for their turn. Common examples include pointing a finger while trying to interrupt and holding a palm straight up to keep a person from interrupting. During online communication, abbreviations such as *BRB* ("be right back") and *JAS* ("just a second") serve as textual substitutes for gestural regulators.

Adaptors are touching gestures often unconsciously made that serve a psychological or physical purpose (Ekman & Friesen, 1969). For example, you smooth your hair to make a better impression while meeting a potential new romantic partner.

Posture The fourth kinesic is your body posture, which includes straightness of back (erect or slouched), body lean (forward, backward, or vertical), straightness of shoulders (firm and broad or slumped), and head position (tilted or

 Video
macmillanhighered.com/reflectrelate4e

Adaptors
Watch this clip online to answer the questions below.

Are some types of body language contagious? Have you ever been in a situation in which you were influenced by the body movements of another person? Has this mirroring of body language been helpful to you? Are there some situations in which adapting to the physical cues of others hasn't been helpful to you?

◐ Our postures are determined by conditions and tools. In Western cultures, where many people work in offices, the chair greatly influences body posture. In agrarian and pastoral societies, where people spend most of their lives working outside, body postures are shaped accordingly. In Asia and Africa, for example, a common posture is the deep squat. (Left) Royalty-Free/Corbis; (right) Robert Harding World Imagery/Getty Images

skills practice

Communicating Immediacy

Using kinesics to communicate immediacy during interpersonal encounters

① Initiate an encounter with someone whom you want to impress as an attentive and involved communicator (such as a new friend or a potential romantic partner).

② While talking, keep your facial expression pleasant. Don't be afraid to smile!

③ Make eye contact, especially while listening, but avoid prolonged staring.

④ Directly face the person, keep your back straight, lean forward, and keep your arms open and relaxed (rather than crossing them over your chest).

⑤ Use illustrators to enhance important descriptions, and regulators to control your exchange of turns.

straight up). Your posture communicates two primary messages to others: immediacy and power (Mehrabian, 1972). **Immediacy** is the degree to which you find someone interesting and attractive. Want to nonverbally communicate that you like someone? Lean forward, keep your back straight and your arms open, and hold your head up, facing the person when talking. Want to convey dislike? Lean back, close your arms, and look away.

Power is the ability to influence or control other people or events (discussed in detail in Chapter 9). Imagine attending two job interviews in the same afternoon. The first interviewer sits upright, with a tense, rigid body posture. The second interviewer leans back in his chair, with his feet up on his desk and his hands behind his head. Which interviewer has more power? Most Americans would say the second. In the United States, high-status communicators typically use relaxed postures (Burgoon et al., 1996), but in Japan, the opposite is true. Japanese display power through erect posture and feet planted firmly on the floor.

COMMUNICATING THROUGH VOICE

Grammy winner T-Pain has collaborated with an enviable who's who list of rap, hip-hop, and R&B stars: Ludacris, Lil Wayne, Chris Brown, Kanye West, and a host of others. But what makes T-Pain unique, and his songs so instantly recognizable, is his pioneering work with the pitch-correction program Auto-Tune. He was one of the first musicians to realize that Auto-Tune could be used not only to subtly correct singing errors but to alter one's voice entirely. Running his vocals through the program, his normally full, rich voice becomes thin and reedy sounding, jumping in pitch precisely from note to note without error. The result is a sound that is at once musical yet robotic. The style is so popular that he even released an iPhone app called "I Am T-Pain," allowing fans to record and modify their own voices so that they could sound like him.

The popularity of T-Pain's vocal manipulations illustrates the impact that **vocalics**—vocal characteristics we use to communicate nonverbal messages—has on our impressions. Indeed, vocalics rival kinesics in their communicative power (Burgoon et al., 1996) because our voices communicate our social, ethnic, and individual identities to others. Consider a study that recorded people from diverse backgrounds answering a series of small-talk questions, such as "How are you?" (Harms, 1961). People who listened to these recordings were able to accurately judge participants' ethnicity, gender, and social class, often within only 10 to 15 seconds, based solely on their voices. Vocalics strongly shape our perception of others when we first meet them. If we perceive a person's voice as calm and smooth (not nasal or shrill), we are more likely to view him or her as attractive; form a positive impression; and judge the person as extraverted, open, and conscientious (Zuckerman, Hodgins, & Miyake, 1990).

When we interact with others, we typically experience their voices as a totality—they "talk in certain ways" or "have a particular kind of voice." But people's voices are actually complex combinations of four characteristics: tone, pitch, loudness, and speech rate.

○ Rapper T-Pain regularly uses the pitch-correction program Auto-Tune to dramatically alter his voice, giving it an unnatural, computerized tone. What impressions do you think he is trying to convey by changing his voice? Have you ever consciously modified or "corrected" your natural voice? Gary Gershoff/WireImage/Getty Images

Tone The most noticeable aspect of T-Pain's vocals is their unnatural, computerized tone. Tone is the most complex of human vocalic characteristics and involves a combination of richness and breathiness. You can control your vocal tone by allowing your voice to resonate deep in your chest and throat—achieving a full, rich tone that conveys an authoritative quality while giving a formal talk, for example. By contrast, letting your voice resonate through your sinus cavity creates a more whiny and nasal tone—often unpleasant to others. Your use of breath also affects tone. If you expel a great deal of air when speaking, you convey sexiness. If you constrict the airflow when speaking, you create a thin and hard tone that may communicate nervousness or anxiety.

English-speakers use vocal tone to emphasize and alter the meanings of verbal messages. Regardless of the words you use, your tone can make your statements serious, silly, or even sarcastic, and you can shift tone extremely rapidly to convey different emphases. For example, when talking with your friends, you can suddenly switch from your normal tone to a much more deeply chest-resonant tone to mimic a pompous politician, then nearly instantly constrict your airflow and make your voice sound more like SpongeBob SquarePants. In online communication, we use italics to convey tone change ("I can't *believe* you did that").

Pitch You're introduced to two new coworkers, Rashad and Paul. Both are tall and muscular. Rashad has a deep, low-pitched voice; Paul, an unusually high-pitched one. How do their voices shape your impressions of them? If you're like most people,

Assignment:
Pitch and Perceptions

Place students in groups and ask them to take turns reading the following sentence aloud, placing emphasis on the different italicized word each time they say the sentence: 1. *Will* you come to the store with me tonight? 2. Will *you* come to the store with me tonight? 3. Will you *come* to the store with me tonight? 4. Will you come to the *store* with me tonight? 5. Will you come to the store with *me* tonight? 6. Will you come to the store with me *tonight*? Then discuss how the simple change in inflection and pitch of one word entirely changes the meaning.

self-reflection

Think about someone you know whose voice you find funny, strange, or irritating. What is it about this person's voice that fosters your negative impression? Is it ethical to judge someone solely from his or her voice? Why or why not?

you'll conclude that Rashad is strong and competent, while Paul is weak (Spender, 1990). Not coincidentally, people believe that women have higher-pitched voices than men and that women's voices are more "shrill" and "whining" (Spender, 1990). But although women across cultures do use higher pitch than men, most men are capable of using a higher pitch than they normally do but *choose* to intentionally limit their range to lower pitch levels to convey strength (Brend, 1975).

Loudness Consider the following sentence: "Will John leave the room" (Searle, 1965). Say the sentence aloud, each time emphasizing a different word. Notice that emphasizing one word over another can alter the meaning from statement to question to command, depending on which word is emphasized ("WILL John leave the room" versus "Will JOHN leave the room").

Loudness affects meaning so powerfully that people mimic it online by USING CAPITAL LETTERS TO EMPHASIZE CERTAIN POINTS. Indeed, people who extensively cap are punished for being "too loud." For example, a member of a music Web site I routinely visit accidentally left his Caps Lock key on while posting, and all of his messages were capped. Several other members immediately pounced, scolding him, "Stop shouting!"

Speech Rate The final vocal characteristic is the speed at which you speak. Talking at a moderate and steady rate is often considered a critical technique for effective speaking. Public-speaking educators urge students to "slow down," and people in conversations often reduce their speech rate if they believe that their listeners don't understand them. But MIT computer science researcher Jean Krause found that speech rate is not the primary determinant of intelligibility (Krause, 2001). Instead, it's pronunciation and articulation of words. People who speak quickly but enunciate clearly are just as competent communicators as those who speak moderately or slowly.

COMMUNICATING THROUGH TOUCH

Using touch to communicate nonverbally is known as **haptics,** from the ancient Greek word *haptein*. Touch is likely the first sense we develop in the womb, and receiving touch is a critical part of infant development (Knapp & Hall, 2002). Infants deprived of affectionate touch walk and talk later than others and suffer impaired emotional development in adulthood (Montagu, 1971).

Touch can vary based on its duration, the part of the body being touched, and the strength of contact, and these varieties influence how we interpret the physical contact (Floyd, 1999). Scholars distinguish between six types of touch. We use **functional-professional touch** to accomplish some type of task. Examples include touch between physicians and patients, between teachers and students, and between coaches and athletes. **Social-polite touch** derives from social norms and expectations. The most common form of social-polite touch is the handshake, which has been practiced as a greeting in one form or another for over 2,000 years (Heslin, 1974). Other examples include light hugging between friends or relatives, and the light cheek kiss. We rely on **friendship-warmth touch**—for example, gently grasping a friend's arm and giving it a squeeze—to

focus on CULTURE

Touch and Distance

Cultures vary in their norms regarding appropriate touch and distance, some with lots of touching and close distance during interpersonal encounters and others with less (Hall, 1966). Often, these differences correlate with latitude and climate. People living in cooler climes tend to be low contact, and people living in warmer areas tend to be high contact (Andersen, 1997). The effect of climate on touch and distance is even present in countries that have both colder and hotter regions. Cindy, a former student, describes her experience juggling norms for touch and distance:*

> I'm a Mexican American from El Paso, Texas, which is predominantly Latino. There, most everyone hugs hello and good-bye. And I'm not talking about a short slap on the back—I mean a nice encompassing *abrazo* (hug). While I can't say that strangers greet each other this way, I do recall times where I've done it. Growing up, it just seemed like touching is natural, and I never knew how much I expected it, maybe even relied on it, until I moved.
>
> I came to Michigan as a grad student. My transition here was relatively smooth, but it was odd to me the first time I hung out with friends and didn't hug them hello and good-bye. A couple of times on instinct I did greet them this way, and I'll never forget the strange tension that was created. Some people readily hugged me back, but most were uneasy. Quickly I learned that touching was unacceptable.
>
> Now I find that I hold back from engaging people in this manner. I feel like I'm hiding a part of myself, and it is frustrating. Nonetheless, this is the way things are done here, and I've had to adjust. Fortunately, I now have a few friends who recognize my need to express myself in this way and have opened themselves up to it. I'm grateful for that, and through these people a piece of me and my identity is saved.

discussion questions

- What has your culture taught you about the use of touch and distance? Are you a high- or low-contact person?
- When communicating with people from other cultures, how do you adapt your use of touch and distance?

*Cindy's narrative was provided voluntarily to the author with full permission for publication.

---

express our like for another person. **Love-intimacy touch**—cupping a romantic partner's face tenderly in your hands, giving him or her a big, lingering hug—lets you convey deep emotional feelings. **Sexual-arousal touch,** as the name implies, is intended to physically stimulate another person. Finally, **aggressive-hostile touch** involves forms of physical violence, like grabbing, slapping, and hitting—behaviors designed to hurt and humiliate others.

Cultural upbringing has a strong impact on how people use and perceive touch. For example, many Hispanics use friendship-warmth touch more frequently than do Europeans and Euro-Americans. Researchers in one study monitored casual conversations occurring in outdoor cafés in two different locales: San Juan, Puerto Rico, and London, England. They then averaged the number of touches between conversational partners. The Puerto Ricans touched each other an average of 180 times per hour. The British average? Zero (Environmental Protection Agency, 2002).

**Assignment:
Violating Personal
Space Norms**

Ask students to engage in a personal space violation outside of class. For example, students could break a personal space rule with a friend or violate elevator norms in a public space. Students should describe their behavior, why it was a violation, and others' reactions to it in a short paper. Share the examples in class, and discuss various informal rules for nonverbal expectations.

 Video

macmillanhighered.com
/reflectrelate4e

Proxemics
Watch this clip online to answer the questions below.

When first meeting someone you are romantically interested in, which proxemics zones do you use? Why? In the video, what prompts the woman to place her coat on the empty chair next to her? What message is the man sending as he changes chairs?

Want to see more? Check out LaunchPad for a clip on **haptics.**

Because people differ in the degree to which they feel comfortable giving and receiving touch, consider adapting your use of touch to others' preferences, employing more or less touch depending on your conversational partner's behavior responses to your touching. If you are talking with a "touchy" person, who repeatedly touches your arm gently while talking (a form of social-polite touch), you can probably presume that such a mild form of touch would be acceptable to reciprocate. But if a person offers you no touch at all, not even a greeting handshake, you would be wise to inhibit your touching.

COMMUNICATING THROUGH PERSONAL SPACE

The fourth nonverbal communication code, **proxemics** (from the Latin *proximus*, meaning "near"), is communication through the use of physical distance. Edward T. Hall, one of the first scholars to study proxemics, identified four communication distances: intimate, personal, social, and public (Hall, 1966). **Intimate space** ranges from 0 to 18 inches. Sharing intimate space with someone counts among the defining nonverbal features of close relationships (see Figure 8.1). **Personal space** ranges between 18 inches and 4 feet and is the distance we occupy during encounters with friends. For most Americans and Canadians, personal space is about your "wingspan"—that is, the distance from fingertip to fingertip when you extend your arms. **Social space** ranges from about 4 to 12 feet. Many people use it when communicating in the workplace or with acquaintances and strangers. In **public space,** the distance between persons ranges upward from 12 feet, including great distances; this span occurs most often during formal occasions, such as public speeches or college lectures.

In addition to the distance we each claim for ourselves during interpersonal encounters, we also have certain physical areas or spaces in our lives that we

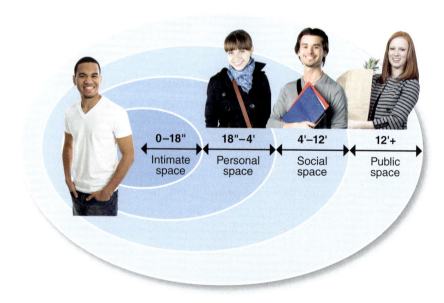

figure 8.1 **Physical Distance in Communication**

consider our turf. **Territoriality** is the tendency to claim physical spaces as our own and to define certain locations as areas we don't want others to invade without permission (Chen & Starosta, 2005). Human beings react negatively to others who invade their perceived territory, and we respond positively to those who respect it (King, 2001). Imagine coming back to your dorm room and finding one of your roommate's friends asleep in your bed. How would you respond? If you're like most people, you would feel angry and upset. Even though your roommate's friend is not violating your personal space (distance from your body), he or she is inappropriately encroaching on physical space that you consider your territory.

What can you do to become more sensitive to differences in the use of personal space? Keep in mind that, as noted earlier in this chapter, North Americans' notions of personal space tend to be larger than those in most other cultures, especially people from Latin America or the Middle East. When interacting with people from other cultures, adjust your use of space in accordance with your conversational partner's preferences. Realize, also, that if you're from a culture that values large personal space, others will feel most comfortable interacting at a closer distance than you're used to. If you insist on maintaining a large personal space bubble around yourself when interacting with people from other cultures, they may think you're aloof or distant or that you don't want to talk with them.

COMMUNICATING THROUGH PHYSICAL APPEARANCE

On the hit TLC show *Say Yes to the Dress*, Randy Fenoli and other sales associates at Kleinfeld Bridal in New York City help prospective brides find the ideal wedding dresses for what is (for many people) "the most important day of their lives." The show involves not just finding a dress but finding the dress that fits a bride's ideal image for how she should look. However, the show is not just about superficial allure. Instead, the choice of dress and accessories conveys a powerful communicative

self-reflection

Which locations in your physical spaces at home and work do you consider your most valued territories? How do you communicate this territoriality to others? What do you do when people trespass? Have your reactions to such trespasses caused negative personal or professional consequences?

On *Say Yes to the Dress*, a bride's dress choice is not merely a fashion statement but a statement about who she is as a person. Similarly, your daily physical appearance is a form of nonverbal communication that expresses how you want others to see you. Courtesy of TLC

Discussion Prompt: Perceptions of Physical Appearance

Create a slide show by searching Google Images for pictures of various kinds of people. Look for stereotypes such as "the hipster," "the biker dude," and "the nerd." Show the pictures in class and have students share their immediate perceptions of the individuals in the photos. What is their job? What do they enjoy doing? You could have students rate their intelligence, likability, and so forth. Have them consider how quickly perceptions are formed based on appearance.

message to others about the bride's self-identity. As Randy notes, "One of the most important things I tell brides is that you should always choose a gown that really represents *who you are*, because what you're doing at a wedding is telling a story about who you are as a person, and as a couple" (Herweddingplanner.com, 2011).

Although weddings are an extreme example in terms of the emphasis placed on how we look, our **physical appearance**—visible attributes such as hair, clothing, and body type—profoundly influences all our interpersonal encounters. In simple terms, how you look conveys as much about you as what you say. And beauty counts. Across cultures, people credit individuals they find physically attractive with higher levels of intelligence, persuasiveness, poise, sociability, warmth, power, and employment success than they credit to unattractive individuals (Hatfield & Sprecher, 1986).

This effect holds in online environments as well. For example, the physical attractiveness of friends who post their photos on your Facebook page has noteworthy effects on people's perceptions of *your* attractiveness (Walther, Van Der Heide, Kim, Westerman, & Tong, 2008). That is, if you have attractive friends' photos on your page, people will perceive you as more physically and socially attractive; if you have unattractive friends, you'll seem less attractive to others.

What physical appearance characteristics does it take to be judged attractive? Standards of beauty are highly variable, both across cultures and across time periods. But one factor that's related to attractiveness across cultures is *facial symmetry*—the degree to which each side of your face precisely matches the other. For example, this can include whether someone's eyes are the same shape or whether someone's ears are at the exact same height. People with symmetrical faces are judged as more attractive than people with asymmetrical faces (Grammer & Thornhill, 1994), although perfect facial symmetry may be seen as artificial and unattractive (Kowner, 1996).

Your clothing also has a profound impact on others' perceptions of you. More than 40 years of research suggests that clothing strongly influences people's judgments about profession, level of education, socioeconomic status, and even personality and personal values (Burgoon et al., 1996). The effect that clothing has on perception makes it essential that you consider the appropriateness of your dress, the context for which you are dressing, and the image of self you wish to nonverbally communicate. When I worked for a Seattle trucking company, I was expected to wear clothes that could withstand rough treatment. On my first day, I "dressed to impress" and was teased by coworkers and management for dressing as if I were an executive at a large corporation. But expectations like this can change in other situations. During job interviews, for example, dress as nicely as you can. Being even moderately formally dressed is one of the strongest predictors of whether an interviewer will perceive you as socially skilled and highly motivated (Gifford, Ng, & Wilkinson, 1985).

COMMUNICATING THROUGH OBJECTS

Take a moment to examine the objects that you're wearing and that surround you: jewelry, watch, cell phone, computer, art or posters on the wall, and so forth.

---

self-reflection

Consider your physical appearance, as shown in photos on your Facebook page or other personal Web sites. What do your face, hair, clothing, and body communicate to others about who you are and what you're like? Now examine friends' photos on your pages. How might their appearance affect others' perceptions of you?

These **artifacts**—the things we possess that influence how we see ourselves and that we use to express our identity to others—constitute another code of nonverbal communication. As with our use of posture and of personal space, we use artifacts to communicate power and status. For example, by displaying expensive watches, cars, or living spaces, people "tell" others that they're wealthy and influential (Burgoon et al., 1996).

COMMUNICATING THROUGH THE ENVIRONMENT

A final way in which we communicate nonverbally is through our **environment,** the physical features of our surroundings. As the photo of the Google office illustrates, our environment envelops us, shapes our communication, and implies certain things about us, often without our realizing it.

Two types of environmental factors play a role in shaping interpersonal communication: fixed features and semifixed features (Hall, 1981). *Fixed features* are stable and unchanging environmental elements, such as walls, ceilings, floors, and doors. Fixed features define the size of a particular environment, and size has an enormous emotional and communicative impact on people. For example, the size of structures communicates power, with bigger often being better. In corporations, it's often assumed that larger offices equal greater power for their occupants; and historically, the square footage of homes has communicated the occupant's degree of wealth.

Semifixed features are impermanent and usually easy to change; they include furniture, lighting, and color. We associate bright lighting with environments that are very active and soft lighting with environments that are calmer and more intimate. Color also exerts a powerful effect on our mood and communication: we experience blues and greens as relaxing, yellows and oranges as arousing and energizing, reds and blacks as sensuous, and grays and browns as depressing (Burgoon et al., 1996).

Examine the layout of this Google office space. What do the features of the room—including wall stickers, stuffed animals, and colorful balls—say about Google's company culture and the people who work there?
Maurice Tsai/Bloomberg via Getty Images

Functions of Nonverbal Communication

[How we use nonverbal behaviors in communication]

Triumph. Exultation. Unbridled joy. These meanings are communicated from every aspect of Brandi Chastain's nonverbal expression. On July 10, 1999, Chastain scored the penalty kick that earned the United States the Women's World Cup victory. As tens of millions of viewers watched, she tore her jersey off and dropped to her knees. But even as Chastain celebrated, her decision to communicate in this manner sparked controversy. Although male players routinely removed and waved their jerseys to mark

self-reflection

Look around the room you're in right now. How does this room make you feel? How do the size of the space, furniture, lighting, and color contribute to your impression? What kind of interpersonal communication would be most appropriate for this space—personal or professional? Why?

○ This photo was taken immediately after Brandi Chastain scored the penalty kick that won the 1999 World Cup. Her gesture of tearing off her jersey and falling to her knees communicated many intense emotions and started a media controversy—all without her saying a word. Roberto Schmidt/AFP/Getty Images

victories, female players weren't supposed to present themselves publicly in this way. As Faye Wattleton, president of the Center for Advancement of Women, notes, a substantial double standard exists: what's acceptable nonverbally for men is often viewed with "collective horror" when women do it. In the aftermath, Chastain's choice would ignite public consternation, influence fashion, and alter athletic rules. Photos appeared on the covers of *Time*, *Newsweek*, and *Sports Illustrated*. A man on the street confronted Chastain, demanding, "Why did you do that!? I can't let my daughter walk around in a jog bra!" Some pundits suggested that the gesture was a marketing ploy: the sports bra Chastain wore displayed Nike's trademark "swoosh." In the fashion season following, sports-bra sales skyrocketed. And soccer officials banned the "tearing off the jersey" gesture—for women *and* men.

In 2012, ESPN conducted an online poll of the "greatest moment in U.S. women's sports." The women's World Cup victory was the overwhelming winner. But even though it's been more than a decade since this iconic event, people still question Chastain about her behavior, interpreting it in ways other than what she intended. As she notes, "Everybody is going to have their opinion about it. . . . But it was just a 'YES!' Twenty-something years of playing the game, and this was the most perfect moment."

Like Chastain, when we're caught up in an emotional moment, good or bad, we think of our nonverbal expression as something that just happens, a simple and direct reflection of our inner states. But nonverbal communication serves *many* different functions in our lives. Within interpersonal encounters, nonverbal communication serves at least five functions: it expresses emotions, conveys meanings, presents ourselves to others, helps manage interactions, and defines relationships (Argyle, 1969).

EXPRESSING EMOTION

When Brandi Chastain described her nonverbal behavior as being "just a 'YES!'" she highlighted arguably the most elemental function of nonverbal communication: the expression of emotion. We communicate emotion nonverbally through **affect displays**—intentional or unintentional nonverbal behaviors that display actual or feigned emotions (Burgoon et al., 1996). In everyday interactions, affect displays are presented primarily through the face and voice. Intentional use of the face to communicate emotion begins during late infancy, when babies learn to facially communicate anger and happiness to get what they want (Burgoon et al., 1996). Unintentional affect displays begin even earlier. Infants in the first few weeks of life instinctively and reflexively display facial expressions of distress, disgust, and interest. As adults, we communicate hundreds, if not thousands, of real and faked emotional states with our faces.

People also use vocalics to convey emotions. Consider how you communicate love through your voice. What changes do you make in pitch, tone, volume, and speech rate? How does your "loving" voice differ from your "angry" voice? Most people express emotions such as grief and love through lowered vocal pitch, and hostile emotions—such as anger and contempt—through loudness (Costanzo, Markel, & Costanzo, 1969). Pitch conveys emotion so powerfully that the source of the sound (human voice or other) is irrelevant, and words aren't necessary. Researcher Klaus Scherer (1974) mimicked voice patterns on a music synthesizer and had listeners judge the emotion conveyed. Participants strongly associated high pitch with emotions such as anger, fear, and surprise, and they linked low pitch with pleasantness, boredom, and sadness.

CONVEYING MEANINGS

In the wake of her triumph, much of the debate regarding Chastain centered around what she "meant" by her behavior. Was she making a "feminist statement"? Was it a "marketing ploy"?

Just as we use words to signify unique meanings, we often use nonverbal communication to directly convey meanings. Your boss flips you a thumbs-up gesture following a presentation, and you know she means "Good job!" A friend makes a two-finger *V* at a campus rally, and you recognize it as an emblem for peace.

At other times we use nonverbal communication more indirectly, as a means for accenting or augmenting verbal communication meanings (Malandro & Barker, 1983). We do this in five ways, the first of which is by *reiterating*. Nonverbal communication is used to reiterate or repeat verbal messages, as when you say "Up!" and then point upward. Second, we *contradict* our verbal messages with our nonverbal communication. For example, a friend may ask if you're angry, but you respond by scowling and angrily shouting "No, I'm not angry!" Third, we use nonverbal communication to *enhance* the meaning of verbal messages, such as when you tell an intimate "I love you" while smiling and offering a gentle touch to emphasize the point. Fourth, we sometimes use nonverbal communication to *replace* verbal expressions, such as when you shake your head instead of saying no. Finally, we use nonverbal communication to *spotlight* certain parts of verbal messages, such as when you increase the loudness of just one word: "STOP hitting your brother with that light saber!"

PRESENTING SELF

Think about your interactions with your manager at work. How do you let him or her know—without words—that you're a dedicated and hardworking

Assignment: Perceptions of Artifacts
Ask students to choose a personal belonging that is important to them (a favorite hat, cell phone, wedding ring) and briefly write down why this artifact is important. Then ask for volunteers willing to display their belongings. Show the objects, and ask the class to indicate their perceptions of the items. How does the class's perception match up to the owners' perceptions? Are the volunteers surprised by the results?

Teaching Tip: Communicating through the Environment
Many students do not realize that colors have powerful meanings in different cultures. While white is associated with weddings and purity in the United States, it is associated with mourning in Japan. List various colors, and have students provide what meanings and feelings they associate with each. Then share the meanings from various cultures available at www.empower-yourself-with-color-psychology.com/cultural-color.html.

Teaching Tip: Conveying Meaning

Albert Mehrabian's research (1972) suggests that 93 percent of our communication is transmitted nonverbally (38 percent in paralinguistic clues, or the way something is said, and 55 percent in facial expressions), while 7 percent is transmitted verbally through our words. Yet Burgoon et al. (1996) suggests that only about 65 percent of our meaning comes from nonverbal communication. Ask students to discuss which estimate seems to best fit their experiences and explain why.

skills practice

Professional Self-Presentation

Presenting yourself in a professional fashion in the workplace.

❶ Display a pleasant facial expression, make good eye contact, lean forward, and exhibit upright posture.

❷ Use a moderately resonant and breathy vocal tone, medium pitch and volume, and moderate speech rate.

❸ Adapt your use of proxemics to others' needs for personal space, and respect their territory.

❹ Adjust your touching to match others' preferences.

❺ Keep appointments or allow flexibility regarding punctuality.

❻ Ensure that your physical appearance and artifacts are appropriate, asking your coworkers' and manager's opinions if you're uncertain.

---

employee? Chances are, you employ almost all the nonverbal codes previously discussed, simultaneously. You convey attentiveness through focused eye contact and pleasant facial expression, and you communicate seriousness through moderate speech rate and pitch. You likely avoid crowding your boss and touching him or her. You also dress appropriately for the office and try to obey workplace norms regarding how you decorate your work space.

Now imagine that your manager confides in you a recent diagnosis of terminal illness. How would you use nonverbal communication to convey a different self—one who's compassionate and supportive? You'd likely adopt a facial expression conveying sadness and concern. You'd slow your speech rate and lower the pitch of your voice to convey empathy. You'd decrease your interpersonal distance to communicate support. And you might touch your boss lightly on the elbow or gently clasp his or her shoulder to signify caring.

As these examples suggest, nonverbal communication can help us present different aspects of our self to others. We all use nonverbal communication codes to create our identities during interpersonal encounters. An important part of being a competent nonverbal communicator is recognizing the need to shift our nonverbal communication quickly to present ourselves in different ways when the situation demands—for example, dedicated employee one moment, concerned fellow human being another.

MANAGING INTERACTIONS

Nonverbal communication also helps us manage interpersonal interactions. For example, during conversations, we use regulators, eye contact, touch, smiling, head nods, and posture shifts to signal who gets to speak and for how long (Patterson, 1988). While chatting with a friend, you probably look at him or her anywhere from 30 to 50 percent of your talk time. Then, when you're approaching the end of your conversational turn, you invite your friend to talk by decreasing your pitch and loudness, stopping any gestures, and focusing your gaze on the other person. As your friend begins speaking, you now look at your partner almost 100 percent of his or her talk time, nodding your head to show you're listening (Goodwin, 1981).

During conversations, we also read our partners' nonverbal communication to check their level of interest in what we're saying—watching for signals like eye contact, smiles, and head nods. Yet we're usually unaware that we're doing this until people behave in unexpected ways. For example, if a partner *fails* to react to something we've said that we consider provocative or funny, we may shoot them a glance or frown to express our displeasure nonverbally.

Nonverbal communication also helps us regulate others' attention and behavior. For example, a sudden glance and stern facial expression from a parent or babysitter can stop a child from reaching for the forbidden cookie jar. In my sons' school, the principal gains students' attention by clapping loudly three times, a pattern that students then repeat back to him, falling silent afterward to listen for an important announcement.

DEFINING RELATIONSHIPS

You're sitting at a local diner, eating lunch and people-watching. Two couples are sitting in nearby booths. One couple sits with one partner very close to the other. They cuddle, touch, and occasionally kiss. When they're not touching, they're smiling and gazing at each other. The couple sitting at the next booth over is behaving very differently. The man sits up tall and straight, his arms extended on both sides of the table. He glares at his partner, interrupts her, and doesn't look at her when she's talking. Her eyes are downcast, her hands are folded in her lap, and she speaks softly. What does the nonverbal communication of each of these couples tell you about the degree of intimacy in their relationship? the partners' relative dominance? A final function of nonverbal communication is to define the nature of our interpersonal relationships. In particular, we use our nonverbal communication to create intimacy and define dominance or submissiveness in our relationships (Burgoon & Hoobler, 2002).

Intimacy   One crucial function nonverbal communication serves is to create **intimacy,** the feeling of closeness and "union" that exists between us and our partners (Mashek & Aron, 2004). For example, in her novel *Written on the Body*, acclaimed British author Jeanette Winterson (1993) offers a vivid and poignant description of how the nonverbal code of touch defines intimacy:

> Articulacy of fingers, the language of the deaf. Who taught you to write on my back? Who taught you to use your hands as branding irons? You have scored your name into my shoulders, referenced me with your mark. The pads of your fingers have become printing blocks, you tap a message on to my skin, tap meaning into my body. Your Morse code interferes with my heart beat. I had a steady heart before I met you, I relied upon it, it had seen active service and grown strong. Now you alter its pace with your rhythm, you play upon me, drumming me taut. (p. 89)

But intimacy isn't defined solely through touch. Physical closeness, shared gaze, soft voices, relaxed postures, sharing of personal objects, and, of course, spending time together—each of these nonverbal behaviors highlights and enhances intimacy. Consider just a few specifics. Smiling and gazing are associated with intimacy (Floyd & Burgoon, 1999), something vividly illustrated in the Beaver family photo in our chapter opening. Individuals share more personal space with intimates and liked others than with strangers, and use proximity to convey affection (Floyd & Morman, 1999). Studies that have instructed people to communicate liking to others have found that the primary way people do so is through increasing gaze, smiling, and leaning forward (Palmer & Simmons, 1995). Conversely, one can communicate lack of intimacy and greater formality through distance, lack of eye contact, decreased vocal expressiveness, precise articulation, and tense postures (Burgoon & Hoobler, 2002).

▶ Think about the functions nonverbal communication is playing in this photo. Can you tell what emotions are being expressed? What about the relationships and interactions between the women? What does this tell you about the influence of nonverbal communication in our daily experiences? © Paula Lerner/Aurora

In general, more intimate relationships—particularly romantic bonds—show higher levels of nonverbal involvement across all of the codes (more eye contact, more touch, more smiling, closer distance, and so forth). For romantic couples, the level of nonverbal involvement is a direct indicator of the relationship's health (Patterson, 1988). Think back to the highly engaged couple in the diner booth. Although you don't know who they are, what they're saying, or what culture they're from, you could reasonably conclude that they have a healthy relationship, based solely on their nonverbal behavior.

Teaching Tip: Dominance and Submissiveness

Students often think of dominance as a behavior that is detrimental to relationships. Further, they often believe that symmetrical relationships with equal bases of power are preferred over complementary relationships with unequal bases of power. Place students in pairs and ask them to discuss when dominance is necessary in relationships (e.g., parents giving a child important safety rules) and when complementary relationship types could function better than symmetrical relationship types.

Dominance and Submissiveness Recall the physically distant couple in the other diner booth. Rather than conveying intimacy, their nonverbal communication displays dominance and submissiveness. **Dominance** refers to the interpersonal behaviors we use to exert power and influence over others (Burgoon & Dunbar, 2000). Larger-than-normal use of space; access to other people's space, time, and possessions; one-sided use of touch (giving more, receiving less); indirect body orientation; direct gaze and staring; frowning and scowling; and silence—all of these codes signal the dominance of the person who employs them (Carney, Hall, & Smith LeBeau, 2005). And gender has little effect—these behaviors are perceived as dominant when displayed by either men or women (Carney et al., 2005).

In contrast, **submissiveness** is the willingness to allow others to exert power over us. We communicate submissiveness to others nonverbally by engaging in behaviors that are opposite those that express dominance, such as taking up less space; letting others control our time, space, and possessions; smiling more; and permitting others to interrupt us.

Test Your Nonverbal Dominance Knowledge

Knowing which behaviors people perceive as dominant is an important part of being a competent nonverbal communicator (Carney et al., 2005). Review the following list of behaviors, identify and rank the top five nonverbal cues that you think communicate dominance, and check your answers.

To take this quiz online, visit LaunchPad: macmillanhighered.com/reflectrelate4e.

_____ (a) Using a loud voice while you talk

_____ (b) Exhibiting confident and self-assured facial expressions

_____ (c) Initiating the shaking of an interaction partner's hand

_____ (d) Having your arms crossed or folded on your chest during an encounter

_____ (e) Displaying unresponsive facial expressions toward your conversational partner

_____ (f) Using broad, large, and expansive hand gestures while you talk

_____ (g) Showing facial disgust

_____ (h) Paying attention to your conversational partner

_____ (i) Manipulating objects during the conversation (e.g., playing with your pencil or fiddling with a piece of paper)

_____ (j) Engaging in "invasive" behaviors with your conversational partner, such as standing too close, touching, and pointing

Note: Items in this *Self-Quiz* are derived from Table 1 of Carney et al. (2005).

Scoring: The most to least dominating nonverbal cues: b, c, f, j, and g.

Competently Managing Your Nonverbal Communication

Ways to improve your nonverbal expression

As you interact with others, you use various nonverbal communication codes naturally and simultaneously. Similarly, you take in and interpret others' nonverbal communication instinctively. Look again at the Beaver family photo (on p. 248). While viewing this image, you probably don't think, "What's Samson's mouth doing?" or "Gee, Frances's arm is touching Samson's shoulder." When it comes to nonverbal communication, although all the parts are important, it's the overall package that delivers the message.

Given the nature of nonverbal communication, we think it's important to highlight some general guidelines for how you can competently manage your nonverbal communication. In this chapter, we've offered very specific advice for improving your use of particular nonverbal codes. But we conclude with three principles for competent nonverbal conduct, which reflect the three aspects of competence first introduced in Chapter 1: effectiveness, appropriateness, and ethics.

First, when interacting with others, remember that people view your nonverbal communication as at least as important as what you say, if not more so. Although you should endeavor to build your active listening skills (Chapter 6) and use of cooperative language (Chapter 7), bear in mind that people will often assign the greatest weight to what you do nonverbally.

making relationship choices

Dealing with Mixed Messages

1 BACKGROUND

Receiving mixed messages—when verbal and nonverbal communication clash—is a common dilemma in relationships. To explore ways to deal with mixed messages, read the case study in Part 2; then, drawing on all you know about interpersonal communication, work through the problem-solving model in Part 3.

 Visit LaunchPad to check out the other side of the story (Part 4). For the best experience, complete all parts in LaunchPad: **macmillanhighered.com /reflectrelate4e**.

2 CASE STUDY

You, Dakota, and Tad are good friends. On the occasions that the three of you are not hanging out together, you're in touch through text messages, Instagram, and so on. Despite your collective closeness, romance has never arisen. This is partly because the three of you have always been involved with other people.

Over the past six months, however, you've all been through breakups. In the wake of this, things have started to get weird. It began a few weeks ago, when the three of you met for lunch. Dakota was all dressed up, and when you asked, "What's the occasion?" she was evasive. She kept leaning toward Tad, making extensive eye contact, smiling, touching his arm and leg (although each instance seemed accidental), and even suggested that she and he take more classes together next semester. You're pleased, because you like the two of them immensely and think they'd make a good couple. Tad, however, seems completely clueless, which is not surprising; it has long been a joke between the three of you that Tad can't tell when someone is hitting on him.

After lunch, you corner Tad and say, "Dakota is totally crushing on you!" Tad is shocked and adamantly denies it. He is so persuasive that you begin to doubt your own observations. You decide to e-mail Dakota. The two of you have always been honest and open with each other, so you tell Dakota what you saw. She responds with a teasing, "As if I'd ever crush on Tad ;)!" Now you're *really* confused.

In the days that follow, you increasingly sense that Dakota wants a romantic involvement with Tad. Everything about her nonverbal communication suggests intimacy. But whenever you raise the issue, Dakota denies it, responding, "You've got an overactive imagination." You start getting irked by the mixed messages. Are you really imagining things? Should you push her to tell you the truth? Making matters worse, Tad has finally clued in to her behavior, and he confides to you that although he's worried about getting burned again (his breakup with his ex, Jessica, was ugly), he is starting to fall for Dakota.

Later that evening, you get a call from Dakota. After chatting for a few minutes, the issue of Tad comes up. Dakota says, "I know I've been dodging your questions about Tad, but . . . do you think he likes me?"

3 YOUR TURN

Think about all you've learned thus far about interpersonal communication. Then work through the following five steps. Remember, there are no "right" answers, so think hard about what is the *best* choice! (P.S. Need help? See the *Helpful Concepts* list.)

step 1

Reflect on yourself. What are your thoughts and feelings in this situation? What attributions are you making about Dakota, based on her interpersonal communication? Are your attributions accurate? Why or why not?

step 2

Reflect on your partner. Using perspective-taking and empathic concern, put yourself in Dakota's shoes. What is she thinking and feeling in this situation?

step 3

Identify the optimal outcome. Think about all the information you have regarding Dakota, Tad, and their relationship, as well as what role, if any, you should have in this situation. Given all these factors, what's the best, most constructive relationship outcome possible? Be sure to consider not just what's best for you (as their friend) but what's best for Dakota and Tad as well.

step 4

Locate the roadblocks. Taking into consideration your own thoughts and feelings, those of Dakota and Tad, and all that has happened in this situation, what obstacles are keeping you from achieving the optimal outcome?

step 5

Chart your course. What can you say to Dakota to overcome the roadblocks you've identified and achieve your optimal outcome?

HELPFUL CONCEPTS

The ambiguity of nonverbal communication, **224**

Mixed messages, **225**

Immediacy, **232**

Friendship-warmth touch, **234–235**

Intimacy, **243–244**

4 THE OTHER SIDE

Visit LaunchPad to watch a video in which Dakota tells her side of the case study story. As in many real-life situations, this is information to which you did not have access when you were initially crafting your response in Part 3. The video reminds us that even when we do our best to offer competent responses, there is always another side to the story that we need to consider.

For romantic couples, the level of nonverbal involvement is a direct indicator of the relationship's health. Paul Schutzer/Getty Images

Second, be sensitive to the demands of interpersonal situations. For example, if an interaction seems to call for more formal or more casual behavior, adapt your nonverbal communication accordingly. Remind yourself, if necessary, that being interviewed for a job, sharing a relaxed evening with your roommate, and deepening the level of intimacy in a love relationship all call for different nonverbal messages. You can craft those messages through careful use of the many different nonverbal codes available to you.

Finally, remember that verbal communication and nonverbal communication flow with each other. Your experience of nonverbal communication from others and your nonverbal expression to others are fundamentally fused with the words you and they choose to use. As a consequence, you cannot become a skilled interpersonal communicator by focusing time, effort, and energy only on verbal or only on nonverbal elements. Instead, you must devote yourself to both, because it is only when both are joined as a union of skills that more competent interpersonal communication ability is achieved.

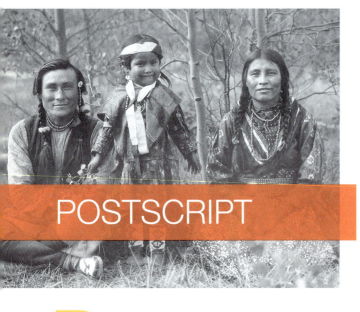

POSTSCRIPT

Reflect on the postures, dress, use of space, eye contact, and facial expressions depicted in the Beaver family photo. Then think about how nonverbal communication shapes your life. What judgments do you make about others, based on their scowls and smiles? their postures? their appearance and voice? Do you draw accurate conclusions about certain groups of people based on their nonverbal communication? How do others see you? As you communicate with others throughout a typical day, what do your facial expressions, posture, dress, use of space, and eye contact convey?

We began this chapter with a family of smiles. The smile is one of the simplest, most commonplace expressions. Yet like so many nonverbal expressions, the smile has the power to fundamentally shift interpersonal perceptions. In the case of the Beaver family, seeing the smiles that talking with a friend evoked 100 years ago helps erase more than a century of Native American stereotypes. But the power of the Beaver family's smiles goes beyond simply remedying a historical distortion. It highlights the power that even your simplest nonverbal communication has in shaping and shifting others' perceptions of you.

LaunchPad for *Reflect & Relate* offers videos and encourages self-assessment through adaptive quizzing. Go to **macmillanhighered.com/reflectrelate4e** to get access to:

 LearningCurve Adaptive Quizzes

 Video clips that help you understand interpersonal communication

key terms

- nonverbal communication, 223
- mixed messages, 225
- nonverbal communication codes, 229
- ▶ kinesics, 230
- ▶ emblems, 231
- ▶ illustrators, 231
- ▶ regulators, 231
- ▶ adaptors, 231
- immediacy, 232
- power, 232
- ▶ vocalics, 233
- ▶ haptics, 234
- functional-professional touch, 234
- social-polite touch, 234
- friendship-warmth touch, 234
- love-intimacy touch, 235
- sexual-arousal touch, 235
- aggressive-hostile touch, 235
- ▶ proxemics, 236
- intimate space, 236
- personal space, 236
- social space, 236
- public space, 236
- territoriality, 237
- physical appearance, 238
- artifacts, 239
- environment, 239
- ▶ affect displays, 240
- intimacy, 243
- dominance, 244
- submissiveness, 244

▶ You can watch brief, illustrative videos of these terms and test your understanding of the concepts in LaunchPad.

key concepts

Principles of Nonverbal Communication

- **Nonverbal communication** includes all unspoken behavioral displays and generally carries more meaning than verbal communication.
- Both culture and gender shape people's perceptions and use of nonverbal communication.

Nonverbal Communication Codes

- Although seven different **nonverbal communication codes** exist, the behaviors that most people associate with nonverbal communication—such as facial expressions, gestures, and body posture—are **kinesics.** Four different forms of gestures are commonly used: **emblems, illustrators, regulators,** and **adaptors.**
- Something as seemingly simple as body posture can communicate substantial information regarding **immediacy** and **power** to others.
- Different features of the voice contribute to the nonverbal code of **vocalics.**
- People vary their duration, placement, and strength of touch (known as **haptics**) to communicate a range of meanings, including **functional-professional touch, social-polite touch, friendship-warmth touch, love-intimacy touch, sexual-arousal touch,** and **aggressive-hostile touch.**
- Forms of physical distance, or **proxemics,** include **intimate, personal, social,** and **public space.** All human beings experience **territoriality** and resent perceived invasions of personal domains.
- Like it or not, our **physical appearance** strongly molds others' impressions of us.
- We use personal **artifacts** to portray who we are to others and to communicate information regarding our worth, status, and power.
- Features of our physical **environment**—such as furnishings—also send distinct messages about status and mood.

Functions of Nonverbal Communication

- Our nonverbal communication serves many purposes. One of the most common is **affect displays,** which function to show others how we are feeling.
- We can harness all of the nonverbal communication codes to send powerful messages of **intimacy, dominance,** and **submissiveness** to others.

chapter review

Conflict is a normal part of all relationships.

When Amy Chua's *Battle Hymn of the Tiger Mother* hit bookstores, a firestorm of controversy erupted regarding her parenting.[1] Chua boasts of never letting daughters Sophia and Lulu watch TV or play computer games, drilling them in piano and violin for hours daily, and demanding that they never get a grade below an A. Although Chua intended *Tiger Mother* to be humorous and satirical, critics decried her behavior as abusive. Blogger Betty Ming Liu even declared, "Parents like Amy Chua are the reason Asian-Americans like me are in therapy." But Chua's book is about more than just parenting rules; it's a tale of power, conflict, and the negative outcomes of approaching disagreements destructively (Cullen, 2011).

Throughout her book, Chua describes her need to wield power over others. While on vacation in Greece, Chua demands that the entire family (including husband Jed and her parents) delay sightseeing of local ruins until after Lulu rehearses her violin. The marathon practice session that follows results in everyone missing their planned activities. "I wouldn't wish the misery that followed on anyone," Chua laments, not seeming to realize it was an outcome of her decision making (pp. 90–91).

Chua's approach to conflict involves demanding that others do what she wants, then verbally abusing them if they don't do so. When Lulu refuses to practice piano, Chua insults

---

[1] All content that follows is adapted from Chua (2011), Choi (2011), Cullen (2011), and Liu (2011).

9 / Managing Conflict and Power

Erin Patrice O'Brien

her for "being lazy, cowardly, self-indulgent, and pathetic!" When Jed intervenes, reminding her that Lulu has a different musical skill set than her prodigy sister, Sophia, Chua sarcastically snipes, "Even losers are special in their own special way" (pp. 60–61).

The conflicts escalate for years, culminating in a public blowup at a restaurant. When Lulu refuses to try caviar, Chua taunts her: "There is nothing more common and low than an American teenager who won't try things. You're boring, Lulu—*boring*." Lulu explodes, "I HATE YOU! You don't love me. You make me feel bad about myself every second. You've wrecked my life. I can't stand to be around you. You're a terrible mother. You're selfish. You don't care about anyone but yourself!" Chua retaliates in kind, "You're a terrible daughter!" (pp. 204–206).

Although Chua attributes her behavior to her Chinese heritage, research suggests otherwise. Temple University psychologist Laurence Steinberg studied thousands of Latino, Euro-, African, and Asian American families and found that authoritarian parents occur in *all* ethnic groups. Chinese caregivers are *not* more likely than others to aggressively abuse power or manage conflict by insulting others (Choi, 2011). Steinberg concludes, "One can't talk about Chinese households as if there isn't variability there . . . that can be misleading" (Choi, 2011, para. 13).

Managing conflict and power in Chua's fashion leads to decidedly negative outcomes. Such behaviors within family settings elevate anxiety, depression, and psychosomatic problems, and children whose parents bully them are less self-assured and socially poised as a result. Late in her book, Chua seems to realize this as she reflects on the destructive legacy of her communication choices: "I don't know how my daughters will look back on all this twenty years from now. Will they tell their own children, 'My mother was a controlling fanatic who even in India made us practice before we could see Bombay and New Delhi?' Or will they have softer memories?" (p. 91).

It's easy to read Amy Chua's book, or watch videos of her appearance on *The Colbert Report*, and laugh at the extremity of her conflict style. Even she makes fun of the things she said and did while fighting with her daughters. But when we face a bullying parent, find ourselves locked in battle with a lover, or get trapped in an intractable disagreement with a friend, the pain becomes personal. The words people most commonly associate with interpersonal conflict are *destruction, heartache,* and *hopelessness* (Wilmot & Hocker, 2010).

Yet conflicts don't have to be hopeless, because we're not helpless. Each of us has the ability to choose constructive approaches to managing conflicts that will help create positive outcomes for everyone involved. In this chapter, we explore interpersonal conflict and how best to manage it. You'll learn:

- The nature of conflict
- The role power plays in conflict
- Different approaches for handling interpersonal conflict
- The impact of gender, culture, and technology on conflict
- Resolutions and long-term outcomes of conflict
- The challenges to resolving conflict in close relationships, and how to overcome them

chapter outline

253 Conflict and Interpersonal Communication

256 Power and Conflict

261 Handling Conflict

270 Conflict Endings

274 Challenges to Handling Conflict

279 Managing Conflict and Power

Conflict and Interpersonal Communication

Most conflicts occur between people who know each other

We like to think of conflict as unusual, an unpleasant exception to the normal routine of our relationships. Each conflict seems freshly painful and unprecedented. "I can't believe it!" we tweet, text, or post on Facebook, "We had a *terrible* fight last night!" Friends immediately fire back messages echoing their shock: "OMG, really?!" Observing other couples, we judge their relationships by how much they fight: couples who argue too much are "doomed to fail," whereas those who rarely disagree must be "blissfully happy."

But such beliefs are mistaken. Conflict is a normal part of *all* relationships (Canary, 2003). Dealing with other human beings (and their unique goals, preferences, and opinions) means regularly having your wants and needs run up against theirs, triggering disputes (Malis & Roloff, 2006). On average, people report seven conflicts a week, mostly with relatives, friends, and lovers with whom they've argued before (Benoit & Benoit, 1990). Thus the challenge you face is not how to avoid conflict, or how to live a conflict-free life, but how to constructively manage the conflicts that *will* arise in your interpersonal relationships.

WHAT IS CONFLICT?

Almost any issue can spark conflict—money, time, sex, religion, politics, love, chores, and so on—and almost anyone can get into a conflict: family members, friends, lovers, coworkers, or casual acquaintances. Despite such variations, all

Teaching Tip: Brainstorming about Conflict

As a class, create a list of words associated with conflict. Discuss patterns that emerge. Many of the terms are likely to be negative, so encourage students to think about positive relational outcomes of conflict as well. Then provide the text definition of conflict as well as its four features. How does the list match up?

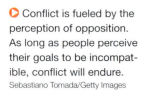 Conflict is fueled by the perception of opposition. As long as people perceive their goals to be incompatible, conflict will endure.
Sebastiano Tomada/Getty Images

conflicts share similar attributes. **Conflict** is the process that occurs when people perceive that they have incompatible goals or that someone is interfering in their ability to achieve their objectives (Wilmot & Hocker, 2010). Four features characterize most conflicts: they begin with perception, they involve clashes in goals or behaviors, they unfold over time as a process, and they are dynamic.

Conflict Begins with Perception Conflict occurs when people perceive incompatible goals or actions (Roloff & Soule, 2002). Because conflict begins with perception, perceptual errors (see Chapter 3) shape how our conflicts unfold. As we'll discuss later in this chapter, we blame others more than ourselves during conflicts, and perceive them as uncooperative and ourselves as helpful. These self-enhancing errors can lead us to manage conflict in ways that create unsatisfying outcomes.

Conflict Involves Clashes in Goals or Behaviors At the heart of conflicts are clashes in goals or behaviors (Zacchilli, Hendrick, & Hendrick, 2009). Some conflicts revolve around incompatible goals, ranging from everyday leisure activity disputes ("I want to go out dancing!" versus "I want to stay home and play video games!") to serious arguments regarding personal values ("I want our children to be raised Jewish!" versus "I want them to be Catholic!"). Other disputes break out when one person's actions clash with another's. A friend texts you repeatedly while you're studying, and you fire back a nasty message; your manager demands that you work over a holiday weekend, and you refuse.

Conflict Is a Process Although people often describe conflict as a series of unrelated events ("I sent her this carefully crafted e-mail, and for no reason, she blasted me in response!"), conflict is a process that unfolds over time. Its course is determined by the communication choices we make: everything we say and do during a conflict influences everything our partner says and does, and vice versa.

Moreover, most conflicts proceed through several stages, each involving decisions and actions that affect the conflict's direction and consequences for the individuals involved. In its most basic form, the process of conflict involves people perceiving that a conflict exists, choosing an approach for how to handle the conflict, and then dealing with the conflict resolutions and outcomes that follow. Conflict is not a one-time-only event: how you handle a conflict with someone will have consequences for your future interactions and relationship with that person.

Conflict Is Dynamic Because conflict typically unfolds over a series of exchanged messages, it is ever changing and unpredictable. Research looking at the dynamic nature of conflict finds that in 66.4 percent of disputes, the focus shifts substantially as the conflict progresses (Keck & Samp, 2007). A fight over your father's snide remark regarding your job quickly becomes a battle about his chronic disapproval of you. Or a dispute regarding your roommate eating your leftovers becomes an argument about her failure to be a supportive friend. When a conflict shifts topic, it can devolve into **kitchen-sinking** (from the expression, "throwing everything at them but the kitchen sink"), in which combatants hurl insults and accusations at each other that have little to do with the original disagreement. For example, a couple fighting over whether one of them was flirting with their server at a restaurant may say things like: "What about the time when you completely forgot our anniversary?!" and "Oh yeah?! Well, at least my family is intelligent!"

Since conflict often dynamically branches out into other troublesome topics, managing conflict is extremely challenging—you can never fully anticipate the twists and turns that will occur. But remember: you have total control over what *you* say and do, and that can influence how someone responds. If you think a conflict is getting completely off track, choose your communication carefully to help bring it back on topic.

CONFLICT IN RELATIONSHIPS

Most conflicts occur between people who know each other and are involved in close relationships, such as romantic partners, friends, family members, and coworkers (Benoit & Benoit, 1990). Unlike people who don't know each other well, people in close relationships experience prolonged contact and frequent interaction, which set the stage for disagreements over goals and behaviors.

In close relationships, conflicts typically arise from one of three issues (Peterson, 2002): *irritating partner behaviors* (e.g., a family member has an annoying personal habit, or your partner interrupts you while you're working), *disagreements regarding relationship rules* (e.g., you and your partner disagree about texting with ex-partners, or family members disagree about inviting friends on

---

self-reflection

Think of a relational partner with whom you have the same conflict over and over again. What effect does this conflict have on your relationship? In what ways do you contribute to its continuance? How might you change your communication to end this repetitive cycle?

**Class Note:
Positive Conflict**

To illustrate the positives of conflict, have students consider this analogy: a small amount of salt is needed to balance the sugar level in cookies. Similarly, although we don't want too much "salt" in our relationships, it can be useful to balance the sweet. Why would this be? What role does conflict play in relationships? When can conflict improve relationships?

family vacations), and *personality clashes* (e.g., you have a sunny disposition but your friend is a complainer, or you're organized and ambitious but your partner is carefree and lazy).

Relationship partners often develop consistent patterns of communication for dealing with conflict that either promote or undermine their happiness. For example, happily married couples are more likely than unhappily married couples to avoid personal attacks during conflicts and instead focus their discussion on the differences at hand (Peterson, 2002). Such patterns are self-perpetuating: happy couples remain motivated to behave in ways guaranteed to keep them happy, and because they believe they can solve their problems, they are more likely to work together to resolve conflict (Caughlin & Vangelisti, 2000). In contrast, dissatisfied couples often choose to avoid important conflicts. Their failure to deal directly with their problems further fuels their unhappiness (Afifi, McManus, Steuber, & Coho, 2009).

Managing conflicts in close relationships presents unique challenges. We feel connected to our intimate partners, and disputes threaten that sense of connection (Berscheid, 2002). *Your conflicts with loved ones are guaranteed to be intense and emotionally draining experiences.* Conflicts also powerfully affect your *future* encounters and relationships. For example, if you and a sibling fight via text message, this conflict will shape not only how the two of you will communicate when you are next face-to-face but how you'll feel about your relationship moving forward. As scholar Donald Peterson (2002) notes, "Every conflict and every resolution, as well as every failure at resolution, becomes a part of your overall relationship history" (p. 363).

Power and Conflict

Power influences who will prevail in conflicts

In Suzanne Collins's futuristic novel *The Hunger Games* (2008), North America has become Panem, consisting of a wealthy Capitol city surrounded by twelve outlying districts.[2] Following suppression of a mass rebellion by the districts, the Capitol creates the annual Hunger Games. Children from each district are selected and pitted against each other in a fight to the death that is televised live. Child participants are chosen lottery-style, and for district residents there is no choice: to not participate in the lottery means death for all. As Katniss Everdeen, the story's central character, describes it:

> Taking kids from our districts, forcing them to kill one another while we watch—this is the Capitol's way of reminding us how totally we are at their mercy. Whatever words they use, the real message is clear: look how we take your children and sacrifice them and there's nothing you can do. If you lift a finger, we will destroy every last one of you. (p. 18)

The dominant theme of *The Hunger Games* is **power**: the ability to influence or control people and events (Donohue & Kolt, 1992). Understanding power is

---

[2]All material that follows is adapted from Collins (2008).

chapter 9 / Managing Conflict and Power   257

◐ In *The Hunger Games*, Effie Trinket wields the Capitol's power by escorting children to the Hunger Games, a televised competition in which youth are forced to fight to the death. When main character Katniss Everdeen volunteers to take her younger sister's place in the Games, she exercises her own power and influences the sequence of events that follow. © Lionsgate Photographer: Murray Close/Photofest

critical for constructively managing conflict, because people in conflict often wield whatever power they have to overcome the opposition and achieve their goals. In conflicts in which one party has more power than the other—like the Capitol has over the districts—the more powerful tend to get what they want.

POWER'S DEFINING CHARACTERISTICS

Most of us won't ever experience power wielded as brutally as in *The Hunger Games*. But power does permeate our everyday lives and is an integral part of interpersonal communication and relationships. Power determines how partners relate to each other, who controls relationship decisions, and whose goals will prevail during conflicts (Dunbar, 2004). Let's consider power's defining characteristics, as suggested by scholars William Wilmot and Joyce Hocker (2010).

Power Is Always Present   Whether you're talking on the phone with a parent, texting your best friend, or spending time with your lover, power is present in all your interpersonal encounters and relationships. Power may be balanced (e.g., friend to friend) or imbalanced (e.g., manager to employee, parent to young child). When power is balanced, **symmetrical relationships** result. When power is imbalanced, **complementary relationships** are the outcome.

Although power is always present, we're typically not aware of it until people violate our expectations for power balance in the relationship, such as giving orders or talking down to us. Your dorm-floor resident adviser tells you (rather than asks

self-reflection

Think of a complementary personal relationship of yours in which you have more power than the other person. How does the imbalance affect how you communicate during conflicts? Is it ethical for you to wield power over the other person during a conflict to get what you want? Why or why not?

you) to pick him up after class. Your work supervisor grabs inventory you were stocking and says, "No—do it *this* way!" even though you were doing it properly. According to **Dyadic Power Theory** (Dunbar, 2004), people with only moderate power are most likely to use controlling communication. Because their power is limited, they can't always be sure they're going to get their way. Hence, they feel more of a need to wield power in noticeable ways (Dunbar, 2004). In contrast, people with high power feel little need to display it; they *know* that their words will be listened to and their wishes granted. This means that you're most likely to run into controlling communication and power-based bullying when dealing with people who have moderate amounts of power over you, such as mid-level managers, team captains, and class-project group leaders, as opposed to people with high power (in such contexts), like vice presidents, coaches, or faculty advisers.

Power Can Be Used Ethically or Unethically Power itself isn't good or bad—it's the way people use it that matters. Many happy marriages, family relationships, and long-term friendships are complementary. One person controls more resources and has more decision-making influence than the other. Yet the person in charge uses his or her power only to benefit both people and the relationship. In other relationships, the powerful partner wields his or her power unethically or recklessly. For example, a boss threatens to fire her employee unless he sleeps with her, or an abusive husband tells his unhappy wife that she'll never see their kids again if she leaves him.

Power Is Granted Power doesn't reside within people. Instead, it is granted by individuals or groups who allow another person or group to exert influence over them. For example, a friend of mine invited his parents to stay with him and his wife for the weekend. His parents had planned on leaving Monday, but come Monday morning, they announced that they had decided to stay through the end of the week. My friend accepted their decision even though he could have insisted that they leave at the originally agreed-on time. In doing so, he granted his parents the power to decide their departure date without his input or consent.

Power Influences Conflicts If you strip away the particulars of what's said and done during most conflicts, you'll find power struggles underneath. Who has

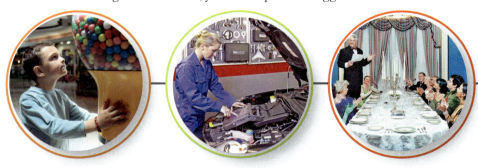

Assignment: Symmetrical and Complementary Relationships

Ask students to write a short paper analyzing power differentials in a close relationship. Have them describe the characteristics of the power in this relationship and what makes it symmetrical or complementary. How is the power in this relationship present, used ethically or unethically, or granted? Have you ever wished that you could change the power in this relationship? Why or why not? What strategies could you use for these changes? What improvements or challenges would you expect from these changes?

more influence? Who controls the resources, decisions, and feelings involved? People struggle to see whose goals will prevail, and they wield whatever power they have to pursue their own goals. But power struggles rarely lead to mutually beneficial solutions. As we'll see, the more constructive approach is to set aside your power and work collaboratively to resolve the conflict.

POWER CURRENCIES

Given that power is not innate but something that some people grant to others, how do you get power? To acquire power, you must possess or control some form of **power currency,** a resource that other people value (Wilmot & Hocker, 2010). Possessing or controlling a valued resource gives you influence over individuals who value that resource. Likewise, if individuals have resources you view as valuable, you will grant power to them.

Five power currencies are common in interpersonal relationships. **Resource currency** includes material things such as money, property, and food. If you possess material things that someone else needs or wants, you have resource power over them. Parents have nearly total resource power over young children because they control all the money, food, shelter, clothing, and other items their children need and want. Managers have high levels of resource power over employees, as they control employees' continued employment and salaries.

Expertise currency comprises special skills or knowledge. The more highly specialized and unique the skill or knowledge you have, the more expertise power you possess. A Stuttgart-trained Porsche mechanic commands a substantially higher wage and choicer selection of clients than a minimally trained Quick Lube oil change attendant.

A person who is linked with a network of friends, family, and acquaintances with substantial influence has **social network currency.** Others may value his or her ability to introduce them to people who can land them jobs, talk them up to potential romantic partners, or get them invitations to exclusive parties.

Personal characteristics that people consider desirable—beauty, intelligence, charisma, communication skill, sense of humor—constitute **personal currency.** Even if you lack resource, expertise, and social network currency, you can still achieve a certain degree of influence and stature by being beautiful, funny, or smart.

▶ **Video**

macmillanhighered.com /reflectrelate4e

Expertise Currency
Watch this clip online to answer the questions below.

What types of expertise currency do you have? When are they beneficial to you? Have there been any times when your expertise worked to your disadvantage? If so, how?

Want to see more? Check out LaunchPad for clips illustrating all the power currencies, including **resource, social network, personal,** and **intimacy.**

◯ Power expresses itself in the form of different power currencies. As shown here, these include resource currency, expertise currency, social network currency, personal currency, and intimacy currency. (Left to right) Britt Erlanson/Getty Images; Peter Dazeley/Getty Images; Britt Erlanson/Getty Images; Rick Diamond/Getty Images; Lou Bopp/StockShop/Aurora

When Cristina Fernández de Kirchner became Argentina's 55th president in 2007, she was one of only a handful of women currently serving as an elected head of state. How does this disparity reflect the wider difference between men's and women's political influence in the world? STR/AFP/Getty Images

Finally, you acquire **intimacy currency** when you share a close bond with someone that no one else shares. If you have a unique intimate bond with someone—a lover, friend, or family member—you possess intimacy power over him or her, and he or she may do you a favor "only because you are my best friend."

POWER AND GENDER

To say that power and gender are intertwined is an understatement. Throughout history and across cultures, *the* defining distinction between the genders has been men's power over women. Through patriarchy, which means "the rule of fathers," men have used cultural practices to maintain their societal, political, and economic power (Mies, 1991). Men have built and sustained patriarchy by denying women access to power currencies.

Although many North Americans presume that the gender gap in power has narrowed, the truth is more complicated. The World Economic Forum's 2014 report examined four "pillars" of gender equality: economic opportunity, educational access, political representation, and physical health (Bekhouche, Hausmann, Tyson, & Zahidi, 2014). Across 142 nations representing over 90 percent of the world's population, the gaps between women and men in terms of education and health *have* largely been closed. Women now have 94 percent of the educational opportunities of men, and 96 percent of the health and medical support. But they still dramatically lack both economic and political power. Women have only 60 percent of the economic opportunities and resources that men share, and a paltry 21 percent of the political representation. Iceland, Finland, Norway, and Sweden top the list of the most gender-equal nations on the planet. Where do Canada and the United States rank? Nineteenth and 20th overall, but in terms of political empowerment, the United States ranks 54th and Canada, 42nd.

How does lack of power affect women's interpersonal communication? As gender scholar Cheris Kramarae (1981) notes, women with little or no power "are not as free or as able as men are to say what they wish, when and where they wish. . . . Their talk is often not considered of much value by men" (p. 1). By contrast, what men say and do is counted as important, and women's voices are muted. In interpersonal relationships, this power difference manifests itself in men's tendency to expect women to listen attentively to everything they say, while men select the topics they wish to attend to when women are speaking (Fishman, 1983). Whereas men may feel satisfied that their voices are being heard in their relationships, women often feel as though their viewpoints are being ignored or minimized, both at home and in the workplace (Spender, 1990).

POWER AND CULTURE

Views of power differ substantially across cultures. Power derives from the perception of power currencies, so people are granted power not only according to which power currencies they possess but also according to the degree to which those power currencies are valued in a given culture. In Asian and Latino cultures, high value is placed on resource currency; consequently, people without wealth, property, or other such material resources are likely to grant power to those who possess those resources (Gudykunst & Kim, 2003). In contrast, in northern European countries, Canada, and the United States, people with wealth may be admired or even envied, but they are not granted unusual power. If your rich neighbor builds a huge mansion, you might be impressed. But if her new fence crosses onto your property, you'll confront her about it ("Sorry to bother you, but your new fence is one foot over the property line"). Members of other cultures would be less likely to say anything, given her wealth and corresponding power.

Handling Conflict

How you approach conflict affects the outcomes

I was flying home after spending spring break with my folks. The jet provided so little space between seats that if someone in front of you leaned back, you couldn't have your tray table out. Across the aisle was "Mike," a large-bellied businessman writing furiously on his laptop. An hour into the flight, the man sitting in front of him, "Tom," suddenly leaned his seat back and began reading a book. Of course, the moment he did so, the tray table on the back of his seat jammed into Mike's belly, and the seat back forced his laptop closed.

> "*Excuse* me!" snapped Mike, "I'm using my computer—can you lean your seat forward?"
> "But I want to lean back," said Tom, staying where he was.
> "But I'm trying to use my computer, and I can't if you're leaning back!" snarled Mike.
> "Your computer isn't my problem! I have the right to lean back if I want!" exclaimed Tom. Mike then buzzed the flight attendant, who approached Tom.
> "Sir, if you could just move your seat forward a little, he can use his computer."
> Tom went berserk. "WHY DOES IT HAVE TO BE ME WHO COMPROMISES? I'M NOT MOVING!" he shouted. The attendant then offered a different seat to Mike, who proceeded to shove Tom's seat back when exiting so that it hit him in the head.

What would you have done in this situation? Would you have avoided the conflict by pretending that you weren't being inconvenienced? Would you have demanded that your desires be met? Would you have freaked out? Or would you have attempted to work collaboratively, seeking an agreeable compromise or a solution that met both of your needs?

In situations in which others are interrupting your goals or actions, your most important decision is how to handle the conflict (Sillars & Wilmot, 1994). *Your choice about what you'll say and do will shape everything that follows—whether the situation will go unresolved, escalate, or be resolved.* Your communication choices

---

Assignment:
Conflict Strategy Types
Conflict is often the plot for newer TV comedies such as *New Girl* and *Modern Family* and even classics such as *Seinfeld* and *Friends*. As an essay assignment, students should analyze a conflict on one of their favorite shows. They should describe the scenario and provide examples of specific conflict strategies the characters used. What was constructive or destructive in the conflict? How could the characters have improved the situation?

also influence whether your relationship with the other person (if one exists) will be damaged or grow stronger.

In this section, we examine the approaches people use for handling conflict. In addition, we look at the impact that gender, culture, and technology have on the selection of these approaches.

APPROACHES TO HANDLING CONFLICT

People generally handle conflict in one of five ways: avoidance, accommodation, competition, reactivity, or collaboration (Lulofs & Cahn, 2000; Zacchilli et al., 2009). Before reading about each approach, take the *Self-Quiz* online to find out how you typically approach conflict.

Avoidance   One way to handle conflict is **avoidance:** ignoring the conflict, pretending it isn't really happening, or communicating indirectly about the situation. One common form of avoidance is **skirting,** in which a person avoids a conflict by changing the topic or joking about it. You think your lover is having an affair and raise the issue, but he or she just laughs and says, "Don't you know we'll always be together, like Noah and Allie from *The Notebook*?" Another form of avoidance is **sniping**—communicating in a negative fashion and then abandoning the encounter by physically leaving the scene or refusing to interact further. You're fighting with your brother through Skype, when he pops off a nasty comment ("I see you're still a spoiled brat!") and signs off before you have a chance to reply.

Avoidance is the most frequently used approach to handling conflict (Sillars, 1980). People opt for avoidance because it seems easier, less emotionally draining, and lower risk than direct confrontation (Afifi & Olson, 2005). But avoidance poses substantial risks (Afifi, McManus, Steuben, & Coho, 2009). One of the biggest is **cumulative annoyance,** in which repressed irritation grows as the mental list of grievances we have against our partner builds (Peterson, 2002). Eventually, cumulative annoyance overwhelms our capacity to suppress it and we suddenly explode in anger. For example, you constantly remind your teenage son about his homework, chores, personal hygiene, and room cleanliness. This bothers you immensely because you feel these matters are his responsibility, but you swallow your anger because you don't want to make a fuss or be seen by him as nagging. One evening, after reminding him twice to hang up his expensive new leather jacket, you walk into his bedroom to find the coat crumpled in a ball on the floor. You go on a tirade, listing all the things he has done to upset you in the past month.

A second risk posed by avoidance is **pseudo-conflict,** the perception that a conflict exists when in fact it doesn't. For example, you mistakenly think your romantic partner is about to break up with you because you see tagged photos of him or her arm in arm with someone else on Facebook. So you decide to preemptively end your relationship even though your partner actually has no desire to leave you (the photos were of your partner and a cousin).

Despite the risks, avoidance can be a wise choice for managing conflict in situations in which emotions run high (Berscheid, 2002). If everyone involved is

---

Online Self-Quiz: How Do You Approach Conflict? To take this self-quiz, visit LaunchPad: macmillanhighered.com/reflectrelate4e

Assignment: Avoidance
Ask students to write a short reflection journal on a time when they avoided conflict. Why did they make this choice? Did they use skirting or sniping? What were the results? Can avoiding conflict sometimes be a good strategy? How do the concepts of suppressing and venting emotions (from Chapter 4) affect avoidance as a way to handle conflict?

self-reflection

Recall a conflict in which you chose avoidance. Why did you make this choice? What consequences ensued? Were there any positive outcomes? If you could relive the encounter, what, if anything, would you say and do differently to obtain more positive results?

angry, and yet you choose to continue the interaction, you run the risk of saying things that will damage your relationship. It may be better to avoid through leaving, hanging up, or not responding to texts or messages until tempers have cooled.

Accommodation Through **accommodation,** one person abandons his or her own goals and acquiesces to the desires of the other person. For example, your supervisor at work asks you to stay an extra hour tonight because a coworker is showing up late. Although you had plans for the evening, you cancel them and act as if it's not a problem.

If you're like most people, you probably accommodate people who have more power than you. Why? If you don't, they might use their power to control or punish you. This suggests an important lesson regarding the relationship between power and conflict: people who are more powerful than you probably won't accommodate your goals during conflicts.

Another factor that influences people's decision to accommodate is love. Accommodation reflects a high concern for others and a low concern for self; you want to please those you love (Frisby & Westerman, 2010). Hence, accommodation is likely to occur in healthy, satisfied close relationships, in which selflessness is characteristic (Hendrick & Hendrick, 1992). For example, your romantic partner is accepted into a summer study-abroad program in Europe. Even though you had planned on spending the summer together, you encourage him or her to accept the offer.

Competition Think back to the airline conflict. Each of the men involved aggressively challenged the other and expressed little concern for the other's perspective or goals. This approach is known as **competition:** an open and clear discussion of the goal clash that exists and the pursuit of one's own goals without regard for others' goals (Sillars, 1980).

The choice to use competition is motivated in part by negative thoughts and beliefs, including a desire to control, a willingness to hurt others in order to gain, and a lack of respect for others (Bevan, Finan, & Kaminsky, 2008; Zacchilli et al., 2009). Consequently, you'll be less likely to opt for competition when you are in a conflict with someone whose needs you are interested in and whom you admire. Conversely, if people routinely approach conflict by making demands to the exclusion of your desires, they likely do not respect you (Hendrick & Hendrick, 2006).

At a minimum, competitive approaches can trigger *defensive communication* (described in Chapter 7)—someone refusing to consider your goals or dismissing them as unimportant, acting superior to you, or attempting to squelch your disagreement by wielding power over you (Waldron, Turner, Alexander, & Barton, 1993). But the primary risk of choosing a competitive approach is **escalation,** a dramatic rise in emotional intensity and increasingly negative and aggressive communication, just like in the airplane dispute. If people in conflict both choose competition, and neither is willing to back down, escalation is guaranteed. Even initially trivial conflicts can quickly explode into intense exchanges.

▶ **Video**

macmillanhighered.com
/reflectrelate4e

Accommodation
Watch this clip online to answer the questions below.

In this video, how does one partner accommodate the other? When have you found it most wise to accommodate in a conflict situation?
 Want to see more? Check out LaunchPad for clips illustrating **avoidance, sniping, competition,** and **collaboration.**

▶ The day after Thanksgiving is traditionally the first day of the winter holiday shopping season. On Black Friday, as it's known, shoppers aggressively compete for limited-supply products or deals. Can you recall a time when you've handled a conflict in a potentially tense situation?
AP Photo/The News Tribune/Russ Carmack

self-reflection

Call to mind someone you know who consistently approaches conflict with reactivity. How has this shaped your willingness to broach issues of disagreement? impacted your feelings? Given the relationship between reactivity and respect, is it possible to sustain a healthy, close relationship with a reactive person? Why or why not?

Reactivity   A fourth way people handle conflict is by not pursuing any conflict-related goals at all; instead, they communicate in an emotionally explosive and negative fashion. This is known as **reactivity,** and it is characterized by accusations of mistrust, yelling, crying, and becoming verbally or physically abusive. Reactivity is decidedly nonstrategic. Instead of avoiding, accommodating, or competing, people simply flip out. For example, one of my college dating partners was intensely reactive. When I noted that we weren't getting along and suggested taking a break, she screamed "I *knew* it! You've been cheating on me!" and hurled a vase of roses I had given her at my head. Thankfully I ducked out of the way, but it took the campus police to calm her down. Her behavior had nothing to do with "managing our conflict." She simply *reacted*.

Similar to competition, reactivity is strongly related to a lack of respect (Bevan et al., 2008; Zacchilli et al., 2009). People prone to reactivity have little interest in others as individuals and do not recognize others' desires as relevant (Zacchilli et al., 2009).

Collaboration   The most constructive approach to managing conflict is **collaboration:** treating conflict as a mutual problem-solving challenge rather than something that must be avoided, accommodated, competed over, or reacted to. Often the result of using a collaborative approach is *compromise*, in which everyone involved modifies his or her individual goals to come up with a solution to the conflict. (We'll discuss compromise more on pages 271–272.) You're most likely to use collaboration when you respect the other person and are concerned about his or her desires as well as your own (Keck & Samp, 2007; Zacchilli et al., 2009). People who regularly use collaboration feel more trust, commitment, and overall satisfaction with their relationships than those who don't (Smith, Heaven, & Ciarrochi, 2008). Whenever possible, opt for collaboration.

To use a collaborative approach, try these suggestions from Wilmot and Hocker (2010). First, *attack problems, not people.* Talk about the conflict as something separate from the people involved, saying, for instance, "This issue has really come between us." This frames the conflict as the source of trouble and unites the people trying to handle it. At the same time, avoid personal attacks while being courteous and respectful, regardless of how angry you may be. This is perhaps the hardest part of collaboration, because you likely *will* be angry during conflicts (Berscheid, 2002). Just don't let your anger cause you to say and do things you shouldn't. If someone attacks you and not the problem, don't get sucked into trading insults. Simply say "I can see you're very upset; let's talk about this when we've both had a chance to cool off," and end the encounter before things escalate further.

Second, *focus on common interests and long-term goals.* Keep the emphasis on the desires you have in common, not the issue that's driving you apart. Use "we" language (see Chapter 7) to bolster this impression: "I know we both want what's best for the company." Arguing over positions ("I want this!" versus "I want that!") endangers relationships because the conflict quickly becomes a destructive contest of wills.

Third, *create options before arriving at decisions.* Be willing to negotiate a solution rather than insisting on one. To do this, start by asking questions that will elicit options: "How do you think we can best resolve this?" or "What ideas for solutions do you have?" Then propose ideas of your own. Be flexible. Most

skills practice

Collaboration
Using collaboration to manage a conflict

❶ During your next significant conflict, openly discuss the situation, emphasizing that it's an understandable clash between goals rather than people.

❷ Highlight common interests and long-term goals.

❸ Create several solutions for resolving the conflict that are satisfactory to both of you.

❹ Combine the best elements of these ideas into a single, workable solution.

❺ Evaluate the solution you've collaboratively created, ensuring that it's fair and ethical.

table 9.1 Competitive versus Collaborative Conflict Approaches

Situation	Competitive Approach	Collaborative Approach
Roommate hasn't been doing his or her share of the housework.	"I'm sick and tired of you never doing anything around here! From now on, you are doing all the chores!"	"We've both been really busy, but I'm concerned that things are not getting done. Let's make a list of all the chores and figure out how to fairly divide them up."
Coworker is draining large blocks of your work time by socializing with you.	"It's obvious that you don't care about your job or whether you get fired. But I need this job, so stop bugging me all the time and let me get my work done!"	"I enjoy spending time with you, but I'm finding I don't have enough time left to get my work done. Let's figure out how we can better balance hanging out and working."
Romantic partner wants you to abandon a beloved pastime because it seems too dangerous.	"I've been racing dirt bikes long before I met you, and there's no way I'm giving them up. If you really loved me, you'd accept that instead of pestering me to quit!"	"Sorry my racing worries you; I know the reason you're concerned is because you care about me. Let's talk about what we can both do so I don't worry you so much."

Media Note: Analyzing Family Conflict in *This Is Where I Leave You*

In the film *This Is Where I Leave You* (2014), based on the book by Jonathan Tropper, adult siblings honor their mother's request to sit shiva for a week after their father dies. The family members' conversations throughout this week display several of the conflict approaches outlined in the text. Ask your students to watch the film, or portions of it, and provide a verbal or written analysis of the many conflict episodes.

self-reflection

In your experience, do women and men deal with conflict differently? If so, how? Does your gender identity perfectly predict how you approach conflicts when they arise? What risks are associated with presuming that men and women will always deal with conflicts according to their gender?

collaborative solutions involve some form of compromise, so be willing to adapt your original desires, even if it means not getting everything you want. Then combine the best parts of the various suggestions to come up with an agreeable solution. Don't get bogged down searching for a "perfect" solution—it may not exist.

Finally, *critically evaluate your solution*. Ask for an assessment: "Is this equally fair for both of us?" The critical issue is livability: Can everyone live with the resolution in the long run? Or is it so unfair or short of original desires that resentments are likely to emerge? If anyone can answer yes to the latter question, go back to creating options (Step 3) until you find a solution that is satisfactory to everyone.

GENDER AND HANDLING CONFLICT

Traditional gender socialization creates challenges for men and women as they seek to constructively resolve conflicts. Women are encouraged to avoid and suppress conflict and to sacrifice their own goals to accommodate others (Wood, 1998). Consequently, many women have little experience in constructively pursuing their goals during a dispute. Men, in contrast, learn to adopt competitive or even violent approaches to interpersonal clashes, as such approaches suggest strength and manliness (Wood, 1998). At the same time, they're taught not to harm women. Thus, during a contentious exchange with a woman, men face a dilemma: Compete or avoid? Many men handle the dilemma by downplaying conflicts or simply leaving the scene instead of seeking constructive resolution.

Given that gender can sometimes interfere with constructive conflict management, reconsider how you approach conflict with men and women. When experiencing conflicts with women, encourage the open expression of goals to allow for a collaborative solution. Above all, avoid assuming that no conflict exists just because the other person hasn't voiced any concerns. When managing conflicts with men, be aware of the male emphasis on competitive approaches. Stress collaboration, and as you communicate, steadfastly avoid forms of communication that may escalate the conflict, such as personal criticism, insults, or threats.

◉ In *Mad Men,* advertising agency employee Peggy Olson often represses her emotions in order to avoid conflict with her coworkers. How does this behavior match or contradict your own experiences of conflict management styles? Carin Baer/© AMC/Everett Collection

CULTURE AND HANDLING CONFLICT

The strongest cultural factor that influences your conflict approach is whether you belong to an individualistic or a collectivistic culture (Ting-Toomey, 1997). People raised in collectivistic cultures often view direct messages regarding conflict as personal attacks (Nishiyama, 1971) and consequently are more likely to manage conflict through avoidance or accommodation. People from individualistic cultures feel comfortable agreeing to disagree and don't necessarily see such clashes as personal affronts (Ting-Toomey, 1985). They are more likely to compete, react, or collaborate.

Given these differences, how might you manage conflict effectively across cultures? If you're an individualist embroiled in a dispute with someone from a collectivistic culture, consider the following practices (Gudykunst & Kim, 2003):

- Recognize that collectivists may prefer to have a third person mediate the conflict (Kozan & Ergin, 1998). Mediators allow those in conflict to manage their disagreement without direct confrontation, thereby helping to maintain harmony in the relationship, which is especially important to collectivists.

Media Note:
Conflict in Marriage
To provide more insight on conflict and gender, have your students view video clips of Dr. John Gottman discussing his well-known research on marriage, conflict, and divorce at www.youtube.com/TheGottmanInstitute. There are also videos of Dr. Gottman discussing the "Four Horsemen of the Apocalypse"—criticism, contempt, defensiveness, and stonewalling—and other useful insights on managing conflict at www.youtube.com/watch?v=1o30Ps-_8is.

focus on CULTURE

Accommodation and Radical Pacifism

You're walking down the street, and a man approaches you and demands your wallet. You immediately give it and then ask him whether he also wants your coat. Or you badly want an open position at work. When you find out that a coworker also wants it, you inform your supervisor that you no longer want the job and encourage her to give it to your colleague instead.

As the biblical verse "When a man takes your coat, offer him your shirt as well" (Luke 6:29) suggests, one way to deal with conflict is an extreme form of accommodation known as *radical pacifism*. Although it is often associated with antiwar movements (Bennett, 2003), radical pacifism embodies a broader philosophy about the nature of interpersonal connections between human beings and how conflict is best resolved. Those practicing radical pacifism believe in a moral obligation to behave in selfless and self-sacrificial ways that quickly end conflicts and assist others. During interpersonal conflict, this means discovering what someone else wants and needs, then aiding that person in attaining those goals, even if it means sacrificing your own.

The practice of radical pacifism cuts across countries, ethnicities, and social classes; it is primarily rooted in the religion of cultures. For example, in the Buddhist text *Kakacupama Sutta* ("The Simile of the Saw"), the Buddha entreats his followers, "Even if bandits were to sever you savagely limb by limb with a two-handled saw, he who gave rise to a mind of hate towards them would not be carrying out my teaching. . . . [Instead] you should abide with a mind of loving kindness" (Bodhi & Nanamoli translation, 1995). Amish church elders embracing radical pacifism share a similar view: "Even if the result of our pacifism is death at the hands of an attacker during a violent conflict, so be it; death is not threatening to us as Christians. Hopefully the attacker will have at least had a glimpse of the love of Christ in our nonviolent response" (Pennsylvania Dutch Country Welcome Center, n.d.).

discussion questions

- What are your beliefs regarding radical pacifism?
- Do you have an ethical obligation to accommodate others when their interests clash with yours? At what point, if any, does this obligation end?

268 **part 2** / Interpersonal Skills

Teaching Tip: Culture Differences in Conflict

To expand your students' understanding of conflict and culture, remind them that it might be too simplistic to consider only the differences between individualistic and collectivistic cultures. A family's cultural heritage is not the sole determinant for the way family members communicate because not all members of an ethnic group identify with, and engage in, the cultural practices of their group (Gudykunst & Lee, 2001). Instead, Gudykunst (1994) recommends that we look at one's tendency toward independent (viewing selves as unique individuals) or interdependent (interconnected to their ingroups) self-construals.

- Use more indirect verbal messages. For example, sprinkle your comments with "maybe" and "possibly," and avoid blunt responses such as "no."
- Let go of the situation if the other person does not recognize that the conflict exists or does not want to deal with it.

If you're a collectivist in contention with someone from an individualistic culture, the following guidelines may help:

- Recognize that individualists often separate conflicts from people. Just because you're in conflict doesn't mean that the situation is personal.
- Use an assertive style, and be direct. For example, use "I" messages and candidly state your opinions and feelings.
- Manage conflicts when they arise, even if you'd much rather avoid them.

TECHNOLOGY AND HANDLING CONFLICT

Evenings at my house are filled with the musical chiming of text-message alerts, as my sons chat with friends and girlfriends. But I can always tell when a fight is brewing. The messaging suddenly accelerates, then there's an actual phone call,

© The New Yorker 1999 Peter Seiner from cartoonbank.com. All Rights Reserved.

followed by a quick scurry up the stairs for privacy. Asking if everything's OK, I always get the same response, "Yes—we're just *fighting*!"

Given how much of our daily communication occurs via technology, it's no surprise that conflicts occur through text- or instant-messaging, e-mail, and Web posts. Nearly two-thirds of college students (61.2 percent) report using mediated channels to engage in conflicts, the most popular form being text-messaging (Frisby & Westerman, 2010). When asked why they choose mediated channels rather than face-to-face contact, respondents report "geographical distance" as the most common reason. Without the means for immediately seeing someone, texting becomes a tempting alternative for handling conflict.

Unfortunately, such media are not well suited for resolving conflicts. The inability to see nonverbal reactions to messages makes people less aware of the consequences of their communication choices (Joinson, 2001). As a result, people are more likely to prioritize their own goals, minimize a partner's goals, and use hostile personal attacks in pursuit of their goals online than face-to-face (Shedletsky & Aitken, 2004).

Thus the first and most important step in managing conflict constructively is to *take the encounter offline*. Doing so can dramatically reduce the likelihood of attributional errors and substantially boost empathy. When college students were asked which channel should be used for handling conflict, they noted that "face-to-face is so much better" because it allows you "to know how the other person feels with their facial expressions" (Frisby & Westerman, 2010, p. 975). If meeting face-to-face isn't an option at the time, you can try to stall the encounter by saying, "I think this is best handled in person. When can we get together and talk?" If you can't (or don't want to) meet, then switch to a phone call. That way, you'll at least have vocal cues to gauge a partner's reaction and enhance your empathy.

If, however, you're in a situation in which you must deal with the conflict online, try these suggestions (Munro, 2002):

1. *Wait and reread.* All conflict—whether it's online or off—begins with a triggering event: something said or done that elicits anger, challenges goals, or blocks desired actions. When you receive a message that provokes you, don't respond right away. Instead, wait for a while, engage in other activities, and then reread it. This helps you avoid communicating when your anger is at its peak. It also provides the opportunity for reassessment: often, in rereading a message later, you'll find that your initial interpretation was mistaken.

2. *Assume the best and watch out for the worst.* When you receive messages that provoke you, presume that the sender meant well but didn't express him- or herself competently. Give people the benefit of the doubt. Keep in mind all you know about the challenges of online communication: anonymity and online disinhibition, empathy deficits, and people's tendency to express themselves inappropriately. At the same time, realize that some people enjoy conflict. Your firing back a nasty message may be exactly what they want.

Media Note: Handling Conflict Online
The popular 2010 movie *The Social Network* includes several examples of technology's influence on conflict, such as the consequences of blogging about a break up, online gossip, and the power of cyberbullying when Mark and his friends develop an algorithm for ranking the attractiveness of their female classmates online. Have students discuss how the movie's characters violate the book's suggestions for handling conflict online.

skills practice

Online Conflict
Effectively working through conflict online

❶ Wait before responding to a message or post that provokes you.

❷ Reread and reassess the message.

❸ Consider all the factors that may have caused the other person to communicate this way.

❹ Discuss the situation offline with someone you trust.

❺ Craft a competent response that begins and ends with supportive statements, uses "I" language, expresses empathy, and emphasizes mutuality rather than just your own perspective and goals.

3. *Seek outside counsel.* Before responding to online conflict messages, discuss the situation *offline* (ideally, face-to-face) with someone who knows you well and whose opinion you trust and respect. Having an additional viewpoint will enhance your ability to perspective-take and will help you make wise communication decisions.

4. *Weigh your options carefully.* Choose cautiously between engaging or avoiding the conflict. Consider the consequences associated with each option, and which is most likely to net you the long-term personal and relationship outcomes you desire. Ask yourself: Will responding at this time help resolve the conflict or escalate things further?

5. *Communicate competently.* When crafting your response, draw on all you know about competent interpersonal communication. That is, use "I" language, incorporate appropriate emoticons, express empathy and use perspective-taking, encourage the other person to share relevant thoughts and feelings, and make clear your willingness to negotiate mutually agreeable solutions. Perhaps most important, start and end your message with positive statements that support rather than attack the other person's viewpoints.

Conflict Endings

Learn about short-term and long-term conflict outcomes

In Antoine Fuqua's stylish thriller *The Equalizer* (2014), Denzel Washington plays Robert, a man with a peerless set of fighting skills coupled with a compulsion to see justice done. When Robert learns that a pair of rogue cops are extorting money from the business of a coworker, he films them making their demands. Then he confronts the two men and gives them a choice: return the money they stole or suffer the consequences. The officers refuse, at which point Robert demonstrates the physical consequences of their decision—after which they give back the money.

In the real world, we don't all have "equalizers" who follow us around, ensuring through cleverness and force that our daily conflicts end in fairness. Nevertheless, our conflicts do end—albeit not always in the ways we wish. For instance, call to mind the most recent serious conflict you experienced, and consider the way it ended. Did one of you "win" and the other "lose"? Were you both left dissatisfied, or were you each pleased with the resolution? More important, were you able to resolve the underlying issue that triggered the disagreement in the first place, or did you merely create a short-term fix?

Given their emotional intensity and the fact that they typically occur in relationships, conflicts conclude more gradually than many people would like. You may arrive at a short-term resolution leading to the immediate end of the conflict. But afterward, you'll experience long-term outcomes as you remember, ponder, and possibly regret the incident. These outcomes will influence your relationship health and happiness long into the future.

Assignment: Conflict Analysis Paper

Have students write an analysis of a recent conflict with a romantic partner, coworker, family member, or friend. Using concepts and theories from the chapter, students should describe the scenario, how each person handled the conflict, influences on the conflict, and the conflict ending. They should also consider how they could have handled the situation differently and what lessons they will keep in mind for the next time they enter a conflict.

SHORT-TERM CONFLICT RESOLUTIONS

The approach you and your partner choose to handle the conflict usually results in one of five short-term conflict resolutions (Peterson, 2002). First, some conflicts end through **separation,** the sudden withdrawal of one person from the encounter. This resolution is characteristic of approaching conflict through avoidance. For example, you may be having a disagreement with your mother, when she suddenly hangs up on you. Or you're discussing a concern with your roommate, when he unexpectedly gets up, walks into his bedroom, and shuts the door behind him. Separation ends the immediate encounter, but it does nothing to solve the underlying incompatibility of goals or the interference that triggered the dispute in the first place.

However, separation isn't always negative. In some cases, short-term separation may help bring about long-term resolution. For example, if you and your partner have both used competitive or reactive approaches, your conflict may have escalated so much that any further contact may result in irreparable relationship damage. In such cases, temporary separation may help you both cool off, regroup, and consider how to collaborate. You can then come back and work together to better resolve the situation.

Second, **domination**—akin to Denzel Washington taking down the rogue cops in *The Equalizer*—occurs when one person gets his or her way by influencing the other to engage in accommodation and abandon goals. Conflicts that end with domination are often called *win-lose solutions*. The strongest predictor of domination is the power balance in the relationship. In cases in which one person has substantial power over the other, that person will likely prevail.

In *The Equalizer*, Denzel Washington plays a vigilante who ends conflicts by bringing criminals to justice. What methods do you use to end conflicts in your relationships? Scott Garfield/© Columbia Pictures/Everett Collection

In some cases, domination may be acceptable. For example, when one person doesn't feel strongly about achieving his or her goals, being dominated may have few costs. However, domination is destructive when it becomes a chronic pattern and one individual always sacrifices his or her goals to keep the peace. Over time, the consistent abandonment of goals can spawn resentment and hostility. While the accommodating "losers" are silently suffering, the dominating "victors" may think everything is fine because they are used to achieving their goals.

Third, during **compromise,** both parties change their goals to make them compatible. Often, both people abandon part of their original desires, and neither

◐ Conflict resolutions depend on the balance of power in a relationship. For example, many parents end conflicts with their children through domination. Stuart Franklin/Magnum Photos

skills practice

Resolving Conflict
Creating better conflict resolutions

❶ When a conflict arises in a close relationship, manage your negative emotions.

❷ Before communicating with your partner, call to mind the consequences of your communication choices.

❸ Employ a collaborative approach, and avoid kitchen-sinking.

❹ As you negotiate solutions, keep your original goals in mind but remain flexible about how they can be attained.

❺ Revisit relationship rules or agreements that triggered the conflict, and consider redefining them in ways that prevent future disputes.

feels completely happy about it. Compromise typically results from people using a collaborative approach and is most effective in situations in which both people treat each other with respect, have relatively equal power, and don't consider their clashing goals especially important (Zacchilli et al., 2009). In cases in which the two parties do consider their goals important, however, compromise can foster mutual resentment and regret (Peterson, 2002). Suppose you and your spouse want to spend a weekend away. You planned this getaway for months, but your spouse now wants to attend a two-day workshop that same weekend. A compromise might involve you cutting the trip short by a night and your spouse missing a day of his or her workshop, leaving both of you with substantially less than you originally desired.

Fourth, through **integrative agreements,** the two sides preserve and attain their goals by developing a creative solution to their problem. This creates a *win-win solution* in which both people, using a collaborative conflict approach, benefit from the outcome. To achieve integrative agreements, the parties must remain committed to their individual goals but be flexible in how they achieve them (Pruitt & Carnevale, 1993). An integrative agreement for the weekend-away example might involve rescheduling the weekend so that you and your spouse could enjoy both the vacation and the workshop.

Finally, in cases of especially intense conflict, **structural improvements**—people agreeing to change the basic rules or understandings that govern their relationship to prevent further conflict—may result. In cases of structural improvement, the conflict itself becomes a vehicle for reshaping the relationship in positive ways—rebalancing power or redefining expectations about who plays what roles in the relationship. Structural improvements are only likely to occur when the people involved control their negative emotions and handle the conflict collaboratively. Suppose your romantic partner keeps in touch with an ex via Facebook. Although you trust your partner, the thought of an ex chatting with him or her on a daily basis, and tracking your relationship through updates and posted photos, drives you crazy. After a jealousy-fueled fight, you and your partner might sit down and collaboratively hash out guidelines for how often and in what ways each of you can communicate with ex-partners, online and off.

We may try to end a conflict through a "peace offering"—a gift or favor to smooth things over. However, it is important to ensure that the parties involved have all reached a resolution so that no lingering conflict remains. D-BASE/Getty Images

LONG-TERM CONFLICT OUTCOMES

After the comparatively short-term phase of conflict resolution, you may begin to ponder the long-term outcomes. In particular, you might consider whether the conflict was truly resolved, and what the dispute's impact was on your relationship. Research examining long-term conflict outcomes and relationship satisfaction has found that certain approaches for dealing with conflict—in particular, avoidant, reactive, and collaborative approaches—strongly predict relationship quality (Smith et al., 2008; Zacchilli et al., 2009).

The most commonly used conflict approach is avoidance. But because avoidance doesn't address the goal clash or actions that sparked the conflict, tensions will likely continue. People who use avoidance have lower relationship satisfaction and endure longer and more frequent conflicts than people who don't avoid (Smith et al., 2008). Consequently, try not to use avoidance unless you're certain the issue is unimportant. This is a judgment call; sometimes an issue that seems unimportant at the time ends up eating away at you over the long run. When in doubt, communicate directly about the issue.

Far more poisonous to relationship health, however, is reactivity. Individuals who handle conflict by (in effect) throwing tantrums end up substantially less happy in their relationships (Zacchilli et al., 2009). If you or your partner habitually uses reactivity, seriously consider more constructive ways to approach conflict. If you do not, your relationship is likely doomed to dissatisfaction.

In sharp contrast to the negative outcomes of avoidance and reactivity, collaborative approaches generally generate positive long-term outcomes (Smith et al., 2008). People using collaboration tend to resolve their conflicts, report higher satisfaction in their relationships, and experience shorter and fewer disputes. The lesson from this is to always treat others with kindness and respect, and strive to deal with conflict by openly discussing it in a way that emphasizes mutual interests and saves your partner's face.

If collaborating yields positive long-term outcomes, and avoiding and reacting yield negative ones, what about accommodating and competing? This is difficult to predict. Sometimes you'll compete and get what you want, the conflict will be resolved, and you'll be satisfied. Or you'll compete, the conflict will escalate wildly out of control, and you'll end up incredibly unsatisfied. Other times you'll accommodate, the conflict will be resolved, and you'll be content. Or you'll accommodate, and the other person will exploit you further, causing you deep discontent. Accommodation and competition are riskier because you can't count on either as a constructive way to manage conflict for the long term (Peterson, 2002).

Challenges to Handling Conflict

Conflicts can spark destructive communication

You and your mother suffer a disagreement that threatens to tear your family apart. So you text her and schedule a lunch date. Sitting down face-to-face, you both express love and admiration for each other, and you agree that the conflict should be resolved in a mutually satisfying fashion. You then collaboratively brainstorm ideas, and voila!—the perfect solution is discovered! You smile, hug, and part ways, each feeling satisfied with the relationship and contented with the resolution.

Yeah, right. If only resolving conflict could be so easy! Unfortunately, conflict in close relationships is rarely (if ever) as streamlined and stress-free as cooperative partners joining forces to reconcile surmountable differences. Instead, close relationship conflict is typically fraught with challenges. Let's take a look at some of the most potent: self-enhancing thoughts, destructive messages, serial arguments, physical violence, and unsolvable disputes.

SELF-ENHANCING THOUGHTS

Arguably the biggest challenge we face in constructively managing conflict is our own minds. During conflicts, we think in radically self-enhancing ways. In a detailed study of conflict thought patterns, scholar Alan Sillars and his colleagues found that during disputes, individuals selectively remember information that supports themselves and contradicts their partners, view their own communication more positively than their partners', and blame partners for failure to resolve the conflict (Sillars, Roberts, Leonard, & Dun, 2000).

Sillars and his colleagues also found little evidence of complex thought. While conflicts are unfolding, people typically do *not* consider long-term outcomes ("How is this going to impact our relationship?") and do *not* perspective-take ("How is she feeling?"). Instead, their thoughts are locked into simple, unqualified, and negative views: "He's lying!" or "She's blaming me!" (Sillars et al., 2000, p. 491). In only 2 percent of cases did respondents attribute cooperativeness to their partners and uncooperativeness to themselves. This means that in 98 percent of fights, you'll likely think, "I'm trying to be helpful, and my partner is being unreasonable!" However, your partner will be thinking the exact same thing about you.

Self-enhancing thoughts dominate conflict encounters, stifling the likelihood of collaboration. Consequently, *the most important thing you can do to improve your conflict-management skills is to routinely practice critical self-reflection during disputes.* Although you might not ever achieve objectivity or neutrality in your thoughts, you can work toward this goal by regularly going through this mental checklist:

- Is my partner *really* being uncooperative, or am *I* making a faulty attribution?
- Is my partner *really* solely to blame, or have *I* also done something to cause the conflict?
- Is the conflict *really* due to ongoing differences between us, or is it *actually* due to temporary factors, such as stress or fatigue?

DESTRUCTIVE MESSAGES

Think back to the chapter opener when Amy Chua had a fight with Lulu in a restaurant. They both were so irate that they said horrible and unforgivable things to each other. When conflicts escalate and anger peaks, our minds are filled with negative thoughts of all the grievances and resentments we feel toward others (Sillars et al., 2000). These thoughts often leap out of our mouths, in the form of messages that permanently damage our relationships (McCornack & Husband, 1986).

Test Your Understanding of Destructive Thoughts

Recall the most recent, serious conflict you've had with another person. Reflect on the thoughts you had *during* the conflict. Then check each statement that fairly represents a thought you had while the conflict was actually happening. When you're done, score yourself using the key at the bottom.

To take this quiz online, visit LaunchPad: macmillanhighered.com/reflectrelate4e.

_____ This isn't all *my* fault.

_____ All my partner cares about is him- or herself.

_____ My partner just wants to blow the whole thing off and not talk about it anymore.

_____ My partner keeps cutting me off, just like usual.

_____ I'm giving in to what my partner wants, like I always do.

_____ All my partner seems to want to do is verbally attack me, instead of treating me like a human being.

_____ I'm just trying to get my point across.

_____ All I'm doing is trying to please my partner.

_____ My partner is just making a lot of excuses about her or his behavior.

_____ I'm being cooperative, but my partner is being a jerk.

Note: This *Self-Quiz* is adapted from Table 1 of Sillars et al. (2000, p. 488).

Scoring: 0–3: Few self-enhancing thoughts. The lack of partner-blame and self-praise likely helped you make better communication decisions and collaborate with your partner in solving the conflict. 4–6: Moderate number of self-enhancing thoughts. How you thought about your partner and yourself likely impeded you from approaching the conflict in a collaborative fashion. 7–10: Frequent self-enhancing thoughts. By exclusively blaming your partner while holding yourself faultless, you likely behaved in ways that ensured continuation of or escalated the conflict. **NOTE:** If your score is in the "moderate" (4–6) or "frequent" (7–10) ranges, carefully review the suggested steps for critical self-reflection during conflicts described in the text, to help you better perspective-take and empathize during disputes.

Media Note:
Sudden-Death Statements

Films and TV shows often feature sudden-death breakups, such as when Elaine's boyfriend, "The Bad Breaker-Upper," tells her she has a "big head" on *Seinfeld*, and when Rachel breaks up with Ross on *Friends* by saying, "Let's take a break." Discuss the implications of sudden-death statements. Can relationships be repaired after such statements? How does one deal with the regret?

self-reflection

Recall a conflict in which you and the other person exchanged destructive messages, such as sudden-death statements or dirty secrets. What led to them being said? What impact did these messages have on the conflict? How did they affect your relationship?

Sudden-death statements occur when people get so angry that they suddenly declare the end of the relationship, even though breaking up wasn't a possibility before the conflict. When my wife, Kelly, and I had been married for two years, we had a major argument while visiting her parents. A small dispute over family differences quickly escalated into a full-blown conflict. After flinging a number of kitchen-sink messages at each other, we both shouted, "Why are we even together?! We're so different!" Fortunately, this sudden-death statement caused us to calm down. But many couples who blurt out such things during escalation follow through on them.

Perhaps the most destructive messages are **dirty secrets:** statements that are honest in content, have been kept hidden to protect a partner's feelings, and are designed to hurt. Dirty secrets can include acts of infidelity ("I cheated, and it was great!"). They can also include intense criticism of a partner's appearance ("You know how I've always said I like your nose? Well, I hate it!"), and even a lack of feelings ("I haven't been in love with you for years!"). Dirty secrets are designed to hurt, and because the content is true, they can irreparably damage the recipient and the relationship.

Needless to say, destructive messages can destroy relationships. Couples who exchange critical and contemptuous messages during the first seven years of marriage are more likely to divorce than couples who refrain from such negativity (Gottman & Levenson, 2000). Thus, no matter your level of anger or the caustic thoughts that fill your head, it's essential to always communicate toward your partner in a civil, respectful fashion.

SERIAL ARGUMENTS

Another conflict challenge we face in close relationships is **serial arguments:** a series of unresolved disputes, all having to do with the same issue (Bevan, Finan, & Kaminsky, 2008). Serial arguments typically stem from deep disagreements, such as differing relationship expectations or clashes in values and beliefs. By definition, serial arguments occur over time and consist of cycles in which things "heat up" and then lapse back into a temporary state of truce (Malis & Roloff, 2006). During these "quiet" periods, individuals are likely to think about the conflict, attempt to repair the relationship, and cope with the stress resulting from the most recent fight (Malis & Roloff, 2006).

In the movie *Brave* (2012), Merida and her mother, Elinor, engage in serial arguments over Merida's behavior, which Elinor considers unladylike and inappropriate. Eventually, the two resolve the conflict by working together to overcome their differences. © Walt Disney/Everett Collection

According to the **serial argument process model,** the course that serial arguments take is determined by the goals individuals possess, the approaches they adopt for dealing with the conflict, and the consequent perception of whether or not the conflict is resolvable (Bevan, 2014). Specifically, when individuals in close relationships enter into serial arguments with positive goals, such as "creating a mutual understanding" or "constructively conveying relationship concerns," they're more likely to use collaborative conflict strategies for dealing with the argument (Bevan, 2014, p. 774). As a result, the conflict is more likely to be perceived as eventually resolvable in the aftermath, and people are less likely to ruminate about it. In contrast, when individuals enter into serial arguments with goals such as "gaining power over the partner" or "personally wounding the partner in order to win," they're more likely to use competitive strategies, the conflict is more likely to be perceived as unresolvable, and they're more likely to stew about it afterwards.

Serial arguments are most likely to occur in romantic and family involvements, in which the frequency of interaction provides ample opportunity for repetitive disagreements (Bevan et al., 2008). They are also strongly predictive of relationship failure: couples who suffer serial arguments experience higher stress levels and are more likely to have their relationships end than those who don't (Malis & Roloff, 2006).

Although many serial arguments involve heated verbal battles, others take the form of a **demand-withdraw pattern,** in which one partner in a relationship demands that his or her goals be met, and the other partner responds by withdrawing from the encounter (Caughlin, 2002). Demand-withdraw patterns are typically triggered when a person is bothered by a repeated source of irritation, but doesn't confront the issue until his or her anger can no longer be suppressed. At that point, the person explodes in a demanding fashion (Malis & Roloff, 2006).

If you find yourself in a close relationship in which a demand-withdraw pattern has emerged, discuss this situation with your partner. Using a collaborative approach, critically examine the forces that trigger the pattern, and work to generate solutions that will enable you to avoid the pattern in the future.

PHYSICAL VIOLENCE

The most destructive conflict challenge is physical violence, a strategy to which people may resort if they cannot think of a better way to deal with conflict or if they believe no other options are available (Klein, 1998). In the National Violence Against Women Survey (Tjaden & Thoennes, 2000), 52 percent of women and 66 percent of men reported that at some time in their lives they had been physically assaulted during conflicts. Both men and women use violence as a strategy for dealing with conflicts. Approximately 12 percent of women and 11 percent of men surveyed reported having committed a violent act during conflict with their spouse in the preceding year (Barnett, Miller-Perrin, & Perrin, 1997). Moreover, in an analysis of data from 82 violence studies, researcher John Archer found no substantial difference between men and women in their propensity toward violence as a conflict strategy (2000). At the same time, however, women are substantially more likely to be injured or killed, owing to their lesser physical size and strength (Archer, 2000; O'Leary & Vivian, 1990). Physical violence doesn't restrict itself to heterosexual relationships; nearly 50 percent of lesbian and 30 to 40 percent of gay respondents have been victims of violence during interpersonal conflicts at some time in their lives (Peplau & Spalding, 2000).

One outcome of physical violence in close relationships is the **chilling effect,** whereby individuals stop discussing relationship issues out of fear of their partners' negative reactions (Solomon & Samp, 1998). In these relationships, individuals who are "chilled" constrain their communication and actions to a very narrow margin, avoiding all topics and behaviors they believe may provoke a partner (Afifi et al., 2009). The result is an overarching relationship climate of fear, suppression, anxiety, and unhappiness.

If you find yourself in a relationship in which your partner behaves violently toward you, seek help from family members, friends, and law enforcement officials. Realize that your best option might be to end the relationship and avoid all contact with the person. We discuss tactics for dealing with relational violence in more detail in Chapter 10.

If you find that you are inclined to violence in relationships, revisit the anger management techniques described in Chapter 4 as well as the suggestions for constructively handling conflict described earlier in this chapter. Most aggression during conflicts stems from people's perception that they have no other options. Although situations may exist in which there truly are no other options—for example, self-defense during a violent assault or robbery—within most encounters more constructive alternatives are available. If you are unable to control your impulses toward violence, seek professional counseling.

UNSOLVABLE DISPUTES

A final conflict challenge is that some disputes are unsolvable. In the climactic scene of Margaret Mitchell's Civil War classic *Gone with the Wind*, the principal character, Scarlett O'Hara, declares her love for Rhett Butler, only to find that he no longer feels the same about her (Mitchell, 1936).

> "Stop," she said suddenly. She knew she could no longer endure with any fortitude the sound of his voice when there was no love in it. He paused and looked at her quizzically. "Well, you get my meaning, don't you?" he questioned, rising to his feet. "No," she cried. "All I know is that you do not love me and you are going away! Oh, my darling, if you go, what shall I do?" For a moment he hesitated as if debating whether a kind lie were kinder in the long run than the truth. Then he shrugged. "Scarlett, I was never one to patiently pick up broken fragments and glue them together and tell myself that the mended whole was as good as new. What is broken is broken—and I'd rather remember it as it was at its best than mend it and see the broken places as long as I lived. I wish I could care what you do or where you go, but I can't." He drew a short breath, and said lightly but softly: "My dear, I don't give a damn." (p. 732)

As this famous fictional scene illustrates, if one person loves another but the feeling isn't reciprocated, no amount of collaborating will fix things. Part of

---

self-reflection

Think of an unsolvable conflict you've had. What made it unsolvable? How did the dispute affect your relationship? Looking back on the situation, could you have done anything differently to prevent the conflict from becoming unsolvable? If so, what?

[Some conflicts are impossible to solve.]

SELZNICK/MGM/The Kobal Collection/Art Resource

effectively managing conflict is accepting that some conflicts are impossible to resolve. How can you recognize such disputes? Clues include the following: you and the other person aren't willing to change your negative opinions of each other; your goals are irreconcilable and strongly held; and at least one partner is uncooperative, chronically defensive, or violent. In these cases, the only options are to avoid the conflict, hope that your attitudes or goals will change over time, or abandon the relationship, as Rhett Butler did.

Managing Conflict and Power

[Conflicts can be opportunities for positive change] Whether it's big or small, when a dispute arises, you may feel that no one else has ever had the same thoughts and emotions. The anger, fear of escalation, pain of hurtful comments that should have been left unsaid, and uncertainty associated with not knowing the long-term relationship outcomes combine to make the experience intense and draining.

But conflicts and struggles over power needn't be destructive. Though they carry risk, they also provide the opportunity to engineer positive change in the way you communicate with others and manage your relationships. Through conflict, you can resolve problems that, left untouched, would have eroded your relationship

making relationship choices

Dealing with Family Conflict

1 BACKGROUND

Conflict poses complex challenges for interpersonal communication and relationships. Parental expectations, power differences between generations, and the emotional connections within families can make matters even more complex. To understand how you might competently manage such a relationship challenge, read the case study in Part 2; then, drawing on all you know about interpersonal communication, work through the problem-solving model in Part 3.

 Visit LaunchPad to check out the other side of the story (Part 4). For the best experience, complete all parts in LaunchPad: macmillanhighered.com/reflectrelate4e.

2 CASE STUDY

Your parents are old school in their views of parental power: they believe that children should always show deference to elders. Although you're still in college, your brother, Sanjay, is much older and has a family of his own, including a teenage son, Devdas. You have always gotten along well with Devdas, but he has recently been going through a rebellious phase in which he shows little respect for adults, including you. During a recent visit, Devdas was sprawled on the sofa all afternoon, playing video games on the big screen. You asked if you could watch a movie, and he snapped, "Find your own &*$%# TV!" You did not mention this incident to the rest of your family in order to avoid escalating the issue.

Your parents decide to spend a week with Sanjay and his family. You're nervous because your mother delights in picking on Devdas about his hair, clothing, and music, and given Devdas's recent attitude, you're afraid he may strike back. Sure enough, toward the end of the week, you get a phone call from your mother, telling you that she and your father ended their visit early and that she wishes no further contact with your brother or his family. She says that Devdas "swore at her for no reason at all." She says, "I have no interest in associating with children who behave like that." Shortly after, you get a text from your brother. He says that your mother is delusional and "made the whole thing up." When you ask whether Devdas might have sworn at your mom, your brother fires back, "Absolutely not! Devdas doesn't even *know* such words!!!" Since you weren't a witness to the encounter, you try to stay neutral.

As the weeks go by, the rift deepens. Devdas refuses to talk about the issue at all, even with you or his parents. Your mother refuses contact with her grandson until he "admits his wrongdoing!"

Now, with the holidays approaching, you receive an e-mail from your parents. They demand that you side with them, saying, "If you continue to support Devdas in this shameful matter, we will be forced to rethink our financial support for your education." Sitting down at your computer, you write back a message.

3 YOUR TURN

Think about all you've learned thus far about interpersonal communication. Then work through the following five steps. Remember, there are no "right" answers, so think hard about what is the *best* choice! (P.S. Need help? See the *Helpful Concepts* list.)

step 1
Reflect on yourself. What are your thoughts and feelings in this situation? What attributions are you making about your mother, Devdas, and their behavior? Are your attributions accurate? Why or why not?

step 2
Reflect on your partner. Using perspective-taking and empathic concern, put yourself in your mother's shoes. Do the same for Devdas. What are they thinking and feeling in this situation?

step 3
Identify the optimal outcome. Think about all the information you have about your communication and relationships with both your mother and Devdas. Consider your own feelings as well as theirs. Given all these factors, what's the best, most constructive relationship outcome possible? Consider what's best for you *and* for your mother and Devdas.

step 4
Locate the roadblocks. Taking into consideration your own thoughts and feelings, those of your mother and Devdas, and all that has happened in this situation, what obstacles are keeping you from achieving the optimal outcome?

step 5
Chart your course. How might you respond to your mother to overcome the roadblocks you've identified and achieve your optimal outcome?

> **HELPFUL CONCEPTS**
> Power principles, **257–259**
> Collaboratively managing conflict, **264–266**
> Conflict resolutions and outcomes, **270–274**
> Critiquing your perceptions and attributions, **274–275**
> Unresolvable conflicts, **278**

4 THE OTHER SIDE

▶ Visit LaunchPad to watch a video in which Devdas tells his side of the case study story. As in many real-life situations, this is information to which you did not have access when you were initially crafting your response in Part 3. The video reminds us that even when we do our best to offer competent responses, there is always another side to the story that we need to consider.

◉ Conflicts do not need to destroy your closest interpersonal relationships. When navigating a challenging conflict with a loved one, remember that renewed intimacy and happiness may be just around the corner. © Peter Coombs/Alamy

or deprived you of greater happiness in the future. The key distinguishing feature between conflict and power struggles that destroy and those that create opportunities for improvement is how you interpersonally communicate.

We've discussed a broad range of communication skills that can help you manage conflict and power more effectively. Whether it's using collaborative approaches, critiquing your perceptions and attributions, knowing when to take a conflict offline, or being sensitive to gender and cultural differences, you now know the skills necessary for successfully managing the disagreements, disputes, and contests that will erupt in your life. It is up to you now to take these skills and put them into practice.

POSTSCRIPT

This chapter began with a woman determined to dominate her children. Amy Chua made headlines and best-seller lists when she boasted of her dictatorial parenting style. Her book, *Battle Hymn of the Tiger Mother*, describes her dysfunctional approaches to managing conflict and power in painful detail, including taunts, tantrums, insults, and accusations.

What messages did you learn growing up about how conflict and power should best be managed? Did the way in which your parents or caregivers dealt with conflicts leave you feeling better about yourself and your relationship with them? Or did it leave a wake of interpersonal destruction and heartache behind?

Satirical or not, Chua's book provides a powerful lesson for us all regarding the relationship between choices, communication, and outcomes. When you consistently choose to manage disputes in unyielding, aggressive ways, the relationship outcomes will be as unsatisfying and unpleasant as the conflict itself.

chapter review

LaunchPad for *Reflect & Relate* offers videos and encourages self-assessment through adaptive quizzing. Go to **macmillanhighered.com/reflectrelate4e** to get access to:

 LearningCurve Adaptive Quizzes

 Video clips that help you understand interpersonal communication

key terms

conflict, 254
kitchen-sinking, 255
▶ power, 256
symmetrical relationships, 257
complementary relationships, 257
Dyadic Power Theory, 258
power currency, 259
▶ resource currency, 259
▶ expertise currency, 259
▶ social network currency, 259
▶ personal currency, 259
▶ intimacy currency, 260
▶ avoidance, 262
skirting, 262
▶ sniping, 262
cumulative annoyance, 262
pseudo-conflict, 262
▶ accommodation, 263
▶ competition, 263
escalation, 263
reactivity, 264
▶ collaboration, 264
separation, 271
domination, 271
▶ compromise, 271
integrative agreements, 272
structural improvements, 272
sudden-death statements, 276
dirty secrets, 276
serial arguments, 276
serial argument process model, 277
demand-withdraw pattern, 277
chilling effect, 278

▶ You can watch brief, illustrative videos of these terms and test your understanding of the concepts online in LaunchPad.

key concepts

Conflict and Interpersonal Communication

- **Conflict** arises whenever people's goals clash or they compete for valued resources.
- Avoid **kitchen-sinking**—hurling insults that have little to do with the original dispute.

Power and Conflict

- Conflict and **power** are closely related.
- Friendships are typically **symmetrical relationships,** whereas parent-child relationships are **complementary relationships.**
- Power is granted to you by others, depending on the **power currency** you possess. Types include **resource, expertise, social network, personal,** and **intimacy.**
- Across cultures and time, men have consolidated power over women by strategically depriving women of access to power currencies.

Handling Conflict

- **Avoidance** can lead to damaging behaviors, including **skirting, sniping, cumulative annoyance,** and the inability to overcome **pseudo-conflict.**
- **Accommodation** is often motivated by the desire to please the people we love.
- **Competition** involves the aggressive pursuit of one's own goals at the expense of others' goals.
- **Reactivity** occurs as a negative, explosive response to conflict.
- **Collaboration** is the best approach to conflict, since it reinforces trust in your relationships and builds relational satisfaction.
- If online conflicts arise, it's best to take the encounter offline.

Conflict Endings

- In the short term, conflicts resolve through **separation, domination, compromise, integrative agreements,** or **structural improvements.**
- In the long term, partners consider the conflict's impact on their relationship.

Challenges to Handling Conflict

- **Sudden-death statements** occur when, in anger, people declare the end of the relationship.
- In close relationships, there is a risk of engaging in **serial arguments,** which may lead to **demand-withdraw patterns.**
- When people believe that no other option exists, they may commit acts of violence.
- Some conflicts are impossible to resolve.

10 Relationships with Romantic Partners

LearningCurve can help you review the material in this chapter. Go to LaunchPad: macmillanhighered.com/reflectrelate4e

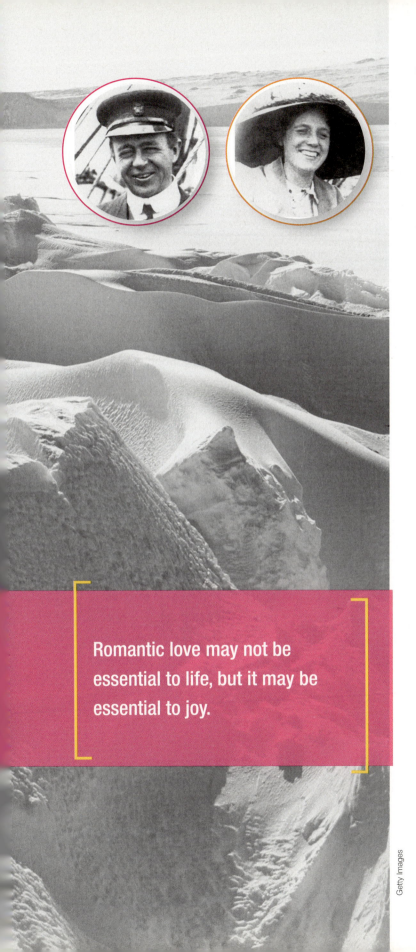

> Romantic love may not be essential to life, but it may be essential to joy.

The temperature was −70°.[1] Although he was only a few miles from his supply depot — and salvation in the form of food and gear — the weather was impassable. Suffering from frostbite and malnutrition, Antarctic explorer Sir Robert Falcon Scott knew two things for certain: he would soon die, and a recovery team would eventually find his body. So he penned a letter to his wife, Kathleen. *"To my widow,"* he began. What followed is one of the most moving testimonials to romantic love ever written.

Scott had led a British team trying to be the first to reach the South Pole. Arriving at their goal on January 17, 1912, they were stunned to find a tent erected on the site. Inside was a note left by Norwegian explorer Roald Amundsen: he had beaten Scott's team by a month. Defeated, Scott and his comrades began the 800-mile return trip, beset by snow blindness, hunger, and exhaustion. The weather worsened, and one by one his team members perished.

Huddled inside his shelter, Scott crafted a note to Kathleen that was at once passionate, practical, upbeat, and astonishingly selfless. Longing and sentiment poured from his pen: "You know I have loved you, you know my thoughts must have constantly dwelt on you . . . the worst aspect of this situation is the thought that I shall not see you again. . . . Oh what a

---

[1] All information and quotes that follow are adapted from the Scott Polar Research Institute. Retrieved from http://www.cam.ac.uk/news/captain-scott%E2%80%99s-final-letters-home-go-on-display

285

10 / Relationships with Romantic Partners

© TopFoto/The Image Works

price to pay — to forfeit the sight of your dear dear face!" He grieved the lost chance to see his son mature: "what dreams I have had of his future." But he praised Kathleen's practicality, and entreated her "to take the whole thing very sensibly as I am sure you will. . . . Make the boy interested in natural history if you can, it is better than games."

Though suffering from frostbite, he remained relentlessly upbeat. "There is a painless end, so don't worry. . . . How much better it has been than lounging in comfort at home." In the most striking passage of all, Scott granted Kathleen romantic liberty: "Cherish no sentimental rubbish about remarriage — when the right man comes to help you in life you ought to be your happy self again. I hope I shall be a good memory."

Eight months later a recovery team reached Scott's encampment. Searching the remnants of his tent, they found Scott's personal journal and his letter to Kathleen. They then built a tomb of ice and snow over the bodies of Scott and his companions, and placed a cross on top to mark the site.

In the years that followed, Scott would be honored across Britain as a tragic hero. Dozens of monuments were raised and memorial funds created to support the families of the fallen. In January 2007, Scott's letters and journal were donated for display at the University of Cambridge. But in the dim light of his tent in March 1912, with storms raging and death approaching, Sir Robert Falcon Scott was just another human being trying to capture in writing the multifaceted complexity of romantic love. To read his words is to be reminded that *love is not singular, but plural*: it is many things at once, including passion, practicality, commitment, respect, sentiment, and selflessness.

286

Throughout time and across cultures, people have fallen in love with each other. When each of us discovers love for ourselves, we honor that legacy, sharing in an experience that is both uniquely and universally human. We also find that romantic love is a multiplicity of elements, some of which seem contradictory. Our affairs may be all about passion, but they also bring with them the rewards (and costs) of companionship. Our love for others may be selfless and giving, yet we're driven to build and sustain only those relationships that benefit us the most, and end those that don't. Although romance may be sentimental and otherworldly, the maintenance of love is decidedly practical. Romantic *relationships* are hard work, entailing constant upkeep to survive the innumerable and unforeseen challenges that threaten them.

In this chapter, the first of three on relationships, you'll learn:

- The defining characteristics of romantic love and relationships
- What drives your attraction to some people and not to others
- How communication changes as your romantic relationships come together . . . and fall apart
- How to communicate in ways that keep your love alive
- The dark side of romantic relationships and how to deal effectively with these challenges

chapter outline

287 Defining Romantic Relationships

293 Romantic Attraction

298 Relationship Development and Deterioration

303 Maintaining Romantic Relationships

311 The Dark Side of Romantic Relationships

319 The Hard Work of Successful Love

Defining Romantic Relationships

People experience different types of love

We often think of romantic relationships as exciting and filled with promise—a joyful fusion of closeness, communication, and sexual connection. When researchers Pamela Regan, Elizabeth Kocan, and Teresa Whitlock (1998) asked several hundred people to list the things they associated most with "being in love," the most frequent responses were trust, honesty, happiness, bondedness, companionship, communication, caring, intimacy, shared laughter, and sexual desire. But apart from such associations, what exactly *is* romantic love? How does it differ from liking? The answers to these questions can help you build more satisfying romantic partnerships.

LIKING AND LOVING

Most scholars agree that liking and loving are separate emotional states, with different causes and outcomes (Berscheid & Regan, 2005). **Liking** is a feeling of affection and respect that we typically have for our friends (Rubin, 1973). *Affection* is a sense of warmth and fondness toward another person, while *respect* is admiration for another person apart from how he or she treats you or communicates with you. **Loving,** in contrast, is a vastly deeper and more intense emotional experience and consists of three components: intimacy, caring, and attachment (Rubin, 1973).

Chapter Theme
The story of this chapter is that romantic love is not a singularity but a plurality. Romantic love is often equated with passion. But many different types of romantic love exist, and being "in love" with someone typically evokes numerous, sometimes contradictory, feelings. To overcome the practical challenges of maintaining a healthy romantic relationship, one must embrace the multidimensional nature of romantic love and work hard to nurture intimacy and commitment.

- *Intimacy* is a feeling of closeness and "union" between you and your partner (Mashek & Aron, 2004).
- *Caring* is the concern you have for your partner's welfare and the desire to keep him or her happy.
- *Attachment* is a longing to be in your partner's presence as much as possible.

The ideal combination for long-term success in romantic relationships occurs when partners both like and love each other.

DIFFERENT TYPES OF ROMANTIC LOVE

Though most people recognize that loving differs from liking, many also believe that to be *in* love, one must feel constant and consuming sexual attraction toward a partner. In fact, many different types of romantic love exist, covering a broad range of emotions and relationship forms. At one end of the spectrum is **passionate love,** a state of intense emotional and physical longing for union with another (Hendrick & Hendrick, 1992). Studies of passionate love suggest six things are true about its experience and expression. First, passionate love quite literally changes our brains. Neuroimaging studies of people experiencing passionate love suggest substantial activation of brain reward centers, as well as activation of the caudate nucleus—an area associated with obsessive thinking (Graham, 2011). In simple terms, people passionately in love often find the experience intensely pleasurable and may have their thoughts circle constantly around their partners. Second, people passionately in love often view their loved ones and relationships in an excessively idealistic light. For instance, many partners in passionate love relationships talk about how "perfect" they are for each other.

Third, people from all cultures feel passionate love. Studies comparing members of individualist versus collectivist cultures have found no differences in

self-reflection

Is passion the critical defining feature of being in love? Or can you fall in love without ever feeling passion? Given that passion typically fades, is romantic love always doomed to fail, or can you still be in love after passion leaves?

People who are passionately in love experience an intense longing to be physically near each other. What other traits or experiences do you associate with passionate love? Philip Jones Griffiths/Magnum Photos

the amount of passionate love experienced (Hatfield & Rapson, 1987). Although certain ethnicities, especially Latinos, are often stereotyped as being more "passionate," studies comparing Latino and non-Latino experiences of romantic love suggest no differences in intensity (Cerpas, 2002).

Fourth, no gender or age differences exist in people's experience of passionate love. Men and women report experiencing this type of love with equal frequency and intensity, and studies using a Juvenile Love Scale (which excludes references to sexual feelings) have found that children as young as age 4 report passionate love toward others (Hatfield & Rapson, 1987). The latter finding is important to consider when talking with children about their romantic feelings. Although they lack the emotional maturity to fully understand the consequences of their relationship decisions, their feelings toward romantic interests are every bit as intense and turbulent as our adult emotions. So if your 6- or 7-year-old child or sibling reveals a crush on a schoolmate, treat the disclosure with respect and empathy rather than teasing him or her.

Fifth, for adults, passionate love is integrally linked with sexual desire (Berscheid & Regan, 2005). In one study, undergraduates were asked whether they thought there was a difference between "being in love" and "loving" another person (Ridge & Berscheid, 1989). Eighty-seven percent of respondents said that there was a difference and that sexual attraction was the critical distinguishing feature of being in love.

Finally, passionate love is *negatively* related to relationship duration. Like it or not, the longer you're with a romantic partner, the less intense your passionate love will feel (Berscheid, 2002).

Although the fire of passionate love dominates media depictions of romance, not all people view being in love this way. At the other end of the romantic spectrum is **companionate love:** an intense form of liking defined by emotional investment and deeply intertwined lives (Berscheid & Walster, 1978). Many long-term romantic relationships evolve into companionate love. As Clyde and Susan Hendrick (1992) explain, "Sexual attraction, intense communication, and emotional turbulence early in a relationship give way to quiet intimacy, predictability, and shared attitudes, values, and life experiences later in the relationship" (p. 48).

Between the poles of passionate and companionate love lies a range of other types of romantic love. Sociologist John Alan Lee (1973) suggested six different forms, ranging from friendly to obsessive and gave them each a traditional Greek name: *storge*, *agape*, *mania*, *pragma*, *ludus*, and *eros* (see Table 10.1 for an explanation of each). As Lee noted, there is no "right" type of romantic love—different forms appeal to different people.

Despite similarities between men and women in their experiences of passionate love, substantial gender differences exist related to one of Lee's love types—*pragma*, or "practical love." Across numerous studies, women score higher than men on *pragma* (Hendrick & Hendrick, 1988, 1992), refuting the common stereotype that women are "starry-eyed" and "sentimental" about romantic love (Hill, Rubin, & Peplau, 1976). What's more, although men are often stereotyped as being "cool" and "logical" about love (Hill et al., 1976), they are much more likely

Discussion Prompt: Romantic Love Types
Place students in small groups, and assign each group a few romantic love types to define and discuss. Students should come up with a list of relationships found in the media—from reality TV programs, sitcoms, movies, celebrity news, politicians—that exhibit the characteristics of their assigned types. Ask groups to share their examples with the class.

table 10.1 **Romantic Love Types**

Type	Description	Attributes of Love
Storge	Friendly lovers	Stable, predictable, and rooted in friendship
Agape	Forgiving lovers	Patient, selfless, giving, and unconditional
Mania	Obsessive lovers	Intense, tumultuous, extreme, and all consuming
Pragma	Practical lovers	Logical, rational, and founded in common sense
Ludus	Game-playing lovers	Uncommitted, fun, and played like a game
Eros	Romantic lovers	Sentimental, romantic, idealistic, and committed

Online Self-Quiz:
Test Your Love Attitudes.
To take this self-quiz,
visit LaunchPad:
macmillanhighered.com
/reflectrelate4e

than women to perceive their romantic partners as "perfect" and believe that "love at first sight is possible" and that "true love can overcome any obstacles" (Sprecher & Metts, 1999).

KEY ELEMENTS OF ROMANTIC RELATIONSHIPS

We know that loving differs from liking and that people experience different types of love. But what exactly does it mean to have a romantic relationship? A **romantic relationship** is a chosen interpersonal involvement forged through communication in which the participants perceive the bond as romantic. Six elements of romantic relationships underlie this definition.

Perception A romantic relationship exists whenever the two partners perceive that it does. As perceptions change, so, too, does the relationship. For example, a couple may consider their relationship "casual dating" but still define it as "romantic" (rather than friendly). Or, a long-term couple may feel more companionate than passionate but still consider themselves "in love." If two partners' perceptions of their relationship differ—for example, one person feels romantic and the other does not—they do not have a romantic relationship (Miller & Steinberg, 1975).

Diversity Romantic relationships exhibit remarkable diversity in the ages and genders of the partners, as well as in their ethnic and religious backgrounds and sexual orientations. Yet despite this diversity, most relationships function in a similar manner. For example, whether a romantic relationship is between lesbian, gay, or straight partners, the individuals involved place the same degree of importance on their relationship, devote similar amounts of time and energy to maintaining their bond, and demonstrate similar openness in their communication (Haas & Stafford, 2005). The exact same factors that determine marital success between men and women (e.g., honesty, loyalty, commitment, and dedication to maintenance) also predict stability and satisfaction within same-sex couples (Kurdek, 2005). As relationship scholar Sharon Brehm sums up, gay and lesbian couples "fall in love in the same way, feel the same passions, experience the same doubts, and feel the same commitments as straights" (Brehm, Miller, Perlman, & Campbell, 2002, p. 27).

Choice We enter into romantic relationships through choice, selecting not only with whom we initiate involvements but also whether and how we maintain these bonds. Contrary to widespread belief, love doesn't "strike us out of the blue" or "sweep us away." Choice plays a role even in arranged marriages: the spouses' families and social networks select an appropriate partner, and in many cases the betrothed retain at least some control over whether the choice is acceptable (Hendrick & Hendrick, 1992).

Commitment Romantic relationships often involve **commitment:** a strong psychological attachment to a partner and an intention to continue the relationship long into the future (Arriaga & Agnew, 2001). When you forge a commitment with a partner, positive outcomes often result. Commitment leads couples to work harder on maintaining their relationships, resulting in greater satisfaction (Rusbult, Arriaga, & Agnew, 2001). Commitment also reduces the likelihood that partners will cheat sexually when separated by geographic distance (Le, Korn, Crockett, & Loving, 2010).

self-reflection

How much do you desire or fear commitment? Are your feelings based on your gender or on other factors? Consider your male and female friends and acquaintances. Do all the men dread commitment and all the women crave it? What does this tell you about the legitimacy of commitment stereotypes?

● Depictions of romantic love are often found in art, movies, literature, poetry, music, and other media, but they rarely detail the everyday interpersonal communication that makes successful relationships work. Erich Lessing/Art Resource, NY

Although men are stereotyped in the media as "commitment-phobic," this stereotype is false. *Both* men and women view commitment as an important part of romantic relationships (Miller, 2014). Several studies even suggest that men often place a higher value on commitment than do women. For example, when asked which they would choose if forced to decide between a committed romance and an important job opportunity, more men than women chose the relationship (Mosher & Danoff-Burg, 2007). Men also score higher than women on measures of commitment in college dating relationships (Kurdek, 2008). These trends aren't new. Throughout fifty years of research, men have consistently reported more of a desire for marriage than have women and described "desire for a committed relationship" as more of a motivation for dating (Rubin, Peplau, & Hill, 1981).

Tensions When we're involved in intimate relationships, we often experience competing impulses, or tensions, between ourselves and our feelings toward others, known as **relational dialectics** (Baxter, 1990). Relational dialectics take three common forms. The first is *openness versus protection*. As relationships become more intimate, we naturally exchange more personal information with our partners. Most of us enjoy the feeling of unity and mutual insight created through such sharing. But while we want to be open with our partners, we also want to keep certain aspects of our selves—such as our most private thoughts and feelings—protected. Too much openness provokes an uncomfortable sense that we've lost our privacy and must share *everything* with our lovers.

The second dialectic is *autonomy versus connection*. We elect to form romantic relationships largely out of a desire to bond with other human beings. Yet if we come to feel so connected to our partners that our individual identity seems to dissolve, we may choose to pull back and reclaim some of our autonomy.

The final dialectic is the clash between our need for stability and our need for excitement and change—known as *novelty versus predictability*. We all like the security that comes with knowing how our partners will behave, how we'll behave, and how our relationships will unfold. Romances are more successful when the partners behave in predictable ways that reduce uncertainty (Berger & Bradac, 1982). However, predictability often spawns boredom. As we get to know our partners, the novelty and excitement of the relationship wears off, and things seem increasingly monotonous. Reconciling the desire for predictability with the need for novelty is one of the most profound emotional challenges facing partners in romantic relationships.

Communication Romantic involvements, like all interpersonal relationships, are forged through interpersonal communication. By interacting with others online, over the phone, and face-to-face, we build a variety of relationships—some of which blossom into romantic love. And once love is born, we use interpersonal communication to foster and maintain it.

---

self-reflection

Do you need to tell a lover everything in order to be truly intimate, or can you keep some parts of yourself private? Should you spend all of your free time together or retain a degree of independence? How can you best keep things from getting stale while staying reliable and trustworthy?

▶ **Video**

macmillanhighered.com /reflectrelate4e

Relational Dialectics
Watch this clip online to answer the questions below.

When have you experienced the tension between being completely open and wishing to keep something private from someone? How did you deal with this tension? Is it ever ethical to keep something private in order to not hurt someone's feelings? Why or why not?

Romantic Attraction

Why we are attracted to some people and not others

In the movie *Silver Linings Playbook* (2012), Bradley Cooper plays Pat Solitano, a former teacher trying to get his life back on track after being institutionalized for bipolar disorder. At dinner with his friend Ronnie, he meets Ronnie's sister-in-law, Tiffany (Jennifer Lawrence), and a spark of attraction immediately kindles. Much to Ronnie and his wife's chagrin, Pat and Tiffany shift the dinner discussion to the psychotropic effects of various medications and end up leaving together. Although Pat had intended reconciliation with his ex-wife, he finds himself inexorably drawn to Tiffany. As the two spend more time together, collaborating on a dance routine for an upcoming competition, they realize they are intensely physically attracted to each other, and have much more in common than their shared mental health challenges.

Every day you meet and interact with new people in class, while standing in line at the local coffee shop, or at gatherings with friends. Yet few of these individuals make a lasting impression on you, and even fewer strike a chord of romantic attraction. What draws you to those special few? Many of the same factors that drew Pat and Tiffany together in *Silver Linings Playbook*: proximity, physical attractiveness, similarity, reciprocal liking, and resources (Aron et al., 2008). These factors influence attraction for both men and women, in both same- and opposite-sex romances (Felmlee, Orzechowicz, & Fortes, 2010; Hyde, 2005).

PROXIMITY

The simple fact of physical proximity — being in each other's presence frequently — exerts far more impact on romantic attraction than many people think. Like Pat and Tiffany, you're likely to feel more attracted to those with

> **Assignment: Applying Relational Dialectics**
>
> After teaching relational dialectics, ask students to write a short essay applying one of the dialectical tensions to a past or current romantic relationship or one they have observed. Ask students to carefully define the tension, briefly describe the relationship, and provide thorough examples of the tension. Students can also describe how the couple coped or dealt with the tension in the relationship.

◀ In *Silver Linings Playbook*, Pat and Tiffany become immediately attracted to each other because of their similar experiences with mental illness. Have you ever become romantically interested in someone because of a shared experience or interest? JoJo Whilden/© Weinstein Company/Everett Collection

▶ You're more likely to be attracted to people you're around a lot, but the effect of proximity on attraction depends on your experience with the people. At least one study has found that people feel most negatively toward those whom they find bothersome and those whom they live nearest to. © LWA-Dan Tardif/Corbis

self-reflection

How much daily contact do you have with people of other ethnicities, based on where you live, work, and go to school? Do you date outside your ethnic group? How has the frequency with which you've had contact with diverse others shaped your dating decisions?

whom you have frequent contact and less attracted to those with whom you interact rarely, a phenomenon known as the **mere exposure effect** (Bornstein, 1989).

Proximity's pronounced effect on attraction is one reason that mixed-race romantic relationships are much rarer than same-race pairings in the United States. Despite this nation's enormous ethnic diversity, most Americans cluster into ethnically homogeneous groups, communities, and neighborhoods. This clustering reduces the likelihood that they will meet, regularly interact with, and eventually become attracted to individuals outside their own cultural group (Gaines, Chalfin, Kim, & Taing, 1998). Those who do form interethnic romances typically have living arrangements, work situations, or educational interests that place them in close proximity with diverse others, fostering attraction (Gaines et al., 1998).

PHYSICAL ATTRACTIVENESS

It's no secret that many people feel drawn to those they perceive as physically attractive. In part this is because we view beautiful people as competent

▲ Although people lust after gorgeous others, most of us end up in long-term relationships with those we perceive to be our equal in physical attractiveness. (Left to right) © Rhoda Sidney/The Image Works; Sarune Zerba/Getty Images; © Arnold Gold/New Haven Register/The Image Works; Dubova/Shutterstock

chapter 10 / Relationships with Romantic Partners

◯ Approximately 50 percent of students surveyed think interracial dating is acceptable, but this masks substantial race and gender differences. While 81 percent of European American and 75 percent of African American men express willingness to date outside their ethnicity, the majority of European American and African American women report negative attitudes toward interracial dating.
Monkey Business Images/Shutterstock

communicators, intelligent, and well adjusted, a phenomenon known as the **beautiful-is-good effect** (Eagly, Ashmore, Makhijani, & Longo, 1991). But although most of us find physical beauty attractive, we tend to form long-term romantic relationships with people we judge as similar to ourselves in physical attractiveness. This is known as **matching** (Feingold, 1988). Research documents that people don't want to be paired with those they think are substantially "below" or "above" themselves in looks (White, 1980).

SIMILARITY

No doubt you've heard the contradictory clichés regarding similarity and attraction: "Opposites attract" versus "Birds of a feather flock together." Which is correct? Scientific evidence suggests that we are attracted to those we perceive as similar to ourselves (Miller, 2014). This is known as the **birds-of-a-feather effect.** One explanation for this phenomenon is that people we view as similar to ourselves are less likely to provoke uncertainty. In first encounters, they seem easier to predict and explain than do people we perceive as dissimilar (Berger & Calabrese, 1975). Thus, we feel more comfortable with them.

Similarity means more than physical attractiveness; it means sharing parallel personalities, values, and likes and dislikes (Markey & Markey, 2007). Having fundamentally different personalities or widely disparate values erodes attraction between partners in the long run. At the same time, differences in mere tastes and preferences have no long-term negative impact on relationship health, as long as you and your partner are similar in other, more important ways. For example, I love heavier music, such as Pantera, Mastodon, and Tool; my favorite recent album is Black Crown Initiate's *The Wreckage of Stars*. My wife *hates* this stuff! But we've been happily married for more than 25 years because we have very similar personalities and values. Differences in tastes don't predict relationship success, so you shouldn't dismiss potential romantic partners because of their minor likes and dislikes.

Discussion Prompt: Attraction and Similarity

Before teaching the section on physical attractiveness, place students in small groups and ask the following: Do birds of a feather flock together, or do opposites attract? Ask them to take a stance and provide a rationale to the class. You could also divide the groups into male and female to see if that provides different perspectives on similarity and attraction.

self-reflection

When you find out that someone really likes you, how does this impact your feelings toward him or her? Have you ever fallen for someone who you knew didn't like you? What does this tell you about the importance of reciprocal liking in shaping attraction?

RECIPROCAL LIKING

A fourth determinant of romantic attraction is one of the most obvious and often overlooked: whether the person we're attracted to makes it clear, through communication and other actions, that the attraction is mutual, known as **reciprocal liking** (Aron et al., 2008). Reciprocal liking is a potent predictor of attraction; we tend to be attracted to people who are attracted to us. Studies examining people's narrative descriptions of "falling in love" have found that reciprocal liking is *the* most commonly mentioned factor leading to love (Riela, Rodriguez, Aron, Xu, & Acevedo, 2010).

RESOURCES

A final spark that kindles romantic attraction is the unique resources that another person offers. Resources include such qualities as sense of humor, intelligence, kindness, supportiveness, and whether the person seems fun to be with. These attributes are viewed as valuable by both straight persons and gay men and lesbians (Felmlee et al., 2010). But what leads *you* to view a person's resources as desirable?

Social exchange theory proposes that you'll feel drawn to those you see as offering substantial benefits (things you like and want) with few associated costs (things demanded of you in return). Two factors drive whether you find someone initially attractive: whether you perceive the person as offering the kinds of rewards you think you deserve in a romantic relationship (affection, emotional support, money, sex), and whether you think that the rewards the person can offer you are superior to those you can get elsewhere (Kelley & Thibaut, 1978). In simple terms, you're attracted to people who can give you what you want and who offer better rewards than others.

Once you've experienced attraction because of perceived rewards, **equity**—the balance of benefits and costs exchanged by you and the other person—determines whether a relationship will take root (Stafford, 2003). Romantic partners are happiest when the balance of giving and getting in their relationship is equal for both, and they're least happy when inequity exists (Hatfield, Traupmann, Sprecher, Utne, & Hay, 1985).

What is *inequity*? People in relationships have a strong sense of proportional justice: the balance between benefits gained from the relationship versus contributions made to the relationship (Hatfield, 1983). Inequity occurs when the benefits or contributions provided by one person are greater than those provided by the other. People who get more rewards from their relationships for fewer costs than their partners are *overbenefited*; those who get fewer rewards from their relationships for more costs than their partners are *underbenefited*. Overbenefited individuals experience negative emotions such as guilt, while underbenefited partners experience emotions such as sadness and anger (Sprecher, 2001).

Equity strongly determines the short- and long-term success of romantic relationships. One study found that during a several-month period, only 23 percent of equitable romances broke up, whereas 54 percent of inequitable romantic relationships broke up (Sprecher, 2001).

TECHNOLOGY AND ROMANTIC ATTRACTION

The enormous range of communication technologies available to us these days has refined and enhanced the attraction process. You can establish virtual proximity to attractive others by befriending them on social networking sites (Facebook, Tumblr) and then exchanging daily (or even hourly) updates and posts. You can assess a prospective partner's similarity to you and the rewards he or she could offer you by interacting with the person through text-messaging or simply by checking his or her personal Web pages and online profiles. You can assess physical attractiveness by viewing online photo albums and video clips. On dating sites such as Match.com, OkCupid, and eHarmony, or even on free sites such as Craigslist, you can enter a set of search parameters—desired age, profession, appearance, interests, gender identity, sexual orientation—and immediately see a broad range of potential partners.

But despite the conveniences they offer, these technologies also evoke tensions. For one thing, you have to decide how honest to be in your online self-presentations (Ellison, Heino, & Gibbs, 2006). Because so many people now use online communication to gauge one another, you may feel great pressure to present yourself as highly attractive, even if that means providing a distorted self-description. In a survey of more than 5,000 online dating service users, misrepresentation of self was commonplace (Hall, Park, Song, & Cody, 2010). Men were more likely than women to exaggerate their education level and income, and women were more likely to lie about their weight. And both men and women over 50 routinely distorted their ages to appear younger. Correspondingly, people view others' online dating profiles skeptically. Users liken profiles to résumés; that is, they are vehicles for marketing one's "best self," rather than accurate glimpses into one's authentic identity (Ellison, Heino, & Gibbs, 2006). Just as people lie on

Teaching Tip: Matching and Attraction
For an interesting look at the matching hypothesis, check out Taylor, Fiore, Mendelsohn, and Cheshire's article (2011) titled "'Out of My League': A Real-World Test of the Matching Hypothesis," in *Personality and Social Psychology Bulletin, 37*(7), 942–954. This experiment with actual online daters found that the matching hypothesis was not entirely supported. The authors discovered evidence for matching based on physical attractiveness, self-worth, and popularity; however, it differed based on stages of the dating process and other related variables.

🟠 The dating app Tinder has drawn controversy from critics, who claim that the matchmaking system is superficial and based overwhelmingly on physical appearance. What differences have you found to exist between online dating and asking someone out on a date in person? Jetta Productions/Getty Images

their résumés, so, too, do online daters presume that others will lie in their profiles. As one online dating service user describes, "Everyone is so wonderful over the Internet. What the Internet doesn't tell you is that, 'I'm defensive, I talk about my problems all the time, I can't manage my money'" (Ellison et al., 2006, p. 435).

If your goal is to forge an offline romantic relationship, distorting your online self-description is ultimately self-defeating (Ellison et al., 2006). When you mislead someone online about your appearance or other personal attributes and then take your romance offline, your partner *will* discover the truth. Such unpleasant revelations are commonplace: one study found that 86 percent of people using online dating sites report having met others who they felt had misrepresented their physical attractiveness (Gibbs, Ellison, & Heino, 2006). When people feel misled, the outcome is often a damaged impression, negative emotion (such as resentment or anger), and an injured or even ruined relationship (McCornack & Levine, 1990). Clearly, the most ethical and practical thing you can do in your online self-descriptions is to accentuate your attractive attributes without resorting to distortion or dishonesty. If you feel you may be crossing the line into deception, have a trustworthy friend check your online description and assess its authenticity.

Relationship Development and Deterioration

How couples come together and separate

Romantic relationships come together and apart in as many different ways and at as many different speeds as there are partners who fall for each other (Surra & Hughes, 1997). Many relationships are of the "casual dating" variety—they flare quickly, sputter, and then fade. Others endure and evolve with deepening levels of commitment. But all romantic relationships undergo stages marked by distinctive patterns in partners' communication, thoughts, and feelings. We know these transitions intuitively: "taking things to the next level," "kicking it up a notch," "taking a step back," or "taking a break." Communication scholar Mark Knapp (1984) modeled these patterns as ten stages: five of "coming together" and five of "coming apart."

COMING TOGETHER

Knapp's stages of coming together illustrate one possible flow of relationship development (see Figure 10.1). As you read through the stages, keep in mind that these suggest turning points in relationships and are not fixed rules for how involvements should or do progress. Your relationships may go through some, none, or all of these stages. They may skip stages, jump back or forward in order, or follow a completely different and unique trajectory.

figure 10.1 **Stages of Coming Together**

Initiating During the **initiating** stage, you size up a person you've just met or noticed. You draw on all available visual information (physical attractiveness, body type, age, ethnicity, gender, clothing, posture) to determine whether you find him or her attractive. Your primary concern at this stage is to portray yourself in a positive light. You also ponder and present a greeting you deem appropriate. This greeting might be in person or online. More than 16 million people in the United States have used online dating sites to meet new partners (Heino, Ellison, & Gibbs, 2010).

Experimenting Once you've initiated an encounter with someone else (online or face-to-face), you enter the **experimenting** stage, during which you exchange demographic information (names, majors, where you grew up). You also engage in *small talk*—disclosing facts you and the other person consider relatively unimportant but that enable you to introduce yourselves in a safe and controlled fashion. As you share these details, you look for points of commonality on which you can base further interaction. This is the "casual dating" phase of romance. For better or worse, *most involvements never progress beyond this stage*. We go through life experimenting with many people but forming deeper connections with very few.

Intensifying Occasionally, you'll progress beyond casual dating and find yourself experiencing strong feelings of attraction toward another person. When this happens, your verbal and nonverbal communication becomes increasingly intimate. During this **intensifying** stage, you and your partner begin to reveal previously withheld information, such as secrets about your past or important life dreams and goals. You may begin using informal forms of address or terms of endearment ("honey" versus "Joe") and saying "we" more frequently. One particularly strong sign that your relationship is

> **Assignment: Relationship Stages**
>
> As an essay assignment, have students choose a romantic relationship from literature, film, television, or their personal experience to analyze using Knapp's relational stages of coming together or coming apart. Students should write a brief description of the relationship in general. Then, in the analysis, they should carefully define each stage the couple experienced and provide examples. Encourage students to discuss how the relationship both conformed to and defied Knapp's stages.

"Conversation? I thought we were just meeting for coffee."

© Michael Maslin/The New Yorker Collection/www.cartoonbank.com

Video

macmillanhighered.com /reflectrelate4e

Integrating
Watch this clip online to answer the questions below.

How many of your relationships have progressed to the integrating stage? How did you know when they reached that stage? What verbal and nonverbal behaviors do two people in the integrating stage of their relationship use?

Want to see more? Check out VideoCentral for clips illustrating **experimenting** and **bonding**.

intensifying is the direct expression of commitment. You might do this verbally ("I think I'm falling for you") or online by marking your profile as "in a relationship" rather than "single." You may also spend more time in each other's personal spaces, as well as begin physical expressions of affection, such as hand-holding, cuddling, or sexual activity.

Integrating   During the **integrating** stage, your and your partner's personalities seem to become one. This integration is reinforced through sexual activity and the exchange of belongings (items of clothing, music, photos, etc.). When you've integrated with a romantic partner, you cultivate attitudes, activities, and interests that clearly join you together as a couple—"*our* song" and "*our* favorite restaurant." Friends, colleagues, and family members begin to treat you as a couple—for example, always inviting the two of you to parties or dinners. Not surprisingly, many people begin to struggle with the dialectical tension of *connectedness versus autonomy* at this stage. As a student of mine once told his partner when describing this stage, "I'm not me anymore; I'm *us*."

Bonding   The ultimate stage of coming together is **bonding,** a public ritual that announces to the world that you and your partner have made a commitment to each other. Bonding is something you'll share with very few people—perhaps only one—during your lifetime. The most obvious example of bonding is marriage.

Bonding institutionalizes your relationship. Before this stage, the ground rules for your relationship and your communication within it remain a private matter, to be negotiated between you and your partner. In the bonding stage, you import into your relationship a set of laws and customs determined by governmental authorities and perhaps religious institutions. Although these laws and customs help solidify your relationship, they can also make your relationship feel more rigid and structured.

▶ There are many ways for couples to bond, but the key is that both partners agree and make a deep commitment to each other.
(Left) Norm Betts/Bloomberg News/Getty Images; (right) Digital Vision/Punchstock/Getty Images

In *Orange Is the New Black*, the main character, Piper, and her girlfriend, Alex, break up and get back together repeatedly. Have you ever experienced a relationship that ended and then started again?
Jessica Miglio/© Netflix/Everett Collection

COMING APART

Coming together is often followed by coming apart. One study of college dating couples found that across a three-month period, 30 percent broke up (Parks & Adelman, 1983). Similar trends occur in the married adult population: the divorce rate has remained stable at around 40 percent since the early 1980s (Hurley, 2005; Kreider, 2005). This latter number may surprise you because the news media, politicians, and even academics commonly quote the divorce rate as "50 percent."[2] But studies that have tracked couples across time have found that 6 out of 10 North American marriages survive until "death does them part" (Hurley, 2005). Nevertheless, the 40 percent figure translates into a million divorces each year.

In some relationships, breaking up is the right thing to do. Partners have grown apart, they've lost interest in each other, or perhaps one person has been abusive. In other relationships, coming apart is unfortunate. Perhaps the partners could have resolved their differences but didn't make the effort. Thus, they needlessly suffer the pain of breaking up.

Like coming together, coming apart unfolds over stages marked by changes in thoughts, feelings, and communication (see Figure 10.2). But unlike coming together, these stages often entail emotional turmoil that makes it difficult to negotiate skillfully. Learning how to communicate supportively while a romantic relationship is dissolving is a challenging but important part of being a skilled interpersonal communicator.

Discussion Prompt: Bonding & Same-Sex Marriage

A much debated topic in the United States is the legality of same-sex marriage. While most states now allow such marriages, others ban them. This difficult conversation may not be right for every class, but a potentially interesting angle on this controversial topic is how such laws influence the bonding stage. What challenges and benefits does marriage offer? How would laws restricting marriage affect the communication and relationships of couples at this stage?

Discussion Prompt: Coming Apart

Time magazine reported that divorce is less likely among college graduates because "it's easier for the college-educated, with their dominance of the knowledge economy, to get married and stay married" (Luscombe, 2010). This claim was due, in part, to college-educated individuals developing conflict resolution and negotiation skills. What other elements may lead college-educated individuals to stay married? Ask students to consider how aspects of romantic attraction may apply, such as proximity, similarity, and resources.

---

[2]The "50 percent" claim came from a U.S. Census Bureau calculation that computed the divorce rate by dividing the number of marriages in a given year by the number of divorces. But this calculation is obviously flawed because the people marrying in a particular year are not usually the same people who are getting divorced.

| Differentiating | Circumscribing | Stagnating | Avoiding | Terminating |

figure 10.2 Stages of Coming Apart

Differentiating In all romantic relationships, partners share differences as well as similarities. But during **differentiating**—the first stage of coming apart—the beliefs, attitudes, and values that distinguish you from your partner come to dominate your thoughts and communication ("I can't *believe* you think that!" or "We are *so* different!").

Most healthy romances experience occasional periods of differentiating. These moments can involve unpleasant clashes and bickering over contrasting viewpoints, tastes, or goals. But you can move your relationship through this difficulty—and thus halt the coming-apart process—by openly discussing your points of difference and working together to resolve them. To do this, review the constructive conflict skills discussed in Chapter 9.

Circumscribing If one or both of you respond to problematic differences by ignoring them and spending less time talking, you enter the **circumscribing** stage. You actively begin to restrict the quantity and quality of information you exchange with your partner. Instead of sharing information, you create "safe zones" in which you discuss only topics that won't provoke conflict. Common remarks made during circumscribing include "Don't ask me about that" and "Let's not talk about that anymore."

Stagnating When circumscribing becomes so severe that almost no safe conversational topics remain, communication slows to a standstill, and your relationship enters the **stagnating** stage. You both presume that communicating is pointless because it will only lead to further problems. People in stagnant relationships often experience a sense of resignation; they feel stuck or trapped. However, they can remain in the relationship for months or even years. Why? Some believe that it's better to leave things as they are rather than expend the effort necessary to break up or rebuild the relationship. Others simply don't know how to repair the damage and revive the earlier bond.

Avoiding During the **avoiding** stage, one or both of you decide that you can no longer be around each other, and you begin distancing yourself physically. Some people communicate avoidance directly to their partner ("I don't want to see you anymore"). Others do so indirectly—for example, by going out when the partner's at home, screening cell-phone calls, ignoring texts, and changing their Facebook status from "in a relationship" to "single."

Terminating In ending a relationship, some people want to come together for a final encounter that gives a sense of closure and resolution. During the **terminating** stage, couples might discuss the past, present, and future of the relationship. They often exchange summary statements about the past—comments on

---

skills practice

Differentiating
Overcoming the challenge of differentiating

1. Identify when you and your romantic partner are differentiating.

2. Check your perception of the relationship, especially how you've punctuated encounters and the attributions you've made.

3. Call to mind the similarities that originally brought you and your partner together.

4. Discuss your concerns with your partner, emphasizing these similarities and your desire to continue the relationship.

5. Mutually explore solutions to the differences that have been troubling you.

Media Note: Terminating and Technology

As a class or individually, view iBreakUp.net, a Web site that claims to be the "premiere full-service relationship separation service." Have students consider whether or not they would use this site to terminate a romantic relationship. If so, under what circumstances? How would they feel if a partner ended a relationship in this manner? What other types of technology are appropriate or inappropriate for breakups?

"how our relationship was" that are either accusations ("No one has ever treated me so badly!") or laments ("I'll never be able to find someone as perfect as you"). Verbal and nonverbal behaviors indicating a lack of intimacy are readily apparent, including physical distance between the two individuals and reluctance to make eye contact. The partners may also discuss the future status of their relationship. Some couples may agree to end all contact going forward. Others may choose to maintain some level of physical intimacy even though the emotional side of the relationship is officially over. Still others may express interest in "being friends."

Many people find terminating a relationship painful or awkward. It's hard to tell someone else that you no longer want to be involved, and it is equally painful to hear it. Draw on your interpersonal communication skills to best negotiate your way through this dreaded moment. In particular, infuse your communication with empathy—offering empathic concern and perspective-taking (see Chapter 3). Realize that romantic breakups are a kind of death and that it's normal to experience grief, even when breaking up is the right thing to do. Offer supportive communication ("I'm sorry things had to end this way" or "I know this is going to be painful for both of us"), and use grief management tactics (see Chapter 4). Conversations to terminate a relationship are never pleasant or easy. But the communication skills you've learned can help you minimize the pain and damage, enabling you and your former partner to move on to other relationships.

self-reflection

Have most of your romantic relationships ended by avoiding? Or have you sought the closure provided by terminating? In what situations is one approach to ending relationships better than the other? Is one more ethical?

Maintaining Romantic Relationships

[Strategies to sustain romances, even long-distance ones]

My parents have been happily married for sixty years. Growing up with them as my relational role models, I got the impression that love just "happened." They made it look *easy*, and I entered into my teen years thinking that people fell in love, got along, and experienced enduring love. But as I aged and negotiated the pitfalls of my own romances, I realized that what I had presumed about my parents' relationship was completely wrong. Their love wasn't a magical, mystical union that just existed. It was *actively maintained*, day in and day out. I began to notice how they went out of their way to compliment each other, give each other little gifts, and lift each other's spirits through humor; how they assured each other of their feelings and commitment, and how they pitched in to help each other out with daily chores and tasks, regardless of fatigue or mood; how they shared everything with each other—all their hopes, dreams, and vulnerabilities—and how they accepted each other for who they really are. I realized that their "enduring love"—which had looked so effortless to me as a child—was actually the result of hard work.

My parents work tirelessly to maintain their relationship by staying positive, offering assurances, sharing tasks, and practicing self-disclosure. What strategies have you used to maintain a romantic relationship? Courtesy of Steven McCornack

○ Constant, daily maintenance is needed to keep romantic relationships alive and healthy. (Top to bottom) © Andrew Fox/Alamy; Ian Berry/Magnum Photos; © Russell Underwood/Corbis; © Bernard Annebicque/Sygma/Corbis

To this point we've talked a good deal about the nature of love, and we've traced the stages through which many romances progress. Now let's shift focus to a more practical concern: how you can use interpersonal communication to maintain a satisfying, healthy romantic relationship.

MAINTENANCE STRATEGIES

Like me when I was growing up, many people believe that love just happens—that once it strikes, it endures. But a basic rule of romantic love is that maintenance is necessary to keep relationships from deteriorating (Stafford, 2003). **Relational maintenance** refers to using communication and supportive behaviors to sustain a desired relationship status and level of satisfaction (Stafford, Dainton, & Haas, 2000). Across several studies, communication scholar Laura Stafford has observed seven strategies that satisfied couples—no matter their ethnicity or sexual orientation—routinely use to maintain their romances (Stafford, 2010). (See Table 10.2 for an overview of these categories.)

Positivity Positivity includes communicating in a cheerful and optimistic fashion, doing unsolicited favors, and giving unexpected gifts. Partners involved in romantic relationships cite positivity as *the* most important maintenance tactic for ensuring happiness (Dainton & Stafford, 1993). This holds true for men and women in straight relationships (Stafford, 2010), and for same-sex partners in gay and lesbian romances (Haas & Stafford, 2005). You use positivity when:[3]

- You try to make each interaction with your partner enjoyable
- You try to build your partner up by giving him or her compliments
- You try to be fun, upbeat, and romantic with your partner

You undermine positivity when:

- You constantly look for and complain about problems in your relationship without offering solutions
- You whine, pout, and sulk when you don't get your way
- You criticize favors and gifts from your partner

Assurances The second most powerful maintenance tactic in boosting relationship satisfaction is assurances: messages that emphasize how much a partner means to you, demonstrate how important the relationship is, and describe a secure future together. Assurances may be expressed directly, such as saying "I love you" or "I can't see myself ever being with anyone but you." You may also communicate assurances more indirectly, by emphasizing the value you place on your time together—for example, sending a text message saying "I can't wait to see you again" (Rabby, 1997). You use assurances when:

---

[3]All bulleted items that follow are adapted from the revised relationship maintenance behavior scale of Stafford (2010).

- You regularly tell your partner how devoted you are to your relationship
- You talk about future plans and events to be shared together (anniversaries, vacations, marriage, children)
- You do and say things to demonstrate the depth of your feelings for your partner

You undermine assurances when:

- You flirt with others and talk about how attractive they are in front of your partner
- You tell your partner not to count on anything long term
- You systematically avoid pledging love or fidelity to your partner

Sharing Tasks The most frequently practiced form of maintenance is sharing tasks. This involves taking mutual responsibility for chores and negotiating an equitable division of labor. Although this may sound like something that only serious, cohabiting, or married couples face, sharing tasks is relevant for all couples and includes responsibilities like providing transportation to work or campus, running errands, and making reservations for dinner. You share tasks when:

- You try to pitch in equally on everyday responsibilities
- You ask your partner how you can help out
- You make an effort to handle tasks before your partner asks you to do them

You undermine task sharing when:

- You strategically avoid having to do your share of the work
- You never ask your partner how you can help out
- You expect your partner to run errands and do chores for you, without reciprocating

Acceptance Part of what builds a strong sense of intimacy between romantic partners is the feeling that lovers accept us for who we really are, fully and completely, and forgive us our flaws. Acceptance involves communicating this affirmation and support. You convey acceptance when:

- You forgive your partner when he or she makes mistakes
- You support your partner in his or her decisions
- You are patient with your partner when he or she is irritable or in a bad mood

You undermine acceptance when:

- You hold grievances and grudges against your partner
- You tell your partner that you wish he or she were different
- You critique your partner's appearance, personality, beliefs, and values

---

Assignment: Analyzing Relationship Maintenance
People often make the mistake of choosing relational maintenance strategies that they prefer for *themselves* as opposed to what their partner prefers. For a journal assignment or short essay, ask students to analyze how relational maintenance was used in a past or current close relationship (romantic or friendship): What strategies do you prefer for yourself? What strategies do you think your partner prefers? What strategies worked best in the relationship? What improvements could you make in maintaining the relationship?

 Video

macmillanhighered.com/reflectrelate4e

Relational Maintenance
Watch this clip online to answer the questions below.

Maintaining a relationship after a conflict can be a challenging situation. How is the couple in the video handling the situation? What maintenance strategies are they using? What maintenance strategies do you think are especially important after a fight? on a daily basis?

▶ When romantic partners take an interest in each other's favorite activities, they support each other and deepen the level of intimacy in their relationship. Tanya Constantine/Blend Images/Getty Images

Self-Disclosure   An essential part of maintaining intimacy is creating a climate of security and trust within your relationship. This allows both partners to feel that they can disclose fears and feelings without repercussion. To foster self-disclosure, each person must behave in ways that are predictable, trustworthy, and ethical. Over time, consistency in behavior evokes mutual respect and the perception that self-disclosure will be welcomed. You use self-disclosure when:

- You tell your partner about your fears and vulnerabilities
- You share your feelings and emotions with your partner
- You encourage your partner to disclose his or her thoughts and feelings, and offer empathy in return

table 10.2 Romantic Relationship Maintenance Strategies

Maintenance Strategy	Suggested Actions
Positivity	Be cheerful and optimistic in your communication.
Assurances	Remind your partner of your devotion.
Sharing Tasks	Help out with daily responsibilities.
Acceptance	Be supportive and forgiving.
Self-Disclosure	Share your thoughts, feelings, and fears.
Relationship Talks	Make time to discuss your relationship and really listen.
Social Networks	Involve yourself with your partner's friends and family.

You undermine self-disclosure when:

- You disparage your partner's perspective
- You routinely keep important information hidden from your partner
- You betray your partner by sharing confidential information about him or her with others

Relationship Talks Romantic maintenance includes occasionally sitting down and discussing the status of your relationship, how you each feel about it, and where you both see it going. Relationship talks allow you to gauge how invested you each are and whether you agree on future plans and goals. They also provide a convenient forum for expressing and resolving concerns, and forestalling future conflict. You encourage relationship talks when you:

- Set aside time in your schedule to chat about your relationship
- Openly and respectfully share your relationship concerns with your partner
- Encourage your partner to share his or her feelings about the relationship with you

You undermine relationship talks when you:

- React defensively and egocentrically whenever your partner shares relationship concerns
- Avoid or refuse to have relationship talks with your partner
- Actively ridicule the need to discuss the relationship

Social Networks Romances are more likely to survive if important members of a couple's social networks approve of the relationship (Felmlee, 2001). For example, communication scholars Malcolm Parks and Mara Adelman (1983) measured how much support romantically involved individuals received from their partner's friends and family, what percentage of their partner's network they had met, and how often they communicated with these people. Using these factors and others, Parks and Adelman were able to predict with 88 percent accuracy which relationships would survive. What were the strongest determinants of whether couples stayed together? Support from family and friends, and regular communication with one's partner.

Fostering healthy relationships with surrounding friends and family appears especially crucial for those involved in interethnic relationships (Baptiste, 1990), and for gay and lesbian couples. Approximately 67 percent of interethnic marriages end in divorce, compared with an overall divorce rate of 40 percent, the largest reasons being lack of network support and cultural disapproval (Gaines & Agnew, 2003). Gay and lesbian couples report having supportive environments—such as churches or clubs—and being treated "the same" as straight couples by their friends and family as especially important for their relationship stability and satisfaction (Haas & Stafford, 1998). You foster supportive social networks when you:

- Tell your partner how much you like his or her friends and family
- Invite your partner's friends or family members to share activities with the two of you
- Willingly turn to family members of both partners for help and advice when needed

You undermine social networks when you:

- Make critical and disparaging remarks regarding your partner's friends and family
- Intentionally avoid encounters with your partner's friends and family
- Demand that your partner choose between spending time with you and spending time with friends and family

MAINTAINING ROMANCE ACROSS DISTANCE

A common challenge to maintaining romantic relationships is geographic separation. At any one time, nearly half of college students are involved in romances separated by geography, and 75 percent will experience a long-distance dating relationship while in school (Aylor, 2003).

People often think that long-distance relationships are doomed to fail. However, long-distance romantic relationships have actually been found to be *more* satisfying and stable than those that are geographically close (Stafford, 2010). On measures of love, positivity, agreement, and overall communication quality, geographically distant couples score *higher* than local partners (Stafford & Merolla, 2007). Why? Stafford (2010) offers several reasons. Couples separated by distance often constrain their communication to only that which is positive, steadfastly shying away from troublesome topics that provoke conflict. Geographically distant couples also idealize their partners more. When you're not around your partner every day, it's easy to cherish misconceptions about his or her "perfection." And visits between partners are typically occasional, brief in duration, and passionate. This amplifies the feeling that all their time together is intense and positive—an unsustainable illusion when people see each other regularly (Sahlstein, 2004).

The most difficult maintenance challenge long-distance couples face is not the separation but the eventual reunion. Almost all couples separated by distance express a desire to be near each other again, and they anticipate that being together will result in dramatic relationship improvements (Stafford, Merolla, & Castle, 2006). But the reality is more complicated. Couples who are reunited following separation are twice as likely to break up, compared with those who remain long distance (Stafford & Merolla, 2007). Rather than being "all bliss, all the time," living locally presents a blend of rewards and costs (Stafford, Merolla, & Castle, 2006). On the plus side, couples get to spend more time together, savoring each other's company and sharing in the "little" things they missed when apart. On the minus side, partners' cherished illusions about each other are shattered. Reunited couples report realizing for the first time their lover's negative characteristics, such as laziness, sloppiness, immaturity, or failure to invest effort in the relationship.

Discussion Prompt: Long-Distance Relationships & Technology

Have students consider some of the positive aspects that long-distance relationships with loved ones can provide, such as both parties learning self-reliance skills. Once some of the positive facets are considered, have students discuss how to maintain successful long-distance relationships. How have they used technology such as Skype, Viber, FaceTime, or Facebook to keep up with friends, family, and other long-distance significant others?

skills practice

Technology and Maintenance
Using technology to maintain romance

❶ Send your partner a text message or e-mail that has no purpose other than to compliment him or her.

❷ Post a message on your partner's Facebook page, saying how excited you are about seeing her or him soon.

❸ During a high-stress day for your partner, send an e-mail or text message that says "Just thinking of you."

❹ Recall a friend or family member whom your partner has been concerned about, and send an e-mail or text message to your partner inquiring about how the person is doing.

❺ Think of a task your partner has been wanting you to do, complete it, then text-message your partner to let her or him know you took care of it.

They describe a substantial reduction in autonomy, experienced as a loss of time and space for themselves, loss of interaction with friends and family, and irritation with having to be accountable to their partner. Reunited couples also report increased conflict, as formerly "taboo" topics become regularly discussed and fought over.

Despite the challenges, you can have a happy and enduring long-distance romance. Here are some suggestions to help maintain such relationships:

1. While separated, use technology to regularly communicate with your partner. Using text messages, e-mail, IM, Facebook, and Skype has a significant impact on improving relationship health (Dainton & Aylor, 2002).

2. When communicating with your distant partner, follow the maintenance strategies discussed on pages 304–308. In particular, focus on the two most important for maintaining satisfaction—positivity and assurances—and keep your interactions upbeat, positive, and filled with discussions of shared future plans and dreams.

3. When you permanently reunite, expect a significant period of adjustment— one that is marked by tension (as you rebalance autonomy versus connection), disappointment (as idealistic illusions of your partner are replaced by the reality), and conflict (as you begin talking about topics you shelved during the separation). Avoid expecting everything to be perfect, and use the strategies you've learned in our discussion of conflict (Chapter 9) to manage difficult dilemmas when they arise.

DECIDING WHETHER TO MAINTAIN

In my favorite movie of all time, *Eternal Sunshine of the Spotless Mind* (2004), Joel (Jim Carrey) and Clementine (Kate Winslet) are lovers struggling to maintain a bittersweet romance (Bregman, Golin, Gondry, & Kaufman, 2004). Clementine, an outgoing self-described "high-maintenance girl," is the opposite of quiet, bookish Joel, who communicates more with his private journal than with her. Following a fight, Clementine impetuously visits a clinic that specializes in memory erasure and has Joel expunged from her mind. Despondent, Joel follows suit. But the two meet again and find themselves attracted to each other. Eventually discovering the truth—that they aren't strangers at all but longtime lovers—they face a momentous decision: Do they invest the time and energy necessary to maintain their romance a second time, knowing that they failed so terribly before that they chose to destroy their memories? Or do they end it before their history of relational disaster can repeat itself?

Romantic relationships aren't always about happiness and celebration. No matter how much you love your partner, you will still experience unpleasant moments, such as feeling irked, bored, or trapped. In fact, on any given day, 44 percent of us are likely to be seriously annoyed by a close relationship partner (Kowalski, Walker, Wilkinson, Queen, & Sharpe, 2003). Though such experiences are normal, many people find them disturbing and wonder whether they should end the relationship.

▶ In *Eternal Sunshine of the Spotless Mind*, Joel and Clementine decide to take another shot at their relationship despite the risks.
Focus Features/Everett Collection

As one way to work through this decision, familiarize yourself with the characteristics of couples whose relationship has survived—like my parents. Four factors, each of which we've discussed, appear to be most important in predicting survival of a romantic relationship. First is *the degree to which the partners consider themselves "in love."* Couples are more likely to stay together if they think of themselves as in love, are considering marriage or a lifelong commitment, rate their relationship as high in closeness, or date each other exclusively (Hill et al., 1976). In *Eternal Sunshine*, this was the factor that eventually leads Joel and Clementine to decide to stay together: the realization that despite all they've suffered—including purging of their memories—they still love each other. Second is *equity*. Romantic relationships are happiest and most stable when the balance of giving and getting is equal for both partners (Hatfield et al., 1985). Third is *similarity*. Highly similar couples are more likely to stay together than couples who are dissimilar (Hill et al., 1976). Fourth is *network support*. A romance is more likely to endure when the couple's social networks approve of the relationship (Felmlee, 2001; Parks & Adelman, 1983). To determine how well your relationship meets these criteria, ask yourself the following questions:

1. Are you still in love with your partner?
2. Is your relationship equitable?
3. Do you and your partner share values and personality traits?
4. Do your family and friends support your relationship?

If you answer yes to these questions, your relationship may warrant investment in maintenance. But remember: *deciding whether to maintain a struggling relationship or to let it go is a choice only you can make*. Friends, family members, pop-culture relationship experts, and even textbooks can't tell you when to keep or when to leave a romantic involvement. Romantic relationships are in many ways practical endeavors. Your decision to maintain or end a struggling romance should be based on a long-term forecast of your relationship. Stacking your relationship up against those four criteria can give you insight into whether your relationship has a solid foundation on which to invest further effort.

The Dark Side of Romantic Relationships

Addressing issues related to romance

In Kaui Hart Hemmings's novel *The Descendants* (2008), attorney Matt King is the descendant of native Hawaiian royalty, whose wife Joanie is in an irreversible coma. Suddenly a single parent, Matt must try to reconnect emotionally with two daughters from whom he has long been detached. Complicating matters further, he discovers that Joanie—whom he had considered his best friend, sparring partner, and closest confidante—was cheating on him before the accident and had planned to divorce him. In the climactic scene of the book, he puts the pain of her betrayal to rest:

> I bow my head and speak to Joanie softly. "I'm sorry I didn't give you everything you wanted. I wasn't everything you wanted. You were everything I wanted. Every day. Home. There you are. Dinner, dishes, TV. Weekends at the beach. You go here. I go there. Parties. Home to complain about the party." I can't think of anything else. Just our routine together. "I forgive you," I say. Why is it so hard to articulate love, yet so easy to express disappointment? (Hemmings, 2011, pp. 235–236)

Romantic love inspires us to strive toward a host of ideals, including compassion, caring, generosity, and selflessness. But romance has a dark side as well. As scholar

In *The Descendants*, Matt King is able to move on and come to terms with his wife's betrayal by bonding with his daughters. Have you ever felt betrayed by a romantic partner? If so, what strategies did you use to cope with this betrayal?
Merie Weismiller Wallace/TM and copyright © Fox Searchlight Pictures. All rights reserved/Everett Collection

Robin Kowalski pointedly puts it, "people in romantic relationships do a lot of mean and nasty things to one another" (Kowalski et al., 2003, p. 472). And when they do, the result is often unparalleled pain and despair. In this section, we explore some of the most troubling issues related to romance—betrayal, jealousy, intrusion, and violence—and discuss communication strategies for addressing them.

BETRAYAL

As illustrated in *The Descendants*, betrayal is one of the most devastating experiences that can occur in a close involvement (Haden & Hojjat, 2006). **Romantic betrayal** is defined as an act that goes against expectations of a romantic relationship and, as a result, causes pain to a partner (Jones, Moore, Scratter, & Negel, 2001). Common examples include *sexual infidelity* (engaging in sexual activity with someone else), *emotional infidelity* (developing a strong romantic attachment to someone else), *deception* (intentional manipulation of information), and *disloyalty* (hurting your partner to benefit yourself). But any behavior that violates norms of loyalty and trustworthiness can be considered betrayal.

In romantic relationships, partners inevitably behave in ways that defy each other's expectations and cause disappointment. But betrayal is different. Betrayal is *intentional*. As a result, it typically evokes two intense, negative reactions in betrayed partners. The first is an overwhelming sense of relational devaluation—the realization that our partner does not love and respect us as much as we thought he or she did (Leary, 2001). This sense of devaluation, which is triggered most by sexual infidelity and deception, is difficult to overcome and often leads us to abandon our relationships. The second is a profound sense of loss. In the wake of betrayal, we may feel that all the time and effort we invested in our partner and the relationship were a waste, and that intimacy, commitment, and trust have been permanently destroyed (Haden & Hojjat, 2006). Consequently, when you are betrayed by a lover, expect to feel grief over the loss of the relationship that was. (See Chapter 4 for more on grief management.)

self-QUIZ

How Often Do You Betray Romantic Partners?

Read each statement, and rate how often you have done the activity: 1 (never), 2 (once), 3 (a few times), 4 (several times), 5 (many times). Get your score by adding up your answers.

To take this quiz online, visit LaunchPad: macmillanhighered.com/reflectrelate4e.

_____ Snubbing a romantic partner when you are with a group you want to impress

_____ Gossiping about a romantic partner behind his or her back

_____ Making a promise to a romantic partner with no intention of keeping it

_____ Telling others information given to you in confidence by a romantic partner

_____ Lying to a romantic partner

_____ Failing to stand up for a romantic partner when he or she is being criticized or belittled by others

Note: Information in this *Self-Quiz* adapted for romantic relationships is from Jones and Burdette (1994).

Scoring: 6–14 = You're an infrequent betrayer; 15–23 = You're a moderate betrayer; 24–30 = You're a frequent betrayer.

chapter 10 / Relationships with Romantic Partners 313

◓ Sometimes relationships start out great but deteriorate as a result of poor communication choices. In *Gone Girl*, Amy and Nick's passionate love eventually gives way to mutual hatred and betrayal. Merrick Morton/TM & copyright © 20th Century Fox Film Corp. All rights reserved/Everett Collection

Sexual Infidelity The most destructive form of romantic betrayal is sexual infidelity. A partner who cheats on you has broken a fundamental sacrament—the spoken or unspoken pledge to remain faithful. Not surprisingly, many people react to infidelity with a strong urge to leave their partner. One study found that more than 20 percent of American women and men would consider divorce if a spouse passionately kissed someone else, more than 30 percent would consider divorce if their spouse had a romantic date with another person, and more than 60 percent would consider divorce if their spouse had a serious (sexual) affair (Shackelford & Buss, 1997). Whether or not a sexual dalliance is planned matters little: cheaters' original intentions have no impact on subsequent feelings of blame by their partner (Mongeau, Hale, & Alles, 1994). At the same time, method of discovery has a pronounced effect on subsequent outcomes, including whether the relationship will endure, as well as whether the betrayed person will forgive the betrayer (Afifi, Falato, & Weiner, 2001). Relationships are most likely to survive sexual infidelity, and cheaters are most likely to be forgiven by their partner, when they confess their betrayals without being asked. In contrast, when the infidelity is discovered by catching the cheater in the act, relationships are unlikely to survive (83 percent of such relationships end), and forgiveness is low (Afifi et al., 2001).

For college students in dating relationships, the two strongest predictors of sexual infidelity appear to be a *ludus* (see Table 10.1, p. 290, Romantic Love

self-reflection

Think about Buss's dilemma. Which would you find more upsetting: discovering that your romantic partner had formed an emotional attachment outside of the relationship or that he or she had been sexually unfaithful? If your partner did betray you in one of these ways, how would you respond?

▼ Most people discover lies indirectly, through hearing about them from a third party or stumbling across damning evidence. Thinkstock/Getty Images

Types) love attitude and high sexual sensation-seeking: students who "enjoy playing the game of love with a number of different partners" and who also "like wild and uninhibited sexual encounters" are more likely to sexually cheat on dating partners than those who don't possess such preferences (Wiederman & Hurd, 1999). In addition, across a broad range of specific sexual behaviors, including kissing and fondling, performing oral sex, receiving oral sex, and engaging in sexual intercourse, male dating partners are more likely to cheat than female dating partners (Wiederman & Hurd, 1999).

Although both men and women view infidelity as treasonous, their perceptions diverge when they're asked to compare sexual with emotional cheating. Infidelity researcher David Buss presented study respondents with the following dilemma (Buss, Larsen, Westen, & Semmelroth, 1992). Imagine you discover that your partner has become interested in someone else. What would distress you more: your partner forming a deep emotional attachment to that person, or your partner enjoying passionate sex with that person? Sixty percent of men said that sex would upset them more, but 83 percent of women said they'd find the emotional attachment more distressing. The same pattern of results was found in samples of men and women from Sweden, the Netherlands, Germany, Korea, and Japan (Buss et al., 1999; Buunk, Angleitner, Oubaid, & Buss, 1996; Wiederman & Kendall, 1999).

Deception As defined in Chapter 7, deception involves misleading your partner by intentionally withholding information, presenting false information, or making your message unnecessarily irrelevant or ambiguous (McCornack, 1997). Despite media images depicting romantic partners catching each other in lies, most people discover lies indirectly, through hearing about them from a third party or stumbling across damning evidence, such as a text message or e-mail (Park, Levine, McCornack, Morrison, & Ferrara, 2002). When partners discover a lie, the experience typically is emotionally intense and negative. One study looking at the emotional and relational aftermath of lies found that 16 percent of people who recalled having discovered a lie reported breaking up because of it (McCornack & Levine, 1990). That decision was usually determined by the severity of the lie. If the lie was "important" (for example, lying about relationship feelings), people were more likely to end their involvement (McCornack & Levine, 1990).

Dealing with Betrayal The truth about romantic betrayal is that no simple solution or skill set will remedy the sense of devaluation and loss that results. The strongest predictor of what happens afterward is the seriousness of the betrayal. If a betrayal permanently stains your perception of your partner, the relationship probably won't survive. If you believe you can eventually overcome the pain, then your relationship has a chance.

People struggling to cope with betrayal commonly adopt one of four general communication approaches (Rusbult, 1987). You can actively confront the betrayal, seeking to understand the conditions that led to it and jointly working with your partner to change those causes. You can quietly stand by your partner, choosing to forgive and forget and trusting that, in time, your love will heal the pain you feel. You can stand by your partner but simmer with pain and rage, venting your anger by constantly reminding the person of his or her transgression or withholding sex or other rewards. Or you can simply end the relationship, believing that the emotional costs associated with the betrayal are too substantial to surmount.

Regardless of which approach you take, the hard truth is that after a betrayal, your relationship will never be the same, and it will never be "better" than it previously was in terms of trust, intimacy, and satisfaction. You can certainly rebuild a strong and enduring relationship, but it will always be scarred. As my therapist friend Joe says, "You will *never* get over it. You just learn to live with it."

JEALOUSY

A second problem for romantic relationships is **jealousy**—a protective reaction to a perceived threat to a valued relationship (Hansen, 1985). Most scholars agree that jealousy isn't a singular emotion but rather a combination of negative emotions—primarily anger, fear, and sadness (Guerrero & Andersen, 1998).

Jealousy especially plagues users of online social networking sites like Facebook. Such sites open the possibility for people other than your romantic partner to post provocative photos, write enticing posts on your wall, and send alluring messages, all of which can trigger your partner's jealousy. Imagine how you'd feel if you saw such communication on your partner's page. Studies of Facebook have found that jealousy is one of the most frequent problems reported by users (Morrison, Lee, Wiedmaier, & Dibble, 2008). Jealousy can intensify even further if site users engage in what communication scholar Kelly Morrison calls **wedging**. Through wedging, a person deliberately uses messages, photos, and posts to try and "wedge" him- or herself between partners in a romantic couple because he or she is interested in one of the partners (Morrison et al., 2008).

The most effective way to deal with jealousy is *self-reliance*: allowing yourself to feel jealous but not letting whatever sparked your jealousy to interrupt you. You should continue your current activities and give yourself time to cool off (Salovey & Rodin, 1988). Avoid communicating with your partner until you're able to do so in a cooperative and constructive fashion. When you *are* ready to talk, don't be afraid to candidly acknowledge your own jealousy and discuss your perception of threat with your partner: "I saw that post from your old girlfriend,

---

Teaching Tip: Jealousy Online

For some interesting readings on jealousy and technology, see Christofides, Muise, and Desmarais's (2009) study in *Cyber Psychology, Behavior, and Social Networking*, which indicates that the more time college students spend on Facebook, the more likely they will be to feel jealous toward their romantic partner. Additionally, check out two further studies in *Cyber Psychology, Behavior, and Social Networking*: Clayton's (2014) "The Third Wheel: The Impact of Twitter Use on Relationship Infidelity and Divorce" and Fox and Warber's (2014) "Social Networking Sites in Romantic Relationships: Attachment, Uncertainty, and Partner Surveillance on Facebook." Then discuss students' experiences of jealousy due to online communication and how they have dealt with it.

skills practice

Dealing with Jealousy
Communicating more competently when jealousy strikes

❶ Identify a situation in which your jealousy is sparked.

❷ Continue your current activities, not letting the jealousy-evoking event distract you from completing what you are doing.

❸ Avoid immediate communication with your partner.

❹ While you're finishing what you are doing, practice the Jeffersons strategy, counting to 10 or 100 until you cool off.

❺ Initiate communication with your partner, using your cooperative language skills and explaining to him or her why the event caused you to feel jealous. Solicit your partner's perspective.

focus on CULTURE

Infidelity Internationally

In Japan it's called "going off the path," and in Israel it's "eating to the side" (Druckerman, 2007). But regardless of differences in lingo, the suffering that ensues from sexual betrayal is similar around the globe.

Wall Street Journal reporter Pamela Druckerman interviewed people in 10 different countries, gauging their infidelity attitudes and behaviors. She discovered vast cultural differences and some similarities. For example, in Japan, intricate rules of discretion guide how one cheats, whereas in Finland, people are more open in discussing and engaging in adultery. In Russia, Druckerman was struck by its sheer prevalence. One marital therapist told her, "Affairs should be obligatory, because they make for stronger marriages," and an issue of Russian *Cosmopolitan* provided instructional tips to women on how to hide their betrayals from their partners.

Druckerman's observations mirror scientific research. A study of nonmarital sex involving 24 nations and 33,000 respondents found that the top three countries in infidelity acceptance were Russia, Bulgaria, and the Czech Republic (Widmer, Treas, & Newcomb, 1998). What countries were the most infidelity *intolerant*? The Philippines, Ireland, and the United States.

Despite cultural differences, however, Druckerman notes at least three betrayal universals (as cited in Corner, 2007). First, across cultures, people who cheat prefer to cheat with someone who is also seriously involved, making the risks "evenly shared." Second, cheaters typically describe themselves as "not the cheating type." Third, regardless of cultural attitudes or prevalence, sexual betrayal almost always causes intense emotional pain and relationship distress. When asked about the lessons she learned from her study, Druckerman said, "I still very much believe in monogamy as the ideal, but I have become more realistic—or fatalistic—about it. I now think it could easily happen to me. And, if it does, I won't automatically assume my relationship is over."

discussion questions

- What lessons have you learned from your culture regarding the ethics of infidelity? How have these lessons shaped your beliefs? your relationship behaviors?
- If a partner cheated on you, would you assume that your involvement was over, or would you try to repair and rebuild your relationship? What impact would your cultural values have on your decision?

---

and I'm worried that she wants to get back together with you. Am I reading too much into this, or should I really feel threatened?"

RELATIONAL INTRUSION

Sometimes romantic partners try to control you or behave in ways that invade your privacy. In mild cases, they might check up on you—talking with your friends or family to verify your whereabouts. In more extreme instances, they might search your phone or read your e-mail without permission. Such behaviors are known as **relational intrusion:** the violation of one's independence and privacy by a person who desires an intimate relationship (Cupach & Spitzberg, 1998). Intrusion happens in all cultures, is equally likely to be perpetrated by men or women, and occurs both in current relationships and in those in which the partners have broken up (Lavy, Mikulincer, Shaver, & Gillath, 2009).

Within intact romances, two forms of intrusion are common (Lavy et al., 2009). The first is *monitoring and controlling*. A partner may text you constantly to ensure that you are always accounted for and instruct you to be home by a certain time. He or she may follow you or hire a private investigator to conduct surveillance. People who have experienced this behavior say: "My partner wants to know where I am and what I'm doing all the time," and "My partner does not let me meet my family or friends without him being present" (Lavy et al., 2009, p. 995). The second form of intrusion is *invasion of privacy*. This includes nosing or snooping through your belongings, computer, and phone, and asking overly personal and suspicious questions designed to "interrogate" you.

For romances that have ended, intrusion is symptomatic of a person's inability to let go. Of people who report difficulty in dealing with breakups, 79 percent admit behaving intrusively (Dutton & Winstead, 2006). The most common forms of postrelationship intrusion are leaving gifts and messages for the ex-partner, expressing exaggerated levels of affection (such as giving public serenades or posting love poems), physically following the ex-partner around, and showing up uninvited at the ex-partner's home or work. If done repeatedly, these latter behaviors may turn into stalking, which is a criminal offense.

For its recipients, relational intrusion is decidedly negative and threatening. If the relationship is intact, intrusion generates strong negative impressions, uncertainty, and relational turmoil (Lavy et al., 2009). As one victim describes, "He was acting so unfair; I no longer was sure about our relationship" (Lavy et al., 2009, p. 999). For people dealing with postrelationship intrusion, anger and fear are common responses, and the intrusion may spark a desire to seek revenge against or act violently toward the intruding partner (Lavy et al., 2009).

What makes intrusion tricky, however, is that perpetrators typically perceive their behaviors *positively*, as reflecting love, loyalty, or just the desire to stay in touch (Cupach & Spitzberg, 2004). Consequently, they tend to minimize or deny the harms created by their undesirable actions.

How can you best deal with intrusion? Realize first that intrusion is absolutely unacceptable and unethical. No one has the right to impose themselves on another in an unwanted fashion. If you're on the receiving end of intrusion, talk with your partner or ex directly about his or her behavior, and firmly express your discontent and discomfort. Use "I" language, avoid "you" language, and make it clear that your privacy is being violated and that the intrusive behavior is unacceptable ("I feel really uncomfortable receiving this gift" or "I am really upset by this, and I feel that my privacy is being invaded"). Most important, keep your language respectful and polite. Avoid lashing out verbally, especially if you're angry, as it will only escalate the situation. If the person's behavior persists, contact local authorities to ask for help. If you find yourself engaging in intrusive behaviors, stop immediately. The fact that *you* view your actions as well intentioned is irrelevant. If you are making a partner or ex feel uncomfortable, you are behaving unethically. If you don't know how to stop, seek counseling from a licensed therapist.

DATING VIOLENCE

Assignment: Antiviolence Campaigns

Although students are often uncomfortable discussing dating violence in front of others, it is important for them to know about the variety of resources available. Assign students to groups, and have them research organizations online and on their campus that have been developed to prevent violence (such as Loveisrespect.org). Ask students to present their findings to the class. Then discuss the importance of preventing physical and emotional abuse.

Scott and I became friends in grad school, when we both served as instructors with a campus karate club. Scott was originally from Southern California, where he was a kickboxing champion.[4] He was 6 foot 3, was all muscle, and had a very long reach, something I learned the hard way when he caught me with an unexpected back-fist on my nose while sparring!

Soon after our friendship began, Scott met Pam, and the two fell for each other hard and fast. But within a few weeks, Scott confessed to me several concerns: Pam was extremely jealous and constantly accused him of cheating. She called him names, swore at him, and ridiculed his sexual performance. She demanded that he no longer go out with his friends, and when he refused, she threatened to leave him. Visiting him one afternoon, I was stunned to see the glass frame of his black-belt certificate shattered. "Yeah," he admitted, "Pam threw it at me the other night." When she learned that Scott was confiding in me, Pam told him a series of lies to alienate him from me: I had "stolen money from him," I had "hit on her," I was "gay and wanted him to myself" (never mind that the last two were contradictory). But Scott stayed with her until she put him in the hospital with a broken nose and third-degree burns across his face. She had demanded that he quit karate, and when he refused, she had hit him in the face with a heated clothes iron. When I asked why he didn't fight back, or at least defend himself (given his abundant skills), he looked at me in disbelief. "I can't hit *a girl*, man. I'm not that kind of guy!"

Dating violence affects millions of people, and as Scott's story shows, despite common beliefs, dating violence knows no demographic boundaries: men and women of all ages, sexual orientations, social classes, ethnicities, and religions experience violence in romantic relationships. According to the National Center for Victims of Crimes (2008), 21 percent of college students report having experienced such violence. In addition to physical injuries (and in extreme cases, death), victims of dating violence are more likely than others to suffer from substance abuse, low self-esteem, suicidal thoughts, and eating disorders (Ackard & Neumark-Sztainer, 2002).

If you haven't experienced a violent relationship, it's easy to think, "Well, the person should have seen it coming!" But this is false, for at least two reasons (Eisikovits & Buchbinder, 2000). First, violence doesn't happen all at once—it typically escalates slowly over time. Also, it often doesn't evolve into full-blown physical violence until relationships are firmly established, making victims all that much more vulnerable because of their love and commitment. Second, potential abusers often mask their jealousy, violent anger, and excessive need for control in the early stages of a relationship, making it difficult to discern "warning signs" (see Table 10.3 for a detailed list). In Scott's case, both of these reasons played a role in making him vulnerable. Pam seemed perfectly "normal" in the first few weeks of their relationship. She was funny, attractive, smart, and outgoing. By the time the first incidents occurred, he was already in love. And the destructiveness of her behaviors escalated slowly—starting with minor jealous tantrums, and only

---

[4] Although the facts of this story are true, the names and demographic information have been changed to protect the identities of the parties involved.

table 10.3 **Five Common Warning Signs of an Abusive Partner**

An abusive partner will . . .
(1) isolate you from others Examples: restricting your contact with friends and family, showing extreme paranoid jealousy regarding perceived romantic rivals, or telling you lies about friends and family
(2) use power to control you Examples: insisting they make all decisions about leisure activities, including sex; exploding into anger when you "disobey" them; demanding knowledge of your whereabouts; or displaying violence, such as throwing or breaking objects
(3) frequently threaten you in various ways Examples: threatening to leave you or hurt themselves if you leave, threatening violence against past lovers or perceived romantic rivals, threatening to lie about you to others or file false charges against you, or threatening violence
(4) use emotionally abusive language Examples: criticizing your weight, appearance, intelligence, career, or sexual skill; calling you names; swearing at you; or ridiculing your pain when they've hurt you
(5) shift the blame to you Examples: blaming you for their jealousy, violence, and destructiveness, or tricking you into behaving badly so they can exploit your guilt
Source: Adapted from "Symptoms: Indicators of Abusive Relationships," An Abuse, Rape, and Domestic Violence Aid and Resource Collection (AARDVARC). Retrieved from www.aardvarc.org/dv/symptoms.shtml.

evolving into violence after many months. As a consequence, Scott didn't perceive Pam's abusiveness as particularly "severe" until she put him in the hospital.

What should *you* do if you find yourself in a relationship with a violent partner? First and foremost, let go of the belief that you can "heal" your partner through love, or "save" him or her by providing emotional support. Relationship repair strategies will not prevent or cure dating violence. Your only option is to extricate yourself from the relationship. As you move toward ending the involvement, keep in mind that the most dangerous time comes immediately after you end the relationship, when the abuser is most angry. So, make sure you cut all ties to the abuser, change your phone number, and have ready a *safety plan*: a road map of action for departing the relationship that provides you with the utmost protection. For information on how to develop such a plan, or for help in dealing with an abusive relationship, call the National Domestic Violence Hotline, 1-800-799-SAFE, or visit www.thehotline.org.

The Hard Work of Successful Love

Love is not singular, but plural

Romantic relationships are most satisfying and stand a greater chance of surviving when you and your partner view your bond without illusions and embellishments. When you do this, when you look love square in the face, you'll find that it isn't one simple, clear, obvious thing. Instead, love is complex. Love is triumph *and* heartache.

making relationship choices

Managing Jealousy about a Partner's Ex

1 BACKGROUND

Dealing with jealousy in a romantic relationship is challenging, but it becomes even more so when the relationship is rather volatile and you're unsure about your partner's level of commitment. To understand how you might competently manage such a relationship challenge, read the case study in Part 2; then, drawing on all you know about interpersonal communication, work through the problem-solving model in Part 3.

 Visit LaunchPad to check out the other side of the story (Part 4). For the best experience, complete all parts in LaunchPad: **macmillanhighered.com/reflectrelate4e**.

2 CASE STUDY

Your relationship with Javi is the most passionate you've ever had, and you consider yourself head-over-heels in love. You two share a powerful sexual connection, fueled in part by the fact that Javi is extremely physically attractive.

On the down side, Javi is undeniably high-maintenance. Although affectionate and funny, Javi has a volatile temper. You've learned the hard way that if you raise an issue that Javi perceives as problematic, huge drama with lots of yelling, and then sulking, is likely to ensue. More concerning, however, is Javi's flirtatiousness. Javi loves being the center of attention and frequently flirts with others, sometimes right in front of you. Javi also sends mixed signals about commitment, saying "I love you!" one day and "I hope you're not getting too serious on me!" the next.

Your friends think Javi is "ridiculously hot." They also think Javi is "trouble." Nevertheless, you're happy with your relationship because you've never experienced this intensity of connection before, and you think Javi may actually be your soul mate.

Recently, a few incidents have sparked worry. Javi didn't return any of your texts one night and afterwards said, "My phone battery was dead." The thing is, you borrowed Javi's phone earlier that evening and it was fully charged. There also have been instances in which Javi's phone has gone off but Javi either ignored it or said, "It's a solicitor." You know this latter excuse is bogus because Javi is on a do-not-call list.

Tonight, you and Javi are having fun at a party, when Javi's ex, Pau, shows up. Although you're jealous, you tell Javi that it's fine to talk to Pau because you're busy with your own friends. You keep an eye on the two of them, however, and sure enough, after a few minutes, you see them flirting. Your jealousy escalates as you see them sitting close together and laughing like they're still a couple! What's more, they can't seem to keep their hands off each other. Although the touches are all technically friendly and innocent, they imply a degree of intimacy that further fuels your jealousy.

As you two are driving back to your apartment, you're fuming about Javi and Pau. Noticing your demeanor, Javi explodes: "You know, you can be really annoying sometimes! You tell me to talk to Pau, and then you get all mad when I do! What's your problem?"

3 YOUR TURN

Think about all you've learned thus far about interpersonal communication. Then work through the following five steps. Remember, there are no "right" answers, so think hard about what is the *best* choice! (P.S. Need help? See the *Helpful Concepts* list.)

step 1
Reflect on yourself. What are your thoughts and feelings in this situation? What attributions are you making about Javi? Are your attributions accurate? Why or why not?

step 2
Reflect on your partner. Using perspective-taking and empathic concern, put yourself in Javi's shoes. What is Javi thinking and feeling in this situation?

step 3
Identify the optimal outcome. Think about all the information you have about your communication and relationship with Javi and the situation surrounding the encounter with Pau. Consider your own feelings as well as Javi's. Given all these factors, what's the best, most constructive relationship outcome possible? Consider what's best for you *and* for Javi.

step 4
Locate the roadblocks. Taking into consideration your own and Javi's thoughts and feelings and all that has happened in this situation, what obstacles are keeping you from achieving the optimal outcome?

step 5
Chart your course. What can you say to Javi to overcome the roadblocks you've identified and achieve your optimal outcome?

HELPFUL CONCEPTS
Romantic love types, **288–290**

Deciding whether to maintain or end, **309–311**

Jealousy, **315–316**

Relational intrusion, **316–317**

Dating violence, **318–319**

4 THE OTHER SIDE

Visit LaunchPad to watch a video that will expose you to Javi's side of the case study story. As in many real-life situations, this is information to which you did not have access when you were initially crafting your response in Part 3. The video reminds us that even when we do our best to offer competent responses, there is always another side to the story that we need to consider.

▶ The positive communication decisions you make with your partner have a profound effect on the overall happiness and health of your bond. While successful, satisfying love is something you must consciously work at, it is also one of life's greatest joys. Yadid Levy/Anzenberger/Redux Pictures

It is passion *and* peaceful companionship. It is joy *and* grief. And keeping love alive is hard work. Some days, your love for your partner will take your breath away. On others, everything he or she does will annoy you. Most days, it will fall somewhere in between.

Romantic relationships endure because *partners choose to communicate in ways that maintain their relationship.* It's the everyday communication and effort that you and your partner invest that will most enable you to build a satisfying, intimate bond—and sustain it if that's what you choose to do. Enduring couples succeed at love by working at it day in and day out—helping each other with studying or the dishes, cheering each other with kind words following disheartening days at school or work, nursing each other through illness, and even holding each other close as one partner lets go of life.

POSTSCRIPT

We began this chapter with the dying words of a doomed explorer. As Sir Robert Falcon Scott huddled inside his tent, awaiting death, he penned a last letter to his "widow." Of all the possible things he could have said during those final moments — the limitless selection of topics and words available to sum up his life — what did he choose to focus on? *Love.*

When the impassable storms of your life rage around you, what shelter does love provide? If you had but a few hours to live and were going to craft a final statement, what view of love would you elaborate?

Scott's letter reminds us that love is not one thing but many. To experience romantic love means to feel passion, practicality, commitment, respect, sentiment, and selflessness — all at the same time. Although no two people ever experience love in exactly the same way, we do share this in common: romantic love may not be essential to life, but it may be essential to joy.

LaunchPad for *Reflect & Relate* offers videos and encourages self-assessment through adaptive quizzing. Go to **macmillanhighered.com /reflectrelate4e** to get access to:

LearningCurve
Adaptive Quizzes

Video clips that help you understand interpersonal communication

key terms

liking, 287
loving, 287
passionate love, 288
companionate love, 289
romantic relationship, 290
commitment, 291
▶ relational dialectics, 292
mere exposure effect, 294
beautiful-is-good effect, 295
matching, 295
birds-of-a-feather effect, 295
reciprocal liking, 296
social exchange theory, 296
equity, 296
initiating, 299
▶ experimenting, 299
intensifying, 299
▶ integrating, 300
▶ bonding, 300
▶ differentiating, 302
circumscribing, 302
▶ stagnating, 302
avoiding, 302
terminating, 302
▶ relational maintenance, 304
romantic betrayal, 312
jealousy, 315
wedging, 315
relational intrusion, 316

▶ You can watch brief, illustrative videos of these terms and test your understanding of the concepts in LaunchPad.

key concepts

Defining Romantic Relationships

- **Liking, loving, passionate love,** and **companionate love** are all distinct.
- A **romantic relationship** often involves **commitment** and **relational dialectics.**

Romantic Attraction

- Attraction is strongly influenced by proximity. The **mere exposure effect** is one reason for the comparative rarity of interethnic romances.
- We often attribute positive characteristics to physically appealing people, known as the **beautiful-is-good effect.** We tend to engage in **matching** when forming long-term romantic relationships.
- **Social exchange theory** suggests that attraction to others is driven in part by the resources they can offer you. For relationships to survive, **equity** must exist.

Relationship Development and Deterioration

- When coming together, couples commonly go through **initiating** and **experimenting.** Some couples move to **intensifying** and **integrating.** Few relationships progress to **bonding.**
- **Differentiating** leads partners to believe that their differences are insurmountable, and they may begin **circumscribing** or even **stagnating.**
- Many relationships end by **avoiding,** although some couples may conduct a **terminating** discussion.

Maintaining Romantic Relationships

- Long-term couples use several **relational maintenance** tactics.
- Long-distance romantic relationships can create unique maintenance issues.

The Dark Side of Romantic Relationships

- **Romantic betrayal** is the gravest threat to relationships.
- **Wedging** occurs when someone deliberately interferes in a relationship.
- If a romantic partner uses behaviors that invade your privacy, it is called **relational intrusion.**
- Dating violence affects both men and women of all ages and ethnicities. If you experience such abuse, reach out for professional help.

chapter review

LearningCurve can help you review the material in this chapter. Go to LaunchPad: macmillanhighered.com/reflectrelate4e

11 Relationships with Family Members

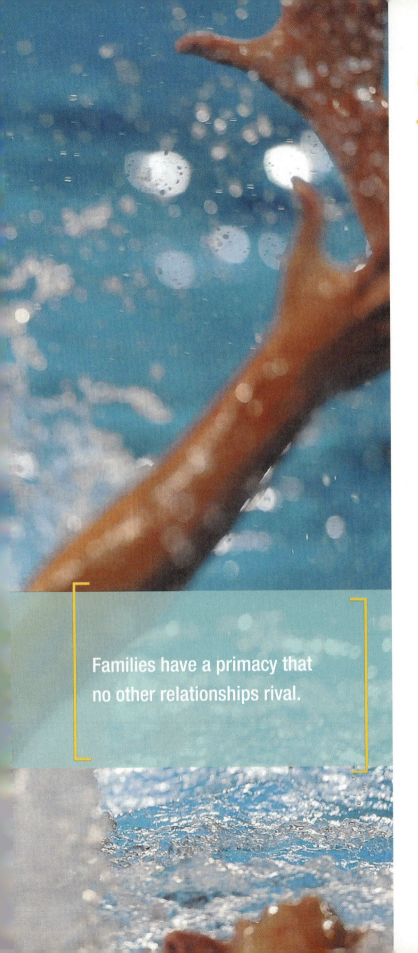

Families have a primacy that no other relationships rival.

She's one of the greatest water polo players ever.[1] She is an NCAA Women's Player of the Year, a 2012 Olympic gold medalist, a three-time World Champion, and a World Cup Champion. But when Brenda Villa is asked about her abilities and accomplishments, she is quick to credit her family, especially her mother: "I get my confidence and 'swagger' from my mom. She's one tough woman. She always supports me but is unafraid to tell me when I'm not being humble."

Brenda grew up in Commerce, California, a working-class suburb of Los Angeles. At a young age, her mother enrolled her in swimming classes. Brenda excelled and gravitated to water polo after seeing her older brother, Edgar, compete. Although her parents had no experience with the sport, they encouraged Brenda's interest. "They taught me that you should always be open to new things."

Growing up, four themes were foundational in the Villa family: *support*, *honesty*, *sacrifice*, and *love*. As Brenda describes, "Both my parents worked full time. Yet they were at all my swim meets, water polo games, school activity nights, and assemblies. They knew that I was committed to both school and sports, and they supported me in every way so that I could achieve my goals." Her parents are also scrupulously honest with her, in good times and bad. "They know when I need a kick in the butt and when I need

---

[1] All information that follows is adapted from personal interviews with the author, July 2011, and published with permission.

325

11 / Relationships with Family Members

MCT/Newscom

someone to listen. Recently I was feeling sorry for myself after missing a penalty shot at a tournament. My mother found out from my boyfriend, and the next thing you know I get a comforting text message from my dad and a phone call from my mom. She reminded me that it's my choice to continue to play and if I'm going to dwell on mistakes that I shouldn't play anymore. She wants me to be the champion I am—no fear. Gotta love her!"

The Villa family is always willing to sacrifice for one another. For example, Brenda's training camps for the U.S. team were in Chula Vista, a two-hour commute from Commerce. Her parents drove her, without debate or resentment. As Brenda describes, "I don't remember asking my parents to do this—they just did it. And I never realized how hard it was for them. My mother would accompany my dad because she was afraid he would fall asleep on the drive home. I didn't appreciate the depth of their sacrifice at the time, as a kid, but now that I'm older, I'm so thankful that they put me first." The willingness to sacrifice communicated a powerful message of love. "Their love is unconditional. It warms my heart to think that my mom would accompany my dad just to keep him awake. *That's* love!"

Though she's one of America's most talented and celebrated female athletes, Brenda Villa remains humble about her accolades. As the Women's Sports Foundation notes, "[Brenda] seems unaware of the splash she has made as role model and hero to Latina athletes. Maybe she's just too busy and too modest by nature" (Lewellen, 2008). But the truth is, Brenda doesn't think of herself as role model—she thinks of her *parents* that way. "I look at their 30-plus years of marriage and how they still always put their kids first. I hope to be as selfless as them with my own children."

Families have a primacy that no other relationships rival. Family members are the first people we see, hear, touch, and interact with. As we grow from infancy to childhood, we learn from family the most basic of skills: how to walk, talk, feed, and clothe ourselves. As we develop further, our families teach us deeper lessons about life akin to those learned by Brenda Villa from her parents: the importance of support, honesty, sacrifice, and love. As our relationships broaden to include friendships and romances, we still use kinship as a metaphor to describe closeness: "How close are we? We're like *family*!" (Rubin, 1996). But family relationships are also compulsory. We don't *choose* our families—we are brought into them by birth, adopted into them by law, or integrated into them by remarriage. When problems arise in our family relationships, the stress is unrivaled. One survey of adults found that the greatest source of emotional strain the preceding day was "family" (Warr & Payne, 1982). When the same sample was asked to name the greatest source of pleasure from the previous day, the answer was identical: "family." Day in and day out, family relationships provide us with our greatest joys and most bitter heartaches (Myers, 2002).

In this chapter, we look at the most influential and enduring of our close involvements: family relationships. You'll learn:

- The defining features of family
- The different ways in which families communicate
- Communication strategies to maintain healthy family relationships
- Challenges that families face, and how to manage them

> **chapter outline**
>
> **327** Defining Family
>
> **334** Communicating in Families
>
> **337** Maintaining Family Relationships
>
> **344** Family Relationship Challenges
>
> **349** The Primacy of Family

Defining Family

Family identity is created through communication

When many of us think of family, iconic TV images come to mind, like the Johnsons in *Black-ish* or the Dunphys from *Modern Family*. These images are simple and comforting: families consist of happily married couples raising their biological children, bonded by love and united in facing any challenges that confront them (Braithwaite et al., 2010).

But families today are more diverse than such depictions suggest. Between 1970 and 2010, the percentage of households composed of married couples with biological children in the United States declined from 40 percent to just 20 percent (Tavernise, 2011). In Canada, this kind of family declined from 55 percent in 1981 to 39.2 percent in 2011 (Statistics of Canada, 2012). Instead, couples are increasingly living together rather than getting married, making marriage less common than at any prior time in history (Cherlin, 2004). Rising divorce rates over the past half century have also decreased the average size of households, as families divide into smaller units and re-form into blended arrangements featuring stepparents and stepchildren. Adding to this complexity, individual families are constantly in flux, as children move out, then lose jobs and move back in with parents; grandparents join the household to help with day care or receive care themselves; and

Chapter Theme

This chapter is about the primacy of family. Family ties run deep, and as a consequence, all of the normal, everyday ups and downs we face in interpersonal relationships seem amplified when experienced within our families. Although our culture often depicts families in caricatured, uniformly positive ways, family relationships are characteristically marked by emotional intensity and ambivalence. Successfully navigating the sea of interpersonal challenges that families present requires skill and effort.

In *Black-ish*, the Johnson family members have differing personality types that often create conflict between them, but in the end, they are a supportive family with a strong bond. ABC/Photofest

Discussion Prompt: What Does "Family" Mean?

Ask students: What is a family? How do you personally define it? Have students Think-Ink-Pair-Share about their definitions of family. You will likely find that students have come up with a list of identifiers (*legal*, *birth*, *blood*) and related concepts (*closeness, love, conflict*), and that they have very different perceptions of what constitutes a family. Some prefer more liberal versions of self-defined families, while others prefer more textbook definitions. Then, define *family* and discuss the characteristics of families.

spouses separate geographically to pursue job opportunities (Crosnoe & Cavanagh, 2010).

DEFINING CHARACTERISTICS OF FAMILY

The enormous diversity in contemporary families requires a broad, inclusive definition. **Family** is a network of people who share their lives over long periods of time and are bound by marriage, blood, or commitment; who consider themselves as family; and who share a significant history and anticipated future of functioning in a family relationship (Galvin, Brommel, & Bylund, 2004). This definition highlights six characteristics that distinguish families from other social groups.

First, families possess a strong sense of family identity, created by how they communicate (Braithwaite et al., 2010). The way you talk with family members, the stories you exchange, and even the manner in which members of your family deal with conflict all contribute to a shared sense of what your family is like (Tovares, 2010).

Second, families use communication to define boundaries, both inside the family and to distinguish family members from outsiders (Afifi, 2003; Koerner & Fitzpatrick, 2006). As we'll discuss later, some families constrict information that flows out ("Don't talk about our family problems with anyone else"). Some also restrict physical access to the family—for example, by dictating with whom family members can become romantically involved ("No son of mine is going to marry a Protestant!"). Others set few such boundaries: a family may welcome friends and neighbors as unofficial members, such as an "uncle" or "aunt" who isn't really related to your parents (Braithwaite et al., 2010). For instance, my sons grew up knowing and referring to our good friend Tim Levine as "Uncle Tim," even though he isn't a blood relation. A family may even welcome others' children, such as the neighbors across the street whom you think of as your "family away from home." If remarriage occurs and stepfamilies form, these boundaries are renegotiated (Golish, 2003).

Third, the emotional bonds underlying family relationships are intense and complex. Family members typically hold both warm *and* antagonistic feelings toward one another (Silverstein & Giarrusso, 2010). As author Lillian Rubin (1996) notes, family relationships have "an elemental quality that touches the deepest layers of our inner life and stirs our most primitive emotional responses" (p. 256). Consider the strength of feeling that arises in you when you get into an argument with a parent or sibling, or when you celebrate an important milestone (a graduation, a wedding, a new job) with family members.

chapter 11 / Relationships with Family Members 329

◯ Although every family possesses its own distinct identity, all families hold certain things in common. Whether bound together by marriage, blood, or commitment, each family has a profound shared history made up of the small, everyday moments they spend together. (left) © Tony Avelar/Christian Science Monitor/The Image Works; (right) © The Star-Ledger/Aristide Economopoulos/The Image Works

Fourth, families share a history (Galvin et al., 2004). Such histories can stretch back for generations and feature family members from a broad array of cultures. These histories often set expectations regarding how family members should behave ("We Ngatas have always been an honest bunch, and we're not about to change that now"). Families also share a common future: they expect to maintain their bonds indefinitely. For better or worse, everything you say and do becomes a part of your family history, shaping future interactions and determining whether your family relationships are healthy or destructive.

Fifth, family members may share genetic material (Crosnoe & Cavanagh, 2010). This can lead to shared physical characteristics as well as similar personalities, outlooks on life, mental abilities, and ways of relating to others. For example, some studies suggest that interpersonal inclinations such as shyness and aggressiveness are influenced by genes (Carducci & Zimbardo, 1995).

Finally, family members constantly juggle multiple and sometimes competing roles (Silverstein & Giarrusso, 2010). Within your family, you're not just a daughter or son, but perhaps a sibling, a spouse, or an aunt or uncle as well. By the time you reach middle age, you may simultaneously be a parent, spouse, grandparent, daughter or son, *and* sibling—and each of these roles carries with it varying expectations and demands. This makes communicating competently within families challenging.

TYPES OF FAMILIES

No "typical" family type exists. Instead, families come in many different forms (Braithwaite et al., 2010). But even these forms are not fixed: you may experience several different family structures as you progress through life and as our larger society evolves. For example, 60 years ago, the **nuclear family**—a wife, a husband,

self-reflection

With whom do you share more intense emotional bonds: family members, friends, lovers, or coworkers? Do you always feel positively toward your family, or do some members consistently trigger negative emotions in you? What does this tell you about the intensity and complexity of emotional bonds in family relationships?

Assignment: Brainstorming for Types of Families

In groups, have students identify famous media families for each family type, such as the Johnsons from *Black-ish* (nuclear), the Gilmore girls (single-parent mother), Jake and Alan from *Two and a Half Men* (single-parent father), and Molly's family in *Mike and Molly* (extended). Ask students to discuss the communication styles of these families and the different types of conflict unique to each type. As a class, discuss the following: Are families accurately represented in current media? How do media families compare to real-life ones?

self-reflection

What type of family did you grow up with? What makes you collectively a family—the fact that you are biologically related? live in the same household? share a strong emotional bond? Now think about other people's families. Are there those that consider themselves families that you don't? If so, why?

and their biological or adopted children—was the most common family type in North America. Today, it is in the minority. Instead, families may include children or not; have one parent or two; be headed by heterosexual, lesbian, gay, bisexual, or transgendered people; include other relatives, such as grandparents; include stepparents and stepsiblings; or consist of any other combination you can imagine! While we discuss the family types further, consider how your family experiences align with or depart from these depictions. But perhaps most importantly, keep this in mind: *what matters most is not the "type" of family you have but whom you consider part of your family in terms of love, respect, and communication.*

When relatives such as aunts, uncles, parents, children, and grandparents live together in a common household, the result is an **extended family.** By the year 2050, 100 million people in the United States will be over the age of 65, and many of these individuals will be sharing a household with relatives. Numerous Italian American, African American, and Asian American families fall into this category.

Approximately half of marriages in the United States and Canada are remarriages for one or both partners (Coleman, Ganong, & Fine, 2000). This often creates a **stepfamily** in which at least one of the adults has a child or children from a previous relationship (Ganong & Coleman, 1994). Stepfamilies are often called "blended" or "remarried" families. More than 50 percent of children born throughout the twenty-first century will grow up in stepfamilies (Crosnoe & Cavanagh, 2010).

Some couples live together prior to or instead of marriage. These **cohabiting couples** consist of two unmarried, romantically involved adults living together in a household, with or without children. Cohabitation is steadily increasing in Western societies (Adams, 2004). This is partly due to an increase in cohabitation among middle-aged and older adults, many of whom were formerly married but now want the relational flexibility that cohabitation affords (Silverstein & Giarrusso, 2010).

In a **single-parent family,** only one adult resides in the household, possessing sole responsibility as caregiver for the children. As of 2011, 27 percent of children in the United States (U.S. Census Bureau, 2011) and about 19 percent of children in Canada (Statistics Canada, 2012) were growing up in single-parent households.

A final family type is the **voluntary kin family:** a group of people who lack blood and legal kinship but who nevertheless consider themselves "family." Oftentimes such families arise from distance, dissatisfaction with, or estrangement from blood and legal relatives. In such cases, three types of voluntary kin families arise

No matter who is in them, families are some of the most central and formative interpersonal relationships that we have. (Left to right) Mylan Canon/The New York Times/Redux Pictures; © Inti St Clair/Getty Images; Creatas/Getty Images; Francisco Romero/Getty Images; Erin Patrice O'Brien/Getty Images; Jose Luiz Pelaez Inc/Getty Images

(Braithwaite et al., 2010). The most frequent form is the *supplemental family*, in which dissatisfaction with family relationships leads people to begin labeling other close people in their lives as "family," even though they retain contact with their blood and legal relatives. For example, my college girlfriend, Michelle, developed close relationships with my parents while we were dating—even closer than her own family—and consequently starting calling my parents "Mom" and "Dad," and talking about my family as "her second family." In contrast, people who create a *substitute family* have no contact whatsoever with blood or legal relatives—either because of estrangement or death—and replace their relatives entirely with a group of individuals considered to be "family." Finally, within a *convenience family*, people may, for a particular time span, come to think of a group of people as their "family," although the ties between them are temporary. For instance, students who study abroad may live in a household in which the residents become "family" for that time period, only to have the relationships splinter after everyone returns home. The same thing may happen within institutionalized settings—for example, during lengthy stays in rehab—when people in an intensive, residential counseling facility bond together, only to have those ties fray upon completion of the therapy.

FAMILY STORIES

Characteristics and types define families from the outside looking in. But from the inside, one of the most powerful ways we define our collective family identity is to share stories (Tovares, 2010). For example, when I was growing up, family storytelling was a nightly ritual. Some tales were from my parents' college days, like the time my dad and his buddies filled a friend's dorm room from floor to ceiling with wadded-up newspaper. Others were created from shared family experiences, like when I fed my scrambled eggs to my dog, Lottie, because I didn't want to eat them, and she regurgitated them in front of my mom, incriminating me. Even now, when we get together for visits, we relive and retell these stories and others like them, enjoying the sense of family history they provide.

Family stories are narrative accounts shared repeatedly within a family that retell historical events and are meant to bond the family together (Stone, 2004). Such stories organize collective memories about significant events in the past, and link those occurrences to the present and future in ways that provide

Assignment: Sharing Family Stories

Have your students read the article "What Kids Learn from Hearing Family Stories" at www.theatlantic.com/education/archive/2013/12/what-kids-learn-from-hearing-family-stories/282075. Ask them to write one of their favorite family stories in about a page. Students should indicate why the story is significant in their family and how it affects family communication. They should also think back to the article and indicate what they learned from hearing family stories. Then, have students share their stories in groups and discuss the following: Why are stories important? How do they shape families?

🔶 Sharing old photographs can bring family stories to life by providing lasting, powerful images of family relationships. Do you associate any particular images or other mementos with your favorite family stories?
Michel Gaillard/REA/Redux Pictures

family members with a deep sense of meaning regarding their relationships with one another (Frost, 2012). Importantly, it's not just the content of the stories that bonds families together; it's the activity of storytelling. Family members often collaborate in telling stories: adding details, disagreeing, correcting discrepancies, and confirming perspectives (Kellas, 2005).

When people tell family stories, they typically lace their narratives with opinions and emotions that make clear how they feel about other family members (Vangelisti, Crumley, & Baker, 1999). These evaluations have a powerful effect on closeness: the regular sharing of stories that cast relational partners in a positive light and that have "happy endings" substantially boosts relationship satisfaction and mental health (Frost, 2012). However, family stories aren't always positive; some criticize family values, condemn specific family members' actions, or discourage dissent. These stories may also involve family histories of abandonment, abuse, or parental oppression, and corresponding lessons about how not to parent (Goodsell, Bates, & Behnke, 2010). Although families share many types of stories, three stand out as especially potent in affirming family identity: *courtship stories*, *birth stories*, and *survival stories* (Stone, 2004).

Courtship Stories One of my family's most poignant stories tells how my dad serenaded my mom from the courtyard of her dorm at Pomona College while she stood on her balcony, listening. Forty-five years later, my parents and I visited Pomona. While driving around campus, Mom suddenly shouted "Stop!" and leapt from the car. Dad and I followed her into a well-worn building, only to find her standing in the very courtyard that I had heard described so many times. Mom stood there, gazing at the balcony where she'd listened to Dad's song more than four decades earlier. "There it is," she whispered, "the spot where your father serenaded me," and her eyes filled with tears.

Some families share *courtship stories* about how the parents fell in love. Courtship stories emphasize the solidity of the parents' relationship, which children find reassuring. But perhaps most important, such stories give children a framework for understanding romantic love by suggesting what one should feel about love and how to recognize it when it occurs (Stone, 2004).

Birth Stories Families may also share *birth stories*, which describe the latter stages of pregnancy, childbirth, and early infancy of a child. Birth stories help children understand how they fit into the family ("You'll always be the baby"), which roles they're expected to play ("Firstborns are always so independent"), and what their parents hope and dream for them ("We knew from the moment you were born that you'd accomplish great things!").

Unlike biological children, adopted children often have little knowledge of their birth or birth parents. Consequently, the stories that adoptive parents create about how and why the children entered their adoptive families—known as *entrance stories*—are important in providing the child with a sense of personal identity and self-esteem (Krusiewicz & Wood, 2001). Entrance stories also help heal the broken bond with birth parents by giving the child an explanation of why the adoption occurred. For example, one of the most common and constructive entrance stories involves framing the birth mother's decision as altruistic: "the loving, painful decision of an amazing, caring woman" (Krusiewicz & Wood, 2001, p. 793).

Survival Stories   *Survival stories* relate the coping strategies family members have used to deal with major challenges. Survival in these stories may be physical, as in the accounts that combat soldiers and famine victims tell. Or survival may refer to a family member's ability to prevail by achieving a level of financial stability or other forms of success. Survival stories give children the sense that they come from a tough, persevering family, which prepares them to face their own difficulties. For example, the mother of water polo star Brenda Villa (featured in our chapter opener) emigrated from Mexico when she was only 18, following the death of her father.[2] She came to the United States to earn money and help support her family back home. This story of struggle and hardship inspired Brenda to work hard and achieve her own goals.

Telling Family Stories   The breadth and depth of your family experiences provide a rich resource to share with family members. But not all shared experiences are ones your family members would like to relive. To ensure that family stories strengthen, rather than erode, family relationships, select experiences that cast the family and individual members in a positive light and that emphasize unity rather than discord. When sharing stories with younger family members, keep in mind that they will learn values from your story (Tovares, 2010). Ask yourself whether the story sends the message you intend about your family's values.

Stories that cast individual family members in a humorous light require special care. Although such stories may be perfectly appropriate to share, make sure that the "target" family member enjoys and agrees to the telling. For example, you might repeatedly revisit the time your brother brought home an exceptionally strange date or recount the day your father accidentally drove the car through the garage wall while miraculously avoiding injury. Avoid sharing stories that breach personal confidences ("John never told any of you what really happened, but here it is!") or that make sport of family members in ways they don't enjoy. When in doubt, simply (but privately) ask the family member whether he or she wants you to share the story. If the answer is no keep silent.

> **Assignment: Sharing Rituals and Traditions**
> In addition to stories, rituals and traditions are important for creating family identity. Ask students to interview a family member about a ritual or tradition that is unique to their family. What is the function of the tradition? How was it started? What role does culture play in this tradition? How does it function to create roles, share values, or encourage family goals? How do these traditions connect generations? How are they carried on through family stories?

> **self-reflection**
> What are the most memorable family stories that were shared with you during your upbringing? What lessons did they teach you about your family and the values that you share? Did the stories function to bring you together as a family or drive you apart?

---

[2] Excerpted from interview with author, July 13, 2011. Published with permission.

Communicating in Families

Communication patterns determine how families converse

The award-winning 2014 film *Boyhood* follows the development of its central character, Mason, across 12 years of actual, real-world time (the movie was filmed with the same actors over more than a decade). As time passes within the story line, Mason's family structure changes again and again, as Mason's mother marries, gets divorced, remarries, and gets divorced. Mason's first stepfather is authoritarian, abusive, and not at all interested in discussion. He expects everyone to share his viewpoint and enforces it by telling Mason's mother to "back me up!" In contrast, Mason's biological father, Mason Sr., who stays in touch with his kids across the years, emphasizes open communication and diverse opinions. In one scene, Mason Sr. is out driving with Mason and his sister, but when the kids aren't sharing openly enough, Mason Sr. pulls the car to the curb and confronts them:

> Mason Sr.: "No no no! That's *not* how we are going to talk to one another, all right? I will *not* be that guy. You *cannot* put me in that category, you know, the 'biological father who I spend every other weekend with, and make polite conversation, while he drives me places and buys me stuff'—no! Talk to me!"
>
> Mason Jr.: "But, Dad, why is it all on *us*, though? You know, what about *you*? How was *your* week? Who do *you* hang out with? Do *you* have a girlfriend? What have *you* been up to?
>
> Mason Sr.: (smiling) "I see your point. So, we should just let it happen more natural."
>
> Both kids: "Yeah!"
>
> Mason Sr.: "That's what you're saying. OK, that's what we'll do, starting now."

▶ In *Boyhood*, Mason experiences several different family communication patterns, from his friendly, supportive biological father to his two abusive and controlling stepfathers. What is the dominant communication pattern in your family?
IFC Films/Photofest

Like the families depicted in *Boyhood*, our own families' communication is guided by shared beliefs about how families should converse. These beliefs, and the resulting interpersonal communication, are known as family communication patterns (Koerner & Fitzpatrick, 2002). *Family communication patterns* evolve from two communication dimensions, which we'll discuss next.

COMMUNICATION DIMENSIONS

According to **Family Communication Patterns Theory** (Koerner & Fitzpatrick, 2006), two dimensions underlie the communication between family members. The first is **conversation orientation,** the degree to which family members are encouraged to participate in unrestrained interaction about a wide array of topics. Families with a *high conversation orientation* are like Mason's biological father: they believe that open and frequent communication is essential to an enjoyable and rewarding family life. Consequently, they interact often, freely, and spontaneously, without many limitations placed on time spent together and topics discussed.

In contrast, families with a *low conversation orientation* are like Mason's stepfather: they view interpersonal communication as something irrelevant and unnecessary for a satisfying, successful family life. Such families interact only infrequently and limit their conversations to a few select topics—weather, daily activities, current events, and the like. Disclosure of intimate thoughts and feelings between family members is discouraged, as is debate of attitudes and perspectives.

The second dimension is **conformity orientation,** the degree to which families believe that communication should emphasize similarity or diversity in attitudes, beliefs, and values. Like Mason's stepfather, *high conformity families* use their interactions to highlight and enforce uniformity of thought. Such families are sometimes perceived as more "traditional" because children are expected to obey parents and other elders, who (in turn) are counted on to make family decisions. Members of these families tend to prioritize family relationships over outside connections, such as friendships and romantic involvements. Moreover, they are expected to sacrifice their personal goals for the sake of the family.

Low conformity families, akin to Mason's biological father, communicate in ways that emphasize diversity in attitudes, beliefs, and values, and that encourage uniqueness, individuality, and independence. These families typically view outside relationships as equally important to those within the family, and they prioritize individual over family interests and goals. In low conformity families, children contribute to family decision making, and members view the family as a vehicle for individual growth rather than a collective in which members must sacrifice their own interests for the good of the whole.

FAMILY COMMUNICATION PATTERNS

According to communication scholars Ascan Koerner and Mary Anne Fitzpatrick (2006), conversation and conformity dimensions give rise to four possible family communication patterns: *consensual, pluralistic, protective,* and *laissez-faire.*

Assignment: Your Family Pattern
Have students write a journal entry or short paper about which family communication pattern best represents their family. Students should provide examples of behaviors and experiences to demonstrate the pattern, and explain the benefits and drawbacks of the pattern in their family.

Online Self-Quiz: What Communication Pattern Does Your Family Have? To take this self-quiz, visit LaunchPad: macmillanhighered.com/reflectrelate4e

▶ Sitting down and sharing a meal often gives families the opportunity to catch up on daily events, discuss issues large and small, make decisions, and even deal with conflicts. When your family has a meal together, what do you talk about? How does this align with what you perceive as your family communication pattern? © Ariel Skelley/Blend Images/Corbis

▶ **Video**

macmillanhighered.com/reflectrelate4e

Consensual Families
Watch this clip online to answer the questions below.

How does the family in the video exhibit both high conversation and high conformity orientations? In what types of situations has your own family used a more "consensual" approach to communication? Why?

Consensual Families Families high in both conversation and conformity are **consensual families.** In such families, members are encouraged to openly share their views with one another as well as debate those beliefs. Consensual family communication is marked by high disclosure; attentive listening; and frequent expressions of caring, concern, and support toward one another (Rueter & Koerner, 2008). At the same time, consensual family members are expected to steadfastly share a single viewpoint. Parents in such households typically exert strong control over the attitudes, behaviors, and interactions of their children (Rueter & Koerner, 2008). For example, parents may encourage their children to share their thoughts and feelings about important issues ("What do you think we should do?"), but then make clear that only one perspective (the parents') is acceptable. Because of their emphasis on conformity, consensual families perceive conflict as intensely threatening. Consequently, they address conflicts as they occur and seek to resolve them as constructively as possible to preserve family unity.

Pluralistic Families Families high in conversation but low in conformity are **pluralistic families.** They communicate in open and unconstrained ways, discussing a broad range of topics and exploring them in depth. Pluralistic families enjoy debating the issues of the day, and judge one another's arguments on their merit rather than on whether they mesh with other members' attitudes. People in pluralistic families typically don't try to control other family members' beliefs or attitudes (Rueter & Koerner, 2008). Since parents don't feel compelled to wield power over their children, children's contributions to family discussions and decision making are treated as relevant and equally valid. For example, parents in a pluralistic family might ask for their children's opinions regarding a job opportunity ("Should Mom accept the offer from TelCo?") or a family vacation ("Where should we go this year?"). Pluralistic families deal directly with conflict, seeking to resolve disputes in productive, mutually beneficial ways. They may, for instance, establish "official" times (such as mealtimes or family meetings) when members can vent their concerns and work collaboratively to settle them. For this reason, pluralistic family members report the highest rates of conflict resolution of any of the four family types.

Protective Families **Protective families** are low on conversation and high on conformity. Communication in these families functions to maintain obedience and enforce family norms, and little value is placed on the exchange of ideas or the development of communication skills. Parent-child power differences are firmly enforced, and children are expected to quietly obey. Sayings such as "Children should be seen and not heard" and "Children should speak when spoken to" reflect this mind-set. Parents invest little effort in creating opportunities for family discussion, and the result is low levels of disclosure among family members (Rueter & Koerner, 2008). Protective families avoid conflict because it threatens the conformity they value and because they often lack the skills necessary to manage conflicts constructively. Members may tell each other "Don't make waves" or "You don't want to cause trouble."

Laissez-Faire Families Families low in both conversation and conformity are **laissez-faire families.** Few emotional bonds exist between their members, resulting in low levels of caring, concern, and support expressed within the family (Rueter & Koerner, 2008). Their detachment shows itself in a lack of interaction and a decided disinterest in activities that might foster communication or maintenance of the family as a unit. Similar to parents in pluralistic families, laissez-faire parents believe that children should be independent thinkers and decision makers. But this belief derives from their disinterest in their children's thoughts and decisions. Such parents tend to leave it up to their children to form their own opinions regarding sexual behavior, drug and alcohol use, and educational achievement. Because members of such families interact infrequently, they either rarely get embroiled in conflict. If a disagreement does erupt, they either avoid it or (if they feel strongly invested in the issues at stake) compete to "win" the debate.

▶ **Video**
macmillanhighered.com
/reflectrelate4e

Protective Families
Watch this clip online to answer the questions below.

In your view, what are the potential advantages and disadvantages of protective families? Do you think family patterns might change as children grow older?

Want to see more? Check out LaunchPad for clips illustrating **pluralistic families** and **laissez-faire families.**

Maintaining Family Relationships

> All family relationships need constant maintenance

When Arizona caseworker Heather Shew-Plummer met Steven and Roger Ham, she knew they would be ideal adoptive parents.[3] They were "patient, loving, fun and ceaseless advocates for kids." Shew-Plummer helped the Hams adopt a young Hispanic boy, Michael. But Michael worried about his four younger siblings, who were still in foster care. "These kids obviously loved one another," Steven says. "I knew they had to be together, and I was going to make that happen." Eventually, the couple adopted *all* of Michael's siblings and worked to reassure the children about the family's stability by telling them, "*This* [family] is forever." Seeing their success, caseworkers began placing children of all ethnicities, ages, and abilities with the Hams. They now have 14.

---

[3]All information that follows is adapted from Bland (2011).

▶ Steven and Roger Ham work hard to maintain open, honest, and supportive communication with their adopted children. What strategies have you used to maintain positive relationships with your family members? Courtesy of Steven Ham

Critical to their family success is the positive atmosphere Steven and Roger create. "They are really supportive of anything I do," says their daughter Vanessa, and their constant encouragement traverses many varied activities: basketball, karate, ROTC, and cheerleading. The Hams also emphasize open, honest communication. Some of their kids are old enough to remember their troubled previous lives, and the Hams discuss their pasts forthrightly, helping the children to grieve and move forward. "Children should be able to come to you about anything," Steven says. But more than anything else, the Ham family focuses on love. "A loving home is a loving home," Roger says. "Our kids have two parents who love them; not all of their friends do."

The story of the Ham family reminds us of a simple truth: *we create our families through how we communicate*. Although you're only one member of your family, the interpersonal choices you make—and what you say and do as a result—ripple outward. To help boost your family's closeness and happiness, use your interpersonal communication skills to maintain your family relationships, and work carefully to balance ongoing family tensions.

MAINTENANCE STRATEGIES FOR FAMILIES

Many people take their family relationships for granted. Instead of communicating in ways designed to maintain these relationships, people assume that "your family is always there for you" (Vogl-Bauer, 2003). But all family relationships need constant maintenance to be sustained. As illustrated by Steven and Roger Ham, three of the most important strategies for maintaining family relationships are positivity, assurances, and self-disclosure (Vogl-Bauer, 2003).

Positivity The most powerful maintenance tactic for families is *positivity* (Stafford, 2010). In family settings, this means communicating with your family members in an upbeat and hopeful fashion. To implement positivity in your family encounters, start doing favors for other family members without being asked, and unexpectedly gift them in little ways that show you care. Invest energy into making each encounter with family members enjoyable. Avoid complaining about family problems that have no solutions; ridiculing family members; whining or sulking when you don't get your way; and demanding that caregivers, siblings, or other kin give you favored treatment.

Assurances The second way you can bolster your family relationships is by offering regular *assurances* of how much your family means to you. Let other family members know that you consider your relationship with each of them unique and valuable, and that you are committed to maintaining these bonds well into the future ("I love you," "I will always be here for you," "I miss you," or "I can't wait to be home again so I can spend time with you"). Avoid devaluing family relationships in front of others ("They're *just* my family") and commenting on how other families are superior to yours ("I'd give anything to have other parents").

Self-Disclosure *Self-disclosure* in family relationships means sharing your private thoughts and feelings with family members and allowing them to do the same without fear of betrayal. You do this by treating other family members in ways that are consistent, trustworthy, and ethical. Ways to practice self-disclosure include making time in your schedule to talk with parents, siblings, or children about how they are doing; encouraging them to share their feelings and concerns with you; and offering your perspective in a cooperative, respectful way. It also means avoiding communication practices that undermine disclosure, such as betraying confidences, refusing to make time for family conversation, reacting defensively when family members share their feelings with you, disparaging family members' viewpoints, and hiding things from your family.

TECHNOLOGY AND FAMILY MAINTENANCE

My parents live two thousand miles away from me, in an isolated valley in southern Oregon. But we "talk" several times each week by e-mail—exchanging cartoons, photos, and articles of interest. My son Kyle, a student at the University of Chicago, Skypes with my wife and me every Sunday. And my other two sons, Colin and Conor, are constantly exchanging photos, movie clips, reddit and subreddit links, and music suggestions with me online—even though they both live in East Lansing, Michigan, and I teach at the University of Alabama in Birmingham.

Although some lament that technology has replaced face-to-face interaction and reduced family intimacy ("Families are always on the computer and never *talk* anymore"), families typically use online and face-to-face communication in a complementary, rather than substitutive, fashion. Families who communicate frequently via e-mail, text, Twitter, Instagram, Facebook, and IM *also* communicate frequently face-to-face or on the phone. They typically choose synchronous

---

Making You Noise
—for my mother

The day before you are deaf completely, I will make you noise. I will bring birds, bracelets, chimes to hang in the wind. We will drive from Idaho to Washington again, and I will read to keep you awake, and I will tap little poems on the backs of your arms, your neck to be sure you hear me. I will play spoons on your body in restaurants, smack my lips, heave you sighs, each one deeper than the rest. We will finally shout. And then, as quiet slips in, settling over, I will speak. I will keep speaking. I will sing you nonsense songs until you go to sleep.

By Francesca Bell

Discussion Prompt: Family Maintenance Online
Many students use social media to communicate with their family. Ask students to discuss the following: Do you add your family members as friends to your social media networks? Why or why not? Has being friends with family members on social media caused conflict? Do you monitor your communication with others because of this? How has technology changed the way you communicate with your family?

skills practice

Technology and Family Maintenance
Ways to communicate positivity and assurances to family members

1. Send an e-mail to a family member with whom you've been out of touch, letting him or her know you care.

2. Offer congratulations via text message or e-mail to a family member who has recently achieved an important goal.

3. Post a message on the Facebook page of a family member with whom you've had a disagreement, saying that you value his or her opinions and beliefs.

4. Send an e-card to a long-distance family member, sharing a message of affection.

5. Post a supportive response to a family member who has expressed concerns via Twitter or Facebook.

Teaching Note: Positives and Negatives of Dialectical Tensions

Students often think that one side of a dialectic tension is detrimental to the relationship, while the other side is beneficial (e.g., openness is "good," while protection is "bad"). Emphasize the importance of both sides and the "tug and pull" in a dialectic. Discuss why we need to have *both* sides in a relationship. For example, why is protection sometimes important? Are there times when one side is more necessary and functional than others?

---

modes of communication (face-to-face, phone) for personal or urgent matters, and asynchronous modes (e-mail, text, Facebook) for less important issues (Tillema, Dijst, & Schwanen, 2010). What's more, technology, especially the use of cell phones, allows families to connect, share, and coordinate their lives to a degree never before possible, resulting in boosted intimacy and satisfaction (Kennedy, Smith, Wells, & Wellman, 2008). Similarly, families whose members are geographically separated but who use online communication to stay in touch report higher satisfaction, stronger intimacy, more social support, and reduced awareness of the physical separation, compared to families who don't (McGlynn, 2007).

Despite being comparatively "old school," e-mail is the dominant electronic way families communicate. Interpersonal scholar Amy Janan Johnson and her colleagues found that more than half of college students reported interacting with family members via e-mail in the preceding week and that the primary purpose of these e-mails was relationship maintenance (Johnson, Haigh, Becker, Craig, & Wigley, 2008). Students used e-mail to maintain *positivity* ("Have a great day!"), provide *assurances* ("I love you and miss you!"), and *self-disclose* ("I'm feeling a bit scared about my stats exam tomorrow").

Of course, the biggest advantage of online communication is that, unlike face-to-face and phone, it lets you get in touch with family members at any time (Oravec, 2000). For example, my folks and I live in different time zones, making it difficult to find times we can talk. But we still share day-to-day events and interests via e-mail and text messages. Rarely a day goes by when I don't receive a message from my mom detailing their dog Teddy's latest feat of canine intelligence, or from my dad about his progress on his MG "project car." Such messages make us feel close, even though we're thousands of miles apart.

DEALING WITH FAMILY DIALECTICS

Within all families, tension exists between competing impulses, known as **relational dialectics** (see Chapter 10). Two dialectics are especially pronounced in families: *autonomy versus connection* and *openness versus protection*. As we mature, each of us must balance our desire for autonomy against the connection that we share with our families and the corresponding expectations and obligations regarding who we "should" be as family members. We also face frequent decisions regarding how openly we should communicate with other family members, as well as how much information about our families we should share with those outside the family unit. Balancing these tensions is challenging. However, you can strike a balance by applying the following techniques.

Balancing Autonomy and Connection

Even though you may feel intensely connected to your family, you probably also struggle to create your own separate identity. You may enjoy the feeling of intimacy that connectedness brings, while resenting how your family seems blind to your true abilities: "My family insists on seeing me only as an athlete" or "My family doesn't think I can make mature decisions because I'm the youngest."

The tension between autonomy and connection in families is especially difficult to manage during adolescence (Crosnoe & Cavanagh, 2010). As children move

◭ As in any relationship, conflict is an unavoidable part of family life.
(Left) © Bubbles Photolibrary/Alamy; (right) © ImageShop/Alamy

through their teen years, they begin to assert their independence from parents. Their peers eventually replace parents and other family members as having the most influence on their interpersonal decisions (Golish, 2000).

How can you best manage the tension between autonomy and connection in your family? Use two additional relationship maintenance strategies discussed in Chapter 10—sharing tasks and cultivating social networks. In this case, however, it is important to strike a balance between family relationships and outside relationships. First, for sharing tasks, you need to balance your dependence on family members to help you carry out everyday chores with a reliance on yourself and people outside your family. Too much dependence on family members—especially for tasks you could accomplish on your own—can erode your self-reliance, self-confidence, and independence (Strauss, 2006).

Second, examine your social networks (including your family), and assess the degree to which family members constitute the closest people in your life. As with sharing tasks, a balance between family relationships and outside connections is ideal. If you have few or even no close ties with anyone outside of the family sphere, you may feel intensely dependent on your family and experience a corresponding loss of autonomy. Likewise, having no close ties to any family members can create a sense of independence so extreme that you feel little emotional bond with your family.

Balancing Openness and Protection Families also experience tension between openness and protection. In any close relationship—family bonds included—we want both to share personal information and to protect ourselves from the possible negative consequences of such sharing (Afifi & Steuber, 2010). In families, the tension between these two needs is even more pronounced. For example, your family may be extremely close, and as a consequence almost

self-reflection

Who has more influence in shaping your relationship decisions: your family or your friends? Whom do you look to for emotional support in times of need? Has the degree to which you depend on your family versus your friends changed over time? If so, why?

Assignment: Privacy in Your Family

Ask students to write an essay applying the ideas of Communication Privacy Management Theory. What were the family privacy rules in your family of origin? How has privacy been beneficial or detrimental in your family? What changes did you experience in openness during different transitions in your childhood? Would you change or maintain the same privacy rules with your own children in your current or future families?

focus on CULTURE

Autonomy and Class: Helicopter Parents

Robyn Lewis's sons may attend college, but it doesn't mean her involvement in their lives has lessened (ABCnews.go.com, 2005). She creates daily to-do lists for them, checks their grades and bank accounts online, proofreads their papers, and screens their e-mail. "It's nice to have someone who serves as a secretary-mom," says son Brendan. Robyn's response? "I think that's great—a secretary helps keep the boss focused and organized, right?"

In the United States, people have different views of how families should balance autonomy with connection, and these differences often cut along class lines. Middle- and upper-income parents (such as Lewis) are more inclined to view their role as cultivating their children's talents in a highly orchestrated fashion (Lareau, 2003). Organized activities, created and controlled by parents, dominate these children's lives. In extreme form, these children have little or no autonomy, as parents "hover" over all aspects of their lives like helicopters. Technology facilitates such hovering: parents can check up on their kids 24/7 through Facebook, text-messaging, and e-mail.

Lower-income parents, however, tend to view their role as allowing their children to mature without adult interference (Lareau, 2003). These children often have more independence in their leisure activities—they are free to roam their neighborhoods and play with friends, for example—as opposed to participating in arranged "playdates." And when they enter college or the work world, their parents continue to let them develop primarily on their own.

Public elementary and secondary schools in the United States strongly endorse intense connection between parents and children, and they structure their curricula and school-related activities accordingly (Lareau, 2003). But many believe that such intense connectedness does a disservice to children, especially as they mature (Strauss, 2006). For instance, Linda Walter, administrator at Seton Hall University, maintains that "many young adults entering college have the academic skills they need to succeed, but are lacking in self-reliance" (Strauss, 2006).

discussion questions

- How has your parents' or caregivers' approach to balancing autonomy and connection influenced their relationship with you? Are they "helicopters"?
- What are the advantages and disadvantages of the way your parents or caregivers balanced your connection with them and your autonomy?

---

anything that you tell one family member quickly becomes common knowledge. This creates a dilemma when you want to share something with only one family member. Do you disclose the information, knowing that within a week's time your entire family will also know it, or do you withhold it?

According to **Communication Privacy Management Theory** (Petronio, 2000), individuals create informational boundaries by carefully choosing the kind of private information they reveal and the people with whom they share it. These boundaries are constantly shifting, depending on the degree of risk associated with disclosing information. The more comfortable people feel disclosing, the more likely they are to reveal sensitive information. Inversely, people are less likely to share when they expect negative reactions to the disclosure (Afifi & Steuber, 2010).

Within families, these boundaries are defined by **family privacy rules:** the conditions governing what family members can talk about, how they can discuss such topics, and who should have access to family-relevant information (Petronio & Caughlin, 2006). In some families, members feel free to talk about any topic, at any time, and in any situation. In other families, discussion of more sensitive topics such as politics and religion may be permissible only in certain settings. Your family might talk about religion immediately after attending services together or debate political issues over dinner, but you might not discuss such matters during breakfast or on the golf course. Or, some topics may be permanently excluded from your family discussion altogether: personal sexual history, assault, or abuse; severe legal or financial woes; or extreme health problems. Breaking a family privacy rule by forcing discussion of a "forbidden" topic can cause intense emotional discomfort among other family members and may prompt the family to exclude the "rule breaker" from future family interactions. Keep this in mind before you force discussion of an issue that other family members consider off-limits.

Family privacy rules govern *how* family members talk about topics as well, including what's considered an acceptable opinion and how deeply family members can explore these opinions. It may be acceptable to talk at any time about the personal lives of your various family members, for instance, but only if your comments are positive. Or it may be permissible to discuss religion after church, but only if you have a certain viewpoint.

Additionally, family privacy rules identify the people with whom family members can talk. If your family holds a particular religious or political viewpoint that is at odds with surrounding neighbors' views, you might be instructed to avoid these topics when conversing with neighborhood friends ("This stays within the family," or "Don't talk about this at school").

Although family privacy rules help members know how to balance openness and protection, they can also amplify tension within families as people age. When children grow up, the parent-child relationship often shifts from being authority based to being friendship based (Silverstein & Giuarrusso, 2010). As this occurs, people may feel pressure to change long-standing privacy rules. For example, even if your family has never openly discussed severe illness, you may feel compelled to talk about this topic if your mother starts displaying early symptoms of Alzheimer's disease.

How can you improve your family privacy rules and, in doing so, bring about a better balance of openness and protection? First, remember that all families have approved and taboo conversation topics, certain viewpoints they promote over others, and people whom they include or exclude from receiving information about the family. Effective family privacy rules aren't "one size fits all." Instead, they should strike the balance between openness and protection that best fits your family. Second, be respectful of the varying opinions and preferences individual family members have regarding openness and protection. Keep in mind that if your family communication pattern is low on conversation orientation and high on conformity orientation, any push for a change in privacy rules may strike others as a threat to the family.

Finally, if you believe that your family privacy rules should be altered to allow greater openness or increased protection, avoid abrupt, dramatic, and

skills practice

Changing Family Communication Rules
Changing communication about an important issue that's being avoided

❶ Identify an important issue that your family currently avoids discussing.

❷ Select one family member who might be open to talking about this concern.

❸ Initiate a discussion with this person, using competent and cooperative language.

❹ Mutually create a plan for how the issue can be raised with other family members and what exactly you both will say.

❺ Implement your plan, one additional family member at a time.

self-reflection

What topics, if any, are off-limits for discussion within your family? Why are these topics taboo? What would be the consequences of forcing a discussion on these issues? How does not being able to talk about these things with family members make you feel about your family?

demanding calls for change—"We need to learn how to talk more openly about sex!" Such pronouncements will likely offend family members and put them on the defensive. Instead, identify a single family member who you think might share your views. Discuss your desire for change with him or her by using your interpersonal competence skills and cooperative language (Chapters 1 and 7). Ask this person's opinion on the possibility of modifying your family's privacy rules, and invite him or her to suggest ideas for implementing the change. If he or she agrees that change is needed, identify an additional family member who might also concur. Then initiate a three-way discussion. Changes in long-standing family privacy rules—especially for low conversation, high conformity families—are best accomplished slowly, through interactions with one family member at a time.

Family Relationship Challenges

Managing stepfamily transitions and family conflicts

We like to think of family relationships as simple, straightforward, and uniformly positive. Family consists of the most supportive people in our lives—individuals whom we like, love, and depend on. For many people this is true. But family relationships also face daunting challenges. Three of the most difficult to navigate are stepfamily transition, parental favoritism, and interparental conflict.

STEPFAMILY TRANSITION

Transitioning to a stepfamily is a common challenge, given that approximately half of the marriages in the United States and Canada involve a remarriage for one or both partners (Coleman, Ganong, & Fine, 2000). While most people

Discussion Prompt: Stepfamilies in the Media
Ask students to brainstorm for *present* examples of stepfamilies in films and on television. Don't be surprised if students come up with very few examples (e.g. Jay and Gloria on *Modern Family*). Then ask them to consider older examples (*Step-by-Step*, *Sister Sister*, *Brady Bunch*). Encourage a discussion about why there are currently so few examples. Should stepfamilies be better represented in the media? What are the challenges *and* benefits of stepfamilies?

▶ In the classic TV series *The Brady Bunch*, widowed architect Mike Brady marries Carol Martin, creating a new stepfamily. Mike, Carol, and their children have trouble transitioning at first, but they eventually accept that they are all one family. As Carol tells her new son Bobby, "The only 'steps' in this house are those, the ones that lead up to your bedroom." The Everett Collection

enter into stepfamilies with the best intentions for a new start, not all stepfamily members experience the transition equally. Adolescents tend to have more difficulty transitioning into a stepfamily than do preadolescents or young adults. Studies have found that children in stepfamilies have more frequent behavioral problems, turbulent relationships, and lower self-esteem than do children in first-marriage families (Golish, 2003).

The majority of stepfamilies confront very similar challenges, including negotiating new family privacy rules, dealing with discrepancies in conflict-management styles, and building solidarity as a family unit (Golish, 2003). But the most frequent and perplexing challenge is **triangulation:** loyalty conflicts that arise when a coalition is formed, uniting one family member with another against a third family member (Schrodt & Afifi, 2007). Two forms of triangulation are common within stepfamilies: children feeling caught between their custodial and their noncustodial parent, and stepparents feeling caught between the children in their stepfamily (Golish, 2003). Family members caught in triangulation feel torn between different loyalties. As one daughter described her triangulation between her birth parents, "I would carry things from her, she'd say stuff about him, and he'd do the same and talk about her. It's kind of hard to get both sides of it. So I avoided them for a while. . . . I just felt that I was caught in the middle" (Golish, 2003, p. 52). Such triangulation has pronounced negative effects: children who feel "caught between parents" report higher levels of stress and anxiety, and substantially less satisfaction with their parent-child relationships, than do children who aren't triangulated (Schrodt & Shimkowski, 2013).

Given such challenges, how can you help ease the transition to a stepfamily, should you experience it? Try these suggestions:

1. *Go slow, but start early.* Except for the couple getting married, the relationships between other stepfamily members are involuntary. Yet stepfamily members often feel pressure to immediately become intimate (Ganong, Coleman, Fine, & Martin, 1999). This can cause stress and anxiety, as no one enjoys feeling forced to be close to others. To avoid this, *go slow* in building ties with your stepparents, stepchildren, or stepsiblings. Take the time to get to know one another, forging relationships in the same way you would any other interpersonal involvements—by having fun and doing things together. If possible, *start early* in creating these bonds—ideally as soon as it becomes certain that a stepfamily will form. Not doing so can lead to tension and conflict later, when the stepfamily formally becomes a family unit.

2. *Practice daily maintenance.* Research on stepfamilies emphasizes the importance of displaying affection, attending important activities and events, engaging in everyday talk, and sharing humorous stories—the behaviors fundamental to all families (Afifi, 2003). Try to express your support for your new family members by doing at least some of these things every day.

3. *Create new family rituals.* A critical part of building a new family identity is creating *stepfamily rituals*: events or activities shared between stepfamily

self-reflection

Call to mind an instance of triangulation within your family, your stepfamily, or the family of someone you know. Who was involved? Why was the coalition formed? What impact did the triangulation have on the relationships among the triangulated people? the family as a whole?

self-reflection

Does your family or stepfamily have rituals? Which rituals mean the most to you, and why? How does the regular practice of these rituals affect how you feel about your family or stepfamily?

members that function to define the group as a family. This can be sharing a weekly dinner or attending religious services together. Whatever form it takes, the most constructive stepfamily rituals are those that bring stepfamily members together as a family but still recognize and value what was important from the previous families (Schrodt, 2006).

4. *Avoid triangulating family members.* You may feel it's strategic or even enjoyable to team up and triangulate against a stepparent or stepsibling, but such behavior damages your relationship with them and creates family stress (Schrodt & Afifi, 2007). If you're the one caught in the middle of triangulation, confront the perpetrators. Using your interpersonal skills (cooperative language, competent interpersonal communication), respectfully explain to them how their behavior is making you feel and the damage it is doing to the family. Remind them that stepfamilies are difficult enough to maintain without also having to deal with alliances, loyalty struggles, and power battles. Ask them to please stop.

5. *Be patient.* Whenever families experience a major transition, there is always a lengthy period of adjustment. In the case of remarriage, it typically takes anywhere from three to five *years* for a stepfamily to stabilize as a family unit (Hetherington, 1993). Expect that new relationship bonds are going to take a long time to develop, that you will feel uncertain about your new family roles, and that disputes will arise over privacy rules and personal boundaries (Golish, 2003).

PARENTAL FAVORITISM

Few things matter more to children than expressions of affection from parents (Floyd & Morman, 2005). Such displays include verbal statements ("I love you"),

Some parents manage to equally allocate their resources and affection, while others struggle to disguise their preference for one child over another. What impact might favoritism have on a family's relationship and communication? © St. Petersburg Times/Kathleen Flynn/The Image Works

chapter 11 / Relationships with Family Members   347

How Much Family Favoritism Exists?

Call to mind a family whose favoritism you would like to assess (yours or someone else's). Then mark which of the statements below you agree with. Total the number to calculate your score, and use the key to assess the degree of favoritism in that family.

To take this quiz online, visit LaunchPad: macmillanhighered.com/reflectrelate4e.

Parents, stepparents, or caregivers . . .

_____ punish one child less than others for misbehavior.

_____ openly display more pride in the accomplishments of one child than in those of others.

_____ obviously enjoy sharing time and activities more with one child than with others.

_____ are more sensitive to the thoughts and feelings of one child than to those of others.

_____ give more money and valuable gifts to one child than to others.

_____ are more likely to do favors for one child than for others.

_____ are more supportive of the decisions made by one child than of those made by others.

_____ are more likely to give in to the requests and demands of one child over others.

_____ display more affection and love toward one child than toward others.

_____ listen to and respect the opinions of one child more than those of others.

Note: This *Self-Quiz* is adapted from the Sibling Inventory of Differential Experience (SIDE), Daniels (1986).

Scoring: 0–2 = low favoritism; 3–6 = moderate favoritism; 7–10 = high favoritism.

---

nonverbal contact (hugs, cuddling), gifts, favors, and other resources that make children feel adored and appreciated. But when there is more than one child in the family, competition between children for parental affection becomes a natural part of family life (Golish, 2003).

Many parents respond to this age-old dilemma by equally allocating their affection and resources. However, some parents engage in **parental favoritism:** whereby one or both parents allocate an unfair amount of valuable resources to one child over others. This may include intangible forms of affection, such as statements of love, praise, undue patience (letting one child "get away with anything"), and emotional support. Or it may involve tangible resources, such as cash loans, college tuition, cars, or job offers. For example, when my friend "Susan" was growing up, her father blatantly favored her sister over her. He bought her sister a BMW for her 16th birthday but refused to loan Susan his car when she needed to get to work. Susan's father paid her sister's out-of-state college tuition but refused to contribute toward Susan's community college education. When she finally confronted him about his lifelong favoritism, his response was clear: "Your sister *deserves* all I've given her because I love her more than you."

Parental favoritism has profound and enduring effects. Because favored children garner more of their parents' resources, they are more likely than their siblings to be professionally successful as adults (Hertwig, Davis, & Sulloway, 2002).

Media Note: Parental Favoritism
A *Time* magazine article "Playing Favorites" (Kluger, 2011) said: "Never mind what your parents told you. They have a favorite child—and if you have kids, so do you. Why it's hardwired into all of us." Comedies like *Modern Family* and *Everybody Loves Raymond* regularly depict such favoritism. Parents often choose favorites based on physical appearance, gender, birth order, and similarities with the parent. Ask students the following: Do you believe your parents (or friends' parents) have a favorite child? Do any of the above-mentioned reasons apply? Why? What difficulty has favoritism caused in your family?

Favored children also report a greater sense of well-being and life satisfaction in adulthood than do disfavored children (Suitor et al., 2009). At the same time, the *relational* consequences are devastating, especially for siblings. Studies show that siblings from households in which favoritism occurred feel and express substantially less warmth and more hostility toward one another than those from households where it did not. Similarly, siblings from favoritism families are substantially less close and report more conflict than those who grew up in equitable families (Suitor et al., 2009). This is true regardless of family size, gender of siblings, or the family's ethnicity.

What's the best approach for dealing with parental favoritism? First, realize that favoritism is never the fault of the favored child. The sad truth is that some parents play favorites. If you're a disfavored child, avoid blaming your sibling. If you feel unmanageable resentment toward your favored sibling, seek counseling. Second, carefully consider whether it is worth confronting your parents. Unfortunately, challenging parental unfairness is unlikely to bring about positive outcomes. For one thing, you can't control your parents' behavior. Some parents may not even realize they favor one child over others, especially if their favoritism is subtle (for example, differential praise, attention, or emotional support). In such cases, challenging parents for being "unfair" will only hurt their feelings and create a rift between you, them, and the favored sibling. Alternatively, if your parents recognize and relish their preferential treatment, confrontation may lead them to defend their behavior in ways that hurt your feelings further.

Instead, focus on maintaining your sibling relationship by regularly practicing positivity, assurances, and self-disclosure. If you're a favored child, realize that your siblings may resent you and all you've gained. Discuss this openly with them, and look for opportunities to "balance things out" between you and them through acts of generosity and support. To repair the relational damage done by their father, for instance, Susan's sister began quietly funneling financial support to Susan to help her pay for nursing school. Although Susan and her father no longer speak, she and her sister are quite close. This is an unusual outcome, only achieved through both sisters' hard work to overcome the bitter wedge driven between them in their youth.

INTERPARENTAL CONFLICT

One of the most potent family challenges is **interparental conflict:** overt, hostile interactions between parents in a household. While such constant fighting is harmful to the parents' relationship, the impact on children in the household is worse. Interparental conflict is associated with children's social problems, including lower levels of play with peers and lower friendship quality (Rodrigues & Kitzmann, 2007). Such children are also more likely to imitate their parents' destructive interaction styles and, consequently, are more at risk for aggressive and delinquent behaviors (Krishnakumar, Buehler, & Barber, 2003).

But the most devastating effects of interparental conflict are relational. Adolescents who perceive a high frequency of interparental conflict are more likely to report feelings of jealousy and fears of abandonment in their romantic relationships

(Hayashi & Strickland, 1998). Interparental conflict also negatively impacts late teen and adult perceptions of interpersonal trust, love attitudes, sexual behaviors, relationship beliefs, cohabitation, and attitudes toward marriage and divorce (Rodrigues & Kitzmann, 2007).

Why do children suffer so many profound and negative outcomes from fights between parents? One explanation is the **spillover hypothesis:** emotions, affect, and mood from the parental relationship "spill over" into the broader family, disrupting children's sense of emotional security (Krishnakumar et al., 2003). Children living in households torn by interparental conflict experience a chronic sense of instability—not knowing when the next battle will erupt and if or when their parents will break up. This gives them a deep-seated sense of emotional insecurity related to relationships (Rodrigues & Kitzmann, 2007), which manifests in their own intimate involvements, months and even years later. Of course, the spillover hypothesis works both ways: children growing up in households in which parents actively *support* each other's parenting efforts and *calmly discuss* disagreements are more likely to be satisfied in their relationships with their parents, and report better mental health overall, including lower levels of stress and anxiety (Schrodt & Shimkowski, 2013).

What can you do to manage interparental conflict and its outcomes? If you're the child of parents who fight, encourage them individually to approach their conflicts more constructively. Share with them all you know about conflict from Chapter 9: effective approaches for managing conflict, the negative role of self-enhancing thoughts, the dangers associated with destructive messages, and the trap of serial arguments. If you feel that you are suffering negative outcomes from having grown up in a conflict-ridden household, seek therapy from a reputable counselor. And if you're a parent with children, realize this: *everything you say and do within the family realm—including interactions you have with your spouse or partner—spills over into the emotions and feelings of your children.*

The Primacy of Family

> Family ties run so deep that we often use kinship as a metaphor to describe closeness in other relationships

As with romantic relationships, the day-to-day work of maintaining family bonds isn't especially glamorous. Birth, adoption, marriage, or remarriage may structure your family, but the quality of your family relationships is defined by whether you invest time and energy in your interpersonal communication. Such efforts don't have to be complex: a story told to your child or shared with a sibling, gratitude expressed to a parent, an affectionate e-mail sent to a grandparent—all of these simple acts of communication keep your family bonds alive and thriving.

Yet we often neglect to communicate with family members in these ways, in part because such relationships lack the sparkle, excitement, and drama of romances. When we dismiss, look past, or simply take for granted our families, we're like Dorothy in *The Wizard of Oz*—running away from Auntie Em and the farm, thinking we'll do just fine on our own.

---

skills practice

Managing Interparental Conflict
Helping parents better manage their conflicts

❶ Following a significant conflict between parents or caregivers, reach out to each person individually, letting them know you're available to talk.

❷ Encourage them to be mindful of how negative emotions and flawed attributions shape their conflict perceptions and decisions.

❸ Remind them of the relational damage wrought by destructive messages.

❹ Help them identify the causes of the conflict.

❺ List goals and long-term interests they have in common.

❻ Use these points of commonality to collaboratively create solutions that will prevent similar conflicts in the future.

❼ Evaluate these solutions in terms of fairness for both of them.

making relationship choices

Struggling with Family Transitions

1 BACKGROUND

One of the biggest challenges family members face is transitioning from a family to a stepfamily. To understand how you might competently manage such a relationship challenge, read the case study in Part 2; then, drawing on all you know about interpersonal communication, work through the problem-solving model in Part 3.

 Visit LaunchPad to check out the other side of the story (Part 4). For the best experience, complete all parts in LaunchPad: **macmillanhighered.com/reflectrelate4e**.

2 CASE STUDY

Your parents married young, and it was a bad match. Your dad is cold, authoritarian, and a strict disciplinarian. You respect and fear him more than you love him. In contrast, your mom is affectionate and outgoing. She's your principal source of emotional support, and the two of you are very close.

During your childhood, your dad dominated the family. His decisions were law, and family discussions were rare. Your parents fought constantly over his need for control, and your mom eventually divorced him and gained custody.

Despite the divorce, your dad continued to believe that the family would someday reunite. This fantasy was shattered when your mom married Stephan. Stephan is the opposite of your dad; he is open, funny, and kind. He places enormous value on talking things through as a family and welcomes your opinion, even when it differs from his. Slowly you adjust to having a diversity of views encouraged and your opinion valued. You come to adore Stephan, and relish the warm, witty, and varied discussions of your stepfamily.

Your dad remains bitter about your mom's remarriage. He constantly mocks Stephan in e-mails to you. He also plies you for personal information about your mother and her marriage. You feel like a spy. When you tell your mom about your dad's prying, she is furious, and a huge fight erupts between them. The tension is resolved when you leave for college because your parents cease contact with each other.

You're home for the weekend, visiting your dad. When the topic of your mom arises, your dad stuns you by confessing that he still loves her. He says he realizes now that they will never be together, and he blames Stephan for "ruining everything!" He demands that you choose between him and Stephan. He threatens to move away and sever ties with you unless you cut off contact with Stephan, saying, "Knowing you've replaced me with another father reminds me of all I've lost!" Later, when you call your mom and tell her what happened, she says, "Good! He *should* leave. I know *I'm* happier without him in my life. You will be, too!" The next day, your dad shoots you a text, asking whether you've made a decision yet.

3 YOUR TURN

Think about all you've learned thus far about interpersonal communication. Then work through the following five steps. Remember, there are no "right" answers, so think hard about what is the *best* choice! (P.S. Need help? See the *Helpful Concepts* list.)

step 1
Reflect on yourself. What are your thoughts and feelings in this situation? What attributions are you making about your dad? Are your attributions accurate? Why or why not?

step 2
Reflect on your partner. Using perspective-taking and empathic concern, put yourself in your dad's shoes. What is he thinking and feeling in this situation?

step 3
Identify the optimal outcome. Think about all the information you have about your communication and relationship with your dad and the situation surrounding your parents' divorce and your mom's remarriage. Consider your own feelings as well as your dad's. Given all these factors, what's the best, most constructive outcome possible? Consider what's best for you *and* for your dad.

step 4
Locate the roadblocks. Taking into consideration your own and your dad's thoughts and feelings and all that has happened in this situation, what obstacles are keeping you from achieving the optimal outcome?

step 5
Chart your course. What can you say to your dad to overcome the roadblocks you've identified and achieve your optimal outcome?

HELPFUL CONCEPTS

Protective and pluralistic families, 336–337
Maintenance strategies for families, 338–339
Balancing openness and protection, 341–344
Triangulation, 345–346
Interparental conflict, 348–349

4 THE OTHER SIDE

▶ Visit LaunchPad to watch a video in which your dad tells his side of the case study story. As in many real-life situations, this is information to which you did not have access when you were initially crafting your response in Part 3. The video reminds us that even when we do our best to offer competent responses, there is always another side to the story that we need to consider.

351

But life is *not* a skip down the yellow brick road. When we battle metaphorical witches in the form of hardship, disappointment, and even tragedy, it's our family members who often lock arms with us. They're the ones who help us charge forward, even though we're afraid or discouraged. The truth about our family relationships stands like the wizard behind the curtain. When you step forward boldly and pull the curtain back, it's revealed. There is no place like home.

POSTSCRIPT

We began this chapter with a world champion and the family that encouraged her to excel. Throughout her life, Brenda Villa's parents have been a source of inspiration and motivation. Through their support, honesty, sacrifice, and love, they created the foundation on which Brenda has built the most successful water polo career in U.S. history.

To whom do you turn to listen—or to provide you with a necessary kick in the butt—when you're feeling sorry for yourself? From whom did you get the confidence and swagger to face the competitions that life presents?

The story of Brenda Villa and her parents reminds us of a simple truth regarding the primacy of family. The successes, victories, and medals we achieve in our lives may be won through our own efforts, but they were made possible by the people who raised us.

LaunchPad for *Reflect & Relate* offers videos and encourages self-assessment through adaptive quizzing. Go to **macmillanhighered.com /reflectrelate4e** to get access to:

 LearningCurve Adaptive Quizzes

 Video clips that help you understand interpersonal communication

key terms

- family, 328
- nuclear family, 329
- extended family, 330
- stepfamily, 330
- cohabiting couples, 330
- single-parent family, 330
- voluntary kin family, 330
- family stories, 331
- Family Communication Patterns Theory, 335
- conversation orientation, 335
- conformity orientation, 335
- ▶ consensual families, 336
- ▶ pluralistic families, 336
- ▶ protective families, 337
- ▶ laissez-faire families, 337
- relational dialectics, 340
- Communication Privacy Management Theory, 342
- family privacy rules, 343
- triangulation, 345
- parental favoritism, 347
- interparental conflict, 348
- spillover hypothesis, 349

▶ You can watch brief, illustrative videos of these terms and test your understanding of the concepts in LaunchPad.

key concepts

Defining Family

- Given the diversity in contemporary **family** structures, scholars define *family* in very inclusive ways. Families come in myriad forms, including **nuclear, extended, step-, cohabiting couples, single-parent,** and **voluntary kin families.**
- Families solidify their sense of identity by sharing **family stories.** These narrative accounts of birth, courtship, and survival bind children, parents, and other relatives together.

Communicating in Families

- Regardless of the structure of a family, **Family Communication Patterns Theory** suggests that most families' communication is determined by two dimensions: **conversation orientation** and **conformity orientation.**
- These two dimensions often lead to four family communication patterns: **consensual, pluralistic, protective,** and **laissez-faire.** Such families have very different communication beliefs and practices, which shape interpersonal relationships among family members.

Maintaining Family Relationships

- Three of the most important strategies for maintaining family relationships are positivity, assurances, and self-disclosure. Technology is making it easier for family members to communicate such maintenance strategies, especially when distance separates them.
- The ways family members deal with dialectical tensions can be understood through **Communication Privacy Management Theory.** These boundaries are defined by **family privacy rules:** the conditions governing what family members can talk about, how they can discuss such topics, and who should have access to family-relevant information.

Family Relationship Challenges

- A common challenge in stepfamily transition is **triangulation.** Such loyalty conflicts can make individuals feel torn between family members.
- **Parental favoritism** can include both intangible and tangible forms of affection and often drives a wedge between siblings, in addition to other long-term effects.
- Dealing with **interparental conflict** is one of the hardest family communication challenges. Such fights can have long-term and devastating effects on both parents and the children, as explained by the **spillover hypothesis.**

Our friends keep us grounded and provide us with support in times of crisis.

He is the only animated character in history to have a wax likeness in Madame Tussauds New York museum. He has inspired albums, video games, and theme park rides. The media franchise controlling his image is an $8 billion global industry. But the story of SpongeBob SquarePants is not one of a solitary sea sponge sitting alone at the bottom of the ocean. Instead, it's a tale of friendship and the deep and recognizable connections that exist between the characters.

SpongeBob is the brainchild of marine biologist and animator Stephen Hillenburg. While working at the Ocean Institute in California, Hillenburg created a comic titled "The Intertidal Zone," to educate students about oceanic animal life. Inspired to expand the characters into an animated feature, he pitched the plan to Nickelodeon executives, accompanied by Hawaiian music and an underwater terrarium. Nickelodeon funded the project, and the series was born.

At the center of the show are the friendships SpongeBob shares with Sandy, Squidward, and Patrick. Sandy is a consistent voice of reason, supporting SpongeBob when he gets into trouble by offering useful advice. In "MuscleBob Buffpants" (season 1, episode 11a), for instance, Sandy helps SpongeBob with his strength training, although her exercise regimen proves too daunting (SpongeBob ends up buying inflatable muscle arms instead). The support goes both ways. In "House Sittin' for Sandy" (season 8, episode

© Paramount Pictures/Photofest

12 / Relationships with Friends

165a), she asks SpongeBob to take care of her Treedome while she is away. When the result is disastrous, Sandy forgives him.

Although Squidward delights in insulting SpongeBob, beneath his gruff exterior he seems to harbor genuine affection for his spongy friend. In the episode "Squidville" (season 2, episode 26b), Squidward becomes so enraged by SpongeBob's reef-blower play that he explodes, "I would rather tear out my brain stem, carry it to the middle of the nearest four-way intersection, and skip rope with it than go on living where I do now!" But when he moves away, he finds himself missing his former neighbor.

SpongeBob's *best* friend is Patrick. Whether it's chasing jellyfish, selling chocolates, or playing "Robot-Pirate Island" in an empty cardboard box, they do almost everything together. At the core of their friendship is emotional support. In "Big Pink Loser" (season 2, episode 23a), Patrick is heartbroken when he realizes he has never won an award. SpongeBob immediately steps up, coaching Patrick through the task of opening a jar. When Patrick finally (after many failed attempts) succeeds, they mutually celebrate Patrick's "triumph."

SpongeBob's friendships are not without challenges, however. He betrays Sandy by mocking squirrels as part of his comedy act ("What's up with that squirrel fur? I guess fleas need a home, too!"). Patrick gets SpongeBob into trouble at school by drawing an insulting picture of the teacher, then allowing SpongeBob to take the blame. SpongeBob is consumed with jealousy when Patrick replaces him as Grandma Sponge's "baby." But despite these difficulties, the friends always manage to maintain their relationships.

SpongeBob SquarePants has won multiple Emmys, Kids' Choice Awards, and BAFTA Children's Awards. Images of SpongeBob have been embraced by groups as diverse as American schoolchildren and Egyptian revolutionaries. But the resonance of the show lies within a text deeper than its silliness. When we watch SpongeBob, we're reminded of the complexities of our own friendships. Our friends are people who are similar to us, but annoy us. They help us and have our backs, but also hurt us. They lift us up but can also tear us down. Ultimately, though, our friends are the people we choose to share our lives with because, beyond everything else, *we enjoy their companionship*.

It may strike you as strange to think of your friendships as similar to those of an animated sea sponge who lives in a pineapple. Nevertheless, the friendships that fill our lives are akin to SpongeBob's in important ways. We are drawn to our friends through the realization of shared interests. We count on our friends to provide support. We build our friendships by disclosing our thoughts, feelings, and vulnerabilities, while trusting our friends to not betray us. At the same time, our friendships can be difficult to define. They lack the permanence of family bonds and the clear constraints and expectations of romantic involvements. This makes them more fragile and confusing than other close relationships.

In this chapter, we look at friendship. You'll learn:

- How friendships are unique and distinct
- Varied types of friendships you'll experience
- Ways you can communicate so that your friendships survive and thrive
- Challenges to friendships and how to overcome them

chapter outline

357 The Nature of Friendship

363 Types of Friendships

368 Maintaining Friendships

372 Friendship Challenges

379 The Importance of Friends

The Nature of Friendship

Friendships are both delicate and deep

Like family and romantic bonds, friendship plays a crucial role in our lives. Friendship is an important source of emotional security and self-esteem (Rawlins, 1992). Friendship facilitates a sense of belonging when we're young, helps solidify our identity during adolescence, and provides satisfaction and social support when we're elderly (Miller, Hefner, & Scott, 2007). But what exactly *is* friendship?

FRIENDSHIP DEFINED

Friendship is a voluntary interpersonal relationship characterized by intimacy and liking (McEwan, Babin Gallagher, & Farinelli, 2008). Whether it's casual or close, short or long term, friendship has several distinguishing characteristics.

Friendship Is Voluntary We have greater liberty in choosing our friends than we do in choosing partners for any other relationship type (Sias et al., 2008). Whether a friendship forms is determined largely by the people involved, based on their mutual desire to create such a relationship. This is different from romantic, workplace, and family involvements. Consider romantic relationships. You may face substantial familial or cultural constraints in your choice of romantic partners. You may be expected (or allowed) to date only people of a certain age, gender, ethnicity, religion, or income level. You may even have a spouse chosen *for* you in an arranged marriage. In the workplace (discussed in our Appendix), you are required to work collaboratively with certain people, whether you like them or not. And in your family, you're bound to others through birth, adoption, or the creation of a stepfamily. These ties are involuntary. As French

Chapter Theme

This chapter is about the intimacy and intricacy of friendship. We forge friendships freely from shared interests. We then struggle to maintain them in the face of challenges, including separation, betrayal, and attraction. Although they lack the ties of family and the expectations of romance, our friendships form a bulwark against life stress. When lovers, family members, or coworkers cause us pain, we turn to our friends for caring and support.

self-reflection

What constraints, if any, do you face in whom you can choose as friends? Who puts these limits on you? In your experience, do you have more, or less, freedom in choosing friends than lovers? How does this influence your choice of friends?

▶ In the TV show *Community*, the study group at Greendale College meets purely by chance. Despite their frequent bickering, they become loyal friends and support one another through many adventures. How did you meet your closest friends? NBC/Photofest

Assignment: Characterizing Friendships

When assigning the reading for this chapter, ask students to write a short reflective paper on this statement from scholar William Rawlins: "Friendships are permeated with ambiguities." What does it mean to them? If they consider the many types of friendships, how they are created, and all the different rules for each, is it even possible to fully define friendship? What characteristics of a friendship would they add to the ones listed in the book? This short paper should encourage some interesting insights when discussing the chapter.

poet Jacques Delille (1738–1813) put it, "Fate chooses your relations, you choose your friends."

Friendship Is Driven by Shared Interests

Similarity is the primary force that draws us to our friends (Parks & Floyd, 1996). This is true across ages, genders, sexual orientations, and ethnicities. One practical implication of this is that when your interests and activities change, so do your friendships. If you change your political or religious beliefs or suffer an injury that prevents you from playing a beloved sport, friendships related to those things may change as well. Some friendships will endure—the focus of the relationship shifting to new points of commonality—but others will fade away. One of the most common reasons for friendships ending is a change in shared interests and beliefs (Miller et al., 2007).

Friendship Is Characterized by Self-Disclosure

We consider most people in our lives "acquaintances." Only a select few rise to the level of "friends." What distinguishes the two groups? *Self-disclosure*. Both men and women report that being able to freely and deeply disclose is *the* defining feature of friendship (Parks & Floyd, 1996). Self-disclosure between friends means sharing private thoughts and feelings, and believing that "we can tell each other anything." The relationship between friendship and self-disclosure is reciprocal as well. The more you consider someone a friend, the more you will disclose; and the more you disclose, the more you will consider that person a friend (Shelton, Trail, West, & Bergsieker, 2010).

Friendship Is Rooted in Liking   We feel affection and respect for our friends. In other words, we *like* them (Rubin, 1973). We also enjoy their company; pleasure in sharing time together is a defining feature of friendships (Hays, 1988). At the same time, because friendships are rooted in liking—rather than love—we're not as emotionally attached to our friends as we are to other intimates, and we're not as emotionally demanding of them. Correspondingly, we're expected to be more loyal to and more willing to help romantic partners and family members than friends (Davis & Todd, 1985).

Friendship Is Volatile   Friendships are less stable, more likely to change, and easier to break off than family or romantic relationships (Johnson, Wittenberg, Villagran, Mazur, & Villagran, 2003). Why? Consider the differences in depth of commitment. We're bonded to friends by choice, rooted in shared interests. But we're bonded to families by social and legal commitment, and to lovers by deep emotional and sexual attachment. These loyalties mean we may choose or forgo professional opportunities to preserve romances or stay close to family. But most of us will choose to pursue our careers over staying geographically close to friends (Patterson, 2007).

FRIENDSHIP FUNCTIONS

Friendships serve many functions in our lives. Two of the most important are that they help us fulfill our need for *companionship*—chances to do fun things together and receive emotional support—and they help us *achieve practical goals*—deal with problems or everyday tasks (de Vries, 1996). These functions are not mutually exclusive, as many friendships facilitate both.

Communal Friendships   One of the functions friendships serve is enabling us to share life events and activities with others. Compared to family and work relationships, friendship interactions are the least task oriented and tend to revolve around leisure activities, such as talking or eating (Argyle & Furnham, 1982). Scholar William Rawlins (1992) describes friendships that focus primarily on sharing time and activities together as **communal friendships**. Communal friends try to get together as often as possible, and they provide encouragement and emotional support to one another during times of need. Because emotional support is a central aspect of communal friendship, only when both friends fulfill the expectations of support for the relationship does the friendship endure (Burleson & Samter, 1994).

Agentic Friendships   We also look to friends for help in achieving practical goals in both our personal and our professional lives. Friends help us study for exams, fix cars, set up computers, and our complete professional projects. Friendships

---

self-reflection

Call to mind your three closest friends in middle school. Then do the same for high school. Now think about your three closest friends today. Are the lists the same? How have they changed? Why? What does this tell you about the volatility of friendships?

Assignment: Types of Friends

Play the LaunchPad clips on **communal friendships** and **agentic friendships**. Place students in pairs, and ask them to Think-Ink-Pair-Share about an example of each type of friendship: What are the differences in the relationships? (Have them be as specific as possible.) Are some friendships a mix of both categories? Do friends ever change categories?

self-reflection

Do you have more communal or agentic friends? How do you communicate differently with the two types of friends? Which type of friend do you depend on more, day to day? Why?

▶ In *Dallas Buyers Club*, Ron Woodroof forms an agentic friendship with Rayon, a transgender woman. Both are HIV positive, and they start a business selling unapproved drugs that fight HIV. Can you recall a time when an agentic friend helped you achieve a significant goal? Anne Marie Fox/© Focus Features/Everett Collection

▶ **Video**

macmillanhighered.com
/reflectrelate4e

Communal Friendships
Watch this clip online to answer the questions below.

Why are the men in this video considered communal friends? How much do factors like gender, culture, shared interests, and self-disclosure influence your communal friendships?

Want to see more? Check out LaunchPad for a clip illustrating **agentic friendships**.

in which the parties focus primarily on helping each other achieve practical goals are known as **agentic friendships** (Rawlins, 1992). Agentic friends value sharing time together—but only if they're available and have no other priorities at the moment. They also aren't interested in the emotional interdependence and mutual sharing of personal information that characterize communal friendships. They're available when the need arises, but beyond that, they're uncomfortable with more personal demands or responsibilities. For example, an agentic friend from work may gladly help you write up a monthly sales report, but she may feel uncomfortable if you ask her for advice about your romantic problems.

FRIENDSHIP ACROSS THE LIFE SPAN

The importance we attribute to our friendships changes throughout our lives. Up through fourth grade, most children look to their family as their sole source of emotional support (Furman & Simon, 1998). If a child suffers a disappointment at school, has a frightening dream, or just wants to share the events of the day, he or she will turn to parents or siblings. But during adolescence, children slowly transfer their emotional attachment from their family to friends (Welch & Houser, 2010). For example, by seventh grade, young people rely just as much on same-sex friends as they do on family for support. By tenth grade, same-sex friends have become the principal providers of emotional support. This trend continues into early adulthood: for college students, friends are the primary relationship for fulfilling relational needs (McEwan et al., 2008).

By middle adulthood, many people form long-term romantic commitments and start families of their own. Consequently, their romantic partners and children become the primary providers of companionship, affection, and support. The importance of friendships begins to wane (Carbery & Buhrmester, 1998). This is especially the case for married men, who before marriage tend to spend most of their time with male friends (Cohen, 1992). Late in life, however, the pattern shifts back once more, as spouses and siblings pass on and children form their own families. For the elderly, friendships are the most important relationships for providing social support and intimacy (Patterson, 2007).

FRIENDSHIP, CULTURE, AND GENDER

People from different cultures have varied expectations regarding friendships. For example, most Westerners believe that friendships don't endure, that you'll naturally lose some friends and gain others over time (Berscheid & Regan, 2005). This belief contrasts sharply with attitudes in other cultures, in which people view friendships as deeply intimate and lasting. As just one example, when asked to identify the closest relationship in their lives, Euro-Americans tend to select romantic partners, whereas Japanese tend to select friends (Gudykunst & Nishida, 1993).

Friendship beliefs and practices across cultures are also entangled with gender norms. In the United States and Canada, for instance, friendships between women are often stereotyped as communal, whereas men's friendships are thought to be agentic. But male and female same-sex friendships are more similar than they are different (Winstead, Derlaga, & Rose, 1997).[1] Men and women rate the importance of both kinds of friendships equally (Roy, Benenson, & Lilly, 2000), and studies of male friendships in North America have found that companionship is the primary need met by the relationship (Wellman, 1992).

At the same time, Euro-American men, unlike women, learn to avoid direct expressions of affection and intimacy in their friendships with other males. Owing to traditional masculine gender roles, a general reluctance to openly show emotion, and homophobia (among other factors), many men avoid verbal and nonverbal intimacy in their same-sex friendships, such as disclosing personal feelings and vulnerabilities, touching, and hugging (Bank & Hansford, 2000). But in many other cultures, both men and women look to same-sex friends as their primary source of intimacy. For example, in southern Spain, men and women report feeling more comfortable revealing their deepest thoughts to same-sex friends than to spouses (Brandes, 1987). Traditional Javanese (Indonesian) culture holds that marriage should not be too intimate and that a person's most intimate relationship should be with his or her same-sex friends (Williams, 1992).

FRIENDSHIP AND TECHNOLOGY

As with other interpersonal relationships, communication technologies such as social networking sites, Instagram, Snapchat, Twitter, smartphones, e-mail, and text-messaging have reshaped the way people create friendships. In the past, people forged friendships slowly. They took time to discover the values and

Assignment: Friendship Survey
Researchers Blieszner and Adams (1992) asked participants, "What does friendship mean to you?" They discovered that social and individual characteristics, such as age or stage of life, influence a person's view of friendship. Instruct students to conduct a quick friendship survey by asking several males and females, ranging in age and life experience, the same question. How do male and female responses differ, or how are they similar? Do age or life experiences affect the individuals' responses?

self-reflection
Think of friends you only know and interact with online, and compare them with the friends who populate your offline world. Which friends do you consider closer? When you're confronted with a challenging problem or personal crisis, which friends do you turn to for support? Why?

---

[1] As defined in Chapter 2, *gender* is the composite of social, psychological, and cultural attributes that characterize us as male or female (Canary, Emmers-Sommer, & Faulkner, 1997). *Sex* refers to the biological sex organs with which we're born. When communicating, people orient to gender, not sex (which they typically don't see!). But use of the terms *sex* and *gender* by scholars is often inconsistent (Parks, 2007). For example, within the friendship literature, male-female friendships are referred to as *opposite-sex* and male-male and female-female friendships as *same-sex*, rather than *opposite-gender* and *same-gender*. Consequently, in this section, we use the terms *cross-sex* and *same-sex*.

▶ Communication technologies have reshaped the way people create and maintain friendships. Even while socializing with friends face-to-face, it is now possible to stay connected to friends who aren't present. How do you maintain friendships using online communication? Nick David/Getty Images

interests of their neighbors, coworkers, and acquaintances, and only then built friendships with those who shared their values and interests. Now, however, you can form friendships quickly and with more people—some whom you may never actually meet in person—simply by friending them on Facebook or other online communities (Stafford, 2005). This provides a valuable resource to people suffering from chronic shyness. They can interact with others and garner social and emotional support without suffering the anxiety that direct face-to-face contact may cause (Pennington, 2009).

Of course, just because someone is your "Facebook friend" doesn't necessarily mean that they're a "real" friend. For example, 80 percent of Facebook users report that their real-world friends are also Facebook friends (Pennington, 2009). But the inverse isn't true. Most people have dozens of friends, four (or so) close friends, and one (or more) "best" friend—yet well over three *hundred* Facebook friends (Pennington, 2009). The vast bulk of these "friends" aren't friends at all but instead coworkers, acquaintances, neighbors, family, and the like.

Communication technologies make it possible for friends to stay constantly connected with one another. For better or worse, you can now keep your friends updated 24/7 on the latest news in your life through posts and messages. Interestingly, much like within families, technology does not replace in-person interaction. People who regularly use cell phones to call and text their friends are *more* likely to also seek face-to-face encounters (Wang & Andersen, 2007).

Despite all of this technology, people continue to recognize the superiority of offline relationships and communication. Studies comparing offline versus online friendships find that offline friendships have higher degrees of intimacy, understanding, interdependence, and commitment (Chan & Cheng, 2004). Additionally, people prefer face-to-face interactions with friends when discussing deeply personal or troubling topics (Pennington, 2009).

Types of Friendships

Characteristics and roles of different friends

Across our lives, each of us experiences many different types of friendships. Some are intensely close; others less so. Some are with people who seem similar to us in every conceivable way; others with those who, at least "on paper," seem quite different. But when we consider all of the various friendships that arise and decay, two stand out from the rest as unique, challenging, and significant: best friends and cross-category friends.

BEST FRIENDS

Think of the people you consider *close* friends—people with whom you exchange deeply personal information and emotional support, with whom you share many interests and activities, and around whom you feel comfortable and at ease (Parks & Floyd, 1996). How many come to mind? Chances are you can count them on one hand. A study surveying over 1,000 individuals found that, on average, people have four close friends (Galupo, 2009).

But what makes a close friend a *best* friend? Many things. First, best friends are typically same-sex rather than cross-sex (Galupo, 2009). Although we may have close cross-sex friendships, comparatively few of these relationships evolve to being a "best." Second, best friendship involves greater intimacy, more disclosure, and deeper commitment than does close friendship (Weisz & Wood, 2005). People talk more frequently and more deeply with best friends about their relationships, emotions, life events, and goals (Pennington, 2009). This holds true for both women *and* men. Third, people count on their best friends to listen to their problems without judging and to "have their back"—provide unconditional support (Pennington, 2009). Fourth, best friendship is distinct from close friendship in the degree to which shared activities commit the friends to each other in substantial ways. For example, best friends are more likely to join clubs together, participate on intramural or community sports teams together, move in together as roommates, or spend a spring break or another type of vacation together (Becker et al., 2009).

Finally, the *most* important factor that distinguishes best friends is unqualified provision of **identity support:** behaving in ways that convey understanding, acceptance, and support for a friend's valued social identities. **Valued social identities** are the aspects of your public self that you deem the most important in defining who you are—for example, musician, athlete, poet, dancer, teacher, mother, and so on. Whoever we are—and whoever we dream of being—our best friends understand us, accept us, respect us, and support us, no matter what. Say that a close friend who is a pacifist suddenly announces that she is joining the army because she feels strongly about defending our country. What would you say to her? Or imagine that a good friend tells you that he is actually not gay but transgendered and henceforth will be living as a woman in accordance with his true gender. How would you respond? In each of these cases, *best* friends would distinguish themselves by supporting such identity shifts even if they found

self-reflection

Call to mind your most valued social identities. Which friends provide the most acceptance, respect, and support of these identities? Which friends do you consider closest? What's the relationship between the two? What does this tell you about the importance of identity support in determining friendship intimacy?

them surprising. Research following friendships across a four-year time span found that more than any other factor—including amount of communication and perceived closeness—participants who initially reported high levels of identity support from a new friend were more likely to describe that person as their *best* friend four years later (Weisz & Wood, 2005).

CROSS-CATEGORY FRIENDSHIPS

Given that friendships center on shared interests and identity support, it's no surprise that people tend to befriend those who are similar demographically (with regard to age, gender, economic status, etc.). As just one example, studies of straight, gay, lesbian, bisexual, and transgendered persons find that regardless of sexual orientation or gender identity, people are more likely to have close friendships with others of the same ethnicity (Galupo, 2009). But people also regularly defy this norm, forging friendships that cross demographic lines, known as **cross-category friendships** (Galupo, 2009). Such friendships are a powerful way to break down ingroup and outgroup perceptions and purge people of negative stereotypes. The four most common cross-category friendships are cross-sex, cross-orientation, intercultural, and interethnic.

Cross-Sex Friendships   One of the most radical shifts in interpersonal relationship patterns over the past few decades has been the increase in platonic (nonsexual) friendships between men and women in the United States and Canada. In the nineteenth century, friendships were almost exclusively same-sex, and throughout most of the twentieth century, cross-sex friendships remained a rarity (Halatsis & Christakis, 2009). For example, a study of friendship conducted in 1974 found that, on average, men and women had few or no close cross-sex friends (Booth & Hess, 1974). However, by the mid-1980s, 40 percent of men and 30 percent of women reported having close cross-sex friendships (Rubin, 1985). By the late 1990s, 47 percent of tenth- and twelfth-graders reported having a close cross-sex friend (Kuttler, LaGreca, & Prinstein, 1999).

Most cross-sex friendships are not motivated by sexual attraction (Messman, Canary, & Hause, 1994). Instead, both men and women agree that through cross-sex friendships, they gain a greater understanding of how members of the other sex think, feel, and behave (Halatsis & Christakis, 2009). For men, forming friendships with women provides the possibility of greater intimacy and emotional depth than is typically available in male-male friendships (Monsour, 1997).

Despite changing attitudes toward cross-sex friendships, men and women face several challenges in building such relationships. For one thing, they've learned from early childhood to segregate themselves by sex. In many schools, young boys and girls are placed in separate gym classes, asked to line up separately

◯ In addition to the benefits that come with friendship, such as companionship and shared interests, cross-category friends are often exposed to cultural experiences they may not have otherwise encountered. (Top to bottom) David Alan Harvey/Magnum; Noel Vasquez/Getty Images; Wayne Miller/Magnum Photos; © Ann Cutting/Alamy; SassyStock/Fotosearch

In *New Girl,* main character Jess forms a close friendship with her male loftmates. Though they all have very different personalities and interests, they bond through shared humor. Adam Taylor/© Fox/Everett Collection

Online Self-Quiz:
What Kind of Friend Are You? To take this self-quiz, visit LaunchPad:
macmillanhighered.com /reflectrelate4e

Discussion Prompt: Cross-Sex Friendships
Bleske-Rechek and colleagues (2012, p. 593) claim, "Attraction between cross-sex friends is common, and it is perceived more often as a burden than as a benefit." Show the clip from *When Harry Met Sally* when Harry explains his theory of why women and men cannot be friends (http://movieclips .com/VBD2c-when-harry-met -sally-movie-cant-be-friends/). Ask students: Do you agree with Harry? What are the advantages of cross-sex friendships? What are the disadvantages? Can a cross-sex friendship provide insight on romantic relationships?

for class, and instructed to engage in competitions pitting "the boys against the girls" (Thorne, 1986). It's no surprise, then, that young children overwhelmingly prefer friends of the same sex (Reeder, 2003). As a consequence of this early-life segregation, most children enter their teens with only limited experience in building cross-sex friendships. Neither adolescence nor adulthood provides many opportunities for gaining this experience. Leisure-oriented activities such as competitive sports, community programs, and social organizations—including the Boy Scouts and Girl Scouts—are typically sex segregated (Swain, 1992).

Another challenge is that our society promotes same-sex friendship and cross-sex coupling as the two most acceptable relationship options for men and women. So no matter how rigorously a pair of cross-sex friends insist that they're "just friends," their surrounding friends and family members will likely meet these claims with skepticism or even disapproval (Monsour, 1997). Family members, if they approve of the friendship, often pester such couples to become romantically involved: "You and Jen have so much in common! Why not take things to the next level?" If families disapprove, they encourage termination of the relationship: "I don't want people thinking my daughter is hanging out casually with some guy. Why don't you hang out with other girls instead?" Romantic partners of people involved in cross-sex friendships often vehemently disapprove of such involvements (Hansen, 1985). Owing to constant disapproval from others and the pressure to justify the relationship, cross-sex friendships are far less stable than same-sex friendships (Berscheid & Regan, 2005).

Cross-Orientation Friendships A second type of cross-category friendship is *cross-orientation*: friendships between lesbian, gay, bisexual, transgendered, or queer (LGBTQ) people and straight men or women. As within all friendships, cross-orientation friends are bonded by shared interests and activities and provide each other with support and affection. But these friendships also provide unique rewards for the parties involved (Galupo, 2007). For straight men and women, forming a cross-orientation friendship can help correct negative stereotypes about persons of other sexual orientations and the LGBTQ community as a whole. For LGBTQ persons, having a straight friend can provide much-needed emotional and social support from outside the LGBTQ community, helping to further insulate them from societal homophobia (Galupo, 2007).

Although cross-orientation friendships are commonplace on television and in the movies, they are less frequent in real life. Although LGBTQ persons often have as many cross-orientation friends as same-orientation friends, straight men and women overwhelmingly form friendships with other straight men and women (Galupo, 2009). The principal reason is homophobia, both personal and societal. Straight persons may feel reluctant to pursue such friendships because they fear being associated with members of a marginalized group (Galupo, 2007). By far, the group that has the fewest cross-orientation friendships is straight men. In fact, the average number of cross-orientation friendships for straight men is *zero*: most straight men do not have a single lesbian, gay, bisexual, or transgendered friend (Galupo, 2009). This tendency may perpetuate homophobic sentiments because these men are never exposed to LGBTQ persons who might amend their negative attitudes. The Focus on Culture box "Cross-Orientation Male Friendships" on page 367 explores the challenges of such relationships in depth.

Intercultural Friendships A third type of cross-category friendship is *intercultural*: friendships between people from different cultures or countries. Similar to cross-sex and cross-orientation affiliations, intercultural friendships are both challenging and rewarding (Sias et al., 2008). The challenges include overcoming differences in language and cultural beliefs, as well as negative stereotypes. Differences in language alone present a substantial hurdle. Incorrect interpretations of messages can lead to misunderstanding, uncertainty, frustration, and conflict (Sias et al., 2008). The potential rewards of intercultural friendships, however, are great and include gaining new cultural knowledge, broadening one's worldview, and breaking stereotypes (Sias et al., 2008).

As noted throughout this chapter, the most important factor that catapults friendships forward is similarity in interests and activities. However, the defining characteristic of intercultural interactions is *difference*, and this makes formation of intercultural friendships more challenging (Sias et al., 2008). How can you overcome this? By finding, and then bolstering, some significant type of ingroup similarity. For example, a good friend—who is Japanese—and I—of Irish descent—founded our friendship on a shared love of EDM (electronic dance music). But the strongest predictor of whether someone will have an intercultural friendship is prior intercultural friendships. People who have had close friends

focus on CULTURE

Cross-Orientation Male Friendships

As *New York Times* writer Douglas Quenqua notes, the biggest stereotype regarding gay and straight male friendships is "the notion that gay men can't refrain from hitting on straight friends."[1] This is false. In a poll of men involved in gay-straight friendships, Quenqua found little evidence of sexual tension. He did find several other barriers confronting such relationships, however. The most prominent was peer pressure from friends on both sides to not socialize with someone of a different orientation.

The other barriers were perceptual and communicative. Straight men often view gay men solely in terms of their sexual orientation, making it difficult to connect with them on other levels. As Matthew Streib, a gay journalist in Baltimore, describes, "It's always about my gayness for the first two months. First they have questions, then they make fun of it, then they start seeing me as a person." In addition, many straight men feel uncomfortable talking about their gay friends' romantic involvements. Without being able to discuss this critical topic, the friends necessarily face constraints in how close they can become.

One context that *has* proven conducive to close cross-orientation friendships is the military. Sociologist Jammie Price found that the straight and gay men with the closest friendships were those who had fought side by side (1999). Having learned to depend on each other for survival built a bond that far transcended differences in sexual orientation.

But regardless of barriers or bonds, one thing is consistent in cross-orientation male friendships: lack of consistency. As Douglas Quenqua concludes, "For every sweeping statement one can make about such friendships, there is a real-life counter example to undermine the stereotypes. As with all friendships, no two are exactly alike."

discussion questions

- What are the biggest barriers blocking you from maintaining or forming cross-orientation friendships?
- What, if anything, could be done to overcome these barriers?

[1] All quoted material that follows is excerpted from Quenqua (2009).

---

from different cultures in the past are substantially more likely to forge such friendships in the future (Sias et al., 2008). This is because they learn the enormous benefits that such relationships provide, and lack fear and uncertainty about "outgroupers."

Interethnic Friendships The final type of cross-category friendship is an *interethnic* friendship: a bond between people who share the same cultural background (for example, American) but who are of different ethnic groups (African American, Asian American, Euro-American, and so forth). Similar to cross-orientation and intercultural friendships, interethnic friendships boost cultural awareness and commitment to diversity (Shelton, Richeson, & Bergsieker, 2009). In addition, interethnic friends apply these outcomes broadly. People who develop a close interethnic friendship become less prejudiced toward ethnicities of *all* types as a result (Shelton et al., 2009).

The most difficult barriers people face in forming interethnic friendships are attributional and perceptual errors. Too often we let our own biases and stereotypes stop us from having open, honest, and comfortable interactions with

Teaching Tip: Challenges of Interethnic Friendships
In her book *Why Are All the Black Kids Sitting Together in the Cafeteria?* (2003), Beverly Daniel Tatum discusses the ways in which children's friendships change as they enter into adolescence. While children find interethnic friendships easier during childhood, the onset of adolescence and identity development makes such relationships challenging. Ask students to share their experiences with interethnic friendships. How have they changed through the years? What makes them difficult? What makes them rewarding? How can they be encouraged?

people from other ethnic groups. We become overly concerned with the "correct" way to act and thus end up behaving nervously. Such nervousness may lead to awkward, uncomfortable encounters and may cause us to avoid interethnic encounters in the future, dooming ourselves to friendship networks that lack diversity (Shelton et al., 2010).

How can you overcome these challenges and improve your ability to form interethnic friendships? Review Chapter 3's discussion of attributional errors and perception-checking. Look for points of commonality during interethnic encounters that might lead to the formation of a friendship—such as a shared interest in music, fashion, sports, movies, or video games. Keep in mind that sometimes encounters *are* awkward, people *don't* get along, and friendships *won't* arise—and it has nothing to do with ethnic differences.

Maintaining Friendships

Ways to sustain enduring and happy friendships

In the movie *Zombieland* (2009), four people known by the monikers of their former hometowns struggle to survive in a postapocalyptic world (Fleischer, Reesee, & Werrick, 2009). The central character, Columbus, is a self-described loner who never had close ties to friends or family. As he puts it, "I avoided people like they were zombies, even before they *were* zombies!" To deal with the challenge of constant flesh-eater attacks, he develops a set of rules, including Rule #1: *Cardio* (stay in shape to stay ahead of zombies); Rule #17: *Don't be a hero* (don't put yourself at risk to save others); and Rule #31: *Always check the backseat* (to avoid surprises). As time passes, he bands together with three other survivors—Tallahassee, Wichita, and Little Rock—and learns

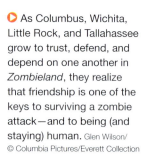

As Columbus, Wichita, Little Rock, and Tallahassee grow to trust, defend, and depend on one another in *Zombieland*, they realize that friendship is one of the keys to surviving a zombie attack—and to being (and staying) human. Glen Wilson/© Columbia Pictures/Everett Collection

that they, too, have trust issues, regrets regarding their former lives, and fears about the future (above and beyond zombie attacks). As they travel across the country together, they learn to trust, support, defend, and depend on one another. This leads to a friendship that eventually deepens to a family-like bond. Columbus even chooses to bend Rule #17 to save Wichita, by being a hero. As he narrates in the final scene, "Those smart girls in the big black truck and that big guy in that snakeskin jacket—they were the closest to something I'd always wanted, but never really had—a family. I trusted them and they trusted me. Even though life would never be simple or innocent again, we had hope—we had each other. And without other people, well, you might as well be a zombie!"

It's true. We *need* our friends. Most of us don't need them for survival, as we don't face daily zombie attacks. But our friends do provide a constant and important shield against the stresses, hardships, and threats of our everyday lives. We count on friends to be there when we need them and to provide support; in return, we do the same. This is what bonds us together.

At the same time, friendships don't endure on their own. As with romantic and family involvements, friendships flourish only when you consistently communicate in ways that maintain them. Two ways that we keep friendships alive are by following friendship rules and by using maintenance strategies.

FOLLOWING FRIENDSHIP RULES

In *Zombieland*, Columbus follows a set of rules that allow him to survive. In the real world, one of the ways we can help our friendships succeed is by following **friendship rules**—general principles that prescribe appropriate communication and behavior within friendship relationships (Argyle & Henderson, 1984). In an extensive study of friendship maintenance, social psychologists Michael Argyle and Monica Henderson observed 10 friendship rules that people share across cultures. Both men and women endorse these rules, and adherence to them distinguishes happy from unhappy friendships (Schneider & Kenny, 2000). Not abiding by them may even cost you your friends: people around the globe describe failed friendships as ones that didn't follow these rules (Argyle & Henderson, 1984). The 10 rules for friendship are:

1. *Show support.* Within a friendship, you should provide emotional support and offer assistance in times of need, without having to be asked (Burleson & Samter, 1994). You also should accept and respect your friend's valued social identities. When he or she changes majors, tries out for team captain, or opts to be a stay-at-home mom or dad, support the decision—even if it's one you yourself wouldn't make.

2. *Seek support.* The flip side of the first rule is that when you're in a friendship, you should not only deliver support but *seek* support and counsel when needed, disclosing your emotional burdens to your friends. Other than sharing time and activities, mutual self-disclosure serves as the glue that binds friendships together (Dainton, Zelley, & Langan, 2003).

Discussion Prompt: Evaluating Friendship Rules

Place students in groups, and ask them to rank Argyle and Henderson's 10 rules of friendship in order of importance. Then ask them to provide an explanation for which rule they think is the most and least important. Have them share examples of when a friendship ended because of a broken rule. Have groups share their rankings and rationale with the class and discuss types of relationship repair that could help alleviate the damage of a broken rule.

self-reflection

Consider the 10 universal rules that successful friends follow. Which of these rules do you abide by in your own friendships? Which do you neglect? How has neglecting some of these rules affected your friendships? What steps might you take to better follow rules you've previously neglected?

3. *Respect privacy.* At the same time that friends anticipate both support and disclosure, they also recognize that friendships have more restrictive boundaries for sharing personal information than do romantic or family relationships. Recognize this, and avoid pushing your friend to share information that he or she considers too personal. Also resist sharing information about yourself that's intensely private or irrelevant to your friendship.

4. *Keep confidences.* A critical feature of enduring friendships is trust. When friends share personal information with you, do not betray their confidence by sharing it with others.

5. *Defend your friends.* Part of successful friendships is the feeling that friends have your back. Your friends count on you to stand up for them, so defend them when they are being attacked—whether it's online or off, face-to-face or behind their back.

6. *Avoid public criticism.* Friends may disagree or even disapprove of each other's behavior on occasion. But airing your grievances publicly in a way that makes a friend look bad will only hurt your friendship. Avoid communication such as questioning a friend's loyalty in front of other friends or commenting on a friend's weight in front of a salesperson.

7. *Make your friends happy.* An essential ingredient to successful friendships is striving to make your friends feel good while you're in their company. You can do this by practicing positivity: communicating with them in a cheerful and optimistic fashion, doing unsolicited favors for them, and buying or making gifts for them.

8. *Manage jealousy.* Unlike long-term romantic relationships, most friendships aren't exclusive. Your close friends will likely have other close friends, perhaps even friends who are more intimate with them than you are. Accept that each of your friends has other good friends as well, and constructively manage any jealousy that arises in you.

9. *Share humor.* Successful friends spend a good deal of their time joking with and teasing each other in affectionate ways. Enjoying a similar sense of humor is an essential aspect of most long-term friendships.

10. *Maintain equity.* In enduring, mutually satisfying friendships, the two people give and get in roughly equitable proportions (Canary & Zelley, 2000). Help maintain this equity by conscientiously repaying debts, returning favors, and keeping the exchange of gifts and compliments balanced.

MAINTENANCE STRATEGIES FOR FRIENDS

Most friendships are built on a foundation of shared activities and self-disclosure. To maintain your friendships, strive to keep this foundation solid by regularly doing things with your friends and making time to talk.

skills practice

Friendship Maintenance
Using interpersonal communication to maintain a friendship

❶ Think of a valued friendship you wish to maintain.

❷ Make time each week to talk with this person, whether online or face-to-face.

❸ Have fun together and share stories.

❹ Let your friend know that you accept and respect his or her valued social identities.

❺ Encourage disclosure of thoughts and feelings.

❻ Avoid pushing for information that he or she considers too personal.

❼ Negotiate boundaries around topics that are best avoided.

❽ Don't share secrets disclosed by your friend with others.

❾ Provide emotional support and assistance when needed, without having to be asked.

❿ Defend your friend online and off.

◯ Two important ways you can maintain your friendships are sharing activities and being open in your communication with your friends. Nina Leen/Time & Life Pictures/Getty Images

Sharing Activities Through *sharing activities*, friends structure their schedules to enjoy hobbies, interests, and leisure activities together. But even more important than the actual sharing of activities is the perception that each friend is willing to make time for the other. Scholar William Rawlins notes that even friends who don't spend much time together can still maintain a satisfying connection as long as each perceives the other as "being there" when needed (Rawlins, 1994).

Of course, most of us have several friends but only finite amounts of time available to devote to each one. Consequently, we are often put in positions in which we have to choose between time and activities shared with one friend versus another. Unfortunately, given the significance that sharing time and activities together plays in defining friendships, your decisions regarding with whom you invest your time will often be perceived by friends as communicating depth of loyalty (Baxter et al., 1997). In cases in which you choose one friend over another, the friend not chosen may view your decision as disloyal. To avert this, draw on your interpersonal communication skills. Express gratitude for the friend's offer, assure him or her that you very much value the relationship, and make concrete plans for getting together another time.

Self-Disclosure A second strategy for friendship maintenance is self-disclosure. All friendships are created and maintained through the discussion of thoughts, feelings, and daily life events (Dainton et al., 2003). To foster disclosure with your friends, routinely make time just to talk—encouraging them to share their thoughts and feelings about various issues, whether online or face-to-face. Equally important, avoid betraying friends—sharing with others personal information friends have disclosed to you.

As with romantic and family relationships, it's important to balance openness in self-disclosure with protection (Dainton et al., 2003). Over time, most friends learn that communication about certain issues, topics, or even people is best avoided to protect the relationship and preclude conflict. As a result, friends negotiate communicative boundaries that allow their time together and communication shared to remain positive. Such boundaries can be perfectly healthy as long as both friends agree on them and the issues being avoided aren't central to the survival of the friendship. For example, several years ago a male friend of mine began dating someone who I thought treated him badly. His boyfriend, whom I'll call "Mike," had a very negative outlook, constantly complained about my friend, and belittled him and their relationship in public. I thought Mike's communication was unethical and borderline abusive. But whenever I expressed my concern, my buddy grew defensive. Mike just had an "edge" to his personality, my friend said, and I "didn't know the real Mike." After several such arguments, we agreed that, for the sake of our friendship, the topic of Mike was off-limits. We both respected this agreement—thereby protecting our friendship—until my friend broke up with Mike. After that, we opened the topic once more to free and detailed discussion.

Friendship Challenges

Dealing with friendship betrayal, geographic distance, and attraction

Assignment: Friendship Challenges

As a journal assignment, have students write about a time when they faced a friendship challenge, such as betrayal or geographic separation. How did they deal with the difficulty? Did the challenge end the friendship? What other friendship challenges have occurred in their relationships?

Ashlee and Rachel were best friends throughout high school.[2] As Ashlee describes, "Rachel was brilliant, confident, blunt, and outgoing. She liked to mock people, but she could make me laugh like nobody else, and she loved the same things I did." After graduation, they were parted by distance: Rachel went to Stanford, while Ashlee attended the University of Washington. Although they regularly texted and e-mailed, they grew apart. The following summer they were reunited, this time as a foursome: Rachel was dating Mike (a friend from high school), and Ashlee was dating Ahmed, a Lebanese transfer student. The four hung out regularly, waterskiing, going to movies, and partying.

One day, after Mike bought a new iPhone, he offered his old one to Ashlee. Arriving home, Ashlee found that her SIM card wasn't compatible, so she started manually clearing Mike's information. When she got to his text in-box, she was stunned to see this message from Rachel: "Ashlee and Ahmed are the perfect couple: stupid sorority slut and steroided camel jockey." As Ashlee describes, "My heart just stopped. I literally sat there, shaking. I thought it was a joke, until I scrolled down and found *hundreds* of similar messages." Text after text slammed

---

[2] All information in this example is true. The names and personal information of the people in question have been altered for confidentiality. This example is used with permission from "Ashlee."

Ashlee and mocked Ahmed's ethnicity. Later that night, crying hysterically, Ashlee summoned the courage to text Rachel: "I cleared out Mike's phone and found all your texts about me and Ahmed. You two are *horrible*. I want nothing to do with either of you." Rachel immediately texted back, "How dare you read our messages! Those were private! Whatever, Ashlee—I'm sorry you're angry, but Mike and I were just messing around. You're completely overreacting." In the aftermath, Ashlee returned Mike's iPhone and refused all contact with Rachel. Back at school that fall, Ashlee received an e-mail with the subject line, "please don't delete." The message read: "I don't even know where to begin. I know I messed up, but I can't lose you as a friend. We've been best friends forever, and I'd hate to lose you over something this dumb. I know I'm asking a lot of you to forgive me, but please think about it." Ashlee deleted the message.

To this point, we've talked about friendships as involvements that provide us with abundant and important rewards. Although this is true, friendships also present us with a variety of intense interpersonal challenges. Three of the most common are friendship betrayal, geographic distance, and attraction.

BETRAYAL

Given the value friends place on mutual support and defending each other, it's no surprise that betrayal is the most commonly reported reason for ending a friendship (Miller, Hefner, & Scott, 2007). Acts of friendship betrayal include breaking confidences, backstabbing (criticizing a friend behind his or her back), spreading rumors or gossip, and lying—all of which violate the friendship rules discussed earlier. When friends violate these rules, it's difficult for friendships to survive. Similar to romantic betrayal, friends who are betrayed experience an overwhelming sense of relationship devaluation and loss (Miller et al., 2007). And—as with the Ashlee and Rachel example—betrayal often leads people to realize things about their friends' characters that simply can't be tolerated.

How can you better manage friendship betrayal when it occurs? If it's a friendship of any closeness, expect to experience grief as you suffer the loss of trust, intimacy, and the image of your friend you once held dear. Revisit the suggestions for grief management offered in Chapter 4, especially the value of *emotion-sharing*—talking about your experience directly with people who have gone through the same thing. Avoid lashing out at the betrayer or seeking revenge, both of which will simply make matters worse.

When you're able, ponder whether you can or should repair the friendship. Ask yourself the following questions to help guide your decision. First, how serious was the betrayal? Not all betrayals are of equal standing, so think carefully about whether this incident is something you can learn to

In *The Social Network* (2010), Facebook entrepreneurs Mark Zuckerberg and Eduardo Saverin disagree over the financial future of their start-up, which leads to a falling-out that destroys their friendship. Have you ever felt betrayed by a friend? If so, how did you respond? © Columbia Pictures/Everett Collection

skills practice

Managing Friendship Betrayal

If you find yourself in a situation in which a friend betrays you:

❶ Manage the intense anger and grief you experience.

❷ Avoid seeking revenge or verbal retaliation.

❸ Contact others who have experienced similar betrayals, and discuss your experience with them.

❹ Evaluate the betrayal, including how serious it is, what caused it, whether it's a one-time event or part of a behavioral pattern, and whether you would have done something similar.

❺ Assess the value of your friendship, compared with the damage of the betrayal.

❻ End or repair the friendship based on your analysis.

---

live with or not. Second, what was the context preceding and surrounding the betrayal? Did *you* do something to provoke the betrayal? Would you have done the same thing in the same situation—or *have* you done similar things in the past? Be careful about blaming others for behaviors that you caused, holding double standards, and judging friends in ways you wouldn't wish to be judged yourself. Third, do the benefits of continuing the friendship outweigh the costs? Use the friendship rules as a guide: Does your friend follow most of these rules, most of the time? If so, he or she may actually be a desirable friend. Fourth, is this betrayal a one-time event or part of a consistent pattern? Everyone falls from grace on occasion; what you want to avoid is a person who habitually abuses your trust. Last, and perhaps most important, does this betrayal reveal something about your friend's character that you simply can't live with? Be honest with yourself and realize that some friendships are best left broken following betrayal. In Ashlee's case, despite years of having Rachel as her best friend—and the corresponding energy, time, and emotional investment—the betrayal revealed multiple aspects of Rachel's character that Ashlee simply couldn't tolerate, including sexism, racism, phoniness, and viciousness.

GEOGRAPHIC SEPARATION

A contributing factor to Ashlee and Rachel's falling-out was their geographic separation, which led them to grow apart. Separation is one of the most common and intense challenges friends face (Wang & Andersen, 2007). Upwards of 90 percent of people report having at least one long-distance friendship, and 80 percent report having a close friend who lives far away (Rohlfing, 1995). Physical separation prevents friends from adequately satisfying the needs that form

"Are you multitasking me?"

© William Haefeli/The New Yorker Collection/www.cartoonbank.com

the foundation of their relationship, such as sharing activities and practicing intimate self-disclosure.

Although most friends begin long-distance separations with the intention of seeing each other regularly, they rarely visit solely for the sake of reuniting. Instead, they tend to see each other only when there's some other reason for them to be in the same area. This is because long-distance friends often don't have the money or time to travel only to visit a friend (Rohlfing, 1995). Instead, they visit when other commitments, such as professional conferences, visits with relatives, or class reunions, bring them together. Such contacts often leave friends feeling empty because their time together is so limited.

Which friendships tend to survive geographic distance, and which lapse? In friendships that survive, the two people feel a particularly strong *liking*—affection and respect—for each other. Friendships between individuals who "enjoy knowing each other" and "have great admiration for each other" are most likely to endure.

Friends who overcome separation also accept change as a natural part of life and their relationship. If you get together with a good friend you haven't seen in a long while, you both will likely have changed in terms of profession, attitudes, and appearance. Friends who are comfortable with such changes and offer identity support tend to have relationships that survive. Friends who want their friends to "always stay the same" don't.

Moreover, friendships that survive separation involve friends who have a strong sense of shared history. In their conversations, they frequently celebrate the past as well as anticipate sharing events in the future. This sense of shared past, present, and future enables them to "pick up where they left off" after being out of touch for a while. Successful long-distance friendships thus involve feeling a sense of relationship continuity and perceiving the relationship as solid and ongoing.

How can you communicate in ways that foster these qualities in your own long-distance friendships? Use technology (Skype, Facebook, phone, text, etc.) to regularly communicate with your friends. Focus your communication on activities and interests that you share. Doing this alleviates the feeling of loss that comes with the inability to actually spend time together (Rabby, 1997). So, for example, if a friend who now lives far away used to be your daily workout or jogging buddy, send her regular e-mails or texts updating her on your marathon training and inquiring about her performance in local races.

Also, remind your long-distance friends that you still think of them with affection and hold them in high regard. Look for opportunities to appropriately express your feelings for a friend, such as, "I miss our Thursday night movie watching! Have you seen any good films lately?" In addition, devote some of your communication to fondly recounting events and experiences you have shared in your past, as well as discussing plans for the future. Such exchanges bolster the sense of relational continuity critical to maintaining friendships.

Finally, when your long-distance friends go through dramatic life changes—as they inevitably will—communicate your continued support of their valued social identities. For instance, a close friend you haven't seen in a while may

skills practice

Using Technology to Overcome Distance
Maintaining long-distance friendships through online communication

❶ Think of a close friend who lives far away.

❷ In your online interactions, focus your message content on common interests, making sure to ask about your friend's continued participation in these things.

❸ Send text messages saying you're thinking of and missing her or him.

❹ Craft e-mails that fondly recap past shared experiences.

❺ Forward Web links with ideas for future activities you can share together.

❻ When your friend discloses major life changes, provide support in the quickest fashion possible, whether by text message, e-mail, phone call, or all three.

Friendship Distance-Durability

This quiz helps you determine whether a friendship is durable enough to survive the challenge of geographic distance. Place a check mark next to each statement with which you agree. Then total your check marks and use the scoring key at the bottom to determine your friendship distance-durability.

To take this quiz online, visit LaunchPad: **macmillanhighered.com/reflectrelate4e**.

- _____ My friend and I share a great deal of personal history.
- _____ I feel a strong sense of warmth and fondness toward my friend.
- _____ I have great respect for my friend as a person.
- _____ I don't expect my friend to be the exact same person in the future as he or she is now.
- _____ Having this person as my friend makes me happy.
- _____ Even if we've been out of touch for a while, my friend and I always seem to be able to pick up where we left off when we communicate again.
- _____ I welcome future changes in my friend's beliefs, values, and attitudes—even if they're different from mine—as long as these changes bring him or her happiness.
- _____ My friend is the kind of person I would like to be.
- _____ My friend and I enjoy sharing numerous stories from our past that remind us of how close we've been.
- _____ I anticipate that as my friend ages, he or she will develop new and varied interests.

Scoring: 0–3 = Low durability; friendship may have difficulty surviving geographic separation; 4–6 = Moderate durability; friendship may be able to handle separation; 7–10 = High durability; friendship has strong potential for enduring across time and distance.

abandon previously shared religious beliefs, adopt new political viewpoints, or substantially alter his or her looks. In making these and other kinds of significant changes, your friend may look to you for identity support, as a friend. A good long-distance friend of mine, Vikram, occupied a job for several years that required a fair degree of professional contact with me, allowing us the opportunity (and excuse) to communicate regularly. Then he accepted a new position with a different company. This new opportunity represented a dramatic professional advancement for him, but it also meant we would have far fewer opportunities to interact once he started the new job. When he broke the news to me, he expected a certain degree of rancor on my part. Instead, I surprised him by expressing my firm support and excitement regarding his decision, even though I knew that, owing to this change, our paths wouldn't cross nearly as often.

ATTRACTION: ROMANCE AND FWB RELATIONSHIPS

A final challenge facing friends is attraction to each other beyond friendship: romantic, sexual, or both. Men typically report more of a desire for romantic involvement with their platonic friends than do women (Schneider & Kenny, 2000). However, one study found that 87 percent of college women and 93 percent of college men reported feeling sexually attracted to a friend at some point in their lives (Asada, Morrison, Hughes, & Fitzpatrick, 2003).

Within cross-sex friendships, the issue of attraction is always a challenge, even when no such attraction exists between the friends. This is because people in their surrounding networks—and the broader culture at large—presume that such attraction *will* exist between men and women, and often pester cross-sex friends about it (Halatsis & Christakis, 2009). But when attraction does blossom between friends, same-sex or cross-sex, pursuing a sexual or romantic relationship brings its own challenges. Friends who feel attracted to each other typically report high uncertainty as a result, regarding both the nature of their relationship and whether or not their friend feels the same way (Weger & Emmett, 2009).

Friends cope with attraction by doing one of three things. Some friends simply repress the attraction, most commonly out of respect for their friendship (Messman et al., 2000). Friends who seek to repress attraction typically engage in *mental management*—they do things to actively manage how they think about each other so that the attraction is diminished (Halatsis & Christakis, 2009). These may include pacts and promises to not pursue the attraction, a strict avoidance of flirting, and the curtailing of activities (such as going out drinking) that might inadvertently lead to sexual interaction (Halatsis & Christakis, 2009). Alternatively, some friends act on their attraction by either developing a full-fledged romantic involvement or trying to blend their friendship with sexual activity through a "friends-with-benefits" arrangement.

Romance between Friends Many friends who develop an attraction opt to pursue a romantic relationship. The first and most powerful cue of such desire is a radical increase in the amount of time the friends spend flirting with each other (Weger & Emmett, 2009). Although people in Western cultures like to think of friendships and romantic relationships as strictly separate, many enduring and successful romances evolve from friendships. One of the strongest predictors of whether or not a friendship can successfully transition to romance is simply whether the friends already possess romantic beliefs that link friendship with love (Hendrick & Hendrick, 1992).

Although it's commonly believed that pursuing a romantic relationship will "kill the friendship" if or when the romance fizzles, the results are actually mixed. People who were friends prior to a romance are much more likely to be friends following a failed romance than those who were not friends first (Schneider & Kenny, 2000). However, postromance friendships tend to be less close than those with friends who have always been platonic. How can you successfully transition from friendship to romance, or back again? First, *expect difference*. Romantic relationships and friendships are fundamentally different in expectations, demands, commitment, and corresponding emotional intensity. Don't presume that your feelings, those of your partner, or the interplay between you two will be the same. Second, *emphasize disclosure*. Relationship transitions tend to evoke high

▶ Adam attempts to follow the rules of his FWB relationship by giving Emma a bouquet of carrots instead of flowers in *No Strings Attached* (2011). However, like many FWB relationships, Adam and Emma eventually have to deal with the romantic impulses they feel toward each other. Dale Robinette/© Paramount Pictures/Everett Collection

Discussion Prompt: Friends with Benefits

Hughes, Morrison, and Asada (2005) found seven distinctive rules that FWBs establish to maintain the relationship: guidelines for negotiation, sex, communication, secrecy, permanence, emotions, and friendship. As a class, discuss the rules that may be developed for an FWB relationship. What are some examples that could fall under each category? Is it important to create rules for maintaining an FWB relationship?

self-reflection

Have you had an FWB relationship? If so, what were the pros and cons? Did you and your friend establish rules for the relationship? If so, what were they? How well did you both follow those rules?

uncertainty, as partners worry about what the other thinks and feels, and wonder where the relationship is going. To reduce this uncertainty, share your feelings in an open and honest fashion, and encourage your partner to do the same. Finally, *offer assurances*. Let your partner know that whether you two are friends or lovers, you stand by him or her, and your relationship, regardless. This is especially important when transitioning back to friendship from romance, as your partner may believe that your relationship is now over.

Friends with Benefits Some friends deal with sexual attraction by forming a "friends-with-benefits" (FWB) relationship. In **FWB relationships,** the participants engage in sexual activity, but not with the purpose of transforming the relationship into a romantic attachment (Hughes, Morrison, & Asada, 2005). FWB relationships appear to be widespread. Studies suggest that around 50 percent of college students have had such a relationship (Mongeau, Ramirez, & Vorrell, 2003).

Those who form FWB relationships do so for two reasons: they welcome the lack of commitment (and all its attendant sacrifices), and they want to satisfy sexual needs (Asada et al., 2003). Both men and women cite these same reasons, contradicting stereotypes that women seek only emotional satisfaction in relationships while men want only sex.

Most partners in FWB relationships develop rules regarding emotional attachment, communication, and sex (Hughes et al., 2005). For example, they commonly strike an agreement to not fall in love. And they establish rules governing the frequency of phone calling, e-mailing, and text-messaging, as well as sex rules regarding safer sex practices, frequency of sex, and sexual exclusivity. But despite these rules, the majority of FWB relationships fail eventually, costing the participants their original friendship as well as the sexual arrangement. Why? Participants tend to develop romantic feelings despite their best efforts to avoid them, and many decide that the FWB relationship doesn't satisfy them enough emotionally (Hughes et al., 2005).

The Importance of Friends

Friends provide essential emotional security

Friendships are both delicate and deep. On the one hand, they're the most transitory of our close relationships. They come and go across our life span, depending on where we're living, going to school, and working; and how our personal interests shift and evolve. As a simple test of this, make a list of the five closest friends in

For much of our lives, friendships are *the* most important close relationships we have.

Discussion Prompt: Friendship Challenges
Play the "Making Relationship Choices" video for your students when engaging in a discussion about the challenges of friendship. This video depicts a college-age woman who joins the Peace Corps in Africa and discovers that when she returns to the United States, she doesn't have much in common with her old friends, who were primarily interested in fashion and status. Ask students to discuss the challenges that they have faced when dealing with newly discovered differences in their friendships. How did they deal with these challenges?

Assignment: Rewards and Costs in Friendship
Social Exchange Theory (SET) suggests that relationships are full of rewards and costs. Ask students to write an essay describing a friendship and explaining the rewards and costs associated with the relationship. While it is easy to analyze another's shortcomings, students should also consider the rewards and costs that *they* offer to the relationship: What makes you a cost to a relationship? How can you improve your own communication style in the relationship? What maintenance strategies would most enhance your friendship?

making relationship choices

Choosing between Friends

 BACKGROUND

Maintaining friendships can be challenging. But when a close friend changes in ways that put her at odds with your other friends, you may be forced to choose between them. To understand how you might competently manage such a relationship challenge, read the case study in Part 2; then, drawing on all you know about interpersonal communication, work through the problem-solving model in Part 3.

 Visit LaunchPad to check out the other side of the story (Part 4). For the best experience, complete all parts in LaunchPad: **macmillanhighered.com /reflectrelate4e**.

2 CASE STUDY

For years you've hung around with the same group of friends. Your ringleader is Karina. She's brilliant and beautiful. She always dresses immaculately, with perfect hair, nails, and makeup. She has a caustic wit and enjoys mocking other people's fashion sense.

But Karina has another side: she is deeply caring. When your Mom was diagnosed with terminal cancer, your other friends avoided visiting. Not Karina. She hung out with your Mom for hours, cracking jokes and sharing funny YouTube videos. After your mother died, it was Karina who supported you in your grief.

One night, Karina gathers everyone together and announces, "Guess what!? I'm joining the Peace Corps!" Your friend John breaks the bewildered silence by joking, "Yeah, right! Who's gonna do your nails!?" Everyone laughs except Karina. She's serious.

Karina serves for two years as a youth development coordinator in Malawi. You hear from her occasionally through e-mail. She shares with you the difficulties of her assignments, the kindness of the people, and the beauty of the landscape. During her absence, you remain close to your other friends—partying, shopping, and taking classes together.

Then Karina is back! Meeting her at the airport, you're staggered by her appearance. She has lost 20 pounds and wears no makeup. She is unusually quiet, and, as time passes, it's clear that Karina has changed. Gone is the glam girl who tossed nasty and hilarious remarks at people. Instead, she is thoughtful and pensive. Rather than partying or shopping, she spends her free time volunteering at a homeless shelter.

You're not sure what to make of her. On the one hand, she's a nicer person than before, and always available for support. On the other hand, she is so *serious* all the time! And she seems really uncomfortable around your other friends. Does she still care about *you*? Is she still interested in being *your* friend?

Although you're on the fence, your friends are unanimous: they can't *stand* the "new" Karina. One night John hosts a party, and Karina again opts to skip. The gathering quickly devolves into a "hate on Karina" fest. One by one, everyone vents their dislike of her "ugly new look" and how "quiet and boring she is." Everyone (except you) agrees the time has come to cut her from the group. You remain silent until John notices and asks, "You're awfully quiet. What do you think?"

3 YOUR TURN

Think about all you've learned thus far about interpersonal communication. Then work through the following five steps. Remember, there are no "right" answers, so think hard about what is the *best* choice! (P.S. Need help? See the *Helpful Concepts* list.)

step 1
Reflect on yourself. What are your thoughts and feelings in this situation? What attributions are you making about Karina? about John and your other friends? Are your attributions accurate? Why or why not?

step 2
Reflect on your partner. Using perspective-taking and empathic concern, put yourself in Karina's shoes. Do the same for John and your other friends. What are they thinking and feeling in this situation?

step 3
Identify the optimal outcome. Think about all the information you have about your communication and relationships with both Karina and your other friends. Consider your own feelings as well as everyone else's. Given all these factors, what's the best, most constructive relationship outcome possible? Consider what's best for you *and* for Karina and the others.

step 4
Locate the roadblocks. Taking into consideration your own and Karina's thoughts and feelings, those of your other friends, and all that has happened in this situation, what obstacles are keeping you from achieving the optimal outcome?

step 5
Chart your course. What can you say to John to overcome the roadblocks you've identified and achieve your optimal outcome?

HELPFUL CONCEPTS

Best friends, 363–364

Identity support, 363–364

Friendship rules, 369–370

Betrayal, 373–374

4 THE OTHER SIDE

Visit LaunchPad to watch a video in which Karina tells her side of the case study story. As in many real-life situations, this is information to which you did not have access when you were initially crafting your response to John in Part 3. The video reminds us that even when we do our best to offer competent responses, there is always another side to the story that we need to consider.

your life right now, in rank order. Then make the same list based on your closest friends five years ago. Chances are, at least some of the names and rankings will have changed.

But at the same time, friendships are deep. For much of our lives, friendships are *the* most important close relationships we have. Our friends keep us grounded and provide us with support in times of crisis. When lovers betray or abandon us, or family members drive us crazy, it's our friends we turn to for support. When everything else seems wrong with the world, and our lives seem mired in misadventure, we find solace in the simple truth shared by Clarence the Angel in the movie *It's a Wonderful Life*: No one is a failure who has friends.

POSTSCRIPT

We began this chapter with an animated sea sponge who lives in a pineapple. Although SpongeBob SquarePants may be an internationally famous kids' cartoon, it also is a tale of friendships and the corresponding complexities, rewards, and challenges that come with such interpersonal involvements.

Which friends of *yours* support and "coach" you in your times of need? Whom do you share your time and passionate interests with? Whom can you count on to forgive you when you inevitably let that person down?

Although the relationships between SpongeBob and his friends may be comical, they mirror the friendships we experience in our own lives. Like us, the characters were drawn to each other through shared interests. And like the bonds we forge with our friends, theirs remain cemented through communication, companionship, humor, and support.

LaunchPad for *Reflect & Relate* offers videos and encourages self-assessment through adaptive quizzing. Go to **macmillanhighered.com/reflectrelate4e** to get access to:

 LearningCurve Adaptive Quizzes

 Video clips that help you understand interpersonal communication

key terms

friendship, 357
communal friendships, 359
agentic friendships, 360
identity support, 363
valued social identities, 363
cross-category friendships, 364
friendship rules, 369
FWB relationships, 378

You can watch brief, illustrative videos of these terms and test your understanding of the concepts in LaunchPad.

key concepts

The Nature of Friendship

- Unlike family relationships, **friendships** are voluntary.
- Depending on the functions being fulfilled, friendships may be primarily **communal** or **agentic.**
- Age, culture, gender, and life situations all influence our view of friendship.
- While technology allows us to communicate with friends 24/7, our closest friends are often those that we spend time with online and off.

Types of Friendships

- We have many types of friends, but we often consider a smaller number our *close* and *best friends*. The latter are distinguished by providing unwavering **identity support** for our **valued social identities** over time.
- **Cross-category friendships**—cross-sex, cross-orientation, intercultural, and interethnic—are a powerful way to break down ingrouper and outgrouper perceptions.

Maintaining Friendships

- Across cultures, people agree on **friendship rules,** the basic principles that underlie the maintenance of successful friendships. Friends who follow these rules are more likely to remain friends than those who don't.
- Two of the most important maintenance strategies for friends are sharing activities and self-disclosure.

Friendship Challenges

- Friendship betrayal often leads to an overwhelming sense of relationship devaluation and loss.
- One of the greatest challenges friends face is geographic separation. Communication technologies can help such friends overcome distance by allowing for regular interaction and maintaining a sense of shared interests.
- Some people form sexual relationships with their friends, known as friends-with-benefits or **FWB relationships.** Both men and women enter these relationships to satisfy sexual needs. Most of these relationships fail, owing to unanticipated emotional challenges.

chapter review

Appendix
Relationships in the Workplace

© DoD/Roger-Viollet/The Image Works

 LearningCurve can help you review the material in this chapter. Go to LaunchPad: **macmillanhighered.com/reflectrelate4e**

Appendix Theme

The story of this appendix is that our professional relationships are often deeply personal. The people we meet, collaborate with, and labor beside in the workplace become more than just coworkers. They become our colleagues, confidants, friends, and sometimes even romantic partners. Although interpersonal communication in the workplace presents unique challenges, including interacting across power imbalances and handling bullying bosses, well-maintained workplace relationships make our professional lives more productive and our personal lives happier.

We like to think of our personal and professional lives as separate. Our personal lives consist of "real" relationships: romantic partners, family members, friends. Our work lives exist in a parallel universe of less meaningful interactions. But this division is a pretense. We spend most of our adult waking hours working and spend more time interacting with coworkers than with any other type of relationship partner (Sias & Perry, 2004). This makes our workplace relationships more important than we often care to admit. Indeed, workplace relationship health predicts both professional and personal outcomes. When our workplace communication and relationships are satisfying, we achieve more professionally and feel happier at home. When our workplace communication and relationships slip into dysfunction, on-the-job productivity and relationships outside the workplace suffer.

In this chapter, we look at interpersonal communication and relationships in the workplace. You'll learn:

- How workplace relationships compare with other types of interpersonal relationships
- Tactics for fostering healthy relationships with peers at work
- Strategies for communicating competently with supervisors and subordinates
- Suggestions for coping with challenges to workplace relationships

The Nature of Workplace Relationships

How organizations' cultures, networks, and climates work

Whether it's a church, a branch of the military, a corporation, or a nonprofit charity, an organization exists and functions because coworkers communicate and form relationships with one another (Contractor & Grant, 1996). All of the information sharing, decision making, and emotional and practical support that occurs in the workplace does so in the context of coworker relationships (Sias, Krone, & Jablin, 2002). Consequently, interpersonal communication and relationships are an organization's lifeblood.

Any affiliation you have with a professional peer, supervisor, subordinate, or mentor can be considered a **workplace relationship.** These involvements differ along three dimensions: *status*, *intimacy*, and *choice* (Sias & Perry, 2004). First, most organizations are structured hierarchically in terms of status, with people ranked higher or lower than others in organizational position and power. Thus, a defining feature of workplace relationships is the equality or inequality of relationship partners. Second, workplace relationships vary in intimacy. Some remain strictly professional, with interpersonal communication restricted to work-related concerns. Others become deeply personal. Third, workplace relationships are defined by choice—the degree to which participants willingly engage in them. Although most of us don't get to handpick our coworkers, we do choose which coworkers we befriend.

Like all interpersonal involvements, workplace relationships provide us with both benefits and costs. On the plus side, workplace relationships can enhance our professional skills through the insights others provide, and increase the speed with which we rise through the organizational hierarchy (Sias & Perry, 2004). They make work more enjoyable, bolster our commitment to the organization, improve morale, and decrease employee turnover (Sias & Cahill, 1998). On the negative side, workplace relationships can spawn gossip and cliques (Albrecht & Bach, 1997). They also can add additional stress to our lives by forcing us to shoulder not only our own professional burdens but the personal challenges of our workplace friends.

As we've stressed throughout this book, interpersonal relationships are forged and maintained within the broader context of social networks and surrounding ethnic, religious, and socioeconomic class cultures. Workplace relationships are no exception. However, in addition to being shaped by all of the previously mentioned forces, workplace relationships are also strongly influenced by each organization's unique culture, networks, climate, and technology.

THE CULTURE OF THE WORKPLACE

Like many teens growing up in the United States, my first two jobs were in chain restaurants—six months at an ice cream parlor and three years at a pizza restaurant. The two workplaces couldn't have been more different. The ice cream parlor had a strict behavior code, and violations were grounds for termination. Managers snapped orders at employees and rarely socialized with them outside the

---

appendix outline

A-1 The Nature of Workplace Relationships

A-7 Peer Relationships

A-10 Mixed-Status Relationships

A-16 Challenges to Workplace Relationships

A-22 Workplace Relationships and Human Happiness

self-reflection

Think of the relationships you have with people at work. What makes them "good" or "bad"? When you compare the benefits and drawbacks of your close workplace relationships, how does this affect your feelings about the organization?

Activity: Observing Organizational Culture

Place students in groups and ask them to discuss the culture of their school. Have students make observations about their classrooms, their department, their professors, and so on. Ask them: What artifacts are important? What is significant about the physical structure and layout of particular offices and the overall campus? What about school mascots, mottoes, and stories?

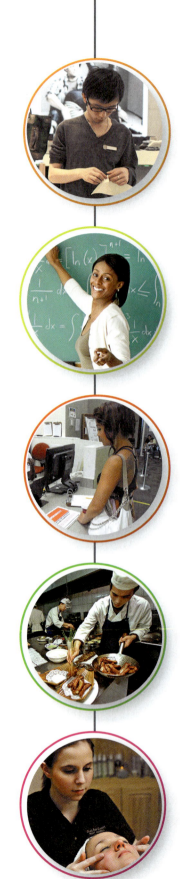

workplace. Few people developed close friendships with coworkers. The pizza restaurant was the opposite. Workers socialized after hours, and supervisor-subordinate relationships were friendly. A sense of camaraderie permeated the restaurant, and management encouraged close friendships through outside activities, including a softball team and waterskiing parties.

In the same way that different cultures have unique traditions, each workplace possesses a distinct set of beliefs regarding how things are done and how people should behave, known as its **organizational culture** (Katz & Kahn, 1978). Organizational culture influences everything from job satisfaction and organizational commitment to service quality and staff turnover (Glisson & James, 2002). An organization's culture derives from three sources, the first of which is *workplace values*: beliefs people share about work performance, dedication to the organization, and coworker relationships. For example, both places I worked in my youth stressed the values of employee excellence and productivity. But the ice cream parlor discouraged friendships between coworkers, whereas the pizza restaurant encouraged such relationships. Other examples of workplace values include beliefs regarding corporate responsibility to the environment, commitment to stakeholders (customers, employees, business partners, shareholders, etc.), and worker integrity.

Workplace values create *workplace norms*—guidelines governing appropriate interpersonal communication and relationships (Eisenberg & Goodall, 2004). In each organization, expectations evolve regarding the frequency and tone of communication. In some organizations, informality is the norm. For example, you might be encouraged by your supervisor to challenge his or her ideas, regardless of your place in the hierarchy. In other organizations, people are expected to strictly observe authority.

The final influence on an organization's culture is its *workplace artifacts*—the objects and structures that define the organization (Schein, 1985). Workplace artifacts include everything from the physical layout of your work space to dress codes and even motivational items, such as hallway posters urging you to always perform at your best.

When you join an organization, you are socialized into its culture through formal and informal encounters with established coworkers (Miller, 1995). During my first day as a dishwasher at the ice cream parlor, for example, my trainer (another dishwasher) told me, "People work here for one reason: the paycheck." My training at the pizza restaurant was conducted by the manager. He encouraged me to stay after work and enjoy free food and drink with my coworkers, an activity he called "new employee training."

NETWORKS IN THE WORKPLACE

Just as each of us has social networks of acquaintances, friends, and family members linked through communication, workplaces also have systems of

◀ The values, norms, and artifacts of an organization constitute its culture. (Top to bottom) Ryan Pyle/The New York Times/Redux Pictures; Jose Luis Pelaez Inc/Getty Images; Geri Engberg/The Image Works; Liu Jin/AFP/Getty Images; Rolf Hicker/Getty Images.

communication linkages, known as **organizational networks** (Miller, 1995). Organizational networks are defined by three characteristics: the nature of the information that flows through them, the media or channels through which the information flows, and the frequency and number of connections among people in a network, also known as *network density*.

In each organizational network, the types of information flowing through the network are diverse (Farace, Monge, & Russell, 1977). In some parts of the network, participants exchange work-related information. For instance, people in product development may interact regularly with people in marketing to create the right advertising campaign for a new product. In other parts of the network, participants share personal information. The "rumor mill"—by which coworkers pass along gossip and speculate about one another's professional and personal lives—is an example.

The second characteristic is the media or channels through which people in workplaces exchange information. These include face-to-face encounters, cell-phone conversations, instant-messaging, and e-mail exchanges. Some networks may be **virtual networks**—groups of coworkers linked solely through e-mail, social networking sites, Skype, and other online services. Virtual networks are increasingly prevalent, as the cost of fuel for transportation skyrockets and more people opt to *telecommute* (work from home and communicate with coworkers via phone and computer). For example, 2.6 percent of the U.S. workforce (3.3 million people) consider home their "primary place of work," and the number of people who telecommute either part or full time has increased a whopping 79.7 percent since 2005 (Global Workplace Analytics, 2013).

Last, networks are defined by their density: how connected each member of the network is to other members. In dense networks, every worker regularly interacts with every other network member. By contrast, members of loose networks may have contact with just one or two other members. Density is influenced by a variety of factors, including job requirements (some jobs simply don't allow for much interaction between network members), physical layout of the work space (whether network members are widely separated or clustered together), and organizational culture (some workplaces encourage frequent interaction; others discourage it). However, two of the strongest factors are familiarity and intimacy: networks in which members have known one another for a long time and are personally close tend to be denser.

Organizational networks come in many forms. Some are formally defined by the organization—the supervisors to whom you report, the employees you oversee, the peers with whom you collaborate. Others are informal and are created by coworkers themselves. Sometimes **workplace cliques** emerge—dense networks of coworkers who share the same workplace values and broader life attitudes (Jones, 1999). Within any workplace, a number of cliques may exist: a clique of "slackers" who do the minimum work necessary, a "fast track" clique of ambitious young workers, an "old boys" clique of longtime employees, and so forth.

Workplace cliques educate new employees about whom they can trust and which networks they should belong to, helping people quickly assimilate into the

Media Note:
***The Office* Culture**
The TV show *The Office* depicts the everyday lives of employees working for a branch of the Dunder Mifflin Paper Company. Have students discuss the culture of this organization (view clips at www.nbc.com/the-office). What are the values, norms, or artifacts that are important to this branch of Dunder Mifflin? Ask students to consider a present or past job. Did the culture directly affect their job satisfaction?

Teaching Note:
Workplace Cliques
Although cliques are often thought of as negative, they can have benefits, too. Ask students to think about some of the cliques they were part of in jobs or other organizations (student groups, charities, etc.). What were some of the pros of these cliques? Did the members of these groups teach you things you may not have learned in training? Were there any cons related to the cliques?

Assignment:
Group Climates

Ask students to write a short paper analyzing a past or current group project. What made the group a success or failure? Was the group a supportive or defensive climate? Describe some of the specific behaviors. What changes could have been made to improve the climate of the group?

Media Note:
Organizational Climates

In the film *The Devil Wears Prada* (2006), Miranda Priestly (Meryl Streep), editor-in-chief of *Runway* magazine, makes the organizational climate in her office one that is hard for most employees to bear. Show students a clip and ask them to discuss: How would you describe the climate of this organization? Is it defensive or supportive? Using Table A.1, what suggestions could Miranda consider to make her organizational climate more supportive?

self-reflection

What is your organization's climate like? Is it supportive, defensive, or somewhere in between? What could you do differently to improve the climate?

---

organizational culture. They also provide information about how things work in the organization. For example, when the copier breaks down or you need to expedite a shipment, members of a workplace clique can provide you with the assistance you need. But cliques can have disadvantages. For example, they may espouse workplace values contrary to those advocated by the organization—priding themselves on being "rebels," or disparaging bosses behind their backs. Worse, they may encourage unethical workplace behavior, such as punching a friend's time card to cover up the fact that the friend is absent.

Regardless of the form that organizational networks take, they are the principal wellsprings from which people get their workplace information. As a consequence, it's vital to keep two things in mind. First, *the private is public in the workplace*. Because all workplace relationships occur within organizational networks, your communication and behavior will serve as material for discussion among network members. Presume that everything you say and do will be shared throughout your organization.

Second, *the organizational networks to which you belong can strongly determine the kinds of opportunities—and obstacles—you'll encounter as you advance in your career*. For this reason, it's important to build interpersonal ties with coworkers who are both respected and connected. Try to develop relationships with *organizational insiders*, workers who are reputable, knowledgeable, and connected to dense organizational networks. The coworkers you befriend will strongly determine your experiences in the organization.

ORGANIZATIONAL CLIMATES

Think about an organization with which you're currently involved, as a paid worker, volunteer, or member. How would you describe the overall emotional tone of the place—that is, the way it *feels* to be there? Is it supportive, warm, and welcoming? detached, cool, and unfriendly? somewhere in between? This overarching emotional quality of a workplace is known as its **organizational climate** (Kreps, 1990). Organizational climate is created primarily through interpersonal communication—the amount of trust, openness, listening, and supportiveness present in the interactions between organizational members (Mohammed & Hussein, 2008).

Two types of organizational climates exist (Kreps, 1990). In a **defensive climate,** the environment is unfriendly, rigid, and unsupportive of workers' professional and personal needs. For example, supervisors may use communication as a way to strategically control others and to strictly enforce company hierarchy. Employees may resist change, be closed-minded toward new ideas or outside input, and negatively perceive any dissent. In contrast, workers in a **supportive climate** describe the workplace as warm, open, and supportive. Workers communicate honestly, collaborate to solve problems, share credit, practice empathy, and encourage people to treat one another with respect, despite any imbalance in power.

Organizational climates are rarely purely defensive or supportive. Instead, most fall somewhere in between. In addition, organizations may have different

appendix / Relationships in the Workplace   A-5

Collaboration, not only in communication but in using teamwork to accomplish tasks and projects, is a way to create a supportive climate. © Jack Kurtz/The Image Works

climates within different units, depending on workers' personalities, job demands, and supervisor communication styles (Elçi & Alpkan, 2009).

As just one person in your organization, you obviously don't have sole control over the climate. Nevertheless, organizational climate is built from the ground up: it is the sum total of individuals' interpersonal behavior in the workplace. Consequently, everything you say and do in your workplace contributes to its climate. See Table A.1 for tips on how to encourage a supportive organizational climate.

table A.1   Creating a Supportive Climate

These suggestions will help you build supportiveness in the workplace. They are especially important if you are a supervisor or manager.

1. *Encourage honest communication.* Workplace climates are most supportive when people view one another as honest and open.

2. *Adopt a flexible mind-set.* Be open to others' ideas, criticisms, and suggestions. Examine your own ideas for weaknesses. Avoid using absolutes ("This is the only option").

3. *Collaborate rather than control.* Avoid trying to manipulate others. Instead, ask for their ideas and perspectives.

4. *Describe challenges rather than assign blame.* When problems arise at work, talk about them in neutral terms rather than pointing fingers.

5. *Offer concern rather than professional detachment.* When coworkers or employees seek your support on personal dilemmas, demonstrate empathy, respect, and understanding.

6. *Emphasize equality.* Avoid pulling rank on people. When you have power over others, it's vital to treat them with respect.

Video

macmillanhighered.com /reflectrelate4e

Defensive Climate
Watch this clip online to answer the questions below.

How did the coworkers in this video create a defensive climate? What influence do you think their workplace culture had on creating their organizational climate?

Want to see more? Check out LaunchPad for a clip illustrating **supportive climate.**

skills practice

Collaborating via Technology
Using technology to collaboratively meet organizational challenges

① Identify a challenge faced by your group or organization.

② Create an online discussion group or community related to this issue.

③ Describe the problem in neutral terms, avoiding assignment of blame.

④ E-mail or text-message everyone in your work unit, inviting them to post potential solutions.

⑤ Encourage open and honest assessment of ideas.

TECHNOLOGY IN THE WORKPLACE

The use of computer-based communication technologies is now standard within workplaces; everyone from executives to maintenance workers uses texting, Twitter, and instant-messaging to coordinate professional activities (Berry, 2006). E-mail has largely replaced written memos and much of telephone and face-to-face interactions. In many corporate workplaces, e-mail is the *primary* communication medium; daily business could not occur without it (Waldvogel, 2007).

Computer-mediated communication in the workplace provides substantial advantages over face-to-face and phone interactions, especially when complex decision making requires input from multiple employees, some of whom may be long-distance (Berry, 2006). For example, hosting meetings online through live chat or posting to a common site ensures more active and equal participation than usually takes place at face-to-face meetings. People can contribute to the interaction without concern for interrupting or talking over others. The conversations are also more democratic: people in authority can't "stare down" those with whom they disagree, suppressing their input; and those who suffer from shyness feel more comfortable contributing. In addition, online discussions provide participants with freedom from time and geographic constraints. People can chime in on the conversation whenever they like over a period of days or even weeks, and participants can join or leave the discussion without having to physically move—an enormous benefit to those who are geographically distant. Online discussions are often more informative, detailed, and factual than face-to-face conversations, as participants have the opportunity to fact-check the information in each of their comments before they post them. Keep these advantages in mind if you're in a position to guide such decision-making discussions.

But the biggest advantage of communication technologies within the workplace is that they *connect* workers in a relational fashion. Online chat has usurped gossiping in the break room or talking on the telephone as the leading way employees build and bolster interpersonal ties (Riedy & Wen, 2010). Technologies allow workers to form and maintain friendships with coworkers they previously would not have been able to, including workers in other divisions of the company or other parts of the country or world (Quan-Haase, Cothrel, & Wellman, 2005).

As with anything, the benefits of workplace technologies are accompanied by certain disadvantages, the most pronounced of which is the near-constant distraction provided by online games, apps, and social networking sites. Workers in the United States now spend almost two hours *a day* **cyberslacking:** using their work computers to game, Web surf, update Facebook, e-mail, and instant-message about personal interests and activities, when they should be focused on work tasks (Garrett & Danziger, 2008). Employees higher in organizational status, male, and under the age of 30 are most likely to cyberslack (Garrett & Danziger, 2008). The lost productivity costs of cyberslacking are enormous. As just one example, companies lose an estimated $1 billion annually each March, as a result of people tracking results of the NCAA men's basketball tournament while at work (Garrett & Danziger, 2008).

Companies combat cyberslacking by using programs that track employee computer use—often without employees' knowledge. Tracking programs monitor what sites employees visit, screen e-mail for potentially inappropriate messages, and record images of employees' screens at periodic intervals (Riedy & Wen, 2010). Importantly, you're *not* protected by using a personal account rather than a company account while cyberslacking. Court cases in which employees have sued employers for violation of privacy have upheld the right of companies to access private employee accounts, arguing that employees do not have a reasonable expectation of privacy when using the employer's computer and Internet access (Riedy & Wen, 2010). When you're at work, remember this simple rule: *everything and anything you do on a company computer is considered company property—and you will be held accountable for it.*

Peer Relationships

[Peers provide personal and practical support]

What do Usher, Kanye West, and Heather Headley have in common with the Human League, Sting, and Earth, Wind, & Fire? They've all had songs written and produced by Terry Lewis and James "Jimmy Jam" Harris.[1] The two have collaborated to produce more than 40 number-one singles, over 100 gold and platinum albums, more than a dozen movie soundtracks, and even the music for the NBA All-Star Game. But through all the fame and fortune they've achieved, the two still view each other primarily as musical coworkers and collaborators. "The number one thing is that we don't do anything alone," notes Jimmy Jam. "We approach each project as equal partners."

Our most meaningful and intimate workplace relationships are those with our **professional peers**—people holding positions of organizational status and power similar to our own. Peers are the most important source of personal and practical support for employees in any type of organization, whether it's a bank, a hospital, or a band (Rawlins, 1992). Similar to Jimmy Jam and Terry Lewis, we also develop close peer relationships in the workplace. After all, our peer relationships are not simply professional; they're often intensely personal.

TYPES OF PEER RELATIONSHIPS

Although peer relationships strongly shape the quality of our work lives, not all peer relationships are the same (Fritz & Dillard, 1994). *Information peers* are equivalent-status coworkers with whom our communication is limited to

**Activity:
Peers at Work**
Play the LaunchPad clip on professional peers, and place students in groups to create response videos on maintaining peer relationships. Students should familiarize themselves with the strategies for maintaining peer relationships provided on pages A-9–A-10 before starting. Have students share their videos with the class and discuss the benefits and challenges of maintaining peer relationships in the workplace. This can also be done as an in-class role play.

Video

macmillanhighered.com/reflectrelate4e

Professional Peers
Watch this clip online to answer the questions below.

What is the difference between being friendly with peers at work and being friends with coworkers? How does your communication reflect such differences? Do you develop the same type of peer relationships with face-to-face coworkers as with virtual ones? Why or why not?

---

[1]The information that follows is adapted from Johnson (2004) and Kimpel (2010).

Music producers Terry Lewis and James "Jimmy Jam" Harris have had remarkable success in working together as professional peers. What do you think are some of the benefits and complications of working closely with someone who is also a friend?
Rick Diamond/Getty Images

self-reflection

How many of your workplace peers do you consider friends rather than simply coworkers? Are there any you think of as best friends? How do your relationships with peers at work affect your feelings about your job and the organization?

work-related content. Information-peer relationships are typically created through assignment rather than choice, and as a result, they lack trust and intimacy. Although these relationships are common, especially in large corporations, many people view information peers as less open and less communicatively skilled than collegial or special peers (Myers, Knox, Pawlowski, & Ropog, 1999).

Collegial peers are coworkers whom we consider friends. When we communicate with collegial peers, we talk about work and personal issues, and we feel moderate levels of trust and intimacy toward these individuals. Scholars sometimes describe these relationships as "blended" because they incorporate elements of both professional and personal relationships (Bridge & Baxter, 1992).

Special peers are equivalent-status coworkers with whom we share very high levels of emotional support, career-related feedback, trust, self-disclosure, and friendship (Sias et al., 2002). The rarest type of peer relationship, special peers are considered best friends in the workplace.

Professional peer relationships can evolve from lesser to greater levels of intimacy over time. The first and most significant relationship transition is from information peer to collegial peer (Sias & Cahill, 1998). Workers who spend extended periods of time together, are placed in proximity with each other, or socialize together outside of the workplace inevitably form stronger bonds with each other. However, sharing time and activities together is not enough to ensure that a coworker relationship will evolve from information peer to collegial peer. Like personal friendships, perceived similarity in interests, beliefs, and values is what decisively pushes a workplace relationship from acquaintanceship to friendship (Sias & Cahill, 1998).

The evolution of the relationship from information peer to collegial peer is similar for **virtual peers**—coworkers who communicate mainly through phone, e-mail, Skype, and other communication technologies. For virtual peers, the progression from information peer to collegial peer hinges on how much time the peers spend interacting and working on shared tasks together. Given the familiarity that many modern workers have with communication technologies and the availability of such technologies in the workplace, it's commonplace for virtual peers to become virtual friends.

The transition from collegial peer to special peer is different, however. Perceived similarity, shared time and tasks, and socializing are all important, but are not sufficient to push coworker friendships to the level of best friend (Sias & Cahill, 1998). Instead, the evolution of a coworker friendship to a higher state of intimacy is usually spurred by negative events in partners' personal lives (serious illness, marital discord) or serious work-related problems that require an exceptional level of social support.

MAINTAINING PEER RELATIONSHIPS

Like other interpersonal bonds, peer relationships remain healthy through the energy and effort you and your peers invest in maintenance. One important tactic that helps maintain your peer relationships is positivity, discussed in Chapters 10 and 11. A positive perspective and upbeat communication with your peers help offset the stress and demands everyone faces in the workplace. Practicing positivity in the workplace means communicating with your peers in a cheerful and optimistic fashion and doing unsolicited favors for them.

Openness also plays an important role. Openness means creating feelings of security and trust between you and your peers. You can create such feelings by behaving in predictable, trustworthy, and ethical ways in your relationships with peers. This means following through on your promises, respecting confidences, and demonstrating honesty and integrity in both your personal and your professional behavior.

Two additional tactics will help you maintain your collegial- and special-peer relationships (Sias et al., 2002). Like assurances given to a romantic partner, assurances given to collegial and special peers help demonstrate your commitment to them. Since choice is what distinguishes close peer relationships from casual ones, a critical part of maintaining these relationships is routinely stressing to your collegial and special peers that your relationships are based on choice rather than professional assignment. This can be accomplished

○ No matter your workplace setting, you can maintain your peer relationships by using positivity, openness, and assurances, and by remembering that peer relationships require a blend of personal and work conversational topics. Michael Goulding, The Orange County Register/Newscom

Online Self-Quiz: Test Your Maintenance of Peer Relationships. To take this self-quiz, visit LaunchPad: macmillanhighered.com /reflectrelate4e

indirectly by inviting peers to join you in activities outside the workplace, which implies that you consider them friends and not just coworkers. More directly, you can straightforwardly tell collegial and special peers that you think of them primarily as friends.

Second, collegial- and special-peer relationships grow stronger when the people involved treat each other as whole human beings with unique qualities and do not strictly define each other as just coworkers. Certainly, you will discuss work, but since your relationships with collegial and special peers are blended, you will also discuss your personal lives.

Mixed-Status Relationships

Communicating with superiors and subordinates

Most organizations are hierarchical, with some people holding positions of power over others. Relationships between coworkers of different organizational status are called **mixed-status relationships,** and they provide the structural foundation on which most organizations are built (Farace et al., 1977).

Mixed-status relationships take many forms, including officer-subordinate, trainer-trainee, and mentor-protégé. But when most of us think of mixed-status relationships, what leaps to mind are *supervisory relationships*, ones in which one person outranks and supervises another (Zorn, 1995). Most of these relationships are assigned rather than chosen.

◉ In *Brooklyn Nine-Nine*, Detective Rosa Diaz has a strong working friendship with her supervisor, Captain Ray Holt. Despite their different workplace status, Diaz and Holt respect each other greatly. What has been your experience with mixed-status relationships at work? Fox Network/Photofest

Supervisory relationships are less likely than peer relationships to evolve into friendships because of the power imbalance (Zorn, 1995). In most friendships, people downplay any difference in status and emphasize their equality. Supervisors by definition have more power. They direct their subordinates' efforts, evaluate their performance, and make decisions regarding their pay and job security.

While some supervisors and subordinates can become friends, many organizations discourage or even forbid friendships between supervisors and their subordinates because it's assumed that such relationships will impair a supervisor's ability to objectively assess a subordinate's work performance (Zorn, 1995). Research on organizational decision making supports this assumption. Managers are less likely to give negative feedback to employees they like than to those they dislike (Larson, 1984). This occurs for two reasons. First, we are reluctant to give friends who work under

"No, Thursday's out. How about never—is never good for you?"
© The New Yorker Collection 1993 Robert Mankoff from cartoonbank.com

us negative feedback because of the relationship consequences that may ensue—our friend may become angry or accuse us of unfairness. Second, as we saw in Chapter 3, our perceptions of others are substantially biased by whether we like them or not. Consequently, if we're in the supervisory position, our affection for a subordinate friend may lead us to judge his or her performance more generously than others.

MANAGING UP

Persuading superiors to support our work-related needs and wants is achieved through **upward communication**—communication from subordinates to superiors—and is conducted with an eye toward achieving influence. People feel more satisfied with their work lives when they believe that their supervisors listen and are responsive to their concerns (Eisenberg & Goodall, 2004).

Organizational communication scholar Eric Eisenberg argues that the most effective form of upward communication is **advocacy** (Eisenberg & Goodall, 2004). Through advocacy, you learn your superior's communication preferences and how to design messages in ways that will appeal to him or her. Advocacy is based on six principles. First, *plan before you pitch*. Most spontaneous appeals to supervisors ("Can I have a raise?" "Will you sign me up for that software course?") are rejected. To avoid this, take time to craft your request before you pitch it.

Second, *know why your supervisor should agree with you*. Your supervisor has the power to make decisions, so the burden is on you to present a compelling case. In your message, connect your goals to something your supervisor thinks is important. For example, "If you sign me up for this course, I'll be able to maintain our new database."

Third, *tailor your message*. Think about successful and unsuccessful attempts to influence your supervisor. Compare the different approaches you and other

▶ **Video**
macmillanhighered.com
/reflectrelate4e

Advocacy
Watch this clip online to answer the questions below.

How well did the employee design his message according to the six suggested principles for advocacy? How would the employee revise his message for a superior who was an action-oriented listener, a content-oriented listener, or a time-oriented listener?

Want to see more? Check out LaunchPad for clips illustrating **upward communication** and **downward communication**.

skills practice

Advocacy
Sharpening your advocacy skills

1. Identify a situation in which you might use advocacy to influence someone who has more power than you.
2. Consider the person's communication and decision-making preferences.
3. Create messages that embody advocacy principles.
4. Assess whether your messages are compelling.
5. Revisit your situation, but this time, imagine the person strongly disagrees with you.
6. Generate new messages to counter possible objections.
7. Choose the messages that will best help you advocate.

Assignment:
Workplace Communication
Have students watch the VideoCentral clips on **defensive climate, downward communication,** and **upward communication.** Ask them to choose one of the videos and write an improvement paper analyzing the workplace interaction. What could the employees and the managers have done differently to improve the communication? Have students experienced similar interactions in their workplaces? If so, what have they done to repair the situation?

---

people have used, and consider their efficacy. Does your supervisor respond more favorably to statistics or to an anecdote? to details or to generalities? Based on your supervisor's preferences, tailor your evidence and appeal accordingly.

Fourth, *know your supervisor's knowledge*. Many attempts at upward communication fail because subordinates present information at an inappropriate level. For example, they present their request in overly abstract terms, wrongly assuming that their supervisor is familiar with the subject. Or they present their appeal in a simplistic form, inadvertently coming across as condescending. To avoid this, know your supervisor's knowledge of the subject before you broach it. You can find this out by talking to other workers who are familiar with your supervisor.

Fifth, *create coalitions before communicating*. Most arguments made by one person are unconvincing, particularly when presented by a subordinate to a supervisor. Try to strengthen your argument with support from others in your organization. Remember to present such information as a helpful and personal observation ("Just to make sure I wasn't completely off about the situation, I checked with Joan, Denise, and Erika, and they all agreed") rather than as a threat to your supervisor's authority ("For your information, three other people feel the same way I do!"). Be sure to get approval beforehand from the people whose opinions you plan to cite. Some may not want their viewpoints referenced, and to use their sentiments as support for your arguments without their approval is highly unethical.

Finally, *competently articulate your message*. You can plan and tailor a message all you want, but if you're unable to articulate it, your supervisor probably won't take it seriously. Before you talk with your supervisor, revisit the information on competent interpersonal communication described in Chapters 1 and 7 to brush up on your skills.

COMMUNICATING WITH SUBORDINATES

When you communicate upward, you're typically trying to influence your supervisors. But when you're the supervisor, *you* have the influence. When you present a request or demand to your subordinates, you don't have to worry about using advocacy. You can simply tell them what to do and use whatever language you want. Or can you?

Having formal authority in an organization gives you freedom in the messages you use when interacting with subordinates, known as **downward communication.** But with this freedom comes responsibility. Although many people in power positions exploit their freedom by bullying or harassing employees (as we'll discuss shortly), what distinguishes competent downward communication is the willingness of empowered people to communicate without relying on their power in order to appeal to subordinates in positive, empathic, respectful, and open ways.

Competent Downward Communication A supervisor's communication sets the tone for his or her subordinates or organization. When a supervisor communicates competently, the effects radiate downward; employees are more motivated, more satisfied with their work, and more productive (Eisenberg &

focus on CULTURE

The Model Minority Myth

Karen Chan had worked in the finance department of a midsize retail chain for seven years when a new supervisor was hired. Karen was shocked when he talked about her ethnicity. "My boss would make comments like, 'I can always count on you to get the budget right, because I know Asians are good with numbers.'" Her supervisor's downward communication began to influence the perception of other department heads, who sought Karen's input on complicated financial questions. "I actually majored in English, and when I chose finance as a career, it wasn't because I was a quantitative expert. I knew I had an eye for detail, and I appreciated the foundation finance would provide for a long-term career in business."

Karen decided to confront her boss. She quickly learned that her boss was behaving out of ignorance. "He didn't mean to deliberately hurt me, but I didn't want him to continue doing it. I may want to make a switch to operations or marketing, and my boss's comments were cornering me into a finance career within the firm." They both agreed to communicate about these slips as they occurred.

Note: Information regarding Karen Chan, including quotes, is excerpted from Hyun (2005).

Many Asian Americans, like Karen Chan, are victims of the model minority myth—the belief that certain immigrant groups have overcome all the barriers to success and are self-effacing, reliable, hardworking, and technically proficient (Asian American Career Center, n.d.; Hyun, 2005). Writer Jane Hyun (2005) of the NAACP encourages workers who feel they are being stereotyped as "model minorities" to discuss the matter directly with their supervisors, much as Karen did. Importantly, you should not try to combat the stereotype by acting irresponsible, loud, or wild. Most employers value workers who are reliable, hardworking, and technically proficient, so you don't want to behave in ways contrary to these attributes.

discussion questions

- How does your culture shape your supervisor's downward communication with you?
- What impact does this communication have on your work? on your workplace satisfaction?

Goodall, 2004). But when a supervisor communicates incompetently, frustration and dissatisfaction build quickly. If you're a manager, you have not only organizational power and status but the power of your interpersonal communication to shape the morale and performance of all the workers under you, simply through how you communicate with them.

Competent downward communication can be achieved by observing five principles (Eisenberg & Goodall, 2004). First, routinely and openly emphasize the importance of communication in workplace relationships with subordinates. For example, some supervisors engage in both informal and formal interactions with subordinates—hallway chats, impromptu office visits, weekly status updates, or team meetings. They also clearly and concisely explain instructions, performance expectations, and policies.

Second, listen empathically. Respond positively to your employees' attempts at upward communication rather than perceiving such attempts as a threat to power. Listen to subordinates' suggestions and complaints and demonstrate a reasonable willingness to take fair and appropriate action in response to what they are saying.

self-reflection

Think about the most skilled supervisor you know. Which aspects of this supervisor's communication make him or her so competent—openness? ability to explain things? honesty and integrity? willingness to listen?

Third, when communicating wants and needs to subordinates, frame these messages as polite requests ("Do you think you could . . .") or persuasive explanations ("Here's why we need to get this done in the next week . . ."). By contrast, incompetent downward communication involves using power to make threats ("Do this now or else!") and demands ("Take care of that customer now!").

Fourth, be sensitive to your subordinates' feelings. For instance, if a reprimand is in order, try to make it in private rather than in front of other workers. Keep such exchanges focused on behaviors that need to change rather than making judgments about the subordinate's character or worth: "John, I noticed that you arrived late to the last three staff meetings. I'm worried that late arrivals disrupt the meetings and cause us to lose time. What ideas do you have for ensuring that you get to meetings on time?"

Last, share relevant information with employees whenever possible. This includes notice of impending organizational changes as well as explanations about why the changes are coming. For example: "Our company hasn't been meeting its forecasted revenues, so several units, including ours, are being sold to another company. We'll have an opportunity to accept jobs here or move to the company that's acquiring us. As soon as I know more about what this change means for all of us, I'll share that information."

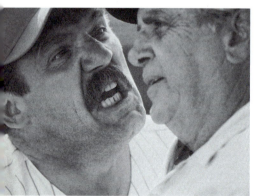

◯ A supervisor's downward communication shapes the morale and performance of all the workers under her or him. (Top) James Hardy/Getty Images; (bottom) Bruce Ayres/Getty Images

Compliments and Criticism Two challenges of downward communication are (1) how to effectively praise subordinates and (2) how to constructively criticize them. Offering subordinates praise for their workplace accomplishments fosters a healthy organizational climate. Studies repeatedly show that employees rank "appreciation" and "supervisory recognition" at the top of their list of factors motivating them to work hard, and that feeling unappreciated at work is a leading cause of employee turnover (Forni, 2002).

Complimenting your subordinates is most effectively done when the compliments are focused on a subordinate's work—his or her achievements, expertise, attitude, cooperativeness, and so forth. Avoid compliments about personal matters—like a subordinate's appearance. Regardless of your intention, something as innocuous as complimenting the stylishness of a subordinate's hairstyle or the beauty of his or her skin may make the person feel uncomfortable. In some organizations, such compliments can trigger charges of sexual harassment or discrimination.

Praise is best presented privately rather than publicly, except in formal contexts, such as recognition dinners and award ceremonies. Many supervisors enjoy spontaneously singling out particular employees for praise in front of their coworkers ("Everyone, let's give Samantha a round of applause—she was our unit sales leader again this past month!"). These supervisors incorrectly believe that such praise improves morale, but it can do the opposite. When someone is publicly singled out in a context in which such recognition is unexpected, that person's status is elevated. This might be merited, but it could foster resentment and envy among the person's peers and ultimately undermine the organization's climate.

Of course, criticizing subordinates is no easier. Especially challenging is providing constructive criticism to high-achieving employees, who often have little experience receiving criticism and expect only praise (Field, 2005). But offering constructive criticism isn't as difficult as you might think. Instead, it requires you to draw on the many skills you have mastered in previous chapters.

Begin by using your knowledge of emotion management from Chapter 4, remaining calm, kind, and understanding throughout the exchange. Open your interaction with positive remarks, and end your comments with similar commendations: "It was obvious you worked really hard on designing that presentation" or "This isn't the end of the world—just something I'd like you to work on for future presentations."

Second, follow the guidelines for competent interpersonal communication described in Chapter 1, and cooperative language detailed in Chapter 7. Informatively, honestly, and clearly identify the issue or behavior that concerns you, describing it neutrally rather than personalizing it or leveling accusations. For example, instead of saying "You clearly don't realize how you came across," say "I think the way you defended our team's work yesterday may not have been the most effective approach." Rather than "You shouldn't have gone in unprepared like that," say "There seemed to be an expectation in the room of more precise data on projected sales."

Strive to experience and express empathy toward your subordinate through perspective-taking and empathic concern (Chapter 3), showing that you understand how he or she may feel: "The same thing has happened to me before" rather than "I would never let something like that happen." Keep in mind how you have felt when receiving criticism from your superiors, and adapt your communication accordingly.

Finally, avoid belaboring the error that has been made, and instead focus most of your talk time on ideas for avoiding such missteps in the future. Although you have the authority to dictate corrections, subordinates respond more favorably when supervisors negotiate solutions with them. Offer your subordinate specific ideas, but frame them as suggestions, asking for his or her opinion. The goal of constructive criticism is not only to correct the errant behavior but to create a mutual consensus with your subordinate.

MAINTAINING MIXED-STATUS RELATIONSHIPS

As we've seen, communicating competently in mixed-status relationships presents numerous challenges—whether you're trying to influence a superior, praise a subordinate, or provide constructive criticism to an employee whose performance is inadequate. But a broader challenge is maintaining these relationships. Maintaining mixed-status relationships requires you to do two things (Albrecht & Bach, 1997). First, with your supervisor and subordinates, *develop and follow communication rules for what's appropriate to talk about as well as when and how to communicate.* For example, supervisors who think their subordinates agree with them on how they should communicate tend to rate those subordinates higher on overall performance than subordinates who hold different beliefs about communication (Albrecht & Bach, 1997). Communication rules govern matters such as how often a supervisor and subordinate meet to discuss work projects, whether communications are formal or informal, and which channels (e-mail, instant-messaging, texting, printed memos, face-to-face conversations) are the most appropriate.

Second, *communicate in consistent and reliable ways.* This means displaying a stable and professional manner with supervisors and subordinates, rather than allowing personal problems or moods to influence your communication. It also means being punctual, following through on appointments and promises, and keeping confidences. Consistency builds trust, an essential component of any interpersonal relationship; a perception that you're "trustworthy" will feed into other positive perceptions of you as well, including your integrity, openness, and competence (Albrecht & Bach, 1997).

Challenges to Workplace Relationships

Dealing with bullying, romance, and harassment

After my freshman year at the University of Washington, I dropped out of school and went to work driving for a local trucking company. My boss, Rob, delighted in tormenting me. During my initial hiring interview, I made the mistake of telling him how desperately I needed the job, so he knew from the beginning that he had substantial power over me. Several times a week he would call me into his office to verbally abuse me for his amusement— insulting me and swearing at me and then laughing because he knew I couldn't do anything about it. Rob would assign me impossible tasks, then punish me when I didn't complete them "on time." For example, he'd send me to the docks to unload a 45-foot trailer filled with sofas but wouldn't let me use a hand truck or forklift. After I'd spent an hour struggling with enormous and weighty boxes, he'd come down and yell at me for "being slow." He assigned me to a truck that had bad brakes. Once, after parking at a delivery ramp, I came out from signing paperwork to see my truck rolling away down the alley. Like a scene from a bad comedy, I had to run after my truck, desperately trying to catch up to it so I could jump in and stop it with the emergency brake. But Rob's favorite sport was to threaten to fire me, just to make me beg him for my job (which I did). After six months of daily bullying, I decided that the financial costs of unemployment were preferable to the abuse I was suffering, and I quit.

Maintaining workplace relationships is hard. We must constantly juggle job demands, power issues, and intimacy, all while communicating in ways that are positive and professional (Sias, Heath, Perry, Silva, & Fix, 2004). Yet sometimes even more intense challenges arise. Three of the most common, and difficult to manage, are workplace bullying, the development of romantic relationships with coworkers, and sexual harassment.

WORKPLACE BULLYING

In the course of your professional lives, many of you will experience situations similar to what I went through with Rob, my trucking boss. **Workplace bullying** is the repeated unethical and unfavorable treatment of one or more persons by others in the workplace (Boddy, 2011). Bullying occurs in a variety of ways, including shouting, swearing, spreading vicious rumors, destroying the target's property or work, and excessive criticism. It is also perpetrated through passive means, such as the silent treatment, exclusion from meetings and gatherings, and ignoring of requests (Tracy, Lutgen-Sandvik, & Alberts, 2006). In nearly one-fifth of cases, workplace bullying involves physical violence, including hitting, slapping, and shoving (Martin & LaVan, 2010). When bullying occurs online, it is known as *cyberbullying*. The most frequently reported forms of workplace cyberbullying are withholding or deleting important information sent via e-mail, and spreading gossip or rumors through text messages, e-mails, and online posts (Privitera & Campbell, 2009). Perpetrators of workplace bullying usually combine several of these tactics to intimidate their victims. The most common forms are detailed in Table A.2 on page A-18.

Workplace bullying has devastating effects on the target's physical and psychological health. Bullying typically generates feelings of helplessness, anger, and despair. It can even cause health problems, such as sleep disorders, depression, and chronic fatigue (Tracy et al., 2006). The associated costs to companies for workplace bullying are huge: they include disability and workers' compensation claims, lawsuits, low-quality work, reduced productivity, high staff turnover, increased absenteeism, and deteriorated customer relationships (Tracy et al., 2006).

skills practice

Workplace Bullying
Responding more effectively to workplace bullying

❶ Consider the situation, and yourself, from the bully's perspective.

❷ List the bully's behaviors and possible motivations for them.

❸ Plan your responses. For each behavior, what would you say or do? Factor in the bully's motivations.

❹ Assess the effectiveness of your responses. Would your responses likely generate positive or negative outcomes? What are the organizational repercussions of your responses?

❺ Use your planned responses the next time the bully behaves badly.

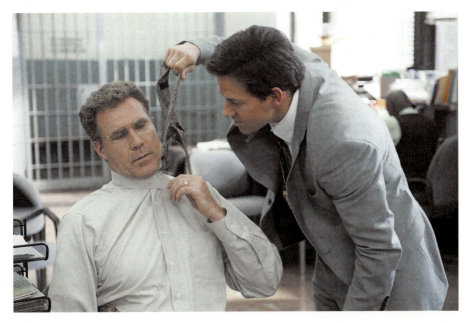

◀ In the movie *The Other Guys* (2010), frustrated detective Terry Hoitz (Mark Wahlberg) regularly bullies his partner, Allen Gamble (Will Ferrell), a forensic accountant in his office. Although presented for laughs in the film, workplace bullying has been shown to decrease productivity and can cause depression and other anxiety-related health problems. Macall B. Polay/© Columbia Pictures/Everett Collection

table A.2 Common Forms of Workplace Bullying

Form	Description
Isolation	Restrict employees' interaction with coworkers; isolate their work area from others; exclude them from group activities and off-site social gatherings.
Control of Important Information	Prevent important information from reaching workers; provide false job-related information to them; block or delete their correspondence, e-mail, telephone calls, and work assignments.
Constraint of Professional Responsibilities	Assign workers to tasks that are useless, impossible, or absurd; intentionally leave them with nothing to do.
Creation of Dangerous Work Conditions	Distract workers during critical tasks to put them in peril; assign them tasks that endanger their health or safety; refuse to provide appropriate safety measures for their job.
Verbal Abuse	Make disdainful, ridiculing, and insulting remarks regarding workers' personal characteristics (appearance, intelligence, personality, etc.); spread rumors and lies about them.
Destruction of Professional Reputation	Attack workers' professional performance; exaggerate the importance of their work errors; ignore or distort their correct decisions and achievements.

Source: Adapted from Escartín, Rodríguez-Carballeira, Zapf, Porrúa, and Martín-Peña (2009).

Unfortunately, workplace bullying is common: 25–30 percent of U.S. employees are bullied at some point during their work lives—10 percent at any given time (Keashly & Neuman, 2005). In one-third of cases, the bullying occurs despite existence of official antibullying workplace policies (Martin & LaVan, 2010). One reason that bullying is so widespread is that when bullied workers share their stories of abuse with others, they typically aren't believed (Tracy et al., 2006). The types of abuse that occur are often so outrageous that people simply can't accept them as true. Adding to this, workplace bullies typically put on an act for their supervisors: behaving in a supportive fashion when they are being watched and being abusive when the boss is not around (Tracy et al., 2006). Workplace bullies can be such good actors that even trial juries believe them. In 73 percent of legal cases in which bullied employees took bullying supervisors to court, juries found in favor of the supervisors (Martin & LaVan, 2010).

How can you cope with workplace bullying? Some people simply quit and find another job (Bies & Tripp, 1998). Of course, this is not an option for everyone, since most people depend on their income, and new job opportunities can be limited. Others give in to the bullying, choosing to ignore it or tough it out because the perceived costs of challenging the abusive supervisor are too high. For example, if you take your complaints to your supervisor's boss, that person may side with your supervisor—leading to an escalation in the bullying. Another option is to use your interpersonal communication skills and directly confront the bully (Bies & Tripp, 1998). In private, point out which actions you feel are abusive and ask the bully to stop. Some bullies may back off when they are confronted. At least one study of workplace bullying found that, although the most frequently reported strategy for dealing with workplace bullies was avoiding or ignoring them, respondents who confronted their abusers saw improvements in their subsequent interactions (Keashly, Trott, & MacLean, 1994).

WORKPLACE ROMANCES

A second challenge to workplace relationships is the development of romantic feelings for coworkers. The workplace is a natural venue for romantic attraction to unfold, as many of the elements that foster attraction are present: a wide variety of attractive and available partners, large amounts of time spent together, physical proximity, and similarity in interests and attitudes (Appelbaum, Marinescu, Klenin, & Bytautas, 2007). Over 80 percent of North American employees have experienced a romantic relationship at work (Schaefer & Tudor, 2001), and 10 million new workplace romances are forged each year (Pierce & Aguinis, 2009), usually among peers.

Historically, companies have discouraged workplace romances, believing that they lead to favoritism, lack of worker motivation, decreased efficiency and productivity, and increased risk of sexual harassment lawsuits (Appelbaum et al., 2007). But many workplaces have begun to shift their views and policies, as research supports that romantic involvement does not hurt worker productivity

self-reflection

If you have had a workplace romance, what were the biggest challenges you faced? How did you and your partner meet these challenges? If you haven't had a workplace romance, what are your perceptions of such romances? Do you approve or disapprove of them? How could they affect your organization?

On *Grey's Anatomy*, hospital intern Meredith Grey begins a relationship with her supervisor, surgeon Derek Shepherd, before they realize that they are coworkers. Over several seasons, they come apart and get together again repeatedly, due to the combined pressures of the workplace and their personal problems. ABC/Photofest

Media Note: Workplace Romances

Clips from the TV show *Grey's Anatomy* can provide examples of workplace romances that affect the partners' workplace performance and stability (http://abc.go.com/shows/greys-anatomy). What advice would students give to the doctors on *Grey's Anatomy* or even a friend who is in a workplace romance? What are some rules students would encourage them to follow? How should those involved balance their workplace relationship and their romantic relationship?

(Boyd, 2010). From the worker's perspective, workplace romance is typically viewed positively. Romantically involved workers are usually perceived by people in their organization as friendly and approachable (Hovick, Meyers, & Timmerman, 2003), and having romances in the workplace is seen as creating a positive, work climate (Riach & Wilson, 2007). Relationship outcomes are often positive, too: married couples who work in the same location have a 50 percent *lower* divorce rate than those employed at different workplaces (Boyd, 2010).

Despite these positives, workplace romances face challenges. Involvement in a romance can create the perception among coworkers that the partners are more interested in each other than in their work, leading to rumors and gossip (Albrecht & Bach, 1997). As a consequence, you can't cultivate a workplace romance without expecting the relationship to become a focus of workplace gossip.

The negative outcomes associated with workplace romances are more pronounced for women than for men. Women are more likely than men to suffer unfavorable work evaluations based on romantic involvement, are judged more negatively by their colleagues following workplace romance breakups, and are more likely to be terminated by their companies for workplace affairs (Riach & Wilson, 2007). When such relationships are mixed status—in particular, if a woman is under the direct supervision of a man—others in the organization often conclude that the woman used the relationship to enhance her career. In contrast, men in workplace romances often win their coworkers' admiration (Dillard, 1987).

How can you successfully overcome the challenge of maintaining a workplace romance should you become involved in one? First, leave your love at home, so to speak, and communicate with your partner in a strictly professional fashion during work hours. When romantic partners maintain a professional demeanor toward each other and communicate with all their coworkers in a consistent and positive fashion, the romance is usually ignored or even encouraged (Buzzanell, 1990).

Second, use e-mail, text messages, Facebook, and instant-messaging judiciously to maintain your relationship. When used properly, these technologies enable romantic partners to communicate frequently and in a way that maintains professional decorum (Hovick et al., 2003). However, electronic messages exchanged in the workplace should never contain overly intimate or controversial messages. Although many workers use their business accounts for personal reasons, it is wise to write messages that comply with official policies, no matter who the recipient is. Electronic messages are not secure. Anyone with the motivation and know-how can gain access to the messages you and your partner exchange. And, as noted earlier in the chapter, if the message was produced during work time, your company has a legal right to access it.

SEXUAL HARASSMENT

Sometimes sexual or romantic interest in the workplace is one sided. Although most people are willing to abandon their attraction once they realize it's unrequited, some exploit their organizational power to pursue it. In some instances, sexual pursuit is merely a vehicle for abusively wielding power over others in the workplace. Consider the case of Leigh-Anne Goins, who took a job as an office manager before pursuing her dream of earning a graduate degree. Her job quickly became a nightmare, as she describes:[2]

> For the first few months my job was wonderful. I was in charge of the office, and I was making supervisory decisions. Then my boss's true colors came out. He began coming up behind me and putting his hands on my shoulders, leaning in and talking into my ear. I thought, *no . . . I'm imagining things*. I should have bailed, but I had to pay my rent and I was trying to save money for school. The final straw came when I purchased some brownies and offered one to my boss in addition to my other coworkers. My boss said no because he was dieting. I offered one last time, just to be polite, and he responded by covering his mouth like he was going to tell a secret and whispering so that only I could see and hear, "You're my brownie," and licking his lips at me. That was the final straw, being called the boss's "brownie."

Many people think the problem of sexual harassment in the workplace has been solved. It hasn't. In 2011, 11,364 charges of sexual harassment were made. (U.S. Equal Employment Opportunity Commission, 2011). These charges represent only a small portion of actual instances, since the majority of sexual harassment incidents go unreported.

Although most people condemn sexual harassment in the workplace, enormous differences exist in perceptions of what constitutes harassment. The most commonly cited definition of **sexual harassment** is one created by the U.S. Equal Employment Opportunity Commission (1980):

> Unwelcome sexual advances, requests for sexual favors, and other verbal or physical conduct of a sexual nature constitute sexual harassment when (1) submission to such conduct is made either explicitly or implicitly a term or condition of an individual's employment, (2) submission to or rejection of such conduct by an individual is used as the basis for employment decisions affecting such individual, or (3) such conduct has the intention or effect of unreasonably interfering with an individual's work performance or of creating an intimidating, hostile, or offensive working environment.

This definition suggests that two types of harassment occur in the workplace. The first is *quid pro quo harassment*—a person in a supervisory position asking for or demanding sexual favors in return for professional advancement or

Online Self-Quiz: Test Your Perception of Sexual Harassment. To take this self-quiz, visit LaunchPad: macmillanhighered.com /reflectrelate4e

Activity: Sexual Harassment in the Workplace
Pass a notecard to each student and provide the following instructions: "Do not put your name on the card. On the front side write if you are male or female and provide an example of sexual harassment that you have experienced while on the job or on a team. On the back side indicate 'read' or 'do not read.'" Collect the cards and read out loud the ones marked "read." Ask students to discuss the forms of harassment and ways to handle and prevent future occurrences. Note: This may bring up challenging topics that require a carefully managed conversation.

---
[2] All information regarding the experience of Leigh-Anne Goins is from L.-A. Goins (personal communication with author, March 2005). Published with permission.

protection from layoffs or other undesirable events (Gerdes, 1999). Much more prevalent than quid pro quo harassment, however, is *hostile climate harassment* (Tyner & Clinton, 2010). As Leigh-Anne Goins experienced, hostile climate harassment is sexual behavior intended to disrupt a person's work performance.

Sexual harassment has a devastating effect. Victims of sexual harassment report feeling angry, afraid, and depressed (Cochran, Frazier, & Olson, 1997). Harassment victims are more likely than others to develop substance abuse and other health problems, including weight loss and sleep and stomach disorders (Clair, 1998). Not surprisingly, they also suffer a host of professional problems, including missed work, lower productivity, and ostracism by coworkers who blame them for inviting the harassment (Hickson, Grierson, & Linder, 1991).

The most common way of coping with sexual harassment is to avoid the harasser, ignore the harassment, or interpret the harassment in ways that minimize its seriousness—"It's not a big enough deal to pursue," "He was only flirting," "That's just the way things work here," or "It was all a harmless joke" (Clair, 1993). Some workers confront the harasser, describing his or her actions as inappropriate or threatening or pursuing legal action. Confronting harassers is strongly encouraged as a matter of principle, but the practical consequences can be difficult to manage. In sexual harassment cases, people in the organization often side with the person in the position of authority (Fitzgerald, 1993).

If you are experiencing sexual harassment, remember that fewer than 5 percent of sexual harassment victims report the problem to an authority (Fitzgerald, 1993). The decision not to report will likely perpetuate the harassment because it can teach harassers that their behavior is OK. The best long-term solution for addressing sexual harassment is to challenge it when it occurs and believe that the harassers deserve to be punished. If you're not sure what to do, contact the Equal Employment Opportunity Commission. Go to www.eeoc.gov for detailed information on how to handle such situations, or call 1-800-669-4000 or the TTY phone number for those who are deaf or hard of hearing: 1-800-669-6820.

Workplace Relationships and Human Happiness

Happiness at work can affect other areas of our lives

self-reflection

Would you continue working if you didn't need to? Why or why not? If you chose not to work, what consequences can you envision for your life? How would not having a job affect your sense of purpose? your happiness?

In his book *The Pursuit of Happiness* (2002), psychologist David Myers comments on the role that workplace relationships play in his life:

Through our work we identify with a *community*. My sense of community is rooted in the network of supportive friends who surround me on our department team, in the institution whose goals we embrace, and in the profession we call our own. (p. 130)

For many of us, our motivation to work transcends the desire to bring home a paycheck. Although we need the money our jobs provide, we also want to feel that our work is meaningful and important. When asked, "Would you continue

◐ Through our work we identify with a community.
Horace Bristol/Time & Life Pictures

working, even if you inherited a huge fortune that made working unnecessary?" three out of four Americans answered yes (Eisenberg & Goodall, 2004). This isn't just an American value: people in nearly every industrialized nation report lower satisfaction with their lives if they're unemployed, regardless of their financial standing (Myers, 2002).

But it's not the work itself that fulfills us; it's the coupling of the professional with the personal, the creation of a coworker community. Day in and day out, we endure work stress and intense demands with those who surround us—our supervisors, subordinates, and peers. These people aren't just coworkers; they can be companions, friends, and sometimes even best friends or lovers. When these relationships are healthy, the effects spread to every part of our lives. We're happier in life and more productive on the job. Those around us find us more pleasant to work with, and the organization as a whole thrives. When it comes to workplace relationships, the professional is profoundly personal.

Assignment: Best Job Ever
Ask students to write a paper about the best job they have ever had: What made you take pleasure in this job? Did you enjoy this job because of your peers or because you had a great boss? Did you love to go to work because of the shared values you had with the organization, the new technology available, or the open and inviting communication? Relate your favorite job to the concepts you have learned throughout the chapter.

review

LaunchPad for *Reflect & Relate* offers videos and encourages self-assessment through adaptive quizzing. Go to **macmillanhighered.com/reflectrelate4e** to get access to:

 LearningCurve Adaptive Quizzes

 Video clips that help you understand interpersonal communication

key terms

- workplace relationship, A-1
- organizational culture, A-2
- organizational networks, A-3
- virtual networks, A-3
- workplace cliques, A-3
- organizational climate, A-4
- ▶ defensive climate, A-4
- ▶ supportive climate, A-4
- cyberslacking, A-6
- ▶ professional peers, A-7
- virtual peers, A-8
- mixed-status relationships, A-10
- ▶ upward communication, A-11
- ▶ advocacy, A-11
- ▶ downward communication, A-12
- workplace bullying, A-17
- sexual harassment, A-21

▶ You can watch brief, illustrative videos of these terms and test your understanding of the concepts in LaunchPad.

key concepts

The Nature of Workplace Relationships

- Our **workplace relationships** are shaped by many forces. Two of the most powerful are **organizational culture** and **organizational networks**. Most workers learn their organization's culture during new employee socialization and by interacting with members of various networks.
- Organizational networks are the principal source of workplace information for most employees. **Virtual networks** also exist, particularly for workers who telecommute from home.
- When members of networks share common beliefs and personal values, they sometimes form **workplace cliques.** Cliques can provide useful insider information to new employees, but they can also be disruptive.
- The overall emotional tone of your organization, known as the **organizational climate,** can be rigid and cold in a **defensive climate,** open and warm in a **supportive climate,** or somewhere in between.
- While technology in the workplace connects workers in a relational fashion, it also creates opportunities for **cyberslacking.**

Peer Relationships

- Our closest workplace relationships are with our **professional peers.** Friendships between peers evolve from frequent interaction and common interests. The same is true for **virtual peers.**

Mixed-Status Relationships

- The primary interpersonal dynamic in **mixed-status relationships** is power. The difference in power makes forming friendships across status lines challenging.
- Much of **upward communication** is designed to gain influence. Although people use different tactics, the most effective is **advocacy**—designing a message that is specifically tailored to the viewpoints of your superior.
- When engaging in **downward communication,** it's important to communicate in positive, empathic, respectful, and open ways.

Challenges to Workplace Relationships

- **Workplace bullying** can occur in a variety of ways, including cyberbullying. Such bullying affects the target's physical and psychological health.
- Even though romances in the workplace are common, they offer both positives and challenges.
- Sexual harassment has devastating effects on victims.

GLOSSARY

accommodation: (p. 263) A way of handling conflict in which one person abandons his or her goals for the goals of another. For example, Louis gives in to Martel over where they should park their cars: "You can have the driveway. I'm tired of arguing about it."

action-oriented listeners: (p. 174) Those who prefer to receive brief, to-the-point, accurate information for decision making or for initiating a course of action. For example, a supervisor who requires brief summaries from department heads and does not want to bat around details in long meetings.

actor-observer effect: (p. 76) A tendency to credit external forces as causes for our behaviors instead of internal factors. For instance, Leon says he snapped at a coworker because she was slow instead of blaming his own impatience.

adaptors: (p. 231) Touching gestures, often unconsciously made, that serve a physical or psychological purpose. For example, twirling hair while reading, jingling pocket change, and fingering jewelry may be gestures that provide comfort, signal anxiety, or are simply unconscious habits.

advocacy: (p. A-11) Communication from a subordinate intended to influence a superior in an organization. For example, you convince your manager to try a new product line.

affect displays: (p. 240) Intentional or unintentional nonverbal behaviors that reveal actual or feigned emotions, such as a frown, a choked sob, or a smile intended to disguise fear.

agentic friendships: (p. 360) Friendships in which the parties are primarily focused on helping each other achieve practical goals, such as those among peers in a study group or colleagues at work.

aggressive-hostile touch: (p. 235) A touch designed to hurt and humiliate others, involving forms of physical violence like grabbing, slapping, and hitting.

aggressive listening: (p. 181) Listening in order to find an opportunity to attack or collect information to use against the speaker, such as when a father encourages his son to describe his ambitions just to ridicule the son's goals. (Also known as *ambushing*.)

algebraic impressions: (p. 89) Impressions of others that continually change as we add and subtract positive or negative information that we learn about them.

anger: (p. 117) The negative primary emotion that occurs when you are blocked or interrupted from attaining an important goal by what you see as the improper action of an external agent.

appropriateness: (p. 21) A measure of communication competence that indicates the degree to which your communication matches the situational, relational, and cultural expectations regarding how people should communicate.

artifacts: (p. 239) Things we possess that influence how we see ourselves and that we use to express our identity to others. Jewelry, for instance, can indicate economic means, marital status, religious affiliation, style preferences, and taste.

assimilation: (p. 138) Attempting to be accepted into the dominant culture.

attending: (p. 165) The second stage of the listening process in which a listener devotes attention to received information. For example, you may *hear* a radio but *attend* only when a favorite song comes on.

attention focus: (p. 115) Preventing unwanted emotions by intentionally devoting your attention only to aspects of an event or encounter that you know will not provoke those emotions. For example, you disregard your uncle's snide comments while forcing all your interest on your aunt's conversation.

attributional complexity: (p. 153) Acknowledging that other people's behaviors have complex causes that may reflect cultural differences.

attributions: (p. 74) Rationales we create to explain the comments or behaviors of others. For example, Ryan reasons that Jason's quietness in class means that Jason is shy.

avoidance: (p. 262) A way of handling conflict by ignoring it, pretending it isn't really happening, or communicating indirectly about the situation. For example, Martel hides behind the newspaper as Louis shouts, "Your car is blocking mine again. How many times do I have to ask you to park it to the side?" See also **skirting; sniping.**

G-1

avoiding: (p. 302) A relational stage in which one or both individuals in a couple try to distance themselves from each other physically. For example, Owen changes jobs to have an excuse to travel away from home frequently.

back-channel cues: (p. 168) Nonverbal and verbal responses that signal you've paid attention to and understood specific comments—for example, saying "Okay, got it" after someone details extensive driving directions, or nodding in agreement.

beautiful-is-good effect: (p. 295) A tendency for physical attractiveness to create the perception of competency and intelligence. For example, a witness is viewed favorably and seems credible because she is good-looking.

birds-of-a-feather effect: (p. 295) A tendency to be attracted to others if we perceive them as similar to ourselves.

blended emotions: (p. 108) Two or more primary emotions experienced at the same time. For instance, Melinda feels fear and anger when her daughter is not home by curfew.

bonding: (p. 300) A relational stage in which an official public ritual unites two people by the laws or customs of their culture. For example, Ruth marries Owen in her hometown church.

catharsis: (p. 118) Within the field of interpersonal communication, the assumption that openly expressing emotions enables you to purge them.

channel: (p. 7) The sensory dimension (sound, sight, touch, scent, or taste) used to transmit information during communication. For example, you may apologize by showing someone a sad facial expression, lightly touching his shoulder, and saying "I'm so sorry."

chilling effect: (p. 278) An outcome of physical violence in which individuals stop discussing relationship issues out of fear of their partner's negative reactions.

chronic hostility: (p. 118) A persistent state of simmering or barely suppressed anger and near-constant state of arousal and negative thinking.

circumscribing: (p. 302) A relational stage in which partners avoid talking about topics that produce conflict. For instance, whenever Owen mentions he's interested in moving, Ruth becomes upset and changes the subject.

Co-cultural Communication Theory: (p. 138) A theory that the people who have more power within a society determine the dominant culture.

co-cultures: (p. 138) Members of a society who don't conform to the dominant culture in terms of language, lifestyle, or even physical appearance.

cohabiting couples: (p. 330) Two unmarried adults who are involved romantically and live together with or without children.

collaboration: (p. 264) A way of handling conflict by treating it as a mutual problem-solving challenge. For example, Martel and Louis brainstorm ways to solve the problem they have with their shared parking area until they come up with an agreeable solution.

collectivistic cultures: (p. 144) Cultures that emphasize group identity, interpersonal harmony, and the well-being of ingroups. Collectivist cultures also value the importance of belonging to groups that look after members in exchange for loyalty. Contrast **individualistic culture.**

commitment: (p. 291) A strong psychological attachment to a partner and an intention to continue the relationship long into the future.

communal friendships: (p. 359) Voluntary relationships focused on sharing time and activities together.

communication: (p. 6) The process through which people use messages to generate meanings within and across contexts, cultures, channels, and media.

communication accommodation theory: (p. 153) The idea that people are especially motivated to adapt their language when they seek social approval, wish to establish relationships with others, and view others' language use as appropriate.

communication apprehension: (p. 214) The fear or anxiety associated with interaction that keeps someone from being able to communicate cooperatively.

communication plans: (p. 214) Mental maps that describe exactly how communication encounters will unfold. For example, before calling to complain about her telephone bill, Marjorie mentally rehearses how she will explain her problem and what objections she might face.

Communication Privacy Management Theory: (p. 342) The idea that individuals create informational boundaries by choosing carefully the kind of private information they reveal and the people with whom they share it.

communication skills: (p. 21) Repeatable goal-directed behaviors and behavioral patterns that enable you to improve the quality of your interpersonal encounters and relationships. See also **appropriateness; interpersonal communication competence.**

companionate love: (p. 289) An intense form of liking defined by emotional investment and deeply intertwined lives.

competition: (p. 263) A way of handling conflict by an open and clear discussion of the goal clash that exists and the pursuit of one's own goals without regard for others' goals. For example, Martel and Louis yell back and forth about whose car should have the driveway parking spot and whose should be parked out front.

complementary relationships: (p. 257) Relationships characterized by an unequal balance of power, such as a marriage in which one spouse is the decision maker.

compromise: (p. 271) When, during a conflict, both parties change their goals to make them compatible. For example, though Matt wants to see the sci-fi thriller and Jane wants to see the new animated film, they agree to go to an adventure comedy.

conflict: (p. 254) The process that occurs when people perceive that they have incompatible goals or that someone is interfering in their ability to achieve their objectives.

conformity orientation: (p. 335) The degree to which family members believe communication should emphasize similarity or diversity in attitudes, beliefs, and values.

connotative meaning: (p. 197) Understanding of a word's meaning based on the situation and the shared knowledge between communication partners (i.e., not the dictionary definition). For instance, calling someone *slender* suggests something more positive than the word *skinny* or *scrawny* does, though all three words mean "underweight." Contrast **denotative meaning.**

consensual families: (p. 336) Families characterized by high levels of conformity and conversation orientation. For example, Dan's parents encourage their son to be open but also expect him to maintain family unity through agreement or obedience.

constitutive rules: (p. 193) Guidelines that define word meaning according to a particular language's vocabulary. For instance, "pencil" is *Bleistift* in German and *matita* in Italian.

content-oriented listeners: (p. 175) Those who prefer to be intellectually challenged by messages—they prefer complex, detailed information. For example, a supervisor reviews the success of a fundraising event by requesting data analyzing the effectiveness of her team's publicity campaign instead of asking to hear about team members' experiences.

contexts: (p. 7) Situations in which communication occurs. Context includes the physical locations, backgrounds, genders, ages, moods, and relationships of the communicators, as well as the time of day.

conversation orientation: (p. 335) The degree to which family members are encouraged to participate in unrestrained interaction about a wide array of topics.

Cooperative Principle: (p. 205) The idea that we should make our verbal messages as informative, honest, relevant, and clear as is required, given what the situation requires. For example, listening closely to your friend's problem with a coworker and then responding with support would demonstrate the Cooperative Principle; interrupting your friend to brag about your new laptop would not.

cooperative verbal communication: (p. 204) Producing messages that are understandable, taking active ownership for what you're saying by using "I" language, and making others feel included.

cross-category friendships: (p. 364) Voluntary relationships that cross demographic lines.

culture: (p. 136) The established, coherent set of beliefs, attitudes, values, and practices shared by a large group of people.

cumulative annoyance: (p. 262) A buildup of repressed irritations that grows as the mental list of grievances we have against our partner grows. For example, Martel's anger about where Louis parks his car is a reaction to several other incidents in which Louis was inconsiderate.

cyberslacking: (p. A-6) Using work computers for personal interests and activities, such as playing games, surfing the Internet, updating Facebook, sending e-mail, or instant-messaging, instead of focusing on work tasks.

deactivation: (p. 116) Preventing unwanted emotions by systematically desensitizing yourself to emotional experience. For example, Josh insulates himself with numbness after his wife's death.

deception: (p. 211) Deliberately using uninformative, untruthful, irrelevant, or vague language for the purpose of misleading others.

defensive climate: (p. A-4) A workplace atmosphere that is unfriendly, rigid, or unsupportive of workers' professional and personal needs. Contrast **supportive climate.**

defensive communication: (p. 213) Impolite messages delivered in response to suggestions, criticism, or perceived slights. For instance, when Stacy asks

Lena to slow down her driving, Lena snaps back, "I'm not going that fast. If you don't like the way I drive, ride with someone else."

demand-withdraw pattern: (p. 277) A way of handling conflict in which one partner in a relationship de-mands that his or her goals be met, and the other partner responds by withdrawing from the encounter.

denotative meaning: (p. 197) The literal, or dictionary, definition of a word. Contrast **connotative meaning.**

dialects: (p. 194) Variations on language rules shared by large groups or particular regions; this may include differences in vocabulary, grammar, and pronunciation. For example, in various regions of the United States, carbonated beverages are called *soda, pop,* or *Coke.*

differentiating: (p. 302) A relational stage in which the beliefs, attitudes, and values that distinguish you from your partner come to dominate your thoughts and communication. For example, Ruth and Owen argue over whose family they are going to visit for Thanksgiving and how much time each has spent fixing up the house.

dirty secrets: (p. 276) Truthful but destructive messages used deliberately to hurt someone during a conflict. For example, Judith tells her sister, "That boy you like—Craig? I heard him tell Elaine you laugh like a horse."

dismissive attachment: (p. 46) An attachment style in which individuals have low anxiety but high avoidance: they view close relationships as comparatively unimportant, instead prizing self-reliance.

display rules: (p. 148) Cultural norms about how people should and should not express emotion—that is, guidelines for when, where, and how to manage emotion displays appropriately. This includes specific aspects of nonverbal communication—how broadly you should smile, the appropriateness of shouting for joy in public, and so on.

dominance: (p. 244) The interpersonal behaviors we use to exert power or influence over others. Dominance may occur through nonverbal behavior, as in crowding threateningly into a person's intimate zone, staring someone down, or keeping another person waiting.

domination: (p. 271) When one person gets his or her way in a conflict by influencing the other to engage in accommodation and abandon goals. For example, Jane wants to see the new animated film, but Matt refuses by saying that it is either his choice or no movie at all.

downward communication: (p. A-12) Messages from a superior to subordinates. For example, the CEO of a company calls the regional managers together for a strategy session. Contrast **upward communication.**

dyadic: (p. 11) Communication involving only two people.

Dyadic Power Theory: (p. 258) The idea that people with only moderate power are most likely to use controlling communication.

eavesdropping: (p. 180) Intentionally listening in on private conversations.

effectiveness: (p. 22) The ability to use communication to accomplish interpersonal goals.

embarrassment: (p. 50) A feeling of shame, humiliation, and sadness that comes from losing face.

emblems: (p. 231) Gestures that symbolize a specific verbal meaning within a given culture, such as the "thumbs up" or the "V for victory" sign.

emotion: (p. 103) An intense reaction to an event that involves interpreting the meaning of the event, becoming physiologically aroused, labeling the experience as emotional, attempting to manage your reaction, and communicating this reaction in the form of emotional displays and disclosures.

emotional contagion: (p. 105) The rapid spreading of emotion from person to person, such as anger running through a mob.

emotional intelligence: (p. 113) The ability to accurately interpret your and others' emotions and use this information to manage emotions, communicate them competently, and solve relationship problems.

emotion management: (p. 114) Attempts to influence which emotions you have, when you have them, and how you experience and express them.

emotion-sharing: (p. 105) Disclosing your emotions to others.

empathy: (p. 92) Understanding of another person's perspective and awareness of his or her feelings in an attempt to identify with them. For instance, Gill doesn't agree with Mike's protest against the new policies at work, but he can see why Mike is worried and angry.

empathy mind-set: (p. 93) Beliefs about whether empathy is something that can be developed and controlled.

encounter avoidance: (p. 115) Preventing unwanted emotions by keeping away from people, places, and activities likely to provoke them. For example, Jessica infuriates Roxanne, so Roxanne moves out of their shared apartment.

encounter structuring: (p. 115) Preventing unwanted emotions by intentionally avoiding discussion of difficult topics in encounters with others. For instance, Natalie and Julie avoid talking about living expenses because Natalie is jealous of Julie's income.

environment: (p. 239) A nonverbal code that represents the physical features of our surroundings.

equity: (p. 296) The balance of benefits and costs exchanged by you and the other person that determines whether a romantic relationship will take root (after attraction is established).

escalation: (p. 263) A dramatic rise in emotional intensity and increasingly negative communication during conflict, such as teasing that inflates to a heated exchange of insults.

ethics: (p. 23) The set of moral principles that guide our behavior toward others. Ethical communication consistently displays respect, kindness, and compassion.

ethnocentrism: (p. 152) The belief that your own culture's beliefs, attitudes, values, and practices are superior to those of all other cultures. For example, Americans, accustomed to lining up, who consider cultures that don't use waiting lines to be disorganized are displaying ethnocentrism. Contrast **world-mindedness.**

experimenting: (p. 299) A relational stage in which two people become acquainted by sharing factual or demographic information about themselves and making light conversation or small talk. For instance, after Ruth is introduced to Owen, they talk about their jobs and where they went to school, and they discover they both like jazz.

expertise currency: (p. 259) Power that comes from possessing specialized skills or knowledge, such as being able to use CPR if someone stops breathing.

extended family: (p. 330) A family type consisting of a group of people who are related to one another—such as aunts, uncles, cousins, or grandparents—and who live in the same household.

face: (p. 50) The self we allow others to see and know; the aspects of ourselves we choose to present publicly. For instance, you dress up and speak carefully for an important social occasion, though in private you're very casual.

family: (p. 328) A network of people who share their lives over long periods of time and are bound by marriage, blood, or commitment; who consider themselves as family; and who share a significant history and anticipated future of functioning in a family relationship.

Family Communication Patterns Theory: (p. 335) The idea that two dimensions—**conformity orientation** and **conversation orientation**—underlie the communication between family members. See also **conformity orientation; conversation orientation.**

family privacy rules: (p. 343) The conditions governing what family members can talk about, how they can discuss such topics, and who should have access to family-relevant information.

family stories: (p. 331) Narratives of family events retold to bond family members. For example, Katie's mother often recounts how Katie was born on the day of a crippling blizzard.

fearful attachment: (p. 46) An attachment style in which individuals are high in both attachment anxiety and avoidance: they fear rejection and thus shun relationships, preferring to avoid the pain they believe is an inevitable part of intimacy.

feedback: (pp. 9, 168) Verbal and nonverbal messages that receivers use to indicate their reaction to communication, such as a frown or saying, "I disagree." See also **interactive communication model.**

feelings: (p. 105) Short-term emotional reactions to events that generate only limited arousal, such as the fleeting nostalgia you experience hearing a familiar song.

feminine cultural values: (p. 150) Values that emphasize compassion and cooperation—on caring for the weak and underprivileged and boosting the quality of life for all people.

fields of experience: (p. 9) Beliefs, attitudes, values, and experiences that each communicator brings to an interaction.

friendship: (p. 357) A voluntary relationship characterized by intimacy and liking.

friendship rules: (p. 369) General principles for appropriate communication and behavior within friendships, such as keeping a confidence and showing support.

friendship-warmth touch: (p. 234) A touch used to express liking for another person, such as an arm across another's shoulders, a victory slap between teammates, or playful jostling between friends.

functional-professional touch: (p. 234) A touch used to accomplish a task, such as a physical therapist positioning a client's arm or a dancer gripping his partner's waist for a lift.

fundamental attribution error: (p. 76) The tendency to attribute someone's behavior solely to his or her personality rather than to outside forces.

FWB relationships: (p. 378) Friendships negotiated to include sexual activity but not with the purpose of transforming the relationship into a romantic attachment.

gender: (p. 27) The composite of social, psychological, and cultural attributes that characterize us as male or female.

Gestalt: (p. 87) A general sense of a person that's either positive or negative. See also **halo effect; horn effect.**

grief: (p. 123) Intense sadness that follows a substantial loss (such as the death of a loved one).

halo effect: (p. 88) A tendency to interpret anything another person says or does in a favorable light because you have a positive Gestalt of that person.

haptics: (p. 234) A nonverbal code that represents messages conveyed through touch. See also **friendship-warmth touch; functional-professional touch; love-intimacy touch; sexual-arousal touch; social-polite touch.**

hearing: (p. 164) The sensory process of taking in and interpreting sound.

high-context cultures: (p. 147) Cultures that presume listeners share their viewpoints. People in such cultures talk indirectly, using hints to convey meaning. Vague, ambiguous language—and even silence—is often used, the presumption being that because individuals share the same contextual view, they automatically know what another person is trying to say. Contrast **low-context cultures.**

honesty: (p. 206) Truthful communication, without exaggeration or omission of relevant information. Failing to tell someone something can be as dishonest as an outright lie.

horn effect: (p. 89) A tendency to interpret anything another person says or does in a negative light because you have a negative Gestalt of that person.

identity support: (p. 363) Behaving in ways that convey understanding, acceptance, and support for a friend's valued social identities.

I-It: (p. 13) A type of perception and communication that occurs when you treat others as though they are objects that are there for your use and exploitation—for example, when you dismiss someone by saying, "I don't have time for your stupid questions. Figure it out yourself."

"I" language: (p. 207) Communication that uses the pronoun *I* in sentence construction to emphasize ownership of one's feelings, opinions, and beliefs—for example, "I'm frustrated because I think I'm doing more than you are on this project" instead of "You're really underperforming on this project." See also **"we" language; "you" language.**

illustrators: (p. 231) Gestures used to accent or illustrate a verbal message. For example, a fisherman holds his hands apart to show the size of his catch, or someone points emphatically at a door while saying, "Leave!"

immediacy: (p. 232) As expressed in your posture, the degree to which you find someone interesting and attractive.

impersonal communication: (p. 13) Messages that have negligible perceived impact on your thoughts, emotions, behaviors, or relationships, such as commenting about the television schedule or passing someone and saying, "How's it going?" without looking up.

implicit personality theories: (p. 85) Personal beliefs about different types of personalities and the ways in which traits cluster together. For instance, Bradley assumes that Will is a disorganized procrastinator because of Will's casual, friendly manner.

individualistic cultures: (p. 143) Cultures that value independence and personal achievement; individual goals over group or societal goals. Contrast **collectivistic cultures.**

ingroupers: (p. 79) People you consider fundamentally similar to yourself because of their interests, affiliations, or backgrounds. Contrast **outgroupers.**

initiating: (p. 299) A relational stage in which two people meet and form their first impressions of each other. For instance, Owen introduces himself in an e-mail to Ruth after reading her profile on an online dating site, and she responds with her telephone number.

instrumental goals: (p. 18) Practical aims you want to achieve or tasks you want to accomplish through a particular interpersonal encounter.

integrating: (p. 300) A relational stage in which two people become a couple and begin to share an identity. For example, Ruth and Owen share an apartment together and spend time with each other's families.

integrative agreements: (p. 272) When, during a conflict, the two sides preserve and attain their goals by developing a creative solution to their problem. For example, because Matt and Jane can't agree on what film to see, they decide they'd both be happier going to a comedy club.

intensifying: (p. 299) A relational stage characterized by deeper self-disclosures, stronger attraction, and intimate communication. For example, Owen and

Ruth have been dating for more than a year and talk with excitement about a future together.

interaction: (p. 7) A series of messages exchanged between people, whether face-to-face or online.

interactive communication model: (p. 8) A depiction of communication messages that are exchanged back and forth between a sender and a receiver and are influenced by feedback and the fields of experience of both communicators.

intercultural competence: (p. 152) The ability to communicate appropriately, effectively, and ethically with people from diverse backgrounds.

interparental conflict: (p. 348) Overt, hostile interactions between parents in a household.

interpersonal communication: (p. 11) A dynamic form of communication between two (or more) people in which the messages exchanged significantly influence their thoughts, emotions, behaviors, and relationships.

interpersonal communication competence: (p. 21) The ability to communicate consistently in appropriate, effective, and ethical ways.

interpersonal impressions: (p. 86) Ideas about who people are and how we feel about them. For instance, when Sarah and Georgia met, Georgia thought Sarah was unfriendly and conceited because she didn't say much.

interpersonal process model of intimacy: (p. 60) The idea that the closeness we feel toward others in our relationships is created through two things: self-disclosure and responsiveness of listeners to such disclosure.

interpretation: (p. 73) The stage of perception in which we assign meaning to the information we have selected. For instance, Randy thinks a man running down the sidewalk hurries because he is late, but Shondra infers that the man is chasing someone.

intimacy: (pp. 58, 243) A feeling of closeness and "union" that exists between us and our relationship partners.

intimacy currency: (p. 260) Power that comes from sharing a close bond with someone that no one else shares. For example, you can easily persuade a close friend to change her mind because she is fond of you.

intimate space: (p. 236) The narrowest proxemic zone—0 to 18 inches of space—between communicators.

intrapersonal communication: (p. 11) Communication involving only one person, such as talking to yourself.

I-Thou: (p. 13) A way to perceive a relationship based on embracing fundamental similarities that connect you to others, striving to see things from others' points of view, and communicating in ways that emphasize honesty and kindness.

jealousy: (p. 315) A protective reaction to a perceived threat to a valued relationship. For instance, Tyler is jealous when his girlfriend, Mary, flirts with Scott.

Jefferson strategy: (p. 119) A strategy to manage anger that involves counting slowly to 10 before responding to someone who says or does something that makes you angry. (The strategy was named after the third president of the United States.)

kinesics: (p. 230) A nonverbal code that represents messages communicated in visible body movements, such as facial expressions, body postures, gestures, and eye contact.

kitchen-sinking: (p. 255) A response to a conflict in which combatants hurl insults and accusations at each other that have very little to do with the original disagreement. For example, although Mary and Pat are arguing about the budget, Mary adds, "I'm sick of the mess you left in the garage and these papers all over the family room."

laissez-faire families: (p. 337) Families characterized by low levels of conformity and conversation orientation. For example, Samantha's parents prefer limited communication and encourage their daughter to make her own choices and decisions.

liking: (p. 287) A feeling of affection and respect typical of friendship.

linear communication model: (p. 8) A depiction of communication messages that flow in one direction from a starting point to an end point.

linguistic determinism: (p. 198) The view that the language we use defines the boundaries of our thinking.

linguistic relativity: (p. 199) The theory that languages create variations in the ways cultures perceive and think about the world.

listening: (p. 163) The five-stage process of receiving, attending to, understanding, responding to, and recalling sounds and visual images during interpersonal encounters.

listening functions: (p. 171) The five general purposes that listening serves: to comprehend, to discern, to analyze, to appreciate, and to support.

listening styles: (p. 174) Habitual patterns of listening behaviors, which reflect one's attitudes, beliefs, and predispositions about listening. See also **action-oriented listeners; content-oriented listeners; people-oriented listeners; time-oriented listeners.**

long-term memory: (p. 168) The part of your mind devoted to permanent information storage.

looking-glass self: (p. 39) Sociologist Charles Horton Cooley's idea that we define our self-concepts through thinking about how others see us. For example, a young girl who believes that others consider her poor in sports formulates an image of herself as uncoordinated even though she is a good dancer.

love-intimacy touch: (p. 235) A touch indicating deep emotional feeling, such as two romantic partners holding hands or two close friends embracing.

loving: (p. 287) An intense emotional commitment based on intimacy, caring, and attachment.

low-context cultures: (p. 147) Cultures in which people tend not to presume that others share their beliefs, attitudes, and values. They strive to be informative, clear, and direct in their communication. In such cultures, people make important information obvious, rather than hinting or implying. Contrast **high-context cultures.**

masculine cultural values: (p. 149) Values that include the accumulation of material wealth as an indicator of success, assertiveness, and personal achievement.

mask: (p. 50) The public self designed to strategically veil your private self—for example, putting on a happy face when you are sad or pretending to be confident while inside you feel shy or anxious.

matching: (p. 295) A tendency to be attracted to others whom we perceive to be at our own level of attractiveness. For example, Michael dates Jennifer because she is pretty but not unapproachably gorgeous.

media: (p. 7) Tools used to exchange messages, including everything from newspapers, blackboards, and photographs to computers, smartphones, and television.

mental bracketing: (p. 167) Systematically putting aside thoughts that aren't relevant to the interaction at hand if your attention wanders when listening—for example, by consciously dismissing your worries about an upcoming exam in order to focus on a customer's request at work.

mere exposure effect: (p. 294) A phenomenon in which you feel more attracted to those with whom you have frequent contact and less attracted to those with whom you interact rarely. For example, the more June sees of Tom, the more attracted to him she becomes.

message: (p. 7) The package of information transported during communication.

meta-communication: (p. 15) Verbal or nonverbal communication about communication—that is, messages that have communication as their central focus.

misunderstanding: (p. 207) Confusion resulting from the misperception of another's thoughts, feelings, or beliefs as expressed in the other individual's verbal communication.

mixed messages: (p. 225) Verbal and nonverbal behaviors that convey contradictory meanings, such as saying "I'm so happy for you" in a sarcastic tone of voice.

mixed-status relationships: (p. A-10) Associations between coworkers at different levels of power and status in an organization, such as a manager and a salesclerk.

mnemonics: (p. 171) Devices that aid memory. For example, the mnemonic *Roy G. Biv* is commonly used to recall the order of the seven colors in the rainbow.

monochronic time orientation: (p. 151) A view of time as a precious resource that can be saved, spent, wasted, lost, or made up, and that can even run out. Contrast **polychronic time orientation.**

moods: (p. 105) Low-intensity states of mind that are not caused by particular events and typically last longer than emotions—for example, boredom, contentment, grouchiness, serenity.

naming: (p. 199) Creating linguistic symbols to represent people, objects, places, and ideas.

narcissistic listening: (p. 183) A self-absorbed approach to listening in which the listener redirects the conversation to his or her own interests. For example, Neil acts bored while Jack describes a recent ski trip, interrupting Jack and switching the topic to his own recent car purchase.

negativity effect: (p. 88) A tendency to place emphasis on the negative information we learn about others.

noise: (p. 8) Environmental factors that impede a message on the way to its destination.

nonverbal communication: (p. 223) The intentional or unintentional transmission of meaning through an individual's nonspoken physical and behavioral cues.

nonverbal communication codes: (p. 229) Different ways to transmit information nonverbally: artifacts, chronemics, environment, haptics, kinesics, physical appearance, proxemics, and vocalics.

nuclear family: (p. 329) A family type consisting of a wife, a husband, and their biological or adopted children.

online communication: (p. 24) Interaction through communication technology, such as social networking sites, e-mail, text- or instant-messaging, Skype, chatrooms, and even massively multiplayer online video games like *World of Warcraft.*

organization: (p. 72) The step of perception in which we mentally structure selected sensory data into a coherent pattern.

organizational climate: (p. A-4) The overarching emotional quality of a workplace environment. For example, employees might say their organization feels warm, frenetic, unfriendly, or serene.

organizational culture: (p. A-2) A distinct set of beliefs about how things should be done and how people should behave.

organizational networks: (p. A-3) Communication links among an organization's members, such as the nature, frequency, and ways information is exchanged. For example, you have weekly face-to-face status meetings with your boss or receive daily reminder e-mails from an assistant.

outgroupers: (p. 79) People you consider fundamentally different from you because of their interests, affiliations, or backgrounds. Contrast **ingroupers.**

paraphrasing: (p. 169) An active listening response that summarizes or restates others' comments after they have finished speaking.

parental favoritism: (p. 347) When one or both parents allocate an unfair amount of valuable resources to one child over others.

passion: (p. 121) A blended emotion of joy and surprise coupled with other positive feelings, such as excitement, amazement, and sexual attraction.

passionate love: (p. 288) A state of intense emotional and physical longing for union with another.

people-oriented listeners: (p. 174) Those who view listening as an opportunity to establish commonalities between themselves and others. For example, Carl enjoys Elaine's descriptions of the triumphs and difficulties she's had learning to snowboard.

perception: (p. 71) The process of selecting, organizing, and interpreting information from our senses.

perception-checking: (p. 94) A five-step process to test your impressions of others and to avoid errors in judgment. It involves checking your punctuation, knowledge, attributions, perceptual influences, and impressions.

personal currency: (p. 259) Power that comes from personal characteristics that others admire, such as intelligence, physical beauty, charm, communication skill, or humor.

personal idioms: (p. 193) Words and phrases that have unique meanings to a particular relationship, such as pet names or private phrases with special meaning. For example, Uncle Henry was known for his practical jokes; now, years after his death, family members still refer to a practical joke as "pulling a Henry."

personality: (p. 85) An individual's characteristic way of thinking, feeling, and acting based on the traits he or she possesses.

personal space: (p. 236) The proxemic zone that ranges from 18 inches to 4 feet of space between communicators. It is the spatial separation most often used in the United States for friendly conversation.

physical appearance: (p. 238) A nonverbal code that represents visual attributes such as body type, clothing, hair, and other physical features.

pluralistic families: (p. 336) Families characterized by low levels of conformity and high levels of conversation orientation. For example, Julie's parents encourage her to express herself freely, and when conflicts arise, they collaborate with her to resolve them.

polychronic time orientation: (p. 151) A flexible view of time in which harmonious interaction with others is more important than being on time or sticking to a schedule. Contrast **monochronic time orientation.**

positivity bias: (p. 88) A tendency for first impressions of others to be more positive than negative.

power: (pp. 232, 256) The ability to influence or control events and people.

power currency: (p. 259) Control over a resource that other people value. See also **expertise currency; intimacy currency; personal currency; resource currency; social network currency.**

power distance: (p. 145) The degree to which people in a culture view the unequal distribution of power as acceptable. For example, in some cultures, well-defined class distinctions limit interaction across class lines, but other cultures downplay status and privilege to foster a spirit of equality.

prejudice: (p. 141) When stereotypes effect rigid attitudes toward groups and their members.

preoccupied attachment: (p. 46) An attachment style in which individuals are high in anxiety and low in avoidance; they desire closeness but are plagued with fear of rejection.

primary emotions: (p. 107) Six emotions that involve unique and consistent behavioral displays across cultures: anger, disgust, fear, joy, sadness, and surprise.

professional peers: (p. A-7) People who hold jobs at the same level of power and status as your own.

protective families: (p. 337) Families characterized by high levels of conformity and low levels of conversation orientation. For example, Brian's parents expect their son to be respectful, and they discourage family discussions.

provocateurs: (p. 181) Aggressive listeners who intentionally bait and attack others in online communication. For example, a group member stirs up trouble in a chatroom by criticizing the study group leader and then humiliates other respondents.

proxemics: (p. 236) A nonverbal code for communication through physical distance. See also **intimate space; personal space; public space; social space.**

pseudo-conflict: (p. 262) A mistaken perception that a conflict exists when it doesn't. For example, Barbara thinks Anne is angry with her because Anne hasn't spoken to her all evening, but Anne is actually worried about a report from her physician.

pseudo-listening: (p. 181) Pretending to listen while preoccupied or bored.

public space: (p. 236) The widest proxemic zone. It ranges outward from 12 feet and is most appropriate for formal settings.

punctuation: (p. 73) A step during organization when you structure information you've selected into a chronological sequence that matches how you experienced the order of events. For example, Bobby claims his sister started the backseat argument, but she insists that he poked her first.

Rational Emotive Behavior Therapy (REBT): (p. 111) A therapy developed by psychologist Albert Ellis that helps neurotic patients systematically purge themselves of the tendency to think negative thoughts about themselves.

reactivity: (p. 264) A way of handling conflict by not pursuing conflict-related goals at all and communicating in an emotionally explosive and negative fashion instead.

reappraisal: (p. 116) Actively changing how you think about the meaning of emotion-eliciting situations so that their emotional impact is changed. For instance, though previously fearful of giving a speech, Luke reduces his anxiety by repeating positive affirmations and getting excited about the chance to share what he knows.

recalling: (p. 170) The fifth stage of the listening process in which a listener is able to remember information after it's received, attended to, understood, and responded to.

receiver: (p. 8) The individual for whom a message is intended or to whom it is delivered.

receiving: (p. 164) The first stage of the listening process in which a listener takes in information by seeing and hearing.

reciprocal liking: (p. 296) When the person we're attracted to makes it clear, through communication and other actions, that the attraction is mutual.

regulative rules: (p. 193) Guidelines that govern how we use language when we verbally communicate—that is, spelling and grammar as well as conversational usage. For example, we know how to respond correctly to a greeting, and we know that cursing in public is inappropriate.

regulators: (p. 231) Gestures used to control the exchange of conversational turns during interpersonal encounters—for example, averting eyes to avoid someone, or zipping up book bags as a class to signal to a professor that the lecture should end.

relational dialectics: (pp. 292, 340) Opposing tensions between ourselves and our feelings toward others that exist in interpersonal relationships, such as the tension between wishing to be completely honest with a partner yet not wanting to be hurtful.

relational intrusion: (p. 316) The violation of one's independence and privacy by a person who desires an intimate relationship.

relational maintenance: (p. 304) Communication and supportive behaviors partners use to sustain a desired relationship. They may show devotion by making time to talk, spending time together, and offering help or support to each other.

relationship goals: (p. 18) Goals of building, maintaining, or terminating relationships with others through interpersonal communication.

resource currency: (p. 259) Power that comes from controlling material items others want or need, such as money, food, or property.

responding: (p. 168) The fourth stage of the listening process in which a listener communicates his or her attention and understanding—for example, by nodding or murmuring agreement.

romantic betrayal: (p. 312) An act that goes against expectations of a romantic relationship and, as a result, causes pain to a partner.

romantic relationship: (p. 290) An interpersonal involvement two people choose to enter into that is perceived as romantic by both. For instance, Louise is in love with Robert, and Robert returns her affections.

salience: (p. 72) The degree to which particular people or aspects of their communication attract our attention.

schemata: (p. 74) Mental structures that contain information defining the characteristics of various concepts (such as people, places, events), as well as how those characteristics are related to one another. We often use schemata when interpreting interpersonal communication. When Charlie describes his home as "retro," Amanda visualizes it before she even sees it.

secure attachment: (p. 46) An attachment style in which individuals are low on both anxiety and avoidance; they are comfortable with intimacy and seek close ties with others.

selection: (p. 72) The first step of perception in which we focus our attention on specific sensory data, such as sights, sounds, tastes, touches, or smells.

selective listening: (p. 178) Listening that takes in only those parts of a message that are immediately salient during an interpersonal encounter and dismisses the rest.

self: (p. 37) The evolving composite of who one is, including self-awareness, self-concept, and self-esteem.

self-awareness: (p. 37) The ability to view yourself as a unique person distinct from your surrounding environment and reflect on your thoughts, feelings, and behaviors.

self-concept: (p. 39) Your overall idea of who you are based on the beliefs, attitudes, and values you have about yourself.

self-concept clarity: (p. 39) The degree to which you have a clearly defined, consistent, and enduring sense of self.

self-disclosure: (p. 60) Revealing private information about yourself to others.

self-discrepancy theory: (p. 41) The idea that your self-esteem results from comparing two mental standards: your *ideal* self (the characteristics you want to possess based on your desires) and your *ought* self (the person others wish and expect you to be).

self-esteem: (p. 40) The overall value, positive or negative, you assign to yourself.

self-fulfilling prophecies: (p. 39) Predictions about future encounters that lead us to behave in ways that ensure the interactions unfold as we predicted.

self-monitoring: (p. 22) The process of observing your own communication and the norms of the situation in order to make appropriate communication choices.

self-presentation goals: (p. 18) In interpersonal encounters, presenting yourself in certain ways so that others perceive you as being a particular type of person.

self-serving bias: (p. 77) A biased tendency to credit ourselves (internal factors) instead of external factors for our success. For instance, Ruth attributes the success of a project to her leadership qualities rather than to the dedicated efforts of her team.

sender: (p. 8) The individual who generates, packages, and delivers a message.

separation: (p. 271) A sudden withdrawal of one person from an encounter. For example, you walk away from an argument to cool off, or you angrily retreat to your room.

serial argument process model: (p. 277) The course that serial arguments take is determined by the goals individuals possess, the approaches they adopt for dealing with the conflict, and the consequent perception of whether or not the conflict is resolvable.

serial arguments: (p. 276) A series of unresolved disputes, all having to do with the same issue.

sexual-arousal touch: (p. 235) An intentional touch designed to physically stimulate another person.

sexual harassment: (p. A-21) Unwelcome sexual advances, physical contact, or requests that render a workplace offensive or intimidating.

sexual orientation: (p. 28) Enduring emotional, romantic, sexual, or affectionate attraction to others that exists along a continuum ranging from exclusive heterosexuality to exclusive homosexuality and that includes various forms of bisexuality.

short-term memory: (p. 168) The part of your mind that temporarily houses information while you seek to understand its meaning.

single-parent family: (p. 330) A household in which one adult has the sole responsibility to be the children's caregiver.

skirting: (p. 262) A way of avoiding conflict by changing the topic or joking about it. For example, Martel tries to evade Louis's criticism about where Martel parked his car by teasing, "I did you a favor. You walked twenty extra steps. Exercise is good for you."

sniping: (p. 262) A way of avoiding conflict by communicating in a negative fashion and then abandoning the encounter by physically leaving the scene or refusing to interact further, such as when Martel answers Louis's criticism about where he parked his car by insulting Louis and stomping out the door.

social comparison: (p. 38) Observing and assigning meaning to others' behaviors and then comparing their behavior to ours (when judging our own actions). For example, you might subtly check out how others are dressed at a party or how they scored on an exam to see if you compare favorably.

social exchange theory: (p. 296) The idea that you will be drawn to those you see as offering substantial benefits with few associated costs. For example, Meredith thinks Leonard is perfect for her because he is much more attentive and affectionate than her previous boyfriends and seems so easy to please.

social network currency: (p. 259) Power that comes from being linked with a network of friends, family, and acquaintances with substantial influence, such as being on a first-name basis with a sports celebrity.

social penetration theory: (p. 56) Altman and Taylor's model that you reveal information about yourself to others by peeling back or penetrating layers.

social-polite touch: (p. 234) A touch, such as a handshake, used to demonstrate social norms or culturally expected behaviors.

social space: (p. 236) The proxemic zone that ranges from 4 to 12 feet of space between communicators. It is the spatial separation most often used in the United States in the work place and for conversations between acquaintances and strangers.

speech acts: (p. 201) The actions we perform with language, such as the question, "Is the antique clock in your window for sale?" and the reply, "Yes, let me get it out to show you."

spillover hypothesis: (p. 349) The idea that emotions, affect, and mood from the parental relationship "spill over" into the broader family, disrupting children's sense of emotional security.

stagnating: (p. 302) A relational stage in which communication comes to a standstill. For instance, day after day, Owen and Ruth speak only to ask if a bill has been paid or what is on television, without really listening to each other's answers.

stepfamily: (p. 330) A family type in which at least one of the adults has a child or children from a previous relationship.

Stereotype Content Model: (p. 141) A model in which prejudice centers on two judgments made about others: how warm and friendly they are, and how competent they are. These judgments create two possible kinds of prejudice: benevolent and hostile.

stereotyping: (p. 90) Categorizing people into social groups and then evaluating them based on information we have in our schemata related to each group.

structural improvements: (p. 272) When people agree to change the basic rules or understandings that govern their relationship to prevent further conflict.

submissiveness: (p. 244) The willingness to allow others to exert power over you, demonstrated by such gestures as a shrinking posture or lowered eye gaze.

sudden-death statements: (p. 276) Messages, communicated at the height of a conflict, that suddenly declare the end of a relationship, even if that wasn't an option before—for example, "It's over. I never want to see you again."

supportive climate: (p. A-4) A workplace atmosphere that is supportive, warm, and open. Contrast **defensive climate.**

supportive communication: (p. 124) Sharing messages that express emotional support and that offer personal assistance, such as extending your sympathy or listening to someone without judging.

suppression: (p. 114) Inhibiting thoughts, arousal, and outward behavioral displays of emotion. For example, Amanda stifles her anger, knowing it will kill her chances of receiving a good tip.

symbols: (p. 192) Items used to represent other things, ideas, or events. For example, the letters of the alphabet are symbols for specific sounds in English.

symmetrical relationships: (p. 257) Relationships characterized by an equal balance of power, such as a business partnership in which the partners co-own their company.

terminating: (p. 302) A relational stage in which one or both partners end a relationship. For instance, Ruth asks Owen for a divorce once she realizes their marriage has deteriorated beyond salvation.

territoriality: (p. 237) The tendency to claim personal spaces as our own and define certain locations as areas we don't want others to invade without permission, such as spreading out personal items to claim the entire library table.

time-oriented listeners: (p. 174) Those who prefer brief, concise encounters to save time.

transactional communication model: (p. 9) A depiction of communication in which each participant equally influences the communication behavior of the other participants. For example, a salesperson who watches his customer's facial expression while describing a product is sending and receiving messages at the same time.

triangulation: (p. 345) Loyalty conflicts that arise when a coalition is formed, uniting one family member with another against a third family member.

uncertainty avoidance: (p. 144) How cultures tolerate and accept unpredictability.

Uncertainty Reduction Theory: (p. 78) A theory explaining that the primary compulsion during initial encounters is to reduce uncertainty about our communication partners by gathering enough information about them that their communication becomes predictable and explainable.

understanding: (p. 168) The third stage of the listening process in which a listener interprets the meaning of another person's communication by comparing newly received information against past knowledge.

upward communication: (p. A-11) Messages from a subordinate to a superior. For instance, a clerk notifies the department manager that inventory needs to be reordered. Contrast **downward communication**.

valued social identities: (p. 363) The aspects of your public self that you deem the most important in defining who you are—for example, musician, athlete, poet, dancer, teacher, or mother.

venting: (p. 114) Allowing emotions to dominate your thoughts and explosively expressing them, such as shrieking in happiness or storming into an office in a rage.

verbal aggression: (p. 210) The tendency to attack others' self-concepts—their appearance, behavior, or character—rather than their positions.

verbal communication: (p. 191) The exchange of spoken or written language with others during interactions.

virtual networks: (p. A-3) Groups of coworkers linked solely through e-mail, social networking sites, Skype, and other online services.

virtual peers: (p. A-8) Coworkers who communicate mostly through phone, e-mail, Skype, and other communication technologies.

vocalics: (p. 233) Vocal characteristics we use to communicate nonverbal messages, such as volume, pitch, rate, voice quality, vocalized sounds, and silence. For instance, a pause might signal discomfort, create tension, or be used to heighten drama.

voluntary kin family: (p. 330) A group of people who lack blood and legal kinship but who consider themselves "family."

warranting value: (p. 53) The degree to which online information is supported by other people and outside evidence.

wedging: (p. 315) When a person deliberately uses online communication—messages, photos, and posts—to try to insert him- or herself between romantic partners because he or she is interested in one of the partners.

"we" language: (p. 208) Communication that uses the pronoun *we* to emphasize inclusion—for example, "We need to decide what color to paint the living room" instead of "I need you to tell me what color paint you want for the living room." See also **"I" language; "you" language**.

workplace bullying: (p. A-17) The repeated unethical and unfavorable treatment of one or more persons by others in the workplace.

workplace cliques: (p. A-3) Dense networks of coworkers who share the same workplace values and broader life attitudes.

workplace relationships: (p. A-1) Any affiliation you have with a professional peer, supervisor, subordinate, or mentor in a professional setting.

world-mindedness: (p. 152) The ability to practice and demonstrate acceptance and respect toward other cultures' beliefs, values, and customs. Contrast **ethnocentrism**.

"you" language: (p. 207) Communication that states or implies the pronoun *you* to place the focus of attention on blaming others—such as "You haven't done your share of the work on this project." Contrast **"I" language; "we" language**.

REFERENCES

ABCnews.go.com. (2005, October 21). Do "helicopter moms" do more harm than good? Retrieved from http://abcnews.go.com/2020/Health/story?id=1237868&page=1

Ackard, D. M., & Neumark-Sztainer, D. (2002). Date violence and date rape among adolescents: Associations with disordered eating behaviors and psychological health. *Child Abuse and Neglect, 26,* 455–473.

Adams, B. N. (2004). Families and family study in international perspective. *Journal of Marriage and Family, 66,* 1076–1088.

Adamson, A., & Jenson, V. (Directors). (2001). *Shrek* [Motion picture]. United States: DreamWorks SKG.

Afifi, T. D. (2003). "Feeling caught" in stepfamilies: Managing boundary turbulence through appropriate communication privacy rules. *Journal of Social and Personal Relationships, 20*(6), 729–755.

Afifi, T. D., McManus, T., Hutchinson, S., & Baker, B. (2007). Parental divorce disclosures, the factors that prompt them, and their impact on parents' and adolescents' well-being. *Communication Monographs, 74,* 78–103.

Afifi, T. D., McManus, T., Steuber, K., & Coho, A. (2009). Verbal avoidance and dissatisfaction in intimate conflict situations. *Human Communication Research, 35,* 357–383.

Afifi, T. D., & Olson, L. (2005). The chilling effect and the pressure to conceal secrets in families. *Communication Monographs, 72,* 192–216.

Afifi, T. D., & Steuber, K. (2010). The cycle of concealment model. *Journal of Social and Personal Relationships, 27*(8), 1019–1034.

Afifi, W. A., Falato, W. L., & Weiner, J. L. (2001). Identity concerns following a severe relational transgression: The role of discovery method for the relational outcomes of infidelity. *Journal of Social and Personal Relationships, 18*(2), 291–308.

Albrecht, T. L., & Bach, B. W. (1997). *Communication in complex organizations: A relational approach.* Fort Worth, TX: Harcourt Brace.

Allegrini, E. (2008, November 15). James Edgar's Santa Claus—the spirit of Christmas. *The Enterprise.* Retrieved from http://www.enterprisenews.com/article/20081116/News/311169851/?Start=1

Allport, G. W. (1954). *The nature of prejudice.* Cambridge, MA: Addison-Wesley.

Altman, I., & Taylor, D. A. (1973). *Social penetration: The development of interpersonal relationships.* New York, NY: Holt, Rinehart & Winston.

Andersen, P. A. (1997). Cues of culture: The basis of intercultural differences in nonverbal communication. In L. A. Samovar & R. E. Porter (Eds.), *Intercultural communication: A reader* (8th ed., pp. 244–255). Belmont, CA: Wadsworth.

Anderson, N. H. (1981). *Foundations of information integration theory.* Orlando, FL: Academic Press.

Andrews, Jennifer. Personal interview with author, December 2014. Published with permission.

APA Online. (n.d.). *Just the facts about sexual orientation & youth: A primer for principals, educators, & school personnel.* Retrieved from http://www.apa.org/pi/lgbc/publications/justthefacts.html

Apatow, J., & Feig, P. (2011). *Bridesmaids.* United States: Universal Pictures.

Appelbaum, S. H., Marinescu, A., Klenin, J., & Bytautas, J. (2007). Fatal attractions: The mismanagement of workplace romance. *International Journal of Business Research, 7*(4), 31–43.

Arasaratnam, L. A. (2006). Further testing of a new model of intercultural communication competence. *Communication Research Reports, 23,* 93–99.

Arasaratnam, L. A., & Banerjee, S. C. (2007). Ethnocentrism and sensation seeking as variables that influence intercultural contact-seeking behavior: A path analysis. *Communication Research Reports, 24*(4), 303–310.

Archer, J. (2000). Sex differences in aggression between heterosexual partners: A meta-analytic review. *Psychological Bulletin, 126,* 651–680.

Argyle, M. (1969). *Social interaction.* New York, NY: Atherton Press.

Argyle, M., & Furnham, A. (1982). The ecology of relationships: Choice of situations as a function of relationship. *British Journal of Social Psychology, 21,* 259–262.

Argyle, M., & Henderson, M. (1984). The rules of friendship. *Journal of Social and Personal Relationships, 1,* 211–237.

Argyle, M., & Lu, L. (1990). Happiness and social skills. *Personality and Individual Differences, 11,* 1255–1261.

Aron, A., Fisher, H., Strong, G., Acevedo, B., Riela, S., & Tsapelas, I. (2008). Falling in love. In S. Sprecher, A. Wenzel, & J. Harvey (Eds.), *Handbook of relationship initiation* (pp. 315–336). New York, NY: Psychology Press.

Arriaga, X. B., & Agnew, C. R. (2001). Being committed: Affective, cognitive, and conative components of relationship commitment. *Personality and Social Psychology Bulletin, 27,* 1190–1203.

Asada, K. J. K., Morrison, K., Hughes, M., & Fitzpatrick, S. (2003, May). *Is that what friends are for? Understanding the motivations, barriers, and emotions associated with friends with benefits relationships.* Paper presented at the annual meeting of the International Communication Association, San Diego, CA.

Asch, S. E. (1946). Forming impressions of personality. *Journal of Abnormal and Social Psychology, 41,* 258–290.

Asian American Career Center. (n.d.). *Goldsea career success.* Retrieved from http://goldsea.com/Career/career.html

Aylor, B. A. (2003). Maintaining long-distance relationships. In D. J. Canary & M. Dainton (Eds.), *Maintaining relationships through communication: Relational, contextual, and cultural variations* (pp. 127–139). Mahwah, NJ: Erlbaum.

Bakke, E. (2010). A model and measure of mobile communication competence. *Human Communication Research, 36,* 348–371.

Balderrama, A. (2010, May 6). Are you paying attention to your online reputation? Employers are. *The Work Buzz.* Retrieved from http://www.theworkbuzz.com/featured/online-reputation

Bane, R. (2010, August 12). How splintered is your attention? [Blog post]. Retrieved from http://www.baneofyourresistance.com/2010/08/12/how-splintered-is-your-attention-take-the-quiz-and-find-out

R-1

Bank, B. J., & Hansford, S. L. (2000). Gender and friendship: Why are men's best same-sex friendships less intimate and supportive? *Personal Relationships, 7*, 63–78.

Baptiste, D. A., Jr. (1990). Therapeutic strategies with black-Hispanic families: Identity problems of a neglected minority. *Journal of Family Psychotherapy, 1*, 15–38.

Barker, L. L. (1971). *Listening behavior*. Englewood Cliffs, NJ: Prentice Hall.

Barker, L. L., & Watson, K. W. (2000). *Listen up.* New York, NY: St. Martin's Press.

Barker, V. & Ota, H. (2011). Mixi diary versus Facebook photos: Social networking site use among Japanese and Caucasian American females. *Journal of Intercultural Communication Research, 40*(1), 39–63.

Barnes, S. B. (2001). *Online connections: Internet interpersonal relationships*. Cresskill, NJ: Hampton Press.

Barnett, O. W., Miller-Perrin, C. L., & Perrin, R. D. (1997). *Family violence across the life-span: An introduction*. Thousand Oaks, CA: Sage.

Barnlund, D. C. (1975). *Private and public self in Japan and the United States*. Tokyo, Japan: Simul Press.

Barry, D. (2011, May 15). A sports executive leaves the safety of his shadow life. *The New York Times*. Retrieved from http://www.nytimes.com

Bartholomew, K., & Horowitz, L. M. (1991). Attachment styles among young adults: A test of a four-category model. *Journal of Personality and Social Psychology, 61*(2), 226–244.

Baxter, L. A. (1990). Dialectical contradictions in relationship development. *Journal of Social and Personal Relationships, 7*, 69–88.

Baxter, L. A., Mazanec, M., Nicholson, J., Pittman, G., Smith, K., & West, L. (1997). Everyday loyalties and betrayals in personal relationships. *Journal of Social and Personal Relationships, 14*, 655–678.

Baym, N., Campbell, S. W., Horst, H., Kalyanaraman, S., Oliver, M. B., Rothenbuhler, E., Weber, R., & Miller, K. (2012). Communication theory and research in the age of new media: A conversation from the CM café. *Communication Monographs, 79*(2), 256–267.

Beach, W. A. (2002). Between dad and son: Initiating, delivering, and assimilating bad cancer news. *Health Communication, 14*, 271–298.

Bear. (2011). In *Merriam Webster online*.

Becker, J. A. H., Johnson, A. J., Craig, E. A., Gilchrist, E. S., Haigh, M. M., & Lane, L. T. (2009). Friendships are flexible, not fragile: Turning points in geographically-close and long-distance friendships. *Journal of Social and Personal Relationships, 26*(4), 347–369.

Beer, J. S., John, O. P., Scabini, D., & Knight, R. T. (2006). Orbitofrontal cortex and social behavior: Integrating self-monitoring and emotion-cognition interactions. *Journal of Cognitive Neuroscience, 18*, 871–879.

Bekhouche, Y., Hausmann, R., D'Andrea Tyson, L., & Zahidi, S. (2014). World economic forum: Gender gap report, 2014. Retrieved from http://reports.weforum.org/global-gender-gap-report-2014

Bell, Francesca (2008). Making you noise. In *Nimrod International Journal: Memory: Lost and Found*. Tulsa: The University of Tulsa.

Bell, R. A., Buerkel-Rothfuss, N. L., & Gore, K. E. (1987). Did you bring the yarmulke for the Cabbage Patch Kid? The idiomatic communication of young lovers. *Human Communication Research, 14*, 47–67.

Bennett, S. H. (2003). *Radical pacifism: The War Resisters League and Gandhian nonviolence in America, 1915–1963*. Syracuse, NY: Syracuse University Press.

Benoit, P. J., & Benoit, W. E. (1990). To argue or not to argue. In R. Trapp & J. Schuetz (Eds.), *Perspectives on argumentation: Essays in honor of Wayne Brockriede* (pp. 55–72). Prospect Heights, IL: Waveland Press.

Berger, C. R., & Bradac, J. J. (1982). *Language and social knowledge: Uncertainty in interpersonal relations*. London, UK: Edward Arnold.

Berger, C. R., & Calabrese, R. J. (1975). Some explorations in initial interaction and beyond: Toward a developmental theory of interpersonal communication. *Human Communication Research, 1*, 99–112. doi:10.1111/j.1468-2958.1975.tb00258.x

Berkowitz, L., & Harmon-Jones, E. (2004). Toward an understanding of the determinants of anger. *Emotion, 4*, 107–130.

Berry, G. R. (2006). Can computer-mediated asynchronous communication improve team processes and decision-making? *Journal of Business Communication, 43*(4), 344–366.

Berscheid, E. (2002). Emotion. In H. H. Kelley et al. (Eds.), *Close relationships* (2nd ed., pp. 110–168). Clinton Corners, NY: Percheron Press.

Berscheid, E., & Peplau, L. A. (2002). The emerging science of relationships. In H. H. Kelley et al. (Eds.), *Close relationships* (2nd ed., pp. 1–19). Clinton Corners, NY: Percheron Press.

Berscheid, E., & Regan, P. (2005). *The psychology of interpersonal relationships*. Upper Saddle River, NJ: Pearson Education.

Berscheid, E., & Walster, E. (1978). *Interpersonal attraction* (2nd ed.). Reading, MA: Addison-Wesley.

Bevan, J. L. (2014). Dyadic perceptions of goals, conflict strategies, and perceived resolvability in serial arguments. *Journal of Social and Personal Relationships, 31*(6), 773–795.

Bevan, J. L., Finan, A., & Kaminsky, A. (2008). Modeling serial arguments in close relationships: The serial argument process model. *Human Communication Research, 34*, 600–624.

Bianconi, L. (2002). *Culture and identity: Issues of authenticity in another value system*. Paper presented at the XII Sietar-EU Conference, Vienna, Austria.

Bies, R. J., & Tripp, T. M. (1998). Two faces of the powerless: Coping with tyranny in organizations. In R. M. Kramer & M. A. Neale (Eds.), *Power and influence in organizations* (pp. 203–219). Thousand Oaks, CA: Sage.

Birdwhistell, R. L. (1970). *Kinesics and context: Essays on body motion communication*. Philadelphia: University of Pennsylvania Press.

Blakely, G. L., Blakely, E. H., & Moorman, R. H. (1995). The relationship between gender, personal experience, and perceptions of sexual harassment in the workplace. *Employee Responsibilities and Rights Journal, 8*, 263–274.

Bland, K. (2011). Phoenix gay dads adopt, raise 12 happy kids. *The Arizona Republic*. Retrieved from http://www.azcentral.com/news/azliving/articles/2011/05/02/20110502gay-dads-ham-family-12-adopted-kids.html?page=1

Blieszner, R., & Adams, R. G. (1992). *Adult friendship*. Newbury Park, CA: Sage.

Bochner, S., & Hesketh, B. (1994). Power distance, individualism/collectivism, and job related attitudes in a culturally diverse work group. *Journal of Cross-Cultural Psychology, 25*, 233–257.

Boddy, C. R. (2011). Corporate psychopaths, bullying and unfair supervision in the workplace. *Journal of Business Ethics, 100*, 367–379.

Bodenhausen, G. V., Macrae, C. N., & Sherman, J. W. (1999). On the dialectics of discrimination: Dual processes in social stereotyping. In S. Chaiken & Y. Trope (Eds.), *Dual process theories in social psychology* (pp. 271–290). New York, NY: Guilford Press.

Bodhi, B., & Nanamoli, B. (1995). *The middle length discourse of the Buddha: A translation of the Majjhima Nikaya.* Somerville, MA: Wisdom Publications.

Bodie, G. D., & Worthington, D. L. (2010). Revisiting the listening styles profile (LSP-16): A confirmatory factor analytic approach to scale validation and reliability estimation. *The International Journal of Listening, 24,* 69–88.

Booth, A., & Hess, E. (1974). Cross-sex friendship. *Journal of Marriage and the Family, 36,* 38–46.

Bornstein, R. F. (1989). Exposure and affect: Overview and meta-analysis of research, 1968–1987. *Psychological Bulletin, 106,* 265–289.

Bowlby, J. (1969). *Attachment and loss: Vol. 1. Attachment.* New York, NY: Basic Books.

Boyd, C. (2010). The debate over the prohibition of romance in the workplace. *Journal of Business Ethics, 97,* 325–338.

Braithwaite, D. O., Bach, B. W., Baxter, L. A., DiVerniero, R., Hammonds, J. R., Hosek, A. M., Willer, E. K., & Wolf, B. M. (2010). Constructing family: A typology of voluntary kin. *Journal of Social and Personal Relationships, 27*(3), 388–407. doi: 10.1177/0265407510361615

Brandes, S. (1987). Sex roles and anthropological research in rural Andalusia. *Women's Studies, 13,* 357–372.

Bregman, A., Golin, S. (Producers), Gondry, M. (Director), & Kaufman, C. (Writer). (2004). *Eternal sunshine of the spotless mind* [Motion picture]. United States: Focus Features.

Brehm, S. S., Miller, R. S., Perlman, D., & Campbell, S. M. (2002). *Intimate relationships* (3rd ed.). Boston, MA: McGraw-Hill.

Brend, R. (1975). Male-female intonation patterns in American English. In B. Thorne & N. Henley (Eds.), *Language and sex: Difference and dominance* (pp. 84–87). Rowley, MA: Newbury House.

Brewer, M. B. (1993). Social identity, distinctiveness, and in-group homogeneity. *Social Cognition, 11,* 150–164.

Brewer, M. B. (1999). The psychology of prejudice: Ingroup love or outgroup hate? *Journal of Social Issues, 55,* 429–444.

Brewer, M. B., & Campbell, D. T. (1976). *Ethnocentrism and intergroup attitudes: East African evidence.* Beverly Hills, CA: Sage.

Bridge, K., & Baxter, L. A. (1992). Blended relationships: Friends as work associates. *Western Journal of Communication, 56,* 200–225.

Brody, L. R., & Hall, J. A. (2000). Gender, emotion, and expression. In M. Lewis & J. M. Haviland (Eds.), *Handbook of emotions* (2nd ed., pp. 338–349). New York, NY: Guilford Press.

Brontë, E. (1995). *Wuthering Heights.* Oxford: Oxford University Press. (Original work published 1848)

Brown, R. (1965). *Social psychology.* New York, NY: Free Press.

Bruess, C. J. S., & Pearson, J. C. (1993). "Sweet pea" and "pussy cat": An examination of idiom use and marital satisfaction over the life cycle. *Journal of Social and Personal Relationships, 10,* 609–615. doi: 10.1177/0265407593104009

Bruner, J., & Taguiri, R. (1954). The perception of people. In G. Lindzey (Ed.), *Handbook of social psychology* (Vol. 1, pp. 601–633). Cambridge, MA: Addison-Wesley.

Buber, M. (1965). *The knowledge of man: A philosophy of the interhuman.* New York, NY: Harper & Row.

Bulfinch, T. (1985). *The golden age of myth and legend.* London: Bracken Books. (Original work published 1855)

Bunkers, S. S. (2010). The power and possibility in listening. *Nursing Science Quarterly, 23*(1), 22–27.

Burgoon, J. K., Buller, D. B., & Woodall, W. G. (1996). *Nonverbal communication: The unspoken dialogue* (2nd ed.). New York, NY: McGraw-Hill.

Burgoon, J. K., & Dunbar, N. E. (2000). An interactionist perspective on dominance-submission: Interpersonal dominance as a dynamic, situationally contingent social skill. *Communication Monographs, 67,* 96–121.

Burgoon, J. K., & Hoobler, G. D. (2002). Nonverbal signals. In M. L. Knapp & J. A. Daly (Eds.), *Handbook of interpersonal communication* (3rd ed., pp. 240–299). Thousand Oaks, CA: Sage.

Burgoon, M. (1995). A kinder, gentler discipline: Feeling good about being mediocre. In B. R. Burleson (Ed.), *Communication yearbook 18* (pp. 464–479). Thousand Oaks, CA: Sage.

Buriel, R., & De Ment, T. (1997). Immigration and sociocultural change in Mexican, Chinese, and Vietnamese American families. In A. Booth, A. C. Crouter, & N. Landale (Eds.), *Immigration and the family: Research and policy on U.S. immigrants* (pp. 165–200). Mahwah, NJ: Erlbaum.

Burleson, B. R., & MacGeorge, E. L. (2002). Supportive communication. In M. L. Knapp & J. A. Daly (Eds.), *Handbook of interpersonal communication* (pp. 374–422). Thousand Oaks, CA: Sage.

Burleson, B. R., & Samter, W. (1994). A social skills approach to relationship maintenance: How individual differences in communication skills affect the achievement of relationship functions. In D. J. Canary & L. Stafford (Eds.), *Communication and relational maintenance* (pp. 61–90). New York, NY: Academic Press.

Bushman, B. J., & Baumeister, R. F. (1998). Threatened egotism, narcissism, self-esteem, and direct and displaced aggression: Does self-love or self-hate lead to violence? *Journal of Personality and Social Psychology, 75,* 219–229.

Buss, D. M., Larsen, R. J., Westen, D., & Semmelroth, J. (1992). Sex differences in jealousy: Evolution, physiology, and psychology. *Psychological Science, 3,* 251–255.

Buss, D. M., Shackelford, T. K., Kirkpatrick, L. A., Choe, J. C., Lim, H. K., Hasegawa, M., . . . Bennett, K. (1999). Jealousy and the nature of beliefs about infidelity: Tests of competing hypotheses about sex differences in the United States, Korea, and Japan. *Personal Relationships, 6,* 125–150.

Buunk, B. P., Angleitner, A., Oubaid, V., & Buss, D. M. (1996). Sex differences in jealousy in evolutionary and cultural perspective: Tests from the Netherlands, Germany, and the United States. *Psychological Science, 7,* 359–363.

Buzzanell, P. (1990, November). *Managing workplace romance.* Paper presented at the annual meeting of the Speech Communication Association, Chicago, IL.

Cacioppo, J. T., Klein, D. J., Berntson, G. G., & Hatfield, E. (1993). The psychophysiology of emotion. In M. Lewis & J. M. Haviland (Eds.), *Handbook of emotions* (pp. 119–142). New York, NY: Guilford Press.

Campbell, J. D., Trapnell, P. D., Heine, S. J., Katz, I. M., Lavallee, L. F., & Lehman, D. R. (1996). Self-concept clarity: Measurement, personality correlates, and cultural boundaries. *Journal of Personality and Social Psychology, 70,* 141–156.

Campbell, R. G., & Babrow, A. S. (2004). The role of empathy in responses to persuasive risk communication: Overcoming resistance to HIV prevention messages. *Health Communication, 16,* 159–182.

Canary, D. J. (2003). Managing interpersonal conflict: A model of events related to strategic choices. In J. O. Greene & B. R. Burleson (Eds.), *Handbook of communication and social interaction skills*. Mahwah, NJ: Erlbaum.

Canary, D. J., Emmers-Sommer, T. M., & Faulkner, S. (1997). *Sex and gender differences in personal relationships*. New York, NY: Guilford Press.

Canary, D. J., & Hause, K. S. (1993). Is there any reason to research sex differences in communication? *Communication Quarterly, 41,* 129–144.

Canary, D. J., & Zelley, E. (2000). Current research programs on relational maintenance behaviors. In M. E. Roloff (Ed.), *Communication yearbook 23* (pp. 305–339). Thousand Oaks, CA: Sage.

Carbery, J., & Buhrmester, D. (1998). Friendship and need fulfillment during three phases of young adulthood. *Journal of Social and Personal Relationships, 15,* 393–409.

Carducci, B. J., & Zimbardo, P. G. (1995, November/December). Are you shy? *Psychology Today, 28,* 34–41.

Carlson, J. G., & Hatfield, E. (1992). *Psychology of emotion*. Orlando, FL: Harcourt Brace.

Carney, D. R., Hall, J. A., & Smith LeBeau, L. S. (2005). Beliefs about the nonverbal expression of social power. *Journal of Nonverbal Behavior, 29,* 105–123.

Carr, N. (2010). *The shallows: What the Internet is doing to our brains*. New York, NY: W. W. Norton.

Castelli, L., Tomelleri, S., & Zogmaister, C. (2008). Implicit ingroup metafavoritism: Subtle preference for ingroup members displaying ingroup bias. *Personality and Social Psychology Bulletin, 34*(6), 807–818.

Caughlin, J. P. (2002). The demand/withdraw pattern of communication as a predictor of marital satisfaction over time: Unresolved issues and future directions. *Human Communication Research, 28,* 49–85.

Caughlin, J. P., & Vangelisti, A. L. (2000). An individual difference explanation of why married couples engage in demand/withdraw patterns of conflict. *Journal of Social and Personal Relationships, 17,* 523–551.

Cerpas, N. (2002). Variation in the display and experience of love between college Latino and non-Latino heterosexual romantic couples. *Ronald E. McNair Scholarship research report*. University of California, Berkeley.

Chaffee, S. H., & Berger, C. R. (1987). What communication scientists do. In C. R. Berger & S. H. Chaffee (Eds.), *Handbook of communication science* (pp. 99–122). Newbury Park, CA: Sage.

Chan, D. K., & Cheng, G. H. (2004). A comparison of offline and online friendship qualities at different stages of relationship development. *Journal of Social and Personal Relationships, 21*(3), 305–320.

Chaplin, T. M., Cole, P. M., & Zahn-Waxler, C. (2005). Parental socialization of emotion expression: Gender differences and relations to child adjustment. *Emotion, 5,* 80–88.

Chen, G.-M., & Chung, J. (1997). The "Five Asian Dragons": Management behaviors and organization communication. In L. A. Samovar & R. E. Porter (Eds.), *Intercultural communication: A reader* (pp. 317–328). Belmont, CA: Wadsworth.

Chen, G.-M., & Starosta, W. J. (2005). *Foundation of intercultural communication*. Boston, MA: Allyn and Bacon.

Cherlin, A. (2004). The deinstitutionalization of American marriage. *Journal of Marriage and Family, 66,* 848–861.

Chesebro, J. L. (1999). The relationship between listening styles and conversational sensitivity. *Communication Research Reports, 16,* 233–238.

Choi, C. Q. (2011, January 18). Does science support the punitive parenting of "tiger mothering"? *Scientific American*. Retrieved from http://www.scientificamerican.com/article.cfm?id=tiger-mother-punitive-parenting

Chua, A. (2011). *Battle hymn of the tiger mother*. New York, NY: Penguin Press.

Chung, J. H., Des Roches, C. M., Meunier, J., & Eavey, R. D. (2005). Evaluation of noise-induced hearing loss in young people using a web-based survey technique. *Pediatrics, 115,* 861–867.

Clair, R. P. (1993). The use of framing devices to sequester organizational narratives: Hegemony and harassment. *Communication Monographs, 60,* 113–136.

Clair, R. P. (1998). *Organizing silence*. Albany: State University of New York Press.

Clark, R. A., & Delia, J. (1979). Topoi and rhetorical competence. *Quarterly Journal of Speech, 65,* 187–206.

Clayton, R. B. (2014). The third wheel: The impact of Twitter use on relationship infidelity and divorce. *Cyberpsychology, Behavior, and Social Networking, 17*(7), 425–430. doi: 10.1089/cyber.2013.0570

Cleveland, J. N., Stockdale, M., & Murphy, K. R. (2000). *Women and men in organizations: Sex and gender issues at work*. Mahwah, NJ: Erlbaum.

Clopper, C. G., Conrey, B., & Pisoni, D. B. (2005). Effects of talker gender on dialect categorization. *Journal of Language and Social Psychology, 24*(2), 182–206. doi: 10.1177/0261927X05275741

Cochran, C. C., Frazier, P. A., & Olson, A. M. (1997). Predictors of responses to unwanted sexual attention. *Psychology of Women Quarterly, 21,* 207–226.

Cohen, T. F. (1992). Men's families, men's friends: A structural analysis of constraints on men's social ties. In P. M. Nardi (Ed.), *Men's friendships: Vol. 2. Research on men and masculinities* (pp. 115–131). Newbury Park, CA: Sage.

Cole, M., & Cole, S. R. (1989). *The development of children*. New York, NY: Freeman.

Coleman, M., Ganong, L., & Fine, M. (2000). Reinvestigating remarriage: Another decade in progress. *Journal of Marriage and the Family, 62,* 1288–1307.

Collins, N. L., & Feeney, B. C. (2004). An attachment theory perspective on closeness and intimacy. In D. J. Mashek & A. Aron (Eds.), *Handbook of closeness and intimacy* (pp. 163–187). Mahwah, NJ: Erlbaum.

Collins, S. (2008). *The hunger games*. New York, NY: Scholastic Inc.

Conlin, J. (2011, October 2). The freedom to choose your pronoun. *The New York Times*. Retrieved from http://www.nytimes.com

Contractor, N. S., & Grant, S. (1996). The emergence of shared interpretations in organizations: A self-organizing systems perspective. In J. H. Watt & C. A. VanLear (Eds.), *Dynamic patterns in communication processes* (pp. 215–230). Thousand Oaks, CA: Sage.

Cooley, C. H. (1902). *Human nature and the social order*. New York, NY: Scribner.

Corner, L. (2007, June 3). Mrs. Infidelity: Lust in translation author Pamela Druckerman. *The Independent*. Retrieved from http://www.belfasttelegraph.co.uk/lifestyle/mrs-infidelity-lust-in-translation-author-pamela-druckerman-13448101.html

Costanzo, F. S., Markel, N. N., & Costanzo, R. R. (1969). Voice quality profile and perceived emotion. *Journal of Counseling Psychology, 16,* 267–270.

Coupland, N., Giles, H., & Wiemann, J. M. (Eds.). (1991). *Miscommunication and problematic talk*. Newbury Park, CA: Sage.

Covarrubias, P. (2000). Of endearment and other terms of address: A Mexican perspective. In M. W. Lustig & J. Koestner (Eds.), *Among us: Essays on identity, belonging, and intercultural competence* (pp. 9–17). New York, NY: Longman.

Crider, D. M., Willits, F. K., & Kanagy, C. L. (1991). Rurality and well-being during the middle years of life. *Social Indicators, 24*, 253–268.

Crosnoe, R., & Cavanagh, S. E. (2010). Families with children and adolescents: A review, critique, and future agenda. *Journal of Marriage and Family, 72*, 594–611.

Cross, S. E., & Madson, L. (1997). Models of the self: Self-construals and gender. *Psychological Bulletin, 122*, 5–37.

Cullen, J. (2011, April 18). *Battle hymn of the tiger mother*: A remarkably bad book [Book review]. *The Cutting Edge News*. Retrieved from http://www.thecuttingedgenews.com/index.php?article=51839

Cunningham, M. (1988). Does happiness mean friendliness? Induced mood and heterosexual self-disclosure. *Personality and Social Psychology Bulletin, 14*, 283–297.

Cupach, W. R., & Spitzberg, B. H. (1998). Obsessive relational intrusion and stalking. In B. H. Spitzberg & W. R. Cupach (Eds.), *The dark side of close relationships* (pp. 233–263). Hillsdale, NJ: Erlbaum.

Cupach, W. R., & Spitzberg, B. H. (2004). *The dark side of relational pursuit: From attraction to obsession to stalking*. Mahwah, NJ: Erlbaum.

Custudio, J. (2002). The divine Ms. C.H.O.: Margaret Cho on her new stand-up movie, Lea Delaria, Joan Rivers, and the meaning of gay pride. *The Montreal Mirror*. Retrieved from www.montrealmirror.com/ARCHIVES/2002/080102/divers7.html

Dainton, M., & Aylor, B. (2002). Patterns of communication channel use in the maintenance of long-distance relationships. *Communication Research Reports, 19*, 118–129.

Dainton, M., & Stafford, L. (1993). Routine maintenance behaviors: A comparison of relationship type, partner similarity and sex differences. *Journal of Social and Personal Relationships, 10*, 255–271.

Dainton, M., Zelley, E., & Langan, E. (2003). Maintaining friendships throughout the lifespan. In D. J. Canary & M. Dainton (Eds.), *Maintaining relationships through communication: Relational, contextual, and cultural variations* (pp. 79–102). Mahwah, NJ: Erlbaum.

Daly, J. (1975). *Listening and interpersonal evaluations*. Paper presented at the annual meeting of the Central States Speech Association, Kansas City, MO.

Daly, J. A., McCroskey, J. C., Ayres, J., Hopf, T., & Ayres, D. M. (Eds.). (2004). *Avoiding communication: Shyness, reticence, and communication apprehension* (3rd ed.). Cresskill, NJ: Hampton Press.

Daniels, D. (1986). Differential experiences of siblings in the same family as predictors of adolescent sibling personality differences. *Journal of Personality and Social Psychology, 51*(2), 339–346.

Davis, K. E., & Todd, M. L. (1985). Assessing friendship: Prototypes, paradigm cases, and relationship description. In S. Duck & D. Perlman (Eds.), *Understanding personal relationships: An interdisciplinary approach* (pp. 17–38). London, UK: Sage.

Dean, J. (2011). Smartphone user survey: A glimpse into the mobile lives of college students. *Digital New Test Kitchen*. Retrieved from http://testkitchen.colorado.edu/projects/reports/smartphone/smartphone-survey

Delgado-Gaitan, C. (1993). Parenting in two generations of Mexican American families. *International Journal of Behavioral Development, 16*, 409–427.

Delia, J. G. (1972). Dialects and the effects of stereotypes on interpersonal attraction and cognitive processes in impression formation. *Quarterly Journal of Speech, 58*, 285–297.

Devine, P. G. (1989). Stereotypes and prejudice: Their automatic and controlled components. *Journal of Personality and Social Psychology, 56*, 5–18.

de Vries, B. (1996). The understanding of friendship: An adult life course perspective. In C. Magai & S. McFadden (Eds.), *Handbook of emotion, aging, and the life course* (pp. 249–268). New York, NY: Academic Press.

Dillard, J. (1987). Close relationships at work: Perceptions of the motives and performance of relational participants. *Journal of Social and Personal Relationships, 4*, 179–193.

Dindia, K. (2006). Men are from North Dakota, women are from South Dakota. In K. Dindia & D. J. Canary (Eds.), *Sex differences and similarities in communication* (2nd ed., pp. 3–18). New York, NY: Lawrence Erlbaum.

Dindia, K., & Allen, M. (1992). Sex differences in self-disclosure: A meta-analysis. *Psychological Bulletin, 112*, 106–124.

Domingue, R., & Mollen, D. (2009). Attachment and conflict communication in adult romantic relationships. *Journal of Social and Personal Relationships, 26*, 678–696.

Donohue, W. A., & Kolt, R. (1992). *Managing interpersonal conflict*. Newbury Park, CA: Sage.

Dreyer, A. S., Dreyer, C. A., & Davis, J. E. (1987). Individuality and mutuality in the language of families of field-dependent and field-independent children. *Journal of Genetic Psychology, 148*, 105–117.

Druckerman, P. (2007). *Lust in translation*. New York, NY: Penguin Press.

Duan, C., & Hill, C. E. (1996). The current state of empathy research. *Journal of Counseling Psychology, 43*, 261–274.

Dunbar, N. E. (2004). Dyadic power theory: Constructing a communication-based theory of relational power. *Journal of Family Communication, 4*(3/4), 235–248.

Duncan, S., Jr., & Fiske, D. W. (1977). *Face-to-face interaction: Research, methods, and theory*. New York, NY: Wiley.

Dutton, L. B., & Winstead, B. A. (2006). Predicting unwanted pursuit: Attachment, relationship satisfaction, relationship alternatives, and break-up distress. *Journal of Social and Personal Relationships, 23*(4), 565–586.

Eagly, A. H., Ashmore, R. D., Makhijani, M. G., & Longo, L. C. (1991). What is beautiful is good, but . . . : A meta-analytic review of research on the physical attractiveness stereotype. *Psychological Bulletin, 110*, 109–128.

Ebbeson, E., Duncan, B., & Konecni, V. (1975). Effects of content of verbal aggression on future verbal aggression: A field experiment. *Journal of Experimental Social Psychology, 11*, 192–204.

Eisenberg, E. M., & Goodall, H. L., Jr. (2004). *Organizational communication: Balancing creativity and constraint* (4th ed.). Boston, MA: Bedford/St. Martin's.

Eisikovits, Z., & Buchbinder, E. (2000). *Locked in a violent embrace*. Thousand Oaks, CA: Sage.

Ekman, P. (1972). Universals and cultural differences in facial expressions of emotion. In J. R. Cole (Ed.), *Nebraska Symposium on Motivation, Vol. 19* (pp. 207–283). Lincoln: University of Nebraska Press.

Ekman, P. (1976). Movements with precise meanings. *Journal of Communication, 26,* 14–26.

Ekman, P., & Friesen, W. V. (1969). The repertoire of nonverbal behavior: Categories, origins, usage, and coding. *Semiotica, 1,* 49–98.

Ekman, P. & Friesen, W. V. (1975). *Unmasking the face: A guide to recognizing emotions from facial clues.* Englewood Cliffs, NJ: Prentice-Hall.

Elçi, M., & Alpkan, L. (2009). The impact of perceived organizational ethical climate on work satisfaction. *Journal of Business Ethics, 84,* 297–311.

Ellis, A., & Dryden, W. (1997). *The practice of rational emotive behavior therapy.* New York, NY: Springer.

Ellison, N. B., Steinfield, C., & Lampe, C. (2007). The benefits of Facebook "friends:" Social capital and college students' use of online social network sites. *Journal of Computer-Mediated Communication, 12*(4), article 1. Retrieved from http://jcmc.indiana.edu/vol12/issue4/ellison.html

Ellison, N., Heino, R., & Gibbs, J. (2006). Managing impressions online: Self-presentation processes in the online dating environment. *Journal of Computer-Mediated Communication, 11*(2), article 2. Retrieved from http://jcmc.indiana.edu/vol11/issue2/ellison.html

Englehardt, E. E. (2001). Introduction to ethics in interpersonal communication. In E. E. Englehardt (Ed.), *Ethical issues in interpersonal communication: Friends, intimates, sexuality, marriage, and family* (pp. 1–27). Orlando, FL: Harcourt College.

Environmental Protection Agency. (2002, September). Cross-cultural communication. Retrieved from http://www.epa.gov/superfund/community/pdfs/12ccc.pdf

Escartín, J., Rodríguez-Carballeira, A., Zapf, D., Porrúa, C., & Martín-Peña, J. (2009). Perceived severity of various bullying behaviours at work and the relevance of exposure to bullying. *Work & Stress, 23*(3), 191–205.

Farace, R. V., Monge, P. R., & Russell, H. M. (1977). *Communicating and organizing.* Reading, MA: Addison-Wesley.

Feingold, A. (1988). Matching for attractiveness in romantic partners and same-sex friends: A meta-analysis and theoretical critique. *Psychological Bulletin, 104,* 226–235.

Felmlee, D. H. (2001). No couple is an island: A social network perspective on dyadic stability. *Social Forces, 79,* 1259–1287.

Felmlee, D., Orzechowicz, D., & Fortes, C. (2010). Fairy tales: Attraction and stereotypes in same-gender relationships. *Sex Roles, 62,* 226–240.

Fenigstein, A., Scheier, M. F., & Buss, A. H. (1975). Public and private self-consciousness: Assessment and theory. *Journal of Consulting and Clinical Psychology, 43,* 522–527.

Fiedler, K., Pampe, H., & Scherf, U. (1986). Mood and memory for tightly organized social information. *European Journal of Social Psychology, 16,* 149–165.

Field, A. (2005). Block that defense! Make sure your constructive criticism works. *Harvard Management Communication Letter, 2*(4), 3–5.

Field, A. E., Cheung, L., Wolf, A. M., Herzog, D. B., Gortmaker, S. L., & Colditz, G. A. (1999). Exposure to the mass media and weight concerns among girls. *Pediatrics, 103,* 36.

Fischer, A. H., Rodriguez Mosquera, P. M., van Vianen, A. E. M., & Manstead, A. S. R. (2004). Gender and culture differences in emotion. *Emotion, 4,* 87–94.

Fisher, B. A. (1983). Differential effects of sexual composition and interactional context on interaction patterns in dyads. *Human Communication Research, 9,* 225–238.

Fishman, P. M. (1983). Interaction: The work women do. In B. Thorne, C. Kramarae, & N. Henley (Eds.), *Language, gender, and society* (pp. 89–101). Cambridge, MA: Newbury House.

Fiske, S. T., Cuddy, A. J. C., Glick, P., & Xu, J. (2002). A model of (often mixed) stereotype content: Competence and warmth respectively follow from perceived status and competition. *Journal of Personality and Social Psychology, 82,* 878–902.

Fiske, S. T., & Taylor, S. E. (1991). *Social cognition* (2nd ed.). New York, NY: McGraw-Hill.

Fitzgerald, L. F. (1993). Sexual harassment: A research analysis and agenda for the 1990s. *Journal of Vocational Behavior, 42,* 5–27.

Fleischer, R. (Director), Reese, R., & Wernick, P. (Writers). (2009). *Zombieland* [Motion picture]. United States: Sony Pictures.

Floyd, K. (1999). All touches are not created equal: Effects of form and duration on observers' interpretations of an embrace. *Journal of Nonverbal Behavior, 23,* 283–299.

Floyd, K., & Burgoon, J. K. (1999). Reacting to nonverbal expressions of liking: A test of interaction adaptation theory. *Communication Monographs, 66,* 219–239.

Floyd, K., & Morman, M. T. (1999). The measurement of affectionate communication. *Communication Quarterly, 46,* 144–162.

Floyd, K., & Morman, M. T. (2005). Fathers' and sons' reports of fathers' affectionate communication: Implications of a naïve theory of affection. *Journal of Social and Personal Relationships, 22*(1), 99–109.

Forgas, J. P., & Bower, G. H. (1987). Mood effects on person perception judgments. *Journal of Personality and Social Psychology, 53,* 53–60.

Forgas, J. P. (1998). Mood effects on the fundamental attribution error: On being happy and mistaken. *Journal of Personality and Social Psychology, 75,* 318–331.

Forni, P. M. (2002). *Choosing civility: The twenty-five rules of considerate conduct.* New York, NY: St. Martin's Griffin.

Foss, S. K., Foss, K. A., & Trapp, R. (1991). *Contemporary perspectives in rhetoric* (2nd ed.). Prospect Heights, IL: Waveland Press.

Fox, J., & Warber, K. M. (2014). Social networking sites in romantic relationships: Attachment, uncertainty, and partner surveillance on Facebook. *Cyberpsychology, Behavior, and Social Networking, 17*(1), 3–7. doi: 10.1089/cyber.2012.0667

Fox, K. R. (1992). Physical education and development of self-esteem in children. In N. Armstrong (Ed.), *New directions in physical education: II. Towards a national curriculum* (pp. 33–54). Champaign, IL: Human Kinetics.

Fox, K. R. (1997). The physical self and processes in self-esteem development. In K. Fox (Ed.), *The physical self* (pp. 111–139). Champaign, IL: Human Kinetics.

Frederikse, M. E., Lu, A., Aylward, E., Barta, P., & Pearlson, G. (1999). Sex differences in the inferior parietal lobule. *Cerebral Cortex, 9,* 896–901.

Frijda, N. H. (2005). Emotion experience. *Cognition and Emotion, 19,* 473–497.

Frisby, B. N., & Westerman, D. (2010). Rational actors: Channel selection and rational choices in romantic conflict episodes. *Journal of Social and Personal Relationships, 27,* 970–981.

Fritz, J. H., & Dillard, J. P. (1994, November). *The importance of peer relationships in organizational socialization.* Paper presented at the annual meeting of the Speech Communication Association, New Orleans, LA.

Frost, D. M. (2012). The narrative construction of intimacy and affect in relationship stories: Implications for relationship quality, stability, and mental health. *Journal of*

Social and Personal Relationships, 30(3), 247–269, doi: 10.1177/0265407512454463

Fuendeling, J. M. (1998). Affect regulation as a stylistic process within adult attachment. *Journal of Social and Personal Relationships, 15,* 291–322.

Furger, R. (1996). I'm okay, you're online. *PC World, 14,* 310–312.

Furman, W., & Simon, V. A. (1998). Advice from youth: Some lessons from the study of adolescent relationships. *Journal of Social and Personal Relationships, 15,* 723–739.

Furr, R. M., & Funder, D. C. (1998). A multimodal analysis of personal negativity. *Journal of Personality and Social Psychology, 74,* 1580–1591.

Gaines, S. O., Jr., & Agnew, C. R. (2003). Relationship maintenance in intercultural couples: An interdependence analysis. In D. J. Canary & M. Dainton (Eds.), *Maintaining relationships through communication: Relational, contextual, and cultural variations* (pp. 231–253). Mahwah, NJ: Erlbaum.

Gaines, S. O., Jr., Chalfin, J., Kim, M., & Taing, P. (1998). Communicating prejudice in personal relationships. In M. L. Hecht (Ed.), *Communicating prejudice* (pp. 163–186). Thousand Oaks, CA: Sage.

Galupo, M. P. (2007). Friendship patterns of sexual minority individuals in adulthood. *Journal of Social and Personal Relationships, 24,* 139–151.

Galupo, M. P. (2009). Cross-category friendship patterns: Comparison of heterosexual and sexual minority adults. *Journal of Social and Personal Relationships, 26*(6–7), 811–831.

Galvin, K. M., Brommel, B. J., & Bylund, C. L. (2004). *Family communication: Cohesion and change* (6th ed.). New York, NY: Pearson.

Gangestad, S. W., & Snyder, M. (2000). Self-monitoring: Appraisal and reappraisal. *Psychological Bulletin, 126,* 530–555.

Ganong, L. H., & Coleman, M. (1994). *Remarried family relationships.* Thousand Oaks, CA: Sage.

Ganong, L., Coleman, M., Fine, M., & Martin, P. (1999). Stepparents' affinity-seeking and affinity-maintaining strategies with stepchildren. *Journal of Family Issues, 20,* 299–327.

Garcia, P., & Geisler, J. (1988). Sex and age/grade differences in adolescents' self-disclosure. *Perceptual and Motor Skills, 67,* 427–432.

Garrett, R. K., & Danziger, J. (2008). *Gratification and disaffection: Understanding personal Internet use during work.* Paper presented at the annual meeting of the International Communication Association, Montreal, Canada.

Gaucher, D., Wood, J. V., Stinson, D. A., Forest, A. L., Holmes, J. G., & Logel, C. (2012). Perceived regard explains self-esteem differences in expressivity. *Personality and Social Psychology Bulletin, 38*(9) 1144–1156. doi: 10.1177/0146167212445790

Gerdes, L. I. (1999). *Sexual harassment: Current controversies.* San Diego, CA: Greenhaven.

Gettings, J. (2005). Civil disobedience: Black medalists raise fists for civil rights movement. Retrieved from www.infoplease.com/spot/mm-mexicocity.html

Giannakakis, A. E., & Fritsche, I. (2011). Social identities, group norms, and threat: On the malleability of ingroup bias. *Personality and Social Psychology Bulletin, 37*(1), 82–93.

Gibbs, J. L., Ellison, N. B., & Heino, R. D. (2006). Self-presentation in online personals: The role of anticipated future interaction, self-disclosure, and perceived success in Internet dating. *Communication Research, 33,* 1–26.

Gibson, B., & Sachau, D. (2000). Sandbagging as a self-presentational style: Claiming to be less than you are. *Personality and Social Psychology Bulletin, 26,* 56–70.

Gifford, R., Ng, C. F., & Wilkinson, M. (1985). Nonverbal cues in the employment interview: Links between applicant qualities and interviewer judgments. *Journal of Applied Psychology, 70,* 729–736.

Giles, H., Coupland, N., & Coupland, J. (Eds.). (1991). *Contexts of accommodation: Developments in applied linguistics.* Cambridge, UK: Cambridge University Press.

Giles, H., & Street, R. L. (1994). Communicator characteristics and behavior. In M. L. Knapp & G. R. Miller (Eds.), *Handbook of interpersonal communication* (2nd ed., pp. 103–161). Beverly Hills, CA: Sage.

Gleason, L. B. (1989). *The development of language.* Columbus, OH: Merrill.

Glenn, D. (2010, February 28). Divided attention: In an age of classroom multitasking, scholars probe the nature of learning and memory. *The Chronicle of Higher Education.* Retrieved from http://chronicle.com/article/Scholars-Turn-Their-Attention/63746/

Glisson, C., & James, L. R. (2002). The cross-level effects of culture and climate in human service teams. *Journal of Organizational Behavior, 23,* 767–794.

Global Workplace Analytics (2013). Latest telecommuting statistics. Retrieved from http://globalworkplaceanalytics.com/telecommuting-statistics

Goffman, E. (1955). On facework: An analysis of ritual elements in social interaction. *Psychiatry, 18,* 319–345.

Goffman, E. (1959). *The presentation of self in everyday life.* Garden City, NY: Doubleday Anchor Books.

Goffman, E. (1979). Footing. *Semiotica, 25,* 124–147.

Goldsmith, D. J., & Fulfs, P. A. (1999). You just don't have the evidence: An analysis of claims and evidence in Deborah Tannen's *You just don't understand.* In M. E. Roloff (Ed.), *Communication Yearbook 22* (pp. 1–49). Thousand Oaks, CA: Sage.

Goldstein, N. J., Vezich, I. S., & Shapiro, J. R. (2014). Perceived perspective taking: When others walk in our shoes. *Journal of Personality and Social Psychology, 106*(6), 941–960. doi: 10.1037/a0036395

Goldstein, T. (2001). I'm not white: Anti-racist teacher education for white early childhood educators. *Contemporary Issues in Early Childhood, 2,* 3–13.

Goleman, D. (2006). *Social intelligence: The new science of human relationships.* New York, NY: Bantam Dell.

Goleman, D. (2007a, February 20). Flame first, think later: New clues to e-mail misbehavior. *The New York Times.* Retrieved from http://www.nytimes.com

Goleman, D. (2007b, August 24). Free won't: The marshmallow test revisited [Blog post]. Retrieved from http://danielgoleman.info/2007/free-wont-the-marshmallow-test-revisited/

Golish, T. D. (2000). Changes in closeness between adult children and their parents: A turning point analysis. *Communication Reports, 13,* 79–97.

Golish, T. D. (2003). Stepfamily communication strengths: Understanding the ties that bind. *Human Communication Research, 29*(1), 41–80.

Goodsell, T. L., Bates, J. S., & Behnke, A. O. (2010). Fatherhood stories: Grandparents, grandchildren, and gender differences. *Journal of Social and Personal Relationships, 28*(1), 134–154.

Goodwin, C. (1981). *Conversational organization: Interaction between speakers and hearers.* New York, NY: Academic Press.

Gosling, S. D., Gaddis, S., & Vazire, S. (2007, March). *Personality impressions based on Facebook profiles.* Paper presented at the International Conference on Weblogs and Social Media (ICWSM), Boulder, CO.

Gottman, J. M., & Levenson, R. W. (2000). The timing of divorce: Predicting when a couple will divorce over a 14-year period. *Journal of Marriage and Family, 62*, 737–745.

Graham, J. M. (2011). Measuring love in romantic relationships: A meta-analysis. *Journal of Social and Personal Relationships, 28*(6), 748–771.

Grammer, K., & Thornhill, R. (1994). Human facial attractiveness and sexual selection: The role of averageness and symmetry. *Journal of Comparative Psychology, 108*, 233–242.

Grice, H. P. (1989). *Studies in the way of words*. Cambridge, MA: Harvard University Press.

Gross, J. J., & John, O. P. (2002). Wise emotion regulation. In L. Feldman Barrett & P. Salovey (Eds.), *The wisdom in feeling: Psychological processes in emotional intelligence* (pp. 297–319). New York, NY: Guilford Press.

Gross, J. J., Richards, J. M., & John, O. P. (2006). Emotion regulation in everyday life. In D. K. Snyder, J. A. Simpson, & J. N. Hughes (Eds.), *Emotion regulation in couples and families: Pathways to dysfunction and health*. Washington, DC: American Psychological Association.

Gudykunst, W. B., & Kim, Y. Y. (2003). *Communicating with strangers: An approach to intercultural communication* (4th ed.). New York, NY: McGraw-Hill.

Gudykunst, W. B., & Nishida, T. (1993). Closeness in interpersonal relationships in Japan and the United States. *Research in Social Psychology, 8*, 85–97.

Guerin, B. (1999). Children's intergroup attribution bias for liked and disliked peers. *Journal of Social Psychology, 139*, 583–589.

Guerrero, L. K., & Andersen, P. A. (1998). Jealousy experience and expression in romantic relationships. In P. A. Andersen & L. K. Guerrero (Eds.), *Handbook of communication and emotion* (pp. 155–188). San Diego, CA: Academic Press.

Gumperz, J. J., & Levinson, S. C. (Eds.). (1996). *Rethinking linguistic relativity*. New York, NY: Cambridge University Press.

Haas, S. M., & Stafford, L. (1998). An initial examination of maintenance behaviors in gay and lesbian relationships. *Journal of Social and Personal Relationships, 15*, 846–855.

Haas, S. M., & Stafford, L. (2005). Maintenance behaviors in same-sex and marital relationships: A matched sample comparison. *Journal of Family Communication, 5*, 43–60.

Haden, S. C., & Hojjat, M. (2006). Aggressive responses to betrayal: Type of relationship, victim's sex, and nature of aggression. *Journal of Social and Personal Relationships, 23*(1), 101–116.

Halatsis, P., & Christakis, N. (2009). The challenge of sexual attraction within heterosexuals' cross-sex friendship. *Journal of Social and Personal Relationships, 26*(6–7), 919–937.

Hall, E. T. (1966). A system of the notation of proxemics behavior. *American Anthropologist, 65*, 1003–1026.

Hall, E. T. (1976). *Beyond culture*. Garden City, NY: Anchor.

Hall, E. T. (1981). *The silent language*. New York, NY: Anchor/Doubleday.

Hall, E. T. (1983). *The dance of life: The other dimension of time*. New York, NY: Doubleday.

Hall, E. T. (1997a). Context and meaning. In L. A. Samovar & R. E. Porter (Eds.), *Intercultural communication: A reader* (pp. 45–53). Belmont, CA: Wadsworth.

Hall, E. T. (1997b). Monochronic and polychronic time. In L. A. Samovar & R. E. Porter (Eds.), *Intercultural communication: A reader* (8th ed., pp. 277–284). Belmont, CA: Wadsworth.

Hall, E. T., & Hall, M. R. (1987). *Understanding cultural differences*. Yarmouth, ME: Intercultural Press.

Hall, J. A., Carter, J. D., & Horgan, T. G. (2000). Gender differences in nonverbal communication of emotion. In A. H. Fischer (Ed.), *Gender and emotion: Social psychological perspectives* (pp. 97–117). Cambridge, UK: Cambridge University Press.

Hall, J. A., Park, N., Song, H., & Cody, M. J. (2010). Strategic misrepresentation in online dating: The effects of gender, self-monitoring, and personality traits. *Journal of Social and Personal Relationships, 27*(1), 117–135.

Halliwell, E., & Dittmar, H. (2006). Associations between appearance-related self-discrepancies and young women's and men's affect, body satisfaction, and emotional eating: A comparison of fixed-item and participant-generated self-discrepancies. *Personality and Social Psychology Bulletin, 32*, 447–458. doi: 10.1177/0146167205284005

Hammer, M. R., Bennett, M. J., & Wiseman, R. (2003). Measuring intercultural sensitivity: The intercultural development inventory. *International Journal of Intercultural Relations, 27*, 421–443.

Hansen, G. L. (1985). Dating jealousy among college students. *Sex Roles, 12*, 713–721.

Harms, L. S. (1961). Listener judgments of status cues in speech. *Quarterly Journal of Speech, 47*, 164–168.

Harrison, K. (2001). Ourselves, our bodies: Thin-ideal media, self-discrepancies, and eating disorder symptoms in adolescents. *Journal of Social and Clinical Psychology, 20*, 289–323.

Hastorf, A. H., & Cantril, H. (1954). They saw a game: A case study. *Journal of Abnormal and Social Psychology, 49*, 129–134.

Hatfield, E. (1983). Equity theory and research: An overview. In H. H. Blumberg, A. P. Hare, V. Kent, & M. Davies (Eds.), *Small groups and social interaction* (Vol. 2, pp. 401–412). Chichester, UK: Wiley.

Hatfield, E., & Rapson, R. L. (1987). Passionate love: New directions in research. In W. H. Jones & D. Perlman (Eds.), *Advances in personal relationships* (Vol. 1, pp. 109–139). London, UK: Jessica Kingsley.

Hatfield, E. E., & Sprecher, S. (1986). *Mirror, mirror . . . the importance of looks in everyday life*. Albany: State University of New York Press.

Hatfield, E., Traupmann, J., & Sprecher, S. (1984). Older women's perceptions of their intimate relationships. *Journal of Social and Clinical Psychology, 2*, 108–124.

Hatfield, E., Traupmann, J., Sprecher, S., Utne, M., & Hay, M. (1985). Equity in close relationships. In W. Ickes (Ed.), *Compatible and incompatible relationships* (pp. 91–171). New York, NY: Springer-Verlag.

Hauser, T. (2006). *Muhammad Ali: His life and times*. New York, NY: Simon & Schuster.

Hayashi, G. M., & Strickland, B. R. (1998). Long-term effects of parental divorce on love relationships: Divorce as attachment disruption. *Journal of Social and Personal Relationships, 15*, 23–38.

Hayes, J. G., & Metts, S. (2008). Managing the expression of emotion. *Western Journal of Communication, 72*, 374–396.

Hays, R. B. (1988). Friendship. In S. Duck (Ed.), *Handbook of personal relationships: Theory, research, and interventions* (pp. 391–408). Chichester, UK: Wiley.

Heider, F. (1958). *The psychology of interpersonal relations*. New York, NY: Wiley.

Heino, R. D., Ellison, N. B., & Gibbs, J. L. (2010). Relationshopping: Investigating the market metaphor in online dating. *Journal of Social and Personal Relationships, 27*(4), 427–447.

Hemmings, K. H. (2008). *The Descendants.* New York, NY: Random House.

Hendrick, C., & Hendrick, S. S. (1988). Lovers wear rose colored glasses. *Journal of Social and Personal Relationships, 5,* 161–183.

Hendrick, S. S., & Hendrick, C. (1992). *Romantic love.* Thousand Oaks, CA: Sage.

Hendrick, S. S., & Hendrick, C. (2006). Measuring respect in close relationships. *Journal of Social and Personal Relationships, 23,* 881–899.

Heritage, J. C., & Watson, D. R. (1979). Formulations as conversational objectives. In G. Pathas (Ed.), *Everyday language: Studies in ethnomethodology.* New York, NY: Irvington.

Hertwig, R., Davis, J. N., & Sulloway, F. J. (2002). Parental investment: How an equity motive can produce inequality. *Psychological Bulletin, 128,* 728–745.

Herweddingplanner.com (2011, April 29). *Randy Fenoli "Say Yes to the Dress" wedding gown tips with Chantal Patton of www.herweddingplanner.com.* Retrieved from http://www.youtube.com/watch?v=9T-R3LeFjLU

Heslin, R. (1974, May). *Steps toward a taxonomy of touching.* Paper presented at the annual meeting of the Midwestern Psychological Association, Chicago, IL.

Hetherington, E. M. (1993). An overview of the Virginia longitudinal study of divorce and remarriage with a focus on early adolescence. *Journal of Family Psychology, 7,* 39–56.

Hickson, M., III, Grierson, R. D., & Linder, B. C. (1991). A communication perspective on sexual harassment: Affiliative nonverbal behaviors in asynchronous relationships. *Communication Quarterly, 39,* 111–118.

Higgins, E. T. (1987). Self-discrepancy: A theory relating self and affect. *Psychological Review, 94,* 319–340.

Hill, C. T., Rubin, Z., & Peplau, L. A. (1976). Breakups before marriage: The end of 103 affairs. *Journal of Social Issues, 32,* 147–168.

Hodgins, H. S., & Belch, C. (2000). Interparental violence and nonverbal abilities. *Journal of Nonverbal Behavior, 24,* 3–24.

Hodgson, L. K., & Wertheim, E. H. (2007). Does good emotion management aid forgiving? Multiple dimensions of empathy, emotion management and forgiveness of self and others. *Journal of Social and Personal Relationships, 24*(6), 931–949.

Hofstede, G. (1991). *Cultures and organizations.* London, UK: McGraw-Hill.

Hofstede, G. (2001). *Culture's consequences: Comparing values, behaviors, institutions, and organizations across nations* (2nd ed., pp. 79–123). Thousand Oaks, CA: Sage.

Hofstede, G. (2009). The Hofstede Center, National cultural dimensions. Retrieved from http://www.geert-hofstede.com/national-culture.html

Honeycutt, J. M. (1999). Typological differences in predicting marital happiness from oral history behaviors and imagined interactions. *Communication Monographs, 66,* 276–291.

Horne, C. F. (1917). *The sacred books and early literature of the East: Vol. II. Egypt.* New York, NY: Parke, Austin, & Lipscomb.

Hovick, S. R. A., Meyers, R. A., & Timmerman, C. E. (2003). E-mail communication in workplace romantic relationships. *Communication Studies, 54,* 468–480.

Howard, P. E. N., Rainie, L., & Jones, S. (2001, November). Days and nights on the Internet: The impact of a diffusing technology. *American Behavioral Scientist, 45,* 383–405.

Hughes, M., Morrison, K., & Asada, K. J. K. (2005). What's love got to do with it? Exploring the impact of maintenance rules, love attitudes, and network support on friends with benefits relationships. *Western Journal of Speech Communication, 69,* 49–66.

Hunsinger, M., Isbell, L. M., & Clore, G. L. (2012). Sometimes happy people focus on the trees and sad people focus on the forest: Context-dependent effects of mood in impression formation. *Personality and Social Psychology Bulletin, 38*(2) 220–232.

Hurley, D. (2005, April 19). Divorce rate: It's not as high as you think. *The New York Times,* p. F7.

Hyde, J. S. (2005). The gender similarities hypothesis. *American Psychologist, 60,* 581–592.

Hyun, J. (2005). *Breaking the bamboo ceiling: Career strategies for Asians.* New York, NY: HarperCollins.

Infante, D. A. (1995). Teaching students to understand and control verbal aggression. *Communication Education, 44,* 51–63.

Infante, D. A., Chandler, T. A., & Rudd, J. E. (1989). Test of an argumentative skill deficiency model of interspousal violence. *Communication Monographs, 56,* 163–177.

Infante, D. A., Myers, S. A., & Burkel, R. A. (1994). Argument and verbal aggression in constructive and destructive family and organizational disagreements. *Western Journal of Communication, 58,* 73–84.

Infante, D. A., & Wigley, C. J. (1986). Verbal aggressiveness: An interpersonal model and measure. *Communication Monographs, 53,* 61–69.

Institute of International Education (2011, November 14). Open doors 2011: Report on international education exchange. Retrieved from http://www.iie.org/Research-and-Publications/~/media/Files/Corporate/Open-Doors/Open-Doors-2011-Briefing-Presentation.ashx

Ivey, E. (2012). *The snow child.* New York, NY: Back Bay Books.

Jackson, D. C., Malmstadt, J. R., Larson, C. L., & Davidson, R. J. (2000). Suppression and enhancement of emotional responses to unpleasant pictures. *Psychophysiology, 37,* 515–522.

Jackson, M. (2008). *Distracted: The erosion of attention and the coming dark age.* Amherst, NY: Prometheus Books.

Jacobs, S. (1994). Language and interpersonal communication. In M. L. Knapp & G. R. Miller (Eds.), *Handbook of interpersonal communication* (2nd ed., pp. 199–228). Thousand Oaks, CA: Sage.

Jacobs, S., Dawson, E. J., & Brashers, D. (1996). Information manipulation theory: A replication and assessment. *Communication Monographs, 63,* 70–82.

Janusik, L. A. (2007). Building listening theory: The validation of the conversational listening span. *Communication Studies, 58*(2), 139–156.

John, O. P. (1990). The "Big Five" factor taxonomy: Dimensions of personality in the natural language and in questionnaires. In L. A. Pervin (Ed.), *Handbook of personality: Theory and research* (pp. 66–100). New York, NY: Guilford Press.

John, O. P., Donahue, E. M., & Kentle, R. L. (1991). *The Big Five Inventory: Versions 4a and 54.* Berkeley: University of California, Berkeley, Institute of Personality and Social Research.

John, O. P., & Gross, J. J. (2004). Healthy and unhealthy emotion regulation: Personality processes, individual differences, and lifespan development. *Journal of Personality, 72,* 1301–1334.

John, O. P., & Srivastava, S. (1999). The big five trait taxonomy: History, measurement, and theoretical perspectives. In L. Pervin and O. P. John (Eds.), *Handbook of personality: Theory and research* (2nd ed.). New York, NY: Guilford Press.

Johnson, A. J., Haigh, M. M., Becker, J. A. H., Craig, E. A., & Wigley, S. (2008). College students' use of relational management strategies in email in long-distance and geographically close relationships. *Journal of Computer-Mediated Communication, 13,* 381–404.

Johnson, A. J., Wittenberg, E., Villagran, M. M., Mazur, M., & Villagran, P. (2003). Relational progression as a dialectic: Examining turning points in communication among friends. *Communication Monographs, 70*(3), 230–249.

Johnson, H. (2004, April 1). Jimmy Jam: Three decades of hits; one seamless partnership. Retrieved from http://mixonline.com/mag/audio_jimmy_jam

Joinson, A. N. (2001, March/April). Self-disclosure in computer-mediated communication: The role of self-awareness and visual anonymity. *European Journal of Social Psychology, 31,* 177–192.

Jones, D. C., Vigfusdottir, T. H., & Lee, Y. (2004). Body image and the appearance culture among adolescent girls and boys: An examination of friends' conversations, peer criticism, appearance magazines, and the internalization of appearance ideals. *Journal of Adolescent Research, 19,* 323–339.

Jones, S. E., & LeBaron, C. D. (2002). Research on the relationship between verbal and nonverbal communication: Emerging integrations. *Journal of Communication, 52,* 499–521.

Jones, T. E. (1999). *If it's broken, you can fix it: Overcoming dysfunction in the workplace.* New York, NY: AMACOM Books.

Jones, W. H., & Burdette, M. P. (1994). Betrayal in relationships. In A. L. Weber & J. H. Harvey (Eds.), *Perspectives on close relationships* (pp. 243–262). Boston, MA: Allyn and Bacon.

Jones, W., Moore, D., Scratter, A., & Negel, L. (2001). Interpersonal transgression and betrayals. In R. M. Kowalski (Ed.), *Behaving badly: Aversive behavior in interpersonal relationships* (pp. 233–256). Washington, DC: American Psychological Association.

Jourard, S. M. (1964). *The transparent self.* New York, NY: Van Nostrand Reinhold.

Juncoa, R., & Cotton, S. R. (2012). No A 4 U: The relationship between multitasking and academic performance. *Computers & Education, 59*(2), 505–514. doi: http://dx.doi.org/10.1016/j.compedu.2011.12.023

Kagawa, N., & McCornack, S. A. (2004, November). *Collectivistic Americans and individualistic Japanese: A cross-cultural comparison of parental understanding.* Paper presented at the annual meeting of the National Communication Association, Chicago.

Kaharit, K., Zachau, G., Eklof, M., Sandsjo, L., & Moller, C. (2003). Assessment of hearing and hearing disorders in rock/jazz musicians. *International Journal of Audiology, 42,* 279–288.

Kahneman, D. (1973). *Attention and effort.* Englewood Cliffs, NJ: Prentice Hall.

Kassing, J. W. (2008). Consider this: A comparison of factors contributing to employees' expressions of dissent. *Communication Quarterly, 56*(3), 342–355.

Katz, D., & Kahn, R. (1978). *The social psychology of organizations* (2nd ed.). New York, NY: Wiley.

Katz, J. (1983). A theory of qualitative methodology. In R. M. Emerson (Ed.), *Contemporary field research: A collection of readings* (pp. 127–148). Prospect Heights, IL: Waveland Press.

Katz, J., & Farrow, S. (2000). Discrepant self-views and young women's sexual and emotional adjustment. *Sex Roles, 42,* 781–805.

Keashly, L., & Neuman, J. H. (2005). Bullying in the workplace: Its impact and management. *Employee Rights and Employment Policy Journal, 8,* 335–373.

Keashly, L., Trott, V., & MacLean, L. M. (1994). Abusive behavior in the workplace: A preliminary investigation. *Violence and Victims, 9,* 341–357.

Keck, K. L., & Samp, J. A. (2007). The dynamic nature of goals and message production as revealed in a sequential analysis of conflict interactions. *Human Communication Research, 33,* 27–47.

Keesing, R. M. (1974). Theories of culture. *Annual Review of Anthropology, 3,* 73–97.

Kellas, J. K. (2005). Family ties: Communicating identity through jointly told family stories. *Communication Monographs, 72*(4), 365–389.

Kellermann, K. (1989). The negativity effect in interaction: It's all in your point of view. *Human Communication Research, 16,* 147–183.

Kellermann, K. (1991). The conversation MOP: Progression through scenes in discourse. *Human Communication Research, 17,* 385–414.

Kelley, H. H., & Thibaut, J. W. (1978). *Interpersonal relations: A theory of interdependence.* New York, NY: Wiley.

Kelly, A. E., & McKillop, K. J. (1996). Consequences of revealing personal secrets. *Psychological Bulletin, 120,* 450–465.

Kennedy, T. L. M., Smith, A., Wells, A. T., & Wellman, B. (2008, October 19). Networked families: Parents and spouses are using the Internet and cell phones to create a "new connectedness" that builds on remote connections and shared Internet experiences. *Pew Internet & American Life Project.* Retrieved from http://www.pewinternet.org/

Kimpel, D. (2010). ASCAP Rhythm and Soul Heritage Award: Jimmy Jam & Terry Lewis. Retrieved from http://www.ascap.com/eventsawards/awards/rsawards/2005/heritage.aspx

King, S. K. (2001). Territoriality. Retrieved from http://www.huna.org/html/territor.html

Klein, R. C. A. (1998). Conflict and violence in the family: Cross-disciplinary issues. In R. C. A. Klein (Ed.), *Multidisciplinary perspectives on family violence* (pp. 1–13). New York, NY: Routledge.

Klopf, D. W. (2001). *Intercultural encounters: The fundamentals of intercultural communication* (5th ed.). Englewood, CO: Morton.

Kluger, J. (2011, October 3). Playing favorites. *Time.* Retrieved from http://www.time.com/time/magazine/article/0,9171,2094371,00.html

Knapp, M. (1984). *Interpersonal communication and human relationships.* Boston, MA: Allyn & Bacon.

Knapp, M. L., & Hall, J. A. (2002). *Nonverbal communication in human interaction* (5th ed.). Belmont, CA: Wadsworth/Thomson Learning.

Knobloch, L. K. (2005). Evaluating a contextual model of responses to relational uncertainty increasing events: The role of intimacy, appraisals, and emotions. *Human Communication Research, 31*(1), 60–101.

Koerner, A. F., & Fitzpatrick, M. A. (2002). Toward a theory of family communication. *Communication Theory, 12,* 70–91.

Koerner, A. F., & Fitzpatrick, M. A. (2006). Family communication patterns theory: A social cognitive approach. In D. O. Braithwaite & L. A. Baxter (Eds.), *Engaging theories in family communication: Multiple perspectives* (pp. 50–65). Thousand Oaks, CA: Sage.

Koerner, S. S., Wallace, S., Lehman, S. J., & Raymond, M. (2002). Mother-to-daughter disclosure after divorce: A double-edged sword? *Journal of Child and Family Studies, 11,* 469–483.

Kogan, L. (2006, August). The O interview: Gayle and Oprah, uncensored. *O, the Oprah Magazine.* Retrieved from http://www.oprah.com/omagazine/Gayle-King-and-Oprah-Uncensored-The-O-Magazine-Interview/1

Kostiuk, L. M., & Fouts, G. T. (2002). Understanding of emotions and emotion regulation in adolescent females with conduct problems: A qualitative analysis. *The Qualitative Report, 7*, 1–10.

Kotzé, M., & Venter, I. (2011). Differences in emotional intelligence between effective and ineffective leaders in the public sector: An empirical study. *International Review of Administrative Sciences, 77*(2), 397–427.

Koval, P., Laham, S. M., Haslam, N., Bastian, B., & Whelan, J. A. (2012). Our flaws are more human than yours: Ingroup bias in humanizing negative characteristics. *Personality and Social Psychology Bulletin, 38*(3), 283–295.

Kowalski, R. M., Walker, S., Wilkinson, R., Queen, A., & Sharpe, B. (2003). Lying, cheating, complaining, and other aversive interpersonal behaviors: A narrative examination of the darker side of relationships. *Journal of Social and Personal Relationships, 20*, 471–490.

Kowner, R. (1996). Facial asymmetry and attractiveness judgments in developmental perspective. *Journal of Experimental Psychology: Human Perception and Performance, 22*, 662–675.

Kozan, M., & Ergin, C. (1998). Preference for third-party help in conflict management in the United States and Turkey. *Journal of Cross-Cultural Psychology, 29*, 525–539.

Kramarae, C. (1981). *Women and men speaking: Frameworks for analysis*. Rowley, MA: Newbury House.

Krause, J. (2001). *Properties of naturally produced clear speech at normal rates and implications for intelligibility enhancement* (Unpublished doctoral dissertation). Massachusetts Institute of Technology, Cambridge.

Kreider, R. M. (2005). *Number, timing, and duration of marriages and divorces: 2001*. Washington, DC: U.S. Census Bureau.

Kreps, G. L. (1990). *Organizational communication*. New York, NY: Longman.

Krishnakumar, A., Buehler, C., & Barber, B. K. (2003). Youth perceptions of interparental conflict, ineffective parenting, and youth problem behaviors in European-American and African-American families. *Journal of Social and Personal Relationships, 20*(2), 239–260.

Krusiewicz, E. S., & Wood, J. T. (2001). He was our child from the moment we walked in that room: Entrance stories of adoptive parents. *Journal of Social and Personal Relationships, 18*(6), 785–803.

Kubany, E. S., Richard, D. C., Bauer, G. B., & Muraoka, M. Y. (1992). Impact of assertive and accusatory communication of distress and anger: A verbal component analysis. *Aggressive Behavior, 18*, 337–347.

Kuhn, J. L. (2001). Toward an ecological humanistic psychology. *Journal of Humanistic Psychology, 41*, 9–24.

Kurdek, L. A. (2005). What do we know about gay and lesbian couples? *Current Directions in Psychological Science, 14*, 251–254.

Kurdek, L. A. (2008). Differences between partners from Black and White heterosexual dating couples in a path model of relational commitment. *Journal of Social and Personal Relationships, 25*, 51–70.

Kuttler, A. F., LaGreca, A. M., & Prinstein, M. J. (1999). Friendship qualities and social-emotional functioning of adolescents with close, cross-sex friends. *Journal of Research on Adolescence, 9*, 339–366.

LaFollette, H., & Graham, G. (1986). Honesty and intimacy. *Journal of Social and Personal Relationships, 3*, 3–18.

Langdridge, D., & Butt, T. (2004). The fundamental attribution error: A phenomenological critique. *British Journal of Social Psychology, 43*, 357–369.

Lareau, A. (2003). *Unequal childhoods: Class, race, and family life*. Berkeley: University of California Press.

Larsen, R. J., & Ketelaar, T. (1991). Personality and susceptibility to positive and negative emotional states. *Journal of Personality and Social Psychology, 61*, 132–140.

Larson, J. R. (1984). The performance feedback process: A preliminary model. *Organizational Behavior and Human Performance, 33*, 42–76.

Lasswell, H. D. (1948). The structure and function of communication in society. In L. Bryson (Ed.), *The communication of ideas* (pp. 32–51). New York, NY: Harper & Row.

Lavy, S., Mikulincer, M., Shaver, P. R., & Gillath, O. (2009). Intrusiveness in romantic relationships: A cross-cultural perspective on imbalances between proximity and autonomy. *Journal of Social and Personal Relationships, 26*(6–7), 989–1008.

Le, B., Korn, M. S., Crockett, E. E., & Loving, T. J. (2010). Missing you maintains us: Missing a romantic partner, commitment, relationship maintenance, and physical infidelity. *Journal of Social and Personal Relationships, 28*, 653–667.

Leary, M. R. (2001). Toward a conceptualization of interpersonal rejection. In M. R. Leary (Ed.), *Interpersonal rejection* (pp. 3–20). New York, NY: Oxford University Press.

Leary, M. R., Gallagher, B., Fors, E., Buttermore, N., Baldwin, E., Kennedy, K., & Mills, A. (2003). The invalidity of disclaimers about the effects of social feedback on self-esteem. *Personality and Social Psychology Bulletin, 29*(5), 623–636. doi: 10.1177/0146167203251530

Lee, J. A. (1973). *The colors of love: An exploration of the ways of loving*. Don Mills, Ontario, Canada: New Press.

Lee-Flynn, S. C., Pomaki, G., DeLongis, A., Biesanz, J. C., & Puterman, E. (2011). Daily cognitive appraisals, daily affect, and long-term depressive symptoms: The role of self-esteem and self-concept clarity in the stress process. *Personality and Social Psychology Bulletin, 37*(2), 255–268. doi: 10.1177/0146167210394204

Lehrer, J. (2009, May 18). Don't! The secret of self-control. *The New Yorker*. Retrieved from http://www.newyorker.com/reporting/2009/05/18/090518fa_fact_lehrer

Lemerise, E. A., & Dodge, K. A. (1993). The development of anger and hostile interactions. In M. Lewis and J. M. Haviland (Eds.), *Handbook of emotions* (pp. 537–546). New York, NY: Guilford Press.

Lenhart, A., Purcell, K., Smith, A., & Zickuhr, K. (2010). Social media & young adults. *Pew Internet & American Life Project*. Retrieved from http://www.pewinternet.org/Reports/2010/Social-Media-and-Young-Adults.aspx

Leone, C., & Hall, I. (2003). Self-monitoring, marital dissatisfaction, and relationship dissolution: Individual differences in orientations to marriage and divorce. *Self and Identity, 2*, 189–202.

Lev-Ari, S., & Keysar, B. (2010). Why don't we believe non-native speakers? The influence of accent on credibility. *Journal of Experimental Social Psychology, 46*, 1093–1096. doi: 10.1016/j.jesp.2010.05.025

Levine, T. R., McCornack, S. A., & Baldwin Avery, P. (1992). Sex differences in emotional reactions to discovered deception. *Communication Quarterly, 40*, 289–296.

Levinson, S. C. (1985). *Pragmatics*. Cambridge, UK: Cambridge University Press.

Lewellen, W. (2008, July 7). Brenda Villa: The American saint of water polo. *Women's Sports Foundation*. Retrieved from http://66.40.5.5/Content/Articles/Athletes/About-Athletes/B/Brenda-Villa-saint-of-Water-Polo.aspx

Licoppe, C. (2003). Two modes of maintaining interpersonal relations through telephone: From the domestic to the mobile phone. In J. E. Katz (Ed.), *Machines that become us: The social context of personal communication technology* (pp. 171–185). New Brunswick, NJ: Transaction.

Lippa, R. A. (2002). *Gender, nature, and nurture.* Mahwah, NJ: Erlbaum.

Lippmann, W. (1922). *Public opinion.* New York, NY: Harcourt Brace.

Liu, B. M. (2011, January 8). Parents like Amy Chua are the reason why Asian-Americans like me are in therapy [Blog post]. Retrieved from http://bettymingliu.com

Lopes, P. N., Salovey, P., Cote, S., & Beers, M. (2005). Emotion regulation abilities and the quality of social interaction. *Emotion, 5,* 113–118.

Luft, J. (1970). *Group processes: An introduction to group dynamics* (2nd ed.). Palo Alto, CA: National Press Books.

Lulofs, R. S., & Cahn, D. D. (2000). *Conflict: From theory to action* (2nd ed.). Needham Heights, MA: Allyn & Bacon.

Luscombe, B. (2010, November 18). Who needs marriage? A changing institution. *Time.* Retrieved from http://www.time.com/time/magazine/article/0,9171,2032116,00.html

Lustig, M. W., & Koester, J. (2006). *Intercultural competence: Interpersonal communication across cultures* (5th ed.). Boston, MA: Allyn and Bacon.

Macrae, C. N., & Bodenhausen, G. V. (2001). Social cognition: Categorical person perception. *British Journal of Psychology, 92,* 239–255.

Maeda, E., & Ritchie, L. D. (2003). The concept of Shinyuu in Japan: A replication of and comparison to Cole and Bradac's study on U.S. friendship. *Journal of Social and Personal Relationships, 20,* 579–598.

Malandro, L. A., & Barker, L. L. (1983). *Nonverbal communication.* Reading, MA: Addison-Wesley.

Malcolm X. (1964). Personal letter. Retrieved from http://www.malcolm-x.org/docs/let_mecca.htm

Malis, R. S., & Roloff, M. E. (2006). Demand/withdraw patterns in serial arguments: Implications for well-being. *Human Communication Research, 32,* 198–216.

Marikar, S. (2013, December 20). For Millennials, a generational divide. *New York Times.* Retrieved from http://www.nytimes.com/2013/12/22/fashion/Millenials-Millennials-Generation-Y.html?pagewanted=all&_r=1&

Markey, P. M., & Markey, C. N. (2007). Romantic ideals, romantic obtainment, and relationship experiences: The complementarity of interpersonal traits among romantic partners. *Journal of Social and Personal Relationships, 24*(4), 517–533.

Martin, W., & LaVan, H. (2010). Workplace bullying: A review of litigated cases. *Employee Responsibilities and Rights Journal, 22*(3), 175–194.

Marzano, R. J., & Arredondo, D. E. (1996). *Tactics for thinking.* Aurora, CO: Mid Continent Regional Educational Laboratory.

Mashek, D. J., & Aron, A. (2004). *Handbook of closeness and intimacy.* Mahwah, NJ: Erlbaum.

Maslow, A. H. (1970). *Motivation and personality* (2nd ed.). New York, NY: Harper & Row.

Matlin, M., & Stang, D. (1978). *The Pollyanna principle: Selectivity in language, memory, and thought.* Cambridge, MA: Schenkman.

Mauss, I. B., Levenson, R. W., McCarter, L., Wilhelm, F. H., & Gross, J. J. (2005). The tie that binds: Coherence among emotion experience, behavior, and physiology. *Emotion, 5,* 175–190.

Mayer, J. D., & Salovey, P. (1997). What is emotional intelligence? In P. Salovey & J. D. Sluyter (Eds.), *Emotional development and emotional intelligence* (pp. 3–31). New York, NY: Basic Books.

Mayer, J. D., Salovey, P., & Caruso, D. R. (2004). Emotional intelligence: Theory, findings and implications. *Psychological Inquiry, 15*(3), 197–215.

McCornack, S. A. (1997). The generation of deceptive messages: Laying the groundwork for a viable theory of interpersonal deception. In J. O. Greene (Ed.), *Message production: Advances in communication theory* (pp. 91–126). Mahwah, NJ: Erlbaum.

McCornack, S. A. (2008). Information manipulation theory: Explaining how deception works. In L. A. Baxter & D. O. Braithwaite (Eds.), *Engaging theories in interpersonal communication: Multiple perspectives* (pp. 215–226). Thousand Oaks, CA: Sage.

McCornack, S. A., & Husband, R. (1986, May). *The evolution of a long-term organizational conflict: A design logic approach.* Paper presented at the annual meeting of the International Communication Association, Chicago, IL.

McCornack, S. A., & Levine, T. R. (1990). When lies are uncovered: Emotional and relational outcomes of discovered deception. *Communication Monographs, 57,* 119–138.

McCrae, R. R. (2001). Trait psychology and culture. *Journal of Personality, 69,* 819–846.

McCrae, R. R., & Costa, P. T., Jr. (2001). A five-factor theory of personality. In L. A. Pervin and O. P. John (Eds.), *Handbook of personality: Theory and research* (2nd ed., pp. 139–153). New York, NY: Guilford Press.

McCroskey, J. C., & Richmond, V. P. (1987). Willingness to communicate. In J. C. McCroskey & J. A. Daly (Eds.), *Personality and interpersonal communication* (pp. 129–156). Beverly Hills, CA: Sage.

McEwan, B., Babin Gallagher, B., & Farinelli, L. (2008, November). *The end of a friendship: Friendship dissolution reasons and methods.* Paper presented at the annual meeting of the National Communication Association, San Diego, CA.

McGlynn, J. (2007, November). *More connections, less connection: An examination of computer-mediated communication as relationship maintenance.* Paper presented at the annual meeting of the National Communication Association, Chicago, IL.

McGuirk, R. (2011, September 14). Australian passport gender options: "Transgender" will be included. *Associated Press.* Retrieved from http://www.huffingtonpost.com/2011/09/14/australia-passport-gender_n_963386.html

McIntosh, P. (1999). White privilege: Unpacking the invisible knapsack. In E. Lee, D. Menkart, & M. Okazawa-Rey (Eds.), *Beyond heroes and holidays: A practical guide to K–12 anti-racist, multicultural education and staff development* (pp. 79–82). Washington, DC: Network of Educators on the Americas.

McLaughlin, M. L., & Cody, M. J. (1982). Awkward silences: Behavioral antecedents and consequences of the conversational lapse. *Human Communication Research, 8,* 299–316.

McNaughton, D., Hamlin, D., McCarthy, J., Head-Reeves, D., & Schreiner, M. (2007). Learning to listen: Teaching an active listening strategy to preservice education professionals. *Topics in Early Childhood Special Education, 27*(4), 223–231.

Mead, G. H. (1934). *Mind, self, and society.* Chicago, IL: University of Chicago Press.

Mehrabian, A. (1972). *Nonverbal communication*. Chicago, IL: Aldine.

Messman, S. J., Canary, D. J., & Hause, K. S. (1994, February). *Motives, strategies, and equity in the maintenance of opposite-sex friendships*. Paper presented at the Western States Communication Association convention, San Jose, CA.

Messman, S. J., Canary, D. J., & Hause, K. S. (2000). Motives to remain platonic, equity, and the use of maintenance strategies in opposite-sex friendships. *Journal of Social and Personal Relationships, 17*, 67–94.

Metts, S., & Chronis, H. (1986, May). *Relational deception: An exploratory analysis*. Paper presented at the annual meeting of the International Communication Association, Chicago, IL.

Metts, S., & Planalp, S. (2002). Emotional communication. In M. L. Knapp & J. A. Daly (Eds.), *Handbook of interpersonal communication* (pp. 339–373). Thousand Oaks, CA: Sage.

Michalos, A. C. (1991). *Global report on student well-being: Vol. 1. Life satisfaction and happiness*. New York, NY: Springer-Verlag.

Michaud, S. G., & Aynesworth, H. (1989). *The only living witness: A true account of homicidal insanity*. New York, NY: Signet.

Mickelson, K. D., Kessler, R. C., & Shaver, P. R. (1997). Adult attachment in a nationally representative sample. *Journal of Personality and Social Psychology, 73*, 1092–1106.

Mies, M. (1991). *Patriarchy and accumulation on a world scale: Women in the international division of labor*. London, UK: Zed Books.

Miller, G. R., & Steinberg, M. (1975). *Between people: A new analysis of interpersonal communication*. Chicago, IL: Science Research Associates.

Miller, H., & Arnold, J. (2001). Breaking away from grounded identity: Women academics on the Web. *CyberPsychology and Behavior, 4*, 95–108.

Miller, K. (1995). *Organizational communication: Approaches and processes*. Belmont, CA: Wadsworth.

Miller, L., Hefner, V., & Scott, A. (2007, May). *Turning points in dyadic friendship development and termination*. Paper presented at the annual meeting of the International Communication Association, San Francisco, CA.

Miller, R. S. (2014). *Intimate relationships* (7th ed.). New York, NY: McGraw-Hill.

Miller, R. S., Perlman, D., & Brehm, S. S. (2007). Love: Chapter 8. In R. S. Miller, D. Perlman, & S. S. Brehm (Eds.), *Intimate relationships* (pp. 244–275). New York, NY: McGraw-Hill.

Milne, A. A. (1926). *Winnie-the-Pooh*. New York, NY: E. P. Dutton.

Milne, A. A. (1928). *The house at Pooh corner*. New York, NY: E. P. Dutton.

Mister Rogers. (n.d.). *TVAcres*. Retrieved from http://www.tvacres.com/child_mrrogers.htm

Mitchell, M. (1936). *Gone with the wind*. New York, NY: Macmillan.

Mohammed, R., & Hussein, A. (2008, August). *Communication climate and organizational performance*. Paper presented to the Eighth International Conference on Knowledge, Culture & Changes in Organizations, Cambridge University (UK).

Mongeau, P. A., Hale, J. L., & Alles, M. (1994). An experimental investigation of accounts and attributions following sexual infidelity. *Communication Monographs, 61*, 326–344.

Mongeau, P. A., Ramirez, A., & Vorrell, M. (2003, February). *Friends with benefits: Initial explorations of sexual, nonromantic relationships*. Paper presented at the annual meeting of the Western Communication Association, Salt Lake City, UT.

Monsour, M. (1997). Communication and cross-sex friendships across the life cycle: A review of the literature. In B. Burleson (Ed.), *Communication Yearbook 20* (pp. 375–414). Thousand Oaks, CA: Sage.

Montagu, M. F. A. (1971). *Touching: The human significance of the skin*. New York, NY: Columbia University Press.

Morrison, K., Lee, C. M., Wiedmaier, B., & Dibble, J. L. (2008, November). *The influence of MySpace and Facebook events on interpersonal relationships*. Paper presented at the annual meeting of the National Communication Association, San Diego, CA.

Morrison, K., & McCornack, S. A. (2011). *Studying attitudes toward LGBT persons in mid-Michigan: Challenges and goals*. Technical report presented at the annual meeting of the Michigan Fairness Forum, Lansing, MI.

Mosher, C., & Danoff-Burg, S. (2007). College students' life priorities: The influence of gender and gender-linked personality traits. *Gender Issues, 24*(2). doi:10.1007/s12147-007-9002-z

Mulac, A., Bradac, J. J., & Mann, S. K. (1985). Male/female language differences and attributional consequences in children's television. *Human Communication Research, 11*, 481–506.

Mulac, A., Incontro, C. R., & James, M. R. (1985). Comparison of the gender-linked language effect and sex role stereotypes. *Journal of Personality and Social Psychology, 49*, 1098–1109.

Munro, K. (2002). Conflict in cyberspace: How to resolve conflict online. In J. Suler (Ed.), *The psychology of cyberspace*. Retrieved from http://www-usr.rider.edu/~suler/psycyber/conflict.html

Myers, D. G. (2002). *The pursuit of happiness: Discovering the pathway to fulfillment, well-being, and enduring personal joy*. New York, NY: HarperCollins.

Myers, S. A., Knox, R. L., Pawlowski, D. R., & Ropog, B. L. (1999). Perceived communication openness and functional communication skills among organizational peers. *Communication Reports, 12*, 71–83.

National Communication Association (NCA). (1999). *NCA credo for ethical communication*. Retrieved from http://www.natcom.org

National Communication Association (NCA). (n.d.). *The field of communication*. Retrieved from http://www.natcom.org/Tertiary.aspx?id=236

Neuliep, J. W. (2002). Assessing the reliability and validity of the generalized ethnocentrism scale. *Journal of Intercultural Communication Research, 31*, 201–215.

Neuliep, J. W., & McCroskey, J. C. (1997). The development of a U.S. and generalized ethnocentrism scale. *Communication Research Reports, 14*, 385–398.

Nishiyama, K. (1971). Interpersonal persuasion in a vertical society. *Speech Monographs, 38*, 148–154.

Nofsinger, R. E. (1999). *Everyday conversation*. Prospect Heights, IL: Waveland Press.

Oetzel, J., Ting-Toomey, S., Matsumoto, T., Yokochi, Y., Pan, X., Takai, J., & Wilcox, R. (2001). Face and facework in conflict: A cross-cultural comparison of China, Germany, Japan, and the United States. *Communication Monographs, 68*, 235–258.

Ohbuchi, K., & Sato, K. (1994). Children's reactions to mitigating accounts: Apologies, excuses, and intentionality of harm. *Journal of Social Psychology, 134*, 5–17.

O'Keefe, B. J. (1988). The logic of message design. *Communication Monographs, 55*, 80–103.

O'Leary, K. D., & Vivian, D. (1990). Physical aggression in marriage. In F. D. Fincham & T. N. Bradbury (Eds.), *The psychology of marriage: Basic issues and applications* (pp. 323–348). New York, NY: Guilford Press.

Ophir, E., Nass, C. I., & Wagner, A. D. (2012). Cognitive control in media multitaskers. *Proceedings of the National Academy of Sciences.* Retrieved from http://www.pnas.org/content/106/37/15583

Oravec, J. (2000). Internet and computer technology hazards: Perspectives for family counseling. *British Journal of Guidance and Counselling, 28,* 309–324.

Orbe, M. P. (1998). *Constructing co-cultural theory: An explication of culture, power, and communication.* Thousand Oaks, CA: Sage.

Orth, U., Robins, R. W., Trzesniewski, K. H., Maes, J., & Schmitt, M. (2009). Low self-esteem is a risk factor for depressive symptoms from young adulthood to old age. *Journal of Abnormal Psychology, 118,* 472–478.

Oyamot, C. M., Fuglestad P. T., & Snyder, M. (2010). Balance of power and influence in relationships: The role of self-monitoring. *Journal of Social and Personal Relationships, 27*(1), 23–46. doi: 10.1177/0265407509347302

Palmer, M. T., & Simmons, K. B. (1995). Communicating intentions through nonverbal behaviors: Conscious and nonconscious encoding of liking. *Human Communication Research, 22,* 128–160.

Palmer Stadium. (2008). Retrieved from http://football.ballparks.com/NCAA/Ivy/Princeton/index.htm

Park, H. S., & Guan, X. (2006). The effects of national culture and face concerns on intention to apologize: A comparison of the USA and China. *Journal of Intercultural Communication Research, 35*(3), 183–204.

Park, H. S., Levine, T. R., McCornack, S. A., Morrison, K., & Ferrara, M. (2002). How people really detect lies. *Communication Monographs, 69,* 144–157.

Parkinson, B., & Simons, G. (2012). Worry spreads: Interpersonal transfer of problem-related anxiety. *Cognition and Emotion, 26*(3), 462–479. doi: 10.1080/02699931.2011.651101

Parkinson, B., Totterdell, P., Briner, R. B., & Reynolds, S. (1996). *Changing moods: The psychology of mood and mood regulation.* London, UK: Longman.

Parks, M. R. (1994). Communicative competence and interpersonal control. In M. L. Knapp & G. R. Miller (Eds.), *Handbook of interpersonal communication* (2nd ed., pp. 589–620). Beverly Hills, CA: Sage.

Parks, M. R. (2007). *Personal relationships and personal networks.* Hillsdale, NJ: Erlbaum.

Parks, M. R., & Adelman, M. B. (1983). Communication networks and the development of romantic relationships: An expansion of uncertainty reduction theory. *Human Communication Research, 10,* 55–79.

Parks, M. R., & Floyd, K. (1996). Making friends in cyberspace. *Journal of Communication, 46,* 80–97.

Patterson, B. R. (2007). Relationship development revisited: A preliminary look at communication in friendship over the lifespan. *Communication Research Reports, 24*(1), 29–37.

Patterson, M. L. (1988). Functions of nonverbal behavior in close relationships. In S. W. Duck (Ed.), *Handbook of personal relationships* (pp. 41–56). New York, NY: Wiley.

Patterson, M. L. (1995). A parallel process model of nonverbal communication. *Journal of Nonverbal Behavior, 19,* 3–29.

Payne, M. J., & Sabourin, T. C. (1990). Argumentative skill deficiency and its relationship to quality of marriage. *Communication Research Reports, 7,* 121–124.

Pennebaker, J. W. (1997). *Opening up: The healing power of expressing emotions.* New York, NY: Guilford Press.

Pennington, N. (2009, November). *What it means to be a (Facebook) friend: Navigating friendship on social network sites.* Paper presented at the annual meeting of the National Communication Association, Chicago, IL.

Pennsylvania Dutch Country Welcome Center (n.d.). *The Amish: FAQs.* Retrieved from http://www.padutch.com/atafaq.shtml

Peplau, L. A., & Spalding, L. R. (2000). The close relationships of lesbians, gay men and bisexuals. In C. Hendrick & S. S. Hendrick (Eds.), *Close relationships: A sourcebook* (pp. 111–123). Thousand Oaks, CA: Sage.

Pervin, L. A. (1993). Affect and personality. In M. Lewis & J. M. Haviland (Eds.), *Handbook of emotions* (pp. 301–311). New York, NY: Guilford Press.

Peterson, D. R. (2002). Conflict. In H. H. Kelley et al. (Eds.), *Close relationships* (2nd ed., pp. 360–396). Clinton Corners, NY: Percheron Press.

Petronio, S. (2000). The boundaries of privacy: Praxis of everyday life. In S. Petronio (Ed.), *Balancing the secrets of private disclosures* (pp. 37–49). Mahwah, NJ: Erlbaum.

Petronio, S., & Caughlin, J. P. (2006). Communication privacy management theory: Understanding families. In D. O. Braithwaite & L. A. Baxter (Eds.), *Engaging theories in family communication: Multiple perspectives* (pp. 35–49). Thousand Oaks, CA: Sage.

Pew Research Center (2010). Millennials: A portrait of generation next. Retrieved from http://www.pewsocialtrends.org/files/2010/10/millennials-confident-connected-open-to-change.pdf

Phillips, A. G., & Silvia, P. J. (2005). Self-awareness and the emotional consequences of self-discrepancies. *Personality and Social Psychology Bulletin, 31,* 703–713. doi: 10.1177/0146167204271559

Philpott, T. (2004, October). Stop stop-loss. Retrieved from http://www.moaa.org/todaysofficer/columnists/Philpott/Stop.asp

Pierce, C. A., & Aguinis, H. (2009). Moving beyond a legal-centric approach to managing workplace romances: Organizationally sensible recommendations for HR leaders. *Human Resource Management, 48*(3), 447–464.

Planalp, S., & Honeycutt, J. M. (1985). Events that increase uncertainty in personal relationships. *Human Communication Research, 11,* 593–604.

Plutchik, R. (1980). *Emotions: A psycho-evolutionary synthesis.* New York, NY: Harper & Row.

Plutchik, R. (1993). Emotions and their vicissitudes: Emotions and psychopathology. In M. Lewis & J. M. Haviland (Eds.), *Handbook of emotions* (pp. 53–66). New York, NY: Guilford Press.

Pomerantz, A. (1990). On the validity and generalizability of conversation analytic methods: Conversation analytic claims. *Communication Monographs, 57,* 231–235.

Price, J. (1999). *Navigating differences: Friendships between gay and straight men.* Binghamton, NY: Haworth Press.

Privitera, C., & Campbell, M. A. (2009). Cyberbullying: The new face of workplace bullying? *Cyberpsychology & Behavior, 12*(4), 395–400.

Pruitt, D. G., & Carnevale, P. J. (1993). *Negotiation in social conflict.* Monterey, CA: Brooks-Cole.

Przybylski, A. K., & Weinstein, N. (2012). Can you connect with me now? How the presence of mobile communication technology influences face-to-face conversation quality. *Journal of Social and Personal Relationships, 30*(3), 237–246.

Pyszczynski, T., Greenberg, J., Solomon, S., Arndt, J., & Schimel, J. (2004). Why do people need self-esteem? A theoretical and empirical review. *Psychological Bulletin, 130*(3), 435–468.

Quan-Haase, A., Cothrel, J., & Wellman, B. (2005). Instant messaging for collaboration: A case study of a high-tech firm. *Journal of Computer-Mediated Communication, 10.* Retrieved from http://jcmc.indiana.edu/vol10/issue4/quan-haase.html

Quenqua, D. (2009). I love you, man (as a friend). *The New York Times.* Retrieved from http://www.nytimes.com

Rabby, M. K. (1997, November). *Maintaining relationships via electronic mail.* Paper presented at the annual meeting of the National Communication Association, Chicago, IL.

Rahim, M. A., & Mager, N. R. (1995). Confirmatory factor analysis of the styles of handling interpersonal conflict: First-order factor model and its invariance across groups. *Journal of Applied Psychology, 80,* 122–132.

Rainey, V. P. (2000, December). The potential for miscommunication using email as a source of communications. *Transactions of the Society for Design and Process Science, 4,* 21–43.

Ramasubramanian, S. (2010). Testing the cognitive-affective consistency model of intercultural attitudes: Do stereotypical perceptions influence prejudicial feelings? *Journal of Intercultural Communication Research, 39*(2), 105–121.

Ramírez-Sánchez, R. (2008). Marginalization from within: Expanding co-cultural theory through the experience of the *Afro Punk. The Howard Journal of Communications, 19,* 89–104.

Randall, W. S. (1998). *George Washington: A life.* New York, NY: Owl Books, Henry Holt.

Rawlins, W. K. (1992). *Friendship matters: Communication, dialectics, and the life course.* New York, NY: Aldine de Gruyter.

Rawlins, W. K. (1994). Being there and growing apart: Sustaining friendships during adulthood. In D. J. Canary & L. Stafford (Eds.), *Communication and relational maintenance* (pp. 275–294). New York, NY: Academic Press.

Reeder, H. M. (2003). The effect of gender role orientation on same- and cross-sex friendship formation. *Sex Roles, 49,* 143–152.

Regan, P. C., Kocan, E. R., & Whitlock, T. (1998). Ain't love grand: A prototype analysis of the concept of romantic love. *Journal of Social and Personal Relationships, 15,* 411–420.

Reis, H. T., & Patrick, B. C. (1996). Attachment and intimacy: Component processes. In E. T. Higgins & A. W. Kruglanski (Eds.), *Social psychology: Handbook of basic principles* (pp. 523–563). New York, NY: Guilford Press.

Reis, H. T., & Shaver, P. (1988). Intimacy as an interpersonal process. In S. W. Duck (Ed.), *Handbook of personal relationships* (pp. 367–389). New York, NY: Wiley.

Riach, K., & Wilson, F. (2007). Don't screw the crew: Exploring the rules of engagement in organizational romance. *British Journal of Management, 18,* 79–92.

Richards, J. M., Butler, E. A., & Gross, J. J. (2003). Emotion regulation in romantic relationships: The cognitive consequences of concealing feelings. *Journal of Social and Personal Relationships, 20,* 599–620.

Ridge, R. D., & Berscheid, E. (1989, May). *On loving and being in love: A necessary distinction.* Paper presented at the annual convention of the Midwestern Psychological Association, Chicago, IL.

Riedy, M. K., & Wen, J. H. (2010). Electronic surveillance of Internet access in the American workplace: Implications for management. *Information & Communications Technology Law, 19*(1), 87–99.

Riela, S., Rodriguez, G., Aron, A., Xu, X., & Acevedo, B. P. (2010). Experiences of falling in love: Investigating culture, ethnicity, gender, and speed. *Journal of Social and Personal Relationships, 27,* 473–493.

Rintel, E. S., & Pittam, J. (1997). Strangers in a strange land: Interaction management on Internet relay chat. *Human Communication Research, 23,* 507–534.

Ritchie, L. D., & Fitzpatrick, M. A. (1990). Family communication patterns: Measuring interpersonal perceptions of interpersonal relationships. *Communication Research, 17,* 523–544.

Rodrigues, L. N., & Kitzmann, K. M. (2007). Coping as a mediator between interparental conflict and adolescents' romantic attachment. *Journal of Social and Personal Relationships, 24*(3), 423–439.

Rohlfing, M. E. (1995). Doesn't anybody stay in one place anymore? An exploration of the under-studied phenomenon of long-distance relationships. In J. T. Wood & S. Duck (Eds.), *Under-studied relationships: Off the beaten track* (pp. 173–196). Thousand Oaks, CA: Sage.

Roloff, M. E., & Soule, K. P. (2002). Interpersonal conflict: A review. In M. L. Knapp & J. A. Daly (Eds.), *Handbook of interpersonal communication* (3rd ed., pp. 475–528). Thousand Oaks, CA: Sage.

Rosen, L. D., Carrier, L. M., & Cheever, N. A. (2013). Facebook and texting made me do it: Media-induced task-switching while studying. *Computers in Human Behavior, 29,* 948–958. doi: http://dx.doi.org/10.1016/j.chb.2012.12.001

Rosenfeld, H. M. (1987). Conversational control functions of nonverbal behavior. In A. W. Siegman & S. Feldstein (Eds.), *Nonverbal behavior and communication* (2nd ed., pp. 563–602). Hillsdale, NJ: Erlbaum.

Rothbard, M. N. (1999). *Conceived in liberty* (Vol. 4). Auburn, AL: Mises Institute.

Rothbart, M. K., Ahadi, S. A., & Evans, D. E. (2000). Temperament and personality: Origins and outcomes. *Journal of Personality and Social Psychology, 78,* 122–135.

Rowatt, W. D., Cunningham, M. R., & Druen, P. B. (1998). Deception to get a date. *Personality and Social Psychology Bulletin, 24,* 1228–1242.

Roy, R., Benenson, J. F., & Lilly, F. (2000). Beyond intimacy: Conceptualizing sex differences in same-sex friendships. *Journal of Psychology, 134,* 93–101.

Rubin, L. (1985). *Just friends.* New York, NY: Harper & Row.

Rubin, L. B. (1996). Reflections on friendship. In K. M. Galvin & P. J. Cooper (Eds.), *Making connections: Readings in relational communication* (pp. 254–257). Los Angeles, CA: Roxbury.

Rubin, Z. (1973). *Liking and loving: An invitation to social psychology.* New York, NY: Holt, Rinehart & Winston.

Rubin, Z., Peplau, L. A., & Hill, C. T. (1981). Loving and leaving: Sex differences in romantic attachments. *Sex Roles, 7,* 821–835.

Rueter, M. A., & Koerner, A. F. (2008). The effect of family communication patterns on adopted adolescent adjustment. *Journal of Marriage and Family, 70,* 715–727.

Ruppel, E. K. (2014, July 9). Use of communication technologies in romantic relationships: Self-disclosure and the role of relationship development. *Journal of Social and Personal Relationships.* Published online. doi: 10.1177/0265407514541075

Rusbult, C. E. (1987). Responses to dissatisfaction in close relationships: The exit-voice-loyalty-neglect model. In D. Perlman & S. Duck (Eds.), *Intimate relationships: Development, dynamics, and deterioration* (pp. 209–237). Newbury Park, CA: Sage.

Rusbult, C. E., Arriaga, X. B., & Agnew, C. R. (2001). Interdependence in close relationships. In G. J. O. Fletcher & M. S. Clark (Eds.), *Blackwell handbook of social psychology, vol. 2: Interpersonal processes* (pp. 359–387). Oxford, UK: Blackwell.

Sabourin, T. C., Infante, D. A., & Rudd, J. E. (1993). Verbal aggression in marriages: A comparison of violent, distressed but nonviolent, and nondistressed couples. *Human Communication Research, 20*, 245–267.

Sahlstein, E. (2004). Relating at a distance: Negotiating being together and being apart in long-distance relationships. *Journal of Social and Personal Relationships, 21*, 689–702.

Salovey, P., & Rodin, J. (1988). Coping with envy and jealousy. *Journal of Social and Clinical Psychology, 7*, 15–33.

Savicki, V., Kelley, M., & Oesterreich, E. (1999). Judgments of gender in computer-mediated communication. *Computers in Human Behavior, 15*, 185–194.

Schaefer, C. M., & Tudor, T. R. (2001). Managing workplace romances. *SAM Advanced Management Journal, 66*(3), 4–10.

Schein, E. H. (1985). *Organizational culture and leadership*. San Francisco: Jossey-Bass.

Scherer, K. R. (1974). Acoustic concomitants of emotional dimensions: Judging affect from synthesized tone sequences. In S. Weitz (Ed.), *Nonverbal communication: Readings with commentary* (pp. 105–111). New York, NY: Oxford University Press.

Scherer, K. R. (2001). Appraisal considered as a process of multilevel sequential checking. In K. R. Scherer, A. Schorr, & T. Johnstone (Eds.), *Appraisal processes in emotion* (pp. 92–120). Oxford, UK: Oxford University Press.

Schlacpfer, T. E., Harris, G. J., Tien, A. Y., Peng, L., Lee, S., & Pearlson, G. D. (1995). Structural differences in the cerebral cortex of healthy female and male subjects: A magnetic resonance imaging study. *Psychiatry Research, 61*, 129–135.

Schneider, C. S., & Kenny, D. A. (2000). Cross-sex friends who were once romantic partners: Are they platonic friends now? *Journal of Social and Personal Relationships, 17*(3), 451–466.

Schramm, W. (Ed.). (1954). *The process and effects of mass communication*. Urbana: University of Illinois Press.

Schrodt, P. (2006). Development and validation of the Stepfamily Life Index. *Journal of Social and Personal Relationships, 23*(3), 427–444.

Schrodt, P., & Afifi, T. D. (2007). Communication processes that predict young adults' feelings of being caught and their associations with mental health and family satisfaction. *Communication Monographs, 74*(2), 200–228.

Schrodt, P., & Shimkowski, J. R. (2013). Feeling caught as a mediator of co-parental communication and young adult children's mental health and relational satisfaction with parents. *Journal of Social and Personal Relationships, 30*(8), 977–999. doi: 10.1177/0265407513479213

Schumann, K., Zaki, J., & Dweck, C. S. (2014). Addressing the empathy deficit: Beliefs about the malleability of empathy predict effortful responses when empathy is challenging. *Journal of Personality and Social Psychology, 107*(3), 475–493. doi: 10.1037/a0036738

Searle, J. R. (1965). What is a speech act? In M. Black (Ed.), *Philosophy in America* (pp. 221–239). Ithaca, NY: Cornell University Press.

Searle, J. R. (1969). *Speech acts*. Cambridge, UK: Cambridge University Press.

Searle, J. R. (1976). The classification of illocutionary acts. *Language in Society, 5*, 1–24.

Sebold, A. (2002). *The lovely bones*. New York, NY: Little, Brown.

Seta, J. J., & Seta, C. E. (1993). Stereotypes and the generation of compensatory and noncompensatory expectancies of group members. *Personality and Social Psychology Bulletin, 19*, 722–731.

Shackelford, T. K., & Buss, D. M. (1997). Anticipation of marital dissolution as a consequence of spousal infidelity. *Journal of Social and Personal Relationships, 14*, 793–808.

Shannon, C. E., & Weaver, W. (1949). *The mathematical theory of communication*. Urbana: University of Illinois Press.

Shaver, P. R., Wu, S., & Schwartz, J. C. (1992). Cross-cultural similarities and differences in emotion and its representation. In M. S. Clark (Ed.), *Emotion* (pp. 175–212). Newbury Park, CA: Sage.

Shedletsky, L. J., & Aitken, J. E. (2004). *Human communication on the Internet*. Boston, MA: Pearson Education/Allyn and Bacon.

Shelton, J. N., Richeson, J. A., & Bergsieker, H. B. (2009). Interracial friendship development and attributional biases. *Journal of Social and Personal Relationships, 26*(2–3), 179–193.

Shelton, J. N., Trail, T. E., West, T. V., & Bergsieker, H. B. (2010). From strangers to friends: The interpersonal process model of intimacy in developing interracial friendships. *Journal of Social and Personal Relationships, 27*(1), 71–90.

Shoda, Y., Mischel, W., & Peake, P. K. (1990). Predicting adolescent cognitive and self-regulatory competencies from preschool delay of gratification: Identifying diagnostic conditions. *Developmental Psychology, 26*(6), 978–986.

Shweder, R. A. (1993). The cultural psychology of the emotions. In M. Lewis & J. M. Haviland (Eds.), *Handbook of emotions* (pp. 417–431). New York, NY: Guilford Press.

Sias, P. M., & Cahill, D. J. (1998). From co-workers to friends: The development of peer friendships in the workplace. *Western Journal of Communication, 62*, 273–300.

Sias, P. M., Drzewiecka, J. A., Meares, M., Bent, R., Konomi, Y., Ortega, M., & White, C. (2008). Intercultural friendship development. *Communication Reports, 21*(1), 1–13.

Sias, P. M., Heath, R. G., Perry, T., Silva, D., & Fix, B. (2004). Narratives of workplace friendship deterioration. *Journal of Social and Personal Relationships, 21*(3), 321–340.

Sias, P. M., Krone, K. J., & Jablin, F. M. (2002). An ecological systems perspective on workplace relationships. In M. L. Knapp & J. A. Daly (Eds.), *Handbook of interpersonal communication* (pp. 615–642). Thousand Oaks, CA: Sage.

Sias, P. M., & Perry, T. (2004). Disengaging from workplace relationships: A research note. *Human Communication Research, 30*, 589–602.

Sillars, A. L. (1980). Attributions and communication in roommate conflicts. *Communication Monographs, 47*, 180–200.

Sillars, A., Roberts, L. J., Leonard, K. E., & Dun, T. (2000). Cognition during marital conflict: The relationship of thought and talk. *Journal of Social and Personal Relationships, 17*, 479–502.

Sillars, A., Smith, T., & Koerner, A. (2010). Misattributions contributing to empathic (in)accuracy during parent–adolescent conflict discussions. *Journal of Social and Personal Relationships, 27*(6), 727–747.

Sillars, A. L., & Wilmot, W. W. (1994). Communication strategies in conflict and mediation. In J. Wiemann & J. Daly (Eds.), *Communicating strategically: Strategies in interpersonal communication* (pp. 163–190). Hillsdale, NJ: Erlbaum.

Silvera, D. H., Krull, D. S., & Sassler, M. A. (2002). Typhoid Pollyanna: The effect of category valence on retrieval order of positive and negative category members. *European Journal of Cognitive Psychology, 14*, 227–236.

Silversides, B. V. (1994). *The face pullers: Photographing native Canadians, 1871–1939*. Saskatoon, Saskatchewan, Canada: Fifth House.

Silverstein, M., & Giarrusso, R. (2010). Aging and family life: A decade review. *Journal of Marriage and Family, 72,* 1039–1058.

Smith, C. A., & Kirby, L. D. (2004). Appraisal as a pervasive determinant of anger. *Emotion, 4,* 133–138.

Smith, G., & Anderson, K. J. (2005). Students' ratings of professors: The teaching style contingency for Latino/a professors. *Journal of Latinos and Education, 4,* 115–136.

Smith, L., Heaven, P. C. L., & Ciarrochi, J. (2008). Trait emotional intelligence, conflict communication patterns, and relationship satisfaction. *Personality and Individual Differences, 44,* 1314–1325.

Snyder, M. (1974). Self-monitoring of expressive behavior. *Journal of Personality and Social Psychology, 30,* 526–537.

Solomon, D. H., & Samp, J. A. (1998). Power and problem appraisal: Perceptual foundations of the chilling effect in dating relationships. *Journal of Social and Personal Relationships, 15,* 191–209.

Soto, J. A., Levenson, R. W., & Ebling, R. (2005). Cultures of moderation and expression: Emotional experience, behavior, and physiology in Chinese Americans and Mexican Americans. *Emotion, 5,* 154–165.

Spears, R., Postmes, T., Lea, M., & Watt, S. E. (2001). A SIDE view of social influence. In J. P. Forgas & K. D. Williams (Eds.), *Social influence: Direct and indirect processes* (pp. 331–350). Philadelphia: Psychology Press–Taylor and Francis Group.

Spender, D. (1984). Defining reality: A powerful tool. In C. Kramarae, M. Schultz, & W. O'Barr (Eds.), *Language and power* (pp. 195–205). Beverly Hills, CA: Sage.

Spender, D. (1990). *Man made language.* London: Pandora Press.

Spitzberg, B. (1997). A model of intercultural communication competence. In L. A. Samovar & R. E. Porter (Eds.), *Intercultural communication: A reader* (pp. 379–391). Belmont, CA: Wadsworth.

Spitzberg, B. H., & Cupach, W. R. (1984). *Interpersonal communication competence.* Beverly Hills, CA: Sage.

Spitzberg, B. H., & Cupach, W. R. (2002). Interpersonal skills. In M. L. Knapp & J. A. Daly (Eds.), *Handbook of interpersonal communication* (3rd ed., pp. 564–611). Thousand Oaks, CA: Sage.

Sprecher, S. (2001). A comparison of emotional consequences of and changes in equity over time using global and domain-specific measures of equity. *Journal of Social and Personal Relationships, 18,* 477–501.

Sprecher, S., & Metts, S. (1999). Romantic beliefs: Their influence on relationships and patterns of change over time. *Journal of Social and Personal Relationships, 16*(6), 834–851.

Stafford, L. (2003). Maintaining romantic relationships: A summary and analysis of one research program. In D. J. Canary & M. Dainton (Eds.), *Maintaining relationships through communication: Relational, contextual, and cultural variations* (pp. 51–77). Mahwah, NJ: Erlbaum.

Stafford, L. (2005). *Maintaining long-distance and cross-residential relationships.* Mahwah, NJ: Erlbaum.

Stafford, L. (2010). Measuring relationship maintenance behaviors: Critique and development of the revised relationship maintenance behavior scale. *Journal of Social and Personal Relationships, 28,* 278–303.

Stafford, L., & Canary, D. J. (1991). Maintenance strategies and romantic relationship type, gender, and relational characteristics. *Journal of Social and Personal Relationships, 8,* 217–242.

Stafford, L., Dainton, M., & Haas, S. (2000). Measuring routine and strategic relational maintenance: Scale revision, sex versus gender roles, and the prediction of relational characteristics. *Communication Monographs, 67,* 306–323.

Stafford, L., & Merolla, A. J. (2007). Idealization, reunions, and stability in long-distance dating relationships. *Journal of Social and Personal Relationships, 24,* 37–54.

Stafford, L., Merolla, A. J., and Castle, J. (2006). When long-distance dating partners become geographically close. *Journal of Social and Personal Relationships, 23,* 901–919.

Statistics Canada, Government of Canada. (2012). Portrait of families and living arrangements in Canada. Retrieved from http://www12.statcan.ca/census-recensement/2011/as-sa/98-312-x/98-312-x2011001-eng.cfm

Stiff, J. B., Dillard, J. P., Somera, L., Kim, H., & Sleight, C. (1988). Empathy, communication, and prosocial behavior. *Communication Monographs, 55,* 198–213.

Stone, E. (2004). *Black sheep and kissing cousins: How our family stories shape us.* New Brunswick, NJ: Transaction.

Strauss, V. (2006, March 21). Putting parents in their place: Outside class. *The Washington Post,* p. A08.

Streek, J. (1980). Speech acts in interaction: A critique of Searle. *Discourse Processes, 3,* 133–154.

Streek, J. (1993). Gesture as communication I: Its coordination with gaze and speech. *Communication Monographs, 60,* 275–299.

Suitor, J. J., Sechrist, J., Plikuhn, M., Pardo, S. T., Gilligan, M., & Pillemer, K. (2009). The role of perceived maternal favoritism in sibling relations in midlife. *Journal of Marriage and Family, 71,* 1026–1038.

Suler, J. R. (2004). The online disinhibition effect. *CyberPsychology and Behavior, 7,* 321–326.

Sumner, W. G. (1906). *Folkways.* Boston, MA: Ginn.

Surra, C., & Hughes, D. (1997). Commitment processes in accounts of the development of premarital relationships. *Journal of Marriage and the Family, 59,* 5–21.

Swain, S. O. (1992). Men's friendships with women: Intimacy, sexual boundaries, and the informant role. In P. M. Nardi (Ed.), *Men's friendships: Vol. 2. Research on men and masculinities* (pp. 153–172). Newbury Park, CA: Sage.

Tamir, M., & Robinson, M. D. (2007). The happy spotlight: Positive mood and selective attention to rewarding information. *Personality and Social Psychology Bulletin, 33,* 1124–1136. doi: 10.1177/0146167207301030

Tannen, D. (1990). *You just don't understand: Women and men in conversation.* New York, NY: Morrow.

Tannen, D. (1990, June 24). Sex, lies and conversation: Why is it so hard for men and women to talk to each other? *The Washington Post.*

Tardy, C. H. (2000). Self-disclosure and health: Revising Sidney Jourard's hypothesis. In S. Petronio (Ed.), *Balancing the secrets of private disclosures* (pp. 111–122). Mahwah, NJ: Erlbaum.

Tardy, C., & Dindia, K. (1997). Self-disclosure. In O. Hargie (Ed.), *The handbook of communication skills.* London, UK: Routledge.

Tavernise, S. (2011, May 26). Married couples are no longer a majority, census finds. *The New York Times.* Retrieved from http://www.nytimes.com

Tavris, C. (1989). *Anger: The misunderstood emotion.* New York, NY: Touchstone Press.

Thayer, R. E., Newman, J. R., & McClain, T. M. (1994). Self-regulation of mood: Strategies for changing a bad mood, raising energy, and reducing tension. *Journal of Personality and Social Psychology, 67,* 910–925.

The English language: Words borrowed from other languages. (n.d.). Retrieved from http://www.krysstal.com/borrow.html

The National Center for Victims of Crimes. (2008). *Dating violence fact sheet*. Retrieved from http://www.ncvc.org

Thomas, L. T., & Levine, T. R. (1994). Disentangling listening and verbal recall: Related but separate constructs? *Human Communication Research, 21,* 103–127.

Thompson, J. K., Heinberg, L. J., Altabe, M., & Tantleff-Dunn, S. (1999). *Exacting beauty: Theory, assessment, and treatment of body image disturbances*. Washington, DC: American Psychological Association.

Thorne, B. (1986). Boys and girls together . . . but mostly apart: Gender arrangements in elementary schools. In W. Hartup & Z. Rubin (Eds.), *Relationships and development* (pp. 167–184). Hillsdale, NJ: Erlbaum.

Tillema, T., Dijst, M., & Schwanen, T. (2010). Face-to-face and electronic communications in maintaining social networks: The influence of geographical and relational distance and of information content. *New Media & Society, 12*(6), 965–983.

Ting-Toomey, S. (1985). Toward a theory of conflict and culture. In W. B. Gudykunst, L. P. Stewart, & S. Ting-Toomey (Eds.), *Communication, culture, and organizational processes* (pp. 71–86). Beverly Hills, CA: Sage.

Ting-Toomey, S. (1997). Managing intercultural conflicts effectively. In L. A. Samovar & R. E. Porter (Eds.), *Intercultural communication: A reader* (pp. 392–403). Belmont, CA: Wadsworth.

Ting-Toomey, S. (1999). *Communicating across cultures*. New York, NY: Guilford Press.

Ting-Toomey, S. (2005). The matrix of face: An updated face-negotiation theory. In W. B. Gudykunst (Ed.), *Theorizing about intercultural communication* (pp. 211–234). Thousand Oaks, CA: Sage.

Tippett, M. (1994). The face pullers [Review of the book *The face pullers*, by B. V. Silversides]. *Canadian Historical Review, 75,* 1–4.

Tjaden, P., & Thoennes, N. (2000). Full report of the prevalence, incidence, and consequences of violence against women: Findings from the national violence against women survey. *Research Report*. Washington, DC, and Atlanta, GA: U.S. Department of Justice, National Institute of Justice, and U.S. Department of Health and Human Services, Centers for Disease Control and Prevention.

Tovares, A. V. (2010). All in the family: Small stories and narrative construction of a shared family identity that includes pets. *Narrative Inquiry, 20*(1), 1–19.

Tracy, S. J., Lutgen-Sandvik, P., & Alberts, J. K. (2006). Nightmares, demons, and slaves: Exploring the painful metaphors of workplace bullying. *Management Communication Quarterly, 20*(2), 148–185.

Triandis, H. (1988). Collectivism v. individualism: A reconceptualisation of a basic concept in cross-cultural social psychology. In G. K. Verma & C. Bagley (Eds.), *Cross-cultural studies of personality, attitudes and cognition* (pp. 60–95). New York, NY: St. Martin's Press.

Tsai, J. L., & Levenson, R. W. (1997). Cultural influences of emotional responding: Chinese American and European American dating couples during interpersonal conflict. *Journal of Cross-Cultural Psychology, 28,* 600–625.

Turkle, S. (1995). *Life on the screen: Identity in the age of the Internet*. New York, NY: Simon & Schuster.

Turner, J. C., Hogg, M. A., Oakes, P. J., Reicher, S. D., & Wetherell, M. S. (1987). *Rediscovering the social group: A self-categorization theory*. Cambridge, MA: Basil Blackwell.

Tyner, L. J., & Clinton, M. S. (2010). Sexual harassment in the workplace: Are human resource professionals victims? *Journal of Organizational Culture, Communications and Conflict, 14*(1), 33–49.

U.S. Census Bureau. (2010). The next four decades: The older population in the United States: 2010 to 2050. Retrieved from https://www.census.gov/prod/2010pubs/p25-1138.pdf

U.S. Census Bureau. (2012, May 17). Most children younger than age 1 are minorities, census bureau reports. Retrieved from http://www.census.gov/newsroom/releases/archives/population/cb12-90.html

U.S. Equal Employment Opportunity Commission. (1980). Guidelines on discrimination because of sex. *Federal Register, 45,* 74676–74677.

U.S. Equal Employment Opportunity Commission. (2011). *Sexual harassment charges: 1997–2011*. Retrieved from http://www.eeoc.gov/statistics/enforcement/sexual_harassment.cfm

Vallacher, R. R., Nowak, A., Froehlich, M., & Rockloff, M. (2002). The dynamics of self-evaluation. *Personality and Social Psychology Review, 6,* 370–379.

Vangelisti, A. L., Crumley, L. P., & Baker, J. L. (1999). Family portraits: Stories as standards for family relationships. *Journal of Social and Personal Relationships, 16*(3), 335–368.

Vazire, S., & Gosling, S. D. (2004). E-Perceptions: Personality impressions based on personal websites. *Journal of Personality and Social Psychology, 87,* 123–132.

Veale, D., Kinderman, P., Riley, S., & Lambrou, C. (2003). Self-discrepancy in body dysmorphic disorder. *British Journal of Clinical Psychology, 42,* 157–169.

Villaume, W. A., & Bodie, G. D. (2007). Discovering the listener within us: The impact of trait-like personality variables and communicator styles on preferences for listening style. *International Journal of Listening, 21,* 102–123.

Vogl-Bauer, S. (2003). Maintaining family relationships. In D. J. Canary & M. Dainton (Eds.), *Maintaining relationships through communication: Relational, contextual, and cultural variations* (pp. 31–50). Mahwah, NJ: Erlbaum.

Voyer, D. (2011). Sex differences in dichotic listening. *Brain and Cognition, 76*(2), 245–255.

Waldron, H. B., Turner, C. W., Alexander, J. F., & Barton, C. (1993). Coding defensive and supportive communications: Discriminant validity and subcategory convergence. *Journal of Family Psychology, 7,* 197–203.

Waldvogel, J. (2007). Greetings and closings in workplace email. *Journal of Computer-Mediated Communication, 12,* 122–143.

Wallace, P. (1999). *The psychology of the Internet*. Cambridge, UK: Cambridge University Press.

Walther, J. B., & Parks, M. R. (2002). Cues filtered out, cues filtered in: Computer-mediated communication and relationships. In M. L. Knapp & J. A. Daly (Eds.), *Handbook of interpersonal communication* (3rd ed., pp. 529–563). Thousand Oaks, CA: Sage.

Walther, J. B., Van Der Heide, B., Hamel, L., & Schulman, H. (2008, May). *Self-generated* versus *other-generated statements and impressions in computer-mediated communication: A test of warranting theory using Facebook*. Paper presented at the annual meeting of the International Communication Association, Montreal, Canada.

Walther, J. B., Van Der Heide, B., Kim, S. Y., Westerman, D., & Tong, S. T. (2008). The role of friends' appearance and behavior on evaluations of individuals on Facebook: Are we known by the company we keep? *Human Communication Research, 34,* 28–49.

Wang, H., & Andersen, P. A. (2007, May). *Computer-mediated communication in relationship maintenance: An examination of self-disclosure in long-distance friendships.* Paper presented at the annual meeting of the International Communication Association, San Francisco, CA.

Warr, P. B., and Payne, R. (1982). Experiences of strain and pleasure among British adults. *Social Science & Medicine, 16*(19), 1691–1697.

Waterman, A. (1984). *The psychology of individualism.* New York, NY: Praeger.

Watson, K. W., Barker, L. L., & Weaver, J. B., III. (1995). The listening styles profile (LSP-16): Development and validation of an instrument to assess four listening styles. *International Journal of Listening, 9,* 1–13.

Wattleton, Faye. (2008, May 5). *Eyes on Miley's bare back, not on the big picture.* Retrieved from http://ac360.blogs.cnn.com/2008/05/05/eyes-on-miley%E2%80%99s-bare-back-not-on-the-big-picture

Watzlawick, P., Beavin, J. H., & Jackson, D. D. (1967). *Pragmatics of human communication: A study of interactional patterns, pathologies, and paradoxes.* New York, NY: Norton.

Wedge, D., & Shearman, C. (2014). The way back. *Esquire.* Retrieved from http://www.esquire.com/blogs/news/the-way-back-boston-marathon-cruise

Weger, H., & Emmett, M. C. (2009). Romantic intent, relationship uncertainty, and relationship maintenance in young adults' cross-sex friendships. *Journal of Social and Personal Relationships, 26*(6–7), 964–988.

Weinberg, N., Schmale, J. D., Uken, J., & Wessel, K. (1995). Computer-mediated support groups. *Social Work with Groups, 17,* 43–55.

Weisz, C., & Wood, L. F. (2005). Social identity support and friendship outcomes: A longitudinal study predicting who will be friends and best friends 4 years later. *Journal of Social and Personal Relationships, 22*(3), 416–432.

Welch, R. D., & Houser, M. E. (2010). Extending the four-category model of adult attachment: An interpersonal model of friendship attachment. *Journal of Social and Personal Relationships, 27*(3), 351–366.

Wellman, B. (1992). Men in networks: Private communities, domestic friendships. In P. M. Nardi (Ed.), *Men's friendships: Vol. 2. Research on men and masculinities* (pp. 74–114). Newbury Park, CA: Sage.

Wells, G. L., Lindsay, R. C. L., & Tousignant, J. P. (1980). Effects of expert psychological advice on human performance in judging the validity of eyewitness testimony. *Law and Human Behavior, 4,* 275–285.

Wheeless, L. R. (1978). A follow-up study of the relationships among trust, disclosure, and interpersonal solidarity. *Human Communication Research, 4,* 143–145.

White, G. L. (1980). Physical attractiveness and courtship progress. *Journal of Personality and Social Psychology, 39,* 660–668.

Whorf, B. L. (1952). *Collected papers on metalinguistics.* Washington, DC: Department of State, Foreign Service Institute.

Widmer, E., Treas, J., & Newcomb, R. (1998). Attitudes toward nonmarital sex in 24 countries. *Journal of Sex Research, 35,* 349–358.

Wiederman, M. W., & Hurd, C. (1999). Extradyadic involvement during dating. *Journal of Social and Personal Relationships, 16*(2), 265–274. doi: 10.1177/0265407599162008

Wiederman, M. W., & Kendall, E. (1999). Evolution, sex, and jealousy: Investigation with a sample from Sweden. *Evolution and Human Behavior, 20,* 121–128.

Wiemann, J. M. (1977). Explication and test of a model of communicative competence. *Human Communication Research, 3,* 195–213.

Williams, W. L. (1992). The relationship between male-male friendship and male-female marriage: American Indian and Asian comparisons. In P. M. Nardi (Ed.), *Men's friendships: Vol. 2. Research on men and masculinities* (pp. 186–200). Newbury Park, CA: Sage.

Wilmot, W. W., & Hocker, J. L. (2010). *Interpersonal conflict* (8th ed.). Boston, MA: McGraw-Hill.

Winstead, B. A., Derlaga, V. J., & Rose, S. (1997). *Gender and close relationships.* Thousand Oaks, CA: Sage.

Winterson, J. (1993). *Written on the body.* New York, NY: Knopf.

Wolvin, A. D. (1987). *Culture as a listening variable.* Paper presented at the summer conference of the International Listening Association, Toronto, Canada.

Wolvin, A., & Coakley, C. G. (1996). *Listening.* Madison, WI: Brown & Benchmark.

Wood, J. T. (1998). *But I thought you meant . . . : Misunderstandings in human communication.* Mountain View, CA: Mayfield.

Wood, W., Rhodes, N., & Whelan, M. (1989). Sex differences in positive well-being: A consideration of emotional style and marital status. *Psychological Bulletin, 106,* 249–264.

Wu, C. (2011, September 21). Students vote to adopt gender-neutral constitution. *The Student Life.* Retrieved from http://tsl.pomona.edu/articles/2011/9/22/news/356-students-vote-to-adopt-gender-neutral-constitution

Wu, D. Y. H., & Tseng, W. (1985). Introduction: The characteristics of Chinese culture. In W. Tseng & D. Y. H. Wu (Eds.), *Chinese culture and mental health* (pp. 3–13). Orlando, FL: Academic Press.

Yoo, B., Donthu, N., & Lenartowicz, T. (2011). Measuring Hofstede's five dimensions of cultural values at the individual level: Development and validation of the CVS Scale. *Journal of International Consumer Marketing, 23,* 193-210.

YouTube Statistics. (n.d.). Retrieved from http://www.youtube.com/t/press_statistics

Zacchilli, T. L., Hendrick, C., & Hendrick, S. S. (2009). The romantic partner conflict scale: A new scale to measure relationship conflict. *Journal of Social and Personal Relationships, 26,* 1073–1096.

Zahn-Waxler, C. (2001). The development of empathy, guilt, and internalization of distress: Implications for gender differences in internalizing and externalizing problems. In R. Davidson (Ed.), *Anxiety, depression, and emotion: Wisconsin symposium on emotion, Vol. 1* (pp. 222–265). New York, NY: Oxford University Press.

Znaniecki, F. (1934). *The method of sociology.* New York, NY: Farrar & Rinehart.

Zorn, T. E. (1995). Bosses and buddies: Constructing and performing simultaneously hierarchical and close friendship relationships. In J. T. Wood & S. Duck (Eds.), *Under-studied relationships: Off the beaten track* (pp. 122–147). Thousand Oaks, CA: Sage.

Zuckerman, M., Hodgins, H., & Miyake, K. (1990). The vocal attractiveness paradigm: Replication and elaboration. *Journal of Nonverbal Behavior, 14,* 97–112.

Zuckerman, M., Miyake, K., & Hodgins, H. S. (1991). Crosschannel effects of vocal and physical attractiveness and their implications for interpersonal perception. *Journal of Personality and Social Psychology, 60,* 545–554.

Instructor's Annotated Edition

Bleske-Rechek, A., Somers, E., Micke, C., Erickson, L., Matteson, L., Stocco, C., . . . Ritchie, L. (2012). Benefit or burden? Attraction in cross-sex friendship. *Journal of Social and Personal Relationships, 29*(569). doi: 10.1177/0265407512443611

Christofides, E., Muise, A., & Desmarais, S. (2009). Information disclosure and control on Facebook: Are they two sides of the same coin or two different processes? *CyberPsychology & Behavior, 12*(3), 341–345.

Clayton, R. B. (2014). The third wheel: The impact of Twitter use on relationship infidelity and divorce. *Cyberpsychology, Behavior, and Social Networking, 17*(7), 425–430. doi: 10.1089/cyber.2013.0570

Dunleavy, K. N., & Booth-Butterfield, M. (2009). Idiomatic communication in the stages of coming together and falling apart. *Communication Quarterly, 57*(4), 416–432.

Fox, J., & Warber, K. M. (2014). Social networking sites in romantic relationships: Attachment, uncertainty, and partner surveillance on Facebook. *Cyberpsychology, Behavior, and Social Networking, 17*(1), 3–7. doi: 10.1089/cyber.2012.0667

Gudykunst, W. B., & Lee, C. M. (2001). An agenda for studying ethnicity and family communication. *Journal of Family Communication, 1,* 75–85.

Sheldon, P. (2010). Pressure to be perfect: Influence on college students' body esteem. *Southern Communication Journal, 75,* 277–298.

Tatum, B. D. (2013). *"Why are all the black kids sitting together in the cafeteria?" and other conversations about race.* New York, NY: Basic Books.

Vangelisti, A. L., Maguire, K. C., Alexander, A. L., & Clark, G. (2007). Hurtful family environments: Links with individual, relationship, and perceptual variables. *Communication Monographs, 74,* 357–385.

NAME INDEX

Acevedo, B., 293, 296
Ackard, D. M., 318
Adams, B. N., 330
Adams, R. G., 361
Adamson, A., 55
Adelman, M., 301, 307, 310
Afifi, T. D., 61, 256, 262, 278, 328, 341, 342, 345, 346
Afifi, Falato & Weiner, 313
Agnew, C. R., 291, 307
Aguinis, H., A–19
Aitken, J. E., 76, 269
Alberts, J. K., A–17, A–18
Albrecht, T. L., A–1, A–15, A–16, A–20
Alexander, J. F., 213, 214, 263
Alexander, M., 109
Allen, M., 62, 82
Alles, M., 313
Allport, G. W., 79
Alpkan, L., A–5
Altabe, M., 43
Altman, Irwin, 56
Amundsen, Roald, 285
Andersen, P. A., 362, 374
Anderson, K. J., 91
Anderson, N. H., 235
Anderson, P. A., 109, 117, 315
Andrews, Jennifer, 162
Angleitner, A., 314
Appelbaum, S. H., A–19
Arasaratnam, 153
Archer, John, 277
Argyle, M., 240, 359, 369
Arndt, J., 40
Arnold, J., 54
Aron, A., 56, 243, 288, 293, 296
Arredondo, Carlos, 122
Arredondo, D. E., 166
Arriaga, X. B., 291
Asada, K. J. K., 377, 378, 379
Asch, S. E., 87
Ashmore, R. D., 295
Aylor, B. A., 308, 309
Aylward, E., 81
Aynesworth, H., 87
Ayres, D. M., 214
Ayres, J., 214

Babin Gallagher, B., 357, 360
Babrow, A. S., 92
Bach, B. W., 327, 328, 329, 331, A–1
Baker, B., 61

Baker, J. L., 332
Bakke, E., 25
Balderrama, A., 55
Baldwin Avery, P., 211
Bane, R., 166
Bank, B. J., 361
Banks, Tyra, 230
Baptiste, D. A., Jr., 307
Barber, B. K., 348, 349
Barker, L. L., 169, 174, 175, 176, 207, 241
Barker & Ota, 144
Barnes, S. B., 62
Barnett, O. W., 277
Barnlund, D. C., 61
Barry, D., 48n
Barta, P., 81
Barton, C., 213, 214, 263
Bates, J. S., 332
Bauer, G. B., 207
Baumeister, R. F., 183
Baxter, L. A., 292, 327, 328, 329, 331, 371, A–8
Baym et al., 24
Beach, W. A., 124
Beavin, J. H., 7, 13–14, 15, 73
Becker, J. A. H., 340, 363
Beer, J. S., 120
Beers, M., 111, 114
Behnke, A. O., 332
Bekhouche, Hausmann, Tyson, & Zahidi, 260
Belch, C., 223
Bell, Francesca, 339
Bell, R. A., 193
Benenson, J. F., 361
Bennett, M. J., 152
Bennett, S. H., 267
Benoit, P. J., 253, 255
Benoit, W. E., 253, 255
Berger, C. R., 19, 78, 142, 292, 295
Bergsieker, H. B., 56, 62, 359, 367, 368
Berkowitz, L., 117
Berntson, G. G., 104
Berry, G. R., A–6
Berscheid, E., 103, 104, 105, 121, 122, 256, 262, 264, 265, 276, 277, 287, 289, 361, 365
Bevan, J. L., 264, 276, 277
Bianconi, L., 154
Bies, R. J., A–18, A–19
Biggs, Jason, 53
Birdwhistell, R. L., 229
Blieszner, R. A., 361

Bochner, S., 147
Boddy, C. R., A–17
Bodenhausen, G. V., 74, 90, 91, 168
Bodhi, B., 267
Bodie, G. D., 174, 175
Booth, A., 364
Bornstein, R. F., 294
Bower, G. H., 106
Bowlby, J., 45
Boyd, C., A–20
Bradac, J. J., 78, 209, 292
Braithwaite, D. O., 327, 328, 329, 331
Brand, Russell, 50
Brandes, S., 361
Brashers, D., 206
Bregman, A., 309
Brehm, S. S., 291
Brend, R., 234
Brewer, M. B., 80, 83, 91
Bridge, K., A–8
Briner, R. B., 106
Brody, L. R., 112
Brommel, B. J., 328, 329
Brontë, E., 180
Brown, Chris, 232
Brown, R., 105
Bruess & Pearson, 193
Bruner, J., 85
Buber, Martin, 13
Buchbinder, E., 318
Buehler, C., 348, 349
Buerkel-Rothfusws, N. L., 193
Buhrmester, D., 360
Bulfinch, T., 182
Buller, D. B., 231, 232, 233, 238, 239, 240
Bundy, Ted, 87, 89
Bunkers, S. S., 163, 173
Burgoon, J. K., 22, 78, 223, 225, 229, 231, 232, 233, 243
Burielo, R., 148
Burkel, R. A., 214
Burleson, B. R., 124, 359, 369
Bushman, B. J., 183
Buss, A. H., 49
Buss, D. M., 313, 314
Butler, E. A., 114, 116
Butt, T., 76, 77
Buunk, B. P., 314
Buzzanell, P., A–20
Byard, Eliza, 200
Bylund, C. L., 328, 329
Bytautas, J., A–19

I-1

Cacioppo, J. T., 104
Cahn, D. D., 262
Calabrese, 78, 142, 295
Campbell, D. T., 80
Campbell, M. A., A–17
Campbell, R. G., 92
Campbell, S. M., 291
Campbell et al., 40
Canary, D. J., 27, 44, 62, 81, 209, 253, 361n, 364, 370, 377
Cantril, H., 69n, 70
Carbery, J., 360
Carducci, B. J., 329
Carlos, John, 46, 48
Carlson, J. G., 117
Carnevale, P. J., 272
Carney, D. R., 244
Carr, N., 165, 166
Carreon, Claudia, 167
Carrey, Jim, 309
Carter, J. D., 81, 226
Caruso, D. R., 114
Castelli, L., 79
Castle, J., 308
Caughlin, J. P., 256, 277, 343
Cavanagh, S. E., 328, 329, 340
Cerpas, N., 289
Chaffe, S. H., 19
Chalfin, J., 294
Chan, D. K., 362
Chan, Karen, A–13
Chandler, T. A., 181
Chanel, 230
Chaplin, T. M., 112
Chastain, Brandi, 239, 240
Chávez, César, 22
Chen, G. M., 152, 178
Chen, W. J., 152, 194, 225, 226, 237
Cheng, G. H., 362
Cherlin, A., 327
Chesebro, J. L., 175, 176
Cheung, L., 43
Cho, M., 43
Christakis, N., 364, 377
Christofides, E., 315
Chronis, H., 213
Chua, Amy, 251–252, 253, 282
Chung, J., 178
Chung, J. H., 164
Ciarrochi, J., 264, 273
Clair, R. P., A–22
Clark, M., 109
Clark, R. A., 18
Clay, Cassius, 196, 199
Clayton, 315
Cleveland, J. N., 91
Clinton, M. S., A–22
Clopper, Conrey, & Pisoni, 194, 195
Coakley, A. D., 163, 168, 169
Cochran, C. C., A–22
Cody, M. J., 170, 297

Cohen, T. F., 360
Coho, A., 256, 278
Colditz, G. A., 43
Cole, M., 191
Cole, P. M., 112
Coleman, M., 330, 344, 345
Collins, N. L., 45, 46
Collins, Suzanne, 256
Coloe, S. R., 191
Conlin, J., 200
Contractor, N. S., A–1
Cooley, Charles Horton, 39
Cooper, Bradley, 293
Corner, L., 316
Costa, P. T., Jr., 85
Costanzo, F. S., 241
Costanzo, R. R., 241
Cote, S., 111, 114
Cothrel, J., A–6
Coupland, J., 154
Coupland, N., 153
Covarrubias, P., 78
Craig, E. A., 340, 363
Crider, D. M., 108
Crockett, E. E., 291
Crosnoe, R., 328, 329, 340
Cross, S. E., 44
Crumley, L. P., 332
Cullen, J., 251
Cunningham, M., 107
Cunningham, M. R., 50
Cupach, W. R., 21, 23, 316, 317
Custudio, J., 43
Cyrus, Miley, 88

Dainton, M., 304, 309, 369, 371, 372
Daley, John Francis, 209
Daly, J., 169
Daly, J. A., 214
Daniels, D., 347
Danoff-Burg, S., 292
Danziger, J., A–6, A–7
Datta, Arko, 123
Davidson, R. J., 116
Davis, J. E., 208
Davis, J. N., 348
Davis, K. E., 359
Dawson, E. J., 206
Delgado-Gaitan, C., 147
Delia, J., 18
Delia, J. G., 195
Delille, Jacques, 358
De Ment, T., 148
Derlaga, V. J., 361
Deschanel, Emily, 209
Desmarais, S., 315
Des Roches, C. M., 164
Devine, P. G., 91
de Vries, B., 359
Dibble, J. L., 315

DiCaprio, Leonardo, 71
Dijst, M., 340
Dillard, J., 93, A–20
Dillard, J. P., A–7
Dindia, K., 61, 62, 82, 177
Di Verniero, R., 327, 328, 329, 331
Dodge, K. A., 117
Domingue, R., 45, 46
Donohue, W. A., 256
Dreyer, A. S., 208
Dreyer, C. A., 208
Druckerman, P., 316
Druen, P. B., 50
Dryden, W., 111
Duan, C., 93
Dun, T., 274, 275
Dunbar, N. E., 244, 257, 258
Duncan, B., 119
Duncan, S., Jr., 168
Dunleavy & Booth-Butterfield, 194
Dutton, L. B., 317
DuVernay, Ava, 175

Eagly, A. H., 295
Eastwood, Clint, 152
Eavey, R. D., 164
Ebbeson, E., 119
Ebling, R., 148
Edgar, James, 161
Eisenberg, E. M., A–2, A–11, A–12, A–13
Eisikovits, T., 318
Eklof, M., 164
Ekman, P., 107, 109, 148, 231
Elçi, M., A–5
Ellis, A., 111
Ellison, N., 53, 297, 298
Ellison, N. B., 298
Emmers-Sommer, T. M., 27, 81
Emmett, M. C., 377
Englehardt, 23
Ergin, C., 267
Escartin, J., A–18n

Farace, R. V., A–3, A–10
Farinelli, L., 357, 360
Farrow, S., 41
Faulkner, S., 27, 81
Feeney, B. C., 45, 46
Feingold, A., 295
Felmlee, D. H., 296, 307, 310
Fendi, 230
Feningstein, A., 49
Fenoli, Randy, 237
Ferrara, K. M., 314
Fiedler, K., 106
Field, A. E., 43
Finan, A., 264, 276, 277
Fine, M., 330, 344, 345

Firth, Colin, 215
Fischer, A. H., 112
Fisher, B., A., 209
Fisher, H., 293, 296
Fishman, P. M., 260
Fiske, D. W., 168
Fiske, S. T., 141, 142, 165
Fiske, Cuddy, Glick, & Xu, 141, 142
Fitzgerald, L. F., A–22
Fitzpatrick, M. A., 328, 335
Fitzpatrick, S., 377, 378
Fix, B., A–16
Fleischer, R., 368
Floyd, K., 234, 243, 346, 358, 363
Forgas, J. P., 106
Forni, P. M., A–14
Foss, K. A., 192
Foss, S. K., 192
Fouts, G. T., 114–115
Fox, K. R., 40
Fox & Warber, 315
Frazier, P. A., A–22
Frederikse, M. E., 81
Friesen, W. V., 148, 231
Frijda, N. H., 103, 105
Frisby, B. N., 263, 269
Fritsche, J., 79
Fritz, J. H., A–7
Froehlich, M., 39
Frost, D. M., 332
Fuendeling, J. M., 114–115, 116
Fulfs, Patricia, 177
Funder, D. C., 114
Fuqua, Antoine, 270
Furger, R., 124
Furman, W., 360
Furnham, A., 359
Furr, R. M., 114

Gaddis, S., 53
Gaines, S. O., Jr., 294, 307
Galupo, M. P., 363, 364, 366
Galvin, K. M., 328, 329
Gangestad & Snyder, 22
Ganong, L., 330, 344, 345
Ganong, L. H., 330
Garcia, P., 62
Garrett, R. K., A–6, A–7
Gaucher et al., 41
Geisler, J., 62
George VI, 215
Gerdes, L. I., A–22
Gettings, J., 46
Gevinson, Tavi, 42
Gevrey, G., 151
Giannakakis, A. E., 79
Giarrusso, R., 328, 329, 330, 343
Gibbs, J., 298
Gibbs, J., 53, 297, 298
Gibson, B., 50

Gifford, N., 238
Gilbert, Elizabeth, 126
Gilchrist, E. S., 363
Giles, H., 22, 153, 154
Gillath, O., 317
Gilligan, M., 348
Gleason, J. B., 194
Glenn, D., 165
Glisson, C., A–2
Goffman, E., 50, 51n, 180
Goins, Leigh-Anne, A–22
Goldsmith, Daena, 177
Goldstein, T., 83
Goldstein, Vezich, & Shapiro, 94
Goleman, D., 112n, 120
Golin, S., 309
Golish, T. D., 328, 341, 345, 346, 347
Gondry, M., 309
Goodall, H. L., Jr., A–2, A–11, A–12, A–13
Goodsell, T. L., 332
Goodwin, C., 242
Gore, K. E., 193
Gortmaker, S. L., 43
Gosling, S. D., 52, 53
Gottman, J. M., 276
Gottman, John, 267
Graham, G., 213
Graham, Janice, 87
Graham, J. M., 288
Grammer, K., 238
Grant, S., A–1
Greenberg, J., 40
Grice, Paul, 205, 206
Grierson, R. D., A–22
Gross, J. J., 103, 105, 113, 114, 115, 116
Gudykunst, W. B., 27, 48, 79, 136, 261, 268, 361
Gudykunst & Lee, 268
Guerrero, L. K., 109, 117
Guillaume, Alfred, Jr., 49
Gumperz, J. J., 198, 199

Haas, S., 304
Haas, S. M., 290, 304, 307
Haden, S. C., 312
Haier, Richard, 81
Haigh, M. M., 340, 363
Halatsis, P., 364, 377
Hale, J. L., 313
Hall, E. T., 147, 151, 197, 235, 236, 239
Hall, J. A., 81, 112, 226, 230, 234, 244, 297
Hall, Judith, 226
Hall, L. R., 112
Hall, M. R., 147
Halliwell & Dittmar, 41
Ham, Roger, 337
Ham, Steven, 337
Hamel, L., 53–54

Hamlin, D., 163, 168
Hammer, M. R., 152
Hammonds, R. J., 327, 328, 329, 331
Hanks, Tom, 16–17
Hansen, G. L., 315, 365
Hansford, S. L., 361
Harmon-Jones, E., 117
Harms, L. S., 233
Harris, G. T., 81
Harris, James "Jimmy Jam," A–7
Harrison, K., 43
Hastorf, A. H., 69n
Hastorf, Albert, 70
Hatfield, E., 104, 117, 121, 238, 289, 296, 310
Hause, K. S., 209, 364, 377
Hay, M., 296, 310
Hayashi, G. M., 349
Hayes, Isaac, 20
Hayes & Metts, 148
Hays, R. B., 359
Headley, Heather, A–7
Head-Reeves, D., 163, 168
Heath, R. G., A–16
Heaven, P. C. L., 264, 273
Hefner, V., 357, 373
Heider, F., 76
Hein, Ellison, & Gibbs, 299
Heinberg, L. J., 43
Heino, R., 53, 297, 298
Heino, R. D., 298
Hemmings, K. H., 311
Henderson, M., 369
Hendrick, C., 254, 262, 263, 264, 272, 273, 288, 289, 291, 377
Hendrick, R., 263, 288, 289, 291, 377
Hendrick, S. S., 254, 262, 264, 272, 273
Heritage, J. C., 170
Hertwig, R., 348
Herzog, D. H., 43
Hesketh, B., 147
Heslin, R., 234
Hess, E., 364
Hetherington, E. M., 346
Hickson, M., III, A–22
Higgins, E. T., 41
Higginsen, Vy, 101–102, 127
Hill, C. E., 93
Hill, C. T., 292, 310
Hobler, G. D., 78, 223, 225, 229, 243
Hocker, J. I., 253, 254, 257, 259, 265
Hodgins, H., 233
Hodgins, H. S., 223
Hodgson, I. K., 114
Hofstede, G., 143–146, 150
Hogg, M. A., 79
Hojjat, M., 312
Holmstrom, A., 124–125
Honeycutt, J. M., 60, 208
Hopf, T., 214

Horgan, T. G., 81
Horne, C. F., 10
Hosek, A. M., 327, 328, 329, 331
Houser, R. D., 360
Hovick, S. R. A., A–20
Hughes, D., 298
Hughes, M., 377, 378, 379
Hunsinger, Isbell, & Clore, 106
Hurley, D., 301
Husband, S. A., 275
Hussein, A., A–4
Hutchinson, S., 61
Hyde, J. S., 293
Hyun, Jane, A–13

Incontro, C. R., 82
Infante, D., 181, 210, 211, 214
Ivey, Eowyn, 59, 60n

Jablin, F. M., A–1
Jackson, D. C., 116
Jackson, D. D., 7, 13–14, 15, 73
Jackson, M., 165
Jacobs, S., 201, 206
James, L. R., A–2
James, M. R., 82
Janusik, L. A., 170
Jefferson, Thomas, 119
Jenson, V., 55
John, O. P., 85, 103, 113, 114, 115, 116, 120
Johnson, A. J., 340, 359, 363
Johnson, A. N., 61, 269
Jones, D. C., 43
Jones, E., 312
Jones, S. E., 229
Jones, T. E., A–3
Jourard, S. M., 61
Jun, Lingzi, 122
Jun, Lu, 122
Juncoa & Cotton, 165

Kagawa, N., 147–148
Kaharit, K., 164
Kahn, D., A–2
Kahneman, D., 165
Kaminsky, A., 264, 276, 277
Kanagy, C. L., 108
Katz, D., A–2
Katz, J., 19, 41
Kaufman, C., 309
Kazmaier, D., 69–70
Keashly, L., A–18, A–19
Keck, K. L., 264
Keesing, R. M., 27, 48, 136
Kellas, J. K., 332
Kellermann, K., 88, 203
Kelley, H. H., 296

Kelley, M., 53
Kelly, A. E., 62
Kendall, E., 314
Kennedy, John F., 62
Kennedy, T. L. M., 340
Kenny, D. A., 369
Kessler, R. C., 117
Ketelaar, T., 111
Kim, H., 93
Kim, M., 294
Kim, Y. Y., 27, 48, 79, 136, 261
Kinderman, P., 41
King, S. K., 237
Kirby, L. D., 104
Kirchner, Christina Fernández de, 260
Kitzmann, K. M., 348, 349
Klein, D. J., 104
Klein, R. C. A., 277
Klenin, J., A–19
Klopf, D. W., 61
Knapp, M. L., 230, 234
Knapp, Mark, 298
Knight, R. T., 120
Knobloch, J. K., 118
Knox, R. L., A–8
Kocan, Elizabeth, 287
Koener, Ascan, 335
Koerner, A., 76
Koerner, A. F., 328, 335, 336, 337
Koerner, S. S., 61
Koester, J., 83
Kolt, R., 256
Konecni, V., 119
Korn, M. S., 291
Kostiuk, L. M., 114–115
Kotzé, M., 113
Koval et al., 80
Kowalski, R. M., 309, 312
Kowner, R., 238
Kozan, M., 267
Kramarae, Cheris, 260
Krause, J., 234
Kreider, R. M., 301
Kreps, G., A–4
Krishnakumar, A., 348, 349
Krone, K. J., A–1
Krull, D. S., 88
Krusiewicz, E. S., 333
Kubany, E. S., 207
Kurdek, L. A., 290, 292
Kuttler, A. F., 364

LaFollette, H., 213
LaGreca, A. M., 364
Lambrou, C., 41
Lampe, C., 53
Lane, L. T., 363
Langdridge, H., 76, 77
Langen, E., 369, 371, 372
Lareau, A., 342

Larsen, R. J., 314
Larson, C. I., 116
Larson, J. R., 111, A–11
Lasswell, H. D., 8
LaVan, H., A–17, A–18
Lavy, S., 317
Lawrence, Jennifer, 293
Le, B., 291
Leary, M. R., 312
Leary et al., 42
LeBaron, C. D., 229
Lee, C. M., 315
Lee, John Alan, 289
Lee, S., 81
Lee, Y., 43
Lee-Flynn et al., 39, 40
Lehman, S. J., 61
Lehrer, J., 112n
Lemerise, E. A., 117
Leonard, K. E., 274, 275
Levenson, R. W., 105, 148, 276
Levine, T., 211, 328
Levine, T. R., 170, 213, 298, 314
Levinson, S. C., 198, 199, 201
Levi-Ari & Keysar, 195
Lewellen, W., 326
Lewis, Robyn, 342
Lewis, Terry, A–7
Licoppe, 24
Lilly, F., 361
Lil Wayne, 232
Linder, B. C., A–22
Lindsay, R. C. L., 170
Lippa, R. A., 44
Lippmann, Walter, 90
Liston, Sonny, 197
Liu, Betty Ming, 251
Longo, L. C., 295
Lopes, P. N., 111, 114
Loving, J. G., 291
Loving, T. J., 291
Lu, A., 81
Lu, L., 114
Ludacris, 232
Luft, J., 61
Lulofs, R. S., 262
Lustig, M. W., 83
Lutgen-Sandvik, P., A–17, A–18

MacGeorge, E. L., 124
MacLean, L. M., A–19
Macrae, C. N., 74, 90, 91, 168
Madson, L., 44
Makhijani, M. G., 295
Malandro, L. A., 241
Malcolm X, 92, 95
Malis, R. S., 253, 276, 277
Malmstadt, J. R., 116
Manikar, S., 139
Mann, S. K., 209

Manstea, A. S. R., 112
Marinescu, A., A–19
Markel, N. N., 241
Markey, C. N., 295
Markey, P. M., 295
Martin, P., 345
Martin, W., A–17, A–18
Martin-Peña, J., A–18n
Marzano, R. J., 166
Mashek, D. J., 56, 243, 288
Maslow, A., 17–18
Matln, M., 88
Mauss, I. B., 105
Mayer J. D., 114
Mazanee, M., 371
Mazur, M., 359
McCarter, L., 105
McCarthy, J., 163, 168
McClain, T. M., 107
McCornack, S. A., 147, 201, 206, 211, 212, 213, 275, 298, 314
McCrae, R. R., 85
McCroskey, J. C., 153, 214
McEwan, B., 357, 360
McGlynn, J., 340
McGuirk, R., 200
McIntosh, Peggy, 83
McKillop, K. J., 62
McLaughlin, M. L., 170
McManus, T., 61, 256, 262, 278
McNaughton, D., 163, 168
Mead, George Herbert, 37
Mehrabian, A., 232, 242
Mendelsohn & Cheshire, 297
Merolla, A. J., 308
Messman, S. J., 364, 377
Metts, S., 104, 213, 290
Meunier, J., 164
Meyers, R. A., A–20
Michalos, A. C., 108
Michaud, S. G., 87
Michelson, K. D., 117
Mies, M., 260
Mikulincer, M., 317
Miller, G. R., 9, 54, 290
Miller, K., 292, 295, A–2, A–3
Miller, L., 357, 373
Miller, R. S., 291
Miller, Hefner & Scott, 358
Miller-Perrin, C. L., 277
Milne, A. A., 173, 174
Mischel, W., 112–113
Mitchell, Margaret, 278
Miyake, K., 225, 233
Mohammed, R., A–4
Mollen, D., 45, 46
Moller, C., 164
Monge, R. R., A–3, A–10
Mongeau, P. A., 313, 378
Monsour, M., 364, 365
Montagu, M. F. A., 234

Moore, D., 312
Morman, M. T., 243, 346
Morrison, K., 201, 314, 315, 377, 378, 379
Mosher, C., 292
Muhammad Ali, 196, 197, 199
Muise, A., 315
Mulac, A., 82, 209
Mumulo & Wiig, 109
Munro, K., 269
Muraoka, M. Y., 207
Murphy, K. R., 91
Myers, D. G., 11, 29, 108, 327
Myers, David, A–22, A–23
Myers, S. A., 214, A–8

Nanamoli, B., 267
Naslund, Denise, 87
Nass, C. J., 165
Negel, L., 312
Neulip, J. W., 153
Neuman, J. H., A–18
Neumark-Sztainer, D., 318
Newcomb, R., 316
Newman, J. R., 107
Ng, C. F., 238
Nicholson, J., 371
Nishida, J., 361
Nishiyama, K., 267
Nofsinger, R. E., 202
Nowak, A., 39

Oakes, P. J., 79
Oesterreich, E., 53
Oetzel et al., 146
O'Leary, K. D., 277
Olson, A. M., A–22
Olson, L., 262
Ophir, E., 165
Oravec, J., 340
Orbe, 138
Orth, Robius, Trzesniewski, Maes, & Schmitt, 41
Orzechowicz, D., 293, 296
Ott, Janice, 87
Oubaid, V., 314
Oyamot, Fuglestad, & Snyder, 22
Oyelowo, David, 175

Paine, Thomas, 190, 218
Palmer, M. T., 243
Pampe, H., 106
Pardo, S. T., 348
Park, H. S., 314
Park, N., 297
Park & Guan, 144
Parkinson, B., 106
Parkinson & Simons, 105

Parks, M. R., 23, 24, 25, 52, 62, 204, 301, 307, 310, 358, 361n, 363
Patrick, B. C., 60
Patterson, B. R., 359, 361
Patterson, M. L., 223, 242, 244
Pawlowski, D. R., A–8
Payne, M. J., 181
Payne, R., 327
Peake, P. K., 112n
Pearlson, G., 81
Peng, L., 81
Pennebaker, J. W., 62
Pennington, N., 362, 363
Peplau, L. A., 103, 108, 278, 292, 310
Perlman, D., 291
Perrin, R. D., 277
Perry, Katy, 50
Perry, T., 384, A–1, A–16
Pervin, L. A., 110
Peterson, D. R., 255, 256, 271, 272, 274
Petronio, S., 342, 343
Phillips & Silvia, 41
Pierce, C. A., A–19
Pillemer, K., 348
Piper, Christina, 4
Pittam, J., 53
Pittman, G., 371
Planalp, S., 60, 104
Plikuhn, M., 348
Plutchik, R., 107, 108, 109
Pomerantz, A., 20
Pornia, C., A–18n
Pratt, Louisa, 200
Price, Jammie, 367
Prinstein, M. J., 364
Privitera, C., A–17
Pruitt, D. G., 272
Przybylski, D. G., 22
Ptah Hotep, 10
Pyswzcynski, T., 40

Quan-Haase, A., A–6
Queen, A., 309, 312
Quenqua, D., 367

Rabby, M. K., 304, 375
Rabin, Z., 310
Rainey, V. P., 207
Ramasubramanian, 141, 142
Ramirez, A., 378
Randall, W. S., 189
Rapson, R. L., 289
Rawlins, W. K., 357, 359, 360, 371, A–7
Raymond, M., 61
Reeder, H. M., 365
Reese, R., 368
Regan, P., 103, 121, 287, 289, 361, 365

Regan, Pamela, 287
Reicher, S. D., 79
Reis, H. T., 60
Reynolds, S., 106
Rhodes, N., 108
Riach, K., A–20
Richard, D. C., 207
Richards, J. M., 103, 114, 115, 116
Richeson, J. A., 367, 368
Richmond, V. P., 214
Ridge, J. D., 289
Riedy, M. K., A–6, A–7
Riela, S., 293, 296
Riley, S., 41
Rintel, E. S., 53
Roberts, L. J., 274, 275
Rockloff, M., 39
Rodin, J., 315
Rodrigues, I. N., 348, 349
Rodriguez, G., 296
Rodriquez-Carballeira, A., A–18n
Rodriquez Mosquera, P. M., 112
Rohlfing, M. E., 374, 375
Roloff, M. E., 253, 254, 276, 277
Ropog, B. L., A–8
Rose, S., 361
Rosen, Carrier, & Cheever, 166
Rosenfeld, M., 231
Rothbard, M. N., 189
Rowatt, W. D., 50
Roy, R., 361
Rubin, L., 287, 327, 328, 359, 364
Rubin, Z., 292
Rudd, J. E., 181, 211
Rueter, M. A., 336, 337
Ruppel, E. K., 61
Rush, Benjamin, 189
Russell, H. M., A–3, A–10

Sabourin, T. C., 181, 211
Sachau, D., 50
Sahlstein, E., 308
Salovey, P., 111, 114, 315
Samp, J. A., 264, 278
Samter, W., 359, 369
Sandsjo, L., 164
Sapir, Edward, 198, 199
Sassler, M. A., 88
Savicki, V., 53
Scabini, D., 120
Schaefer, C. M., A–19
Scheier, M. F., 49
Schein, E. H., A–2
Scherer, K., 117, 241
Scherf, U., 106
Schimel, J., 40
Schlaepfer, T. D., 81
Schmale, J. D., 124
Schneider, C. S., 369, 377
Schramm, W., 9

Schreiner, M., 163, 168
Schrodt, P., 345, 346
Schrodt & Shimkowski, 345, 349
Schulman, H., 53–54
Schumann, Zaki, & Dweck, 93
Schwanen, S., 340
Schwartz, J. C., 109
Scott, A., 357, 373
Scott, Kathleen, 285–286, 322
Scott, Robert Falcon, 285–286, 322
Scratter, A., 312
Searle, J., 193, 201, 234
Sebold, Alice, 203
Sechrist, J., 348
Seinfield, C., 53
Seligman, Melissa, 3–4, 32
Semmroth, J., 314
Seta, C. E., 91
Seta, J. J., 91
Shackelford, T. K., 313
Shakira, 171
Shakur, Tupac, 90
Shannon, C. E., 8
Sharpe, B., 309, 312
Shaver, P. R., 109, 117, 317
Shaw-Plummer, Heather, 337
Shedletsky, L. J., 76, 269
Sheldon, Pavica, 41
Shelton, J. N., 56, 62, 359, 367, 368
Sherman, J. W., 90, 91
Shoda, Y., 112n
Shweder, R. A., 109
Sias, P. M., 384, A–1, A–8
Sias et al., 366, A–8, A–9
Sillars, A., 76, 170, 262, 263, 274, 275
Sillars, A. L., 261
Silva, D., A–16
Silvera, D. H., 88
Silversides, B. V., 221
Silverstein, M., 328, 329, 330, 343
Simmons, K. B., 243
Simon, V. A., 360
Singh, Ray, 203
Sleight, C., 93
Smith, A., 340
Smith, C. A., 104
Smith, G., 91
Smith, K., 371
Smith, L., 264, 273
Smith, T., 46, 48, 76, 170
Smith LeBeau, L. S., 244
Snyder, M., 22
Solomon, D. H., 278
Solomon, S., 40
Somera, L., 93
Song, H., 297
Soto, J. A., 148
Soule, K. P., 254
Spalding, I. R., 278
Spears, Postmes, Lea, & Watt, 91
Spender, D., 82, 196, 197, 199, 226, 260

Spitzberg, B. H., 21, 23, 316, 317
Sprecher, S., 121, 238, 290, 296, 310
Stadium, Palmer, 69n
Stafford, I., 204, 290, 296, 304, 307, 308, 339, 362
Staib, Eric, 35–36, 66
Stang, D., 88
Stefani, Gwen, 171
Steinberg, M., 9, 290
Steuber, K., 256, 278, 341, 342
Stewart, Jon, 133n
Stiff, J., 93
Stokdale, M., 91
Stone, E., 331, 332
Strauss, V., 341, 342
Streck, J., 231
Streek, J., 10
Street, R. L., 22
Strickland, B. R., 349
Strong, G., 293, 296
Suitor, J. J., 348
Suler, J. R., 120
Sulloway, F. J., 348
Sumner, W. G., 153
Surra, C., 298
Swain, S. O., 365

Taguiri, R., 85
Taing, P., 294
Tamir & Robinson, 106
Tannen, D., 81, 177, 209
Tantleff-Dunn, S., 43
Tardy, C. H., 61, 62
Tatum, Beverly Daniel, 367
Tavernise, S., 327
Tavris, C., 118, 119
Taylor, D., 56
Taylor, S. E., 165
Taylor, S. T., 39, 72, 76, 77
Thayer, R. E., 107
Thibaut, J. W., 296
Thoennes, N., 277
Thomas, L. T., 170
Thorne, B., 365
Thornhill, R., 238
Tien, A. Y., 81
Tillema, T., 340
Timmerman, C. I., A–20
Ting-Toomey, S., 146, 267
Tippett, Maria, 221, 222
Tjaden, P., 277
Tod, M., 359
Tomelleri, S., 79
Tottendell, P., 106
Tousignant, J. P., 170
Tovares, A. V., 328, 331, 333
Townshend, Pete, 165n
T-Pain, 232
Tracy, S. J., A–17, A–18
Trail, T. E., 56

Trapp, R., 192
Traupmann, J., 121, 296, 310
Treas, J., 316
Trinket, Effie, 257
Tripp, T. M., A–18, A–19
Tropper, Jonathan, 265
Trott, V., A–19
Tsai, J. L., 148
Tsapelas, I., 293, 296
Tseng, W., 148
Tudor, T. R., A–19
Turkle, S., 53
Turner, C. W., 213, 214, 263
Turner, J. C., 79
Tyner, I. J., A–22

Uken, J., 124
Usher, 171, A–7
Utne, M., 296, 310

Vallacher, R. R., 39
Van Der Heide, B., 53–54, 238
Vangelisti, A. L., 109, 256, 332
Vangelisti, Maguire, Alexander, & Clark, 109
van Vianen, A. E. M., 112
Vazire, S., 52, 53
Veale, D., 41
Venter, I., 113
Vergara, Sofia, 143
Vigfusdottir, T. H., 43
Villa, Brenda, 325–326, 327, 333, 352
Villagran, M. M., 359
Villagran, P., 359
Villaume, W. A., 175
Vivian, D., 277
Vogl-Bauer, S., 338
Vorrell, M., 378
Voyer, Daniel, 177

Wagner, A. D., 165
Waldron, H. B., 213, 214, 263
Waldvogel, J., A–6
Walker, S., 309, 312
Wallace, P., 76
Wallace, S., 61
Walster, E., 289
Walter, 53
Walther, J. B., 24, 53–54, 238
Wang, H., 362, 374
Warber, 315
Warr, P. B., 327
Washington, Denzel, 270, 271
Washington, George, 189, 218
Waterman, A., 143
Watson, D. R., 170
Watson, K. W., 174, 175, 176, 207
Wattleton, Faye, 240
Watzlawick, P., 7, 13–14, 15, 73
Weaver, J. B., III, 175, 176, 207
Weaver, W., 8
Wedge & Sherman, 122
Weger, H., 377
Weinberg, N., 124
Weisz, C., 363, 364
Welch, R. D., 360
Wellman, B., 340, 361, A–6
Wells, A. T., 340
Wells, G. L., 170
Welts, Rick, 48–50
Wen, J. H., A–6, A–7
Werrick, P., 368
Wertheim, E. H., 114
Wessel, K., 124
West, Kanye, 232, A–7
West, L., 371
West, T. V., 56
Westen, D., 314
Westerman, D., 263, 269
Wetherell, M. S., 79
Wheeless, L. R., 60
Whelan, M., 108
Whie, Betty, 88
White, G. L., 295
White, Walter, 211
Whitlock, Teresa, 287
Whorf, B. L., 137, 194, 198, 199
Widmer, E., 316
Wiederman & Hurd, 313, 314
Wiedmaier, B., 315
Wiemann, J. M., 21, 154

Wigley, C. J., 181, 210, 211
Wigley, S., 340
Wilhelm, F. H., 105
Wilkinson, M., 238
Wilkinson, R., 309
Williams, Pharrell, 171, 361
Willits, F. K., 108
Wilmot, W. W., 253, 254, 257, 259, 261, 265
Wilson, F., A–20
Winslet, Kate, 309
Winstead, B. A., 317, 361
Winterson, Jeanette, 243
Wiseman, R., 152
Wittenberg, E., 359
Wolf, A. M., 43
Wolvin, A. D., 163, 168, 169, 178
Wood, J. T., 266, 333, 363, 364
Wood, Julia, 200
Wood, W., 108
Woodall, W. G., 231, 232, 233, 238, 239, 240
Worthington, D. L., 174, 175
Wu, C., 200
Wu, D. Y. H., 148
Wu, S., 109

Xu, X., 296

Yousafzai, Malala, 133–135, 158
Yousafzai, Ziauddin, 133

Zacchilli, J. L., 254, 262, 264, 272, 273
Zachau, G., 164
Zahn-Waxler, C., 112
Zamenhof, L. L., 193
Zapf, D., A–18n
Zelley, E., 369, 370, 371, 372
Zimbardo, P. G., 329
Znaniecki, F., 19
Zorn, T. E., A–10
Zuckerman, M., 225, 233

SUBJECT INDEX

Acceptance in relational maintenance, 305
Accommodation
 in handling conflict, 263
 radical pacifism and, 267
Action-oriented listeners, 174
Actions, performing, 201
Active listening, 161–162, 163, 183, 186, 245
 in comforting others, 125
 gift of, 183
Active strategies, 78
Actor-observer effect, 76
Adaptors, 231, 232
Advice, 126
Advocacy, A-11, A-12
Affect displays, 240
Affection, 287
Age, happiness and, 108
Agentic friendships, 359–360
Aggression, verbal, 210–211
Aggressive-hostile touch, 235
Aggressive listening, 181–182
Agreeableness, 84, 110, 111, 112
Algebraic impressions, calculating, 89–90
American Dialect Society, 195
America's Next Top Model (TV show), 230
Analyze, listening to, 172
Anchorman (film), 113
Anger, 117–119
Anxiety, attachment, 45
Apologizing, 51
Appreciate, listening to, 172–173
Appropriateness, 21–22
Arguments, serial, 276–277
Arthur (TV show), 83, 85
Artifacts, 229, 239
 perceptions of, 241
 workplace, A-2
Assimilation, 138–139
Assurances
 in family relationships, 339
 in relational maintenance, 304–305
Asynchronous, 120
Attachment, 288
 dismissive, 46
 fearful, 46
 preoccupied, 46
 secure, 46
Attachment anxiety, 45
Attachment avoidance, 45–46
Attending, 165–167
Attention, multitasking and, 166

Attention focus, 115
Attraction, romantic, 293–298
Attractiveness, physical, 294–295
Attributional complexity, 153
Attributions, 74
 external, 75
 improving online, 76
 internal, 75
Attribution theories, 74
Autonomy, balancing connection and, 340–341
Avoidance
 attachment, 45–46
 in coming apart, 302
 in handling conflict, 262–263

The Babadook (film), 163, 164
Back-channel cues, 168
Barriers to cooperative verbal communication, 209–215
Battle Hymn of the Tiger Mother (Chua), 251, 282
Beautiful-is-good-effect, 295
Behaviors, conflict and, 254
Benefits, friends with, 378–379
Benevolent prejudice, 142
Best friends, 363–364
BET, 138
Betrayal, romantic, 312–315
Bias
 positivity, 87–88
 self-serving, 77
The Big Bang Theory (TV show), 13, 113, 201
Biological sex, 44
Birds-of-a-feather effect, 295
Birth stories, 332–333
Bisexuality, 28
Black-ish (TV show), 328
Blended emotions, 108
Body movements, communicating through, 230–232
Bonding, in coming together, 300
Bones (TV show), 209
Boston Marathon, 123
Boyhood (film), 334–335
The Brady Bunch (TV show), 344
Brain plasticity, 165
Brave (film), 276
Breadth, 56–57
Breaking Bad (TV show), 209–210, 211
Bridesmaids (film), 109–110, 111, 112
Brooklyn Nine-Nine (TV show), A-10

Bruce Almighty (film), 113
Bullying, in the workplace, A-17–A-19
BuzzFeed, 229

Caring, 288
Castaway (film), 16–17
Catharsis, 118
Channel, 7
Children, gender-role socialization and, 44
Chilling effect, 278
Chilon of Sparta, 37
Choice in romantic relationships, 291
Chronic hostility, 118
Circumscribing in coming apart, 302
Clarifying, 169–170
Clarity, 206
Climates, organizational, A-4–A-5
Co-cultural Communication Theory, 138
Co-cultures, 137–141
Codes in nonverbal communication, 229–239
Cohabiting couples, 330
The Colbert Report (TV show), 253
Collaboration in handling conflict, 264–266
Collectivism, 143–144
Collegial peers, A-8
Coming apart, 301–303
 avoiding in, 302
 circumscribing in, 302
 differentiating in, 302
 stagnating in, 302
 terminating in, 302
Coming together, 298–300
 bonding in, 300
 experimenting in, 299
 initiating in, 299
 integrating in, 300
 intensifying in, 299–300
Commissive act, 201
Commitment in romantic relationships, 291–292
Communal friendships, 359
Communication
 channels in, 7
 cultural influences on, 143–151
 defensive, 213–214
 defined, 6–7
 downward, A-12
 in families, 334–337

I-9

Communication (*continued*)
  feedback in, 9
  forms used by college students, 7
  impersonal, 13
  interaction in, 7
  intercultural, 29
  interpersonal (*See* Interpersonal communication)
  intrapersonal, 11
  I-thou, 13
  media in, 7
  messages in, 7
  meta, 15
  models of, 8–10
  noise in, 8
  nonverbal (*See* Nonverbal communication)
  online, 29
  receiver in, 8
  in romantic relationships, 292
  salient, 72
  sender in, 8
  with subordinates, A-12–A-15
  supportive, 124, 125
  upward, A-11
  verbal (*See* Verbal communication)
Communication accommodation, 153–155
Communication apprehension, 214–215
Communication plans, 214
Communication Privacy Management Theory, 342–344
Community (TV show), 358
Companionate love, 289
Comparative evaluation, 152
Competition, in handling conflict, 263, 265
Complementary relationships, 257
Compliments, A-14–A-15
Comprehend, listening to, 171–172
Compromise, 271–272
Concealment, 212
Conflict
  challenges to handling, 274–278
  clashes in goals or behaviors and, 254
  culture in handling, 267–268
  defined, 253–255
  as dynamic, 255
  endings in, 270–274
  handling, 261–270
  influence of power on, 258–259
  interpersonal communication and, 253–256
  management of, 279
  perception and, 254
  power and, 256–257
  as a process, 254–255
  in relationships, 255–256
  technology in handling, 268–270
Conflict resolutions
  long-term, 273–274
  short-term, 271–273
Conformity orientation, 335
The Conjuring (film), 163
Connection, balancing autonomy and, 340–341
Connotative meaning, 197
Conscientiousness, 84, 110
Consensual families, 336
Constitutive rules, 193
Content information, 13–14
Content-oriented listeners, 175–176
Context, 7
Control messages, 213
Conversation orientation, 335
Conversations, crafting, 201–203
Cooperative language, 245
Cooperative Principle, 205
Cooperative verbal communication, 204–209
  barriers to, 209–215
  gender and, 208–209
Courtship stories, 332
Crazy, Stupid, Love (film), 15
Critical self-reflection, 38
Criticism, A-14–A-15
Cross-category friendships, 364–365
Cross-orientation friendships, 366, 367
Cross-sex friendships, 364–365
Cultural identity, 49
Culture, 27
  assimilation of, 138–139
  attributional complexity and, 153
  collectivistic, 144
  communication accommodation and, 153–155
  communication of, 137
  creation of intercultural competence and, 152–155
  defined, 135–137
  embracing differences, 155
  friendship and, 361
  in handling conflict, 267–268
  happiness across, 108
  high-context, 147–148
  high-uncertainty-avoidance, 144–145
  individualistic, 143–144
  influence on communication, 143–151
  influences on nonverbal communication, 225–226
  language and, 194–195
  as layered, 137
  as learned, 136–137
  listening styles and, 177–178
  as lived, 137
  low-context, 147–148
  low-uncertainty-avoidance, 145
  masculinity versus femininity and, 149–150
  millennials and technology and, 139
  organizational, A-2
  perception and, 79–81
  power and, 260–261
  power distance and, 145–147
  prejudice and, 141–142
  self and, 46–48/
  uncertainty avoidance and, 144–145
  views of time, 151
  in workplace, A-1–A-2
Cumulative annoyance, 262
Cyberslacking, A-6

Dallas Buyers Club (film), 360
Dating violence, 318–319
Deactivation, 116
Deception, 211–213, 314–315
Declarative act, 201
Defensive climate, A-4
Defensive communication, 213–214
Demand-withdraw pattern, 277
Denotative meaning, 197
Dependability, 84
Depth, 57
The Descendants (film) 311, 312
Destructive messages, 275–276
The Devil Wears Prada (film), A-5
Dialectics
  family, 340–344
  relational, 292, 340
Dialects, 194–195
Differentiating in coming apart, 302
Directive act, 201
Dirty secrets, 276
Discern, listening to, 172
Disclosure, differences in, 61–62
Dismissive attachment, 46
Display rules, 148
Disputes, unsolvable, 278
Distance
  maintaining romance across, 308–309
  touch and, 235
Diversity in romantic relationships, 290–291
Dogmatic messages, 213
Dominance, 245
Domination, 271
Downward communication, A-12
Dyadic Power Theory, 258
Dyads, 11
Dyslexia, 36

Eat, Pray, Love (Gilbert), 126
Eavesdropping, 180–181
Effectiveness, 22–23
Ego protection, 77
eHarmony, 297
e-mail, 5
Embarrassment, 50
Emotional challenges, 117–126
  anger as, 117–119
  expressing, 240–241
  grief as, 122–126

Subject Index I-11

online communication and empathy
    deficits, 119–126
    passion as, 121–122
Emotional contagion, 105, 109
Emotional intelligence, 113–114
Emotional life, living happy, 126
Emotional stability, 84
Emotion displays, 148–149
Emotions
    blended, 108
    defined, 103–105
    feelings and moods and, 103–105
    forces shaping, 109–110
    gender and, 112
    happiness across cultures and, 108
    managing your, 112–116
    music and, 117
    nature of, 103–107
    personality and, 110–112
    preventing, 115–116
    primary, 107
    reappraising, 116
    sharing, 105, 123, 373
    types of, 107–109
Empathic concerns, 93, 120
Empathy, 92, 120
    enhancing, 93
    guidelines for, 142
    offering, 92–94
    in online communication, 119–126
    testing, 93
Empathy mind-set, 93
Encounter avoidance, 115
Encounter structuring, 115
Environment, 229
    communication through, 239, 241
The Equalizer (film), 270, 271
Equity, 296
Eternal Sunshine of the Spotless Mind
    (film), 309, 310
Ethics, 23–24
    power and, 258
Ethnocentrism, 152–153, 154
Everybody Loves Raymond
    (TV show), 347
The Exorcist (film), 163
Experimenting, in coming together,
    299
Expertise currency, 259
Explanations, creating, 74–75
Expressive act, 201
Extended family, 330
External attributions, 75
Extroversion, 84, 110, 112
Eye contact, 230–231, 248

Face, 50
Facebook, 4, 5, 51, 273, 297, 339
Face-to-face interactions, 5
Facial expressions, 230, 248

Families
    communicating in, 334–337
        dimensions in, 335
        patterns in, 335–337
    defining, 327–328
    defining characteristics of, 328–329
    primacy of, 349
    self and, 44–46
    types of, 329–331
Family Communication Patterns
    Theory, 335
Family dialectics, dealing with, 340–344
Family maintenance, technology and,
    339–340
Family privacy rules, 343
Family relationships
    assurances in, 339
    interparental conflict in, 348–349
    maintaining, 337–344
    parental favoritism in, 346–348
    positivity in, 339
    self-disclosure in, 339
    stepfamily transition in, 344–346
Family stories, 331–333
Fearful attachment, 46
Feedback, 9, 120, 168–169
Feelings, moods and, 105–107
Feminine cultural values, 150
Fields of experience, 9
Fixed features, 239
Flexible, language as, 193
Flickr, 51, 228
Flipping, 231
Friendliness, 84
Friends
    with benefits, 378–379
    best, 363–364
    importance of, 379
    romance between, 377–378
Friends (TV show), 276
Friendships
    across the life span, 360–361
    agentic, 359–360
    betrayal and, 373–374
    challenges of, 372–373
    communal, 359
    cross-orientation, 366, 367
    cross-sex, 364–365
    culture and, 361
    defined, 357–358
    functions of, 359–360
    gender and, 361
    geographic separation and, 374–376
    interethnic, 367–368
    liking in, 359
    maintaining, 368–372
    nature of, 357–362
    online, 228
    rules in, 369–370
    self-disclosure in, 358–359, 371–372
    shared interests in, 358

    sharing activities in, 371
    technology and, 361–362
    types of, 363–368
    volatility in, 359
    as voluntary, 357–358
Friendship-warmth touch, 234
Frozen (film), 121
Functional-professional touch, 234
Fundamental attribution error, 76

Game of Thrones (film), 115
Gender, 27–28
    cooperative verbal communication and,
        208–209
    emotions and, 112
    friendship and, 361
    influences on nonverbal communica-
        tion, 226–228
    in listening styles, 176–177
    perception and, 81–83
    power and, 260
    self and, 44
Gender labels, challenging
    traditional, 200
Gender-role socialization, children and, 44
Geographic separation in friendship,
    374–376
Gestalts, 87, 95
    constructing, 87–89
Gestures, 231
Girls (TV show), 178
Goals
    conflict and, 254
    in interpersonal communication, 18
Golden Girls (TV show), 88
Gone Girl (film), 313
Gone with the Wind (film), 278–279
Google, 51
Gran Torino (film), 152, 155
Grief, 122–126
    comforting of others and, 124–125
    managing your, 123–124

Halo effect, 88, 89
Happiness across cultures, 108
Haptics, 229, 234
Hearing, 164
Hearing impairment, 164
A Heart Apart (Seligman & Piper)
Helicopter parents, 342
The Help (film), 79
HERE TV, 138
High-context cultures, 147–148
High power-distance cultures, 146
High self-monitors, 22
High-uncertainty-avoidance cultures,
    144–145
High warranting value, 53
Homosexuality, 28

Subject Index

Honesty, 206
Horn effect, 89
Hostile climate harassment, A-22
Hostile prejudice, 142
Hostility, testing your chronic, 118
How to Lose a Guy in 10 Days (film), 81
Human happiness, workplace relationships and, A-22–A-23
Human needs, interpersonal communication and, 17–18
The Hunger Games (film), 256–257
Hypotheses, 20

I Am Malada (Yousafzai), 135
Ideal self, 41
Identity support, 363
Idioms, personal, 193
I-it, 13
"I" language, 207–208
    versus "you" language, 208
Illustrators, 231
Imgur, 228
Immediacy, communication of, 231, 232
Impairment, hearing, 164
Impersonal communication, 13
    improving, 38
Implicit personality theories, 85
Impressions
    calculating algebraic, 89–90
    forming, of others, 86–87
Inception (film), 71
Indifference messages, 213
Individualism, 143–144
Information
    content, 13–14
    interpreting, 73–77
    organizing, 72–73
    relationship, 14–15
    selecting, 72
    using familiar, 73–74
Ingroupers, 79, 141
Initiating in coming together, 299
Instagram, 5, 228, 339
Instance messaging, 339
Instant messaging, 4, 5
Instructions, attending and, 165–166
Instrumental goals, 18
Integrating in coming together, 300
Integrative agreements, 272
Intelligence, emotional, 113–114
Intensifying in coming together, 299–300
Interactions, 7
    managing, 242
Interactive communication model, 8–9, 10
Interactive strategies, 78
Intercultural communication, 29
Intercultural competence
    creating, 152–155

defined, 152
    world-mindedness in, 152–153
Intercultural friendships, 366–367
Interethnic friendships, 367–368
Internal attributions, 75
Interparental conflict, 348–349
Interpersonal communication, 20–27
    appropriateness in, 21–22
    conflict and, 253–256
    defined, 10–13
    as dynamic, 16
    effectiveness in, 22–23
    ethics in, 23–24
    human needs and, 17–18
    improving online, 24–27
    as intentional, 15–16
    as irreversible, 16
    issues in, 27–29
    motives for, 16–18
    principles of, 13–16
    research in, 19–20
    specific goals in, 17
Interpersonal impressions, 86
Interpersonal process model of intimacy, 60
Interpersonal relationships, dark side of, 29
Interview test, 55
Intimacy, 58, 288
Intimate space, 236
Intrapersonal communication, 11
Intrusion, relational, 316–317
Invisibility, 120
Iroquois Theater (Chicago), 105
Irritating partner behaviors, 255
I-thou communication, 13

Jealousy, 315–316
Jefferson strategy, 119, 123
Johari Window, 58–59
Juvenile Love Scale, 289

Kinesics, 229, 230, 231
The King's Speech (film), 215
Kitchen-sinking, 255

Laissez-faire families, 337
Language
    cooperative, 245
    as cultural, 194–195
    evolution of, 195–196
    as flexible, 193
    governing of, by rules, 193
    as symbolic, 191–192
Lesbian, gay, bisexual, transgendered, or queer (LGBTQ) people, 200, 366
Life span, friendship across, 360–361
Lifetime, 138

Liking, 287–288
    in friendships, 359
    reciprocal, 296
Linear communication model, 8, 10
Linguistic relativity, 199
LinkedIn, 51
Listening
    active, 161–162, 163, 183, 186, 245
    adapting purpose of, 173
    aggressive, 181–182
    to analyze, 172
    to appreciate, 172–173
    attending in, 165–167
    to comprehend, 171–172
    culture and, 177–178
    defined, 163
    to discern, 172
    functions of, 171–173
    gender differences in, 176–177
    narcissistic, 182–183
    preventing incompetent, 178–183
    pseudo-, 181
    recalling in, 170–171
    receiving in, 164
    responding in, 168–170
    selective, 178, 180
    steps in, 163–171
    styles of, 173–178
    to support, 173
    understanding in, 167–168
Long-term conflict resolutions, 273–274
Long-term memory, 168
Looking-glass self, 39
Loudness, 234
Love
    companionate, 289
    hard work of successful, 319
    passionate, 289
Love-intimacy touch, 235
The Lovely Bones (Singh), 203
Loving, 287–288
Low conformity families, 335
Low-context cultures, 147–148
Low power-distance cultures, 146
Low self-monitors, 22
Low-uncertainty-avoidance cultures, 145

Mad Men (TV show), 266
Masculine cultural values, 149
Mask, 50
Match.com, 297
Matching, 295
Mean Girls (film), 24
Meaning
    connotative, 197
    conveying, 241
    denotative, 197
    sharing of, 197

Media, 7
  in shaping self-esteem, 43
Memory
  long-term, 168
  short-term, 168
Mental bracketing, 167
Mere exposure effect, 294
Messages, 7
  destructive, 275–276
  mixed, 225
  understandable, 205–207
Meta-communication, 15
Millennials, 139
Misperceptions, 86
Misunderstanding, dealing with, 206–207
Mixed messages, 225
Mixed-status relationships, A-10–A-16
  maintaining, A-15–A-16
Mnemonics, 171
Model minority myth, A-13
Modern Family (TV show), 143, 261, 327, 344, 347
Monochronic time orientation, 151
Moods, 105
  feelings and, 105–107
Motivation, 21
Mud (film), 90
Multitasking
  attention and, 166
  online, 165
Music, emotions and, 117
My Big Fat Greek Wedding (film), 148

Naming, 199–200
Narcissistic listening, 182–183
National Communication Association
  credo of, 24
  on defining communication, 6–7
  Web site of, 32
National Violence Against Women Survey, 277
NBA All-Star Weekend, 48
Needs
  human, 17–18
  physical, 18
  safety, 18
  self-actualization, 18
  self-esteem, 18
  social, 18
Negativity effect, 88
Networks in workplace, A-2–A-4
Neuroticism, 84, 110, 111, 112
New Girl (TV show), 261, 365
9/11 Memorial, 149
Noise, 8
Noise pollution, 164
Nonverbal communication, 221–223
  as ambiguous, 224
  body movements in, 230–232
  codes of, 229–239

competence in managing, 245
cultural influences on, 225–226
defined, 223
functions of, 239–245
gender influences on, 226–228
meaning in, 225
multiple channels in, 224
personal space in, 236–237
physical appearance in, 237–238
principles of, 223–229
rules in, 224–225
technology and, 228
through objects, 238–239
through the environment, 239
through touch, 234–235
through voice, 232–234
Norms, workplace, A-2
No Strings Attached (film), 378
The Notorious C.H.O. (one-woman show), 43
Nuclear family, 329–330

Objects, communication through, 238–239
The Office (TV show), 169, A-3
OkCupid, 297
Online communication, 29
  empathy deficits and, 119–126
Online competence, 24–27
Online self-presentation
  importance of, 51–54
  improving, 54–55
Openness, 84, 110
  balancing protection and, 341–342
Orange Is the New Black (TV show), 301
Organizational climates, A-4–A-5
Organizational culture, A-2
Organizational networks, A-3
Organizing information, 72–73
The Other Guys (film), A-17
Ought self, 41
Outgroupers, 79, 141

Paranormal Activity (film), 163
Paraphrasing, 169–170
Parental favoritism, 346–348
Parents, helicopter, 342
Passion, 121–122
Passionate love, 288
Passive strategies, 78
Peer relationships, A-7–A-10
  maintaining, A-9–A-10
  types of, A-7–A-9
People-oriented listeners, 174–175
Perception
  calculating algebraic impressions, 89–90
  checking your, 94–95
  conflict and, 254

constructing Gestalts, 87–89
culture and, 79–81
defined, 71–78
forming impressions of others, 86–87
gender and, 81–83
generalizing from traits, 85–86
halos and horns and, 88–89
improving, of others, 92–95
influences on, 79–86
interpreting the information, 73–77
negativity effect and, 88
offering empathy, 92–94
organizing information in, 72–73
personality and, 83–86
practicing responsible, 95
prioritizing traits and, 85
of race, 83
reducing uncertainty, 77–78
in romantic relationships, 290
selecting information, 72
using stereotypes, 90–91
Perception-checking, 142
Personal currency, 259
Personal idioms, 193
Personality, 83–86
  defined, 85
  traits in, 84, 85–86
Personality clashes, 256
Personal space, 236
  communication through, 236–237
Perspective-taking, 92–93, 120
Phone calls, 5
Physical appearance, 229
  communication through, 237–238
Physical attractiveness, 294–295
Physical needs, 17–18
Physical violence, 277–278
Pitch, 233–234
Plan actions, 214–215
Plan contingencies, 215
Pluralistic families, 336–337
Pollution, noise, 164
Pollyanna (Porter), 87–88
Pollyanna effects, 88
Polychronic time orientation, 151
Positivity
  bias in, 87–88
  in family relationships, 339
  in relational maintenance, 304
PostSecret, 59
Posture, 231–232, 248
Power, 232
  conflict and, 256–257
  culture and, 260–261
  defining characteristics of, 257–259
  gender and, 260
  influence on conflict, 258–259
  management of, 279
Power currencies, 259–260
Power distance, 145–147
Praise, giving, 126, A-14–A-15

Subject Index

Prejudice, 141–142
  addressing, 142
  benevolent, 142
  hostile, 142
Preoccupied attachment, 46
Primary emotions, 107
Professional peers, A-7
Prolonged staring, 230
Protection, balancing openness and, 341–342
Protective families, 337
Proxemics, 229, 236
Proximity, 293–294
Pseudo-conflict, 262
Pseudo-listening, 181
Public space, 236
Punctuation, 73

Qualitative approaches, 19–20
Quantitative approaches, 20
Quid pro quo harassment, A-21

Race, perception of, 83
Radical pacifism, accommodation and, 267
Rational Emotive Behavior Therapy (REBT), 111
Reactivity, in handling conflict, 264
Reappraisal, 116
Recalling, 170–171
Receiver, 8
Receiving, 164
Regulative rules, 193
Regulators, 231
Relational dialectics, 292, 340
Relational intrusion, 316–317
Relational maintenance, 304
Relational self, 55–63
Relationship crises, 46
Relationship development, 56
Relationship goals, 18
Relationship information, 14–15
Relationships
  complementary, 257
  conflict in, 255–256
  defining, 243–245
  family (*See* Family relationships)
  managing, 203–204
  peer (*See* Peer relationships)
  romantic (*See* Romantic relationships)
  symmetrical, 257
  workplace (*See* Workplace relationships)
Relationship talks, 307
Relevance, 206
Representative act, 201
Resource currency, 259
Resources in romantic attraction, 296
Respect, 287

Responding, 168–170
Romance
  between friends, 377–378
  workplace, A-19–A-20
Romantic attraction, 293–298
  technology and, 297–298
Romantic betrayal, 312–315
Romantic love, types of, 288–290
Romantic relationships
  choice in, 291
  commitment in, 291–292
  communication in, 292
  dark side of, 311–319
  defining, 287–290
  development and deterioration of, 298–303
  diversity in, 290–291
  key elements of, 290–292
  liking in, 287–288
  loving in, 287–288
  maintaining, 303–311
  perception in, 290
  tensions in, 292
Rookie (online magazine), 42
Rules
  friendship, 369–370
  governing of language by, 193

Safety needs, 18
Salience, 72
Say Yes to the Dress (TV show), 237
Scandal (film), 122
Schemata, 74
Secure attachment, 46
Selection, 72
Selective listening, 178, 180
Self
  components of, 37–43
  culture and, 46–48
  disclosing to others, 59–63
  family and, 44–46
  gender and, 44
  hidden and revealed, 58–59
  improving your, 63
  maintaining your public, 50–51
  opening, to others, 55–58
  presenting your, 48–49, 241–242
  relational, 55–63
  sources of, 43–48
Self-actualization needs, 18
Self-awareness, 37–38
Self-concept, 39–40
Self-concept clarity, 39, 40
Self-disclosure, 60
  in family relationships, 339
  in friendships, 358–359
  in relational maintenance, 306–307
  testing your, 23
Self-discrepancy theory, 41–42
Self-enhancing thoughts, 274–275

in handling conflict, 274–275
Self-esteem, 40–43
  media in shaping, 43
Self-esteem needs, 18
Self-fulfilling prophecies, 39–40
Self-monitoring, 22
Self-presentation goals, 18
Self-serving bias, 77
Selma (film), 175
Semifixed features, 239
Sender, 8
Separation, 271
Serial argument process model, 277
Serial arguments, 276–277
The 70s Show (TV show), 183
Sex, biological, 44
Sex and the City (TV show), 7
Sexual-arousal touch, 235
Sexual harassment, A-20–A-22
Sexual infidelity, 313–314
Sexual orientation, 28
Sharing tasks, in relational maintenance, 305
Sherlock (BBC series), 206
Short-term conflict resolutions, 271–273
Short-term memory, 168
Silver Linings Playbook (film), 293
Similarity, 295
Single-parent family, 330
Sister Sister (TV show), 344
Skirting, 262
Skype, 4
Slang words, 196
Smiles, 248
Sniping, 262
"The Snow Child" (Ivey), 59–60
Social comparison, 38
Social needs, 18
The Social Network (film), 269
Social network currency, 259
Social networks, 5, 307–308
Social penetration theory, 56
Social-polite touch, 234
Social space, 236
South Park (TV show), 20–22
Space, 248
Special peers, A-8
Speech acts, types of, 201
Speech rate, 234
SpongeBob SquarePants, 355–356
Stagnating in coming apart, 302
Step-by-Step (TV show), 344
Stepfamily, 330
Stepfamily transition, 344–346
Stereotype Content Model, 141–142
Stereotypes, 90, 141
  using, 90–91
Stories, family, 331–333
Structural improvements, 272–273
Submissiveness, 245
Subordinates, communication with, A-12–A-15

Sudden-death statements, 276
Superiority messages, 213
Support, listening to, 173
Supportive climate, A-4, A-5
Supportive communication, 124, 125
Suppression, 114
Survival stories, 333
Symbolic, language as, 191–192
Symbols, 192
Symmetrical relationships, 257

Talks, relationship, 307
Technology, 139
    family maintenance and, 339–340
    friendship and, 361–362
    in handling conflict, 268–270
    nonverbal communication and, 228
    romantic attraction and, 297–298
    in the workplace, A-6–A-7
Telemundo, 138
Telephone (game), 171
Telling family stories, 333
Tensions, in romantic relationships, 292
Terminating in coming apart, 302
Territoriality, 237
Texting, 4, 5
Text-messaging, 25
That '70s Show (TV show), 183
This Is Where I Leave You (film), 265
Thought, shaping of, 197–199
Time, views of, 151
Time-oriented listeners, 174
Tinder (dating app), 297
Tone, 233
Touch
    communication through, 234–235
    distance and, 235
Transactional communication model, 9–10
Traumatic brain injury (TBI), 167
Triangulation, 345–346
Tumblr, 51, 297
Tweeting, 5
Twitter, 5, 51, 339
Two and a Half Men (TV show), 330

Uncertainty, reducing, 77–78
Uncertainty avoidance, 144–145
Uncertainty Reduction Theory, 78
Understanding, 167–168
Unsolvable disputes, 278
Upward communication, A-11

Valued social identities, 363
Values, workplace, A-2
Venting, 114–115, 118
Verbal aggression, 210–211
Verbal communication, 189–190
    barriers to cooperative, 209–215
    characteristics of, 191–196
    cooperative, 204–209
    crafting conversations in, 201–203
    defined, 191
    functions of, 196–204
    gender and, 208–209
    "I" language in, 207–208
    managing relationships in, 203–204
    naming in, 199–200
    performing actions in, 201
    power of, 215
    shaping thought in, 197–199
    sharing meaning in, 197
    "we" language in, 208
    "you" language in, 207
Violence
    dating, 318–319
    physical, 277–278
Virtual networks, A-3
Virtual peers, A-8
Vocalics, 229, 233
Voice
    communication through, 232–234
    loudness of, 234
    pitch of, 233–234
    speech rate and, 234
    tone of, 233
The Voice (TV show), 172
Voluntary kin family, 330–331

Warranting theory, 53
Warranting value, 53
Web conference calls, 4
Wedging, 315
"We" language, 208
White Privilege (McIntosh), 83
Words, slang, 196
Workplace
    artifacts in, A-2
    bullying in, A-17–A-19
    cliques in, A-3
    communicating with subordinates in, A-12–A-15
    culture in, A-1–A-2
    mixed-status relationships in, A-10–A-16
    networks in, A-2–A-4
    norms in, A-2
    peer relationships in, A-7–A-10
    romances in, A-19–A-20
    sexual harassment in, A-20–22
    technology in, A-6–A-7
    values in, A-2
Workplace relationships
    challenges to, A-16–22
    human happiness and, A-22–A-23
    nature of, A-1–A-7
World-mindedness, 152–153, 154
World of Warcraft (video game), 24
Wuthering Heights (Brontë), 180

"You" language, 207
    "I" language versus, 208
YouTube, 228

Zombieland (film), 368, 369

LaunchPad Videos in LaunchPad

macmillanhighered.com/reflectrelate4e

- Over 90 video clips illustrate key interpersonal communication concepts.
- Videos marked with an asterisk appear as features in the margins of the text.

Chapter 1: Introducing Interpersonal Communication

channel .... page 7
linear communication model .... page 8
*noise .... page 8
*self-monitoring .... page 22
*transactional communication model .... page 9

Chapter 2: Considering Self

face .... page 50
*mask .... page 50
*self-disclosure .... page 60
self-fulfilling prophecies .... page 39
*social comparison .... page 38

Chapter 3: Perceiving Others

algebraic impressions .... page 89
empathy .... page 92
*halo effect .... page 88
horn effect .... page 89
*punctuation .... page 73
self-serving bias .... page 77
Uncertainty Reduction Theory ..... page 78

Chapter 4: Experiencing and Expressing Emotions

*blended emotions .... page 108
emotional contagion .... page 105
encounter avoidance .... page 115
*encounter structuring .... page 115
*reappraisal .... page 116
*supportive communication .... page 124

Chapter 5: Understanding Culture

assimilation .... page 138
attributional complexity .... page 153
collectivistic cultures .... page 144
display rules .... page 148
*high-context cultures .... page 147
*individualistic cultures .... page 143
low-context cultures .... page 147
*power distance .... page 145

Chapter 6: Listening Actively

*action-oriented listeners .... page 174
*aggressive listening .... page 181
content-oriented listeners .... page 175
narcissistic listening .... page 183
selective listening .... page 178
time-oriented listeners .... page 174

Chapter 7: Communicating Verbally

*connotative meaning .... page 197
defensive communication .... page 213
denotative meaning .... page 197
*"I" language .... page 207
"we" language .... page 208
"you" language .... page 207

Chapter 8: Communicating Nonverbally

*adaptors .... page 231
affect displays .... page 240
emblems .... page 231
haptics .... page 234
illustrators .... page 231
kinesics .... page 230
*proxemics .... page 236
regulators .... page 231
vocalics .... page 233

Chapter 9: Managing Conflict and Power

*accommodation .... page 263
avoidance .... page 262
collaboration .... page 264
competition .... page 263
compromise .... page 271
*expertise currency .... page 259
intimacy currency .... page 260
personal currency .... page 259
power .... page 256
resource currency .... page 259
sniping .... page 262
social network currency .... page 259

Chapter 10: Relationships with Romantic Partners

bonding .... page 300
differentiating .... page 302
experimenting .... page 299
*integrating .... page 300
*relational dialectics .... page 292
*relational maintenance .... page 304
stagnating .... page 302

Chapter 11: Relationships with Family Members

*consensual families .... page 336
laissez-faire families .... page 337
pluralistic families .... page 336
*protective families .... page 337

Chapter 12: Relationships with Friends

agentic friendships .... page 360
*communal friendships .... page 359

Appendix: Relationships in the Workplace

*advocacy .... page A-11
*defensive climate .... page A-4
downward communication .... page A-12
*professional peers .... page A-7
supportive climate .... page A-4
upward communication .... page A-11